World Yearbook of Education 2012

The phenomenon of 'travelling reforms' has become an object of great professional interest and intensive academic scrutiny. The fact that the same set of educational reforms is transferred from one country to another makes scholars wonder whether policy transfer has increased as a result of globalisation. But also the fact that policy makers increasingly import 'best practices' and international standards, and use them as a tool to accelerate reform, has captured the imagination of many that deal with policy studies. An international comparative perspective is key for understanding why reforms travel from one corner of the world to another. Not surprisingly, the study of policy borrowing and lending constitutes one of the core research topics of comparative policy studies, a new area of research that links comparative education with policy studies.

The *World Yearbook of Education 2012* brings together a diverse range of perspectives on education policy through contributions from internationally renowned authors. It reflects on the way policy borrowing and lending is reconfiguring the world of education and offers a new collection of insights into the changes occurring across the globe. It particularly focuses on:

- the political and economic reasons for policy borrowing
- the agencies, international networks and regimes that instigate policy change
- the process of borrowing and lending
- the impact of these systems, agendas and institutions on indigenous settings.

This book will prove invaluable to researchers of globalisation and to policy experts, especially those interested in comparative and international educational studies. It is also essential reading for undergraduate and postgraduate students and anyone involved in the sociology, economics or history of education.

Gita Steiner-Khamsi is Professor of Comparative and International Education at Teachers College, Columbia University, New York, USA.

Florian Waldow is Research Director at the University of Münster, Germany.

World Yearbook of Education Series
Series editors: Terri Seddon, Jenny Ozga, Gita Steiner-Khamsi and Agnès van Zanten

World Yearbook of Education 2012

Policy Borrowing and Lending in Education

Edited by Gita Steiner-Khamsi and Florian Waldow

Routledge
Taylor & Francis Group

LONDON AND NEW YORK

First published 2012
by Routledge
2 Park Square, Milton Park, Abingdon, Oxon OX14 4RN

Simultaneously published in the USA and Canada
by Routledge
711 Third Avenue, New York, NY 10017

Routledge is an imprint of the Taylor & Francis Group, an informa business

British Library Cataloguing in Publication Data
A catalogue record for this book is available from the British Library

ISBN: 978-0-415-61524-2 (hbk)
ISBN: 978-0-203-13762-8 (ebk)

Typeset in Minion
by Keystroke, Station Road, Codsall, Wolverhampton

MIX
Paper from
responsible sources
FSC® C004839

Printed and bound in Great Britain by
CPI Antony Rowe, Chippenham, Wiltshire

Contents

Figures

Tables

Notes on Contributors

Motoko Akiba, PhD, is Associate Professor in the Department of Educational Leadership & Policy Analysis at the University of Missouri, USA. In 2008, she received an NSF CAREER award for a five-year project entitled 'Work Contexts, Teacher Learning Opportunities, and Mathematics Achievement of Middle School Students'. She is author of *Improving Teacher Quality: The U.S. Teaching Force in Global Context* (Teachers College Press, 2009) and numerous journal articles on teacher policy, multicultural teacher education and school safety.

Jason Beech, PhD, is Director, School of Education at the Universidad de San Andrés in Buenos Aires, Argentina, where he also teaches comparative education. He is a researcher of the National Council of Scientific and Technical Research of Argentina (CONICET). A co-editor of the journal *Revista de Política Educativa*, he is the author of the books *Going to School in Latin America* (Greenwood, 2008; with Silvina Gvirtz) and *Global Panaceas, Local Realities: International Agencies and the Future of Education* (Peter Lang, 2011). His main interests are the transfer of specialised knowledge about education in the global educational field and conditions of reception in different local contexts.

Stephen Carney, D. Phil., is Associate Professor of Comparative Education at Roskilde University, Denmark. Australian by birth and trained in England, Stephen Carney's research focuses mainly on educational policy in a comparative context. Much of his work has centred on developing countries. He has published widely within the field of comparative and international education in contexts as diverse as school development and leadership in the Nordic countries, higher education reform in Denmark, community schooling in Nepal and classroom pedagogy in the west of China. In 2010 he received the George Bereday award for his article on globalisation and educational policyscapes that was published in the journal *Comparative Education Review.*

Linda Chisholm, PhD, is Special Advisor to the Minister of Basic Education, South Africa; seconded from the Human Sciences Research Council, where she is a Director in the Research Programme on Education and Skills Development. She is a former editor of the journal *Southern African Review of Education* and co-editor of the books *South–South Cooperation in Education and Development* (Teachers College Press and HSRC, 2009; with Gita Steiner Khamsi) and *Education, Growth,*

Aid and Development (CERC, Hong Kong, 2009; with G. Block and B. Fleisch). She has published numerous books and journal articles on comparative education and education and development in South and Southern Africa.

Roger Dale, PhD, is Professor of Globalisation, Education and Development, University of Auckland, New Zealand, and Professor of Education, Centre for Globalisation, Education and Societies, University of Bristol, UK. He is author of numerous publications on the political sociology of education and the state, and on globalisation and education. He is co-author of *Globalisation, Education and Development* (DfID, 2007) and co-editor of *Globalisation and Europeanisation in Education* (Symposium, 2009), as well as founding co-editor of *Globalisation, Societies and Education*.

Philipp Gonon, Dr. phil., is Professor of Vocational Education and Training at the University of Zürich, Switzerland. Before that he was Professor of Adult Education at the University of Trier in Germany. He is the author of several books and numerous articles on the history and theory of vocational pedagogy, the politics of education and policy studies in an international comparative context. His most recent book, *The Quest for Modern Vocational Education – Georg Kerschensteiner between Dewey, Weber and Simmel* (Lang, 2009), provides a historical account of the apprenticeship model in the twentieth century. He is co-editor of the book series *Studies in Vocational and Continuing Education* and serves as a member of the editorial boards for *Journal of Vocational Education and Training* and *Vocations and Learning*.

Sotiria Grek, PhD, is Lecturer of Social Policy at the School of Social and Political Science, University of Edinburgh, UK. She is currently preparing two book manuscripts, one on *Europeanising Education* (with Martin Lawn, Symposium Publishers) and another on the *EU Government of Education* (Routledge). She is the author of numerous articles on the EU governance of education and the role of international organisations for *Comparative Education, Journal of Education Policy* and *European Education Research Journal.* Previously, she was Research Fellow at the Centre for Educational Sociology, University of Edinburgh.

Anja P. Jakobi, Dr. phil., is Senior Researcher at the Peace Research Institute Frankfurt (PRIF/HSFK), and project director in the Cluster of Excellence research programme 'The Formation of Normative Orders', funded by the German Research Foundation (DFG). In her research, she investigates topics related to international institutions, world society and global political change. Recent publications include *International Organizations and Lifelong Learning: From Global Agendas to Policy Diffusion* (Palgrave, 2009), *Mechanisms of OECD Governance: International Incentives for National Policy Making?* (Oxford University Press, 2010; with Kerstin Martens). Her work has also appeared in journals like *Comparative Education Review, Compare, European Educational Research Journal* and *Zeitschrift für Pädagogik.*

Emmanuel Lista, Research and Teaching Assistant in Comparative Education and in Teacher Education, School of Education, Universidad de San Andrés. He is also local coordinator of 'Escuelas del Bicentenario', a school improvement project of the government of the Province of Buenos Aires. He worked as a consultant for UNICEF in the study 'Educational gaps in the secondary level in Argentina: A study of cases' (forthcoming) and is particularly interested in exploring the recontextualisation of pedagogical discourse as it moves from national policies to the contexts of practice in schools.

Christian Maroy, PhD, is Professor and Canada Research Chair in Education Policies at the University of Montreal, Canada. Previously, he was Professor of Sociology at the University of Louvain and Director of the GIRSEF research centre. He is the author of numerous articles on education policies, new modes of regulation in education, teachers' work and the teaching profession in international journals such as *Journal of Education Policy, Compare, Revue Française de Sociologie, Sociologie du Travail* and *Education et Sociétés*. He is also author of *Ecole, Régulation et Marché: Une comparaison de six espaces scolaires locaux en Europe* (Presses Universitaires de France, 2006).

Ka Ho Mok, PhD, is Chair Professor of Comparative Policy, Associate Vice President (External Relations) and Dean of the Faculty of Arts and Sciences, The Hong Kong Institute of Education, PR China. He is also currently Changjiang Chair Professor, Zhejiang University China and President of the Comparative Education Society of Hong Kong (CESHK). He has researched and published in comparative development and policy studies with a focus on East Asia. His articles have appeared in, among others, *Comparative Education, Comparative Education Review, Compare, Journal of Education Policy, Higher Education, Global Social Policy, The Pacific Review, Higher Education Policy* and *Journal of Contemporary China*. His recent books are entitled *The Search for New Governance of Higher Education in Asia* (Palgrave Macmillan, 2010) and *Social Cohesion in Greater China: Challenges for Social Policy and Governance* (World Scientific and Imperial College Press, 2010).

Michelle Morais de Sá e Silva, PhD, is Coordinator of International Cooperation at the Secretariat for Human Rights, Presidency of the Republic of Brazil. She has done extensive research on conditional cash transfers, policy borrowing and lending, and South–South cooperation. She obtained her doctoral degree from Teachers College, Columbia University, with a dissertation titled 'Conditional Cash Transfers and Education: United in theory, divorced in practice'.

Jeremy Rappleye, D. Phil., is Research Fellow at the University of Tokyo, Graduate School of Education, Japan. He is author of *Exploring Cross-National Attraction in Education* (Oxford Studies in Comparative Education, 2007), *Educational Policy Transfer in an Era of Globalization* (Peter Lang, 2011) and co-editor of *Reimagining Japanese Education* (Symposium, 2011). His research interests focus on the processes and politics of educational transfer, past and present. More recent research includes a number of articles and chapters on the effects of policy transfer in aid-dependent contexts in the developing world.

Julia Resnik, PhD, is Lecturer of Sociology of Education at the School of Education of the Hebrew University, Jerusalem, Israel. Her main research fields include globalisation of educational reforms, multiculturalism and international education.

She is the editor of *The Production of Educational Knowledge in a Global Era* (Sense Publisher, 2008) and author of several articles in *Comparative Education Review*, *Journal of Education Policy*, *British Journal of Sociology of Education* and *British Journal of Educational Studies*. She has been Visiting Fellow at the Institute of Education (London), the Complutense University (Madrid) and the San Andrés University (Buenos Aires).

Natasha Ridge, Ed. D., is currently Executive Director of the Sheikh Saud bin Saqr Al Qasimi Foundation for Policy Research, United Arab Emirates, specialising in education policy. She has published a number of policy papers for the Dubai School of Government and the Emirates Center for Strategic Studies and Research, as well as for UNESCO, including *Teacher Quality, Gender and Nationality: A Crisis for Boys* and *Gender, Education and Development: Global Priorities, Local Realities*. Her latest research focuses on the role of the private sector in public education provision in the GCC. In 2011, she was elected President of the Gulf Comparative Education Society (GCES).

Susan L. Robertson, PhD, is Professor of Sociology of Education, University of Bristol, UK. Previously, she has held academic posts in New Zealand and Australia. She has published numerous papers on critical policy studies, the changing role of the state in education, globalisation, regionalisation and new scalar projects in governing education. She is founding co-editor of the journal *Globalisation, Societies and Education*, and founding Director of the Centre for Globalisation, Education and Societies at the University of Bristol. She is the author of five books including, most recently, *Globalisation and Europeanisation of Education* (Symposium, 2009).

Barbara Schulte, Dr. phil., is Research Fellow at the Centre for East and South-East Asian Studies, Lund University, Sweden. Her record of publications includes an edited volume on transfer issues around the world titled *Locating Transfer: Concepts, Actors, Concepts* (Leipziger Universitätsverlag, 2006; in German); a co-edited volume on European educational systems in crisis, *European Educational Systems: Crisis or Transformation?* (Fundación "la Caixa", 2005; in Spanish); and, most recently, a monograph on the emergence and transformation of vocational education in China, '*Saving the Country': Education and Profession in Republican China* (Campus, 2008; in German). In addition, she has written articles on educational transfer, governance and governmentality, transnational educational actors and organisations, and vocational education, with a particular focus on China.

Kazuhiko Shimizu, PhD, is Vice President of Academic Affairs and Professor at the University of Tsukuba, Japan, Executive Director of the Japanese Educational Research Association and the Japan Society for Educational System and Organization. He is the author of numerous books and articles on higher education reforms, university evaluation systems and educational articulation including *Japan–US Comparison of University Credit Systems* (Kazamashobo, 1998) and *Understanding University Reforms* (Kyodoshuppan, 1999). Previously, he was Visiting Scholar at the University of Pennsylvania, the University of Minnesota-Twin Cities and the University of Missouri-Columbia.

Iveta Silova, PhD, is Associate Professor of Comparative and International Education at Lehigh University, Pennsylvania, USA. Her research and publications cover a range of issues critical to understanding globalisation in general, and educational transformation processes in the post-socialist region in particular. She edited *Globalization on the Margins: Education and Post-Socialist Transformations in Central Asia* (Information Age Publishing, 2011), *Post-socialism Is Not Dead: (Re)reading the Global in Comparative Education* (Emerald, 2010) and *How NGOs React: Globalization and Education Reform in the Caucasus, Central Asia, and Mongolia* (Kumarian Press, 2008; with Gita Steiner-Khamsi). She is author of the monograph *From Sites of Occupation to Symbols of Multiculturalism: Re-conceptualizing Minority Education in Post-Soviet Latvia* (Information Age Publishing, 2006). She is the co-editor (with Noah W. Sobe) for the peer-reviewed journal *European Education: Issues and Studies.*

Noah W. Sobe, PhD, is Associate Professor of Cultural and Educational Policy Studies at Loyola University Chicago, USA. He is the author of *Provincializing the Worldly Citizen: Slavic Cosmopolitanism and Yugoslav Student and Teacher Travel in the Interwar Era* (Peter Lang, 2008), and editor of *American Post-Conflict Educational Reform: From the Spanish-American War to Iraq* (Palgrave, 2009), as well as articles in journals such as *Educational Theory, Harvard Education Review, Current Issues in Comparative Education (CICE), European Education* and *Paedagogica Historica.*

Gita Steiner-Khamsi, Dr. phil., is Professor of Comparative and International Education at Teachers College, Columbia University, New York, USA. She is past President of the Comparative and International Education Society (CIES). Her publications include six books and numerous articles on the politics and economics of policy borrowing, international educational development and policy studies in an international comparative context. She is editor of *Global Politics of Educational Borrowing and Lending* (Teachers College Press, 2004), co-editor of *South–South Cooperation in Education and Development (Teachers College Press and HSRC,* 2009; with L. Chisholm) and co-author of *Educational Import. Local Encounter with Global Forces in Mongolia* (Palgrave Macmillan, 2006; with I. Stolpe).

Keita Takayama, PhD, is Lecturer of Sociology of Education at University of New England, Australia. He has published numerous articles on politics of education reform and policy borrowing in *Asia Pacific Journal of Education, British Journal of Sociology of Education, Comparative Education* and *Comparative Education Review.* In 2011, the Comparative and International Education Society selected his article 'Politics of Externalization in Reflexive Times: Reinventing Japanese Education Reform Discourses through "Finnish PISA Success"' (published in *Comparative Education Review*) for the George Bereday Award.

Florian Waldow, Dr. phil., is Research Director at the University of Münster, Germany, and Recipient of an Emmy-Noether-Grant from the German Research Foundation (DFG). He is author of *Structural Economic Cycles and International Discursive Swings: Educational Policy-Making in Sweden, 1930–2000* (Peter Lang, 2007) and of several journal articles on policy transfer and borrowing, published in

Comparative Education, Zeitschrift für Pädagogik and *Scandinavian Journal of Educational Research*. Previously, he was Lecturer at Humboldt University in Berlin (Centre of Comparative Education), Visiting Fellow at Stockholm University and Research Fellow at Uppsala University, Sweden.

Geoff Whitty, D. Lit(Ed), is Director Emeritus at the Institute of Education, University of London and past President of the British Educational Research Association. His many publications include *Devolution and Choice in Education* (Open University Press, 1998; with Sally Power and David Halpin), *Making Sense of Education Policy* (SAGE Publications, 2002) and *Education and the Middle Class* (Open University Press, 2003; with Sally Power, Tony Edwards and Valerie Wigfall), which won the Society for Educational Studies book prize in 2004. He is now Professor in the School of Management at the University of Bath and a specialist advisor to the UK House of Commons Select Committee for Education.

Series Editors' Introduction

Since 2006, the current series editors of the Routledge *World Yearbook of Education* have taken advantage of its global reach to focus it on different aspects of the problem of globalisation. In doing this, we are responding to shifts in the global, national, local and institutional scale that have been understood and explained in different ways in research and scholarship in the field of education. One key aspect of these shifts is the preoccupation of nation states and transnational agencies with finding new ways of 'doing governing'. As a consequence we see shifts from hierarchy to network as the preferred model, accompanied by outsourcing of services to hybrid public–private organisations, increasing devolution of responsibility for self-management, choice-making and the management of risk to individuals and families and away from state institutions. Governments cease to be enablers of provision; they are re-defined as market regulators or, more recently as drivers of 'integration' of action and delivery with a range of partners in the provision of services – often organised in networks of hybrid public/private providers.

These ideas reflect cross-border movements of people and ideas, the flow of data and experts, and the influence of apparently shared policy agenda for education and other services following increasingly similar design principles in the reconfiguration of education/learning (education as learning). Policy work no longer operates within closed systems through bureaucratically organised, command and control processes. Rather, the work of making/fabricating governing occurs in complex 'systems' in which cooperation and coordination must be managed. Governing through trans-national networks is not constrained by path-dependent thinking at the national scale. In education these changes have been conceptualised as 'top down' globalisation, as globalisation from below, and as combining travelling and local policy pressures.

Recent *World Yearbook of Education* volumes on education in the Arab world, on workplace learning, and on the changing curriculum have tracked and analysed these changes. As we build a reference library through these volumes that offers a global perspective on change in education, located in the very varied contexts in which globalising shifts play out, we have become more and more aware of the significance of the 'governmental technologies' that seek to deliver these shifts and promote or mediate change. Miller and Rose (2008: 55) draw attention to the importance of the 'mundane programmes, calculations, techniques, apparatuses, documents and procedures through which authorities seek to embody and give effect to governmental ambitions', and argue that it is through examination of the interconnections between political projects and such technologies that we can understand how globalising agendas affect and interact with actors, agencies and conditions 'on the ground'.

Data constitute a very important technology, as data make comparison possible. In addition, the shift in governing is dependent on the belief (or perhaps the illusion) among those 'doing' governing that data make systems knowable and transparent. Data support and create new kinds of policy instruments that organise political relations through communication and information (Ozga et al. 2011). These policy technologies make policy borrowing and lending, the topic of this current volume, more important and more prevalent than they have been in the past. This volume not only locates policy borrowing and lending as a key topic in the *World Yearbook of Education*'s continuing engagement with understanding, as well as tracking globalising change in education, but also presents new directions for enquiry into policy borrowing and lending, and offers a variety of perspectives on processes of borrowing and lending as governmental technologies.

We are fortunate, then, to be able to offer a volume on this key topic that is edited by acknowledged experts in the field, with contributions from a range of scholars working in both 'lending' and 'borrowing' contexts. We are also fortunate in the contribution made by Ryan Hathaway, Graduate Research Assistant at Teachers College, Columbia University, who has assisted with reference checking and with other editorial tasks. The editors have ensured that contributors organised their approaches to the topic under a number of analytical categories. First, we are encouraged to consider the range of agencies involved in policy transfer, with attention to the governing capacity exercised by these agencies, before turning to consideration of 'externalisation' as a way of explaining interventions in a range of contexts. We then turn to the issue of selective borrowing and local adaptation – thus offering a shift from top down perspectives on policy borrowing and lending. Finally, the volume engages with travelling policy and the idea of policyscapes, moving the agenda beyond the idea of policy entering national systems to engage with the possibility of emergent transnational/international social system interaction and change.

Given the richness of the material, and the centrality of the topic to understanding the problem of globalisation, we are confident that this volume will be of interest to a wide range of scholars, not only those working in education.

Globalisation researchers will make use of this volume in exploring whether or not there is an international convergence of national educational systems, provisions and practices as a result of transnational policy transfer, or transfer of 'best practices' and 'international standards'. In the globalisation literature, there is much talk about the emergence of international knowledge banks (OECD, World Bank, etc.) that seek to govern through global indicators that monitor national progress. Perspectives from policy borrowing/lending research – such as those in this volume – help to illuminate the fact that these knowledge banks not only describe and then prescribe 'best practice', they often start with the prescription and then, *a posteriori*, conduct an analysis of the local situation, implying that global solutions exist first and then local problems have to be found, invented or identified to suit these global solutions.

Policy researchers will find material here in their enquiries into whether the travelling reforms 'arrive' in identical form or whether it is necessary to differentiate between transfer at the rhetorical level (policy talk) and implementation where it may become heavily indigenised and locally adapted. Scholars of *education politics* may also find common ground here in the analysis of policy borrowing/lending as a political, rather than a rational, act.

Economics of education scholars will find material here from which they may draw conclusions about transfer costs and benefits, especially where imported reform is sometimes adapted to the local realities to such a degree that there is little or no similarity with the 'original'.

Sociologists of education will find material on the extent to which the act of externalisation may disempower some interest groups or policy coalitions at the expense of others and how reference to 'globalisation' or 'international standards' serves as a stamp of approval for a particular group's agenda.

Finally, *historians of education* may respond to this volume by considering the extent to which neither policy transfer nor harmonisation are new phenomena. Regional adaptation or harmonisation was a major feature agenda of colonial education policy.

We commend this volume to scholars from all of these fields of enquiry.

Jenny Ozga, Oxford
Terri Seddon, Melbourne
Gita Steiner-Khamsi, New York
Agnès van Zanten, Paris

References

Miller, P. and Rose, N. (2008) *Governing the present: Administering economic, social and personal life*, Cambridge: Polity Press.

Ozga, J., Dahler-Larsen, P., Segerholm, C. and Simola, H. (eds) (2011) *Fabricating quality in education: Data and governance in Europe*, London: Routledge.

Introduction

1 Understanding Policy Borrowing and Lending

Building Comparative Policy Studies

Gita Steiner-Khamsi

This book deals, in a broad sense, with globalisation in education. More narrowly, it provides critical analyses of 'travelling reforms', that is, reforms that surface in different parts of the world. Globalisation is commonly viewed as an act of deterritorialisation. By implication, globalisation studies investigate the transnational flow of money, communication, beliefs, or, as is the case with comparative educational research, the travel of educational reforms from one cultural context to another.

Is the global circulation of reforms good or bad? The opinions on whether the transnational flow of reforms should be a cause for concern, or for celebration, are deeply divided. Some authors fear that we are abandoning our idiosyncratic conceptions of 'good education', and are gradually converging toward an 'international model of education'. They interpret the proliferation of policy borrowing and lending as proof that global players not only record and monitor national developments, but also impose their own portfolio of 'best practices' on governments. At the other end of the spectrum are authors who applaud travelling reforms, because they supposedly represent 'best practices', or 'international standards', that have been transferred successfully from one country to another. These analysts regard policy planning as a rational undertaking, and view policy transfer as proof of lesson-drawing, and thus one of the more desirable outcomes of evidence-based policy planning. No doubt, the discussion on policy borrowing and lending research is saturated with strong opinions. However, the authors of this book move beyond simplistic normative judgments (good or bad questions), to describe, analyse, and understand policy borrowing and lending in an era of globalisation.

Linkages between Comparative Education and Policy Studies

The contributions which follow are intended to advance comparative policy studies. The preoccupation with travelling reforms has, perhaps more than other research topics, helped to illustrate the substance of, and justify the need for, comparative studies. Methodologically, any cross-national investigation of reforms is, by default, comparative. Nested in the intersection of two large and ever-growing academic fields – comparative education and policy studies – the study of travelling reforms draws on both research traditions. These two research traditions are interdisciplinary in orientation, and typically attract scholars in comparative political science and comparative sociology, who have invigorated research on globalisation and policy transfer.

At the same time, there is a significant gap separating comparative education from policy studies. Two distinct features of each field are particularly relevant for our research topic: while comparative education is transnational in orientation, policy studies is transsectoral. In other words, the focus on understanding local policy contexts against the backdrop of larger transnational or global developments should be considered a prominent feature of comparative education.

Openness towards debates in other policy sectors (social policy, environmental policy, etc.), as well as in the profit and non-profit/non-governmental sectors, is an important characteristic of researchers affiliated with policy studies. An intellectual cross-fertilisation is very much needed. Interaction between the two fields is mutually beneficial, and helps to compensate for some of the conceptual shortcomings of research traditions in each. One positive result would be for debates in comparative education to become more open towards theories concerning the policy process. These theories typically draw from numerous sectors, and are neither confined to government-issued policies, nor restricted to the education sector alone. In turn, there is also much to be gained for policy studies, because the comparative perspective challenges the nationalist – at times parochial – outlook that policy analysts tend to display.

The pace with which reforms currently circumnavigate the globe is truly astounding. Unsurprisingly, there is heightened interest in understanding why, and how, policy makers draw inspiration from a limited number of knowledge banks – OECD, IEA, the World Bank, and UNESCO – in particular. The resemblance between reforms across all levels of the system, and all aspects of education policy, is striking. Across a wide variety of nations and despite vastly different levels of social, political, and economic development, one finds talk of per-capita financing in schools, quality assurance in higher education, lifelong learning, and student-centred teaching (to name just a few), at all levels of the education system. From Ulaanbaatar to Berlin, from Anchorage to Cape Town, the similarities have grown to the extent that policy makers unscrupulously refer to these reforms as 'best practices', or 'international standards', in education, *as if* there existed a clearly defined set of standards, policies, and practices that are universally shared. Nevertheless, *imagined globalisation* in education has affected agenda-setting as significantly as the *real* pressure to harmonise or align the education systems with systems in the same region, or in the same 'educational space' (Nóvoa and Lawn 2002).

A Commitment to Understanding Local Policy Context

Naturally, the group of authors presented in this book shares more than merely a joint interest in comparative policy studies. They also have in common a similar interpretive framework and method of inquiry, that enables them to draw attention to the local meaning, adaptation, and recontextualisation of reforms that had been transferred or imported. They have systematically adopted a lens that lends explanatory power to *local policy contexts*, and makes it feasible to explore the contextual reasons for why reforms, best practices, or international standards, were adopted. For these authors, reforms from elsewhere are not necessarily borrowed for rational reasons, but for political or economic ones. Such an interpretive framework categorically refutes the commonsense, yet naïve, assertion that reforms are imported because they have proven to be good or – even worse – because they represent best practices.

Emphasis on local policy context as the analytical unit for examining policy transfer places greater weight on the agency, process, impact, and timing, of policy borrowing. Very often, an investigation into policy borrowing and lending is triggered by a phenomenon that initially appears to be irrational or contradictory. These inconsistencies end up making sense once we apply an interpretive framework that pays attention to the 'socio-logic' (Schriewer and Martinez 2004) of cross-national policy attraction, or acknowledges the political and economic rationale for policy borrowing. The terrain under scrutiny should be the local policy context. It is this context that provides the clues for understanding why a borrowed reform resonates, what policy issue it pretends to resolve, and which policy actors it managed to mobilise in support of reform.

The interpretive framework used by many of the authors in this book relates to the political, as well as economic, dimensions of policy transfer (see Steiner-Khamsi 2010). Politically, borrowing often has a salutary effect on protracted policy conflict, because it builds coalitions. It enables opposed advocacy groups to combine resources to support a third, supposedly more neutral, policy option borrowed from elsewhere. 'International standards' have become an increasingly common point of reference in such decisions.

Economically, policy borrowing is often a transient phenomenon, because it only exists as long as external funding – contingent upon the import of a particular reform package – continues. Policy borrowing in poor countries is to the education sector what structural adjustment, poverty alleviation, and good governance, are to the public sector at large: a condition for receiving aid. As a requirement for receiving grants or loans at the programmatic level, policy borrowing in developing countries is coercive, and unidirectional. Reforms are transferred from the global North/West to the global South/East.

Interest in exploring the political, *and* economic, reasons for policy borrowing and lending is relatively new. For a long time, policy-transfer researchers focused on the politics of policy borrowing mainly because they were concerned with transatlantic transfer (United States and Europe), transpacific transfer (Asia and North America), or intercontinental transfer. The economic gains that drive policy borrowing and policy lending were ignored. Clearly it is time to study both, and pay attention to policy transfer within, *and* between, both world-systems: the wealthy, and the impoverished.

From a historical perspective, however, one needs to acknowledge that policy transfer between the two world-systems is not new. In fact, it constituted one of the key research areas for scholars immersed in the study of colonial education. One example is the study of 'adapted education' in early twentieth-century British colonial education policy. This model was disseminated to over thirty former British colonies and dependent territories (Steiner-Khamsi and Quist 2000). Interest in understanding the lending or export of policies, and the economic gains associated with disseminating, exporting, or lending 'best practices' and 'international standards' is, upon closer examination, a revitalised, rather than novel, area of colonial education research. Nowadays, those scholars in policy transfer research who live or work in developing countries, and who have adopted a postcolonial or post-developmental research paradigm, hold a keen interest in understanding the political, as well as the economic, dimension of imported reforms.

Something Borrowed, Something Learned?

Twenty years ago, policy exchange between the United Kingdom and the United States peaked, with the busy transfer of neoliberal reforms between the two countries (see Whitty, in this volume). The transfer was well documented, and led one group of researchers to wonder whether anything was learned from the proliferation of choice, standards-based, and quasi-market reforms (Finegold et al. 1993). It may be an opportune moment to reflect, two decades later, on the meaning of policy learning, and its relation to policy borrowing.

The authors that have been assembled for this volume have chosen the term 'policy borrowing and lending' deliberately, so as to situate their work within the broader field of comparative policy studies. In contrast to related terms such as 'policy learning' and 'policy transfer' (produced in political science), or 'diffusion' or 'reception' (generated in sociology, social anthropology, and history), the term policy borrowing and lending emerged in the field of comparative education, and underwent a revival of noticeable magnitude in the past decade. This new interest was the outcome of debate on how global governance affects national educational systems, beliefs, and practices, and was fuelled by the controversy over whether the international convergence of educational systems should be interpreted as a direct result of cross-national lesson-drawing, or other, more coercive, forms of policy transfer. Arguably, new policy instruments such as the adoption of 'best practices', or the alignment of national educational systems with 'international standards', could be viewed as transnational policy transfer, and thus add credence to what David Dolowitz and David Marsh prescribed ten years ago (Dolowitz and Marsh 2000: 14): 'When we are analysing policy change we always need to ask the question: is policy transfer involved?' Authors in comparative education have studied different types of transfer, ranging from voluntary transfer (lesson-drawing, emulation), to coercive transfer (harmonisation, imposition). As mentioned above, scholars have traditionally directed their attention to the study of travelling reforms. It is with good reason that comparative education has been traditionally enamoured with the study of reforms that travel from one country to another. One must be familiar with two or more educational systems to notice that the same reforms pop up again and again in different parts of the world. Above all, one needs to compare.

Today, scholars in comparative education investigate the international dimension that surfaces at various stages of the policy cycle, starting from the stage of problem definition and agenda setting, to policy implementation and evaluation. It has been noted, for example, that the pre-existence of global reform packages disseminated, and sometimes funded, by global actors such as the OECD, the World Bank or the regional development banks, suggests a sequence that is at odds with what is typically assumed in policy planning: local problems are sometimes *created* in line with packaged global solutions, rather than the other way around. Another recent phenomenon that has drawn considerable attention is the proliferation of international knowledge banks containing statistics on national educational systems. Set up by global actors to monitor national progress, these banks promote evidence-based or knowledge-based regulation as a tool to justify the adoption of global reforms.

The educational focus notwithstanding, we find the scholarship produced in public policy (e.g. Sabatier 2007) and comparative social science – particularly comparative political science, sociology, and history – extremely useful for the study of travelling education reforms. In comparative political science, for example, the term 'policy learning' is closely associated with the seminal work of Peter A. Hall (1993), and has been expanded over the past few years to include a fascinating, and interdisciplinary, array of analytical work that deals with the actors, processes, and effects of policy change. Hall frames policy change as social learning, i.e. a 'deliberate attempt to adjust the goals or techniques of policy in response to past experience and new information. Learning is indicated when policy changes as the result of such a process' (Hall 1993: 278).

Hall distinguishes between first-, second- and third-order changes. Incremental or first-order changes represent the most common type of policy learning. The instruments and goals of the policy are preserved, but the policy is pursued with greater vigour, efficiency, and effectiveness. In second-order changes, the policy instruments are altered, but the policy goals are maintained. Finally, third-order changes signal radical or fundamental policy alterations. Comparable to Kuhnian 'paradigm shifts', these third-order changes often result from policy failure and, as a consequence, replace not only the instruments, but also the goals of policy making with new ones. Indicative of second- and third-order changes is the broad range of actors and organisations involved in the social learning process. Known for his analyses of neoliberal thought in the 1980s and 1990s, Hall identified the change in economic policy under British Prime Minister Margaret Thatcher as a third-order change, because the Keynesian mode of policy making was completely revamped, and replaced with a new monetarist approach.

In another early piece on policy learning and change, Colin J. Bennett and Michael Howlett (1992: 275) distinguished between actors, content, and effects of policy learning, and turned their attention to 'who learns, what they learn, and the effects of learning on subsequent policies'. Unsurprisingly, incremental policy learning, considered the standard mode of policy change, does not attract great professional interest or academic scrutiny. On the contrary, most studies on the policy process focus on second- and third-order social learning.

In the same vein, research on policy borrowing and lending focuses on second-order and third-order policy change. More recent literature on policy studies, comparative education, and political science, features the terms 'transfer', or 'policy borrowing and lending', to neutralise the positive connotations associated with 'policy learning'. This work also constitutes an attempt to examine the transsectoral or transnational dimensions involved in transfer processes. As with diffusion studies, research on policy borrowing and lending investigates how policies from one domain or one sub-system (education sector, health sector, economic sector, etc.) are transferred to another, or how they are transplanted from one system or country to another.

This particular area of policy research gained prominence in the context of globalisation studies, and studies on the international convergence of national education systems. Many important research questions arise when a policy borrowing and lending lens is utilised. Such questions include: why is a policy borrowed from another policy domain or system, when a similar reform has already been tested? Why is policy borrowing more likely to occur after political changes, or after changes in administration? Which educational systems tend to be objects of emulation, i.e. serve as reference systems or 'reference societies'? Why are policies transferred that failed in the initial context? Why do emulation and lesson-drawing have a salutary effect on protracted policy conflict? As mentioned previously, the emphasis in this interpretive framework is on local policy context. This framework has also been applied to investigations of the economic reasons politicians and policy makers in developing countries are led to import reforms from the global North or the global West.

Obviously, there is no single term that could adequately contain all of the nuances embedded in a set of concepts as diverse as policy learning, policy change, policy transfer, or policy borrowing and lending. Of all the terms available, we found 'policy borrowing and lending' to be the most appropriate for the following reasons: it is a term that is widely used in comparative education research, includes a notion of agency, is neutral with regard to the purpose and outcome of the policy transfer, and accounts for a focus on the receivers, as well as the senders, in the policy-transfer process. The term also avoids some of the interpretive pitfalls attached to the term policy 'learning', which in educational research, in particular, may carry excessively positive associations about the reasons or purposes of policy transfer.

New Scholarship, New Avenues of Inquiry

The study of cross-national policy borrowing and lending is accompanied by lively intellectual debates. As with all theories, the concepts used in this field have been adjusted, refined, and expanded, over time. Policy borrowing and lending – both as an act (normative aspect), and as an object of study (analytical aspect) – has a long-standing tradition in comparative education. However, it has only gained popularity among social researchers and policy analysts within the past twenty or thirty years. One can find the contributions of three generations of scholars who helped to boost, and sustain, interest in policy-transfer research.

The first generation of scholars introduced fundamental concepts. These include selective policy borrowing and lending (Brian Holmes), externalisation (Bernd Zymek, Jürgen Schriewer), or cross-national policy attraction (David Phillips). These ideas laid the foundation for a particular research paradigm that pays great attention to local policy contexts as the main site for understanding policy transfer.

Building on the new research paradigm that used local policy context as the primary site for analysis, my generation of researchers adapted several concepts, and refined them in ways to make them applicable to the study of travelling reforms. For example, each of the co-editors of the *World Yearbook of Education* examined governance by numbers (Jenny Ozga), travelling pedagogies (Terri Seddon), or the growing influence of non-state actors and backstage advisors in post-bureaucratic states (Agnès van Zanten). The work of Joseph Tobin, Yeh Hsueh and Mayumi Karasawa (2009), and

Kathryn Anderson-Levitt (2003) – anthropologists with a genuine interest in understanding the local meaning attached to imported reforms – has also been influential in comparative policy studies. Several authors in this book – Linda Chisholm, Roger Dale, Philippe Gonon, Christian Maroy, Ka Ho Mok, Susan L. Robertson, Geoff Whitty – are renowned representatives of the second generation. Since the 1990s they have opened up new research areas and introduced new concepts, such as, for example, the study of regional harmonisation of educational policy (Chisholm), methodological nationalism (Dale and Robertson), or policy tourism (Whitty), to list just a few of their accomplishments.

At the same time, these second-generation researchers have expanded the geographic radius to include developing countries, where grants and loans are often tied to the import of specific programmes or reforms. As a result of this conceptual and geographic recalibration we supported, at my home institution, Teachers College, Columbia University, numerous empirical studies and dissertations exploring the politics and economics of policy transfer (see Steiner-Khamsi 2010). The commitment to exploring the agencies, reasons, and impacts of travelling reforms, made it necessary to expand our horizon, and draw on additional theories in the field of policy studies. This conceptual expansion made us recognise that the reliance of policy makers on 'best practices', or 'international standards', is often a political manoeuvre to help build political or economic alliances in support of contested reform agendas. In short, globalisation is not an external force, but rather a domestically induced rhetoric mobilised at particular moments of protracted policy conflict, to generate reform pressure and build policy advocacy coalitions.

Research on policy borrowing and lending grew exponentially over the past decade, producing an abundance of valuable studies. It would have been impossible to include all the third-generation authors who have either introduced new cutting-edge themes, propelled new perspectives, or advanced new interpretations of old topics. This book is only able to present a small selection of promising new research that surfaced in the new millennium. This third generation of scholars in policy-transfer research will set the research agenda in comparative policy studies in the years to come, and is therefore worth discussing in greater detail. I will confine my remarks to four promising research areas that are likely to attract academic curiosity and professional interest in the future:

- the shift from bilateral to international reference frames
- understanding the logic of systems and cases
- methodological repercussions of 'policyscapes'
- deciphering projections in cross-national policy attraction.

The Shift from Bilateral to International Reference Frames

It is noticeable that policy makers increasingly refer to 'international standards', rather than to concrete lessons learned from a particular educational system, when they make their case for policy transfer. The bilateral framework has clearly been broken up into a diverse set of ideas subsumed under the vague label, 'international standards'. This phenomenon has produced four compelling new strands of research on the lifespan of a policy, network analysis as a methodological tool to analyse agency, harmonisation and coercive transfer, and policyscapes.

The Process of Gradual Deterritorialisation over the Lifespan of a Policy

The proliferation of international, rather than bilateral, references may be interpreted as a sign that certain reforms that were disseminated across the globe are now maturing, and eventually will be replaced. The epidemiological model identified three phases of a so-called 'reform epidemic': slow growth, explosive growth, and burnout (Watts 2003). Today we are surrounded by 'well-travelled' reforms: the quasi-market, neoliberal, or hyper-liberal reforms, launched during the Thatcher–Reagan era. These were borrowed by New Zealand and Australia, and then disseminated to other parts of the world. Precisely because they were introduced so long ago, policy makers in late-adopter countries refer to them as international reforms, without considering where they originated. The transformation of a policy over time is succinctly summarised in Robert Cowen's brilliant phrase 'as it moves, it morphs' (Cowen 2009).

A well-documented example of a policy that continued moving and morphing, or gradually became deterritorialised, is the conditional cash transfer (CCT) programme. In this book Morais de Sá e Silva focuses her investigation of conditional cash transfer programmes, which provide incentives to children from poor families to enrol and/or complete school, on three countries – Brazil, Colombia, and the United States. The conditional cash transfer programme is ideal for consideration as a reform package that went global, because it was transferred to over forty countries within the past fifteen years. It resonated for different reasons in various countries, and the design of the programme differed considerably depending upon which version, or at which stage, policy makers borrowed it.

Network Analysis and the Quest for Identifying Agency

Another strand of cutting-edge research that contributes to refining transfer research builds methodologically on social network analysis. Different from diffusion research, which tends to downplay the agency involved in disseminating innovations or reforms, network analysts developed methodological tools to identify actors of transfer. In this book, for example, Barbara Schulte places agency at the centre, enabling her to identify individuals, associations, and institutions that were key disseminators of vocational education reforms in PR China. Her sophisticated methodology uses the variables closeness, betweenness, and connectivity, within the network of the Chinese Association of Vocational Education (CAVE), to understand why local actors were able to draw on CAVE as a quasi-external, credible source of authority for building vocational education. Her method of inquiry allows her to understand why, and how, concepts of vocational education in China were strongly influenced by the network of CAVE members.

Schulte's chapter is important for scholars of policy-transfer research who subscribe to case study methodology as their preferred method of inquiry. Case-study methodology, if applied rigorously, provides access to the inner workings of a case, a system, a country, or an institution. For many of us, it is thorough analysis of the local context that matters most in understanding the agency, rationale, and impact, of policy transfer. Rather than viewing policy makers as helpless recipients of global standards, reforms, and trends, this group of authors acknowledges (active) agency as reflected, among other examples, in selective borrowing and local adaptation.

Harmonisation: A Special Type of Coercive Policy Transfer?

Given the replacement of the bilateral framework with loosely defined international references as the primary form of externalisation, the usefulness of the dichotomies borrowing/lending, reception/diffusion, and import/export, has been called into question. Several authors propose using other terms that are less specific with regard to spatial mobility. One approach to resolving the lack of explicit reference to a particular education system, or reference society, is to acknowledge the existence of a 'referential web' (Vavrus 2004). Another approach is to recognise the blurred trajectories, and label transplanted educational reforms simply as 'travelling policies' (Seddon 2005; Coulby et al. 2006). In this sense, all global educational reforms qualify as travelling policies: one does not know where they come from, or go to; they are at the same time nobody's and everybody's reform. The suspension of the bilateral frame of reference does, however, have larger repercussions for the debate in comparative policy studies.

For borrowing researchers of the first generation, it was vital to interpret the choice of 'reference society', that is, the educational system from where policies, practices and ideas were borrowed. Typically, there were cultural, political, or economic reasons that accounted for the borrower's interest in a particular system. David Phillips (2004), for example, examined the reasons for the cross-national policy attraction of British government officials and scholars towards the educational system in Germany, during the nineteenth century. The range of motivators for one country to seek inspiration from the educational system of another can be extremely diverse. In the United States affinity attracted reformers to the UK model in the early 1990s. However, US education policy makers have also been driven by competition (e.g. the Soviet Union in the late 1950s and early 1960s), or curiosity (e.g. Japan during the 1980s). Nowadays, the league leaders in international student achievement tests, such as Shanghai–China, Finland, or Singapore, receive the most attention.

Arguably, the preoccupation with understanding the choice of reference society has become somewhat obsolete. Studies today deal increasingly with the emergence of new regional and international educational spaces as a result of harmonisation. Examples include the Bologna and Lisbon Protocols in higher education, and the Education for All programmes in developing countries. Governments that sign such agreements must eventually align their policies with those of the larger 'educational space' they have chosen to inhabit.

Iveta Silova's dissertation research (see Silova 2005) examined the shift from the Soviet to the post-Soviet/European educational space, inhabited by Latvia in the 1990s. Using the fascinating case of bilingual education policy, she demonstrated how parallel, or separate, schooling was preserved, even as a multilingual reform was added to comply with the policies of the new European allies. From the perspective of policy-transfer research, harmonisation is only one of many variants of policy borrowing and lending; one that, perhaps more visibly than with other variants, depicts the move away from bilateral, to a regional or international frame of reference.

Several authors in this book, notably Roger Dale and Susan L. Robertson, Sotiria Grek, and Anja P. Jakobi, reflect on harmonisation from a theory perspective. By design, international or regional agreements (Education for All Declaration, Bologna Protocol, Paris Declaration on Aid Effectiveness, etc.) are prescriptive and coercive. Therefore, these authors raise fundamental questions that greatly impact the larger field of comparative policy studies: what does harmonisation do to local policies and practices, and what mechanisms of power are invoked when pressure is exerted to align national structures and policies with a larger educational space? If we acknowledge that global governance is more than merely accrued national governance systems, extrapolated at the international level, we understand the urgency of understanding how transnational social movements, networks, and linkages (including public–private), have diminished state autonomy in agenda setting, policy formulation, and implementation.

Understanding the Logic of Systems and Cases

Many authors in this book have chosen local policy context as the primary site for understanding policy borrowing and lending. A few explicitly link their framework with larger theories. For example, some of us find the theory of self-referential systems (closely associated with the work of Niklas Luhmann) suitable as a lens for analysing the inner workings of a system that precedes, accompanies, or results, from policy transfer. We have applied the theory as an interpretive framework to understand select systems regardless of whether the 'system' constitutes an educational system, a local education authority, a non-governmental organisation, an aid agency, or any other living entity that involves actors. We deliberately use the terms 'case' and 'system' interchangeably, because methodologically a case is a bounded system with its own 'causal web' (Tilly 1997) that connects the large number of variables in the case/system. The synonym, however, only makes sense if case study methodology is carried out rigorously, that is, if the emphasis is placed upon examining the causal web, and the interrelations within one and the same case or bounded system.

A few examples may help illustrate the features of this particular approach to deciphering the logic, or inner workings, of a system or case. In a landmark study on educational knowledge, Schriewer and Martinez (2004) examined flagship educational research journals in three countries: Spain, Russia/Soviet Union, and PR China. They noticed considerable fluctuation with regard to space allocated to international scholarship, as measured in the number and type of foreign bibliographical references made in the journal articles, of the three respective countries. Schriewer and Martinez found that 'socio-logic' (particularly political developments in a given country) was a better predictor of receptiveness towards international scholarship, than an external logic as manifested in the ever-expanding transnational network of educational researchers.

In fact, the era of greatest convergence with regard to educational knowledge was in the 1920s and 1930s, when educational researchers in Spain, the Soviet Union, and China were drawn to the work of John Dewey. Once that brief period was over, Dewey was dropped from the reference list in Soviet educational journals, and replaced by Nadezhda Krupskaya (Lenin's wife). It is striking that against all expectations of international convergence theorists, educational knowledge in the three countries did not become more internationalised after the mid-1980s, when all three opened their ideological boundaries, and increased international cooperation. Even though Schriewer and Martinez's (2004) justification for the case selection leans on a problematic notion of culture and 'civilisation', the design and methodology of the study is compelling and well-suited for analysing international convergence/divergence processes.

Similarly, we drew on the theory of self-referential systems in *How NGOs React*, to analyse the logic of the Soros Foundation Network (Silova and Steiner-Khamsi 2008). We compared the Soros Foundation Network – a combination of donor agency and implementation agency – with other donors operating in the post-socialist region. We found that donor logic was instrumental for shaping the programmatic priorities, implementation modalities, as well as the exit strategies that various organisations pursued in the region. Donor logic also provided clues for understanding how organisations define aid effectiveness, sustainability, and other key concepts in development work. Our study of the Soros Foundation Network was meant to contribute to the larger body of scholarship analysing bilateral and multilateral external assistance, against the backdrop of foreign-policy goals, economic gains, and other rationales for aid (e.g. Alesina and Dollar 2000; Riddell 2007). Examination of Soros Network Foundation's donor logic not only contributed to the larger field of donor logic research, but also showed how the theory of self-referential systems could be enlisted to do so.

Focus on 'socio-logic' (Schriewer and Martinez 2004), or on 'donor logic' (Silova and Steiner-Khamsi 2008), represent just two examples of how the causal web of a bounded system, or case, may be explored. A third type of research that attempts to distil the inner workings of a network focuses on processes of 'translation' that occur when a reform from elsewhere is selectively borrowed, recontextualised, and then implemented, in a new system. In fact, it is accurate to state that the great bulk of policy borrowing and lending research consists of studies on reception, translation, and selective policy borrowing. These are carried out with the intention of understanding the logic of a particular local institution: the educational system of the country under study.

The work on socio-logic, donor logic, or institutional logic, illuminates three research areas in which system theory has much to offer. I see the contours of a fourth nascent field of research: the investigation of 'sector logic', particularly a comparison between the logic of the educational sector, versus the logic of the economic sector. There is nothing exciting about revisiting the discussion on how economic thinking crept into the educational discourse, but it would be novel to examine in greater detail how economic thinking was recontextualised, and adapted, to suit an educational logic as a result of policy transfer. Arguably, the turn of the century saw no scarcity of research literature pointing out the contradictions of market-oriented educational reform when applied to the education sector. It is noticeable that as educational researchers we find it easier to ponder the rationality/irrationality principles of others than our own. The dissection of one's own educational logic is a topic that is likely too close for comfort. Even though educational researchers are masters at defining the key principles, or the 'logic', of the economy (e.g. supply/demand, profit, competition, accountability, etc.), we have shied away from elaborating on the educational logic that is genuine to the education sector.

The new generation of policy borrowing and lending researchers, however, is expected to produce groundbreaking work in this area. For example, the study of transsectoral policy transfer between the economic and the educational sectors in Sweden, produced by Florian Waldow (2007), is a start in this promising new direction. From a system theory perspective, the following research questions are currently understudied: how are policies that are borrowed from other sectors or subsystems (e.g. economy, health sector, church, family) translated, re-interpreted and modified, in the education sector or subsystem? To what extent does this act of translation reflect an 'educational logic'? How does the educational system deal with incongruences, contradictions, and inconsistencies in the subsystem that arise when the transferred policy could not sufficiently be translated or recontextualised to suit the logic of the educational system? For us, these incongruences, contradictions, and inconsistencies are not merely 'loose coupling', or some kind of unpleasant 'noise' that is best ignored. On the contrary, they provide important clues for understanding the idiosyncrasies of a system, case, or an institution, including the education sector.

Methodological Repercussions of 'Policyscapes'

One section of this book is dedicated to the study of travelling reforms or, in a more comprehensive manner, the study of policyscapes. It would be wrong to assume that these two terms – travelling reforms and policyscapes – should be used interchangeably. The latter evokes a 'globalisation optique', and calls for a critical reflection on national educational systems as a unit of analysis. I will reiterate here what I have presented earlier in terms of the innovativeness of the 'policyscapes' as presented by Stephen Carney in his award-winning article, published in 2009 (Carney 2009; see Steiner-Khamsi 2010).

Carney's coinage of the term 'policyscapes' advanced ongoing debates over contextual comparison and case study methodology. How is the case significant? What does it represent? These questions not only provoke unease among qualitative researchers, they are the Achilles' heel of the single country study. Carney's work accounts for many vulnerabilities in the comparative case study method. Most notable are the central questions of what a case stands for, and the fate of nation-state analysis in an era of globalisation.

In his study of educational reforms and practices in Denmark (5 million residents), Nepal (26 million residents), and China (1.3 billion residents), Carney combines vertical with horizontal comparison. The former involves different levels, sites, and actors *within* a country/case, while the latter addresses issues *across* the three countries/cases. Several interpretive frameworks inform his method, notably Arjun Appadurai's notion of flows (Appadurai 1996), as well as James Ferguson's idea of state spatiality encompassing horizontal (across states), and vertical (within nation-states), dimensions (Ferguson 2006). Carney extracts elements from each to coin the term 'policyscapes', denoting how the transnational flow of hyperliberal policies permeates every level, transforms every aspect, and affects each actor, in an educational system.

Precisely because globalisation is ubiquitous, every case enables us to understand the transnational character of educational policies and practices. Any site, level of analysis, or actor within a given case(s), qualifies for comparison. As a corollary, Carney compares three different countries, three different levels (higher education, general education, non-university-based teacher education), and two different areas of reform (governance and management systems, curriculum reform). By comparing different cases, levels, and areas, he stretches the conventional rules of cross-national comparison. The two key questions in contextual comparison – case selection (what do the selected cases stand for?), and comparability (can they be compared?) – are addressed convincingly. The *tertium comparationis* between the three cases – Denmark, Nepal, China – is the transnational dimension, the policyscape. Policyscapes, suggestions regarding multi-level analysis (Mark Bray), vertical case studies (Frances Vavrus and Lesley Bartlett), or video-cued multivocal ethnography (Joseph Tobin), are all methods of inquiry that help us overcome the methodological nationalism implied in many comparative studies, particularly those that deal with cross-national comparison.

Deciphering Projections in Cross-National Policy Attraction

I started out this chapter by highlighting the methodological approach that most authors of this book have in common: we believe that policy borrowing and lending has more to do with what is occurring in the local policy context, than with best practices, or effective policies, that await transfer from somewhere else. Over the past few years, scholars have started to analyse the reception of TIMSS, or PISA, in national media accounts, and also examined the second-guessing and lively public debate over what system variables in a given country's educational system accounted for students' outstanding test results. Arguably, the educational systems of Singapore and Finland (league leaders in TIMSS and PISA, respectively), have received so many accolades for their teacher education systems, that policy makers from Ohio to Japan to Germany project features into these two systems that have nothing to do with reality (Takayama 2010, Waldow 2010).

With this in mind, Florian Waldow and Keita Takayama (both in this book), use a culturalist approach to take study of policy transfer a step further, and examine (national) projections into another country's educational system. Takayama's recent study on how policy makers in Japan reframed policy talk to emulate, at least rhetorically, the 'Finish PISA success', has attracted great attention among comparative education scholars. Similarly, Florian Waldow analysed the reasons for cross-national policy attraction in Germany. He introduced the term 'projections' to denote the (German) socio-logic that shaped the distorted, simplified, and at times contradictory, presentation of the Finnish school system in the media. In the cases of Japan and Germany, policy makers reframed, or 'Finnlandised', ongoing debates in their country, that had little to do with why Finnish students performed exceptionally well in the PISA studies.

As with other researchers that focus on local policy context, Waldow and Takayama use the study of policy projections as a methodological tool for identifying protracted policy conflict in a national context. A forthcoming generation of scholars – perhaps the fourth generation of policy borrowing and lending researchers – will turn their attention to analysing how national policy agendas are projected into so-called 'international standards'. Indeed, it is striking that international standards are defined differently depending on the country, case, or system in which they are employed.

Traditionally, the *World Yearbook of Education* has been closely associated with comparative education research. It bodes well for the future of comparative policy studies that two recognised policy borrowing and lending researchers, Carney and Takayama, were awarded the George Bereday Award for best article in the journal *Comparative Education Research* in two subsequent years, 2010 and 2011 (Carney 2009; Takayama 2010). There seems to be a shared understanding that travelling reforms, a long-standing research area of comparative education, has visibly expanded its target audience over the past few years. No doubt, the study of policy borrowing and lending has generated a heightened interest in the broader educational research and policy studies communities. The fascination with the topic is likely to grow further, given the promising new avenues of research that contributors to this book have proposed.

References

Alesina, A. and Dollar, D. (2000) 'Who gives foreign aid to whom and why?' *Journal of Economic Growth*, 5 (1): 33–63.

Anderson-Levitt, K. (ed.) (2003) *Local Meanings, Global Schooling: Anthropology and world culture theory*, New York: Palgrave.

Appadurai, A. (1996) *Modernity at Large: Cultural Dimensions of Globalization*, Minneapolis: University of Minnesota Press.

Bennett, C. J. and Howlett, M. (1992) 'The lessons of learning: reconciling theories of policy learning and policy change', *Policy Sciences*, 25: 275–294.

Carney, S. (2009) 'Negotiating policy in an age of globalization: exploring educational 'policyscapes' in Denmark, Nepal, and China', *Comparative Education Review*, 53 (1): 63–88.

Coulby, D., Ozga, J., Popkewitz, T. S., and Seddon, T. (eds) (2006) *World Yearbook in Education 2006: Education Research and Policy*, London: Routledge.

Cowen, R. (2009) 'The transfer, translation and transformation of educational processes: And their shape-shifting?' *Comparative Education*, 45 (3): 315–327.

Dolowitz, S. P. and Marsh, D. (2000) 'Learning from abroad: the role of policy transfer in contemporary policy-making', *Governance: An International Journal of Policy and Administration*, 13 (1): 5–24.

Ferguson, J. (2006) *Global Shadows: Africa in the Neo-Liberal World Order*, Durham, NC: Duke University Press.

Finegold, D., McFarland, L., and Richardson, W. (eds) (1993) *Something Borrowed? Something Learned? The Transatlantic Market in Education and Training Programs*, Washington, DC: Brookings.

Hall, P. A. (1993) 'Policy paradigms, social learning, and the State: the case of economic policymaking in Britain', *Comparative Politics*, 25 (3): 275–296.

Nóvoa, A. and Lawn, M. (eds) (2002) *Fabricating Europe: The Formation of an Education Space*, London: Kluwer.

Phillips, D. (2004) 'Toward a theory of policy attraction in education', in G. Steiner-Khamsi (ed.) *The Global Politics of Educational Borrowing and Lending*, New York: Teachers College Press.

Riddell, R. C. (2007) *Does Foreign Aid Really Work?* Oxford: Oxford University Press.

Sabatier, P. A. (ed.) (2007) *Theories of the Policy Process*, Boulder, CO: Westview, 2nd edition.

Schriewer, J. and Martinez, C. (2004) 'Constructions of internationality in education', in G. Steiner-Khamsi (ed.) *The Global Politics of Educational Borrowing and Lending*, New York: Teachers College Press.

Seddon, T. (2005) 'Travelling policy in post-socialist education', *European Educational Research Journal*, 4 (1): 1–4.

Silova, I. (2005) *From Sites of Occupation to Symbols Of Multiculturalism: Transfer of Global Discourse and the Metamorphosis of Russian Schools in Post-Soviet Latvia*, Greenwich, CT: Information Age Publishing.

Silova, I. and Steiner-Khamsi, G. (eds) (2008) *How NGOs React: Globalization and Education Reform in the Caucasus, Central Asia and Mongolia*, Bloomfield, CT: Kumarian Press.

Steiner-Khamsi, G. (2010) 'The politics and economics of comparison', *Comparative Education Review*, 54 (3): 323–342.

Steiner-Khamsi, G. and Quist, H. O. (2000) 'The politics of educational borrowing: reopening the case of Achimota in British Ghana', *Comparative Education Review*, 44 (3): 272–299.

Takayama, K. (2010) 'Politics of externalization in reflexive times: reinventing Japanese education reform discourses through "Finnish success"', *Comparative Education Review*, 54 (1): 51–75.

Tilly, C. (1997) 'Means and ends of comparison in macrosociology', *Comparative Social Research*, 16: 43–53.

Tobin, J., Hsueh, Y., and Karasawa, M. (2009) *Preschool in Three Cultures Revisited: China, Japan, and the United States*, Chicago: University of Chicago Press.

Vavrus, F. (2004) 'The referential web: externalization beyond education in Tanzania', in G. Steiner-Khamsi (ed.) *The Global Politics of Educational Borrowing and Lending*, New York: Teachers College Press.

Waldow, F. (2007) *Ökonomische Strukturzyklen und internationale Diskurskonjunkturen: Zur Entwicklung der schwedischen Bildungsprogrammatik, 1930–2006*, Frankfurt am Main: Peter Lang.

Waldow, F. (2010) 'Der Traum vom "skandinavisch schlau Werden" – Drei Thesen zur Rolle Finnlands als Projektionsfläche in der gegenwärtigen Bildungsdebatte', *Zeitschrift für Pädagogik*, 56 (4): 497–511.

Watts, D. J. (2003) *Six Degrees: The Science of a Connected Age*, New York: Norton.

Part I
Agencies of Transfer

2 Towards a Critical Grammar of Education Policy Movements

Roger Dale and Susan L. Robertson

Over the past two decades there has been an exponential growth in research papers on theorising the movement of policy ideas and practices, including those concerned with education, across national territorial boundaries, and the implications this has for the contexts into which it enters. A series of different terms are used to describe this phenomenon, ranging from policy transfer to policy borrowing, policy learning, policy mobility and policy travel (see Steiner-Khamsi 2004). All have as a common concern an attempt to understand the mobilisation, movement, and spread of education policy and practice across global space. And whilst the movement of policy, largely from central governments into specific localities, is not a new concern in policy studies, particularly those concerned with implementation, it would seem that the dynamics broadly associated with globalisation (cross border flows of ideas, people, technology, ideas, finance) have stimulated a fresh wave of interrogations, reflections and outputs on this topic. In other words, the globalisation of education policy and practice, as transfer, borrowing, learning, and so on, creates explanatory and normative burdens that differ from, and go beyond, those generated by analyses of the movement of policy in a national context.

This insight clearly raises the important issue of what we might learn about processes of globalisation and education that are stimulated by debates over the transfer of policy and practice across national borders. Our aim in this chapter is to elaborate some of the analytic consequences of the changing topology, geography and geology, of those debates. We see these changes as, themselves, consequences of the changes brought about to the world and the study of education policy, and its transfer, by the forces of globalisation. Like others, these changes have transformed the worlds we inhabit and experience, and consequently the ways we might understand those worlds.

Our strategy for opening up a debate about policy transfer is to place centre stage the globalisation of the Bologna Process, a political project aimed at transforming the form, scope and nature of higher education architectures across more than 46 European countries and beyond. We chose to focus on Bologna on the basis that it is possibly the most extensive and successful example of 'policy transfer' in education ever, to think about the globalisation of the education policy and practice more generally. Our strategy will be to consider the picture of Bologna that emerges from the kinds of account of it that draw broadly on the policy transfer/borrowing literature and the frameworks it is based on, and to compare that with an alternative, critical political economy approach to understanding globalisation and education. Our position is broadly that Bologna could not have happened without the changes brought about by globalisation, that it can be seen fundamentally as a response to globalisation in higher education as well as constituting globalisation, and that understanding it entails revising the assumptions on which studies of policy transfer draw. Those assumptions were developed in a context dominated by conceptions of international transfer, and we will suggest that a different approach to the understanding of Bologna, drawing on conceptions of the transnational framing of policy, on the one hand, and on critical policy studies, on the other, can provide a different picture and account of the Process. In essence this involves us in 'problematising the problematic' of policy transfer in the fullest of senses of what this implies; as an approach to framing, naming and explaining the duality of motion and fixity of education policy in a globalising world.

Very briefly, the Bologna Declaration, setting up what became known as the Bologna Process and the European Higher Education Area, was signed in 1999 by the Ministers of Education of 29 European countries, including not only all member states of the European Union but other European countries as well. It is a non-binding intergovernmental agreement whose aims were to enhance the employability and mobility of citizens and to increase the international attractiveness and competitiveness of European higher education. As we will see in our analysis of Bologna, the stated aims/outputs are not necessarily the same as the implicit outcomes (quite apart from the related discussion about the actual aims/outputs). Its basis was a common degree architecture based on two main cycles, a three-year undergraduate degree and a two-year master's degree. Following that beginning, it has continued to grow; in scope – it now has ten 'action lines', all accepted by all members; in membership – it now has 47 members; in 'density' – the Bologna Follow Up Group, composing representatives of all member countries, was set up to advance the process and organise the bi-annual Ministers meetings, while the European Commission plays a major role in funding and enabling the Process; and in scale – versions of Bologna have been adopted across the world. The Bologna Process aims at creating convergence around its various action lines and is not intended to standardise European higher education, while emphasising the importance of diversity.

Our basic procedure will be to articulate different accounts and pictures of Bologna generated and provided by contrasting two possible explanations. One approach we call an 'orthodox policy transfer approach', the second a 'critical policy movements approach'. We will then develop our analysis through deploying a complex, 'doubly articulated' argument. And whilst we will represent this as a series of moves, in reality these are mutually constitutive moments.

Our first move is to bring into view the changing place of education in a globalising world, and the implications of these changes for how we look at, and theorise, these relations. These changes include the role of the state, the rescaling of education governance, the changing role of the national, and transformations in wider agendas shaping the role, scope and place of education in a globally competitive world. In a second move, we specify in more detail the key features of the two contrasting approaches – 'orthodox policy transfer approach' as opposed to a 'critical policy movements approach' – and the explanations each offer of the globalisation of the

Bologna Process as a concrete case of the globalisation of education. Specifically we take the two different literatures as the basis for developing a series of contrasting elements of the two distinct explanatory frameworks, or conceptual grammars, whose individual components have at least elective meta-theoretical affinities with each other. In a third, and final move, we reiterate the key elements of a conceptual grammar for the critical analysis of education policy movements across territorial boundaries.

Move One: Locating Education, and Policy Movements, in a Globalising World

In our first move, we bring into view the changing place and forms of education in a globalising world, and the implications of these changes for how we look at, and theorise these relations. We note that though there is considerable debate over precisely how best to define globalisation (Scholte 2005), there is broad agreement that it is an historical process involving the uneven development and partial and contingent transformation of political, economic and cultural structures, practices and social relations (Hobsbawm 1999; Jessop 1999; Mittelman 2004; Scholte 2005). Crucial in these unfolding processes is the rise of powerful globalising actors; the intensification of capital accumulation; new political, social and class struggles (Harvey 2006); and the denationalisation and transformation of policies, capital, political subjectivities, urban spaces, temporal frameworks (Sassen 2006: 1). Having said this, it is also important to note that globalisation is also taking place within as well as beyond national boundaries.

One of the key effects of globalisation on education is an evident shift away from a predominantly national education system to a more fragmented, multi-scalar and multi-sectoral distribution of activity that now involves new players, new ways of thinking about knowledge production and distribution, and new challenges in terms of ensuring the distribution of opportunities for access and social mobility (Dale and Robertson 2008). One way of conceptualising the changing nature, scope and sites involved in the work of education is to see a new 'functional and scalar division of the labour of education' emerging (see Dale 2003).

More broadly, these emerging social structures of the world demand new knowledges so that we might understand better a new ontology of world order (Cox 2002). Ulrich Beck (2002), for instance, has argued that the global transformation of modernity calls for rethinking the humanities and social sciences. He argues that the study of globality and globalisation has revolutionised the social sciences as these processes call into question the deeply held national assumptions that have historically shaped the development of modern social sciences. Like Cox (2002), what is at issue for Beck (2002) is that it is not possible to understand changes in the nature of the relationship between social structures and our knowledge of the world with tools that are no longer fit for purpose. We require a new lexicon, Beck argues, to describe social phenomena that is not dependent upon what he colourfully refers to as 'zombie' categories – such as 'national states', 'identities', 'classes' and so on.

The Globalisation of Policy and Policy Transfer as Explanation

There has been a lively and continuing debate about the nature, purposes and outcomes of policy borrowing more generally (see Dolowitz and Marsh 2000; James and Lodge 2003; Rose 1993) which enables us to consider the phenomenon and its conceptualisation across wider canvases. Two reasons underlie the basis of the distinction between the policy transfer literature and the approach we will try to advance, and in particular, the way they represent and account for phenomena, such as the Bologna Process. The first is that the possibility of other outcomes than those related to the purpose and outcomes of what is seen as 'transfer' becomes very limited, especially since the dominant theme in the transfer literature seems to be how 'successful' the transfer is, and frequently how effective it is. This is linked to the second reason, which concerns what it is to be explained and how. When the issue of the 'success' of the transplant, and of the reasons for that are so prominent, this inevitably – and rightly in their own terms – frames both the conceptualisation of the problem and the theoretical and methodological tools to be deployed, in order to account for the relative 'success' of the transfer.

A very useful summary of 'conventional political science understanding of policy transfer' has recently been provided by Jamie Peck and Nik Theodore (2010). They suggest that these accounts:

> typically posit the existence of a relatively unstructured policy market within which producer-innovators and consumer-emulators engage in freely chosen transactions, adopting policy products that maximize reform goals. In this rational-actor environment, policy transfers are stylized as a distinctively conspicuous category of boundary-crossing practice, the occurrence of which is (implicitly or explicitly) traced to superior performance in exporting juris-dictions . . . (becoming)' in effect, success stories, and as such . . . objects of emulation and learning. (They are) . . . predominantly concerned with ex post facto evaluations of "successful" transfers, often in situations of observed or alleged convergence, which are typically judged according to surface similarities in policy designs, scripts, and rationales.
>
> (Peck and Theodore 2010: 169)

One basic difference between the two sets of problematisations, then, is that the 'orthodox' literature attempts to address the questions 'How does Bologna work?' and 'What are its domestic effects?', while what we see as the most important questions generated by the Bologna phenomenon are 'What work does it do, and for whom?' and 'What is the framework through which it realises this'? There are both 'internal' and 'external' differences between the 'orthodox' approaches and those we are seeking to advance. On the one hand, seeing Bologna as a form of policy transfer is made very difficult in so far as the 'transferers' and the 'recipients' are essentially the same people – national ministers and ministries responsible for higher education. On the other hand, while, of course, both foci are necessary, rather than focussing on the *context of Bologna* (where did it come from and what makes it like it is?), the orthodox emphasis is very much on '*Bologna as context*' (how does it affect national higher education?).

Globalising European Higher Education Policy: The Intriguing Challenge of How to Explain the Bologna Process

Bologna may be seen as possibly the most extensive and effective means of bringing about levels of convergence of education policy so far witnessed, yet it shares few of the elements and mechanisms that are associated with existing studies of policy transfer. This difference is due largely to the changing circumstances – especially those we short-handedly refer to as globalisation – in which Bologna emerged and developed. Bologna has spawned a very large literature, much of which adopts similar assumptions to, or is more or less explicitly based on, the mainstream policy-transfer literature. We learn a lot from that work about the nature of national higher-education systems, and their responses to attempts to 'modernise' them on a common basis, and about how conceptions of 'the university' are also undergoing sometimes radical changes. However, such approaches do not enable us to capture as effectively as they might what is distinctive about the relationships between globalisation and higher education. They represent in essence a 'stretching' of previous conceptual frameworks that is ultimately limiting of the possibilities of analysis. Many of these studies resemble what we have referred to elsewhere as a set of methodological 'isms', in their adherence to a particular set of assumptions whose validity and relevance are taken for granted, even when the political, economic, social and educational conditions that they were developed to analyse have altered in highly significant and relevant ways.

The basis of our problematisation of the problematic encapsulated in the concept 'policy transfer' is that it assumes and is based on conceptions of the world that are losing their validity as globalisation advances. Our argument will be that for all its sophistication and relevance, this body of work does illustrate clearly what we take to be the under-recognition of the nature and importance of the changes in both the 'real' world and in our tools for analysing it consequent on the changes that are referred to as globalisation.

Move Two: Two Contrasting Perspectives on the Globalisation of the Bologna Process as Policy Movement

As signalled above, we intend to contrast two different approaches to the understanding of the Bologna Process as policy transfer/policy circulation and the kind of explanation they produce. Table 2.1 provides an overview of their differences – around the purpose of theory in explanation, the key meta-assumptions made in the globalisation of education, the level of analysis, criteria for determining effect, process through which movement is explained, and methodology. We do not view these categories as exhaustive, but rather starting points for a discussion and further elaboration. For instance, there are important differences around space and scale that we do not address here but which feature very differently in these two contrasting explanations of Bologna as policy transfer.

The Purpose of Theory: Problem Solving or Critical

We begin the process of contrasting explanations of the globalisation of education policy/policy transfer by pointing to different conceptions of the *purpose* of theory in the two perspectives. The importance of this is announced in Robert Cox's famous declaration that 'all theory is for someone and for some purpose' (1996: 87). We use Cox's distinction between what he refers to as broadly critical theory and a problem solving approach to problematise the key categories that we use to approach the analysis of education in a globalising world.

Using Cox's work on problem solving and critical theory we argue that education policy transfer theories, if and when applied in fundamentally unchanged form to provide accounts of 'post-globalisation' phenomena, such as Bologna, can be seen as essentially 'problem solving' and as offering accounts that limit the range of analytical focus; view the object of inquiry as discrete and disconnected from wider processes; view the movement of policy travel as unidirectional, horizontal, relatively unhindered by topographies, and converging; and whose methodologies reinforce singularity rather than multiplicity and plurality. We argue that policy-transfer accounts of the Bologna Process reveal only partial accounts of the complexity and dynamism of Bologna as policy. A more critical political economy account of the globalisation of Bologna as education policy would bring into view the significance of wider contexts and social relations in framing, constructing, circulating, receiving, contextualising, materialising and institutionalising Bologna, as education policy. For instance, the movement of key elements of the Bologna Process, such as Tuning, into the US and Latin America, the intense debate in the US about Bologna as a possible threat to US hegemony in higher education (see Adelman 2009), the reaction in Australia to the Bologna Process because of what it might mean to its share of the international student market, all have been key dynamics in shaping the forms, directions and consequences of Bologna, well beyond the European higher education area (Jayasuriya 2010; Robertson 2010; Robertson and Keeling 2008). Nor should we see the Bologna Process as being simply about higher education. Rather, it has emerged as an instrument of foreign policy, of trade, labour mobility, as a mechanism

Table 2.1 'Orthodox' and 'critical' explanations of globalisation and education

	'Orthodox policy transfer'	*'Critical policy movements'*
Purpose	Problem solving	Critical
Meta-assumptions	'Isms'	Beyond 'isms'
Scale of analysis	Middle range (empirical and abstraction)	Multi-level (empirical and abstraction)
Criteria for identifying the globalisation of education	Convergence	Change
Process	Diffusion, transmission	Logic of intervention programme ontology
Methodology	Comparison-lite	Incorporated comparison

of state-building, and as a means for Europe to build itself as a region. These developments in turn transform our understandings of higher education, of knowledge, citizenship, rule and sovereignty (Dale 2008). The contours of these changes would also all demand rigorous interrogation. Given this, explanations that tend to depend on perspectives that view the world and its social categories as if they were static and universal, as in problem solving, limit our understanding of these processes. And as Gavin Smith (2006) points out, 'a whole series of key concepts for the understanding of society derive their power from appearing to be just what they always were, and derive their instrumentality from taking on quite different forms' (p. 628). This leads us to the second category for comparison – what we call 'isms'.

Meta-Assumptions: Isms or Beyond Isms?

Elsewhere we have argued that problem-solving as a set of meta-assumptions leads to a set of tendencies or 'isms' in the study of education policy (see Dale and Robertson 2008; Robertson and Dale 2009). Our intention in pointing to these 'isms' in the study of globalisation and education is to suggest they limit our ability to *see* the full extent of changes taking place. By 'ism' we mean the 'tendency to see categories, such a 'education', 'private' or 'knowledge' as 'natural, fixed, and unchanging – or in other words, as ontologically and epistemologically ossified' (Robertson and Dale 2008: 20). We identified four isms at work in analyses of globalisation and education: 'methodological nationalism', 'methodological statism', 'methodological educationism' and 'spatial fetishism' (pp. 21–29) (see also Table 2.1). By 'methodological nationalism' we mean the assumption that the nation state is viewed as the container of society, and that education in this equation is contained solely within this container. By 'methodological statism', we mean the tendency to see that there is a universal form of the state – the Westphalian state – with a common configuration of institutions, and mechanisms of governance. By 'methodological educationism', we refer to the tendency to see it as describing a system that is made up of a universally true configuration of actors and activities. And, by 'spatial fetishism', we mean the tendency to reify and naturalise processes, like globalisation, as in 'globalisation does' or 'the local is', locking us into atemporal and ahistorical analyses (Robertson and Dale 2009: 28).

A fundamental assumption underlying much analysis of the relationship between education and globalisation concerns how far globalisation represents 'something new, distinct and different'; a break or rupture with what has gone before, and how far it represents continuity, albeit with quite harsh differences appearing, with what we have known before. It is notable that in the orthodox approach, globalisation is seen as 'exterior', as part of 'the context' shaping national education systems. Education may be shaped by, directed by, influenced by, dominated by, its contexts but there is rarely the implication that it is, for instance, either on the one hand constituted by its contexts or, on the other, continuous with them, or indeed that education and globalisation are co-constitutive.

Yet even when globalisation is taken as exterior, it is rarely analysed in the sense of a key *context of context*. Here, on the one hand, in the orthodox approach, globalisation is seen as 'exterior'; as too 'big', and complex, and concerned with economic and social issues, to be easily taken into account when looking at the details of education policy and provision. Yet on the other hand, education itself is at least implicitly seen to be too complex, too nationally-culturally informed, too path dependent, too 'nationally controlled' for it to be vulnerable to globalisation, except through the idea of convergence. That is, its sectoral, cultural, institutional, etc. integrity at a national level, and its ties to national purposes, make it a difficult proposition for globalisation. It might be expected to be among the last institutions to be significantly changed by globalisation.

Such assumptions form much of the interpretive frameworks and filters through which, at its broadest, the study of 'the globalisation of education' is approached. For instance, they tend to produce studies and theories of the middle range (in both the senses of that term – empirical and abstraction). In essence, they represent the collective wisdom/assumptions of the isms, what makes the isms so powerful in education. The dominant kind of analysis that this produces is comparison, of national case studies, with 'convergence' the key axis of comparison/measurement. Our argument is not that any of these elements are 'wrong', individually or collectively, but rather that they generate two theoretical/methodological ensembles which are likely to provide very different kinds of questions and answers about the relationships between globalisation and education.

If we turn to the expansion of the Bologna Process beyond its initial launch, an orthodox account might view its extension into the wider European space and beyond as being advanced by the European Universities Association; a European-level association made up of rectors/administrators or their delegates from member states. Whilst it most certainly is the case that the EUA have played a critical role in the development and expansion of Bologna since 1999, to leave our analysis there would be to take at face value a common explanation for the presence, and purpose, of Bologna. It would also mean accepting the view that any changes in the architecture of higher education for signatory countries were largely technical matters. However, these architectures are, in themselves, forms of selectivity for what knowledges are possible, and what are not; why these particular kinds of packaging were central to the development of a competitive Europe, and so on. In essence, the Bologna Process needs to be viewed, not just as a higher-education reform, but a reform that has altered what it means to talk about knowledge, the university, student mobility, a national higher education system, higher education as a public good, and so on.

Scale of Analysis: Middle Range or Multi-Level?

Our argument here is that the 'orthodox' analysis is largely pitched at what is known as a 'middle range'. There are two main axes across which the concept of middle range theory is elaborated, those of abstraction and level of focus.[1] The first runs from the abstract to the concrete, and the second from what is generally referred to as the micro to the macro. Our argument is that studies of the relationships between globalisation and education typically tend to fall around and focus upon the 'middle' of both axes. On the one hand, the size and complexity and inaccessibility typically attributed to 'globalisation' tend to deter or discourage direct analysis of it, both empirically and conceptually. The perceived empirical and theoretical complexity both lead towards the development of middle-range approaches. Empirically, coming to terms with globalisation as a complex whole appears a daunting task. The response to this is often to seek to reduce both its size and complexity. Rather than looking at 'the global' as a whole, there is a tendency to try to reduce it to a more manageable scale, for instance through the use of proxies, such as quantitative scales; or 'intermediate' scales, such as regional rather than global; or choosing particular institutions taken as representative or typical of globalisation, such as McDonaldisation, or international organisations; or focusing on 'a limited range of cases that are unified in space and/or time' (Thelen 1999); or identifying a concept that enables several different cases to be discussed on a similar footing, of which policy transfer could be seen to be an excellent example. So, more generally, we may see that the concept of 'policy transfer', or borrowing, falls clearly into the middle-range category.

Theoretically, the focus tends to be on discerning and describing the 'effects of' globalisation, and in particular using such criteria as 'convergence' as automatic proxies for the 'degree of' globalisation (see below). This eschewing of the search for more complex explanations is reinforced by the tendency to

work our way up inductively from a 'messy' empirical reality and building our explanations from such patterns as we can uncover descriptively . . . (However) without a general theory of some kind to orient this procedure, analysis will generate only localised, 'middle range' hypotheses, which lack the capacity to penetrate aspects of causality or agency which extend more deeply into social space or historical time.

(Rosenberg 2007: 467–468)

The problem with such strategies is, of course, that they tend to become fixed, and to move the analytical gaze away from the substantive targets themselves. They may become perceived not only as sufficient in themselves, but as constituting the theoretical and empirical problematic tout court. It is important to emphasise that there is nothing inherently 'wrong' with middle-range theories and approaches; the problems emerge only when they become taken as sufficient rather than as necessary.

One very useful way of illustrating the consequence of the middle range focus is to consider the priority it gives to the concept of 'context'. This is especially noticeable and important in cases where, following the methodological nationalist assumptions of most comparative education, in studies concerned with the relationship between globalisation and education, it is 'the national' that comes to occupy the middle ground, empirically and analytically. This has a number of consequences, in both areas. In particular, the national becomes seen and represented as the key *context* in the mediation between global structures and local detail. This is perhaps especially the case in comparative studies of education, where the concept of context has been signalled as especially important (see, e.g., Crossley 2000). Here, it is context that mediates and modifies the forces of globalisation, and that gives them local meaning. However, here again, we encounter the problem of the exteriority assumption, that globalisation, national states and education systems are involved in a fundamentally hierarchical, even nested, relationship; this becomes clearer when we see how little 'traffic' there is in these assumptions from local to global. The other element of the problem, which is possibly more important here, is that it means that the 'national' 'context' is by no means still (if it ever was) independent of the forces it is seen to mediate and localise, but to a degree constituted by them. In short, we need to problematise and frame the national rather than to take it as an independent modifying context. In other words (those of Brenner et al. (2010)) we need to identify the context of the (national) context. As they put it, there is a danger that when we are focusing closely on local contingencies and variations, '[w]hat tends to fade into the background . . . is the *context of context* – specifically, the evolving macro-spatial frameworks and interspatial circulatory systems [i.e. 'globalisation'] in which local regulatory projects unfold' (p. 203).

Criteria: Convergence, or Wider Change?

One of the main, almost taken for granted, characteristics of work on the Bologna Process is its national basis; the great majority of studies appear to focus on Bologna's 'effects on' national HE systems and institutions. This in turn influences the research problematic in the direction of the idea of 'convergence'. If so many countries are apparently doing the same things, is one result that they converge over time? As Christoph Knill points out:

> [while] transfer studies investigate the content and process of policy transfer as the dependent variable, [and] while the focus of diffusion research is on the explanation of adoption patterns over time . . . convergence studies place particular emphasis on effects. Transfer and diffusion thus reflect processes which under certain circumstances might result in policy convergence . . . Policy convergence thus describes the end result of a process of policy change over time towards some common point, regardless of the causal processes.
>
> (2005: 4–5)

However, even though, as we have seen, 'convergence' is an officially sanctioned outcome of the Bologna Process, it turns out to be a rather more complex and less helpful concept than appears at first sight. For instance, we need first to ask *what* is converging (input, output, policy, practice, how far, over what period, and with what consequences (Hay 2000). In addition, it is not clear what knowledge of inter-national convergence (of policies, practices, or whatever) tells us on its own. It seems likely to produce an interesting picture rather than one that is useful in policy or analytic terms. And finally, as in the case of making context a key variable, a concentration on the extent of convergence means that other possible forms and outcomes of the relationship between globalisation and education are neglected.

The alternative approaches are based on many of the points we have been making so far about the changing nature and bases of education policy in an era of globalisation. The idea of convergence does reflect the recognition of the extra-national dimension of what is occurring via processes like Bologna, but very much from a perspective that places the national still in the centre, to all intents and purposes unchanged in its scope and authority. The interest is still in whether national systems are changing, rather than in whether what we are witnessing might represent something quite distinct, that does not replace the national, or result in an ultimate merger of all with all where all are alike, or in some kind of lowest common denominator (or more optimistically, highest common factor) solution, but in a novel and distinct entity. And the perspective that arises from a combination of the pictures created by studies of policy transfer, diffusion and convergence is one that makes it difficult to recognise the possibility of Bologna as a form of transnational cooperation, based on common problem perceptions and framings. Such a conception itself rests on a 'context of context' analysis of Bologna. What were the circumstances under which it was possible for what became Bologna to emerge? The more 'immediate' story of the beginnings of Bologna has now been clearly narrated (see Corbett 2005; Croche 2009; Ravinet 2008) and we are well informed about it, and how its history shaped the context that Bologna now is. However, a wider account, of how global changes created opportunity structures for intervention in national education policy making, and especially in national HE policies in Europe, has not been nearly so fully articulated (Dale 2008), nor its consequences fully taken into account in the understanding of Bologna.

Process: Diffusion or Logics of Intervention?

The very term 'diffusion' is suggestive of the theoretical assumptions on which it is based. The essence of this is in the use of an intransitive verb – that is, a verb without a subject – to account for the process being described, which then becomes a process without an agent, a considerable hindrance to effective analysis of the process. This point can be made most clearly though an outstanding and widely quoted theoretical study of diffusion (Strang and Meyer 1993). The essence of the argument is that diffusion occurs through a process of *theorisation*, which 'facilitates communication between strangers by providing a language that does not presume directly shared experience. It provides rationales for adoption that run counter to simple interaction-based processes like direct mimicry and superstitious learning (where adopted practices are temporally rather than causally linked to desired outcomes' (p. 496). However, the problem with agency does not disappear in this argument. There is a strong tendency to make 'theories' the subjects of sentences, with a basic attachment to abstract rationality – the terms in which theorisation is typically couched, and which might be seen to make rational choice on the part of the adopter the key mechanism of diffusion. Thus:

> Theorization specifies why the potential adopter should attend to the behavior of one population and not some other, what effects the practice will have, and why the practice is particularly applicable or needed given the adopter. All this permits the actor to see through the confusing evidence of others' mixed successes and detect the 'true' factors at work. In short, theorization may be regarded as turning diffusion into rational choice.
>
> (p. 500)

Here again, the nature and sources of the theorisation, and the agenc(ies) propelling it, are not alluded to; it is the logic of the theorisation that is the dominant factor, with the authors 'emphasiz[ing] the continuing role of a compelling logic in permitting such movements to gain support, and in defusing self-interested opposition' (p. 495).

Marsh and Sharman (2009) also make the point about diffusion studies typically being based on processes without agents, but they also point out that, by contrast, 'transfer' studies tend to privilege agency, with 'a focus upon who was involved in transfer, how and why' (p. 274). However, there are two other features of policy diffusion and transfer studies that are worth commenting on in this context. One is that, according to Meseguer and Gilardi (2009), most analyses of policy transfer 'make strong *homogenizing assumptions* (such as that) any given mechanism is equally relevant or irrelevant across all cases; it is assumed that all governments are equally keen to engage in learning, are equally reactive to competitive pressures, or equally sensitive to emulative pressures' (p. 531). They go on to argue that there is an implicit model (of diffusion), where each mechanism is sufficient condition for increasing the probability of policy adoption, and in which each mechanism adds to that of the others.

Globalisation's relationship with national education systems does not just 'happen' (as often appears to be the case in studies that use verbs like 'diffusion' intransitively to convey precisely such a sense of freedom from agency, if not spontaneity). It has to be actively brought about, and the 'practical' and theoretical means for doing that always and necessarily rest on what we will refer to as 'logics of intervention'. The question then becomes: 'through what 'logics of intervention' does 'globalisation of education' work? *how* does it contribute to forms of educational provision that are always justified in terms of the *improvements* they will bring about? However, the link between 'educational improvements', and progress and societal improvement, is not automatic and straightforward. Rather, it is mediated and shaped through particular 'logics of intervention', which frame and specify in what ways and through what mechanisms education may be delivered to bring about the desired improvements. The simplest example of *a logic of educational intervention* is the use of curriculum change to bring about educational and wider social change – change what you teach and you will change the learner – a tendency so deep rooted as to seem in no need of explanation.

The logics of Bologna as an intervention are to some extent spelled out in its founding aims – increasing competitiveness, increasing the mobility of labour, increasing the attractiveness of European education, all with a view to improving Europe economically, augmented perhaps by a trickle-down logic. The point here is that understanding Bologna more broadly involves matching the *logic* of intervention to the *means* of intervention – policy transfer – with which in this case its relationship becomes rather complex, given differences of governance and jurisdiction between Europe and member states.

The two approaches differ in the ways that they conceive of the 'how' of the transfer programme, what makes it likely to succeed. In seeking for a way of attempting to find a basis for generalisation of successful (or rejection of unsuccessful) social interventions and innovations, the English sociologist, Ray Pawson (2002), argued that the crucial point is to distinguish between what he calls the 'Programme' and the 'Programme Ontology'. Basically, the Programme is the intervention, or policy, or innovation that is being introduced or implemented with the intention of bringing about beneficial changes in some social phenomenon. The 'Programme Ontology', by contrast, accounts for *how* programmes, policies, etc, actually work. It is essentially the 'theory' of the programme, what makes it work, as opposed to its content alone (and 'the theory' is typically quite likely to be implicit). The clearest example of programme ontology is perhaps that of smoking cures. Pawson argues that it is necessary to compare their ontologies, the ways they are intended to bring about a cessation of smoking; these can vary between hypnotism, nicotine patches, financial rewards, showing lurid videos of poisoned lungs, etc. These all work in different ways, and it is the ways as much as the contents of the programmes that make them effective. According to this perspective it is not 'programmes' that work; rather it is the underlying reasons or resources that they offer subjects that generate change. Causation is also reckoned to be contingent. Whether the choices or capacities on offer in an initiative are acted upon depends on the nature of their subjects and the circumstances of the initiative. The vital ingredients of programme *ontology* are thus its 'generative mechanisms' and its 'contiguous context'' (Pawson 2002: 342). The relevance to the Bologna Process seems clear. Rather than offering a particular foolproof, or indispensable body of content, that was to be taken up as faithfully as possible (in the normal implementation mode), the Bologna Process may, for instance, be more usefully seen as operating as/through a form of 'soft law', offering (its members) reasons and resources that will enable them to generate change in individually distinct but collectively mutually attuned ways.

Methodology: Comparison 'Lite' or Incorporated Comparison

Forms of comparison are central to most studies of the Bologna Process, especially inter-national comparison. However, the forms of comparison practised are not on the whole such as to meet with the approval of the comparative education community, and hence we refer to them as 'comparison-lite'. They are 'comparison-lite' because when we move 'beyond' the national level it is necessary to have some way of constructing a basis for comparability. This necessity inheres in the need to have a basis for assuming that transfers take place both between countries/legislations that can be shown to be sufficiently similar to each other for comparison to be meaningful, and because comparability is essential if we are to be able to judge the value of different polices. Thus, researchers are called on to provide data that allow comparison of policies across nations and that bolster beliefs that policy makers in one country can learn from the success or failure of policy making in another. The 'lite-ness' that this involves is evident from Gail Wilson's (2001) account of uses of comparison in the context of Europe. She comments on the statement that 'Within a more integrated European environment, it is becoming increasingly important to allow access across national and linguistic boundaries so that decision-makers can be provided with a broader, comparative picture of society across the continent' (Matthews and Wilson 2000), '*Such statements imply an approach to the translation of information that will eliminate as much cultural variation as possible in order to produce standardized and comparable data. It is also an approach that obscures the power relations inherent in the production, translation and use of information*' (Wilson 2001: 4, emphasis added). The italicised sentences capture neatly both the essential 'lite-ness' and competitiveness of the comparisons made.

The comparisons can be referred to as competitive, because their purpose is not just to compare, in an analytic sense, but to contrast, in a competitive sense. Such comparison operates as a technology of transnational power – and to provide the basis of reputational competition, between countries and institutions. This has very clear overlaps with what Antonio Nóvoa and Tali Yariv-Mashal (2003) refer to as comparative education as a form of governance, where they 'insist on the importance of comparative approaches as a way to legitimate national policies on the basis of "international measures" . . . which result in the creation and re-creation of 'global signifiers' based on international competition and assessment'.

In essence, this means the purposive elision or standardisation of national differences in pursuit of comparability for the purpose of more efficient and effective government, effectively both making national institutional boundaries more porous and laying the basis for the construction of both reconstructed and reshaped national education sectors and a transnational education sector. In so far as comparative education is complicit in this, it is ironic that that involvement definitively undermines the national basis on which it has rested and taken for granted.

Very briefly, the alternative to this, which is intended to come closer to realising the enormous analytic potential of comparative studies (not confined to the international) within the Bologna Process, is what we call 'theoretically articulated comparison'. The effective use of the comparative method is far from straightforward in studies of globalisation (or Bologna) and education. Within this group we can distinguish explanations that see globalisation as a process, a product, a discourse, a project, and so on. However, in the majority of cases, globalisation is seen as a force external to and affecting individual nation-states and their education systems, and the role of the comparativist is to distinguish between these impacts, and to speculate on their causes. We are thus confronted with a range of studies that are effectively not comparable, because we cannot be sure that they conceive of globalisation – and consequently its relationship with nation states and their education systems – in the same way, irrespective of, and prior to, the nature and effectiveness of the comparisons they make. So, in effect, one of the first moves we should make is to carry out a comparison of the theories that underpin comparative studies and inform the methods they use. This can be the first stage of what we refer to as a process of 'theoretically articulated comparison'.

Cases do not pre-exist theories, nor are they external to them, or independent of them; their 'casing' is always theoretical, even though the theories framing them may be taken for granted, implicit, unarticulated or unrecognised. This is a key element of the difference between articulated and unarticulated (methodological) comparison. Perhaps the commonest form this framing takes in comparative education is its 'methodological nationalism'; the unproblematised assumption that cases are 'naturally' nation-state based.

It is then necessary to interrogate the theoretical construction of the cases on two bases. First, we need to ask, what they are cases *of*. For instance, if we think of the different understandings of globalisation that we mentioned above, we see that each of them sees/constructs globalisation as a case of something different from all the others. Those who see globalisation fundamentally as a discourse will be less interested in the actual practices that might be associated with it than those who see it as a process, for example. Second, we need to consider what we might call their 'explanatory theorem'. What is the logic through which they seek to analyse and elucidate the case that they have constructed? What are the key variables and mechanisms involved, how are they related to each other, in what explanatory sequences/relationships? Having completed these preliminaries, we could then begin to consider how a comparative methodology can be marshalled to both test and maximise the explanatory capacity of the theories.

Move Three: By Way of Conclusion – Towards a Critical Grammar of Education Policy Movement

We are now in a position to draw on the comparisons we have advanced between orthodox 'policy transfer' explanations of Bologna versus a critical account of policy movement in order to lay out the basis for what we think might be some of the elements of a critical grammar of policy movement.

In our discussion of problem-solving versus a critical theory approach to the movement of education policy across borders we argued that a critical theory approach would emphasise their *relational, dialectical* and *co-constitutive* nature. This means placing education policies into a series of contexts – from the production of the policy to its movement and new point of fixity – and that these contexts are themselves understood, not as neutral backdrops or convenient launch and landing places, but as co-constitutive. Here we would be alert to the power of particular ideas to mobilise, materialise and institutionalise political projects in education and other sectors and in constructing pedagogical subjects. And whilst recognising the tendential nature of powerful policies, we also would want to be mindful of the dialectical nature of social events and social outcomes, and that societies themselves are open systems. A critical theory approach also reminds us of the importance of problematising and reflecting upon the tools, or theories, we use to see with – or as we argued, 'problematising the problematic'. This includes locating our theories of the world in those worlds – whose wider 'rules of the game' make possible, visible and commonsensical particular ways of seeing over others. The question that needs posing here is: what kind of work does 'policy transfer' do in constituting social relations and in realising powerful political projects?

This leads to our second point; the need to beware of 'isms' in order to go beyond them. A critical grammar of policy movement would be attentive to the ways in which *categories* are constructed, contain, and order, particular social groups and problems (and not others) making them the object (or not) of education policy interventions and solutions. Naturalising categories enables governing to also take place through the mundane, routine and commonsensical. The purpose of a critical approach is to reveal the constructed nature of categories. In doing so, it brings into view the *power* of some categories to more easily move over topographies, avoiding the frictions of uneven development and difference. The Bologna Process is a good example here of a project able to move across diverse cultural, political and economic topographies and be inserted – its speed of movement and apparent ease of institutionalisation in a new space the result of its multiple faces and the politics of its *contexts of reception*. We also pointed to the need to see key actors and scales of action, such as the state, and the national as a nodal platform for advancing education, as themselves undergoing major changes in geometry, form and reach, with major implications for the sites, structures and subjects of education policy. In other words, we also need to take account of the *context of contexts* which makes some policy problems and their solutions visible and viable, and others not. Jessop (2005) calls this 'structural selectivity'. If policy is moving (as it has), but this time frequently over a more extended (global) space involving national territorial borders, who, how and with what outcomes are education-policy problems and their solutions being constructed, projected, contested and materialised? At the current conjuncture, the movement of education policies and projects across national territorial boundaries raises important questions around the autonomy of national states to determine, and implement, rules for governing which are implicit in the education–state–citizen contract.

The third element of a critical grammar emerged from our discussion on middle-range theory. We argued middle-range theory is premised on a particular conception of the hierarchical nature of the world, and of explanatory frameworks, expressed through the two pairs, simple–complex and abstract–concrete; it 'fixes' theorising at imaginary intermediate points along those two scales, at a point where it is not too simple or too abstract to prevent the emergence of valuable insights and analyses. However, such conceptions assume the relative independence of levels of simplicity or abstraction, rather than the continuity of the two scales. Or, to put it another way, 'simple' depends on a particular conception of 'complex', 'concrete' on a particular conception of 'abstract'. We only know that a theory is a middle-range theory if we know what a more complex and a more abstract theory might look like. In our view this begins to matter when we encounter phenomena that exist at *different levels of complexity* and can be can/need to be *analysed at different levels of abstraction*. Our contention is that the Bologna Process is an excellent example of just such an issue, but more than this, the levels at which it exists themselves interact. One example of this is the existence of 'the global' *in* the local, as well as *exterior* to it, or produced by it – as in the case of Santos's (1995) 'globalised localisms' and 'localised globalisms'.

Fourth, a critical grammar would focus attention on the *logic of intervention* entailed in any policy problem definition and its solution. We mentioned briefly some concrete examples of what we understand by the logic of intervention above, but here we will attempt to elaborate a little further on the assumptions the idea rests on. At their heart is the distinction between *processes, outputs* and *outcomes*, which frequently appear as if they are identical. Very simply, processes are means through which intended or unintended outputs may or may not be effectively produced, and outcomes are the intended or unintended achievements of outputs, that may or may not be effective. It is the distinction between outputs and outcomes that is crucial here. We could take an output as a specific intended goal of a policy – to improve school performance in mathematics, for instance, or to increase the number of foreign students recruited to local universities. Outcomes, by contrast, are the wider goals of the policy – the ultimate purpose of the outputs produced. By focusing on the logic of intervention regarding the Bologna Process, we can see that it is about outcomes rather than outputs. It specifies outputs – the action lines, etc. – but they are seen as means towards a set of outcomes: a stronger Europe, a bigger share of the international market for students, a global presence for Europe, etc. And the logic of intervention applies essentially to outcomes rather than outputs. So, we may see convergent outputs in Bologna, but they should be seen as not only important in themselves, but much more so as a means towards a common outcome.

A fifth element in a critical grammar would problematise claims to convergence, precisely because the specificities of historical institutional structures place limits on replication. Convergence is also a trickier concept than is often recognised. Where it becomes the sole or dominant measure of the success of a policy like Bologna, it tends to crowd out other possible outputs. This isolation of convergence as an output is a logical consequence of the linear, means-end logic that is assumed and followed by many studies of policy transfer; it can be seen to be relevant and measurable. Against this, we favour a more tendential approach, where goals are tendentially generated rather than pre-specified, as in the case of convergence in the linear model. Jessop (2005) offers as an illustration of spatial-scalar divisions of labour (which we may see in the Bologna Process) 'the tendential dissolution of the distinction between foreign and domestic relations' (p. 336). This may clearly be linked to Bologna, as the Process's transnational basis can be substantiated in many more ways than through convergence. For instance, it may lead to increasing differences between conceptions of domestic and external within nation states, as well as changing the nature of external-become-internal relations that is implied by Bologna. As well as crowding out other possible outputs at a national level, a focus on convergence also distracts us from the recognition that 'convergence' can occur at input, output, policy and process levels, as noted above, but needs also to be similarly multiplied when we consider the possible geographical scales of convergence, such as sub-national, national, regional and global.

Finally, a critical grammar would problematise *comparison* as a methodology in the analysis education policy movements. It engages in what we have called *theoretically articulated comparison* (see Dale 2010). In other words, as a conceptual priority, it would spell out the theoretical bases on which the comparison of the cases rests. From there it might ask questions around what is to be learned both substantively and theoretically, but this ought to follow, and not be in place of, theoretically articulated comparison.

Comparative education, as an area of study, has enjoyed a new lease of life under globalisation, and has made a number of moves to respond to the differences that accompany it. However, some of its basic assumptions and propositions have remained in place. In particular, 'lesson-learning', a deeply modernist value, seems to retain a strong position among the rationales for comparative education. Here again, the Bologna Process raises a number of issues that would not have been present in comparative education a quarter of a century ago. It would, for instance, be interesting to harvest responses to the question, 'Who learns what lessons from Bologna?' 'Which practices, at which levels, might others want to emulate?' Interestingly, it is clear from the success of the Bologna global forum, where many countries from outside Europe came to find out more about Bologna, and especially to find out if they might be allowed to join, or be associated with it, that Bologna itself is a process deemed worthy of emulation. However, emulation may not be a wholly correct interpretation of their motivation here; they may not be looking to learn lessons at all, except the lesson that membership of Bologna is likely to be useful in itself, especially given the number of countries already involved – that is, policies may be adopted solely or mainly because they have been adopted by other countries, whether to gain mutual benefits or avoid loss from not being involved (Meseguer and Gilardi 2009). But in the end, our view is that by far the greatest benefit to be gained from comparative studies is the generation of new hypotheses. Properly conducted, comparison is the method that takes us closest to explanation. Lots of red meat here right at the end!

Note

1   It should be noted that there is considerable debate about the concept 'middle range'. There have been multiple different versions of the idea, and it is not wholly clear how its originator, Robert Merton, intended it to be used (see Pawson 2000), though the desire to avoid the twin dangers of American post-war sociology, 'grand theory' and 'abstracted empiricism', was clearly influential, and has continued to inform subsequent discussion. Nevertheless, the continuing popularity of the concept suggests that it does resonate with some of the most basic and challenging problems of social theory and social research, and does fulfil a need in articulating those problems.

References

Adelman, C. (2009) *The Bologna Process for U.S. Eyes: Re-learning Higher Education in the Age of Convergence*, Washington: Institute of Higher Education.

Beck, U. (2002) The cosmopolitan society and its enemies, *Theory, Culture and Society* 19(1–2), 17–44.

Brenner, N., Peck, J. and Theodore, N. (2010) Variegated neoliberalism: geographies, modalities, pathways, *Global Networks* 10(2), 1–41.

Corbett, A. (2005) *Universities and the Europe of Knowledge: Ideas, Institutions and Policy Entrepreneurship in European Union Higher Education Policy, 1955–2005*, Basingstoke: Palgrave Macmillan.

Cox, R. (1996) *Approaches to World Order*, Cambridge: Cambridge University Press.

Cox, R. (2002) *The Political Economy of a Plural World: Critical Reflections on Power, Morals and Civilisation*, London and New York: Routledge.

Croche, S. (2009) The Bologna network: a new sociopolitical area in higher education, *Globalisation, Societies and Education* 7(4), 489–503.

Crossley, M. (2000) Bridging cultures and traditions in the reconceptualisation of comparative and international education. *Comparative Education* 3(3), 319–332.

Dale R. (2003) *The Lisbon Declaration, the Reconceptualisation of Governance and the Reconfiguration of European Educational Space*, paper presented to RAPPE seminar Governance, Regulation and Equity in European Education Systems, Institute of Education, University of London, 20 March.

Dale, R. (2008) Shifting discourses and mediating structures in the co-construction of Europe, knowledge and universities, in B. Jessop, N. Fairclough and R. Wodak (eds) *Education and the Knowledge Based Economy in Europe*, Rotterdam: Sense Publications.

Dale, R. (2010) The comparative method as 'comparativism' in comparative education, a paper presented to the 14th World Congress of Comparative Education Societies, Istanbul, 14–18 June.

Dale, R. and Robertson, S. L. (2008) Beyond methodological 'isms' in comparative education in an era of globalisation, in A. Kazamias and R. Cowen (eds) *Handbook on Comparative Education*, Netherlands: Springer.

Dolowitz, D. and Marsh, D. (2000) Learning from abroad: the role of policy transfer in contemporary policy making, *Governance* 13, 5–24.

Harvey, D. (2006) *Spaces of Global Capitalism: Towards a Theory of Uneven Development*, London: Verso.

Hay, C. (2000) Contemporary capitalism, globalization, regionalization and the persistence of national variation, *Review of International Studies* 26(4), 509–531.

Hobsbawm, E. (1999) *The New Century*, London: Abacus.

James, O. and Lodge, M. (2003) The limitations of 'policy transfer' and 'lesson drawing' for public policy research, *Political Studies Review* 1, 179–193.

Jayasuriya, K. (2010) Learning by the market: regulatory regionalism, Bologna, and accountability communities, *Globalisation, Societies and Education* 8(1), 7–22.

Jessop, B. (1999) The changing governance of welfare: recent trends in its primary functions, scale and modes of coordination, *Social Policy and Administration* 343(4), 348–359.

Jessop, B. (2005) Critical realism and the strategic relational approach, *New Formations* 56, 40–53.

Knill, C. (2005) Introduction: special issue, *Journal of European Public Policy* 12(5), 764–774.

Marsh, D. and Sharman, J. C. (2009) Policy diffusion and policy transfer, *Policy Studies* 30(3), 269–288.

Matthews, B. and Wilson, M. (2000) 'Multilingual metadata to access social science data', *ERCIM News*, 41.

Meseguer, C. and Gilardi, F. (2009) What is new in the study of policy diffusion?, *Review of International Political Economy* 16(3), 527–543.

Mittelman, J. (2004) *Whither Globalization? The Vortex of Knowledge and Ideology*, London: Routledge.

Nóvoa, A. and Yariv-Mashal, T. (2003) Comparative research in education: a mode of governance or a historical journey? *Comparative Education* 39(4), 423–438.

Pawson, R. (2000) Middle-range realism, *European Journal of Sociology* 41, 283–325.

Pawson, R. (2002) Evidence-based policy: the promise of realist synthesis, *Evaluation* 8(3), 340–358.

Peck, J. and Theodore, N. (2010) Mobilizing policy: models, methods and mutations, *Geoforum* 41(2), 169–174.

Ravinet, P. (2008) From voluntary participation to monitored coordination: why European countries feel increasingly bound by their commitment to the Bologna Process, *European Journal of Education* 43(3), 353–366.

Robertson, S. L. (2010) The EU, regulatory state regionalism and new modes of higher education governance, *Globalisation, Societies and Education*, 8(1), 23–37.

Robertson, S. L. and Dale, R. (2008) Researching education in a globalising era: beyond methodological nationalism, methodological statism, methodological educationism and spatial fetishism, in J. Resnik (ed.) *The Production of Educational Knowledge in the Global Era*, Rotterdam: Sense Publications, pp. 19–32.

Robertson, S. L. and Dale, R. (2009) The World Bank, the IMF and the possibilities of critical education, in M. Apple, W. Au and L. A. Gandin (eds) *The Routledge International Handbook of Critical Education*, London: Routledge.

Robertson, S. L. and Keeling, R. (2008) Stirring the Lions: strategy and tactics in global higher education, *Globalisation, Societies and Education* 6(3), 221–240.

Rose, R. (1993) *Lesson Drawing in Public Policy*, Chatham, NJ: Chatham House.

Rosenberg, J. (2007) International relations – the 'higher bullshit': a reply to the globalization theory debate, *International Politics* 44, 450–482.

Santos, B. S. (1995) *Toward a New Common Sense: Law, Science and the Politics of the Paradigmatic Transition*, London: Routledge.

Sassen, S. (2006) *Territory, Authority, Rights*, Princeton, NJ: Princeton University Press.

Scholte, J.-A. (2005) *Globalization: A Critical Introduction*, Basingstoke: Palgrave.

Smith, G. (2006) When 'the logic of capital is the real which lurks in the background': Programme and practice in european 'regional economies', *Current Anthropology* 47(4), 621–639.

Steiner-Khamsi, G. (2004) *The Global Politics of Educational Borrowing and Lending*, New York: Teachers College Press.

Strang, D. and Meyer, J. W. (1993) Institutional Conditions for Diffusion, *Theory and Society* 22, 487–511.

Thelen, K. (1999) Historical institutionalism in comparative politics, *Annual Review of Political Science* 2, 369–404.

Wilson, G. (2001) Power and translation in social policy research, *International Journal of Social Research Methodology: Theory and Practice* 4(4), 319–326.

3 Learning from Meetings and Comparison

A Critical Examination of the Policy Tools of Transnationals

Sotiria Grek

Responses to the increased global significance of education/learning as a policy area have tended to focus on the top-down policy influence of international organisations (IOs) and the transfer of policy from the international to the national level (see, for example Taylor et al. 1997, Ball 1998). However, there has been little attention to date given to education policy learning at the *transnational* level, especially within Europe. Current research (Grek et al. 2009) suggests that education policies by the European Commission (EC) and the Organisation for Economic Cooperation and Development (OECD) are received at the national level as relatively homogeneous, and this prompts questions about their relationship in terms of policy direction over recent years, and especially since the Lisbon Treaty in 2000. Following the emphasis in the Kok Report[1] (2004) on global, free-market – rather than European-based – education policies and programmes (Robertson 2007), as well as the increased significance of the skills and competencies policy agenda (Grek 2009, 2010), this chapter focuses on an enquiry into the nature and direction of policy learning between international organisations, through the examination of international comparative studies as tools in governing education in Europe.

While research in this area is limited (but see Finnemore 1993, Stone 2004, Porter and Webb 2004) the key consideration is that international organisations are not 'mere epiphenomena' of an impersonal policy machinery (Barnett and Finnemore 1999) but purposive actors who, 'armed with a notion of progress, an idea of how to create a better life, and some understanding of the conversion process', have become the 'missionaries of our time' (Barnett and Finnemore 1999: 712). For example, the OECD's transformation into a powerful agent of transnational education governance follows from the comparative turn towards 'a scientific approach to political decision making', which builds on data collection and the ranking and rating of member countries (Martens 2007: 42). This approach highlights not only the significance of the OECD as an education policy agent, but crucially the emergence of a social *matrix* of interrelated governing actors, who classify and construct meaning and articulate and diffuse new norms and principles.

Further, Power (1999, 2003a, 2003b, 2004) and Strathern (2000, 2004) suggest that a 'metrological mood' (Power 2004: 766) has become the mechanism through which education systems are measured and made accountable, and has permeated the structure and public face of international organisations themselves. A related, parallel development is the relatively recent 'evidence-based' or 'evidence-informed' policy-making trend, which builds on the assumption that as more evidence underpins policy, so it will become better and more rational (Davies et al. 2000; Davies 2004; Nutley et al. 2002; Schuller and Burns 2007).

On the other hand, and as a parallel development at a European level, we observe a stark change of the Commission's education policy-making tools, especially since 2000 and the Lisbon Treaty, which heralded an increased emphasis on indicators and benchmarking that were meant to drive change and push the 'growth and jobs' agenda forward. These new policy tools work as governing devices that, through the mutual learning of the policy makers and experts that come together for their development, their negotiations and co-options, together with cross-comparison and competition, draw national systems closer into European and global frameworks and practices. Similarly, although for much longer, the OECD has been cultivating and promoting technical expertise in creating comparable datasets (like the Programme for International Student Assessment – PISA), where countries can potentially measure the success of their education systems against others and shift their policy orientations accordingly. In this new context, notions such as lifelong learning and the knowledge economy have turned education departments in both the Commission and the OECD into central governing hubs. Thus, the development of new policy technologies, combined with the new significance of education redefined as (lifelong) learning, have together greatly enhanced the OECD's and EC's governing capacity, not only in their use of monitoring and measuring, but also in their promotion of particular attitudes and dispositions to learning.

As already suggested, a considerable body of research has focused on the education work of these bodies (see, for example, Henry et al. 2001; Lawn 2003; Lawn and Lingard 2002; Ozga and Lingard 2007; Martens 2007; Pépin 2006; Shore 2000); however, this research does not examine their interaction. International organisations are often seen as monolithic institutions, or actors with similar interests in a similar context, without attention to the complex set of realities that bring them together and apart over time. Thus, important questions about 'what mechanisms work, in what ways, for whom and under what circumstances' (Dale and Robertson 2007: 219) are neglected, as is a detailed investigation of the *extent* and the *means* through which they may or may not unite in pursuit of a common, hegemonic agenda.

Hence, building on the analysis of documents and reports, as well as interview data from the ESRC-funded Transnational Policy Learning project,[2] this chapter investigates the degree to which, especially since the Lisbon Treaty (2000), the organisation and conduct of international comparative studies have increased the collaboration and policy learning between the OECD and the European Commission (EC). It seeks to establish whether commonalities between the two IOs' policy instruments and content simply reflect the dominance of 'rational choice' principles, such as efficiency and equity; or instead, if instances of policy teaching and learning between the two organisations may be identified. It examines the role of *politics* (ideas, interests and strategies) in changing *polities* (administrative adjustments, changes in processes and institutions) and *policies* (policy agendas, content and implementation). I will try to answer these questions through the specific examination of the development of three

OECD studies since the mid-1990s – these are the International Adult Literacy Survey (IALS) (1994–1998); the Adult Literacy and Life Skills Survey (ALL) (2002–2004); and, finally, the Programme for the International Assessment of Adult Competencies (PIAAC) (2011). The chapter will examine the ways constellations of actors or ideas converge in the shaping of the testing regime *prior* to its diffusion to the nation states.

Finally, the idea of policy learning (Bennett 1997; Haas and Haas 1995; May 1992; Raffe and Spours 2007; Steiner-Khamsi 2004) is central here. It is not limited to the idea of instrumental learning, or learning about new policy tools or interventions; instead, it encompasses an idea of social policy learning which entails 'new or reaffirmed understanding of policy problems and objectives' (May 1992: 334) – the social construction of policy priorities. It also takes account of 'political' learning; this involves processes that take place in advocacy coalitions. On the other hand, the idea of policy teaching (Bomberg 2007) is also significant in that it assumes that the learning of specific policy instruments depends not only on 'learners' but also on those agents responsible for promoting and inducing that learning. Although it is important to look at who is learning, what is learned and to what effect, it is equally significant to focus on who is teaching, what is taught and to what effect (Bomberg 2007). It would be interesting therefore to observe the cascading strategies of 'teachers', as well as the take-up of ideas by 'model pupils' (Rinne 2006). PISA offers a good example of such practices; through its promotion, the OECD has been foregrounding skills-focused curricula as one of the secrets of educational success (for a more detailed analysis of the PISA impact in Europe, see Grek 2009; Knodel et al. 2010). As a consequence, and given the focus on lifelong learning as a central policy priority by the EC, the development of PIAAC has been emerging as the new 'post-PISA success' data dream for education steering in Europe and beyond. But how did we get here?

Skills and Competencies: The New Lingua Franca?

> When I started here the focus was very much on trying to gather data on systems. So, the number of students, the features of the programmes, mixing qualitative and quantitative information on systems. In parallel the OECD was already working on skills and more and more this is a trend that is now taking place here and we have all these discussions about what is actually the focus of our work. . . . So that's a progressive shift of work that has taken place over the past ten years I would say, with a very strong emphasis at the policy level in the past three years. Especially in the European Union. The OECD was more advanced in discussing skills, at least skills of adults or skills of young people earlier but in the European Union the policy shift is very, very strong since the last three years. Skills have become a buzz word for many, many things.
>
> (Eu1a)

> We talk in Cedefop about a shift in paradigm from systems that are based in the input – we have this programme that is this length, has these features, works for these students etc. . . . to a focus on outputs or outcomes of systems, the skills, knowledge, competence that they are supposed to produce. And a focus on these

aspects will become increasingly disconnected from the systems themselves because we recognise formal but also informal learning as a way to acquire these.

(Eu2b)

As is clear from above, the emphasis on developing a skills and competencies policy agenda did not occur simultaneously at the headquarters of the OECD and the EU, despite market pressures, such as changes in the labour market and the increasing dominance of the service market industries in Europe and the US. The OECD was first to respond to what was emerging as a requirement by business that education systems prepare a flexible workforce (Lauder et al. 2008, Brown et al. 2001). Although in Europe training and vocational education have been the primary focus of collaborative work since the 1970s (Pépin 2006), the move in emphasis from inputs to outputs has been very recent. In fact, as the second quotation above suggests, skills and competencies have been described as a paradigm shift in education governance in the European Union and its agencies, for example Cedefop, the European Centre for the Development of Vocational Training. This policy area is thus of particular interest, not just for its centrality in working towards 'becoming the most competitive and dynamic knowledge-based economy in the world' (Council of the European Union 2000), but in providing a rich and suitable resource for the interrogation of this governing shift through the testing of the convergence and divergence of discourses and policy tools between the OECD and the EC. More recently, Cedefop has been working closely on the identification of skill needs in Europe through the Skillsnet project[3] as well as through CEDRA, the Cedefop Research Arena.[4] During the last five years, numerous Council Resolutions and Commission staff publications and working documents on the topic have also been published (OJEU 2007, European Commission 2007a, 2007b).

Skills and competencies have been central to the OECD's work, as its highest-profile international assessment, PISA, has suggested. PISA has had a high impact on curriculum reform in several European countries by pushing education systems in the direction of more 'can-do' dispositions towards education, rather than more traditional pedagogic approaches (Grek 2009). PISA also built the OECD's image as a technically competent and scientifically robust organisation for performing such comparative ranking and ordering of national performance (Ozga et al. 2010). In addition, as I will examine further on, the OECD's Definition and Selection of Competencies project (DeSeCo) (1997–2005) was a major effort to provide 'a sound conceptual framework to inform the identification of key competencies, to strengthen international assessments, and to help to define overarching goals for education systems and lifelong learning'.[5] Finally, prior to the development of PIAAC, the OECD had already conducted two international adult skill surveys: the International Adult Literacy Survey (1994–1998) and the Adult Literacy and Life Skills Survey (2002–2006). It is to these two studies that I will now turn, in order to examine their development and reporting as key in the construction of very specific and influential policy directions in education in Europe in the post-Lisbon era.

The International Adult Literacy Survey (IALS)

a new quality standard in measurement

(OECD 2000: 87)

IALS was one of the largest international comparative studies conducted in the 1990s, and unique in its kind as it was the first time ever that an international comparative dimension was added to the construction of a literacy survey instrument. Literacy studies which had already run in the US, like the Young Adult Literacy Assessment (1986), the Survey of Workplace Literacy (1992) and the National Adult Literacy Survey (1992), had US populations as their focus. IALS heralded a new era in the construction and evolution of international comparative studies, since for the first time, it:

1   gave such testing a global dimension, where measurement and comparison against others offered unprecedented visibility and thus exposure;
2   boosted confidence in the construction of measurement tools of this kind, increased their persuasive power in regard to their validity and transparency and created substantial revenues to the research agencies administering them;
3   above all, created a circle of like-minded individuals, a 'magistracy' of influence (Lawn and Lingard 2002), who found in these studies a platform for promoting the problematisation of specific issues, their institutionalisation through their exchanges and the setting up of the study, as well as their legitimation, in the form of advice to failing countries once the results were published.

IALS, having started as a nine-country initiative in 1994 (Canada, France, Germany, Ireland, the Netherlands, Poland, Sweden, Switzerland and the US), grew as five additional countries joined in 1996 (Australia, Flemish Belgium, the UK, New Zealand and Northern Ireland) and, finally, nine other countries or regions joined the study in 1998 (Chile, the Czech Republic, Denmark, Finland, Hungary, Italy, Norway, Slovenia and the Italian-speaking region of Switzerland); by the end of its run, the study had reached the impressive number of 23 participating countries. It was also the first time that such a study established a cycle of data collection, involving three rounds of testing, thereby managing to get more support and momentum as it went on, as well as improve its tools and techniques. The study was led by the OECD, in collaboration with the European Union and UNESCO, and administered by Statistics Canada, the Educational Testing Service (ETS) and the National Centre for Education Statistics (NCES) – all North American agencies.

IALS examined literacy 'as a particular capacity [information-processing compe-tency] and mode of behaviour' and assessed performance levels 'along a continuum' (OECD 2000: iii). Individuals from age 16 to 65 took part in the study, with nationally representative samples, in order to 'provide insights for policy makers responsible for the design of lifelong learning, and social and labour market policies' (OECD 2000: xiii). In other words, high levels of literacy were presented as the essential ingredient of a flourishing society, without which, according to the study, 'globalisation, tech-nological change and organisational development' (OECD 2000: xiii) – the challenges of the twenty-first century – could not be met. Indeed, the report offers an extensive analysis of the knowledge-based economy (KBE), describing it as the move towards high technology industries, but also the rise of intensive users of high technology or industries that have a highly skilled workforce (finance, insurance, communications). This, according to the OECD, has had an impact on the demand for skills, due to changes in employment and changes in work organisation, as 'flexible work practices demand higher skills than those that do not' (Capelli and Rogovsky 1994: 218). Similarly, according to the International Labour Organisation (ILO), 'The skill level and quality of the workforce will increasingly provide the cutting edge in competing in the global economy' (ILO 1999: 202), while, in a similar fashion, the OECD contends that one should 'possess broad foundation skills that must be regularly updated and complemented with specific skills through training and lifelong learning processes' (OECD 2000: 11).

Apart from relating skills to increased earnings, IALS also managed to skilfully connect literacy (and thus the findings of the study) with a range of other outcomes, such as social capital, community engagement, voluntary participation, social cohesion, political participation of women, better health and wider social benefits. 'Health literacy', for example, was to become a new measure of the ability of individuals to lead healthier lives, with literacy being seen as a mediating factor in health disparities (Rudd et al. 2000). Through the masterly build-up of such a discourse, IALS – again, for the first time – was transcending the boundaries of education research, as it claimed to show the 'complex relationships between human capital, economic outcomes and social benefits' (OECD 2000: 84). Thus, with literacy being turned into not only the *sine qua non* of workplace learning, but almost the *sine qua non* of living, IALS was slowly managing to shift education policy into the foreground of the governance of high-achieving, well-to-do societies in Europe and beyond.

Apart from the discursive construction of the new study, it is also interesting to examine its innovative design. IALS was organised as a combination of tools of educational assessment with the application of household survey techniques. The difficulties (and criticisms) faced in terms of management, funding, staffing and establishing the study's quality assurance processes were turned into its advantage, as the organisers of the study were – soon after its completion – to teach these lessons to countries wishing to collect education data in a similar manner. Indeed, since then, Japan, Malaysia, Portugal, Ontario and Vanuatu have also collected data with instruments derived from IALS (Murray et al. 2005). Above all, IALS established 'a new standard for providing a theoretical basis for its measurement framework' (OECD 2000: 87–88) – hence, a new logic. It also followed 'an advanced psychometric approach', moving the focus to psychometric testing, and thus opening up the field to significant commercial interests. Finally, claiming to have achieved 'unprecedented levels of reliability in scoring open-ended items across cultures and languages', the study boasted the decontextualisation of literacy (OECD 2000: 87–88). Thus, it essentially sidelined the New Literacy studies field, which proclaims that literacy has meaning only within its particular context of social practice and does not transfer unproblematically across contexts (Barton and Hamilton 1998). Indeed, the management of the study received a lot of criticism precisely because of the relative lack of literacy specialists involved in its design (Blum et al. 2001: 226), some of whom were taking particular issue with the study's assumption that a valid common definition of literacy across cultures could be established (Hamilton and Barton 2000; Street 1996). In fact, some went as far as to argue that 'those involved in the IALS research are testers and technicians, committed to quantitative methodologies' (Hamilton and Barton 2000: 379). In a similar manner, Harvey Goldstein elsewhere argued that the technical complexity of studies like IALS often acts as a well-built and fixed barrier that protects their designers (usually technical experts), by shielding them away from the critical comments of subject specialists. In fact, Goldstein contends that this is 'fertile ground for the psychometrician to dominate the debate, invoking the high status generally associated with mathematical reasoning', as well as simultaneously attracting 'powerful commercial interests in the shape of largely US testing agencies . . . as providers of sophisticated know-how' (Goldstein 1996). He continues:

> Subject matter specialists are involved in designing questions and tasks but thereafter they assume a much more passive role. If they are brave enough to suggest that some complexities have been overlooked then they may well be dismissed as having not properly understood the technicalities.
>
> (Goldstein 1996)

IALS, despite it being the debut OECD international study, did not lack the 'spectacle' that similar studies, like PISA, were to create few years later. IALS in fact offered a dramatic premiere, one that made it widely known even to those not involved; the protagonist this time was France, which withdrew its results and the country's participation from the first round when the study's findings suggested that three quarters of the French population had an ability level in terms of 'literacy' which prevented them from handling the normal matters of everyday life, like reading a newspaper, writing a letter or understanding a short text. 'With the novelty has come some controversy' (Blum et al. 2001: 123), the OECD suggested, as more objections were raised against the study; it was seen as favouring more 'Anglo-Saxon' populations, at the expense of Latin cultures, due to the origin of the survey in North America. Another criticism was that the translation and adaptation of some items into French had increased their difficulty level. Finally, the French respondents were seen as less motivated than respondents in other countries (Blum et al. 2001).

To conclude, IALS created fertile ground for the OECD to push its education policy agenda, through measurement and comparison that would 'provide empirically grounded interpretation upon which to inform policy decisions' (Kirsch 2001: 1). As Irwin Kirsch, director of the Centre for Global Assessment at the ETS, suggested:

> while the chief benefit of constructing and validating a framework for literacy is improved measurement, a number of other potential benefits are also evident. Namely:
>   – A framework provides a *common language* and a *vehicle* for discussing the definition of the skill area;
>   – Such a discussion allows us to build *consensus* around the framework and measurement goals;

– An analysis of the kinds of knowledge and skills associated with successful performance provides *an empirical basis for communicating a richer body of information to various constituencies*

(Kirsch 2001: 2, my emphasis)

IALS became therefore instrumental not only in linking research, assessment and public policy (Kirsch 2001: 3), but crucially in establishing: first, the problematisation around specific issues (a common language for the participant countries, research agencies, other IOs and, ultimately, the public); second, their institutionalisation (the creation of a consensus of all those involved on priorities and necessary policy directions); and third, their legitimation (it created evidence on the basis of which education reform could be justified). Finally, the study did what all such studies always do – it created the need for the design and delivery of yet another study of its kind. That was the Adult Literacy and Life Skills Survey (ALL).

The Adult Literacy and Life Skills Survey (ALL)

The success of the IALS approach led several national governments to wonder if the methods could be adopted to measure a broader array of skills on an international level.

(Murray et al. 2005: 13)

The first meeting to consider the possibility of mounting the successor to the IALS study, the Adult Literacy and Life Skills survey, took place on European ground, hosted by the Swedish Educational Authority (Skolverket). It was decided to build on IALS in order to create a survey that would look at foundational skills, such as prose literacy, document literacy, numeracy and problem-solving, as well as familiarity with and use of information and communication technologies. Statistics Canada suggested that the study be organised as a computer-based assessment of samples of workers derived from within firms in order to produce 'explicit statistical linkages . . . to isolate the impact of observed skill on economic productivity and indicators of firm success such as employment growth and profitability' (Murray et al. 2005: 13). There was a decision to organise a second meeting of the group, at the University of Amsterdam, in order to discuss the possibility of such a study. However, the operational implications of fielding a computer-based assessment were insurmountable at the time. A third meeting, closer to the study's home this time at the NCER's headquarters in Washington, DC, concluded 'on pragmatic grounds' (ibid.) that the test would be undertaken using the humble paper and pencil method and that the sample would be drawn from households rather than the workplace.

As a result of the two meetings, a Project Advisory Group (PAG) was formed in order to work further in refining the transnational comparability of the measures for numeracy, problem-solving, teamwork and practical cognition. Two subsequent meetings of the international study team were hosted by the US National Center for Education Statistics in Washington in 1998, in order to work on more accurate measures for problem-solving, teamwork and computer literacy, resulting in new development teams being recruited and funded by Statistics Canada, NCES and the

Governments of Sweden and Luxembourg. Additional meetings were held in the US: first, a meeting of all development team leaders in Washington in January 1999 'to help integrate the different assessments and to provide expert feedback' (Murray et al. 2005: 14); second, another meeting of the development team leaders was held in Princeton in August of the same year 'to review the frameworks' (ibid.). Finally, a separate international team developed the background questionnaire for the study.

The sheer number of meetings organised merely to initiate the workings of these groups of experts is such that, analytically, one cannot but underline the significance and impact of meetings in the transfer of ideas at a global level. In fact, it was not simply necessity that pushed their organisation. Instead, meetings became a significant means of pushing the agenda forward, as:

> success in this complex field depends not only on theoretical *and* empirical work, but also on a constant *dialogue and exchange* among the various specialists and stakeholders to assure that an iterative process takes place (e.g., Murray 2003, Schleicher 2003).
>
> (Murray et al. 2005: 33, emphasis in original)

In the end, six countries – Bermuda, Canada, Italy, Norway, Switzerland and the United States – participated in the first round of ALL data collection, fielding the ALL pilot study in 2002 and the main data collection in the first and second quarters of 2003 (Murray et al. 2005). Apart from the OECD which led the study, its development and management were also coordinated by Statistics Canada and the Educational Testing Service (ETS) in collaboration with the National Center for Education Statistics (NCES) of the US Department of Education, the OECD, the Regional Office for Latin America and the Caribbean (OREALC) and the Institute for Statistics (UIS) of UNESCO. The survey instruments were developed by international teams of experts with financing provided by the governments of Canada and the United States. Participating governments absorbed the costs of national data collection and a share of the international overheads associated with the implementation of the study. The study explicitly suggested that 'literacy and education are not synonymous, and that social and economic success depends, in part, on tested skill' (Murray et al. 2005: 17), thus moving the lens to 'on the job' skills and competencies, rather than the measurement of educational inputs. Finally, it was also suggested that:

> Direct measurement of the sort employed in the IALS study requires considerable operational and technical skill and significant financial resources to unilaterally design, validate, collect and analyse. Such resources are *beyond the means of many* of even the most advanced economies to support. IALS has also demonstrated the potential of a *comparative perspective* to shed light on deep relationships underlying the observed phenomena, relationships that remain undetected in *idiosyncratic* national studies.
>
> (Murray et al. 2005: 18, my emphasis)

This is a common argument purported by international organisations when it comes to comparison: they claim that they have a panoramic view of the field, as opposed to the 'idiosyncratic' national level which cannot 'see' very much further than the boundaries of its own culture, people and policies. However, there is a paradox here. What is immediately observed are concerted efforts led by the OECD to establish a field of study and a platform for exchange at the international level, where national actors, be they technical experts or policy makers, can come together to learn from one another. However, the financing of this venture was offered by two governments, those of the US and Canada – hence, the role and impact of the national cannot and should not be underplayed, as is the role of other stakeholders like education authorities (Skolverket is a case in point) or academic institutions (like the University of Amsterdam).

A parallel development to the design and implementation of the ALL study was the development of another project focusing on defining and measuring competences – the Definition and Selection of Competencies: Theoretical and Conceptual Foundations (DeSeCo) project, launched in 1997. It was led and managed by a new actor that appears at the foreground of developments in the field, the Swiss National Statistics Office (BFS), which is located in the heart of Europe, yet at the same time outside of it. DeSeCo was financed by the Swiss, Statistics Canada and the US National Center for Education Statistics, and implemented under the aegis of the OECD. The notion of competencies was relatively new in Europe at the time, however not so new in the US, which had been developing them as an alternative to using traditional tests of cognitive intelligence, because the latter were seen as poor predictors of job performance. The competence approach starts from the opposite end, observing successful and effective job performers to determine how these individuals differ from less successful performers. Competency captures skills and dispositions beyond cognitive ability such as self-awareness, self-regulation and social skills. Thus, competencies are fundamentally behavioural and susceptible to learning (Lucia and Lepsinger 1999; Raven and Stephenson 2001).

DeSeCo was primarily a theory-oriented (Murray et al. 2005) study that would complement the work that was being done in a range of studies, designed either to be implemented in the near future, or taking place at the time. These assessments were TIMSS (the IEA study), IALS, ALL and PISA. More interestingly, DeSeCo, as well as theoretically backing the empirical work that these studies were undertaking, offered another crucial means of support to them, as it facilitated further exchanges and meetings between experts in the field. Indeed, the number and variety of stakeholders involved was wide, as the project brought together 'sociologists, economists, anthropologists, philosophers, psychologists, a historian, education researchers, statisticians, assessment specialists, policy-makers and policy analysts, unionists, employers and other stakeholders' (Murray et al. 2005) representing various sectors and national and international institutions. The project involved an analysis of international studies on indicators of education outcomes (Salganik et al. 1999), followed by a study reviewing scholarly work on the concept of competence (Weinert 2001) and expert opinions by scholars from five different academic disciplines, each of whom was asked to construct a set of theoretically grounded key competencies, and provide comments from policy and practice (Rychen and Salganik 2001). Following the usual organisation of such studies, these experts met for the first time at an international symposium in 1999 which brought together academics and stakeholders from various fields, followed by country consultations organised by the OECD, with the remit to review national experiences in defining, developing, and assessing key competencies (Trier 2003). A second international symposium was then organised in order to work 'towards a consensus on key competencies among a wide range of countries, stakeholders, and interest groups' (Rychen et al. 2003). Finally, DeSeCo's main conclusions and recommendations were submitted in the form of a strategy paper (OECD 2002) to the relevant OECD committees, and the findings were published in DeSeCo's final report entitled 'Key competencies for a Successful Life and a Well-Functioning Society' (Rychen and Salganik 2001). As with IALS, drawing on what the study claimed to be 'a common vision of society as a normative anchoring point', DeSeCo built a 'demand-oriented approach to competence', which 'designates a complex action system encompassing cognitive and non-cognitive components', in order to create today's 'flexible, adaptive, innovative, creative, self-directed, self-motivated and responsible . . . learner, worker, citizen, family member, or consumer' (Murray et al. 2005: 36).

Claiming to use these studies in order to masterfully craft the perfect OECD-envisaged individual is interesting enough in itself; nevertheless, the focus of this analysis is different. What has the policy learning that took place around the construction of these instruments and common visions been? How can one observe and analyse the processes that bring actors together in search of best ideas and policies? Three crucial points need to be raised here, in relation to the ALL and the DeSeCo objectives and impact. Interestingly, both studies, as their designers themselves suggest, moved policy directions and thus policy makers and nations 'towards a common, coherent international discourse on competence and skill development' (Murray et al. 2005: 39). What they have also done – and they themselves proclaim – is create 'a bridge between student and adult competence assessments' (ibid: 42), thus breaking down the boundaries between schooling and the rest of the life course. This is important because after claiming to have achieved decontextualisation, these studies now also make a move towards the de-institutionalisation of learning, and thus bring lifelong learning to the fore of education governance. Finally, both studies created a starting point, on the basis of which all such work needs now to build on, and also established networks of experts in the field – a field which exceeds the limits of achieving educational success to the much larger and all-encompassing idea of reaching personal and societal 'well-being':

> It is important to build future assessment on existing studies, expertise and knowledge, thus *not to reinvent the wheel* . . . DeSeCo and ALL have *established networks of researchers* that can contribute – from different perspectives – to continued research on key competencies and the educational, social, and economic factors that contribute to improve the education and training and to enhanced returns on investments in competencies in terms of *personal, economic, and social well-being.*
>
> (Murray et al. 2005: 43, my emphasis).

The Programme for the International Assessment of Adult Competencies (PIAAC)

[Surveys like PIAAC are important] as they bring people together to discuss a common concept – because all these instruments are validated, they are validated against intercultural variances and so on, so yes, you are in front of some kind of evidence, you cannot deny the facts anymore.

(Eu2b)

[PIAAC] is influential by placing the discussion about skills based on evidence – now if you really look at what they are measuring in terms of skills it can be a very narrow piece from the skills palette of an individual but still having policy makers discuss the skills level of their population or the skill demand of the economy is a big step I think.

(Eu1a)

Following the success of PISA, PIAAC is the new OECD multi-cycle programme of assessment. In contrast to PISA, it is not organised solely by the Education Directorate but by a collaboration of the latter with the OECD's Directorate for Employment, Labour and Social Affairs, in order to provide evidence on adults' competence levels in the participating countries. As the interviewees above (both EU actors) suggest, although still under development, it has already been very influential in building and continuing policy makers' communication and exchanges that had started with IALS and ALL. What is different with PIAAC is that, although European countries, and the EU to a lesser extent, were always at the background of the previous studies, but with no direct or active involvement, this time the European Commission through its agencies has acquired a far more dynamic and committed role in financing and supporting the new OECD initiative.

Already under way, PIAAC was fielded in 2011, aiming to 'help governments to go further in evaluating and designing education and training policies by providing comparative information on skills among their adult populations' (OECD 2010: 7). Twenty-four OECD member countries took part in the first cycle of the Programme, in addition to three non-member countries (Estonia, Malta, Slovenia). The study has received high recognition and is being promoted at the very top level of the OECD as greatly ambitious. As with all previous studies, it is in line with the OECD's economistic view of education and knowledge:

Knowledge and skills are the most valuable assets to present and future generations, as governments seek to maintain global competitiveness, increase the flexibility and responsiveness of labour markets and deal with issues of population ageing. OECD's breakthrough survey on adult competencies, PIAAC, will provide governments with a unique and effective tool to assess where they stand in terms of quantity and quality of the knowledge and skills of their workforce. Equally important, it will provide insights into how skills relate to the social and economic well-being of individuals and nations and also benchmark how effectively education and training systems meet emerging skill demands.

(Angel Gurria, OECD Secretary-General, OECD 2010)

Interestingly, PIAAC is also in line with European aspirations and targets:

> Many countries adhere to national and multi-national statements of intent regarding the achievement of economic performance targets relative to international norms. An example is the declaration from the March 2000 meeting of the European Council in Lisbon . . . Monitoring of progress in meeting such international targets necessarily requires international comparisons.
>
> (Schleicher 2008: 629)

The survey's results will be presented in 2013 and they will be based on interviews with 5,000 adults (16–65 years old) in each participating country, in order to assess their literacy and numeracy skills and 'their ability to solve problems in technology-rich environments'. The test will also collect information in relation to how adults use their skills at work and in the community (OECD 2010: 2).

Unlike PISA, which is designed and analysed by the Australian Council for Educational Research (ACER), the design and implementation of PIAAC is the responsibility of an international consortium of research organisations in North America and Europe, led by the ETS (Educational Testing Service) in the United States. Interestingly, the choice of research centres involved is far more cosmopolitan that ever before: Westat in the US; cApStAn in Belgium; the Research Centre for Education and the Labour Market (ROA) at the University of Maastricht; GESIS-ZUMA Centre for Survey Research; the German Institute for International Education Research (DIPF); and the Data Processing Centre of the International Association for the Evaluation of Educational Achievement (IEA) in Germany.

PIAAC's core features include: literacy in the information age; the use of key work skills through the Job Requirement Approach (JRA) questionnaire; and a background questionnaire, which will measure skill formation and economic and social outcomes (OECD 2004). It is expected that JRA, already applied in the UK Skills Survey, will explain salary variations and employment opportunities based on longer learning trajectories, but also through 'influence skills', such as persuasion and presentation skills. The JRA pilot unfolded in five countries (Australia, France, Greece, Korea and the United States) and its results were presented in an 'International Validation Seminar' at Cedefop in February 2009. According to Mark Keese, senior OECD economist in another joint JRA OECD–Cedefop workshop held in Paris in May 2008, JRA 'will open up a new world for investigating the demand for a range of generic work skills and the implications for education and training policies' (Keese 2008). Cedefop had a very significant role in the development of the JRA; it supported it financially and intellectually, as this lengthy, though very illustrative, interview extract suggests:

> One particular thing in working with the OECD is that there is no requirement for formal cooperation. So usually we cooperate as individuals when we work well together or when we believe in what we are doing. So it is always a bit tricky. So we cannot talk about really a real agenda, a formal agenda for cooperation. I mean if I take the example of PIAAC, we were involved in PIAAC developments via our work in INES,[6] in the INES B Network at the time so we were there

involved in the INES discussions on PIAAC, on the orientations, etc., from the point of view of data collection of course . . . also because of knowing certain persons and they knew our competence and so on in the PIAAC expert group. So we have been participating in the PIAAC expert group for the last year of the development of PIAAC. And in that context we learn about the specific module within PIAAC which is using the Job Requirement Approach and we agreed that from the point of view of Cedefop, because it was analysing the kinds of skills that people use at work, that it was a particularly relevant strand of work within PIAAC. And then we supported it financially. So we supported the development of the tools, the data collection tools and the pilot. And as a result now the JRA is a full module of PIAAC. So this is an example of particular kind of work. But it is like coincidental the way we work on that – we go to a meeting, we think 'oh, it is interesting', we discuss it in the street going to the restaurant in the evening, 'ah, it may be good if we can support it', then they come back to you, we formalise an agreement. If we hadn't been at a particular meeting at a particular time it would never have happened . . . we gave them a 60K euro grant which helped to kick off the initiative and then we supported it. I was also involved in the expert group following the development of the module and the assessment of the pilot. So we also gave them expertise if you like in developing the module, so it was both financial and in terms of expertise or technical support.

(Eu2b)

Cedefop was not the only European agency that supported the development of PIAAC. According to their work programme,[7] the European Commission's Centre for Research in Lifelong Learning (CRELL) has substantially contributed to the development of the PIAAC background questionnaire. In addition, a 'Coordination Group' has been established by the Directorate General for Education and Culture for cooperation with the OECD in the area of adult skills and PIAAC in particular; most importantly, a total amount of 1.05 million euros was budgeted in the 2008 EU budget for the support of European countries in PIAAC. Therefore, we see that apart from the mainly German and American-based research consortium responsible for the study, the European Commission, through its agencies, and in particular Cedefop and CRELL, have been closely engaged in the preparation of PIAAC. But why? According to some:

There is strong push from member states. I mean if you see recent Council's conclusions in the fields of education or even employment there is the need for systematic collaboration between international organisations because member states are a bit fed up funding different initiatives. They fund the OECD research and they also fund the Commission and the research that is done by Commission institutions indirectly. So they have the feeling that at least we should work together and not re-invent the wheel all the time.

(Eu1a)

Others suggest that, rather than financial reasons, there is significant data collection fatigue:

When they were planning PIAAC at some point the member states said 'Look, you know we will want to be on board with PIAAC and we don't want the EU to have a separate initiative [because] we get tired of all this data collection' – so you need to work together.

(Eu4a)

Finally, from the Commission's point of view:

We used to have great competition between the two institutions [OECD and the EC] which was that they were research-based, we were policy-based. And we needed that. They needed the policy aspect to mobilise the European consciousness . . . it was in their interest working with us . . . We had some differences but we are working closer and closer together, we are very, very good friends now, there is no conflict.

(Eu3b)

Conclusions

This chapter has attempted to open the black box of international comparative studies as technologies in the governing of the European education space. Ultimately, it aimed to examine the policy learning that occurs amongst actors during their conception and organisation prior to their actual delivery – thus, it tried to move the discussion from the national to the transnational level, where national actors are still the dominant players, but to a large degree liberated from national constraints and pressures. There is a great deal of scholarly work on policy learning but little has been written on the actual workings of such processes – how policy makers learn, what, when and where. The chapter highlighted the ways that such studies apply specific discourses and techniques first, in order to create interest around an innovative idea which will distinguish them from other research agencies (with whom of course they compete for funds from national governments), so that they can then push specific policy orientations forward. Learning by meeting has emerged as by far the most significant instrument in their efforts to create consensus around measurement goals. Indeed, many of the actors whose participation was discussed, mainly national official statisticians, subject experts and policy makers, would suggest that they are learning from one another. But how? Freeman's work (2006, 2008) on public policy learning is very useful in terms of unfolding these processes, in order to analyse what this learning consists of.

According to Brown and Duguid (2000), networks of practice usually comprise people that belong to the same occupational groups and meet from time to time in order to share their knowledge; they might know each other or they might not, but most of the time there is little reciprocity or willingness to do something with the knowledge they exchange. On the other hand, Haas (1992) has written about 'epistemic communities', 'a network of professionals with recognized expertise and competence in a particular domain and an authoritative claim to policy-relevant knowledge within that domain or issue-area' (Haas 1992: 3), and Wenger and Snyder (2000) have also talked about 'communities of practice', usually a smaller group of people where collaboration and reciprocity are tighter. In a similar manner, one of the interviewees suggested: 'It is always the same people you know, at the end of the day it is a very small community' (Eu1a).

According to Freeman, when one deals with a community of networked members/ actors, then by definition this allows for a different kind of communication, where actors initially bring their own ideas and knowledge. Nonetheless, 'over time, they come to talk increasingly about things they have thought of through their talking; the dialog becomes self-generating. Participants in a dialog are not only learning from each other, but also learning something new' (Freeman 2006: 376). Ultimately, this is the creation of a circle of individuals, a 'magistracy of influence' (Lawn and Lingard 2002) who rarely find themselves in uncharted territory – the principal condition both of and for new decision-making is previous policy (Freeman 2006). The OECD has been time and again capitalising on the premise of a need not to 're-invent the wheel' but instead build on previous work, which in the majority of times is of their own inspiration, authorship and direction. As the quotations at an earlier passage of this chapter suggest, increasingly members of this 'small community' like each other, they learn to work together, they call one another, and finally become friends. We trust to learn from friends, rather than strangers (Forrester 1999), especially when these friends provide us with the information we need. Friends are those that understand our situation and the values which inform our choices (Freeman 2008); they help us deliberate and offer persuasive arguments to be used in more hostile contexts – in a sense, the kind of 'sensitivity' that is predominant in PIAAC documentation in terms of the Lisbon process (and its failings) as well as more 'European' agendas in education policy, such as a focus on mobility and improving vocational education and training.

Further, Freeman gives a very interesting account of how cross-national meetings work in terms: first, of 'status leveling' ('a temporary parity among participants who are equal at least in their status as invitees' (2008: 10)); second, in relation to their situation, as participants usually find themselves away from home, at a place where they lose their ordinary sense of time and space; and third, the fact that meetings are also a *social* situation where dialogue over food and drink are common and for the majority of the participants the time when the 'real' talk takes place (Freeman 2008). Finally, Freeman discusses the role of language for meetings. This is usually English, a 'third-code' language, or the only language in which actors can communicate – a broken English perhaps, one that native English speakers also recognise as a special kind of language, one used by 'Europeans'. However, it is not the physicality of the language that matters here; language acquires a different significance as it becomes a medium of translation and mutual recognition:

> Cross-national talk requires a creative, slightly more abstract grammar and vocabulary than the ones we might ordinarily use to talk about cases we know to those who also inhabit them. Discussion is realized in what might be described as a 'third code', or a language of translation, and this is also partly why it often seems difficult, alien, disorientating as well as exhilarating.
>
> (Freeman 2008: 13)

Therefore, policy learning can be characterised as one of the prime instruments in the exchange of governing knowledge in education in Europe today, as it creates the necessary preconditions for achieving policy understanding, travel, translation and thus, despite local idiosyncrasies and histories, policy consensus. In fact, one could go a step further in the examination of the effects of international comparative studies, especially in relation to using indicators and data to achieve consensus and promote specific kinds of governing knowledge. Nico Stehr has persuasively written on the role and impact of knowledge politics (2004). This chapter has discussed the role of policy learning and the management of statistical knowledge in the creation of international commensurability and a plain field of continuous, unforgiving comparison.

Closely interlinked with the idea of learning by meeting, is the centrality of knowledge in processes of problematisation at the level of transnational education governance. Through the examination of PIAAC and its predecessor studies, we witness an evolving and progressing consensus based on the co-construction of policy knowledge and, crucially, statistical knowledge, in education. The processes of problematisation are thus rooted in knowledge and expertise and their ever-expanding territories – but this is not to say that knowledge here becomes an uncontrollable force which has acquired a life of its own. On the contrary, it is a social construct heavily managed and steered through a series of expert meetings and exchanges – and this is where policy learning becomes intimately entangled with knowledge politics. These European encounters are not limited within the boundaries of one organisation, or even two, as this chapter might have tried to show – sometimes they are not even confined within European boundaries at all. They include a wide range of actors, with different interests and opportunities, who need to be traced every single time one attempts to examine the construction of a policy problem from scratch. Knowledge is the main engine powering the governance of the European education space, since data can be collated, monitored and interpreted by different states and actors, and even used as a basis for forecasting future needs (Grek 2008). Thus, the governance of the European education space is heavily dependent on knowledge and its exchange through processes of policy learning (Grek and Ozga 2010). This is not a neutral, apolitical process; rather, it is heavily political and directed. To a large – and constantly increasing – extent, the management of knowledge appears to determine the orientation of education policy. Thus, it is in the analysis of such processes that one has to look in order to open the black box of international comparative assessments and, ultimately, of education governance in Europe.

Notes

1 This was a report on the EU's 'Lisbon strategy', issued by a high-level group chaired by the former Dutch Prime Minister Wim Kok (2004).
2 Full title of the project is 'Transnational Policy Learning: A comparative study of OECD and EU education policy in constructing the skills and competencies agenda' (2010–2012), funded by the Economic and Social Research Council (ESRC) (RES-000-22-3429), PI Dr. Grek. More info at www.ces.ed.ac.uk/research/TransPol/index.htm
3 www.trainingvillage.gr/etv/Projects_Networks/skillsnet/
4 www.trainingvillage.gr/etv/Projects_Networks/Cedra/
5 www.deseco.admin.ch/
6 This is the OECD CERI International Education Indicators Project (INES), which has been running since 1988 – four networks comprise INES. These are: student achievement outcomes (Network A), labour-market destinations (Network B), school processes (Network

C), and attitudes and expectations (Network D). The Networks meet approximately twice a year in order to collaboratively conceptualise and produce innovative education indicators.
7　http://crell.jrc.ec.europa.eu/WP/workprogramme.htm

References

Ball, S. J. (1998) 'Big policies/small world: an introduction to international perspectives on education policy', *Comparative Education*, 34(2): 119–130.

Barnett, M. and Finnemore, M. (1999) 'The politics, power and pathologies of international organizations', *International Organization*, 53(4): 599–632.

Barton, D. and Hamilton, M. (1998) *Local Literacies*. London: Routledge.

Bennett, C. (1997) 'Understanding ripple effects: the cross-national adoption of policy instruments for bureaucratic accountability', *Governance*, 10: 213–233.

Blum, A., Goldstein, H. and Guerin-Pace, F. (2001) 'International Adult Literacy Survey (IALS): an analysis of international comparisons of adult literacy', *Assessment in Education: Principle, Policy and Practice*, 8(2): 225–246.

Bomberg, E. (2007) 'Policy learning in an enlarged European Union: environmental NGOs and new policy instruments', *Journal of European Public Policy*, 14(2): 248–268.

Brown, J. S. and Duguid, P. (2000) *The Social Life of Information*. Boston: Harvard Business School Press.

Brown, P., Green, A. and Lauder, H. (2001) *High Skills: Globalisation, Competitiveness and Skill Formation*. Oxford: Oxford University Press.

Capelli, P. and Rogovsky, N. (1994) 'New work systems and skill requirements', *International Labour Review*, 133(2): 205–220.

Council of the European Union (2000) *Presidency Conclusions, Lisbon European Council (23 and 24 March 2000)*. Online. Available: http://europa.eu.int./ISPO/docs/services/docs/2000/jan-march/doc_00_8_en.html (accessed 17 September 2006).

Dale, R. and Robertson, S. (2007) 'New arenas of global governance and international organisations: reflections and directions', in K. Martens, A. Rusconi and K. Lutz (eds) *Transformations of the State and Global Governance*. London: Routledge: 217–228.

Davies, H. (2004) 'Is evidence-based government possible?', Jerry Lee lecture, 4th Annual Campbell Collaboration Colloquium, Washington, DC.

Davies, H., Nutley, S., Sandra, M. and Smith, P. (2000) *What Works? Evidence-based Policy and Practice in Public Services*. Bristol: The Policy Press.

European Commission (2007a) *Towards More Knowledge-Based Policy and Practice in Education and Training*, SEC (2007) 1098. Brussels: Commission of the European Communities.

European Commission (2007b) *Key Competences for Lifelong Learning – European Reference Framework*. Luxembourg: Office for Official Publications of the European Communities.

Finnemore, M. (1993) 'International organisations as teachers of norms: UNESCO and science policy', *International Organization*, 47(4): 565–597.

Forrester, J. (1999) *The Deliberative Practitioner: Encouraging Participatory Planning Processes*. Cambridge, MA: MIT Press.

Freeman, R. (2006) 'Learning in public policy', in M. Moran, M. Rein and R. E. Goodin (eds) *The Oxford Handbook of Public Policy*. Oxford University Press: 367–388.

Freeman, R. (2008) 'Learning by meeting', *Critical Policy Analysis*, 2(1): 1–24.

Goldstein, H. (1996) 'Models for reality: new approaches to the understanding of the educational process', in D. Reynolds and S. Farrell (eds) *Worlds Apart? A Review of International Surveys of Educational Achievement Involving England*. London: HMSO.

Grek, S. (2008) 'From symbols to numbers: the shifting technologies of education governance in Europe', *European Education Research Journal*, 7(2): 208–218.

Grek, S. (2009) 'Governing by numbers: the PISA effect in Europe', *Journal of Education Policy*, 24(1): 23–37.

Grek, S. (2010) 'International organisations and the shared construction of policy 'problems': problematisation and change in education governance in Europe', *European Educational Research Journal*, 9(3): 396–406.

Grek, S. and Ozga, J. (2010) 'Re-inventing public education: the new role of knowledge in education policy-making', *Public Policy and Administration*, 25(3): 271–288.

Grek, S., Lawn, M., Lingard, B., Segerholm, C., Simola, H. and Ozga, J. (2009) 'National policy brokering and the construction of the European education space in England, Sweden, Finland and Scotland', *Comparative Education*, 45(1): 5–21.

Haas, P. M. (1992) 'Introduction: epistemic communities and international policy coordination', *International Organization*, 46(1), special issue: 1–35.

Haas, P. M. and Haas, E. B. (1995) 'Learning to learn: improving international governance', *Global Governance*, 1: 255–285.

Hamilton, M. and Barton, D. (2000) 'The International Adult Literacy Survey: what does it really measure?', *International Review of Education–Internationale Zeitschrift für Erziehungswissenschaft–Revue Internationale de l'Education* 46(5): 377–389.

Henry, M., Lingard, B., Rizvi, F. and Taylor, S. (2001) *The OECD, Globalization and Education Policy*. Oxford: Pergamon Press.

International Labour Organisation (1999) *World Employment Report 1998/99: Employability in the Global Economy: How Training Matters*. Geneva: ILO.

Keese, M. (2008) 'Progress with the JRA pilot', presentation at the Joint OECD–Cedefop Workshop on Employers' Surveys as a Tool for Identification of Skill Needs, Paris, 22–23 May. Online. Availiable: www.cedefop.europa.eu/etv/upload/etvnews/news/3501-att1-1-05_progress_with_the_jra_pilot_mark_keese.pdf

Kirsch, I. (2001) The International Adult Literacy Survey (IALS): understanding what was measured, Research Report RR-01-25. Princeton, NJ: Educational Testing Service, Statistics and Research Division.

Knodel, P., Martens, K., de Olano, D. and Popp, M. (eds) (2010) *Das PISA-echo: Internationale Reaktionen auf die Bildungsstudie*, Campus Verlag Gmbh.

Kok, W. (2004) *Facing the Challenge: The Lisbon Strategy for Growth and Employment*, Report from the High Level Group chaired by Wim Kok. Online. Available: http://europa.eu.int/comm/lisbon_strategy/index_en.html.

Lauder, H., Brown, P. and Ashton, D. (2008) 'Globalisation, skill formation and the varieties of capitalism approach', *New Political Economy*, 13(1): 19–35.

Lawn, M. (2003) 'The "usefulness" of learning: the struggle over governance, meaning and the European education space', *Discourse: studies in the cultural politics of education*, 24(3): 325–336.

Lawn, M. and Lingard, B. (2002) 'Constructing a European policy space in educational governance: the role of transnational policy actors', *European Educational Research Journal*, 1(2): 290–307.

Lucia, A. D. and Lepsinger, R. (1999) *The Art and Science of Competency Models: Pinpointing Critical Success Factors in Organizations*. New York: Pfeiffer.

Martens, K. (2007) 'How to become an influential actor: the "comparative turn" in OECD education policy', in K. Martens, A. Rusconi and K. Lutz (eds) *Transformations of the State and Global Governance*. London: Routledge: 40–56.

May P. J. (1992) 'Policy learning and failure', *Journal of Public Policy*, 12(4): 331–354.

Murray, T. S. (2003) 'Reflections on future international assessments', in D. S. Rychen and L. H. Salganik (eds) *Key Competencies for a Successful Life and a Well-Functioning Society*. Göttingen: Hogrefe & Huber.

Murray, T. S., Owen, E. and McGaw, B. (2005) *Learning a Living: First Results of the Adult*

Literacy and Life Skills Survey. Ottawa: Statistics Canada and the Organization for Cooperation and Development.

Nutley, S., Davies, H. and Walter, I. (2002) 'Evidence-based policy and practice: cross-sector lessons from the UK', keynote paper for the Social Policy Research and Evaluation Conference, Wellington, New Zealand, 2–3 July.

OECD (2004) *PIAAC Draft Strategy Paper: Policy Objectives, Strategic Options and Cost Implications*, COM/DELSA/EDU (2004)9. Online. Available: www.oecd.org/document/ 57/0,3343,en_2649_33927_34474617_1_1_1_1,00.html (accessed 27 August 2008).

OECD (2010) The OECD Programme for the International Assessment of Adult Competencies (PIAAC). Paris: OECD.

OECD, Statistics Canada (2000) *Literacy in the Information Age: Final Report of the International Adult Literacy Survey*. Paris: OECD and Ottawa: Ministry of Industry, Canada.

Official Journal of the European Union (2007) *Council Resolution of 15 November 2007 on the new skills for new jobs*, 2007/C 290/01.

Ozga, J. and Lingard, B. (2007) 'Globalisation, education policy and politics', in B. Lingard and J. Ozga (eds) *The Routledge Falmer Reader in Education Policy and Politics*. London: RoutledgeFalmer: 65–82.

Ozga, J., Dahler-Larsen, P., Segerholm, C. and Simola, H. (eds) (2010) *Fabricating Quality in Education: Data and Governance in Europe*. London: Routledge.

Pépin, L. (2006) *The History of European Cooperation in Education and Training: Europe in the Making – an Example*. Luxembourg: Office for Official Publications of the European Communities.

Porter, T. and Webb, M. (2004) 'The role of the OECD in the orchestration of global knowledge networks', paper prepared for the *International Studies Association Annual Meeting*, Montreal.

Power, M. (1999) *The Audit Society: Rituals of Verificatio.1*. Oxford: Oxford University Press.

Power, M. (2003a) 'Auditing and the production of legitimacy', *Accounting, Organizations and Society*, 28: 379–394.

Power, M. (2003b) 'Evaluating the audit explosion', *Law and Policy*, 25(3): 185–202.

Power, M. (2004) 'Counting, control and calculation: reflections on measuring and management', *Human Relations*, 57: 765–783.

Raffe, D. and Spours, K. (eds) (2007) *Policy-making and Policy Learning in 14–19 Education*. London: Bedford Way papers, Institute of Education.

Raven, J. and Stephenson, J. (eds) (2001) *Competence in the Learning Society*. New York: Peter Lang.

Rinne, R. (2006) 'Like a model pupil? Globalisation, Finnish educational policies and pressure from supranational organizations', in J. Kallo and R. Rinne (eds) *Supranational Regimes and National Education Policies: Encountering Challenge*. Turku: Finnish Educational Research Assosiation: 183–216.

Robertson, S. L. (2007) 'Embracing the Global: Crisis and the Creation of a New Semiotic Order to Secure Europe's Knowledge-Based Economy', published by the Centre for Globalisation, Education and Societies, University of Bristol, Bristol BS8 1JA, UK. Online. Available: http://www.bris.ac.uk/education/people/academicStaff/edslr/publications/ 12slr/.

Rudd R. E., Colton T. and Schacht, R. (2000) *An Overview of the Medical and Public Health Literature Addressing Literacy Issues: An Annotated Bibliograph*. National Center for the Study of Adult Learning and Literacy; January 2000. Online. Available: http://www.hsph. harvard.edu/health/literacy/literature.html.

Rychen, D. S., and Salganik, L. H. (eds) (2001) *Defining and Selecting Key Competencies*. Göttingen: Hogrefe and Huber.

the degree of centralisation, standardisation or diversification of curricula among the countries studied.

However, beyond these national particularities, the bureaucratic–professional model is still quite present in all countries studied, and beyond; it has been able to spread not only because of generalised development of 'mass education' but also because of 'institutional mimetic' processes (Meyer et al. 1997), the development of an educator state, and standardised norms generally associated with 'progress' in economic growth, as well as at a social level (i.e. social mobility).

Partial Policy Convergences

For approximately 20 years now there has been significant evolution in modes of institutional regulation in the countries studied; most often they have been fostered by major legislation on education policy (like the Education Reform Act of 1988 in England and Wales, the '"missions" decree' (1997) in the francophone community of Belgium (BFr), and laws on decentralisation and deconcentration, as well as a law of orientation (1989) in France, or a major political turning point like the end of the communist regime in Hungary (1989). Portugal is the country that has witnessed the least evolution.

These evolutions are partially convergent and involve six tendencies:

1   *Increasing autonomy for schools.* The promotion (or maintenance) of a form of increasing 'devolution' of responsibilities to schools is visible everywhere (policies relative to 'self-governing schools' in England, and to the 'autonomy of schools' in France, Portugal, Hungary or BFr).

2   *The search for a balancing point between centralisation/decentralisation.* I observe a tendency to decentralise/deconcentrate decision making in traditionally centralised states towards intermediate or local decision-making authorities (France, Portugal and Hungary) and a tendency to reinforce centralisation in states that were strongly decentralised at the outset, notably as regards major curricular objectives in competencies to be attained (BFr and England). Furthermore, as in England, reinforcement of centralisation has also focused on student, school or system evaluation. However, these processes are accomplished with widely varying means, degrees and time frames.

3   *The rise of external evaluations of schools and school systems.* Increased evaluation is, above all, the result of the central state's policy (voluntarily and/or under pressure from users) and at times ramped up and passed on at intermediate or local levels. The extent of evaluation development, its technical sophistication, its instrumentation as a 'steering' tool and its public diffusion are rather uneven. In fact, it is in England (and to a lesser extent in France) that these strategies have been most well developed, and have really been put to work to guide the system. Thus, in England, the creation of OFSTED (Office for Standards in Education, Children's Services and Skills) and the establishment of systematic inspections have led to detailed performance evaluation and the requirement to develop plans to improve all identified weaknesses, with the threat of mandatory school closings in 'failure' situations ('failing schools'). In France, and to a lesser extent in

Portugal, external institutional evaluation has been promoted on a central level (with, for example, the key role of the Department of Evaluation [DEP] within the French Ministry of Education between 1987 and 1997) or regional level, yet with significant variations in application and follow-up at the level of institutions or regional education bodies. Concretely, these evaluations have had only a minor symbolic impact as a regulatory 'corrective mechanism' on the system and schools. External evaluation has also developed in the BFr and Hungary, but without much concrete effect on daily school life. However, recent laws could reinforce the impact of this 'steering' policy in the near future (Mangez et al. 2009, Bajomi et al. 2009).

4   *Promoting or enlarging parents' 'choice' of school.* Parents' possible choices for their children's school are reinforced or maintained in all the countries studied. This practice may proceed from political pressure and a desire to relax administrative rules, as well as from public authorities' laissez-faire position. In England and Wales, besides parents' and students' greater liberty in choosing a school, the government has promoted information for parents on 'performance'. In the BFr, parents' freedom of choice of schools is accompanied by a mechanism financing the schools according to student enrolment. These institutional arrangements, historically established to guarantee philosophical and religious pluralism, have been maintained by recent policies despite recognition of their negative effects on segregation and inequality. However, a very recent decree tightened and formalised school registration procedures to ensure equality for families in exercising their freedom of choice (see Delvaux and Maroy 2009).

Meanwhile, in France and Portugal, it is, instead, social pressure from parents (notably middle-class parents) that has led to a 'soft' policy that relaxed the assignment of children to schools by local authorities (a policy called 'desectorisation' in France, giving parents the possibility of expressing three to five preferences for secondary schools). The application of this policy has varied depending on the institution and period. Yet this practical or official 'opening up' is taking place at the same time as an attempt to preserve the egalitarian nature of the educational offering (via a common and extensive curriculum and a desire to preserve schools' social and educational mix). In Hungary a school map has long co-existed with a tradition liberalising school choice by parents. It is thus easy to obtain authorisation to enrol children outside the family's residential area.

5   *Diversification of the education offered.* We have also observed a varying tendency to emphasise the range of school offerings as a way to highlight the 'diversity of choices possible' for students and parents. This is true in countries where the curriculum was defined in a centralised and relatively standardised fashion (Portugal, France and Hungary), as well as in England, where decentralisation goes hand-in-hand with the comprehensive school model. In France, for example, the possibility of offering more specialised courses has been authorised, in various ways, at the college level, through 'European classes' and classes '*à horaire aménagé*' (specially scheduled classes), and by incorporating optional disciplines like sports or the arts. In England schools can claim 'specialist' status centred around a domain (commerce, media, etc.) and can benefit from increased funding.

In Portugal, schools can vary the number of class hours of different programme components within pre-established limits (non-disciplinary curriculum
areas, creation of technological courses in secondary instruction and programmes
for students in failing situations). In Hungary and Belgium, certain schools can
specialise in learning foreign languages (bilingual tracks), whereas others specialise to ensure particular treatment for certain categories of students (i.e. special
needs students). The policy of diversifying school offerings may be combined
with policies defining common curricular standards increasingly focussed on core
subjects (as in England and Belgium).

6   *Increasing the controlled regulation of teaching.* A sixth tendency is common to all
     five countries: the tendency to erode teachers' individual professional autonomy,
     now subject to increasingly varied forms of supervision of their practices, through
     training, the greater or lesser presence in the school of pedagogical counsellors
     or inspectors (except in Hungary), good practice codes and pressure to engage
     in teamwork. This lessening of professional autonomy also involves the pro-
     fessional group itself, through a weakening of their unions' positions in certain
     countries (above all in England and Hungary).

Supranational Models and National Educational Policies: Two Models of Post-Bureaucratic Governance

Even if we agree that each of these policies is underpinned by models and debates
specific to each subject or country (concerning the autonomy to manage self-
governing schools, the question of 'free choice', the promotion of a more or less
standardised or diversified curriculum, the centralisation or decentralisation of
systems, etc.), they can also be linked to broader governance models across these
various dimensions. These policies can be related to the 'quasi-market' model or to
the 'evaluative state' model, both of which share certain post-bureaucratic traits as
opposed to the bureaucratic–professional model already presented. By 'governance
models' I mean the theoretical and normative models serving as cognitive and
normative references, especially for decision makers, in defining 'good ways to steer
or govern' the education system. These models include basic values and norms and are
simultaneously instruments for interpreting the real situation and guides for action.[5]

Quasi-Market Regulation

In the quasi-market model, the state does not disappear. It retains the important role
of defining system objectives and the teaching curriculum. Yet it delegates autonomy
to schools (or other local entities) to choose the means to carry out these objectives.
In addition, to improve quality and respond to various user demands, it installs a
quasi-market system. This involves granting users free choice of schools, coupled with
financing schools as a function of their student public (financing on demand) (Bartlett
and Legrand 1993). In other words, schools find themselves competing to meet
centrally defined objectives. Users may choose their 'school provider', which must
submit to a considerable number of centrally defined rules, such as a definition of
programmes and certification. These schools can then have public or private status.

The central state, through a specialised agency (private or public), aims to keep users/clients informed about the performance, efficacy and efficiency of different schools so that the rationality of users' choices puts pressure on school staff to improve their operations. It is also important to stress how a quasi-market differs from a classical economic market: 1) the balance between supply and demand is not achieved through prices; and 2) the state is still a key actor fulfilling several roles, such as entering into agreement with 'new providers', funding the providers, creating a definition of compulsory rules for demand (i.e. age of compulsory schooling) and determining the educational offering (programmes, certification system, etc.).

This model was forged by British economists (Bartlett and Legrand 1993) and has been widely promoted in English-speaking countries by certain neoliberal analysts critical of the bureaucratic model (Chubb and Moe 1990). They believe that since the system's bureaucratic character makes it inefficient, it is necessary to foster competitive pressure from users to improve schools. The diffusion of this model has been mediated by various international networks (of international or academic organisations, and experts in education policies) (Halpin and Troyna 1995; Ball 1998; Whitty and Edwards 1998). Such a model has strongly inspired English policies (as well as, further afield, Australia and New Zealand) (Whitty et al. 1998) and has been the object of an extensive critical literature in the Anglo-Saxon world (see for example, Ball 1993).

The Evaluative State

The evaluative state model, thematised by Neave (1988) and Broadfoot (2000), also supposes that the educational system's objectives and programmes are centrally defined and that teaching units enjoy considerable autonomy in pedagogical, organisational and/or budget management, but are subject to meeting the terms of a contract. The central state negotiates 'targets to reach' with local entities (like schools), delegates responsibilities and increases autonomy regarding the means of reaching these goals, corresponding to the general missions promoted by public trust authorities, taking the public or local school context into account. In addition, a system of external school performance evaluation and symbolic or material incentives, or even sanctions, is established to promote improved performances and fulfilment of the explicit or implicit 'contract' signed between the state and schools. In principle these evaluation activities could be carried out by various specialised bodies, either private (pedagogical consultants) or public (i.e. inspection services). The main point here is that these bodies should have recognised expertise related to various evaluation tools (surveys, statistical analyses, audits, follow-ups, etc.).

The goal then is a process of organisational and professional learning resulting in better education in local schools. Thus, ipso facto, the model implies independent economic and pedagogical management of schools and recognition of their ability to respond to requests, either from authorities in control of education or from users. In any case it involves the spread and acceptance of an 'evaluation culture' that relies as much on institutional self-evaluation by teams seeking to improve their practice and results as on external evaluation and data provided by outside expert bodies (Ozga 2009).

A common feature of these two models is the state's important role: the state defines objectives and oversees maintenance of the system's management. To that end, schools or local entities are granted relative autonomy. Moreover, the state no longer wants to be seen as the sole provider of legitimate instruction.

Beyond these common elements, a major difference between the models should be emphasised: in the quasi-market model, it is above all competitive pressure through the intervention of an 'informed' user parent that encourages the school to improve its educational services. In the evaluative state model, regulation occurs more through evaluation of processes and results and through incentives or sanctions meted out to schools according to their 'progress' and results. This system of 'regulation by results' is supposed to boost schools' organisational or professional expertise. The two models essentially differ, then, concerning the place of competition and the 'market' as vector of quality education. Following the model adopted, policies rely either on the market or on evaluation tools, as incentive and pressure for quality improvement. Therefore, these models of the evaluative state and the quasi-market seem intellectually distinct[6] even though, in practice, they can be combined, as the English case demonstrates.

The Post-Bureaucratic Nature of the Models

These two models can be described as 'post-bureaucratic' for two principal reasons. First, from an organisational point of view, the modes of coordination and control established for guidance are no longer limited to ensuring that practices conform to rules and procedures, as was typical of the bureaucratic model. New tools for coordination and control are appearing and becoming increasingly complex (external evaluations, audits, goal contracts, benchmarks and competitive measures) and they are considered incentives to improve school performance and teacher practice. In particular, we are witnessing an increase in new knowledge-based regulatory instruments (Pons and van Zanten 2007). In other words, knowledge presented in the form of measurements or statistical tables (indicators, assessment charts, statistical analysis of various external evaluations, etc.) is being incorporated into regulatory and coordination instruments (Ozga 2009), and is as important to consider as the regulations to be followed or respected. More generally, managerial rhetoric and new tools, inspired by the theory of new public management (definition of objectives, project, measures of counselling and accompaniment, and self-evaluation) contribute to a shared cognitive and semantic universe, which is also supposed to encourage collaboration and the obtainment of the desired results.

In short, to return to the vocabulary of organisational theory (Mintzberg 1992), coordination is no longer based only on the 'standardisation of procedures' typical of the bureaucratic organisation or the 'standardisation of qualifications' associated with the 'professional organisation'; it is also assured through instruments such as the 'standardisation of results' and processes connected to the 'standardisation of norms' (pp. 17–31). Yet we remain subject to the rule of law and bureaucracy because there are still a vast number of laws, decrees, circulars and rules, as evidenced by the increasing incidence of conflicts decided in court, and more precautions are taken to avoid administrative irregularities. This is why the post-bureaucratic management approach is, indeed, an offshoot of the bureaucratic model, even if it is also somewhat contradictory in nature.

We may speak of post-bureaucratic regulation for a second, perhaps more important, reason. In a post-bureaucratic regulation regime, it is not only the modes of coordination and control that are renewed and become more complicated; a new normative order (*normativité*) and new institutional referents are also coming to the fore. Indeed, the bureaucratic–professional regulation system, dominant in the 1960s, was not merely a means of coordinating educational activity; rather, it also contained normative referents and justifications leading to various definitions of the common good.

The Weberian bureaucracy, in fact, linked a form of legitimisation of state domination to a foundation in reason and the law. Moreover, the professional model (Freidson 2001) employed a reference to finalities and substantive values, more or less internalised as part of the ethos of teachers who believe, for example, either in the value of instruction linked to the aim of individual/citizen emancipation based on reason or the importance of raising children in such a way that they become fully actualised human beings and fully develop their potential. In fact, this model of regulation goes hand in glove with a general conception of school that sees it as an institution in the Durkheimian sense, intended to ensure the socialisation of human beings and their integration into larger reference collectivities, particularly into the nation-state (Durkheim 1922). Certainly, different value rationalities (in a Weberian sense) could conflict and compete within this institutional framework. For example, a school oriented more towards civic responsibility (the 'civic' register: equality of opportunity, citizenship training and nation-building), or 'domestic' values (the family and the local environment), or even an 'industrial' orientation (values of efficiency and functionality with respect to economic needs) (Derouet 1992). However, the bureaucratic dimension of the school (stronger or weaker, depending on the country) serves to bolster recognition of the law and of rules, which is, to return to a Weberian distinction (Kalberg 2010), not only the expression of a formal rationality – i.e. bureaucratic regulation oriented towards an optimal allocation of resources – but also an integral part of a substantial rationality (still in a Weberian sense) that recognises the role of law and regulation for their civic significance.

Yet, as Dubet (2002) effectively demonstrated, in France we are witnessing the 'decline of the institution', notably in the educational world, and the increasing appearance of a system of post-bureaucratic regulation in conjunction with a new vision of the school. A conception of school as a 'system of educational production' (inspired by the economy and theories of organisation), in which the goal is to improve its functioning and results (Maroy 2009b), is substituted for a vision of school as an institution (a notion inspired by law and sociology). The new styles of post-bureaucratic regulations developing today claim to be 'value free' and pure 'instruments of technical coordination' and performance improvement, which may, in theory, combine with various goals and ethical ends and dramatically different policies (from the aim to have all students acquire similar skill sets and knowledge to the aim to improve the performance of an educational elite). But these regulatory modes, apparently purely organisational and instrumental, in fact lead to a new paradoxical normative order, based mainly on an industrial orientation (the results-based regulatory model) or a market approach (model of the quasi-market) orientation, to return to the vocabulary and analytical model of Boltanski and Thevenot (1991), referring to different conceptions of justice.

While concerns about educational equity persist, the system of civic justification is losing ground, in fact, to the extent that the latter stresses laws and procedures to guarantee that all have the same civic status and identical treatment by the authorities within the political community. Now, with post-bureaucratic regulation, the equality of all before impersonal rules and regulations is giving way to instruments offering incentives or disincentives (quasi-market or evaluation) meant to encourage efficacy – that is, results. The reference to a political community is downplayed. Members of an organisation are expected to recognise and value individual or aggregate performances, without the collective coming into play. This leads to a recognition of efficacy, a constant search for better performances and continuous learning oriented toward this objective, and an ability to question one's routines and habits, whether under the pressure of demands from clients free to choose their educational provider (quasi-market) or due to greater or lesser encouragement through evaluation, to reach or exceed certain predetermined standards. Here we risk sliding into a system of 'performativity', in an endless search for improved performance (Ball 2003).

Supranational Models and Differences in National Policies

Educational policies in the five countries studied are more or less inspired by the post-bureaucratic models mentioned. Thus the state evaluator model inspires the simultaneous promotion of institutional autonomy and evaluation and, as far as decentralised countries are concerned, the reinforcement of central objectives and standardisation of the curriculum. At the same time, the traits most inspired by the quasi-market – tolerance or the promotion of free choice, and relative diversification of educational programmes in response to the varied demands of users – were also developed. Clearly, Reguleduc's research tends to show that educational policies are inclined, to varying degrees and at different times, to partially converge, from the viewpoint of models of governance and regulation that they are seeking to establish. On the one hand, certain partial traits of the state evaluator model tend to appear, reinforcing the state's wish to evaluate, control and follow-up on the 'producers' (notably establishments and their agents) and 'products' of their educational systems (students' acquisition of knowledge and skills), especially through evaluation tools. On the other hand, in a much more variable manner, the ingredients of a quasi-market model are introduced through the promotion of measures favouring users' free choice, more rarely by the recognition of the virtues of competition among school establishments. Finally, through strengthening their managerial autonomy, establishments are called upon to mobilise to improve their operations or results, in response to the various needs of their users or to objectives assigned by local or central authorities.

However, these transformations operate to diverse degrees, rhythms and intensities, more or less contradictory or coherent. Therefore, depending on the country, educational policies differ since the models evoked are selected, mixed, filtered and interpreted in various ways. In short, there are a number of processes and actions that mediate the influence of these transnational models. It is these processes of divergence that we are now going to examine.

Selection and Mixture of Models as a Function of National Political Struggles and Political Coalitions in Power

The state evaluator model and the quasi-market model are not exactly equivalent, although both are components of a system of post-bureaucratic regulation. The proof is that the political mixture in favour of one or the other depends on each country's political majorities and particular political history. Therefore, in France, until recently (the election of Nicolas Sarkozy), policy makers did not question the operation of school districts (*carte scolaire*) (except to ease the requirements) and few politicians openly promoted the quasi-market. On the contrary, it was the state evaluator model that seemed to be favoured by successive governments of both the right and the left for 'modernising national education'. Then, with the election of Sarkozy, the quasi-market model began to be promoted. In Belgium, where a quasi-market has long existed in practice due particularly to the importance of 'freedom of education' as the basis of social and symbolic compromises structuring the political system (see Dupriez and Maroy 2003), there is only a half-hearted desire to 'regulate' the quasi-market in terms of its most negative effects, without wishing (or being able to) question it in principle.

In England, New Labour has not questioned the Conservatives' profound reforms after 1988 that introduced a principle of parental choice of school, while putting in place a measure to evaluate results and provide information to parents. A strong emphasis on 'standards' and their improvement, measures of evaluation and support for educational staff to 'compel' them to innovate and improve have been added by New Labour to the quasi-market traits, already installed by the Conservatives.

Contextualisation of Policies

Although they derive from post-bureaucratic models of governance, the educational policies observed are not identical, not only because they are inspired in various ways by the two different models cited, but also because different initial situations may result in contrasting policies even when the reference model is the same. Thus, as we have seen, certain jurisdictions that were very decentralised from the outset, as in England and the French Community of Belgium, tend to recentralise, while others decentralise. This apparently contradictory movement may be explained if we hypothesise a rise of the evaluator-state in all the countries concerned. For such a model to emerge, the states that are initially decentralised must define national curriculum objectives and, moreover, develop evaluation with an emphasis both on preserving and developing framed autonomy of the local schools. In contrast, centralised states, with an already highly standardised curriculum, with national certification examinations, must, above all, increase the autonomy of establishments on the ground and develop the actors and instruments that could ensure a close monitoring of these schools, once they have been externally evaluated.

Policies of providing greater autonomy to educational establishments, coupled with decentralisation of responsibilities towards territorial collectivities or deconcentrated entities of the state, are completely strategic in centralised states such as Portugal or France. In the French Community of Belgium, the autonomy of establishments was already quite developed in certain networks (especially Catholic schools). In fact, the issue for the central authority, in England as in Belgium, is rather to know how to reduce the power and authority of major collective actors who are playing a role at the intermediate level (the 'networks' and 'organisational powers' in the French community of Belgium and the local education authority in England).

Phenomena of Path Dependencies

Neo-institutional researchers have long demonstrated that there exists in public policies a certain 'path dependence' that limits decision makers' possible choices (Campbell 2004). Certain choices or methods appear difficult, indeed impossible, to explore for various reasons, sometimes in conjunction: 1) the 'higher returns' from pursuing a policy previously agreed upon and the excessive cost of alternatives; 2) legislative obstacles that appear difficult to overcome, at least in the short run, and that forbid one choice or another; and 3) normative or cognitive conventions (widespread in the political arena and in the population or in a particular field) that contribute to defining the universe of conceivable or justifiable choices. In short, diverse forms of institutions may constitute forms of limitation or obstacles to 'institutional change'. Institutions produce their own antidote to change.

These phenomena of path dependencies are strongly present in the orientation of national policies, which could explain why changes in regulatory modes in different countries have not always converged.

- In Belgium a voluntary policy of questioning the quasi-market is impossible for a number of reasons, even though, in terms of discourse, a number of political actors denounce the perverse effects of the quasi-market, especially in segregating school establishments. Indeed, a number of obstacles make the questioning of the quasi-market problematic: 1) a legislative obstacle: freedom of education and especially parents' freedom of choice is inscribed in the constitution; 2) freedom of choice is strongly and normatively valued by parents in general, which makes questioning it a politically costly venture; and 3) freedom of education is strongly rooted in the configuration of school actors comprising the school system (the presence of competitive school networks) that are sensitive to their institutional survival. Consequently, any questioning of their autonomy (to regulate the quasi-market) will encounter their opposition. Indeed, in 2008/09, two governmental projects aiming to further regulate the freedom of choice were aborted (Delvaux and Maroy 2009).
- In France the (normative and cognitive) convention of the republican school, valuing school as a social and cultural melting pot, makes it *a priori* more difficult to promote the quasi-market model. Therefore, when the model is promoted today, it is based on its equalising virtues compared to the school district. Furthermore, the structural and material forms of the (strongly centralised)

French school system make the quasi-market model more difficult to defend, due to existing rules that would have to be dismantled (notably concerning the school district, but also with regard to a number of centralised institutions linked to the management of school establishments). On the other hand, institutional entrepreneurs exist that have promised diverse variants of the state evaluator model.

The Phenomena of Translation and Hybridisation

Models do not spread in an identical fashion engendering phenomena of institutional isomorphism purely and simply, as Powell and Di Maggio (1991) or Meyer et al. (1997) claim. Phenomena of translation and institutional bricolage exist concurrently, with a view to adapt supranational models and make them acceptable locally, taking into account the material or institutional constraints existing in national states. Translation is indeed a distinct process from the simple spreading of a model, to the extent that importation of supranational models entails some bricolage work that transforms them, based on the institutional characteristics of the reception location. As Campbell (2004) suggests:

> diffusion studies fail typically to recognise that when institutional principles and practices travel from one site to another, recipients implement or enact them in different ways, and to greater or lesser extent, depending on their local social and institutional context. More specifically, new ideas are combined with already existing institutional practices, and therefore, are translated into local practice in varying degrees and in ways that involve a process very similar to bricolage. The difference is that translation involves the combination of new externally given elements received through diffusion as well as old locally given ones inherited from the past.
>
> (p. 80)

This process explains that European policies are not convergent, despite the influence of supranational models. We can provide several illustrations:

- The state evaluator model has 'become more flexible' and modified in Belgium to take account of the strong institutional autonomy of educational networks. Therefore, for example, external evaluations for all networks are mainly for 'formative' purposes, to encourage improvement and reflection on practices, without, however, any real positive or negative 'sanction' ensuing. The situation is similar in France, where the department (its political managers and administrators) has insisted on the necessary spread of a culture of evaluation among managers and personnel involved in education (Thélot 1993). Clearly, these processes of translation lead to the creation of a form of 'low stake accountability' within these systems. We see that the process of translation and hybridisation of models with existing realities allows for the modulation of social issues they entail for actors in the system. This modulation is essential to avoid the rise of virulent internal opposition to their implementation.

- In Portugal and in Hungary, the quasi-market model is largely attenuated in its implementation, to the extent that what has been put in place is only a form of mitigating the principles of the school district.

Clearly, therefore, we are witnessing partial convergences of national policies that maintain strong specificities, despite the effects of trans- or supranational models, due to three processes: a process of mixing and filtering models, path dependence and processes of translation and hybridisation of models with local elements.

Conclusion

A number of comparative studies have explored the convergence of educational policies, especially in light of the phenomena of globalisation and Europeanisation of educational policies (Ball 1998; Novoa and Lawn 2002). Two theses may be broadly distinguished. One, inspired by the neo-institutionalist approach (Meyer et al. 1997), stresses the tendencies towards institutional mimetism of educational structures and policies, an isomorphism due to the growing hold of institutional models worldwide, although their origin is associated with Western modernity. The recent convergence of policies would also be linked to the role of various supranational bodies (the OECD, the EU, etc.) (Robertson et al. 2002; Rizvi and Lingard 2006) or that of transnational epistemological or professional communities that are contributing to building or spreading cognitive and normative models and matrices likely to influence the construction or the agenda of national policies (Halpin and Troyna 1995; Steiner-Khamsi 2004). In contrast, or in complementary fashion, the hypothesis of path dependencies in the construction of national policies could be defended (Merrien 2002). Reguleduc's results tend to support these two lines of interpretation and, rather than contrast them, I would be inclined to explain them further. Certainly, there are perceptible convergences at the level of policy announcements, but over time there are processes of hybridisation and path dependency.

Indeed, this comparative analysis shows first that we are witnessing significant and partially convergent changes in institutional regulatory modes in educational systems. In fact, everything suggests that national educational policies have been oriented, to various degrees, to two dominant models of governance: the evaluator-state model and the quasi-market model. The common element in both models is the foreshadowing of a system of post-bureaucratic regulation that contrasts with bureaucratic and professional modes of regulation, previously predominant in each of the national contexts to varying degrees. Therefore, the validity of the neo-institutionalist thesis is apparent. Some of this convergence is, doubtless, due to the transnational spread of models of governance. However, these orientations are merely partially convergent. Major dependencies on the path remain. Given political, institutional and symbolic constraints specific to each society, policies refer to various degrees to the available models of governance (quasi-market and evaluative state), and policy orientations are built based on what already exists (the logic of hybridisation), or through superimposing new elements, so that the convergence of European systems will not happen in the near future.

Moreover, my research on the emergence of post-bureaucratic models of regulation leads to a critical consideration of the profound normative consequences of the changes at play: does not the rise of the conception of the school as a 'system of educational production' associated with the development of new modes of post-bureaucratic regulations lead to a watering-down of educational policies on the question of efficacy and adequate measures for educational action? Is this not to the detriment of a more profound and sociological rethinking of the constituent and socialising virtues and functions of educational institutions? The changes encouraged in the educational system and its regulation may also be consistent with performativity, whereby education loses its direction/meaning and its finalities, and where a change in practices, organisational reform, and an improvement in performance are promoted with no further foundation, merely as ends in themselves. The educational system would thus be caught, more than in the past, in the 'iron cage' of formal rationality, against which Max Weber long ago warned us.

Notes

1   Reguleduc's research seeks to understand the changes in regulation at different levels (in particular, national, intermediary and local). The accent is on the articulation of these changes, the combination of regulations such as may be seen in different local academic spaces (Budapest, Charleroi, Lisbon, Lille, London and the Paris region), where, for example, a regulation of the central government, itself influenced by a supranational regulation, operates in conjunction with intermediary regulations coming from one or several local public authorities, or 'market' rules emerge from competitive interdependent relations between local school establishments (see Maroy 2004, 2006, 2009a).

2   This institutional regulation by the national state is obviously not the only source of regulations for the educational system since, clearly, regulations may arise from other levels of social action, from the 'grassroots of the system', as much as from the 'top'. Thus, other regulations may appear coming from supranational bodies, in particular those that are derived, for example, from inter-state coordination mechanisms between European countries (such as the EU Open Method of Coordination) or performance evaluation of educational system results initiated by international organisations, such as the OECD or IEA (of the PISA type, for example). Other regulations may also emanate from public or private local educational authorities. Finally, all regulations are not political in origin and some come from the social dynamics of actors at the 'grassroots' level of the system: thus independent regulations (Reynaud 1993) may derive from the very action of establishments themselves or from parents: middle-class anxiety about their children's academic success or worries about the social and academic ranking of certain educational establishments may increase families' desire to have a choice, as well as competition between schools, leading to 'horizontal' regulations of school strategies through competition or the market (van Zanten 2008; Maroy and van Zanten 2009). But these interwoven regulations, which are not automatically consistent, and do not necessarily contribute to well-adjusted and ordered social systems, will not be considered here.

3   The analysis of the evolution of modes of institutional regulation is based on a study of the principal morphological and institutional characteristics of educational systems in the five countries investigated, and an analysis of educational policies followed in the last 20 years, particularly those affecting secondary school regulation. Each team assembled the literature on the national situation under consideration. Then, all the material was combined.

4   The differences concern, on one hand, the societies where the educational systems operate (differing in terms of socioeconomic development, degree of separation of church and state, and demography), and, on the other hand, the characteristics of the educational systems. Thus, at the start of the period of observation (early 1980), I may contrast the most centralised systems (France, Portugal and Hungary before 1989) with decentralised systems

(Belgium and England); the most integrated curricula (Portugal, Hungary and, to a lesser extent, France) to the most differentiated curricula (Belgium and England); and the systems where the allocation of students to schools is more administrative (Portugal, France and Hungary) to systems where a 'free choice' of school has been a longstanding policy (Belgium). These differences are behind the choice of countries to compare.

5 This idea of a model is close to the concept of *'référentiel d'action publique'* or 'policy paradigm' used in cognitive approaches to public policies, stressing the presence of cognitive and normative references that tend to orient the definition of political actors' problems and solutions in various areas (Muller 2000).

6 This distinction between the quasi-market model and regulation by results is close to that proposed by Harris and Herrington (2006), who distinguish between 'market-based accountability' and 'government-based accountability'.

References

Bajomi, I., Berenyi, E., Neumann, E. and Vida, J. (2009) *Governing Autonomy: from Curricular Policies to Quality Assurance and Student Assessments.* KnowandPol, WP 10 Hungarian Education Team, www.knowandpol.eu, R&D EU Sixth Framework program.

Ball, S. J. (1993) 'Education markets, choice and social class: the market as a class strategy in the UK and the USA'. *British Journal of Sociology of Education* 14(1): 3–19.

Ball, S. J. (1998) 'Big policies/small world: an introduction to international perspectives in education policy'. *Comparative Education* 34(2): 119–130.

Ball, S. J. (2003) 'The teacher's soul and the terrors of performativity'. *Journal of Education Policy* 18(2): 215–28.

Barroso, J. (2000) 'Autonomie et mode de régulation dans le système éducatif'. *Revue Française de Pédagogie* 130: 57–71.

Bartlett, W. and Legrand, J. (1993) 'The theory of quasi-markets', in J. Legrand and W. Bartlett, *Quasi-Markets and Social Policy.* Houndmills: Macmillan Press.

Bidwell, C. E. (1965) 'The school as a formal organization', in J. G. March (ed.), *The Handbook of Organizations.* Chicago: Rand McNally.

Boltanski, L. and Thévenot, L. (1991) *De la justification: Les économies de la grandeur.* Paris: Gallimard.

Broadfoot, P. (2000) 'Un nouveau mode de régulation dans un système décentralisé: l'État Évaluateur'. *Revue Française de Pédagogie* 130: 43–55.

Campbell, J. L. (2004) *Institutional Change and Globalization.* Princeton: Princeton University Press.

Chubb, J. E. and Moe, T. M. (1990) *Politics, Markets and America's Schools.* Washington DC: The Brookings Institution.

Commaille, J and Jobert, B. (1998) *Les métamorphoses de la régulation politique.* Paris: Librairie Générale de Droit et de Jurisprudence.

Dale, R. (2005) 'Globalization, knowledge economy and comparative education'. *Comparative Education* 41(2): 117–149.

Delvaux, B. and Maroy, C. (2009) 'Justice scolaire et libre choix de l'école: le débat récent en Belgique francophone'. *Ethique publique* 11(1): 32–43.

Derouet, J. L. (1992) *École et Justice.* Paris: Métailié.

Draelants, H., Dupriez, V. and Maroy, C. (2003) *Le système scolaire en Communauté Française.* Bruxelles: Centre de Recherche et d'Information Socio-Politique-CRISP.

Dubet, F. (2002) *Le déclin de l'institution.* Paris: le Seuil.

Dupriez, V. and Maroy C. (2003) 'Regulation in school systems: atheoretical analysis of the structural framework of the school system in French-speaking Belgium'. *Journal of Education Policy* 18(4): 375–392.

Durkheim, E. (1922) *Education et Sociologie.* Paris: Presses Universitaires de France.

Freidson, E. (2001) *Professionalism, the Third Logic.* Cambridge: Polity Press.

Green, A. (1990) *Education and State Formation: The Rise of Education Systems in England, France and the USA.* Houndmills: Macmillan Press.

Halpin, D. and Troyna, B. (1995) 'The politics of education policy borrowing'. *Comparative Education* 31(3): 303–310.

Harris, D.N. and Herrington, C.D. (2006) 'Accountability, standards, and the growing achievement gap: Lessons from the past half-century'. *American Journal of Education* 112: 209–238.

Kalberg, S. (2010) *Les valeurs, les idées et les intérêts: Introduction à la sociologie de Max Weber.* Paris: La Découverte.

Mangez, C., Maroy, C., Cattonar, B., Delvaux, B. and Mangez, E. (2009) *The Construction of Steering and Evaluation Policy in French-speaking Belgium: A Cognitive Approach.* KnowandPol, WP 10, Belgian Education Team, www.knowandpol.eu, R&D EU Sixth Framework program.

Maroy, C. (2004) *Regulation and Inequalities in European Education Systems.* Final Report, Reguleduc research project, Commission Européenne, 5ème PCRD, Improving socio-economic knowledge base.

Maroy, C. (2006) *Ecole, régulation et marché: Une comparaison de six espaces scolaires en Europe.* Paris: PUF, collection Education et Société.

Maroy C. (2009a) 'Introduction to the sub-issue: new modes of regulations of education systems'. *Compare: A Journal of Comparative and International Education* 39(1): 67–70.

Maroy, C. (2009b) 'Enjeux, présupposés et implicites normatifs de la poursuite de l'efficacité dans les systèmes d'enseignement', in X. Dumay and V. Dupriez, *L'efficacité dans l'enseignement. Promesses et zones d'ombre,* pp. 209–224. Bruxelles: De Boeck Universités.

Maroy C. and van Zanten, A. (2009) 'Regulation and competition among schools in six European localities'. *Sociologie du Travail* 51: 67–79.

Merrien, F.-X. (2002) 'États-providences en devenir: une relecture critique des recherches récentes'. *Revue Française de Sociologie* 43(2): 211–242.

Meyer, J. W., Boli J., Thomas, G. M. and Ramirez, F. O. (1997) 'World society and the nation-state'. *American Journal of Sociology* 103(1): 144–181.

Mintzberg, H. (1992) *Structure et dynamique des organisations.* Paris: Ed. D'Organisation.

Muller P. (2000) 'L'analyse cognitive des politiques publiques: vers une sociologie politique de l'action publique'. *Revue Française de Sciences Politiques,* 50(2): 189–207.

Neave, G. (1988) 'On the cultivation of quality, efficiency and enterprise: an overview of recent trends in higher education in Western Europe, 1986–1988'. *European Journal of Education* 23(1–2): 7–23.

Novoa, A. and Lawn, M. (eds) (2002) *Fabricating Europe: The Formation of an Education Space.* Dordrecht/Boston/London: Kluwer Academic Publishers.

Ozga, J. (2009) 'Governing education through data in England: from regulation to self-evaluation'. *Journal of Education Policy* 24(2): 149–162.

Pons, X. and van Zanten, A. (2007) *Knowledge Circulation, Regulation and Governance.* KnowandPol project, deliverable 4, www.knowandpol.eu, R&D EU Sixth Framework program.

Powell, W. W. and DiMaggio, P. J. (ed) (1991) *The New Institutionalism in Organisational Analysis.* Chicago: University of Chicago Press.

Reynaud, J. D. (1993) *Les règles du jeu: L'action collective et la régulation sociale.* Paris: A. Colin.

Rizvi, F. and Lingard, B. (2006) 'Globalization and the changing nature of the OECD's educational work', in H. Lauder, P. Brown, J. A. Dillabough and A. H. Halsey, *Education, Globalization & Social Change,* pp. 247–260. Oxford: Oxford University Press.

Robertson S. L., Bonal, X. and Dale, R. (2002) 'GATS and the education service industry: the politics of scale and global reterritorialization'. *Comparative Education Review* 46(4): 472–496.

Steiner-Khamsi, G. (ed.) (2004) *The Global Politics of Educational Borrowing and Lending.* New York: Teachers College Press.

Stoker G. (1998) 'Cinq propositions pour une théorie de la gouvernance'. *Revue Internationale de Sciences Sociales*, 155: 19–30.

Thélot, C. (1993) *L'évaluation du système éducatif.* Paris: Nathan.

van Zanten A. (2008) 'Régulation et rôle de la connaissance dans le champ éducatif en France: du monopole à l'externalisation de l'expertise'. *Sociologie et Sociétés*, 40(1): 69–92.

Vincent, G., Lahire, B., Thin D. (1994) 'Sur l'histoire et la théorie de la forme scolaire', in G. Vincent (dir) *L'éducation prisonnière de la forme scolaire*, pp. 11–48. Lyon: Presses Universitaires de Lyon.

Weber, M. (1922) *Economie et société* (Volume 1). Paris: Presses pocket coll. Agora.

Whitty, G. and Edwards, T. (1998) 'School choice policies in England and the United States : an exploration of their origins and significance'. *Comparative Education* 34 (2): 221–227.

Whitty, G., Power, S. and Halpin, D. (1998) *Devolution & Choice in Education: The School, the State and the Market.* Buckingham: Open University Press.

5 Educational Accountability and Global Governmentality

Noah W. Sobe

This chapter examines the global diffusion of educational accountability policies and practices. I engage with the question of whether – or in what ways – we might consider accountability a form of global governmentality. This chapter does not report the results of an empirical study but rather is designed as a theorising/conceptualising piece. I argue that researchers should closely examine the preferences and behaviours that are normalised through educational accountability policies and practices. I also argue that researchers should examine the ways that educational accountability helps to constitute the global. In developing this argument I discuss a range of work from the field of comparative and international education. The chapter also draws on scholarship on accountability and globalisation from other academic fields. I begin, however, with two vignettes. My purpose is to set the stage and to use these two incidents to begin a discussion of what it means to talk about the global diffusion of educational accountability policies and practices.[1]

An education researcher who worked in a rapidly industrialising area of eastern China in the early 2000s has provided us with an illuminating account of a school inspection. One morning, as part of the process of determining which schools would be placed on the list of the ten best elementary schools in the province, a 70-member evaluation team showed up at one of the schools that had made the list of finalists. The inspectors arrived in a tour bus and six large black cars and spent approximately one hour at the school in question. First they listened to a series of short speeches and then dispersed around the building to observe students engaged in a variety of activities. From Andrew Kipnis (2008), the ethnographer who provides us with all this information, we learn that one common concern about top-tier Chinese elementary schools is that they fail to fully use their sports facilities, art studios and computer rooms, and instead devote all their time to test drills and preparation. Because of this concern, apparently, the regular class schedule was disrupted on the morning of the inspection. The best student athletes were sent to use the athletic facilities, the best chess players were in the chess room, the most competent computer users were in the computer room demonstrating their PowerPoint prowess, and so forth. Kipnis reports that afterwards he learned that the principal had three full-time staff members 'working year-round preparing for the paperwork demands and visits of various audit-conducting government officials' (2008: 278). For this particular one-hour inspection by the 70-member team the equivalent of a local farmer's annual income (approximately 10,000 yuan or US$1,250) had been spent to print brochures and provide bottled water to the visitors.

The second vignette comes from a researcher who spent a year, also in the early 2000s, conducting research in a US elementary school located in Washington state. The 360-student K-6 school he studied had been classified by local educational authorities as low performing, which meant that teachers and administrators were under considerable pressure to improve test scores – under the logic that the aggregation of individual achievement data correlated to the teaching and learning activities that occurred (or failed to occur) in this particular school building. The researcher, P. Taylor Webb (2005), describes the surveillance culture that developed among school staff as the school's scores were widely publicised and took on increasing consequence for the future of the school. However, rather than the emphasis placed on a school's test scores immediately prompting an increased reliance on tests as a diagnostic and instructional mechanism (i.e. a movement towards test-driven instruction as the most noteworthy response to a high stakes testing environment), Webb argues that in the case of this school, most consequential were shifts in the ways that teachers began to reflect on and adjust their own pedagogic practices in relation to new paradigms of visibility. A 'surveillance circulation', Webb writes, 'prompted teachers to develop their own sense of accountability' (2005: 201). Teachers reported feeling like they were being intensely observed and this guided many of the micro-elements of their teaching, such as how the bulletin boards outside their classrooms were arranged and how they supervised the transit of their students through the school hallways. (In regard to the latter, Webb usefully reminds us that it takes a certain leap of faith to accept as universal truth 'the normative logic that quiet students [equals] pedagogical competence' (2005: 201).)

There is much in common and much that is different in these two instances of elementary school audit-accountability-inspection practices, which occurred at roughly the same chronological moment but were geographically separated by the vastness of the Pacific Ocean. One could argue, for example, that in one sense we are pointing to cultural practices that are so different that it is an untenable analytic move to lay them next to one another as I have done above. In commenting on the Chinese elementary school inspection, Kipnis (2008) makes a powerful argument that rather than this being an instance of the extension of neoliberal governance techniques, it speaks more to the continuation of a socialist audit culture that gained its contours and its traction through the complex modernisation that China underwent over the twentieth century. And this modernisation itself represents a distinct assemblage of various and varied elements. Citing Bian (2005), Kipnis (2008) notes that even if we restrict ourselves to discussing the way central planners attempted to manage the Chinese economy just in the decade of the 1950s, we find both cost-accounting systems similar to those found in the US at the time, as well as work-emulation campaigns of the sort common in the Soviet Union. A single hour-long inspection by an evaluating team that prompts an alteration to the school's normal morning routine is, arguably, radically different from the pervasive attention to appearances that was brought to a failing US elementary school over the course of an entire school year.

Alternatively, one could point out that these very different cultural occurrences share a similar *performative* element. The idea here would be that accountability, audits and inspections (concepts I will pull apart in a moment) intrinsically relate to how the work of educators (i.e. those who, in the common US parlance, are 'in the building') gets *communicated* outside – whether that be to policy makers and the education bureaucracy, to the general public, or to some amalgamation of the two. In both of the above vignettes students and staff appear to have exhibited widespread audit complicity even if this was, again in both instances, bracketed by conscious deception. On both sides of the Pacific, then, we witness forms of 'accountability choreography' (Webb 2006) where educational actions are shaped and take shape in relation to a society's expectations of what schools should accomplish. Seen from this angle, differences can be collapsed as variations on a common theme. In fact, the difference between a 'high-performing' Chinese elementary school and a 'low-performing' US school would seem to disintegrate further when we consider the ways that economic anxieties and considerations infiltrate both situations. Just as successful schooling and Chinese top-ten school lists are linked to individual and national success 'in the global economy', it is quite plausible to argue that the contemporary imperative to remedy low-performing US schools directly flows from ideas about competitiveness, again, 'in the global economy'. In fact, the tie between educational equity, economic inclusiveness and global competitiveness that one sees traces of in the George W. Bush administration's No Child Left Behind legislation, appears only to be gaining momentum in the Obama administration's current educational initiatives.

To some extent, the two positions I have sketched out above map onto debates in comparative and international education scholarship on differences between the *local* and the *global*. This is sometimes framed as the question of what is locally specific and historically path-dependent about a schooling system and what elements or features conform to institutional templates and cultural scripts that have, over the past two hundred years, become increasingly globally widespread and increasingly convergent. The remainder of this chapter explores, in connection with these questions, some of the ways researchers have studied the global diffusion of school accountability policies and practices. I also aim to offer suggestions on how future scholarship might productively approach this question. I do not aim to exhaustively review the academic literature on educational accountability, but rather to sketch out several important perspectives on how scholars conceptualise the transit of and presence of educational accountability mechanisms around the globe. As is suggested by the above vignettes, in many ways this issue is deeply linked to the ways one might conceptualise neoliberalism and approach the question of how neoliberal political rationalities figure into (or don't figure into) social, cultural and educational configurations the world over (see Ong 2006). In my conclusion I argue that even as one can accurately speak of broad-scale epistemic shifts, what is actualised in any given situation is a bundling together – a contingent and unstable assembling – of multiple, heterogeneous and sometimes conflicting elements (Foucault and Gordon 1980; Agamben 2009). With accountability policies and practices, as with education policies and practices generally, it is the way that various elements are put into relation with one another that truly matters.

Accountability is an important concept to discuss in a volume that deals with transnational educational borrowing and lending. As noted, it can be viewed as a technology of governance closely tied to neoliberal political rationalities (Rose 1996;

Lindblad et al. 2002, Ranson 2003; Hursh 2005; Ozga 2009). In the UK, the features and consequences of an 'audit culture' have been the subject of scholarly examination since the mid-1990s (Power 1997; Shore and Wright 2000; Strathern 2000); however, the global diffusion of school accountability policies and practices has not yet received adequate research attention (c.f. Dickhaus 2010). As the two vignettes suggest, there is much to gain from examining the specific processes, actors and interests that are folded into accountability policies and practices in particular locations. And, as part and parcel of this, there is much to gain from examining how non-local references and trans-local pressures and enticements factor into the policies and practices that are actualised at any given moment.

Also worthy of further exploration is the question of the extent to which we are witnessing, at the start of the twenty-first century, a global trend toward increased self-organising reflexivity in the self-description and self-observation that school systems are required to engage in. In recent years some globalisation scholars have called for more detailed study of the specific mechanisms, techniques and apparatuses by which things are constituted as 'global' (Ong and Collier 2005; Tsing 2005; Stichweh 2008). This call stands in stark contrast to what a remarkable body of globalisation scholarship takes as an *a priori* assumption: the idea that there is something out there already existing that is 'global'. As Urs Stäheli (2003) insightfully points out, even those who exalt in the subversive power of 'the local' tend to reify 'the global' in their analyses by assuming a universalising global that is an expressive totality. Aihwa Ong and Stephen Collier (2005) make a powerful case that rather than examining 'the changes associated with globalization in terms of broad structural transformations or new configurations of society or culture', attention should be paid to 'the specific range of phenomena that articulate such shifts' (p. 3). In this vein, and analogous to my above argument that researchers need to be attentive to the contingent bundling together of heterogeneous elements, I will also argue in this piece that accountability practices need to be seen in relation to the ways that they are *constitutive of the global* and not an after-effect that is produced by those nebulous and putatively external forces of globalisation. Playing off Foucault's definition of governmentality as the conduct of conduct, I am proposing that accountability can be described as *the monitoring of monitoring*.[2] In this sense it can be considered one of the features of 'global governmentality' (Larner and Walters 2004), for the behaviours, preferences, habits, representations and forms of reflection that it normalises across multiple social levels, agents, institutions and political formations.

Accountability Systems

In a *World Yearbook of Education* chapter from several years back (Sobe 2006) I argued that in US educational research the concept and practice of 'accountability' was linked to the social administration of the individual and to the design of salvational collective narratives. As part of an effort to unsettle the taken-for-grantedness of the early twenty-first century's 'age of accountability', I emphasised the fact that the US had experienced an accountability wave in the late 1960s and early 1970s where the accountableness of federal, state and local governments was linked to social engineering and the employment of science to plan for the future. Illustrative of this particular policy/engineering environment was the pattern of building a mandatory evaluation component into federal educational initiatives, such as the sprawling components of the federal Elementary and Secondary Education Act (also known as Title I and first authorised in 1965 as part of President Lyndon B. Johnson's War on Poverty). Notable in the US educational research literature from this period is the work of Leon Lessinger, who emphasised the importance of demonstrating educational results obtained from resources used (Lessinger 1970; Lessinger and Tyler 1971; Lessinger and Sabine 1973; see also Levin 1974). We even see that in 1971 the National Council of Teachers of English (NCTE) adopted a position statement on accountability that critiqued behaviourist evaluation paradigms and discussed the multi-directional accountability relations that bound teachers of English to their students, the parents, school administrators and the larger community, and vice versa.

The framing of educational accountability as a relationship (i.e. as someone/something being 'accountable' to or for another someone/something) has by no means disappeared from the modern educational lexicon (e.g. Ryan 2005). However, even in the midst of what was referred to as 'the current "accountability" craze' in a 1972 issue of the *Journal of Higher Education* (Cooper 1972), accountability seems to have been concurrently treated as a process. In this second guise accountability is cast predominantly as a technical undertaking. It indexes the production of data and information that, from a certain social engineering perspective, should properly be built into any public policy initiative. A peculiar transit occurs (Sobe 2006) as accountability increasingly comes simply to refer to the collecting and reporting of data. It moves from being a theoretical concept to being an object or set of material practices that occur in the world. One could add that there is then a third step where accountability transitions back into an analytic construct that describes *whether* measurements and data records are being produced. As an illustration of this, consider that in many settings today the question 'What kind of accountability is there?' would be immediately answered with a listing of what data are collected and no reference to relational obligations.

In the educational research literature of the early 2000s it is common to encounter the notion that policy makers, the educational bureaucracy and educational researchers need to join hands to better implement 'accountability systems'. In his 2003 American Educational Research Association (AERA) presidential address titled 'Accountability: Responsibility and Reasonable Expectations', Robert Linn noted that ideas of shared responsibility were too often ignored and that the question of 'who is accountable' was frequently answered too narrowly. Nonetheless, his address spoke at greatest length about broadening the range of outcome measures, together with data on contextual and process variables, that need to be incorporated into accountability systems. The approach I am taking here to an accountability *system* is different in that what concerns me are the ways that educational accountability systems work as social systems. My emphasis here is on social systems as distinctly patterned sets of cultural practices where technical apparatuses and mechanisms gain their meaning in cultural and social spheres of activity.

One of the inaugural approaches to conceptualising accountability as a social system comes from Michael Power (1994) who, in discussing the explosion of auditing practices in Britain, remarked that this entailed the spread of a distinct mentality of administrative control, a pervasive logic which has a life over and above specific practices. One crucial aspect of this is that many more individuals and organizations are coming to think of themselves as subjects of audit.

(Power 1994: 3)

In Power's terms, auditing practices emerge 'when accountability can no longer be sustained by informal relations of trust alone but must be formalized, made visible and subject to independent validation' (pp. 9–10). In an anthropological mode, Power (1997: 123) also refers to auditing as a 'ritual of verification', a characterisation since taken up by many scholars. Shore and Wright (2000) propose that in the UK auditing has migrated across diverse domains much in the manner of what Raymond Williams would refer to as a *keyword*. It has become the 'centre of a new semantic cluster' (Shore and Wright 2000: 60) and exploded beyond its financial meaning to factor into the operations of a wide range of social institutions. As I am suggesting in this piece, in the US and in other settings it is *accountability* that is more popularly the master concept that describes and prescribes a particular mentality of administrative control. Though Power was speaking of auditing practices, the following seems to similarly describe the deeply reaching consequences of our current accountability craze:

Far from being passive, audit actively constructs the contexts in which it operates. The most influential dimension of the audit explosion is the process by which environments are made auditable, structured to the need to be monitored ex-post.

(Power 1994: 7)

Power's key insight is that audit activities do not simply operate *within* a particular context. Rather, the cultural practice we are describing here is much more recursive: over time auditing begins to shape and re-shape the very context itself. Applied to educational accountability, this suggests that we ask whether schooling, learning and pedagogy are increasingly being designed to be monitorable and calculable (on this point, see Taubman 2009). What is particularly important is that auditing/accountability practices are not simply passive forms of observing but that they shape the standards of performance – and beyond this, that they construct the very contexts in which they operate.

Another way to approach accountability practices as a social system is suggested by Marilyn Strathern (2006) in a discussion of the (re)writing of university mission statements in relation to audit practices. Drawing on Power's work, she suggests that 'the whole audit apparatus in Britain amounts to a self-organizing "system"' (p. 192). Strathern points to Niklas Luhmann's theorisation of social systems as holding that systems are axiomatically self-referential, that they define their own boundaries, and that they position everything beyond themselves as their environment. These self-organising properties describe an audit system which

regenerate[s] itself through the auditable accounts it elicits. For it inspects the auditees' *own* auditing methods; auditees are thus turned into ethical self-auditors—typically they do their own audit on themselves before the experts come in.

(Strathern 2006: 191, emphasis in original)

'Educational accountability' as a pure and simple desideratum might be seen as a system in this manner, as a social system that exists in a state of perpetual demand vis-à-vis the education sector (a social system in its own right). Accountability can be justly accused of simplifying the complexity of the entire business of education (see, e.g., Linn 2003, among countless others). However, in Luhmannian terms, the reduction of complexity describes the exact manner in which social systems translate information. As my opening vignettes suggest, a school might 'do accountability' for accountability's sake. This performance (or this creation of an *account*, i.e. a narrative that can be put into circulation/use) is – as we saw on both sides of the Pacific – potentially a distraction from what participants identify as the functional purposes around which the education system is organised.

The fact that accountability is often cloaked as virtuous and innocent makes it an even more important social system to be reckoned with. The difficulty of 'saying no' to accountability has been remarked upon by many educational researchers (e.g. Peterson and West 2003). In its self-description it is merely an 'enabling technology' (Strathern 2006: 192). As constantly evolving and constantly restless (in large part due to the notion that measurements can always be improved and fine-tuned) accountability can begin to define what it means to be an organisation. In education in particular, engaging in accountability practices is more than a means for communicating with other social systems. In certain settings this is one of the ways that a school performs as an organisation. From the point of view of the education system, however, this engagement with another social system is worked into its processes of boundary definition. Taking Luhmann's argument that systems produce the contexts within which they operate, it becomes quite understandable that an education system would relegate accountability to being a feature of the environment. This is not to say that all educators automatically consider accountability practices a nagging distraction or necessary evil. Rather, the point is that this might help us explain why schools seem to exhibit a tendency to externalise and place accountability mechanisms outside their boundaries, as pressure that comes in from the outside. This also helps explain why accountability reporting seems to be treated as a specialised form of communication.

However, as noted above, Strathern's argument suggests (to the social scientists observing all of this) that accountability ought to be considered a self-organising social system that regenerates itself and propels itself forwards. From this perspective, it appears important to understand the ways that accountability is a specialised set of cultural practices. And, accordingly, when we focus our attention on how the education systems interact with accountability systems, more thought needs to be given to 'how one system is mediated by others' (Munro cited in Strathern 2006: 193).

The notion that accountability might be changing the rules by which educational institutions organise themselves seems partially congruent with the reading offered by neo-institutional sociologists who study the global spread of world cultural models. In a recent article in the *Comparative Educational Review*, David Kamens and Connie McNeely (2010) propose that we can explain the growth of international educational testing and national assessment by looking at key ideological forces within the world polity. Positing that it is possible to discuss culture in terms larger than states or nations, world polity analyses typically concentrate on the institutional features of transnational developments (Boli and Thomas 1997). The polity itself is conceptualised as a network of nation-states, international organisations and societies, all of which are in varying degrees informed by world cultural models. According to Kamens and McNeely (2010), three aspects of world culture explain the growth of national assessments and international testing.

First, there is, allegedly, an increasingly isomorphic world educational ideology under which schooling is seen to possess individual and collective benefits that are increasingly linked to concerns about democracy and equity (Fiala 2007). Widespread agreement internationally about the desired outcomes of education, according to Kamens and McNeely (2010), 'legitimates international efforts to make mass education more accountable to society' (p. 11). Second, one can also point to the hegemony of science as generating the notion that the world can be rationalised with the same kinds of cause-effect relations inhering in any place on the planet. It is this logic that underlies the concept of 'best practices'. And, it is this same logic that suggests that the management of an education system be principally concerned with the production and monitoring of achievement data to find out – in an idiom popularised by the US Department of Education – 'what works'. The third explanation, Kamens and McNeely argue, is the very idea that society is something that can be managed. However, rather than the central planning model that we saw in earlier eras, there is an apparent world cultural trend toward devolution and decentralisation. They argue that nowadays wide sectors of society are brought into this management project. Individuals and collective actors are empowered as agents, thus placing an emphasis on 'the ability of a wide variety of actors to make society accountable and effective in achieving socially desired goals' (p. 13). Though the Kamens and McNeely article deals with assessment instruments specifically, it is quite clear that from a neo-institutionalist world polity angle, measurement, testing and calculation consistently circle back to accountability issues and the cultural models that make accountability viable and desirable in the first place.

In my view, a critical and sometimes overlooked dimension of neo-institutionalist arguments is the assumption that the cultural models that propagate and 'succeed' do not necessarily do so for *functional* reasons (Sobe and Ortegón 2009). Rather, it is processes of emulation and coercion that explain the diffusion of institutional forms and world cultural scripts (Dimaggio and Powell 1983). To claim, then, that assessment circles back to issues of accountability is an analytic and not a normative claim. It may be true but it is not *necessarily* true that accountability mechanisms actually make educational institutions more faithfully and more effectively perform their missions. In fact the opposite may just as well be the case.

Across all the scholarly paradigms just discussed there would seem to be general agreement that the accountability systems that we encounter in the contemporary world are not passive mechanisms of observation but are imbued with mythic notions of virtue, collective salvation and promises of further rationalisation and control. However, the question of how the ideational and the sociological dimensions of accountability merge is still unresolved. To be sure, bridging thought and action – or the epistemological and lived experience(s) – is no small task for social theory. Below I will have more to say on this. For now, let us note that Strathern's Luhmannian analysis does not elucidate the historical confluences that undergird accountability practices to the extent that neo-institutionalist accounts do. Yet at the same time, Strathern's approach does show the severe limitations of the neo-institutionalist reliance on the concept of *cultural models* or *cultural scripts* (specified in advance) to explain and predict what is happening in the world. It seems increasingly clear, as indicated by the two vignettes introduced at the beginning of this chapter, that in certain places around the globe today accountability becomes substantially more than a script-that-guides-action but has self-organising features, which means that the translation and simplification of complexities can take on a life of its own.

The Diffusion of Accountability Policies and Practices

In a recent essay, Rudolph Stichweh (2008), working under the assumption that it is tenable to claim that we presently inhabit a world society, has proposed that researchers interested in globalisation direct their attention to the 'eigenstructures' of said world society. Stichweh draws from a concept that is widespread in the field of mathematics to describe characteristic structures that can change in some respects but not others (such as a vector that changes in magnitude but not direction). Under the heading *eigenstructure* he includes formal organisations (qua organisations), epistemic communities (such as Linux developers as a current example), global function systems (e.g. the world economy), as well as world events (such as the Olympics or 9/11). These eigenstructures and world society reciprocally intensify one another. According to Stichweh (2008), these various eigenstructures also produce diversity, conflict and inequality. Conceptualising social change not as the substitution of something new for the old, he proposes that 'new structures overlay old structures but do not extinguish them' (p. 135). Yet, importantly, the diversity that this produces is non-local diversity – it cannot be legitimately described or experienced as purely local. While it would be a brash move to claim that accountability policies and practices fit neatly into his schema, they do represent a structural pattern that is compatible with the emerging system of world society, and the two can reciprocally intensify one another. This is *not*, I would argue, because accountability lends itself to isomorphic inclinations but simply because accountability mechanisms are highly articulated to the global formations discussed previously and are thus privileged by them.

Numerous comparative and international education scholars have demonstrated that adaptation/modification/indigenisation constantly and consistently occur as educational policies and practices move globally. The same can certainly be said of educational accountability. Barbara Dickhaus (2010) has empirically demonstrated this with regard to 'accountability regimes' in her comparative study of recent quality assurance initiatives in the South African and Argentinian higher education sectors. She points in particular to the traditional mode of higher-education governance in each setting as helping to explain how new accreditation initiatives played out. Nonetheless, Dickhaus argues that quality assurance policies have become a hegemonic tool for reorganising the higher-education sector, in part because of the variety of meanings that can be attached to them and the selectivity that goes into the contested process of appropriation and meaning creation.

The role that international organisations play in disseminating accountability techniques and practices is well described in UNESCO's own statements. A 1995 report on the outcome of a meeting related to its 'Monitoring Learning Achievement' initiative noted:

> The Framework of Action that emanated from the Workshop constitutes some key orientations for the MLA Project in the years to come. A wider dissemination of the outcomes at national and at international levels is needed. Support towards the development of a *Monitoring Culture* can only be pursued through national capacity building programmes.
>
> (UNESCO 1995: 4, emphasis in original)

On the one hand, this quote offers a good example of the ways that language and documents are employed in international governmental and non-governmental organisations to fashion normative imperatives (Riles 2000). It also speaks somewhat to the role that international organisations play as producers of world culture and not merely as its implementers (Resnik 2006). Particularly worthy of note is that the project of implementing assessment instruments and the mechanisms for monitoring achievement are discussed in cultural terms. It is no surprise, then, that numerous scholars find it appropriate to refer to accountability *regimes*, very much in the same sense that Foucault used the word to refer to the regnant systems and sensibilities under whose control human societies and cultures find themselves at various points in time.

If scholars of comparative and international education focus exclusively on where precisely this quality assurance mechanism or that assessment strategy was borrowed/ lent from, there is great danger that we will lose the forest for the trees. The analytic task at hand is not to play a game of origins (Sobe 2005). Rather, if our quest is to better understand the cultural, political, social and epistemic configurations and conditions that shape the range of what are possible, impossible, desirable and undesirable options, then we need to ask more questions about how accountability 'works'.

Accountability as Global Governmentality

If governmentality can be described in Foucault's oft-quoted terms as the 'conduct of conduct', then – as I proposed at the outset – in accountability policies and practices we have a similar meta-level operation that falls under the heading of the 'monitoring of monitoring'. As Hindess (2004) proposes, governmentality analyses allow us to better understand how domains that were previously subject to more direct forms of regulation are increasingly being regulated in seemingly less direct ways. Though goods such as individual choice, empowerment and markets are frequently presented as forms of freedom and as strategies for escaping heavy-handed regulation, there is a rich body of Foucault-inspired scholarship featuring scholars such as Nikolas Rose (1999) that argues that, while they are less 'direct' forms of control, the promotion of choice and markets are regulative projects through and through. The political facets of accountability are not difficult to discern, and above we saw several versions of the argument that accountability, with its technical strategies of measurement, emerges in a social engineering context where progressive political futures are seen as able to be planned for and able to be realised. In a penetrating analysis of the increasingly widespread practice of benchmarking Wendy Larner and Richard Le Heron (2004) note that with the development of ISO standards in the 1980s and as this became coupled with Total Quality Management (TQM) notions, 'a technical device began to mutate into a managerial system' (p. 216). By contrast, accountability practices begin and end as managerial even though it can at times seem that the conversations are purely technical.

The monitoring of monitoring is increasingly being enacted in multiple sites by multiple actors. In the US, the National Council for the Accreditation of Teacher Education (NCATE) process for accrediting schools of education represents a massive audit undertaking that principally concerns itself with how the educational institutions concerned collect data, assess it and act upon it (Taubman 2009). NCATE does not define quality itself, nor does it dictate what objectives must be achieved. Rather, it holds schools of education accountable for formulating their own objectives, monitoring their success at achieving these objectives, and initiating 'data-driven change' to ensure fidelity to mission – less direct control perhaps but undeniably still a managerial and institutional steering endeavour. The same pattern holds in certain international domains. The year 2011 has been designated the 'International Year of Youth' by the United Nations, a ceremonial dedication designed to heighten awareness of and focus international attention on a chosen set of issues (on UN dedications generally, see Drori 2005; on the 2011 youth year, see Sobe forthcoming). The UN resolution announcing this declaration presents a veritable laundry list of tasks for governments, civil society, youth-led organisations, the private sector, etc. – such as to provide increased support for youth development, pay greater heed to the social and political rights of youth, and implement programmes designed to foster intergenerational solidarity. We will not be surprised to find that progress monitoring and the implementation of 'monitoring systems' features prominently on this list.

In a 2004 volume titled *Global Governmentality* Larner and Walters aptly note that governmentality scholarship has tended overwhelmingly to take the nation-state as its analytical locale (with the notable exception of studies of colonial governmentality). To speak of 'global governmentality' does not, however, mean that we are taking 'the global' as the extension of/replacement of the nation-state. The term global governmentality might in fact index the very mobility, versatility and ability to be implemented by multiple actors that so integrally characterises Foucault's notion of governmentality in the first place. Ample are the spheres of human activity, regions of the world, and sectors of society that are completely untouched by accountability regimes. Where they do emerge, however, accountability practices and policies seem to exhibit coherent self-organising systemic properties and regulative dimensions that combine with multiple other elements to give accountability in any given place its actuality.

I opened this chapter with two vignettes and proposed that they might be viewed, on certain grounds, as very different cultural practices, or, on other grounds, as strikingly similar cultural practices. On both sides of the Pacific Ocean we saw the business of schooling being altered for the purpose of communicating a certain set of information onward, outward and upward. Yet, the Potemkin quality of the Chinese inspection seemed notably different in its texture than the Washington state example I provided – noting, of course, that in the United States one could probably find ample recent examples where auditors are presented with a completely fabricated account of how a school conducts its operations. There is no question that the actual meaning of the top-school inspection visit and the failing-school surveillance culture is a local matter (in each setting) and one that is produced by local actors, with reverberations that most chiefly affect them. At the same time, it is fair to say that teachers, students, and administrators were enmeshed in an accountability regime in each setting. And, that the regnant systems and sensibilities were not strictly pre-specified and trans-ferred in from outside, but rather took their form only as part of ongoing social processes. The regulative, managerial dimension of each of these sets of accountability practices emerges both as educational accountability continually unfolds, becomes improved and reinforces itself, and as it communicates information across different social spheres. In both respects, educational accountability may be said to lend itself to the constitution of *globe-level* social forms and interactions. Above I suggested that in these two instances educators and policy makers were struggling with ways to demonstrate educational performance in a manner that would reliably lead to success 'in the global economy'. In other settings it may well be a best-practices problematic that gives force to the lesson-learning-unencumbered-by-borders notions that educa-tional accountability mechanisms portend and promise. Global governmentality is a project, mobile and heterogeneous. Educational accountability practices in eastern China and the Pacific Northwest suggest that this 'monitoring of monitoring' is an important, emerging form of global governmentality.

In discussing educational accountability as global governmentality, I am not proposing a unified theory for rethinking global–local issues. The focus on monitoring performance, self-description, self-observation and the translation of such to other domains and interests means that accountability is a special species of global govern-mentality. While perhaps not an eigenstructure of the world system in the strictest sense, accountability may be said to have globalising tendencies in the sense that it helps to produce global systems and, as reward for this service, seems increasingly to be favoured by them.

Notes

1 I am grateful to Iveta Silova, Sophia Rodriguez and Nicole Ortegón as well as the editors for reading earlier drafts of this essay and providing useful feedback.
2 Later in this chapter I draw on Marilyn Strathern's (2006) discussion of Niklas Luhmann's systems theory, in which the concept of observing observations (*Beobachter des Beobachters*) plays a crucial epistemological role. However, my use of the concept of 'the monitoring of monitoring' is not intended to evoke a reference to Luhmann. It is instead an allusion, in a Foucauldian vein, to the ways in which systematic and systemic self-reflection and self-monitoring are themselves monitored and subjected to normative expectations and parameters.

References

Agamben, G. (2009) *'What Is an Apparatus?' and Other Essays*. Palo Alto, CA: Stanford University Press.

Bian, M. L. (2005) *The Making of the State Enterprise System in Modern China: The Dynamics of Institutional Change*. Cambridge, MA: Harvard University Press.

Boli, J. and Thomas, G. M. (1997) 'World Culture in the World Polity', *American Sociological Review*, 62: 171–190.

Cooper, L. G. (1972) 'Decision Ability, Not Accountability', *Journal of Higher Education*, 43: 655–660.

Dickhaus, B. (2010) 'The Selectivity of Translation: Accountability Regimes in Chilean and South African Higher Education', *Globalisation, Societies and Education*, 8: 257–268.

Dimaggio, P. J. and Powell, W. W. (1983) 'The Iron Cage Revisited: Institutional Isomorphism and Collective Rationality in Organizational Fields', *American Sociological Review*, 48: 147–160.

Drori, G. S. (2005) 'United Nations' Dedications: A World Culture in the Making?' *International Sociology*, 20: 175–199.

Fiala, R. (2007) 'Educational Ideology and the School Curriculum', in A. Benavot and C. Braslavsky (eds) *School Knowledge in Comparative and Historical Perspective: Changing Curricula in Primary and Secondary Education*. Hong Kong: CEERC/Springer, 15–34.

Foucault, M. and Gordon, C. (1980) *Power/Knowledge: Selected Interviews and Other Writings, 1972–1977*. New York: Pantheon Books.

Hindess, B. (2004) 'Liberalism – What's in a Name?' in W. Larner and W. Walters (eds) *Global Governmentality: Governing International Spaces*. New York: Routledge, 23–39.

Hursh, D. (2005) 'Neo-Liberalism, Markets and Accountability: Transforming Education and Undermining Democracy in the United States and England', *Policy Futures in Education*, 3: 3–15.

Kamens, D. and McNeely, C. (2010) 'Globalization and the Growth of International Educational Testing and National Assessment', *Comparative Education Review*, 54: 5–25.

Kipnis, A. (2008) 'Audit Cultures: Neoliberal Governmentality, Socialist Legacy, or Technologies of Governing?' *American Ethnologist*, 35: 275–289.

Larner, W. and Le Heron, R. (2004) 'Global Benchmarking: Participating "at a distance" in the Globalizing Economy', in W. Larner and W. Walters (eds) *Global Governmentality: Governing International Spaces*. New York: Routledge, 212–232.

Larner, W. and Walters, W. (eds.) (2004) *Global Governmentality: Governing International Spaces*. New York: Routledge.

Lessinger, L. M. (1970) *Every Kid a Winner: Accountability in Education*. Palo Alto, CA: Science Research Associates College Division.

Lessinger, L. M. and Sabine, C. D. (1973) *Accountability: Systems Planning in Education*. Homewook. IL: ETC Publications.

Lessinger, L. M. and Tyler, R. W. (1971) *Accountability in Education*. Worthington, OH: CA Jones Pub. Co.

Levin, H. M. (1974) 'A Conceptual Framework for Accountability in Education', *The School Review*, 82: 363–391.

Lindblad, S., Ozga, J. and Zambeta, E. (2002) 'Changing Forms of Education Governance in Europe', *European Educational Research Journal*, 1: 615–624.

Linn, R. L. (2003) '2003 Presidential Address. Accountability: Responsibility and Reasonable Expectations', *Educational Researcher*, 32: 3–13.

Ong, A. (2006) *Neoliberalism as Exception: Mutations in Citizenship and Sovereignty*. Durham, NC: Duke University Press.

Ong, A. and Collier, S. J. (2005) *Global Assemblages: Technology, Politics, and Ethics as Anthropological Problems*. Malden, MA: Blackwell.

Ozga, J. (2009) 'Governing Education through Data in England: from Regulation to Self-evaluation', *Journal of Education Policy*, 24: 149–162.

Peterson, P. E. and West, M. R. (eds) (2003) *No Child Left Behind?: The Politics and Practice of School Accountability*. Washington, DC: Brookings Institution.

Power, M. (1994) *The Audit Explosion*. London: Demos.

Power, M. (1997) *The Audit Society: Rituals of Verification*. New York: Oxford University Press.

Ranson, S. (2003) 'Public Accountability in the Age of Neo-liberal Governance', *Journal of Education Policy*, 18: 459–480.

Resnik, J. (2006) 'International Organizations, the "Education-Economic Growth" Black Box, and the Development of World Education Culture', *Comparative Education Review*, 50: 175–195.

Riles, A. (2000) *The Network Inside Out*. Ann Arbor, MI: University of Michigan Press.

Rose, N. (1996) 'Governing "Advanced" Liberal Democracies', in A. Barry, T. Osborne and N. Rose (eds) *Foucault and Political Reason: Liberalism, Neo-Liberalism and Rationalities of Government*. Chicago, IL: University of Chicago Press, 37–64.

Rose, N. S. (1999) *Powers of Freedom: Reframing Political Thought*. Cambridge, UK: Cambridge University Press.

Ryan, K. E. (2005) 'Making Educational Accountability More Democratic', *American Journal of Evaluation*, 26: 532–543.

Shore, C. and Wright, S. (2000) 'Coercive Accountability: The Rise of Audit Culture in Higher Education', in M. Strathern (ed.) *Audit Cultures: Anthropological Studies in Accountability, Ethics, and the Academy*. London: Routledge, 57–89.

Sobe, N. W. (2005) 'Balkanizing John Dewey', in T. S. Popkewitz (ed.) *Modernities, Inventing the Modern Self and Education: The Traveling of Pragmatism and John Dewey*. New York: Palgrave, 135–152.

Sobe, N. W. (2006) 'Accountability in US Educational Research and the Travels of Governance', in J. Ozga, T. S. Popkewitz and T. Seddon (eds) *World Yearbook of Education: Education Research and Policy*. London: Institute of Education, 33–42.

Sobe, N. W. (forthcoming) 'Transnational Governance', in N. Lesko and S. Talburt (eds) *Youth Studies: Keywords and Movements*. New York: Routledge.

Sobe, N. W. and Ortegón, N. D. (2009) 'Scopic Systems, Pipes, Models and Transfers in the Global Circulation of Educational Knowledge and Practices', in F. Rizvi and T. S. Popkewitz (eds) *Education and Globalism*. New York: National Society for the Study of Education (NSSE)/Teachers College Press, 49–66.

Stäheli, U. (2003) 'The Outside of the Global', *New Centennial Review*, 3: 1–22.

Stichweh, R. (2008) 'The Eigenstructures of World Society and the Regional Cultures of the World', in I. Rossi (ed.) *Frontiers of Globalization Research: Theoretical and Methodological Approaches*. New York: Springer, 133–149.

Strathern, M. (ed.) (2000) *Audit Cultures: Anthropological Studies in Accountability, Ethics and the Academy*. London: Routledge.

Strathern, M. (2006) 'Bullet-Proofing: A Tale from the United Kingdom', in A. Riles (ed.) *Documents: Artifacts of Modern Knowledge*. Ann Arbor, MI: University of Michigan Press, 181–205.

Taubman, P. M. (2009) *Teaching by Numbers: Deconstructing the Discourse of Standards and Accountability in Education*. New York: Routledge.

Tsing, A. L. (2005) *Friction: An Ethnography of Global Connection*. Princeton, NJ: Princeton University Press.

UNESCO (1995) *Final Report: Monitoring Learning Achievement, Towards Capacity Building.* Paris: UNESCO.

Webb, P. T. (2005) 'The Anatomy of Accountability', *Journal of Education Policy*, 20: 189–208.

Webb, P. T. (2006) 'The Choreography of Accountability', *Journal of Education Policy*, 21: 201–214.

6 Webs of Borrowing and Lending

Social Networks in Vocational Education in Republican China

Barbara Schulte

The Importance of Being Social

Research on educational borrowing and lending has been largely concerned with transnational or transsectoral transfer of educational ideas, models and policies (see, e.g., Steiner-Khamsi 2004). Most often, the units between which borrowing and lending are seen to take place are those of the nation-state; but scholars have also looked at how, for example, educational reforms are implemented at the subnational level, after having gone through processes of negotiation, adaptation and, at times, hybridisation at various levels.[1] Most recently, scholars have also paid increasing attention to transnational or global communities in which educational knowledge is circulated, both in history and at present. Differently from players within nationally defined boundaries, these communities transgress national borders or circumvent them by linking up the local directly with the global.[2] It can be almost regarded a tradition within the field of comparative education not to dismiss unfaithful copies of original models and reforms as 'failures' or 'distortions', but to explore the cultural dynamics and rationale behind these sometimes unexpected transformations and side effects. The comparative view sharpens the sensibility for how, in different contexts, things are done in their 'own way', to borrow a phrase from one of the forefathers of comparative education, Michael Sadler, who pondered on the balancing act of borrowing from outside while at the same time maintaining the 'characteristic[s] of English life' (quoted in Waterkamp 2006: 22).

When things are done in their own way – who does them? For a long time different outcomes of transfer processes were either structurally explained or attributed to regional, cultural or even civilisational differences, but studies of recent decades have attempted to break up this cultural 'black box of education', where 'things happen, but we do not know how' (Hoffman 1999: 474). Local agency has been moved to the fore, to understand how actors make sense of, for example, educational reforms, and how their sense-making leads to certain action (or non-action). Two different perspectives prevail when looking at these actors: one can look at the categorical attributes they possess; or one can look at their interaction, their social relations.[3] Social network analysis is concerned with the latter.

'A social network is a set of actors (or points, or nodes, or agents) that may have relationships (or edges, or ties) with one another', reads the minimalist definition by Hanneman and Riddle (2005). Exploring social networks can yield important insights about social action. Social networks can illustrate both the flows of ideas (carried by people or organisations) and the flows of power. The nature of the nodes (actors) through which ideas pass can tell us something about how the ideas get processed and changed, and how this has a backlash on actors and their behaviour. Social network analysis, maintain Eugenia Roldán Vera and Thomas Schupp, is 'a methodology used to explain social change' (2006: 407). Moreover, social network analysis can bridge the gap between micro and macro studies of society since it looks both at groups and individuals: 'the network approach investigates the *constraining* and *enabling* dimensions of patterned relationships among social actors within a system' (Emirbayer and Goodwin 1994: 1418; emphasis in original). Social network analysis can also track the paths that travelling agents and ideologies take when transporting models or reforms.[4] It can thus illustrate the intricacy and agency of processes of diffusion and reception, but also the width and hence the power of social movements; social networks have therefore often been described by the metaphors of epidemics and contagion. Social network analysis 'has become a way of articulating the dimension of the "global"' (Roldán Vera and Schupp 2006: 406).

Despite these advantages, particularly when it comes to exploring processes of borrowing and lending, social network analysis has been mostly used only metaphorically in education studies.[5] Although detractors might claim that education studies always lag behind other social science disciplines, or that data compilation for network analysis is simply too tedious, there might be deeper reasons for this lack of professionalism when dealing with social networks in education. On one side, in spite of heavy investment in data collection, social network analysis usually makes a statement solely on the particular network that is being analysed; generally, network analysts cannot – and have no interest in – 'generaliz[ing] to larger populations of such networks' (Hanneman and Riddle 2005).[6] Analysing a particular social network thus does not entail that the results will be representative of society at large. On the other side, to those education researchers who are interested in local agency, social network analysis might look prone to structural determinism if the focus on relationships – rather than on actors – becomes dictatorial. Claims like that by Ronald Burt that 'people and organizations are not the source of action so much as they are the vehicles for structurally induced action' (1992: 5) can deter researchers who believe in autonomous actors as enacting multiple identities and roles, using and mobilising them strategically, while being embedded into certain ideologies about what is true and good, and what is false and bad.

Mustafa Emirbayer and Jeff Goodwin (1994) have pointed out how a number of studies that make use of social network analysis provide insightful descriptions of networks but fail to look beyond them – namely at how and why these social networks came into being in the first place. They stress the importance of surrounding narratives and underlying rationalities, including the normative commitments of the actors themselves, and criticise most network studies for ignoring the structuring influences of cultural and political discourse on actors, that is, the generative power of discourse. Consequently, while the visible, material structures are carved out skilfully, nonmaterial structures such as symbols and narratives remain largely unexplored. Although this categorical neglect of narratives is indeed widespread, it is not necessarily a compulsive side effect of social network analysis. Social network analysis is a tool for examining (and visualising) social interaction; it does not constitute – at least not to most researchers – a fully fledged theory or world view.

Social network analysis can illuminate the 'how' of social relations, and it can explain the longevity or ephemerality of certain phenomena that are created, maintained or abolished through social relations, but it is much less suited to explain the 'why' of ties – here, other conceptualisations have to come into play. For example, the analysis of a social network like the vocational education movement in Republican China might reveal through which channels the idea of vocational guidance was imported from the United States into China; how earlier networks made it highly probable that it would be the US and not some other country that would be selected as reference society; who served as middlemen or brokers; and which nodes were able to have their say before the idea was finally implemented. However, the analysis cannot explain why actors chose to forge these ties in the first place – which ideas in the educational arena made certain ideas and certain foreign models attractive? Or from a system perspective, which interruptions and repercussions created the 'system's internal needs for "supplementary meaning"' (Schriewer and Martinez 2004: 32) and thus made the system externalise to references outside?[7] Social network analysis thus works as a complement to, not a replacement of, existing conceptualisations of borrowing and lending.

What is, technically speaking, social network analysis? As pointed out above, most studies of (comparative) education that purport to analyse social networks are not social network analyses in the strict sense but discuss the network character of certain communities. This is by no means to say that these studies are valueless; on the contrary, many of these discussions might go beyond what social network analysis alone, as a methodological tool, would be able to explain. Social network analysis in the orthodox sense makes use of either of the two following conceptual strategies: it tries to explain social behaviour through the fact of connectivity; or it emphasises the notion of structural equivalence (positional analysis) in showing how certain patterns in relationships can lead to certain social change (Emirbayer and Goodwin 1994). Below, I will concentrate largely on the first of these two options. After nodes and ties of the network under examination have been traced (and entered into a database) as exhaustively as possible, network analysts will most often use software programmes in order to analyse and visualise their network (especially if there is a high number of nodes and ties).[8] The most important characteristics that a network analysis investigates – and I am leaving out quite a few details here – are closeness, betweenness and connectivity within a given network.

Closeness refers to the distance between two given actors or nodes; looking at closeness means investigating how many steps it would take from a given node to reach all other nodes. The length of paths in a network is not simply a matter of mathematics but has profound social consequences:

> Networks that have few or weak connections, or where some actors are connected only by pathways of great length may display low solidarity, a tendency to fall apart, slow response to stimuli, and the like. Networks that have more and stronger connections with shorter paths among actors may be more robust and more able to respond quickly and effectively.
>
> (Hanneman and Riddle 2005)

Clearly, those actors who have at their disposal a high number of short paths to other actors are in a privileged position to communicate and, ultimately, to influence others. Their enhanced opportunities to bargain make them 'central'; they have networking power.

Betweenness is another measure of centrality and power. It investigates how actors or nodes function as mediators or brokers, that is, how they serve to connect other nodes. Brokers possess a high amount of bridging social capital; their importance rises with an increasingly monopolistic position: if they have few competitors, or are connected to 'pendants', that is, nodes/actors that are only connected to this broker (and thus dangle from the diagram), they have a gate-keeping function. At the same time, however, their increased value endangers the robustness of that part of the network that is dangling – if the gatekeeper is removed (e.g. through political action), the network will be split in two.

Connectivity is concerned exactly with this danger – it denotes the minimum number of nodes/ties that need to be removed in order to disconnect different parts of a network. If a network possesses many redundant ties, the individual players may be less valuable, but the network is robust. If the network possesses many indispensable ties, the individual players have high leverage, but the network as such is vulnerable, particularly in politically or economically unstable times. Within a given network, connectivity may vary. If we imagine a subculture, for example, we can expect it to be highly connected internally, but only a few actors will have ties to the rest of the network. These 'cliques', in network terms, constitute a set of nodes where every element of the set is connected to every other member. Depending on the power and the social capital of those members who are connected to the rest of the network, cliques can be imagined both as counter-narratives and resistance movements, or as influential think tanks that are close to the central power nodes.

In the following, I will present findings from my analysis of the vocational education movement in Republican China between 1917 and 1927 (see Schulte 2008).[9] After a more general section on social networks in Republican China, I will focus on the Chinese Association for Vocational Education (*Zhonghua Zhiye Jiaoyushe*; in the following: CAVE), which was founded in 1917 in Shanghai. As will be elaborated in the next section, both period and location were characterised by networks of borrowing and lending, in education as well as in other realms. Processes of transfer at the time were bifurcated, displaying the inherent hierarchies and power relations: Chinese urban elites were actively and excessively engaged in borrowing from other countries (mainly Europe, the US and Japan), reflecting the then prevalent (and latent) intellectual colonialism involved in knowledge transfer. This asymmetry of exchange was then replicated towards China's periphery – transfers from urban to rural, literate to illiterate, men to women, etc. Furthermore, there was a more symmetrical exchange between hitherto little connected sectors, such as education and economy, and transfer across disciplines (such as that of psychology into education). Thus, lending and borrowing took place across national, regional, class, sectoral and disciplinary boundaries. Concomitantly, actors and ideas crossed different physical and ideological worlds.

Republican China and Social Networks

Republican China was a network society. Daily, thousands of new members joined different political, cultural, educational or business organisations and associations. In the two years following the Xinhai Revolution in 1911, when the imperial government was overthrown and eventually gave way to a republic, almost 400 new organisations emerged. The *Tongmenghui* alone, an umbrella association of revolutionary organisations, grew by several thousand new members each day during this period (Ju 2002). Organisations differed in regional and thematic scope: while some were translocal or even transnational (such as the Chinese Red Cross Society), others were interest associations with a specific local focus. Likewise, comprehensive associations like the Science Society of China (*Zhongguo Kexueshe*) (see, e.g., Wang 2002) were operating along with smaller organisations that were devoted to rather specialised fields and topics. While each of these organisations constituted micro-networks themselves, they were yet embedded in a larger network of associations that emerged through multiple memberships across different organisations. In a society whose political, economic and societal future direction was highly uncertain, networking was a safe investment. Besides conveying a sense of belonging (i.e. transmitting bonding social capital), membership in different networks provided bridging social capital, which could turn out extremely valuable in times of change, as a diversity of social connections could guarantee more options when encountering crises.[10]

Historically, social networks in the form of associations were not a new phenomenon, but their rapidly increasing number and professionalisation were a novelty. Prior to the Republican era, China had been far from homogeneous – much in contrast to official accounts of a cultural and, later, national unity. Even in the nineteenth century, when Western powers started to force China open through warfare and unequal treaties, unification and sinicisation were still in the making, with large regions remaining only loosely coupled to the central government. Regional fragmentation was paralleled by a 'secular decline in governmental effectiveness' (Skinner 1977: 19), whereby local affairs were increasingly taken over by nongovernmental networks, due to the growing scale of empire and the decreasing availability of government officials. However, most of these networks were driven by local concerns and often sanctioned by the local government.[11] They were, in a way, closed local systems.

In urban Republican China, in contrast, many social networks were characterised by a high degree of openness. Different from earlier times, when they were mainly expected to regulate what was not sufficiently dealt with by the state, organisations were now eager to win members for their cause, which was often connected to more overarching social movements and ideologies, such as the movement of self-government.[12] Networking became lobbying; Republican Chinese society had become a meeting and market place of ideas and members, particularly in the coastal and, to a large degree, internationalised cities, such as Shanghai, which by the 1920s had become the hub of commercial and cultural activities. Transfer, or borrowing, of ideas and models, both in education and more generally, was facilitated by two factors. On the one hand, a sense of crisis – often articulated in a social-Darwinist fashion as the looming extinction of Chinese culture and race – made politicians, entrepreneurs and academics look towards the outside, particularly Japan and the West. On the other hand, the urge to forge ties with like-minded individuals led to the formation of new alliances, which transgressed traditional boundaries between, for example, the world of the literati and that of the entrepreneurs. Thus, while the initialisation of transfer was built on the will – and the pressure – to externalise (cf. Schriewer and Martinez 2004),[13] its ongoing enactment, adaptation and negotiation evolved through social interaction and networks.

Most Chinese intellectuals and activists towards the end of the Qing dynasty (overthrown in 1911) saw education in a deep crisis. This crisis lay in the perceived irrelevance of education; the solution lay in making it more relevant.[14] Relevance could only be achieved through linking education to reality – which, in the eyes of the modernising elites, was embodied in factories and shipyards. Consequently, vocational education was heralded as the cure for all ills. However, besides merging two hitherto mutually hostile ideological realms – education and entrepreneurship – it was also the people who had to be linked. In 1917, the pedagogue Huang Yanpei (1878–1965) founded CAVE. This association linked Confucian-educated scholars and modern, internationally trained scientists with entrepreneurs, manufacturers, craftspeople, journalists, politicians and political advisors.[15] From an ideological perspective, this alliance was innovative and perhaps daring; from a network perspective, CAVE's members can be seen to have engaged in 'robust action' (cf. Padgett and Ansell 1993). They were involved in several different games at once, they articulated multivocal interests, and thus they made it difficult to attack them: CAVE was joined by Christians, Buddhists and agnostics, and it was populated by monarchists, anarchists, Communists and Nationalists alike. CAVE's founder Huang Yanpei skilfully interacted with both Nationalist and Communist leaders, allegedly even earning the praise of later premier Zhou Enlai, who is said to have accredited Huang with the capacity to 'weave a far-reaching and close-meshed network with individuals from all possible social circles as well as with young students' (quoted in Wang 1983: 53). Thus, CAVE's – and in particular Huang's – 'flexible opportunism' (Emirbayer and Goodwin 1994: 1436) guaranteed its longevity (CAVE still exists today).

Moreover, CAVE's connection to the non-academic world granted it a strategically advantageous position in Chinese (urban) society. Just as the Medici, in Padgett's and Ansell's (1993) much discussed study, drew their success from the novel alliance between patrician elites and 'new men', educationists in CAVE, as quasi-monopolists, reached out to the entrepreneurial world and could thus profit from what Ronald Burt calls a 'structural hole', comprised of 'disconnections or nonequivalencies between players in the arena', which provide 'opportunities for information access, timing, referrals, and control' (1992: 1–2). Burt's structural holes can be compared to Granovetter's almost proverbial 'weak ties' (1973, 1983), which bring the benefit of connecting to (socially) distant but important nodes. But while 'weak ties' are about the type of relationship, a structural hole is about the chasm that is spanned by the relationship – the cause of creating opportunity; in this case, the productive interface of education and entrepreneurship. While many educators, starting towards the end of the nineteenth century, had talked about the need for education to be rendered more pragmatic and realistic, CAVE succeeded in incorporating 'reality' into its network, much in contrast to other educational associations, which remained largely academic in nature. Figure 6.1 shows how the professional profile of members was able to build bridges between gentry and the entrepreneurial world. While there was still a clear binarity between these two worlds, with high professional mobility within each world but not between them, there were 32 individuals who were active in both, namely those who worked in cultural/humanitarian organisations and vocational education. These 32 members constituted the crucial linkages between the two worlds, opening up communication channels that were often non-existent in other associations.

However, profit has its ideational price, which is often (and naturally) neglected in business-oriented approaches like that of Burt: the exploitation of structural holes brings a backlash on what is to be negotiated. If the aim is to draw in entrepreneurs (in the broad sense), the rationale and logic of ideas circulating within the network have to, at least to some extent, turn entrepreneurial as well. This is one of the openings in social network analysis where ideas can – and must – come back in: structural holes, or weak ties, open up opportunities, in the sense of obtaining useful social capital; but since they are so valuable and at the same time so different, they also have the power to transform ongoing debates within the network, especially if these debates are perceived to occur in times of crisis and if hitherto upheld paradigms have become

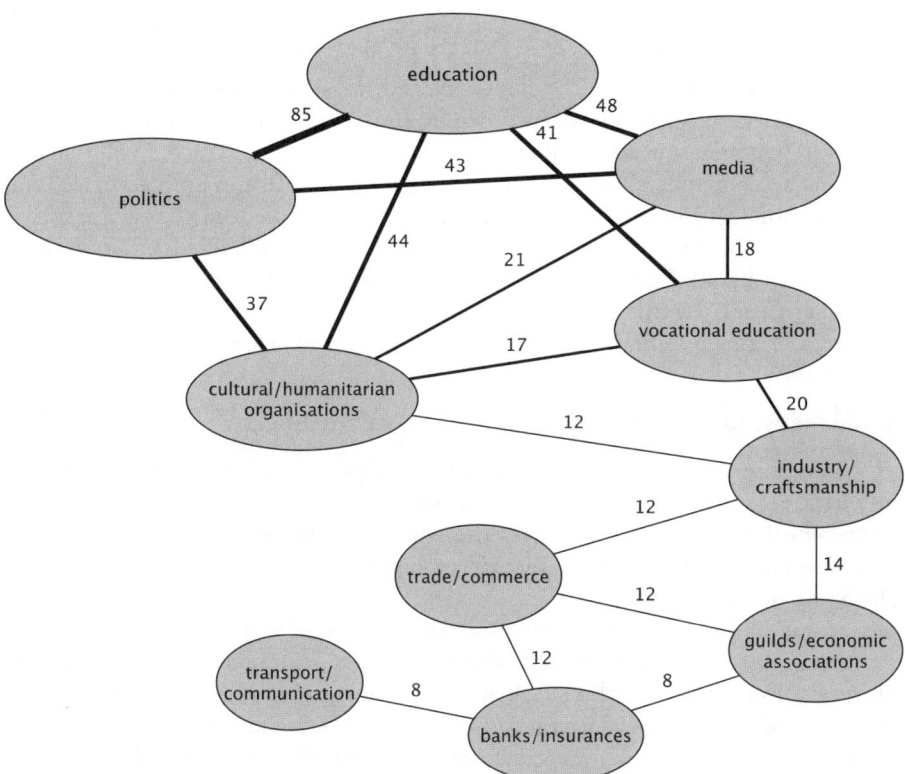

Figure 6.1 Clusters of occupations pursued by identical individuals (numbers of individuals in the overlapping section)

questionable and unstable.[16] In CAVE, this interference from the other side of the hole manifested itself above all in a recourse to vocational morality: bankers bring back moral virtues and civilised behaviour as the gist of (business) education (Shen 1923), while others cite values like honesty, patience and endurance, civility and modesty as well as the readiness to serve as being of central importance to employers, and argue for an integration of these values into vocational education (Pan 1923). Vocational guidance, a newly imported idea from the US, was less about helping an individual find the right job, but more about making this individual accept his or her situation peacefully (Wei 1928). Thus, ideas that were originally designed to support individual development were turned into means of containment and subordination of the individual to the larger interest of society.

What does a more detailed analysis of CAVE's network reveal?

Social Networking for Vocational Education: The Chinese Association of Vocational Education (CAVE)

In the following, I will present, due to limited space, a reductionist picture of CAVE's network,[17] but I will compensate for this shortcoming by illuminating the network from three different perspectives. First, I will outline where its academic members came from in terms of those educational institutions that figured most prominently in training CAVE's future members. Second, I will investigate how CAVE's network spread out geographically, both within China and across the world, to assess the reach of this network both in terms of its potential sources of inspiration (or externalisation), and potential sources of influence (or implementation). Third, I will visualise and discuss the members' network through their involvement in both academic and non-academic institutions, in order to assess, by using the tool of social network analysis, what made CAVE, from the perspective of its embeddedness in existing institutions, special. The nodes in the networks discussed below do not represent individual actors, but (most often) institutions.

Now to the first question: where were members trained before they entered CAVE?

Initial Networks: Academic Training of CAVE Members

CAVE was joined by alumni of quite a number of prestigious academic institutions, both national and international. Figure 6.2 does not show all institutions where members received their education, but only those that contributed four or more members to CAVE. This means that there were eleven institutions (shown in Figure 6.2) from which individuals emerged in smaller or bigger groups to join CAVE, indicating that networking had taken place even before they entered this network of vocational education. Moreover, the network hosted a clique, a foursome consisting of Tsinghua University in Beijing, St. John's College and Nanyang Gongxue, both in Shanghai, and Columbia University. The names of St. John's College and Nanyang Gongxue (or Nanyang Technical College) are less known than Tsinghua or Columbia University today. At the time, these two institutions were crucial breeding grounds for modern knowledge in China. St. John's College was founded in 1882 as a missionary school by the Episcopalians and, particularly after becoming registered in the US as a domestic

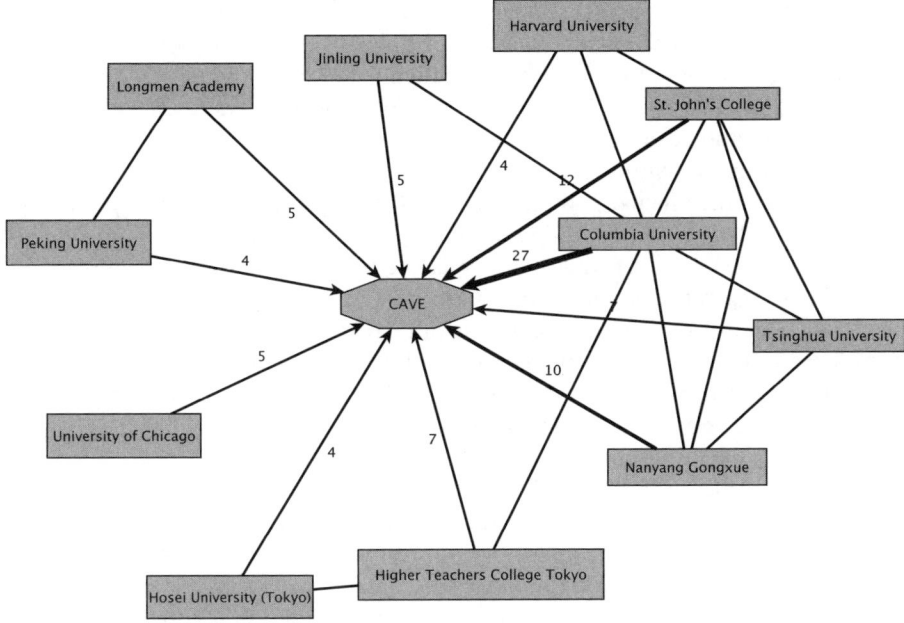

Figure 6.2 Academic institutions where members (four or more) were trained (ties between institutions indicate multiple career paths)

university, trained a large number of later famous politicians, industrialists, diplomats, writers, etc. It was one of the first foreign institutions to teach modern (and thus Western) knowledge in China. Nanyang Technical College was a precursor to Shanghai Jiaotong University and was a genuinely Chinese project. It was founded in 1896 by the influential industrialist, pedagogue and political advisor Sheng Xuanhuai (1844–1916),[18] in response to a perceived lack of know-how in the engineering sciences. Sheng was deeply worried about the fragmentation of Chinese industrial policy and action (in contrast to what he observed as unitary action among foreign powers), and as an antidote initiated the Shanghai Commercial Consultative Association (*Shanghai shangye huiyi gongsuo*) (Fewsmith 1983).

As a teacher at Nanyang Technical College, Sheng taught many later members of CAVE, who, like him, saw China's backwardness not only in its lacking (technical) expertise, but also in its lacking capability and will to carry through concerted, regulated, political and economic action. The mission of CAVE to install, through vocational education, both technical skills and a sense of unity, can be seen as at least partly emanating from the members' early years at Nanyang College. The clique thus linked two eminent universities, one Chinese and one North American, with two institutions, again one Chinese and one North American, which were specifically established to spread 'new learning'. Seen from the perspective of Columbia University, it was placed at the hub of the network. Besides being integrated into this powerful clique of modernisers, Columbia University has the highest number of connections to other universities (five out of eleven possible ties), thus possessing the advantage of having influenced the most cosmopolitan future members, namely those who received their education at several national and international universities. Figure 6.2 also shows that, in absolute numbers, Columbia University contributed the most alumni to the network. A majority of those members who had studied in the US (46 individuals) had at one time been enrolled at Columbia University (27 individuals), of which most studied at Teachers College.

Reports from contemporaries who were anything but sympathetic to Teachers College can confirm its paramount role in influencing Chinese pedagogy. German Carl Heinrich Becker, who in 1931 was in charge of conducting an educational report on China for the League of Nations, complained bitterly, in one of his letters home, about the exaggerated emphasis on pedagogical/didactic questions in American pedagogy, and its 'influence . . . on China', in particular 'the dissolution of all real knowledge into gibberish on the method and psychology of education' (from the seventh letter in the compilation by Kuss 2004: 133).[19] In a subsequent letter, he focuses especially on the role of Teachers College:

> Teachers College at Columbia University has had a downright devastating impact [on China]. I have never experienced the corruptive influence of a single institution on an entire continent so overwhelmingly as that of Teachers College on China. Even with regard to our pedagogical academies, we have realised, in spite of the *Abitur* [higher track secondary school graduation certificate], that the [acquired] disciplinary knowledge does not even suffice for instruction in elementary school. At Teachers College, however, pedagogy, with all its subsections (psychology, sociology, administration, etc.) has been turned into a science which counts as a main subject even for higher level schools. This is, of course, great nonsense. . . . In China, educational colleges have now been established everywhere, whose graduates become higher level teachers without mastering correctly even one single school subject.
>
> (From the eighth letter; Kuss 2004: 151)

Chinese returnees from Teachers College occupied not only mediating and/or powerful positions such as those of translators or (educational) politicians, but they also provided an introduction to prominent figures like John Dewey, in thought and in person, who again exerted a profound influence on the Chinese educational landscape during and after his visit to China (see Schulte 2009).[20]

Networks of Action from a Geographic Perspective

CAVE drew a great part of its inspiration from abroad. As outlined above, Chinese educational culture, to many reform-oriented intellectuals, did not provide sufficient semantic resources to think about amalgamating the needs of the labour market with questions of professional identity and educational training. Other countries looked like convenient suppliers of both ideas and practical solutions.

More than half of the investigated corpus (99 members) had been abroad at least once in their career, either for study or work, or simply for travelling, and all continents were visited by at least one of the actors, although there were obviously vast differences between the popularity of each destination (Figure 6.3; for better clarity,

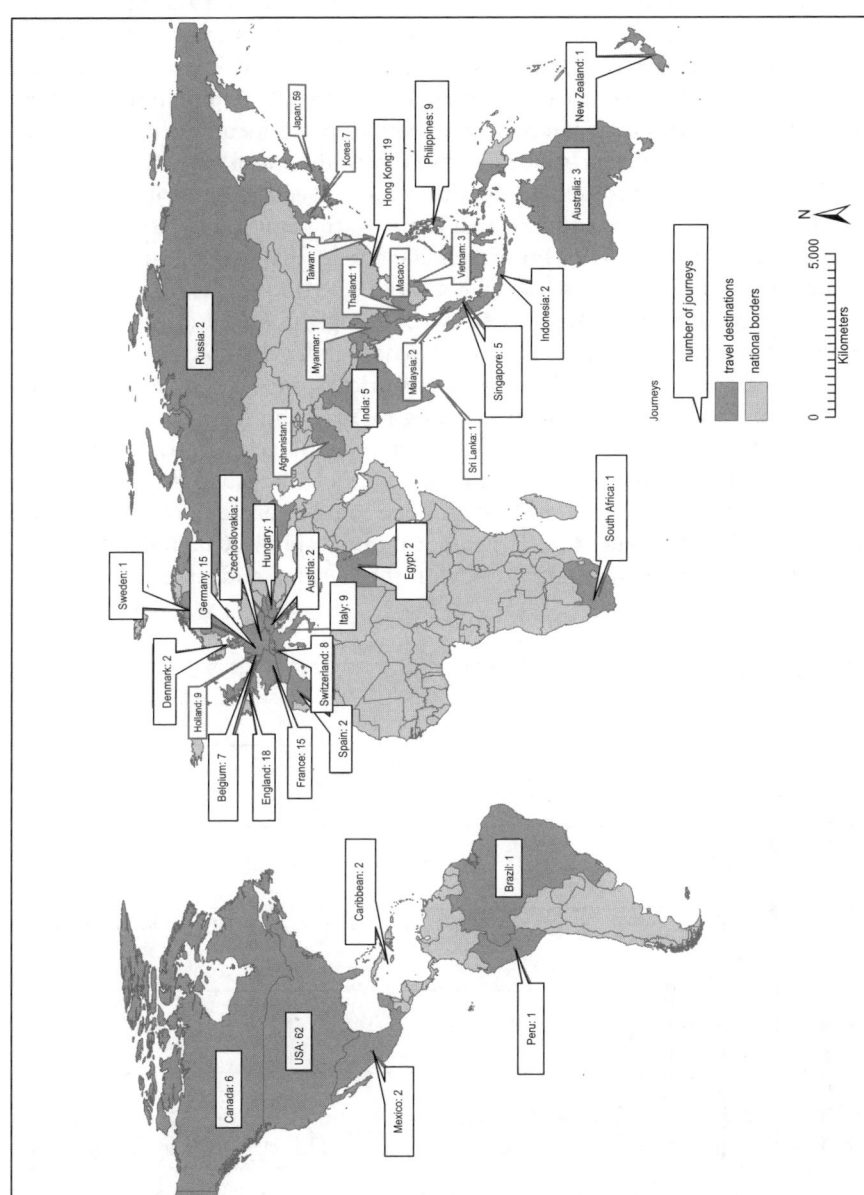

Figure 6.3 World regions to which members travelled (number of journeys)

the journey paths themselves, from China to each destination, are not shown).[21] This number is astounding, considering the fact that those were times of slow transport, scarce resources and (civil) war. The US ranked first as the most visited destination (62 visits), much in parallel with their status as the favourite study destination at the time among those who would become CAVE members, but closely followed by China's neighbour, model and enemy Japan (59 visits), and, at a greater distance, by Hong Kong (19), England (18), France (15), Germany (15) and the Philippines (9).

As illustrative as this map is, it can only visualise the members' international mobility; it cannot explain it. In quantitative terms, the travel pattern can be confirmed if one counts the articles that deal with vocational education in other countries in one of the most important educational journals, the *Educational Review* (*Jiaoyu Zazhi*), between 1909 and 1949. Out of over 200 articles that make clear reference to both vocational education and a foreign country,[22] the US gets the largest share (54 articles), followed by Japan (31), Germany (21), England (15) and Russia (9) (see Figure 6.4).[23] In qualitative terms, the attractiveness of the US model was owed both to historical legacies and practical concerns. Historically, the US was the first country to receive Chinese overseas students, starting in 1872 and thus exerting an early influence through Chinese returnees.[24] Besides, as a vast, largely agrarian country and a successful late-comer among global powers, the US was judged to share similarities with China which, in the eyes of the modernisers, could be exploited for educational transfer. The American model, CAVE member and educationist Guo Bingwen (1879–1969) concludes in his comparative study on the German and American systems,

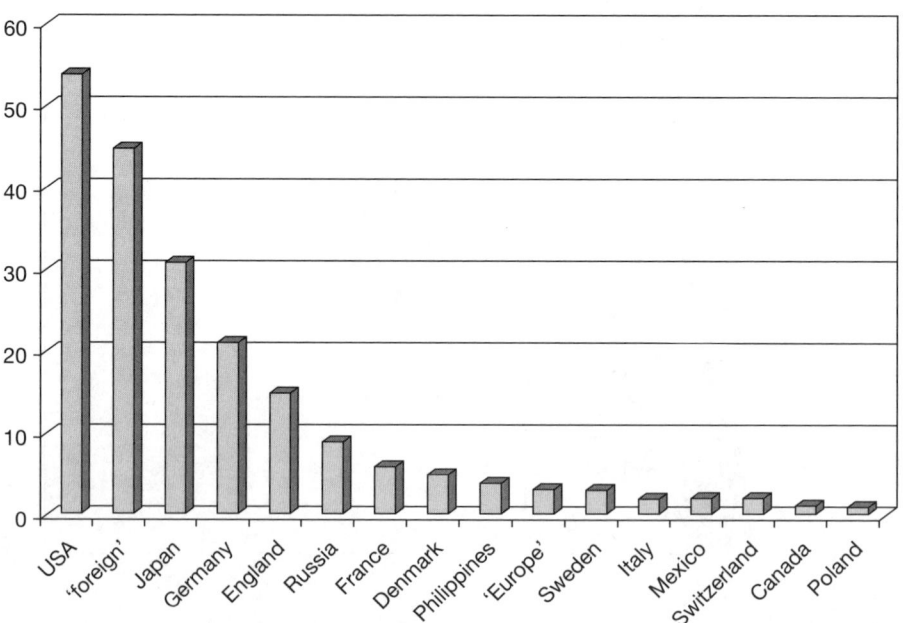

Figure 6.4 Vocational education articles in the *Educational Review* with references to foreign countries (1909–1949)

combines 'the advantages [of vocational education systems] of the entire world and makes use of these' (cited in Qian and Liu 1998: 93).

Likewise, Japan seemed to present both commonalities with and differences from China: being Asian and originally peripheral or 'backward', Japan successfully imported Western models and could thus save the trouble of going through all these models again, as the reformer Zhang Zhidong (1837–1909) remarked already in 1895 (1998: 117). Consequently, and also due to its immediate threat to China after Japan's victory in the Sino-Japanese War in 1895, thousands of Chinese students flocked to Japan, making it 'the first truly large scale modernization-oriented migration of intellectuals in world history' (quoted in Reynolds 1993: 42). Besides, the Japanese model presented an 'Asian alternative' to some and could be used to challenge the perceived US hegemony in educational reform. Similarly, Germany was seen as a suitable example for successfully modernising a 'land of education' (Lu 1916: 15) in a non-American way.

With specific regard to models in vocational education, references to the US or, conversely, to Germany could also signify the conflict between those who were in favour of integrated schools (where vocational education was incorporated into the general curriculum), and those who contested this synchronisation and argued for a more stratified educational system.

The rationality of references cannot be fully explored here (but see Oelsner and Schulte 2006; Schulte 2008). However, this brief discussion shows how outreaching networks like international migration can only be sufficiently understood by taking into account the accompanying systems of meanings, pressures and discourses – or, as Harrison White puts it, '[a] social network is a network of meanings' (1992: 67). A further dimension that could be visualised in migration maps like that in Figure 6.3 (but has not been put to use here) would be the type of ties that reach into each respective country. This could illuminate power flows by, for example, distinguishing between journeys of knowledge-seekers and those of knowledge-carriers. While classic study destinations like the US most often served as sources of information and inspiration, destinations like South Africa were at the receiving end; in this particular case, physician, Christian and CAVE member Diao Xinde (1878–1958) provided medical and mental care for Chinese miners near Johannesburg.

China's interior provinces were certainly placed at the receiving end. The remainder of this subsection looks at where CAVE members carried their knowledge. Most members were born in the wealthier and more educated provinces along the Eastern coast. Even more members received their education there, with a large part (77 members) obtaining additional educational training abroad. A look at where members worked throughout China, however, reveals a more diversified picture (Figure 6.5). While the majority of jobs were still pursued in political, economic and cultural hubs, there was also activity in the hinterland, thus casting an almost nation-wide net of engagement in and for vocational education.

Besides, the number of jobs in urban areas can be artificially high due to frequent changes of employment. Looking at the absolute number of members who had worked in the hinterland at one point in their lives,[25] there were 32 members in all who spent at least part of their professional careers in China's remote areas. The hinterland was also not forgotten with respect to where members founded (mostly

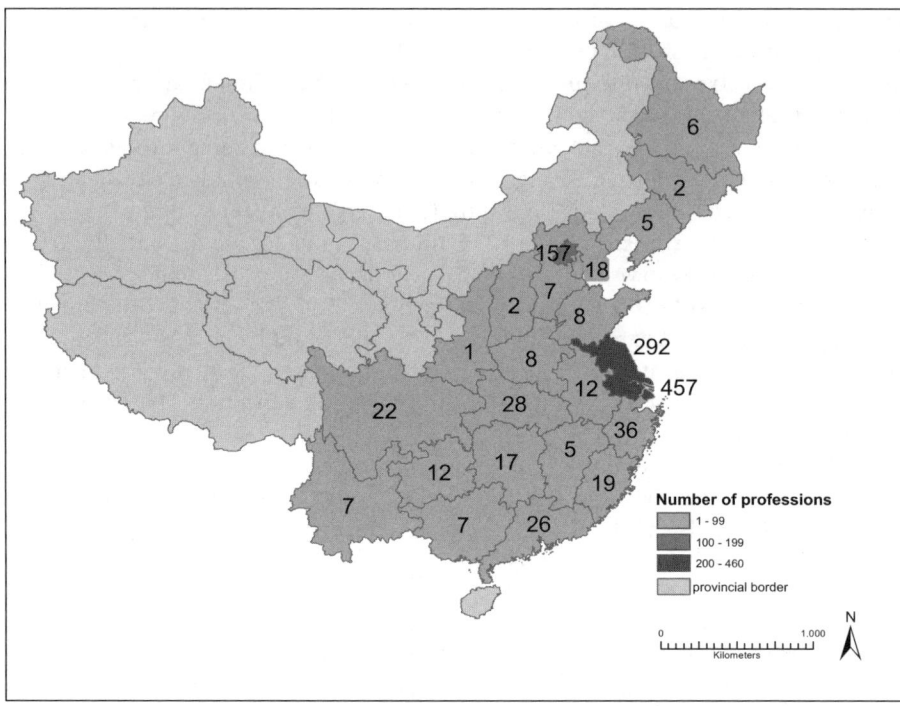

Figure 6.5 Regions in China where members worked

educational) institutions (Figure 6.6). Adding to this the more informal personal contacts that were established between CAVE members and local educators to provide help and support would present the scope of interior engagement as significantly larger, but is difficult to assess quantitatively.

Why did CAVE care about the hinterland at all? Here, again, the narratives and values that circulated in this community come into play. Ruth Hayhoe has diagnosed Chinese intellectuals with being infused by

> a cultural tradition that emphasized a broad geographical participation in intellectual life [that] was a stronger motivating force for a commitment to regional development on the part of the educated youth than the kinds of coercion through national planning or mass organization exercised in the 1950s and 1960s.

> (1992: 68)

If members of CAVE were influenced by such cultural traditions, they did not reflect on them openly. In their attempts to reach and teach those parts of the population that seemed – culturally, economically and politically – distant to them, they voiced their worries about China's fragmentation and centrifugal forces, rather than about its sense of unity. 'The Chinese do not form groups of more than ten persons', and 'China is a nation without organisations', complained, for example, CAVE member

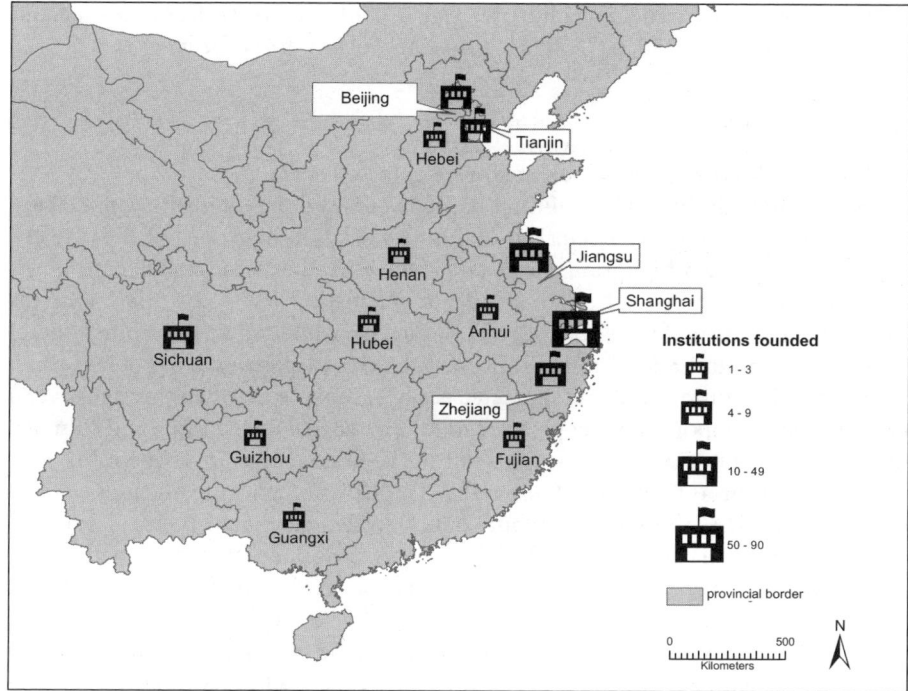

Figure 6.6 Regions in China where members founded institutions

Jiang Hengyuan (alias Jiang Wenyu; 1886–1961), attacking Chinese factionalism that was seen to prevail throughout the country (1933: 2). Regarding the educated strata, he attributed this shortcoming to their widespread arrogance, envy and spirit of exclusion; uneducated strata, by contrast, lacked the will to join forces due to their ignorance and lack of knowledge. Some proponents of the popular education movement within CAVE (such as Wang Maozu (1891–1949) or Tao Xingzhi (1891–1946)) had in mind a genuine democratisation of society, turning individuals into informed and mature citizens.

The largest group within CAVE, however, conceived of this enlightenment project in a one-way manner: culture and modern knowledge were to be passed down to the uneducated, without granting the latter a voice in the process. The pervading imagery when dealing with farmers and workers was that of the child who had to be taken care of (see, e.g., Cai 1921: 7). While in their writings CAVE's educators acknowledged the value of the 'little tradition' (*xiao chuantong*), in practice they showed themselves frustrated by 'bad habits' and 'superstition', which they frequently encountered in non-educated circles. Moreover, they were appalled by those individuals who dared not to conform to the role of the child: emancipated women and Communists (despite the fact that there were a few Communists and women among CAVE's members). Thus, CAVE's 'commitment to regional development', to take up again Hayhoe's (1992) characterisation of Chinese intellectuals, can also be phrased, perhaps a bit exaggeratedly, as internal colonialism. Again, these are speculations about relationships of power and dominion that can be read not directly from the map, but from the discourse in which CAVE's regional networks were embedded.

Institutional Networks

In this last subsection, I will look at a more complex social network that was constituted through the members' multiple engagements at different institutions (Figure 6.7).[26] The most striking characteristic of this network is its high density; the network reveals high closeness, high connectivity and high betweenness. In general, path length – the steps one needs to get from one node, or one institution, to any other node – is short; a high number of nodes can be reached directly, without detour via other nodes. This made communication within the network quick and effective; if a problem arose, the relevant institution could be contacted easily in most cases, often through several people at once (important if people were mobile and often unavailable, and communication media unreliable). As pointed out in the first section, investment in social relations is important in times of instability. The status of many institutions was not only insecure in economic terms, but also often dependent on political patrons. Moreover, particularly in the media business, institutions were existentially competitive: lacking one particular path could mean bankruptcy (e.g. if a publishing house got information regarding future text books later than its competitors).

However, a high number of connections can also be necessary if problem solving is not routinised and institutionalised through reliable administrative structures. From this perspective high closeness is not just convenient for communication but, as a network of mutual help, becomes a prerequisite for any implementation of ideas or reforms. Dense networking can thus be interpreted also as a symptom of an institutional void.[27] Finally, with regard to vocational education as a newly emerging field, a multiplicity of relations can also signify attempts at legitimisation: 'The network that filters information coming to you also directs, concentrates, and legitimates information about you going to others' (Burt 1992: 14). In order, for example, to convince experts or the general public of both the value and the feasibility of vocational education, actors had to be as socially mobile as possible.

The second feature of the network, its high connectivity and robustness, is a commonly found characteristic of networks in Republican China and is also due to the danger that channels could be blocked at any time.[28] CAVE's network was doubly robust. First, many nodes could be removed without affecting the capacity of the network in any serious way: out of 25 players in this network, only eight have less than nine connections; five have even 15 or more connections. Second, ties were often multiply forged. Individuals could be removed (which was the case not only through migration, but also assassination!), and still the tie would not be erased.

Finally, it looks as if the network is replete with brokers: everybody seems to be 'between' everybody else, thus serving a mediating function. But what kind of brokers were they? Most of the relationships are 'overlapping', not 'additive' (Burt 1992: 18), and are thus redundant relationships from a market point of view: they bring no additional value (but make the network more robust). Expectedly, most redundancies can be found in the academic inner circle of the network (universities), with decreasing overlaps in the media, bank business and, at the bottom of the scale, political and

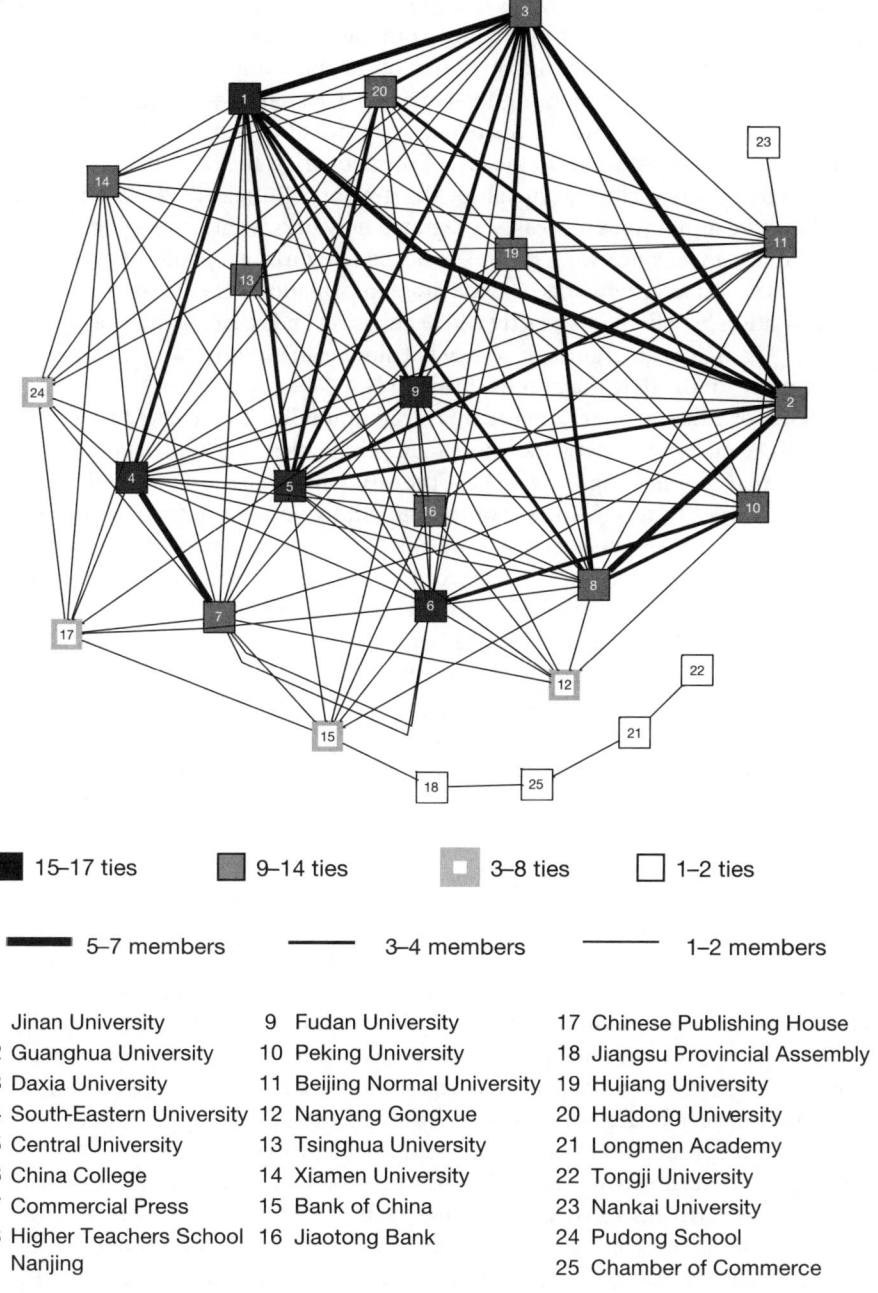

15–17 ties   9–14 ties   3–8 ties   1–2 ties

5–7 members   3–4 members   1–2 members

1 Jinan University	9 Fudan University	17 Chinese Publishing House
2 Guanghua University	10 Peking University	18 Jiangsu Provincial Assembly
3 Daxia University	11 Beijing Normal University	19 Hujiang University
4 South-Eastern University	12 Nanyang Gongxue	20 Huadong University
5 Central University	13 Tsinghua University	21 Longmen Academy
6 China College	14 Xiamen University	22 Tongji University
7 Commercial Press	15 Bank of China	23 Nankai University
8 Higher Teachers School Nanjing	16 Jiaotong Bank	24 Pudong School
		25 Chamber of Commerce

Figure 6.7 Institutional involvement of CAVE's members

economic institutions – the actual seats of power. One feature of the network stands out here: the 'tail' – or pendant – dangling from the network at the bottom of Figure 6.7. This group of institutions contained two of the most important players when it came to making and implementing far-reaching decisions: the Jiangsu Provincial Assembly (*Jiangsu Ziyiju*) and the Shanghai Chamber of Commerce. The only node that links these two institutions to the rest of the network is the Bank of China, which makes the Bank, surprisingly, crucial for the network. Ronald Burt (1992: 17) has pointed out the importance of weakly integrated networks, which makes no intuitive sense at first glance, since we tend to see dense networks as 'good' networks. His argument is that sparse networks provide more information benefits (or, in our case, implementation benefits); it is exactly where cohesion ends that a structural hole can open up. (Again, it is an argument somewhat similar to Granovetter's weak ties but focusing more on the hole than on the bridge.)

The Bank of China was bridging such a structural hole. It connected two realms, politics and economy, to a network whose members, in their self-understanding, were doing just that: connecting their field – (vocational) education – to politics and economy, in order to turn Chinese youth (and adults) into a productive workforce. Or, to put it in a transfer perspective, the Bank of China performed the transsectoral transfer that CAVE's members envisaged, that is, the incorporation of economic reasoning into education. Any member who worked either in the Provincial Assembly or in the Chamber of Commerce virtually passed through the gate of the Bank of China. As much gate-keeping power as that meant for the Bank, it made the network extremely vulnerable – if the Bank was removed, or detached, from the network, the connections to these two important players were lost, and with them those two instances that were capable of bringing the intelligentsia out of their routine of self-referentiality.

Conclusion: More than Meets the Eye

Social network analysis, as I have tried to show with the examples above, can give no definite answer to questions regarding social phenomena and processes. It has to be grounded both in a contextual understanding of the networks in question, and in a conceptual understanding of the social processes that are condensed into these visualisations of nodes and ties. Social reality – as reconstructed by the researcher – is more than meets the eye; along with social ties, it is the sense-making processes that are of importance here. However, social network analysis can also render phenomena more visible which might have remained undetected otherwise.

Strategies in social network analysis have yet to be wed to inquiries into semantic structures, or networks of social meanings. What are the – perhaps conflicting – underlying rationalities and cultural narratives within the network in question? Do these rationales get changed or even replaced through social interaction, what Peter Hall (1993) has framed as paradigm change and social learning? Can networks locate where 'puzzlement', in Hall's sense (1993: 276), takes place; can they show perceived ruptures within sense-making processes which prompt actors to, incrementally or suddenly, shift towards other modes of thinking? There are cases where social network analysis can show, quite convincingly, how a particular constellation in social interaction can have an impact on changing ideas, or changing paradigms, especially if new structural alliances make certain modes of reasoning more likely than before (such as seeing education from an economistic point of view). There is a physical environment and material basis for the mental horizons of actors, which perhaps have been explored too unsystematically in studies that look at educational transfer from a discursive perspective. With the right dosage, social network analysis can help to match the generative power of discourse with the explanatory power of social relations.

Notes

1 See, e.g., the studies on reform in Mongolia by Steiner-Khamsi (2005) and Steiner-Khamsi and Stolpe (2006).
2 See, e.g., the special issue edited by Fuchs (2007) on educational networks in the past, and the article by Ball (2008) on educational networks in the present.
3 Emirbayer and Goodwin call this the 'anticategorical imperative' (1994: 1414).
4 See, e.g., Steiner-Khamsi (2006) on 'late adopters' and Roldán Vera and Schupp (2005) on 'early adopters'.
5 A notable exception is the study by Roldán Vera and Schupp (2005).
6 However, network analysts, especially in business studies, make use of social network analysis to predict social behaviour within that particular network.
7 On the concept of externalisation, see in more detail Schriewer (1990).
8 There is a variety of software programmes available. One of the most commonly used is UCINET (2002); for this chapter, which does without the more complex mathematical operations, I use the software programme yEd for visualisation (yWorks).
9 An English version is in preparation.
10 For a distinction between bonding and bridging social capital, see Putnam (2001).
11 On the evolvement from traditional guilds to modern interest groups, see Fewsmith (1983); on the modernisation of traditional corporate forms of governing in the educational arena, see Schulte (2011b).
12 On self-government, see, e.g., Kuhn (1975).
13 On reference societies within the Chinese educational debate, see Oelsner and Schulte (2006).
14 On the Chinese debate about the uselessness of education, see Schulte (2007, 2011b).
15 For a more detailed profile of CAVE, see Schulte (2008); a condensed summary is available online in Schulte (2010).
16 On policy paradigm change, see Hall (1993).
17 Although CAVE comprised several thousand members several years after its inception, I have focused on a core corpus of 195 individuals, which consisted of all founding members; members with administrative functions (*zhiyuan*); members who had published in the most important periodicals *Educational Review* (*Jiaoyu Zazhi*) and *Education and Vocation* (*Jiaoyu yu Zhiye*); 'special members' (*teyue sheyuan*); and those 'eternal members' (*yongjiu sheyuan*; particularly affluent members) who joined CAVE in the first two years of its inception (membership data from 'Shanghai Shi Jiaoyuju Guanyu Zhonghua Zhiye Jiaoyushe Beian' 1929).
18 It thus preceded the founding of the *Jingshi Daxuetang* in Beijing by two years, whose inception is seen by many as the beginning of modern Chinese education. The time lag is another indicator that it was Shanghai, not Beijing, which served as motor of reform and change.
19 My translation from German; all translations from German and Chinese into English are my own.
20 The English version is forthcoming in Schulte (2011a). See also Su (1996) on how Dewey's ideas were adapted by his disciple Tao Xingzhi.
21 I am grateful to Oliver Oost, who processed my data with GIS (Geographic Information

System) software and produced the maps shown here (the maps were originally in German).

22   As this inquiry has been conducted only with regard to titles, not to the full text – the *Educational Review* published over 10,000 articles during this time period – it can only mirror the broad trend in discussing foreign vocational education models; it eclipses a large number of articles that in some way or another deal with vocational education but do not show this in their titles. For the investigation, all titles that the index lists under the relevant categories (like 'vocational education', 'vocational guidance', etc.; see the index in Wu et al. 2006) were screened for foreign references. Additionally, all titles were searched for key terms (such as 'vocation', 'industry', 'manual labor', 'unemployment', 'commerce', 'technology', etc.); the remaining list was then tested for their relevance for vocational education and for their references to foreign countries. This procedure yielded 204 results.

23   The category 'foreign' comprises articles whose title either refers to 'abroad' in general or to multiple countries; similarly, 'Europe' denotes titles that are on Europe in general or on multiple European countries.

24   For an account of these pioneer students, see LaFargue (1987 [1942]). The US reinvested part of the boxer indemnities (which China had to pay as compensation after the boxer uprising) into educational programmes for Chinese students. On the numbers of students, see Wang (1961: 398).

25   The 'hinterland' is defined here as containing the provinces Yunnan, Henan, Guangxi, Guizhou, Jiangxi, Liaoning, Heilongjiang, Jilin, Shanxi and Shaanxi. Interior regions like Hunan or Sichuan are not included here, since they were much better off both in terms of infrastructure and political/military influence.

26   A tie is created between two institutions when one or several members move from one institution to the other, or work at both institutions simultaneously. The thickness of the line indicates the number of members that performed an identical career move. The shade of the nodes signifies the number of ties. In a more extensive analysis, I have also looked at media networks and networks of organisations in which CAVE was involved; see Schulte (2008: 182–92).

27   On this, and structures of corporate governance in education in Republican China, see Schulte (2011b).

28   See, e.g., Brett Sheehan (2005), who comes to the same conclusion regarding Chinese financial cliques at the time.

References

Ball, S. J. (2008) 'New Philanthropy, New Networks and New Governance in Education', *Political Studies*, 56 (4): 747–65.

Burt, R. S. (1992) *Structural Holes: The Social Structure of Competition*, Cambridge, Mass.: Harvard University Press.

Cai, Y. (1921) 'Putong jiaoyu yu zhiye jiaoyu [General Education and Vocational Education]', *Jiaoyu Zazhi*, 13(1): 1–7.

Emirbayer, M. and Goodwin, J. (1994) 'Network Analysis, Culture, and the Problem of Agency', *American Journal of Sociology*, 99(6): 1411–54.

Fewsmith, J. (1983) 'From Guild to Interest Group: The Transformation of Public and Private in Late Qing China', *Comparative Studies in Society and History*, 25(4): 617–40.

Fuchs, E. (2007) 'Networks and the History of Education', *Paedagogica Historica*, 43(2): 185–97.

Granovetter, M. S. (1973) 'The Strength of Weak Ties', *The American Journal of Sociology*, 78(6): 1360–80.

Granovetter, M. S. (1983) 'The Strength of Weak Ties: A Network Theory Revisited', *Sociological Theory*, 1: 201–33.

Hall, P. A. (1993) 'Policy Paradigms, Social Learning, and the State: The Case of Economic Policymaking in Britain', *Comparative Politics*, 25(3): 275–96.

Hanneman, R. A. and Riddle, M. (2005) *Introduction to Social Network Methods*, University of California, Riverside, available from www.faculty.ucr.edu/~hanneman/nettext/index.html (retrieved January 28, 2010).

Hayhoe, R. (1992) 'Cultural Tradition and Educational Modernization: Lessons from the Republican Era', in R. Hayhoe and W. Zhu (eds), *Education and Modernization: The Chinese Experience*, Oxford: Pergamon Press. 47–72.

Hoffman, D. M. (1999) 'Culture and Comparative Education: Toward Decentering and Recentering the Discourse', *Comparative Education Review*, 43(4): 464–88.

Jiang, H. (1933) 'Jiang xu [Preface by Jiang]', *Zhonghua Zhiye Xuexiao Shiwu Zhounian Jinian [The Fifteenth Anniversary of the Chinese Vocational School]*: Shanghai: Shanghai Municipal Archive, Q 235–3–486, 1–4 (7–8) (May).

Ju, Y. (2002) 'Lun shehui xintai dui beiyang lishi jincheng de yingxiang [The Impact of Social Psyche in the Republic of China under the Northern Governments]', *Lishi Yuekan*, (4): 49–56.

Kuhn, P. A. (1975) 'Local Self-Government under the Republic: Problems of Control, Autonomy, and Mobilization', in F. Wakeman and C. Grant (eds), *Conflict and Control in Late Imperial China*, Berkeley: University of California Press. 256–98.

Kuss, S. (ed.) (2004) *Carl Heinrich Becker in China. Reisebriefe des ehemaligen preußischen Kultusministers 1931/32*, Berliner China-Studien/Quellen und Dokumente, Münster: LIT.

LaFargue, T. E. (1987 [1942]) *China's First Hundred. Educational Mission Students in the United States, 1872–1881*, Washington: Washington State University Press.

Lu, G. (1916) 'Deguo jiaoyu zhi tezhi [The Particularity of German Education]', *Jiaoyu Zazhi*, 8(2; 3): 15–21; 23–28.

Oelsner, V. and Schulte, B. (2006) 'Variationen des Anderen: Die Wahrnehmung ausländischer Bildungsmodelle in der argentinischen und chinesischen Modernisierungsdebatte im späten 19. und frühen 20. Jahrhundert', *Comparativ. Leipziger Beiträge zur Universalgeschichte und vergleichenden Gesellschaftsforschung*, 16(3): 44–67.

Padgett, J. F. and Ansell, C. K. (1993) 'Robust Action and the Rise of the Medici, 1400–1434', *American Journal of Sociology*, 98(6): 1259–319.

Pan, W. (1923) 'Zhiye xuexiao xuesheng ying bei zhi xingxing zhineng [Behaviour and Qualities for Which Vocational Students Have to Be Prepared]', *Jiaoyu yu Zhiye*, (46): 1–4.

Putnam, R. D. (2001) *Bowling Alone: The Collapse and Revival of American Community*, London: Simon & Schuster.

Qian, J. and Liu, G. (1998) 'Lun Zhonghua Zhiye Jiaoyushe zai jindai jiaoyu zhong de diwei he zuoyong [Discussing the Position and the Function of the Chinese Vocational Education Association within Modern Education]', *Huadong Shifan Daxue Xuebao (Jiaoyu Kexueban)*, (4): 89–96.

Reynolds, D.R. (1993) *China, 1898–1912. The Xinzheng Revolution and Japan*, Cambridge, Mass.: Harvard University Press.

Roldán Vera, E. and Schupp, T. (2005) 'Bridges Over the Atlantic: A Network Analysis of the Introduction of the Monitorial System of Education in Early-Independent Spanish America', *Comparativ. Zeitschrift für Globalgeschichte und Vergleichende Gesellschaftsforschung*, (1): 58–93.

Roldán Vera, E. and Schupp, T. (2006) 'Network Analysis in Comparative Social Sciences', *Comparative Education*, 42(3): 405–29.

Schriewer, J. (1990) 'The Method of Comparison and the Need for Externalization: Methodological Criteria and Sociological Concepts', in J. Schriewer and B. Holmes (eds), *Theories and Methods in Comparative Education*, Frankfurt am Main: Lang.

Schriewer, J. and Martinez, C. (2004) 'Constructions of Internationality in Education', in G. Steiner-Khamsi (ed.), *The Global Politics of Educational Borrowing and Lending*, New York: Teachers College Press. 29–53.

Schulte, B. (2007) 'Wenn Wissen auf Reisen geht: Rezeption und Aneignung westlichen Wissens in China', in J. Schriewer (ed.), *Weltkultur und kulturelle Bedeutungswelten: Zur Globalisierung von Bildungsdiskursen.* Frankfurt am Main: Campus. 151–85.

Schulte, B. (2008) *'Zur Rettung des Landes': Bildung und Beruf im China der Republikzeit,* series *Eigene und fremde Welten* 6, Frankfurt am Main: Campus.

Schulte, B. (2009) 'El Dewey Chino: Amigo, demonio y buque insignia', *Encounters on Education/Encuentros sobre Educación/Rencontres sur l'Éducation,* 10: 67–101.

Schulte, B. (2010) *Chinese Actors in Vocational Education,* available from www.ace.lu.se/o.o.i.s/ 22632 (retrieved 30 January 2010).

Schulte, B. (2011a) 'The Chinese Dewey: Friend, Fiend, and Flagship', in R. Bruno-Jofre and J. Schriewer (eds), *The Global Reception of John Dewey's Thought,* London: Routledge (forthcoming).

Schulte, B. (2011b) 'Joining Forces to Save the Nation: Corporate Educational Governance in Republican China', in J. Hsu and R. Hasmath (eds), *The Chinese Corporate State: Past, Present and Future,* London: Routledge (forthcoming).

'Shanghai Shi Jiaoyuju Guanyu Zhonghua Zhiye Jiaoyushe Beian [The Shanghai Office of Education's Files for the Chinese Association for Vocational Education]' (1929): Shanghai: Shanghai Municipal Archive, Q 235–2–1888, 1889, 1890.

Sheehan, B. (2005) 'Myth and Reality in Chinese Financial Cliques in 1936', *Enterprise & Society,* 6(3): 452–91.

Shen, S. (1923) 'Yu yinhangjia taolun shangye jiaoyu [A Discussion about Business Education with Bankers]', *Jiaoyu yu Zhiye,* (41): 5–10.

Skinner, G. W. (1977) 'Introduction: Urban Development in Imperial China', in G. W. Skinner (ed.), *The City in Late Imperial China,* Stanford: Stanford University Press. 3–31.

Steiner-Khamsi, G. (ed.) (2004) *The Global Politics of Educational Borrowing and Lending,* New York: Teachers College, Columbia University.

Steiner-Khamsi, G. (2005) 'Vouchers for Teacher Education (Non)Reform in Mongolia: Transitional, Postsocialist, or Antisocialist Explanations?', *Comparative Education Review,* 49(2): 148–72.

Steiner-Khamsi, G. (2006) 'The Economics of Policy Borrowing and Lending. A Study of Late Adopters', *Oxford Review of Education,* 32 (5): 665–78.

Steiner-Khamsi, G. and I. Stolpe (2006) *Educational Import: Local Encounters with Global Forces in Mongolia,* New York: Palgrave Macmillan.

Su, Z. (1996) 'Teaching, Learning, and Reflective Acting: A Dewey Experiment in Chinese Teacher Education', *Teachers College Record,* 98: 126–52.

UCINET 6 for Windows (2002) Software for Social Network Analysis. Analytic Technologies, Harvard.

Wang, J. (1983) 'Zai shehui li sheng le gen de ren – Mianhuai Huang Yanpei xiansheng [A Person Rooted in Society – My Memories of Huang Yanpei]', *Shehui Kexue,* (7): 52–55.

Wang, Y. C. (1961) 'Intellectuals and Society in China 1860–1949', *Comparative Studies in Society and History,* 3(4): 395–426.

Wang, Z. (2002) 'Saving China through Science: The Science Society of China, Scientific Nationalism, and Civil Society in Republican China', *Osiris,* 17: 291–322.

Waterkamp, D. (2006) *Vergleichende Erziehungswissenschaft. Ein Lehrbuch,* Münster: Waxmann Verlag.

Wei, Q. (1928) 'Zhiye jiaoyu zai Zhongguo xuezhi shang de diwei [The Position of Vocational Education in the Chinese Educational System]', *Jiaoyu yu Zhiye,* (98): 527–34.

White, H. C. (1992) *Identity and Control: A Structural Theory of Social Action,* Princeton: Princeton University Press.

Wu, M., Liu, Z., Ding, Q. and Lin, J. (eds) (2006) *Jiaoyu Zazhi (1909–1948) Suoyin [Index for the Educational Review (1909–1948)]*, Taibei: Psychological Publishing.

yWorks (2011) yEd 3.6.1.1, Tübingen, available from www.yworks.com/en/products_yed_about.html [retrieved February 12, 2011].

Zhang, Z. (1998) 'Youxue di er [Overseas Study, Second Part]', in Z. Zhang (ed.), *Quanxue pian [Encouragement to Study]*, Zhengzhou: Zhongzhou Guji Chubanshe. (Original edition, 1895).

Part II

Externalisation and the Politics of Policy Borrowing and Lending

7 Reimagining Attraction and 'Borrowing' in Education

Introducing a Political Production Model

Jeremy Rappleye

The 'Internationalisation' of Educational Policy?

As the world continues to connect, coalesce, and collide, scholars who reject the traditional parochialism of educational studies are increasingly addressing four key questions, all centring on the apparent 'internationalisation' of educational policy:

- What is driving the marked increase in instances of transnational policy attraction and 'borrowing' in education?
- What do increasingly frequent 'references to elsewhere' suggest about an apparent worldwide convergence of educational policy and practice?
- How should we approach attraction and 'borrowing' theoretically, conceptually, and methodologically?
- What is at stake in our choice of analytical perspective(s)?

Indeed, attraction and 'borrowing' are implicated each time one reads of the pilgrimages of politicians and educational 'experts' to Finland (Salhberg 2006), the prolonged popularity of the New Zealand model (Dale 1999; Steiner-Khamsi 2006), or the embrace of Outcomes Based Education in South Africa (Spreen 2004). It is implicated when reflecting on the larger 'epidemic' (Levin 1998) of policy attraction-cum-reform that washed over the globe in the 1990s and also when interrogating the sudden disappearance of, say, Japan as the global educational 'model' *par excellence* of the 1980s.

Nor have these themes captured the imagination of scholars alone, but continue to become an increasingly common feature of popular coverage of education as well: attraction and 'borrowing' arguably form the primary backdrop for the dramas of *Two Million Minutes* (*New York Times* 2008; Post 2009), set the stage for China's '*Super Kids*' (*New York Times* 2002, 2011), and animate much of the media frenzy following various national 'PISA-shocks' (Takayama 2008a; Waldow 2009). In short, attraction and 'borrowing' are becoming more prominent features of policy discussions, scholarly analyses *and* popular coverage of education as nationally delimited research imaginaries seemingly melt away.

Yet despite the growing prominence and relevance of these four 'core' questions, it is not clear that we yet have a set of coherent answers. With just a few notable exceptions (Phillips and Ochs 2004; Steiner-Khamsi 2004), scholarship has yet to move beyond mere description of specific instances of attraction and 'borrowing'. This attention to difference, however, comes at the cost of recognising similarities of how and why attraction arises, how it enters educational reform discourses and what *effects* it actually has on policy change. There are, of course, good reasons for this focus: attraction unfolds differently according to context, 'borrowings' are sometime unacknowledged (Waldow 2009) and so on. This must not be forgotten. Still, without continued attempts to move beyond mere description and recognise similarity, it seems unlikely that analyses of policy borrowing can advance to engage theoretically, innovate conceptually and formulate some common answers.

It is in this frame then, and around these four questions, that the current chapter operates within and seeks to contribute. This chapter explores instances of *explicit* attraction and intimations of 'borrowing' and offers a new framework for analysing such phenomena. It provides two empirical cases to illustrate the processes involved and then elaborates a synthesis. I suggests that explicit attraction and 'borrowing' are more often than not instances of *political production* on a number of different levels: a carefully scripted, directed, and managed staging for the purpose of *producing* particular policy outcomes.

(Re)Imagining Attraction and 'Borrowing': Theories, Concepts and Methods

Three Current Theoretical and Conceptualisation Perspectives

An exhaustive review of existing research would address the perspectives, potential and paucity of work on attraction and 'borrowing' by each of the dominant theoretical traditions in the field. The focus here, however, will be restricted to the three most prominent and elaborated to date: *actor-centrism*, *systems theory* and *world culture*.[1] Briefly detailing the strengths and weaknesses of each of these positions reveals the advantages of a political production conceptualisation.

The first approach – what I term here actor-centricism – underpins a number of established theories of the policy process. These include the advocacy–coalition framework (Sabatier and Jenkins-Smith 1993) and the 'policy stream' dimension of the widely cited multiple-streams approach (Kingdon 1984). As the name implies, the focus is on actors (either individual, collective or coalitional) that play central roles in shaping the policy process. Within this tradition there appear to be two dominant groups. The first are *realists* who operate from the assumption that actors operate primarily in self-interest, pursuing power, security and/or income – or the prestige, positionality and prominence that provides privileged access to the former. Such perspectives are central to rational-choice models (Ostrom 1986, Chubb and Moe 1990), but also inherent in the notion of, say, 'policy entrepreneurs' (Kingdon 1984). The other group includes those that do not presuppose realist motives, but instead focus attention on, say, how information flows are asymmetrical or how actors view other actors or interact with policy-related information. Attributing these different views to different 'perceptual filters', scholars such as Sabatier and Jenkins-Smith (1993: 194) who elaborate an Advocacy Coalition Framework (ACF), for instance, draw an explicit distinction from the *realist* camp: 'While rational choice frameworks assume self-interested actors rationally pushing relatively simple material interests, the ACF assumes that normative beliefs must be empirically ascertained and does not a priori preclude the possibility of altruistic behavior.'

When applied to policy borrowing, actor-centrism, regardless of whether it is a realist or non-realist variation, pushes for a shifting of the research gaze away from the 'official' policy problematique to actors and their political motives. In doing this, one discovers that attraction and 'borrowing' are, proponents of such an approach contend, less about recognised deficiencies in the 'home' context and/or widespread consensus about the superiority of the provision abroad; more about domestic political agendas, manoeuvrings, and frictions that create the need to look 'elsewhere'. As Steiner-Khamsi (2000: 170) argues, 'educational borrowing serves as a powerful means to displace contested educational reforms . . . reference to successful national educational reforms of other countries gives policy analysts leverage in pushing through a particular policy option'. Hence her call, among others, for research on policy borrowing centring actors, agendas and politics, rather than the content of transfer. Despite this critical and important shift, however, actor-centrism provides little indication, as I argue later, of how politically driven 'references to elsewhere' actually produce a salutory effect on the policy process.

The system theory contribution traces its origins to the work of German sociologist Niklas Luhmann who argued for a perspective privileging spheres of communication, defined and demarcated by boundaries drawn between an internal sphere (*system*) of meaning and order and a wider *environment* of infinite complexity. The particular ways in which the internal sphere reduces the infinite complexity beyond, according to Luhmann, both reflects the distinctive identity of that system but, by the very act of selection and filtering, always also reproduces its own distinctiveness. Schriewer (2003) calls this distinctiveness the 'socio-logic' of the home system, a logic created again and again by selecting elements from its surrounding environment that reinforces the 'Self'. As such, external environmental factors do not actually 'enter' and change the closed communicative/social system in any significant way but are instead acts of *self-reference, externalisations,* or 'supplementary meaning making' that help reinforce long-standing systemic identities. Schriewer (1990, 2000) argues that in education, 'externalizations to "foreign examples" or to "world situations" . . . involve the discursive interpretation of international phenomena for issues of educational policy and ideological legitimation' (Schriewer 2003: 32) rather than signal substantive 'adoption' of external influence.

The implications of this for attraction and 'borrowing' are clear: 'references to elsewhere' function to reinforce either the distinctive identity of the 'home' system or at least particular elements within it. There are obvious parallels here with actor-centric realism discussed previously, producing significant synergy between the two positions. Indeed, in some respects Schriewer's point about self-referential selection producing 'legitimation', fills the void in actor-centric realism: the salutary effect of deploying 'references to elsewhere' are that it bestows legitimacy to the degree that it resonates within the 'home' system. Yet, *systems theory* does not, by itself, call attention to actors nor tell us much about the specifics of deployment, but instead emphasises *systemic* meaning, discoursal formations, semantic constructions and context-specific reception – the (re)infusion of specific system meaning into a foreign 'import'. Nor does it hold out the possibility for substantive change within a communicative/social system: the Luhmann vision, at least to the degree it has been adopted in comparative education, is one of the stasis of systems and meanings within those systems.[2] Yet, can it really be that 'references to elsewhere' have no significant lasting effects beyond reproduction of pre-existing systemic meaning?

The final perspective is provided by world culture theory, which posits the existence of a emerging world culture deriving from growing consensus around a set of 'rationalised myths' about the way that human societies should be organised, educationally and otherwise. Foremost among these 'myths' are the potential of science and a state commitment to 'progress' that, according to world culture proponents reworking Weber, leads to the rationalisation of social phenomena along these lines and thus the structuration of myriad forms of social life around these principles (Meyer et al. 1997; Driori et al. 2003). In effect, institutions such as states, schools and firms are (re)organised to embody, reflect and promote a shared world culture and, when this happens on a global scale, there is thought to be substantive worldwide convergence – *isomorphism* – of institutions, policies and practices, not least in education (McNeely 1995; Baker and LeTendre 2005).

Although the theory was originally developed to attempt to account for the spread of mass schooling globally (Meyer 1977; Meyer et al. 1992), its proponents, especially a younger generation of scholars, have confidently extended world culture tenets into discussions of policy borrowing and lending in recent years. In an article entitled 'The Worldwide Explosion of Internationalized Education Policy' (2005), for example, Wiseman and Baker call attention to a 'policymaking environment already marked by extensive borrowing and copying from one nation to the next' (p. 1). In line with their world culture stance, they argue that 'ideas, or perhaps more accurately ideologies flow down and outward through the world system' and – this is crucial – 'the expansion of internationalizing forces in nations' policy making *is a result of a world culture in education* that continues to flow throughout the world system of nations' (p. 5, emphasis added). In short, world culture theory suggests that 'borrowing' is authentic and substantive, clearly evident in the use of the word 'copying'. Driving external influences and 'internationalising forces' in domestic policy is a shared world culture. Such a divergent vision of attraction and 'borrowing' is, however, one that critics have repeatedly argued is devoid of actor agency, politics and context: is it really that 'world culture' is the primary script from which actors read, leading them to seek 'lessons from elsewhere'? Is the result authentic borrowing that results in substantive change in the home system and thus convergence on a global scale?

The Political Production Model

This recent work provides some insights to the four central questions highlighted at the outset, although leaves significant voids as well. This section builds on these theoretical insights to present a more nuanced picture. I term this conceptualisation the *Political Production Model* to highlight that it applies predominantly to attraction and 'borrowing' emanating from the highest echelons of the political realm (as opposed to, say, the bureaucratic, academic, or media) and attempt to illustrate it with a metaphor of theatre. That is, I argue that attraction and 'borrowing' are political stagecraft: theatrics where particular factions of political players write their own script based on pre-existing *ideological* convictions, then act out the drama of attraction and 'borrowing' with the hopes of producing particular effects among the audience – other policy makers, media, general public and so on.

The starting point for this Political Production Model is a previous piece entitled 'Theorizing Educational Transfer: Toward a Conceptual Map of the Context of Cross-national Attraction' (Rappleye 2006). Therein I argued that mapping the positionality of political actors within education reform debates and ways that they are *externalised* to developments in the 'wider world' helps to reveal the political origins of cross-national attraction. In attempting to disentangle substantive structural change (Phillips 2004) from the way this change was 'framed' rhetorically by a range of actors, the *Contextual Map* drew heavily on previous research to argue that 'references to elsewhere' could come in the form of *legitimation, caution, scandalisation* or *glorification* and are deployed to both catalyse and stymie attempts at reform. The key point was that 'lessons from elsewhere' always arose from and were thus inextricably interwoven in pre-existing reform debates and constellations of actors and competing agendas; attraction always emerged in relation to relative positionality in the reform debates and thus were acts of conscious, skilful, *self-referential* framing.

In some senses, this Map melded together the perspectives provided by actor-centrism and systems theory, in particular the work of Steiner-Khamsi (2000, 2004) and Schriewer (1990, 2000). The argument was that neither actor-centrism nor systems theory alone was sufficient to understand attraction and 'borrowing'. In line with the review above, actor-centrism gave little indication of how 'references to elsewhere' provided a salutary effect on the policy process for particular groups, while system-theory, although it did indicate why these 'references' resonated and functioned rhetorically, still left open the question of both the degree to which actor prestige, positionality, and power sustained the strategy and what the actual effects of such a strategy were. The credit for this synergetic linking belongs to earlier work by Steiner-Khamsi (2000, 2004), but the Map did perhaps combine these theories in a way that provided further clarity and several novel perspectives. While such an approach has stimulated some further thinking (Phillips 2009; Sobe and Ortegon 2009; Takayama 2009), in light of my on-going research, it seems to be, along with the theories that underpin it, somewhat under-elaborated and fails to capture the totality of the attraction and 'borrowing' drama, especially its policy/power effects.

By contrast, the Political Production Model, whilst rooted in this earlier attempt departs from it in two important respects. First, it eschews the notion of a 'map' for a time sequence. It replaces a view of the spatiality of the entire reform debates with a *scripting, production, staging,* and *response/reaction* sequence tracing how a particular political production results in a public staging of 'references to elsewhere' in the wider education reform debates; or to briefly mobilise a different metaphor here, instead of looking at the confluence of all actors and agendas into the larger reform stream as the Map did, the production model traces the 'references to elsewhere' tributaries trickling into this larger reform confluence back 'upstream' to their political headwaters. Second, the Political Production Model integrates the perspectives afforded by post-structuralism, arguing that its optic is necessary to track the effects of these 'references to elsewhere' and intimations of 'borrowing'. Let us explore this second point in more detail since it is the most substantive extension to existing research.

From the review above, it is clear that one of the weaknesses of all current theories, but especially actor-centrism, is that it gives us little indication of what effects 'references to elsewhere' produce. We are told that it affords 'legitimacy' to policy actors, but are the salutary effects limited to this alone? How are we to approach, methodologically, the effects of what is largely the production of a discourse about the superiority of provision 'elsewhere' with a focus on actors alone? Here post-structuralism's attention to the ways that power operates through the *production* of knowledge and operates through discourses that close down alternative ways of thinking is useful.

For Foucault, 'knowledge' could not be decoupled from regimes of power and discoursal 'truths' came to form both individual subjectivity and institutions (e.g. prison, insane asylum) that then served to embody, reproduce, and (re)broadcast this knowledge/power discourse. Foucault was complex and went through several distinctive phases, but a major shift occurred between what Best and Kellner (1991: 46) describe as 'the idealistic archeological Foucault and the materialistic genealogical Foucault'. It was in this later stage that Foucault sought to 'foreground the material context of subject construction' and 'to draw out the political consequences of "subjectification"' (Best and Kellner 1991: 47). In other words, the later genealogical approach attempted to locate the material origins of taken-for-granted 'truths' (discourses) that produce *productive* consequences; those that etch themselves in the subjectivity of individuals, produce institutions, and underpin 'regimes of truth'.

Several scholars have already appropriated this later Foucault to analyse educational policy in similar ways approximated by the Political Production Model. One is Ball (1990), who artfully combines actors, institutions and discourses to describe, for example, the makings of a 'discourse of derision' that clearly originated in conservative political circles in England in the 1970s, then came to powerfully support the sweeping Thatcher reforms of the 1980s. In doing so Ball explicitly calls attention to the policy *effects*:

> This discourse of derision acted to debunk and displace not only specific words and meanings . . . but also the speakers of those words, those 'experts', 'specialists', and 'professionals' referred to as the 'educational establishment'. These privileged speakers have been displaced, their control over meaning lost . . . a new discursive regime has been established and with it new forms of authority.
>
> (Ball 1990: 18)

More recently, and working internationally, Carney and Bista (2009) have further elaborated a similar genealogical approach to describe educational knowledge/discourse/power flows. In appropriating an optic inspired by these earlier works to view the latter response/reaction aspects of the Political Production Model, I argue that we can better locate the effects of 'references to elsewhere' – effects that *(re)produce* power in various ways across several interlocking domains and etch themselves in policy, practice, and even people (subjectivity). That is, using post-structuralism to extend the earlier actor-centric realist and system-theory hybrid (the Map) completes the picture of attraction and 'borrowings' by allowing us to locate the policy effects well after the curtain is drawn on the original production.

To illustrate this empirically, I now turn to explore two recent cases of attraction and 'borrowing', American attraction to Japan in the 1980s and Japanese attraction to England in the 2000s. That such strikingly similar cases of attraction and 'borrowing' unfolded in countries as different historically, culturally, socially, politically and educationally (and so on) as America and Japan, emphasise that the staging of 'attraction' and borrowing is dependent on none of the traditional *contextual* factors that have long enamoured comparative scholars, but instead upon *political* necessity and expediency. The elaboration and comparison of two cases rather than explication of merely one illustrative example helps convey the point that political production is a robust political strategy deployable across space, time, and *a wide diversity of contexts*; neither a 'one-off' aberration nor specific to a particular type of economic, social, cultural or educational configuration. At the same time, comparison *across the diversity* that America and Japan affords (e.g., decentralised versus centralised) allows us to see how variations take place when the same general script is performed within different institutional, political, and educational theatres. It is precisely the similarities *and differences* between America and Japan then that make the following comparison particularly illustrative and illuminating.

Political Production of Attraction and 'Borrowing': Two Empirical Illustrations

Let us begin briefly at the end. That is, before venturing backstage to trace these productions from beginning to end, let us just briefly take the seat amongst the wider audience and glimpse what 'references to elsewhere' productions look like when they emerged on the public stage.

For Americans in the 1980s – the first example explored below – Japanese education burst onto the scene in just a few short years to become the model of educational success *par excellence*, a shining example offering solutions for *A Nation at Risk*. In a major report entitled *A Look at Japanese Education Today* released in 1987, the US Secretary of Education praised Japanese education in the highest terms, arguing explicitly the necessity of 'learning' from Japan:

> Japanese education *works* . . . the Japanese have put their money into a high-quality teaching force and basic education materials, not into frills, large bureaucracies, lavish facilities, innumerable electives, or platoons of specialists . . . Nor do teachers and principals (or parents or other adults) refrain from committing themselves to clear distinctions or from indicating preferred course of action, or imbuing youngsters with a deep sense of good and bad, right and wrong, moral and immoral . . . what seems to work well for Japan in the field of education closely resembles what works best in the United States – and most likely elsewhere. Good education is good education.
>
> (Bennett 1987: 70–71)

Coinciding with the report was a flood of scholarly works and popular coverage of Japanese education on a scale unprecedented in American history (Rappleye 2007);

a 'frenzy' that firmly cemented the image of Japan as a model of educational success and America as image of educational failure for a least a decade, if not much longer.

In Japan in the first decade of the new millennium, English education, in particular the Thatcher reforms of the 1980s, began to be discussed as a model of success for making Japan a 'normal nation' and reviving Japanese society. Consider, as but one example, the praise lavished on English education by then shoo-in for Prime Minister Abe Shinzō in his widely covered (popular) political vision for Japan, entitled *Towards a Beautiful Country* (2006). The crucial final chapter of that volume was entitled 'Education Rebuilding' and opened with a section titled 'The Restoration of Pride through Thatcher's Education Reforms', explaining:

> Prime Minister Thatcher achieved a remarkable reform of consciousness among the English, especially in the forging of a new spirit among the youth . . . [Thatcher] carried out two things in the 1988 Education Reform Act. One was to correct masochistic, skewed educational messages and the other was to raise educational standards . . . Both are major challenges currently facing Japanese education.
>
> (pp. 202–203)[3]

Although the amount of scholarly and popular coverage of English education would reach nowhere near the 'frenzied' levels it did in America (a crucial contrast analysed in conclusion), the ensuing pace and scope of policy change in Japan arguably far outstripped what occurred in America: an Educational Rebuilding Council was inaugurated in October 2006, the Occupation-era Fundamental Law of Education that had stood untouched for 60 years was revised, and three major education bills successfully passed the national legislature in June 2007.

Yet do these 'references' – *precisely the type of references that now permeate the global educational landscape* – represent consensus around superiority of provision 'else-where'? Do they signify authentic attempts to 'borrow' and thus signify substantive policy impact and thus convergence? The Political Production Model suggests otherwise.

The Political Production of 'Lessons from Japan' in America

In America, the political production of Japanese educational success arguably traces its origins to the 1980 US presidential campaign. After a decade of low economic growth and soaring inflation, Ronald Reagan successfully garnered the Republican nomination by promising smaller government, which, according to Reagan, was the cause of national economic stagnation. This view was clearly ideological, predating the oil shocks of the early 1970s, as is clearly evident from his famed 'Time for Choosing' speech in support of Barry Goldwater's 1964 presidential bid that launched Reagan into the national political spotlight. The symbolic target of Reagan's drastically downsizing vision for the US federal government was the Department of Education: he promised that if elected he would abolish it completely (Fiske 1983; Cannon 1991). Reagan also spoke out forcefully in favour of a return to moral standards, favouring mandatory prayers in school, a position that appealed to increasing political clout by Christian groups such as Jerry Falwell's Moral Majority.

After securing the Republican Party nomination, Reagan created an Education Policy Advisory Committee, to draft a set of core policy recommendations along these two lines – downsizing the government and restoring moral 'direction' – policy recommendations that would form the substance of both his presidential campaign and, once elected, his administration. Importantly, Glenn Campbell, the director of the Hoover Institute, often called the 'conservative brain trust' of American politics, chaired the group. Berliner and Biddle (1995: 134), who examined these committee documents, report that in a 'tentative draft' dated October 1980, those policy recommendations clearly laid out the 'myths and themes' that would underpin the entire eight years of Reagan educational policy, most of all the famed *A Nation at Risk* report released in 1983. Here Glenn Campbell becomes the key figure to track.

Once elected, Reagan selected Terrel Bell to be his Secretary of Education, appointing him last in symbolic disdain for the Department of Education. In his memoirs, Bell (1988: 115) describes his desire to create another 'Sputnik-type occurrence' to realise the Reagan–Campbell policy objectives that he was tasked with.[4] The result was an idea to create a National Commission in Excellence in Education (NCEE) that would produce a report on the state of American education and recommendations for reform in short order. Bell describes the immense pressure he was under from superiors to 'stack the commission with the 'right people' (p. 117), to produce a report 'without any dissent' (p. 120), and, importantly, the careful planning that was done to get maximum media coverage: 'we needed network TV, the wire services, and the giants among the nation's newspapers to cover this event if we were to get our message out' (p. 121). To amplify coverage, the decision was made to have President Reagan personally launch the final report of NCEE entitled *A Nation at Risk: The Imperative for Education Reform* that began with those memorable lines: 'Our Nation is at risk. Our once unchallenged preeminence in commerce, industry, science and technological innovation is being overtaken by competitors throughout the world . . .' (NCEE 1983: 6).

Bell's strategy to 'get the message out' arguably succeeded beyond even his own expectations. As Berliner and Biddle (1995) emphasise: '*Never* before had such trenchant rhetoric about education appeared from the White House. As a result, the press had a field day' (p. 40). The report clearly framed education as a national project in the service of economic competitiveness, but also anointed cross-national comparison as one of the central means of determining success and failure in education. Importantly, it also explicitly linked Japanese competitiveness and education for the first time, foreshadowing what was to come: 'The risk is not only that the Japanese make automobiles more efficiently than America . . . it is also that these developments signify a redistribution of trained capability throughout the globe' (NCEE 1983: 7).

'Learning from Japan': CULCON, OERI, and Japanese Education Today

In the early 1980s, trade frictions, an artificially weak yen, and a sizeable negative trade balance drew concern from the US Congress and began to animate the American media. General works began to portray Japan as an economic juggernaut that directly challenged American supremacy, an image most prominent in Ezra Vogel's aptly titled book *Japan as Number One: Lessons for America* (1979). There was certainly a growing fascination and respect for Japanese success in the realm of business and finance (Ouchi 1982) but it was hardly enough to suggest that America had something to learn from Japan in terms of education. As Cummings (1989) recalls, 'in the early 1980s, US elites and educators were largely indifferent to Japanese education' (p. 293).

This all changed in November 1983 when – less than seven months after the April release of *A Nation at Risk* – President Reagan visited Japan to smooth growing trade frictions. The trip was largely symbolic leaving plenty of time to discuss other matters (Kunkel 2003). Education reform became a central topic because Prime Minister Nakasone was in the midst of launching his own Ad Hoc Council on Education Reform as a means of reforming the Japanese system. Cummings (1989) reports, 'perhaps to seek relief from the intractable issues surrounding the trade debate, the two leaders spent considerable time exchanging thoughts about their respective educational systems, and proposed to develop some means to further the exchange' (p. 294). One such means was to rejuvenate the US–Japan Conference on Cultural and Educational Interchange (CULCON), a high-level US–Japan exchange programme started in the 1960s that had become all but defunct. The plan was to provide strong leadership and devote sufficient funds to further the 'educational exchange'.

Upon his return to the US, Reagan selected none other than Glenn Campbell to lead CULCON. The conservative architect of Reagan's education reform agenda and the logic underpinning *A Nation at Risk* was now leading an organisation whose primary mission was to 'learn' from Japanese education. Under the direct auspices of the White House, CULCON had considerable power, access, and resources. Campbell thus commissioned Secretary of Education Bell to form a research team and undertake a study of Japan, becoming the Japan Study Team housed within the Office of Education Research and Improvement (OERI). Bell was soon replaced when Reagan embarked on his second term in early 1985 with the more proactive William Bennett who, with the benefit of hindsight, we know as an outspoken advocate of vouchers and curriculum reform, a fiery critic of the educational bureaucracy and the 'loss of virtue' – his euphemism for moral malaise (Bennett 1992, 2001). Clearly Bennett was firmly within the conservative ideological camp, yet had had little experience in either government or educational policy. Probably for that reason Chester Finn was brought in as a special advisor and Assistant Secretary. A focus on actors thus reveals a direct, clear, consistent policy agenda and its concomitant line of conservative political influence running from Campbell's role in the Education Advisory Policy Committee (1980) through *A Nation at Risk* (1983) to *CULCON* and the OERI Japan Study Team under Bennett and Finn.

The OERI Japan Study Team was led by Robert Leestma and comprised of five members of the US Department of Education. Notably, the Study Team very early on commissioned numerous research papers on various aspects of Japanese education by 18 academics including now familiar names like Lois Peak, Merry White, Catherine Lewis and Harold Stevenson (OERI Japan Study Team [OEJST] 1987). The OERI Japan Study Team and these commissioned consultants/associates enjoyed both generous funds and a high degree of access and assistance on the Japan side as part of the high-level official project, most notably funding for several visits to Japan and high-level assistance provided by the Japanese Ministry of Education. In January 1987, the OERI Japan Study Team, after two years of research, released their final report entitled *Japanese Education Today*. Clearly it carried a high degree of legitimacy as an official US Department of Education (DOE) document and was released at press conferences followed-up with several official DOE summaries and press-releases to 'get the message out' (e.g. McKinney 1987; US Department of Education 1987). The report explicated aspects of Japanese education in one hundred concise pages and, indeed, a carefully reading of the report suggests it as academically sound in its *description* of Japanese education. How then could this be construed as part of a project of *political production*? How could Bennett and Finn manipulate the findings to serve the wider Reagan–Campbell ideological agenda?

The answer lies in the duality of voices clearly evident in *Japanese Education Today* and the clear acts of marking and framing, processes that system-theory suggests are not inconsequential, but instead highly significant and illuminating (Schriewer 2000). The first voice is that of the experienced team of academics who wrote the body of the report. Their voice is mostly one of caution, urging readers to recognise that Japanese educational 'achievements appear to be . . . a product of the nation's unique historical and cultural foundations' (OERI 1987: vii) and thus 'there may not be packaged solutions for cross-national import or export' (p. 66). Yet, despite insights such as these that dot the main text, Bennett and Finn reveal that they both (a) actively confined the research team to a description of the Japanese education system stating explicitly in the Foreword that 'the project was not designed initially in comparative terms' (p. iv) and (b) reserved the right for themselves to take up the task of drawing 'lessons' for American education.

Thus, the second and more crucial voice is that of Secretary of Education William Bennett who indeed undertakes this central task of drawing 'Implications for American Education' in the Epilogue of the report. As already highlighted above, he exudes confidence in the lessons Japanese example affords. Among those 'lessons' was a uniform, core curriculum that 'transmits the shared and inherited culture to the next generation' (Bennett 1987: 70). This, according to Bennett, includes 'moral education' with 'clear distinctions . . . imbuing youngsters with a deep sense of good and bad, right and wrong, moral and immoral' (p. 70). He applauds the fact that Japanese schools 'have not turned into societal multi-service centers, nor are they buffeted by pedagogical or curricular fads' because they 'embody these characteristics that research has ascribed to "effective" schools' (pp. 69–70). Moreover, he draws attention to private outlays for education, praising the Japanese for ensuring 'that they are getting value for money' (p. 71).

Two features of the discourse stand out. First, Japan is set up as a salutary example with references to it serving to shape a particular view of contemporary America. Bennett (1987) writes, for example, 'Japanese education *works* – it has been demonstrably successful in providing modern Japan with – a civilisation in which there is relatively little crime or violence, and a functional society wherein the basic technological infrastructure is sound and reliable' (p. 69). The implicit message was that the US lacks those qualities; a contrast that becomes explicit when he states 'a well-ordered, and purposeful learning environment, including both formal discipline and a high level of individual self-discipline' creates Japanese students who 'have learned what kinds of behaviors are appropriate, where and when. *So should our youngsters'* (70, emphasis added). This is a clear continuation of the crisis theme launched by

A Nation at Risk, but in setting up a 'reference to elsewhere' those same messages could be articulated in novel ways.

Second, the discourse infuses the Reagan–Campbell political discourse into the portrayal of Japanese education. When viewed through system-theory, it is clear that the discourse only includes those elements that allow the political agenda to be articulated, filtering out those that do not resonate. This infusion of *self-reference* is clearly evident in comments above, but also from Bennett's brief, but telling exclusion of the rather awkward fact that Japanese education was highly centralised and directed by a large, powerful central Ministry of Education, the exact opposite of Reagan's attempt to downsize: 'we would not . . . want to emulate the basic organisation of Japanese education that relies heavily on direction and control from the central government' (1987: 69). Bennett is apparently confident that the equity that tends to attend centralised systems was not significant in Japanese educational 'success', but feels the need to mark this explicitly to ensure his primary message is not 'misunderstood'.

In limiting the research group to a descriptive account, the body of *Japanese Education Today* reads like an encyclopaedia of dates and facts. We can surmise that the media and the average citizen would probably have just skimmed the eighty-page main text on the way to Bennett's three-page 'Implications for America' conclusion. The inside cover, however, would also have been an area of major reader traffic. Here are presented the 'Highlights of this Report', a section that argues that 'a close look at Japanese education provides a stimulus for Americans to examine the standards, performance, and potential of their own system', failing to reveal that those were in fact Bennett's personal conclusions, *not* those of the Study Team. Indeed, Chester Finn who writes this opening all but reveals the larger political project by (re)injecting the *Nation at Risk* discourse into the Foreword, stating that the report 'helps me understand more clearly some of the risks and opportunities facing American education. And that, after all, is one of the reasons we undertook the project in the first place' (p. iv). All of this points to a deft political move to co-opt the research to serve the wider political project.

But the story does not end there. The years beginning with the inauguration of the OERI Study team (October 1984) and the release of *Japanese Education Today* (January 1987) became the apogee of the 'lessons from Japan' discourse. This was, of course, bolstered by Japan's economic success and growing international clout, but a closer look suggests much more was at work (Rappleye 2007). A large volume of work, scholarly and popular, ensued that judged America's education system in relation to Japanese 'success' and it is here that we can begin to sketch some of the policy effects of the 'lessons from Japan' construction. First, in the years following *Japanese Education Today* many of the scholars who had written commissioned papers for the OERI Japan Study Team produced works that bore a striking resemblance to the dominant discourse of domestic failure and Japanese 'success'. Consider Merry White's *The Japanese Educational Challenge* (1987), Harold Stevenson and James Stigler's *The Learning Gap: Why Our Schools Are Failing and What We Can Learn from Japanese and Chinese Education* (1992), Lois Peak's *Learning to Go to School in Japan* (1993) and Catherine Lewis's *The Roots of Japanese Educational Achievement* (1995) among others. Leestma and Walberg released *Japanese Educational Productivity* in

1992, a volume whose Preface is written by Chester Finn in which he states: 'It is clear from the critical acclaim of the scholarly community as well as widespread positive reaction from the public, the education profession, and the mass media that *Japanese Education Today* hit the mark we had set for it' (p. x).[5] Around the same time, Finn himself published *We Must Take Charge: Our Schools and Our Future* (1991), and in the first section, entitled 'A Nation Still at Risk', the Japan example is resurrected again to make the case for reform. The *Japanese Education Today* project is clearly the point that binds all of the actors and their works into a single network. These works came, in turn, to embody and extend the discourse and thus the wider political project, pushing 'attraction' to Japanese education well into the mid-1990s.

Moreover, this was only half the story: many more works hit book shelves (e.g. Duke 1986a; Lynn 1988), filled educational journals (e.g. Cantor 1985; Ahearn 1986; Cummings et al. 1986; Duke 1986b; Bartell and Willis 1987; Berliner and Casanova 1987; Lewis 1988; McCormick 1988, 1989; Willis and Bartell 1990) and found their way into the popular media (e.g. *New York Times* 1987a, 1987b, 1988; *Economist* 1986). These must be seen, in light of the history traced above, as not spontaneous 'attraction' but a telling example of the interrelationship of research funds and the production of knowledge, as well as the uncritical adoption of the *problematique* of *politically produced* 'lessons from elsewhere' by scholars, the media and others.[6] All of this points to the type of the response that can be generated by the political production of attraction; carefully planned, ideologically driven political theatre that emerges into the public view as simply salutary (and seemingly spontaneous) references from the highest nodes of the political realm. Let us come back to elaborate this after examining a strikingly similar drama staged in Japan.

The Political Production of 'Lessons from England' in Japan

A long view of the roots of Japan's own political production would reach all the way back to the end of the American-led Allied Occupation in 1952. Concerned with a 'Communist take-over' of Japan (recall that the 'Red Scare' was raging in America at the time, China had just 'fallen'), General Headquarters (GHQ) allowed powerful pre-war conservatives to re-emerge on the political scene as a counterweight to swelling leftist influence (Dower 1999). These conservative figures coalesced in 1955 into the Liberal Democratic Party (LDP), which, given their background, soon took as one its central policy goals the revision of the 'distortions' of the American-led Occupation, in particular the 'Peace Constitution' and the Fundamental Law of Education (FLE) that the Americans had created to replace the pre-war 'ultranationalist' Imperial Rescript. Given the obvious sensitivity of explicitly pushing for remilitarisation implied by a revision to the 'Peace Constitution' so soon, the FLE became *the* major symbolic target. This ideologically driven agenda was a central platform of the LDP throughout its ensuing 50 years of one-party rule, yet conservatives within the party were unable to engineer this coveted FLE revision until only very recently (December 2006).

The more recent origins of the Japanese production is found in the 'achievement crisis debate' that engulfed the country from roughly 1999 to 2003 (Tsuneyoshi 2004). The incisive debate began with a fiery conservative response to the proposed *yutori kyōiku* reforms (reductions in classroom hours and content to allow children 'room' to grow) proposed by MEXT in 1998 that many saw as exacerbating falling educational standards. Clearly much of the fervour was an attempt to halt the enactment of the New Course of Study (2002) that would implement these reforms, but the intimations of 'individuality' underpinning the *yutori* also helped re-ignite the longstanding debates about the 'distortions' of the Occupation (Rappleye and Kariya 2011, Cave 2001). Takayama (2007) has already skilfully detailed how some conservative commentators, largely spontaneously and in an uncoordinated fashion it seems, used the rhetorical devices from America's *Nation at Risk* to push their case for reform during this debate. Those findings are a starting point, but stop short of revealing how several key figures subsequently began scripting a much more ambitious plan, in 2002, after failing to defeat the enactment of *yutori* reforms.[7]

This new political project coalesces around Yagi Hidetsugu, a conservative intellectual who, at the height of the 'achievement crisis debate' had dubbed the *yutori* reforms 'an act of unthinking, unilateral educational disarmament' (Tsuchi 2001).[8] Yagi had previously established, in 1996, a highly controversial *Society for History Textbook Reform*, writing a new history textbook that resorted to the glory and appreciation for Japanese history that had, his group argued, been replaced by the Occupation with an unnecessarily negative, even 'masochistic' view (Rose 2006). In November 2002, less than a year after the New Course of Study promulgating *yutori* was enacted, Yagi, together with other prominent figures from the previous achievement crisis debate, published a volume entitled *The Education Black Papers: What are Schools Teaching Our Children?* (Yagi 2002). The original *Black Papers* were, of course, the reports released in the 1970s by British academics Brian Cox and A. E. Dyson that attacked liberal theories of education and provided much of the legitimacy for Prime Minister Callaghan's now famous Ruskin College speech, crucial opening moves in the drama leading up to Thatcher's 1988 Education Reform Act. As Yagi (2002: 5) clearly explains, not just the name but the wider goals were being purposefully borrowed:

> Today our country's education is in crisis . . . the first step towards improving the system is to spread knowledge of the current educational conditions to every of level of Japanese society. For this reason, we have assembled these 'Black Papers' following the example of those who revamped and normalized English education . . . [to] contribute to the normalization of education in our country in the same way as the Black Papers did in England.

This key phrase 'normalization' derived from the political manifesto of LDP heavyweight Ichiro Ozawa's *Blueprint for a New Japan: The Rethinking of a Nation*, published in 1994, which held that until Japan emerged from the shadow of the Occupation it would never be a 'normal' nation.[9] Yagi and his *Black Papers* project were clearly the origins of the later 'learn from England' discourse.[10]

One of the contributors to the *Black Papers* was Yamatani Eriko, who had been elected to the Lower House of the Japanese legislature in 2000 and served on several influential education-related committees. Here is the clearest link to the official world of policy making. Occupied for most of 2003 with an unsuccessful re-election campaign, Yamatani was finally elected to the more influential Upper House in July 2004.

Crucially however, just four months prior to her re-election, a Committee for the Promotion of the Revising the Fundamental Law of Education had been formed by conservative LDP members at a meeting convened with funds from a conservative, private policy lobbying organisation, the Japan Conference.[11] The group began to grapple with the best way to, once again, approach the long-standing, yet politically sensitive and highly charged issue of reforming the FLE. A veteran Upper House LDP member (Ikuo Kamei) was selected to head the Committee that included a number of major LDP-cum-government figures including, crucially, Abe Shinzō, then Party Secretary of the LDP. The group was actively in search of a politically viable strategy to push through the FLE amendment (Hiranuma 2005). With the arrival of Yamatani in the Upper House, Yagi's *Black Papers* approach quickly came to be known at the highest echelons of the LDP. Evidently the strategy impressed them greatly because within a month, the official decision had been made that Japan had much to 'learn from England'.[12]

'Learning from English Education': The English Education Research Group

Immediately a detailed plan to make those 'lessons' clear was put into action, starting with the formation of the English Education Research Group. The opening act was a well-publicised 'educational tour' to England late September of that same year (2004). The high profile group included all of the main LDP heavyweights who formed the Committee, but most significant in the context of later developments, however, were the remaining two members: Yamatani Eriko and Abe Shinzō. These become the key figures to track.

Although the group of twelve stayed a total of two weeks in England, only seven of those days were devoted to the study of 'English education'. As one might expect they visited a couple of schools, met professors at the University of London, and visited the Department of Education and Skills (DfES). As one might not expect they also visited the Professional Council for Religious Education and the Culham Institute – a private think tank promoting religious education. They met twice with representatives from the Centre for Policy Studies (CPS), the British think tank Thatcher personally established in 1974. They also met not once, but twice, with the International Sales Manager and History Book Division Chief of Longman, the giant textbook publishing house. They paid repeated visits to the Qualifications and Curriculum Authority (QCA) and the Office of Standards in Education (OfSTED). On the final day, they also spent the entire morning with the Secretary of Education, not the then incumbent Charles Clarke, but one of his powerful predecessors: Lord Kenneth Baker, the man who had engineered the Thatcher education reforms. This itinerary clearly matched the mix of agendas they set out with.[13]

Upon their return to Japan, they published their findings in an edited volume entitled *Learning from the Thatcher Reforms: The Road to Educational Normalization: The Report of the English Education Research Group* (Nakanishi 2005).[14] Each of the members has a chapter and the book opens with several pictures of the group at the school visits. Despite not even accompanying the group on the trip, Nakanishi Teramasu, a widely known political historian at Kyoto University, edits the volume, writing front matter that explains:

> Today England is at the forefront of numerous advanced countries in achieving historical educational reform. As a result the vitality of the country has been *rebuilt*, improving both its birth rate and public order . . . What brought this sweeping change? It was education reform, because education is that which can trigger the greatest of changes . . . this also our own 'educational rebuilding'.

Having Nakanishi edit the volume can been seen as move to garner further legitimacy and raising the profile of the volume: he was one of the top three most widely cited intellectuals in Japan (Asahi 2008). As the title of the volume suggests, Ozawa's 1994 'normalization' idea picked up in Yagi's *Black Papers* becomes a cohesive, constant reference throughout the book and the three political agendas the group set out with – revising the FLE, remedying history textbooks and monitoring/raising achievement – become the book's major themes.

In terms of the contributions of our key figures, Yamatani reports that England was able to 'rehabilitate moral values' through 'religion and the strengthening of house-holds' that must be emulated if it is to overcome 'the warping of Japanese society' that resulted from the elimination of religious education under the Occupation (Nakanishi 2005: 111). Abe, for his part, first highlights the similarities he sees between England and Japan: 'Not only problems of masochistic history textbooks, but also the decline in achievement due to the implementation of experiential learning in the form of the yutori education and the Integrated Curriculum were originally the same in England' (p. 241). He explains that by rectifying their textbooks, England has regained a sense of its true identity, but in Japan because 'of the fact that the phrase "respect for tradition" was eliminated by GHQ the result is that the Japanese utterly lack a view of how to foster a sense of self-awareness and identity' (p. 263). Thus, Abe asserts that, like England's 1988 Education Reform Act, 'a restoration of education . . . must begin with a revision of the Basic Law of Education' (p. 264). *Self-reference* is more than obvious.

It was at this point that Abe published *Toward a Beautiful Country* (July 2006), cited at the outset of the chapter. It warned of educational 'ruin', praised English education reform, and called for a 'creative destruction' of the status quo. Once elected in September 2006, Abe moved, as promised, to quickly carry out the reforms he envisaged. In his inaugural speech he announced his intent to create the Education Rebuilding Council, a body that would allow Abe to by-pass the Central Council for Education (CCE), the standing body holding the legal authority to direct national education policies. To lead the Council's powerful Secretariat Prime Minister Abe chose, as one might have guessed, Yamatani Eriko.

The plan to employ the English example appeared to work masterfully. On 22 December, just a month after Abe inauguration, the Fundamental Law of Education was successful revised, tempering references to 'individuality' and adding phrases about 'tradition' and 'love of country'. Although establishing causality of major policy change is, admittedly, difficult to determine and clearly involved much 'horse-trading' and highly opaque behind-the-scenes negotiations (Takayama 2008b), the English example-cum-Educational Rebuilding momentum was clearly significant. Following the revision, the ERC churned out several major reports in quick succession height-ening the pace of reform and providing the major impetus for four major education bills that passed the national legislature in June 2007 including one that aligned textbooks with the newly revised FLE and led to the scrapping of *yutori kyoiku* by late October 2007. In examining the minutes of the ERC, references to England are framed and discussed in a way strikingly similar as they are in the lead up to the ERC, most probably because at the first meeting ERC members each received 'background materials' that included one page summaries of Reagan and Thatcher reforms prepared by the Yamatani-led ERC Secretariat (ERC 2006). This was necessary because *no* English education specialists were appointed to the ERC. Surely this void itself is strong evidence that conservative leaders in Japan had no real intention to learn anything from England in the first place, but only to use the English example to launch a discourse that would help 'get the message out'. Not substantive convergence then, but a carefully planned and executed production of self-reference.

Comparison and Contrast: Elaborating the Political Production Model

The fact that two strikingly similar accounts emerge from countries as different historically, culturally, politically and educationally as America and Japan suggest a robust political strategy deployable across space and time. These accounts make it difficult to support the idea that 'references to elsewhere' derive from non-political contextual factors, spontaneous attraction and/or represent substantive attempts to 'borrow'. Instead, they illustrate how 'references to elsewhere' emanating from the political realm are political theatre where specific actors, driven by ideological and political agendas consciously script opportunities to get their 'message out' by articulating it in 'references to elsewhere'. This self-reference intends to produce salutary effects among the audience; catalysing and shaping substantive policy change along the political group's *pre-existing* ideological lines.

While recognising these overarching similarities, comparing and contrasting the two cases allows us to more fully elaborate the multiple manifestations of the general Political Production Model. Let us consider these in terms of a rather arbitrary division of the processes into four sequential stages underpinned by the metaphor of a stage production.

In the scripting phase, we find powerful political actors coming together to explicitly and articulate a long-standing political goal in the form of a concrete reform proposal. Drafting this script – the act that distinguishes this phase from a more general, diffuse discussion of the need for reform – often coincides with an upcoming election or other time of heightened politically sensitivity, approximating Kingdon's (1984) discussion of the 'politics stream'. This is evident in the Reagan collaboration with Campbell on formulating concrete educational reform recommendations in the run-up to the 1980 US President election. This 'coming together' of actors and opportunity can also, however, take the form of relatively 'minor' politically active actors (what the policy literature sometimes calls *policy entrepreneurs*) selling a script to powerful policy makers who are simultaneously in the market for viable strategies. Yagi's attempts to get Yamatani involved in his *Black Papers* project, then her election to the Upper House that moved the project 'upstream' politically is illustrative.

The subsequent production phase is best conceptualised in two parts. The first step is creation of a 'discourse of crisis' of which *A Nation at Risk* (NCEE 1983) becomes the classic example. The second step becomes the production of a foreign example, such as *Japanese Education Today* (OERI 1987) in America. In the Japanese episode, the 'achievement crisis' debate that raged from 1999 to 2002 meant that the stage was already set for the introduction of a discourse about 'lessons from elsewhere', a space filled by the 'learn from England' discourse of 2005–2006. It is in this *production* phase that a quasi-official institution is created and charged with the mission of gathering, like an actual stage production, the necessary constructive materials on 'elsewhere': (a) background materials are prepared, (b) opinions are 'formulated', aligned, and rehearsed (such at the Committee for the Promotion of the Revising the Fundamental Law of Education), and (c) study trips, like those of the OERI Study Team and the LDP Research Group, gather 'lessons' and legitimacy.

Here a major difference between America and Japan is evident. In America, both the NCEE and OERI Japan Study Team were quickly and relatively easily set up as official and these bodies ultimately used American taxpayer (public) money to fund the *production*. In Japan, the LDP relied exclusively on private funding from a private think-tank/lobbying organisation, the Japan Conference, to launch the production and only achieved a publicly funded body – the Education Rebuilding Council – relatively late. This was probably because in the highly centralised Japanese system it was much more difficult to justify a special policy reform council when the Central Council on Education, as mentioned above, was legally charged with formulating national educational policy; not the case in the highly decentralised American system where there was no competing central policy organ.

Taking this discourse 'public' signifies the beginning of the staging phase, the time when the script is acted out for a public already rendered attentive by the spectre of 'crisis'. Although usually punctuated by a high profile report or reference such as *Japanese Education Today* or Abe's 'Restoration of Pride through Thatcher's Education Reforms' (Abe 2006: last chapter), the players attempt, in line with their overall aims, to propagate this message as widely as possible. Press conferences, press releases, articles in leading intellectual magazines (such as a piece by Abe and others on 'English education' in January 2005 in the widely read Japan monthly *Seiron*), op-ed pieces in major newspapers, references in speeches or popular books (such as Chester Finn's *We Must Take Charge: Our Schools and Our Future* (1991)) and Abe's *Towards a Beautiful Country* (2006) – these are all ways to 'get the message out' onto the 'public' stage and attempt to get it picked up, discussed and thus amplified in the media and scholarly discourse. Crucially, one of the key features of this staging is that, like theatre, marks of the political origins of the project are intentionally removed or hidden from view to add authenticity: usually one finds references to the non-political (scientific) nature of the 'study trips', commentary to the obviousness ('common sense') and/or consensus around the superiority of reforms 'elsewhere', and a pushing aside of critique, negative images, or aspects of 'elsewhere' that are 'off message'. Bennett's Epilogue is illustrative in all of these respects (see Bennett 1987).

The form that the subsequent *response/reaction* phase takes is arguably a derivative of who the target audience is, how well the audience has been prepared ('crisis'), how resonant and convincing the drama is, and how crucial it is to continue to extend the duration of the production in the pursuit of policy reform. Here the focus on differences is again most illuminating. In America, the target audience was individual State administrators, local school districts, and the general public (see Bell 1988). As the

Federal government had no constitutional authority to impose change it had to attempt to induce people to act with a *productive* discourse (this strategy has changed a bit with the huge influx of Federal 'incentives' to comply with Federal initiatives such as No Child Left Behind). Policy change along the lines of the Reagan–Campbell agenda would only come about through generating crisis, closing down alternative ways of thinking (e.g. greater equity as the origins of Japanese 'success'), and extending the discourse until all States had 'come around'.

In contrast to this, the target audience for Abe and like-minded leaders of the LDP was the educational establishment and powerful political leaders. In Japan's highly centralised system, sweeping, even drastic change, could take place if one could successfully gain control the political 'centre' – the minds and machinery of the central government and political and bureaucratic elite. But to do so one needed to both win an election and convince the national legislature of the need for a 'supplementary' reform council, charged with basically the same mission as the Central Council for Education. Given that Abe was a virtual shoo-in for the LDP prime minister following the widely popular Koizumi, the 'lessons from England' discourse was probably directed less at the wider electorate, but more at a smaller group of top-level politicians and bureaucrats. Japan has arguably not moved much toward a 'post-bureaucratic state' (Hook and Hasegawa 2005), so power remains locked in the 'centre' and old legalistic/institutional modes are still fairly dominant. This means that wider dissemination of the discourse was probably less important that convincing a smaller group of policy makers. Once the 'centre' was captured, policy change was swift and there was little need to extend the production, probably the major reason the 'lessons from England' discourse drops off so abruptly in Japan, while it exhibits a long tail in American, extending, as it did, well into the 1990s.

We can further sketch a material and discoursal sphere of reaction/response that inches us closer to specifying policy effects of these types of political productions, the key void in the current literature on attraction and 'borrowing'. On the material level, 'lessons to elsewhere' helps produce political actors' educational credentials and also bind together coalitions of actors. This later point is important, as Steiner-Khamsi (2010) has recently pointed out. In the 'English example', both the long-standing goals of LDP conservatives (FLE revision and textbooks) and more widespread support for reforms to stop a purported drop in achievement can, when articulated skilfully, coalesce to form a powerful political coalition. In America too, Glenn Campbell was more of an advocate of the market, but that political agenda could coalesce, in the Japanese model, with the educationally minded Finn and the moral agenda of Bennett, hence all of those messages appeared simultaneously in Bennett's 'Implications for American Education' (1987). It is the *multi-vocality* afforded by 'lessons from elsewhere' fostered by its opacity and novelty that produce stronger reform coalitions than references to more visible and contentious domestic realities.

In the discoursal sphere, the effects are arguably also two-fold. First, going back to Ball's 'discourse of derision' notion, the production of 'lessons from elsewhere' would seem to be another means to 'debunk and displace' domestic educational specialists. By moving the debate quite literally halfway around the world, educational experts in the domestic context 'have been displaced, their control over meaning lost', though one must admittedly be careful not to overestimate the extent to which 'lessons from elsewhere' play in national reform debates. A second effect is that the 'lessons from elsewhere' discourse gets picked up by (uncritical) scholars and the media, leading to its amplification. This is most clear in the American case. With few exceptions, American scholars in the 1980s worked within the discourse of Japanese 'success' rather than problematising it; more and more detailed description of Japanese education emerged only amplifying the original *political* production. This was repeated in the media. The implication is that political discourses originating in ideology etched themselves into the very form and texture of, supposedly objective, scholarly and media treatment of the time. In this flood of works we recognise the powerful *productive effects* of the discourse, closing out alternative models and taking some basic, embedded assumptions as given 'truth' such as, say, the inadequacy of provision at 'home' and/or linkages between economics and educational success.

This means that there are, in contrast to the claims of systems-theory, real effects, substantive, albeit subtle, in the 'home' system originating not from the 'outside' but from powerful coalitions of actors transmitted via productive discourses on the 'inside' that can push the internal system in new directions. System logic does not always trump actor agency. This might even suggest that we look closer at how powerful actors shape the 'socio-logic' of the system, rather than beginning, as systems theory does, with the assumption that such a 'socio-logic' is widely shared or exists *a priori*.

An obvious question arises along these lines: why do we not see a similar spike in scholarly and media work on English attraction in Japan? Indeed, for the most part, Japanese scholars have come out strongly against the English model (e.g. Fujita 2006, Fukuda 2007, Abe 2007). Perhaps the lack of political need for extension of the production factored, but so might have the fact that by 2006 there was a flood of research from Europe and America warning of the downsides of the Thatcher–Reagan model. American scholars in the 1980s had not the tools afforded by comparison, with which they might have understood the detrimental aspects of the model or detected stagecraft; Japanese scholars did and emerged as much more aware of conservative designs on education based on more *cautious* appraisals of 'lessons from elsewhere'.

Conclusion: Understanding the Stakes

To conclude, let us briefly return and sketch some answers to the four 'core' questions surrounding the 'internationalisation' of education policy raised at the outset. When approached through the Political Production Model – this hybrid of actor-centric realism, systems theory, and post-structuralism – the question of what is driving the marked increase in attraction becomes clear: powerful political coalitions with long-standing ideological agendas are resorting to carefully scripted and executed attempts to use 'references to elsewhere' to drive domestic reform. Steiner-Khamsi (2000, 2004) has come to similar conclusions, though we might now add that attraction is also being amplified and extended by the uncritical acceptance of this production among scholars and the media. In that these 'references' are largely self-referential, we are probably not witnessing nearly the degree of convergence that one might assume from a cursory review of such references: no substantive 'borrowing' is taking place and changes derive from the socio-logic, or at least the 'socio-logic' of the most powerful political actors, of the domestic system. Thus, the 'internation-alisation' of educational policy is probably much more *imagined* than it is currently envisaged.

This leads right into the two remaining questions of how to best approach attraction and 'borrowing' and the crucial question of what is 'at stake'. As shown above, there is a real danger that if picked up uncritically, 'references to elsewhere' are taken at face-value, seen not as productions but as authentic attempts to 'borrow', because they are rebroadcast and amplified. The same thus applies when we, as scholars, analyse attraction and 'borrowing', if these 'references to elsewhere' are thought to signal authentic policy change we are likely to assume, reproduce, and amplify an image of substantive convergence. Moreover, if we read only policy texts and/or political actors' carefully choreographed statements in the *staging* phase that are *by their very nature intended to erase the political origins of the stagecraft*, we emerge with an image largely devoid of politics. If this is, in turn, reproduced in academic theory, what is produced is a false image of our world, one that only replicates and amplifies the *stagecraft* of elite political actors.

Despite these stakes, it is hard to avoid the conclusion that this is precisely what is happening in scholarship that begins from, in particular, a world culture perspective. Return to a representative text highlighted at the outset, consider once again Wiseman and Baker's world culture inspired contribution, *The Explosion of Internationalized Educational Policy* (2005). There, on the opening page, they assume and describe the emergence of a 'policymaking environment already marked by extensive borrowing and copying from one nation to the next'. Have they not mistaken reference for substance? Devoid of concrete examples, a close reading of that chapter suggests these scholars have uncritically picked up political production discourses, imagining authentic, convergent borrowing ('copying') and thus the triumph of a shared 'world culture' *devoid of politics.*

Yet, the present chapter suggests it is in fact *politics* itself that has created their very image by erasing its political origins as far as possible to normalise and thus legitimate policy effects, a perspective lost if we fail to move beyond the proscenium arch: public policy documents and official statements. As this well-worn policy strategy continues, the stakes are thus higher and more immediate than we might have expected: will we, as scholars, unwittingly let our own research imaginaries be etched with these discourses and unwittingly become mere extensions of the dominant political project? Or will we extend the Political Production Model in new directions to critically understand how visions of our world and, indeed, our very range of thought, at once derive from and are delimited by such acts of political theatre?

Notes

1 Other possibilities would include *functionalism* and *historical institutionalism*, both of which have fared rather poorly describing domestic changes linked to developments beyond nation-state borders. Another would be *policy science*, which arguably represents the highest pretension of political science: to apply rational, scientific methods to analyses, formu-lation, and evaluation of public policy. *Macro-realism* (e.g. world systems theory), though it does focus on international influences on nation-states and education, would be the obvious final choice, but it has yet to be applied to the problematique of 'borrowing' and

transfer in any meaningful way (e.g., Clayton 1998, 2004), perhaps because it is more interested in larger structural changes in the global economy, rather than domestic political and/or cultural phenomena (Arnove 2009). Some have hinted at a post-colonial approach to understanding attraction (Takayama and Apple 2008) but it remains largely undeveloped to date.

2 For a more elaborate discussion how system theory has been understood in comparative education in ways that appear to differ from Luhmann see the first chapter of Rappleye (2011).

3 All translations of Japanese in this chapter are my own. Japanese names are rendered in their original form (family name first), in both the text and the references.

4 Bell was, admittedly, not completely bought into the Reagan–Campbell plans to dismantle the Department of Education. His memoirs suggest that he was trying to work for reform momentum, but preferred moderate education reform, instead of the more radical proposals (such as abolishing the DOE) of other Reagan administration ideologues.

5 Supporting the notion that Finn was utilising the Japanese example to push domestic reform are his very recent comments to the *New York Times* on Shanghai's 'stunning' PISA results: 'Wow . . . I am thinking Sputnik' (*New York Times*, 7 December 2010). It is rather amazing that Finn would by-pass the more obvious similarities to Japan's dominant economy and test scores in the 1980s to instead reference Sputnik; 'amazing', that is, until one considers that Finn may not have wanted people to make the connections that all of the fears over the dominance of Japan ultimately came to naught, *except for* producing the critical momentum for Reagan–Campbell's neoliberal education reforms that arguably continued right up through Bush's No Child Left Behind Act.

6 I am not arguing that these studies cited above were in any way unsound academically. The questions I am attempting to raise are: what perspectives of Japanese education or other international contexts did not reach publication because they lacked funds, access, or appeal? But more importantly: what other approaches to domestic education reform were 'displaced' (Steiner-Khamsi 2000) in the rush to 'learn from Japan'?

7 A more recent paper by Takayama and Apple (2008) highlighted the 'learn from England' production I detail here, but largely examined the contents of the 'references' and attempted to initiate a discussion of post-colonial possibilities for 'borrowing' research, not looking at actors or effects as I attempt to do here.

8 Takayama (2007) points out that this exact phrase appears in the U.S. National Commission on Educational Excellence suggesting, fascinatingly, that conservatives in Japan were clearly aware of the reform generated by US Nation at Risk *production* and were trying to generate a similar type of momentum in Japan.

9 See specifically Section II 'Becoming a Normal Nation' (pp. 93–150).

10 There is, of course, the question of why England as opposed to another country was selected, especially since England's economy and international testing results did not immediately present themselves as a shining example. Here I find much value and direct readers to the contributions of Takayama's post-colonialist inspired writings (see in particular Takayama 2008c, Takayama and Apple 2008). Rappleye and Kariya (2011) also provide a historical review of the reasons for the dominance of 'the West' in Japan's imagining of its place in the world.

11 The Committee grew out of the Japan Conference's (*Nihon kaigi*) 'Friendship Conference for Members of the Diet' (*Nihon kaigi kokkai kaigiin nendankai*), a forum for the conservative Japan Conference to share its ideas with influential members of the Diet and vice-versa.

12 Space limitations permit a more detailed, documented account of how this decision was made, but those interested can find it in Rappleye (2011).

13 A full, detailed itinerary of the trip can be found in Nakanishi (2005: 22–23). Further analysis and a fuller description can be found in Rappleye (2011).

14 Nakanishi Teramasu is a vocal and famous conservative professor of history at the University of Kyoto. Despite not going on the trip, he shows little qualms in editing the volume and heavily praises the English system in his introduction.

References

Abe, S. (2006) *Utusukushii kuni he* [Toward a beautiful country]. Tokyo: Bungei shunjū.

Abe, E. (2007) Igirisu 'Kyōiku kaikaku' no kyōkun – 'Kyōiku no ichibaka' ha kodomo no tame ni naranai [The Lessons of English 'Education Reform': 'Marketization of Education' is Not in the Interest of Children]. Tokyo: Iwanami Shoten.

Ahearn, E. (1986) 'Japanese and American Special Education: A World Apart', *International Journal of Special Education*, 1(2): 129–140.

Arnove, R. (2009) 'World-systems Analysis and Comparative Education in the Age of Globalization', in R. Cowen and A. Kazamias (eds) *International Handbook of Comparative Education*, Vol. 2 (pp. 101–120). New York: Springer.

Asahi News Publishing (2008) Daigaku rankingu [University Rankings]. Tokyo: Asahi Shinbunsha.

Baker, D. and LeTendre, G. (2005) *National Differences, Global Similarities: World Culture and the Future of Schooling*. Stanford: Stanford University Press.

Ball, S. (1990) *Politics and Policy Making in Education: Explorations in Policy Sociology*. New York: Routledge.

Bartell, C. and Willis, D. (1987) 'American and Japanese Principals: A Comparative Analysis of Instructional Leadership', *NASSP Bulletin*, 71(502): 18–27.

Bell, T. (1988) *The Thirteenth Man: A Reagan Cabinet Memoir*. New York: Free Press.

Bennett, W. (1987) 'Implications for American Education', *In Japanese Education Today*. Washington, DC: US Department of Education.

Bennett, W. (1992) *The De-Valuing of America: The Fight for Our Culture and Our Children*. New York: Touchstone.

Bennett, W. (2001) *The Broken Hearth: Reversing the Moral Collapse of the American Family*. New York: Doubleday Books.

Berliner, D. and Biddle, B. (1995) *The Manufactured Crisis: Myths, Fraud and the Attack on America's Public Schools*. Cambridge: Perseus Books.

Berliner, D. and Casanova, U. (1987) 'Are We Expecting Enough Effort from Students?', *Instructor*, 97: 16–17.

Best, S. and Kellner, D. (1991) *Postmodern Theory: Critical Interrogations*. New York: Guilford Press.

Cannon, L (1991) *President Reagan: The Role of a Lifetime*. New York: Touchstone/Simon & Schuster.

Cantor, L. (1985) 'Vocational Education and Training: The Japanese Approach', *Comparative Education*, 21(1): 67–76.

Carney, S. and Bista, M. (2009) 'Community Schooling in Nepal: A Genealogy of Education Reform since 1990', *Comparative Education Review*, 53(2): 189–211.

Cave, P. (2001) 'Education Reform in Japan in the 1990s: "Individuality" and Other Uncertainties', *Comparative Education* 37(2): 173–191.

Chubb, J. and Moe, T. (1990) *Politics, Markets, and America's Schools*. Washington, DC: Brookings Institute.

Clayton, T. (1998) 'Beyond Mystification: Reconnecting World-System Theory for Comparative Education', *Comparative Education Review*, 42(4): 479–496.

Clayton, T. (2004) 'Competing Conceptions of Globalization Revisited: Relocating the Tension Between World-Systems Analysis and Globalization Analysis', *Comparative Education Review*, 48: 274–294.

Cummings, W. (1989) 'The American Perception of Japanese Education', *Comparative Education*, 25 (3): 293–302.

Cummings, W., Beauchamp, E., Ishikawa, S., Kobayashi, V. and Ushiogi, M. (1986) *Educational Policies in Crisis*. New York: Praeger.

Dale, R. (1999) 'Specifying Globalization Effects on National Policy: A Focus on the Mechanisms', *Journal of Education Policy*, 14(1): 1–17.

Dower, J. (1999) *Embracing Defeat: Japan in the wake of World War II*. New York: W.W. Norton.

Driori, G., Meyer, J., Ramirez, F. and Schofer, E. (2003) *Science in the Modern World Polity: Institutionalization and Globalization*. Palo Alto: Stanford University Press.

Duke, B. (1986a) *The Japanese School: Lessons for Industrial America*. London: Praeger.

Duke, B. (1986b) 'The Liberalization of Japanese Education', *Comparative Education*, 22(1): 37–45.

Education Rebuilding Council (ERC) (2006) Minutes of the First Meeting of the Education Rebuilding Council (27 November). Tokyo: Educational Rebuilding Council. Available online at: www.kantei.go.jp/jp/singi/kyouiku/3bunka/dai1/1gijiroku.pdf.

Economist (1986, December). Crammed Full, 301: 50–51.

Finn, C. (1991) *We Must Take Charge: Our Schools and Our Future*. New York: Free Press.

Fiske, E. (1983) 'Top Objectives Elude Reagan as Education Policy Evolves', *New York Times*, December 27, 1.

Fujita, H. (2006) Kyōiku Kaikaky no Yukue: Kakusa-shakai ka kyoso shakai ka [Whither Education Reform: Stratified or Symbiotic Society?]. Tokyo: Iwanami Shoten.

Fukuda, S. (2007) Kyosō shitemo gakuryoku ikitomari: igirisu kyōiku no shippai to finurando no seikō [Competition Leads to An Achievement Dead-End: England's Educational Reform Failure and Finland's Success]. Tokyo: Asahi Shinbun-Sha.

Hiranuma, T. (2005) *Hajimeni* [Foreword]. In *Sachyā kaikaku ni manabu kyōiku seijōka he no michi: eikokū kyōiku chosa hōkoko.* [Learning from the Thatcher Reforms, The Road to Educational Normalization: The Report of the English Education Research Group], ed. T. Nakanishi. Tokyo: PHP Kenkyūjō [PHP Research Center].

Hook, G. and Hasegawa, H. (2005) *The Political Economy of Japanese Globalization*. London: Routledge.

Kingdon, J. (1984) *Agendas, Alternatives, and Public Policies*. Boston: Little, Brown.

Kunkel, J. (2003) *America's Trade Policy Toward Japan: Demanding Results*. New York: Routledge.

Leestma, R. and Walberg, H. (eds) (1992) *Japanese Educational Productivity*. Ann Arbor, Michigan: Center for Japanese Studies, University of Michigan.

Levin, B. (1998) 'An Epidemic of Education Policy: (What) Can We Learn From Each Other?', *Comparative Education*, 34 (2): 131–141.

Lewis, C. (1988) 'Japanese First-Grade Classrooms: Implications for U.S. Theory and Research', *Comparative Education Review*, 32(2): 159–172.

Lewis, C. (1995) 'The Roots of Japanese Educational Achievement: Helping Children Develop Bonds to School', *Educational Policy*, 9: 129–151.

Lynn, R. (1988) *Educational Achievement in Japan: Lessons for the West*. Armonk, NY: M.E. Sharpe.

McCormick, K. (1988) 'Vocationalism and the Japanese Education System', *Comparative Education*, 24(1): 37–51.

McCormick, K. (1989) 'Towards a Lifelong Learning Society: The Reform of Continuing Vocational education and Training in Japan', *Comparative Education*, 25(2): 133–149.

McKinney, K. (1987) *A Look at Japanese Education Today*. US Department of Education: Office of Educational Research and Improvement.

McNeely, C. L. (1995) 'Prescribing National Education Policies: The Role of International Organizations', *Comparative Education Review*, 39(4): 483–507.

Meyer, J. (1977) 'The Effects of Education as an Institution', *American Journal of Sociology*, 83 (1): 55–77.

Meyer, J., Ramirez, F. and Soysal, Y. (1992) 'World Expansion of Mass Education, 1870–1970', *Sociology of Education*, 65 (2): 128–149.

Meyer, J. W., Boli, J., Thomas, G. M. and Ramirez, F. O. (1997) 'World Society and the Nation-State', *American Journal of Sociology*, 103 (1): 144–181.

Nakanishi, T. (ed.) (2005) *Sachyā kaikaku ni manabu kyōiku seijōka he no michi: eikokū kyōiku chosa hōkoko.* [Learning from the Thatcher Reforms, The Road to Educational Normalization: The Report of the English Education Research Group] Tokyo: PHP Kenkyūjō [PHP Research Center].

National Commission on Excellence in Education (NCEE) (1983) *A Nation at Risk: the imperative for educational reform, a report to the Nation and the Secretary of Education.* Washington, DC: US Government Printing Office.

New York Times (1987a) 'Study, Drawing Lessons for the US, Cites Rigor of Japanese Schooling' (E. Fiske), *New York Times*, available at: www.nytimes.com/1987/01/04/us/study-drawing-lessons-for-us-cites-rigor-of-japanese-schooling.html?scp=4&sq=Japanese+Education&st=nyt.

New York Times (1987b) 'Learning by Rote: A New Appraisal' (S. Salmans), *New York Times*, available at: www.nytimes.com/1987/04/12/education/learning-by-rote-a-new-appraisal.html?scp=31&sq=Japanese+Education&st=nyt.

New York Times (1988) Education: Lessons (E. Fiske), *New York Times*, available at: www.nytimes.com/1988/06/15/nyregion/education-lessons.html?scp=36&sq=Japanese+Education&st=nyt.

New York Times (2002, 22 November) 'China's Super Kids' (N. Kristof) *New York Times*, p. A-27, available at: http://select.nytimes.com/gst/abstract.html?res=F50E1FFE395D0C718ED DA80994DA404482 [1 May 2006].

New York Times (2008) 'The "Crisis" of US Education (W. Gardner), *New York Times*, available at www.nytimes.com/2008/01/14/opinion/14iht-edgardner.1.9196672.html?_r=1.

New York Times (2010, 7 December) 'Top Test Scores from Shanghai Stun Educators.', available at: www.nytimes.com/2010/12/07/education/07education.html [7 December 2010].

New York Times (2011, 16 January) 'China's Winning Schools' (N. Kristof) *New York Times*, p. WK10, available at: www.nytimes.com/2011/01/16/opinion/16kristof.html

OERI Japan Study Team (1987) *Japanese Education Today.* Washington, D.C.: US Department of Education, Office of Educational Research and Improvement.

Ostrom, E. (1986) 'A Method of Institutional Analysis', in F. X. Kaufman, G. Majone and V. Ostrom (eds) *Guidance, Control, and Evaluation in the Public Sector: The Bielefeld Interdisciplinary Project.* New York: Walter de Gruyter.

Ouchi, W. (1982) *Theory Z: How American Business Can Meet the Japanese Challenge.* New York: Avon.

Ozawa, I. (1994) *Blueprint for a New Japan: The Rethinking of a Nation.* New York: Kodansha.

Peak, L. (1993) *Learning to Go to School in Japan.* Berkeley: University of California Press.

Phillips, D. (2004) 'Toward a Theory of Policy Attraction in Education', in G. Steiner-Khamsi (ed.) *The Global Politics of Educational Borrowing and Lending* (pp. 54–67). New York: Teachers College Press.

Phillips, D. (2009) 'Aspects of Educational Transfer', in R. Cowen and A. Kazamias (eds) *International Handbook of Comparative Education*, Vol. 2 (pp. 1061–1077). New York: Springer.

Phillips, D. and Ochs, K. (eds) (2004) *Educational Policy Borrowing: Historical Perspectives.* Oxford: Symposium Books.

Post, D. (2009) 'Moderated Discussion: Two Million Minutes', *Comparative Education Review*, 53(1): 113–137.

Rappleye, J. (2006) 'Theorizing Educational Transfer: Toward a Conceptual Map of the Context of Cross-national Attraction', *Research in Comparative and International Education*, 1 (3): 223–240.

Rappleye, J. (2007) *Exploring Cross-national Attraction in Education: Some historical comparisons of American and Chinese attraction to Japanese education*. Oxford: Symposium Books.

Rappleye, J. (2011) *Theorizing Educational Transfer in an Era of Globalization: Theory – History – Comparison*. Frankfurt: Peter Lang.

Rappleye, J. and Kariya, T. (2011) 'Reimagining Self/Other: "Catch-up" Across Japan's Three Great Education Reforms', in D. Willis and J. Rappleye (eds) *Reimagining Japanese Educational Change: Borders, Transfer, Circulations, and the Comparative* (pp. 27–45). Oxford: Symposium.

Rose, C. (2006) 'The Battle for Hearts and Minds: Patriotic Education in Japan in the 1990s and Beyond', in N. Shimazu (ed.) *Nationalisms in Japan*. New York: Routledge.

Sabatier, P. and Jenkins-Smith, H. (1993) *Policy Change and Learning: An Advocacy Coalition Approach*. Boulder, CO: Westview Press.

Salhberg, P. (2006) 'Education Reform for Raising Economic Competitiveness', *Journal of Educational Change*, 7 (4): 259–278.

Schriewer, J. (1990) 'The Method of Comparison and the Need for Externalization: Methodological Criteria and Sociological Concepts', in J. Schriewer (ed.) in cooperation with B. Holmes, *Theories and Methods in Comparative Education* (pp. 25–83). Frankfurt/M: Peter Lang.

Schriewer, J. (2000) 'Comparative Education Methodology in Transition: Towards a Science of Complexity?', in J. Schriewer (ed.) *Discourse Formation in Comparative Education* (pp. 3–52). Frankfurt/M: Peter Lang.

Schriewer, J. (2003) 'Globalisation in Education: Process and Discourse', *Policy Futures in Education*, 1(2): 271–283.

Sobe, N. and Ortegon, N. (2009) 'Scopic Systems, Pipes, Models and Transfer in the Global Circulation of Educational Knowledge and Practices', *Yearbook for the National Society for the Study of Education*, 108(2): 49–66.

Spreen, C. A. (2004) 'The Vanishing Origins of Outcomes-Based Education', in D. Phillips and K. Ochs (eds) *Educational Policy Borrowing: historical perspectives* (pp. 221–235). Oxford: Symposium Books.

Steiner-Khamsi, G. (2000) 'Transferring Education, Displacing Reforms', in J. Schriewer (ed.) *Discourse Formation in Comparative Education* (pp. 110–132). Frankfurt: Peter Lang.

Steiner-Khamsi, G. (2004) *The Global Politics of Educational Borrowing and Lending*. New York: Teachers College Press.

Steiner-Khamsi, G., (2006) 'The Economics of Policy Borrowing and Lending: A Study of Late Adopters', *Oxford Review of Education*, 32 (5): 665–678.

Steiner-Khamsi, G. (2010) 'The Politics and Economics of Comparison', *Comparative Education Review*, 54(3): 323–342.

Stevenson, H. and Stigler, J. (1992) *The Learning Gap: Why Our Schools are Failing and What We Can Learn from Japanese and Chinese Education*. New York: Summit Books.

Takayama, K. (2007) 'A Nation at Risk Crosses the Pacific: Transnational Borrowing of the U.S. Crisis Discourse in the Debate on Education Reform in Japan', *Comparative Education Review*, 51(4): 423–446.

Takayama, K. (2008a) 'The Politics of International League Tables: PISA in Japan's Achievement Crisis Debate', *Comparative Education*, 44(4): 387–407.

Takayama, K. (2008b) 'Japan's Ministry of Education "becoming the Right": Neo-liberal Restructuring and the Ministry's Struggles for Political Legitimacy', *Globalisation, Societies, and Education*, 6(2): 131–146.

Takayama, K. (2008c) 'Beyond Orientalism in Comparative Education: Challenging the Binary Opposition between Japanese and American Education', *Asia Pacific Journal of Education*, 28(1): 19–34.

Takayama, K. (2009) 'The Politics of Externalization in Reflective Times: Reinventing Japanese Education Reform Discourses through "Finnish PISA Success"', *Comparative Education Review*, 54(1): 51–75.

Takayama, K. and Apple, M. (2008) 'The Cultural Politics of Borrowing: Japan, Britain, and the Narrative of Educational Crisis', *British Journal of Sociology of Education*, 29(3): 289–301.

Tsuchi, K. (ed.) (2001) *'Kyōiku kaikaku' ha kaikaku ka* [Is 'Education Reform' Truly Reform?]. Tokyo: PHP Kenkyūjō [PHP Research Center].

Tsuneyoshi, R. (2004) 'The New Japanese Educational Reforms and the Achievement "Crisis" Debate', *Educational Policy* 18(2): 364–394.

United States Department of Education (1987, 3 January) Press Release: Japanese Education Offers Lessons for American Schools. Washington: U.S. Department of Education.

Vogel, E. (1979) *Japan as Number One: Lessons for America.* Cambridge, MA: Harvard University Press.

Waldow, F. (2009) 'Undeclared Imports: "Silent Borrowing" in Educational Policy-making and Research in Sweden', *Comparative Education*, 45(4): 477–494.

White, M. (1987) *The Japanese Educational Challenge: A Commitment to Children.* New York: Free Press.

Willis, D. and Bartell, C. (1990) 'Japanese and American Principals: A Comparison of Excellence in Educational Leadership', *Comparative Education*, 26(1): 107–123.

Wiseman, A. and Baker, D. (2005) 'The Worldwide Explosion of Internationalized Educational Policy', in D. Baker and A. Wiseman (eds) *Global Trends in Educational Policy* (pp. 1–22). London: JAI Press.

Yagi, H. (ed.) (2002) *Kyōiku kokushō: gakkō ha wagako ni nani wo oshieteruka?* [The Education Black Papers: What are Schools Teaching Our Children?]. Tokyo: PHP Kenkyūjō [PHP Research Center].

8 Bringing a Political 'Bite' to Educational Transfer Studies

Cultural Politics of PISA and the OECD in Japanese Education Reform

Keita Takayama

Though the field of education policy has always been international, with national education policies in constant interaction with 'examples elsewhere' and with 'international consensus' (Schriewer 2000), it has become considerably more globalised in recent years both qualitatively and quantitatively (Beech 2006b). Today, for instance, intergovernmental organisations have a powerful influence over domestic politics of education reform both in the North and the South, whether or not the transnational impact is 'real' or 'imagined' (Steiner-Khamsi 2004). In particular, the Organisation for Economic Cooperation and Development (OECD) has emerged as 'one of the most powerful agents of transnational education governance' (Grek 2009: 24). In clear contrast to its declining influence in economic policy (Amiya-Nakata 2007; Woodward 2007), in the field of education policy the OECD enjoys a current global presence, contributing to the increasing 'convergence' in education policy around the world (Ball 2008; Bieber and Martens 2011; Grek 2009; Wiseman and Baker 2005).

The Programme for International Student Achievement (PISA) has become the most powerful instrument of the OECD's education agenda (Grek 2009; Kallo 2009; Rizvi and Lingard 2006). Since its inception in 2000, PISA has become a significant media event in many nations including Canada (Stack 2006), Israel (Feniger et al. 2009), Japan (Takayama 2008, 2010a), Finland (Grek 2009; Kallo 2009; Rautalin and Alasuutari 2007, 2009), Germany (Ertl 2006; Grek 2009), Switzerland (Bieber and Martens 2011), and the United Kingdom (Grek 2009). The OECD has created and sustained PISA's global presence through its very proactive public relations strategy designed to create maximum media impact (Kallo 2009). With its league tables publicising 'which countries are progressing in the right direction and which are falling further behind' with respect to student achievement (OECD 2003: 25), PISA steers participating nations towards a particular model of curricular and structural reform that the OECD endorses, though scholars vary in their assessment of this global policy convergence (Bieber and Martens 2011; Grek 2009; Kallo 2009; Wiseman and Baker 2005).

In light of this emerging scholarly interest in the role of the OECD and PISA in national education policies, this chapter assesses the impact of PISA studies on the politics of Japanese education reform. More specifically, it examines how various domestic political actors appropriated the last three rounds of PISA data (PISA 2000, 2003, 2006) for different political purposes. A particular focus will be placed on the domestic politics around the PISA 2003 data release (December 2004), which shocked the nation with the declining international rankings of Japanese students. The PISA 2003 release was the critical turning point in recent Japanese education policy. The 'crisis' generated in the immediate aftermath of the data release forced the Ministry of Education, Culture, Sports, Science and Technology (MEXT) to considerably alter its new reform plan implemented just a few years earlier. It also marked a major change in the role of PISA and the OECD in Japanese education discourse; these entities have become the most powerful source of policy legitimisation. Drawing on the theoretical insights of Cultural Studies, which have received little attention in the discussion of educational transfer, I examine how Japanese national newspapers, the Minister of Education, the MEXT and progressive scholars struggled over the articulation of PISA in the nation's recent education reform debate.

In undertaking this exploration, I aim to re-conceptualise the existing discussion of educational transfer in the field of comparative education. Comparative education researchers, in particular those informed by system theory (see the editors' introductory chapter), have focussed on understanding the mechanisms of transfer, driven by such questions as: 'Why did transfer occur? How was the transfer implemented? Who were the agents of transfer?' (Steiner-Khamsi 2000: 164; see also Beech 2006a, 2006b; Rappleye 2006, 2011; Schriewer 2000; Waldow 2009). Despite considerable conceptual gains made in this school of thought, these scholars tend to circumvent making normative judgments about transfers that they examine and their consequences on educational equality and democracy. Furthermore, despite the increasing political significance of transfer in the politics of education policy, the existing discussion hardly recognises the strategic role that researchers can play in challenging the regressive education reform promoted as part of global policy diffusion. Infusing the current discussion of educational transfer with theoretical insights drawn from Gramscian-informed Cultural Studies, I propose a way to bring a political edge to the comparative studies of educational transfer.

Conceptualising PISA

Antonio Gramsci's (1971) discussion of hegemony illuminates the fundamentally contested nature of policy texts and devices. Hegemony refers to the process through which dominant social groups achieve their political authority through incorporation of the fears, hopes and concerns of subordinated groups. In this process of ideological incorporation, dominant groups appropriate symbols and concepts traditionally associated with dominated groups and insert them into their dominant discourses. Hegemony is thus a process through which dominant groups pull together multiple – often contradictory – discourses and achieve 'collective will' under their leadership. Generated through 'official' policy-making processes, policy texts and devices constitute part of this process of ideological incorporation. This Gramscian perspective highlights the inherently contradictory nature of social policies and organisations – containing both what Michael Apple (2006) elaborates as 'good sense' and 'common sense'. Recognising such appropriation as an opportunity for strategic interventions,

Gramscian scholars urge researchers to disentangle the 'good' from the 'common' sense and advance the former for more progressive outcomes (Fiske 1986; Newman and Clarke 2009).

Indeed, the meanings of policies are never completely closed, inherently internalising possibilities of 'resistance to the hegemonic lines of imposition of the meaning' (Lendvai and Stubbs 2007: 177; see also Fiske 1986). Noemi Lendvai and Paul Stubbs (2007) conceptualise policies as 'translation', a process that involves 'an active readership by various policy actors and policy relevant publics, who are both interpreters as well as creators of "new" meanings' (p. 175). Policy texts and devices form a highly contested space where subordinated groups struggle to disarticulate symbols, images and concepts from the hegemonic discursive networks and rearticulate them back into a different set of networks. Drawing on this insight, I conceptualise PISA as an assemblage of highly contradictory, ambiguous meanings, symbols and texts. It is a contested discursive space where dominant groups struggle to fix their particular assemblage of images, texts and meanings, and where subordinated groups disentangle them and disarticulate and rearticulate their elements into oppositional political discourses (Fiske 1986; Hall 1996b; Newman and Clarke 2009).

The contestation over PISA's meanings is further intensified by the discursive 'leakiness' that its very design and methodology generate. Harry Torrance (2006), for instance, argues that because of the conceptual weakness of the data collection methodology and its large sample size, the data from international academic assessments such as PISA 'can be presented in any number of ways and [which] can be cherry-picked by media and policy makers alike to support whatever is the current agenda' (p. 853). Likewise, Marjaana Rautalin and Pertti Alasuutari (2007) maintain that PISA does not provide any analysis of the factors contributing to country-specific results, leaving the more specific analysis of these results to researchers at the national level. Providing its dataset for secondary analyses, PISA allows researchers in respective nations to focus on particular issues of their interest.

According to an OECD informant in Johanna Kallo's (2009) study, however, this is part of the OECD's media strategy; OECD publications including the PISA findings are designed to allow every journalist in every country to 'always find at least one indicator to write a bad news story and one indicator to write a good news story' (p. 144). It is this carefully crafted ambiguity that enables PISA to 'gain political leverage to mass media' (p. 145), attracting interests of divergent political orientations. As John Fiske (1986) maintains, for media entities such as television programmes or PISA to be popular, they must be 'polysemic', allowing divergent audiences to generate meanings that meet their specific needs.

Another source of PISA's discursive openness is the OECD's internal ideological contradiction. Though the OECD has become a powerful advocate for neoliberal free market and managerialist ideology in recent years (Grek 2009; Rizvi and Lingard 2006), it has historically maintained a social democratic orientation (equity, social cohesion and inclusion) that was strongly manifested in the organisation's policy agenda until the 1980s (Kallo 2009; Papadopoulos 1994). The residue of this tradition, though increasingly eclipsed by economic rationalism, is still identifiable in the organisation's policy orientations, making the OECD replete with 'an ideological cleavage between social-democratic and neo-liberal policy stances' (Rizvi and Lingard 2006:

250). In fact, PISA collects a wide range of data about participating nations' schooling and students including the students' background information (the PISA index of economic, social and cultural status). Using this data, PISA reports have consistently identified socio-economic difference as the strongest single factor associated with student performance (OECD 2001, 2004). In recent years, gender- and ethnicity-based disparities in educational outcome have been added to the PISA dataset, providing valuable data that can be used for progressive educational agendas (OECD 2006, 2009).

It is certainly possible to dismiss the OECD's concern about these equity issues as a rearticulation of social justice and equality into the human capitalist discourse of economic rationalism and social efficiency. As Fazal Rizvi and Bob Lingard (2006: 253–254) argue, these equity issues are no longer framed in the social democratic ideals of redistributive and recognitive justice but are reframed in the human capitalist language of 'social cohesion' deemed fundamental to nations' economic productivity and global competitiveness. To these scholars, therefore, PISA's inclusion of equity issues is part of the OECD's strategy of incorporation to maintain the global hegemony of its human capital driven conception of education. It is a strategy to justify the OECD's global policy discourse that marginalises educational goals not suited for quantification and measurement (e.g. democratic participation and artistic talents) and disseminates a particular form of control mechanism (new public management) that governs individuals, schools and nations by 'numbers' (Grek 2009; Nóvoa and Yariv-Mashal 2003; Ozga and Lingard 2007; Rizvi and Lingard 2006).

These criticisms are important for identifying the larger discursive limits that PISA creates, demonstrating how 'policy ensembles, collections of related policies, exercise power through a production of "truth" and "knowledge"' (Ball 1993: 14, Ball 2008). PISA, along with other OECD indicators on education, provides a set of symbols, images and concepts that construct a particular 'truth' about what education ought to look like in a so-called 'knowledge economy'. The uncritical acceptance of the particular articulation of OECD policy terminologies ('competency', 'measurement', 'accountability', 'knowledge economy') could result in the further legitimation of policy ensembles that move education policy away from 'matters of government (habited by citizens, elections, representation, etc) and place it in the more diffused level of *governance* (habited by networks, peer review, and agreements, etc)' (Nóvoa and Yariv-Mashal 2003: 428). Hence, the discussion of PISA as a way of governing highlights the discursive terrain that the OECD establishes, within which a particular conception of the proper relationship between education, economy and state is normalised. Such a critical, macro perspective allows us to question the particular kind of education reform that the OECD naturalises, enabling us to see how PISA's policy terminologies are ordered and combined in particular ways to displace and exclude other assemblages (Ball 1993, 2008).

However, such critiques drawing partly on Foucauldian discussion of power and governmentality, unless combined with Gramsci's strategic insight discussed earlier, simply perpetuate a totalising reading of PISA and the OECD's impact, creating the problem of 'naïve pessimism' (Ball 1993: 15). Such a reading precludes any discussion of possible multiple meanings and usages that can be generated out of PISA, thereby failing to recognise political actors who struggle to disarticulate PISA's inclusion of equity issues from the dominant human capital/new management discourse and rearticulate it back into a different political discourse that reverses the kind of educational restructuring that the OECD propagates (Fiske 1986; Lendvai and Stubbs 2007; Newman and Clarke 2009). As Bob Lingard and Sotiria Grek (2007: 38) rightly recognise, albeit in passing, PISA provides data around which a counter-hegemonic politics for educational change can be mounted.

Stuart Hall's (1996a, 1996b) approach to the politics of language provides a useful starting point in conceptualising PISA's impact in a way that fully recognises the contradictory political meanings and usages generated on the ground. In this school of thought, a sign is 'multi-accentual', or 'polysemic', within which the 'disarticulation and rearticulation of different ideological accenting' takes place (Hall 1996b: 296; see also Fiske 1986). A sign assumes a particular political meaning only when it is articulated into a particular discourse – a network of words, symbols and meanings (Hall 1996a: 142). The highly ambiguous and contradictory nature of PISA renders it a sliding signifier whose content and substance are variously accentuated in a way that reflects the particular power relations of the specific location in a given time. PISA comes to assume political meanings and roles when it is rearticulated into competing domestic discourses of education reform, forming and affecting the different realities embodied by the various discourses. To put it differently, global policy actors such as PISA and the OECD gain their political agency only when domestic actors activate their agentive capacity using them in their own pre-established domestic political discourses (Rautalin and Alasuutari 2009: 541).

Politics of articulation over PISA in Japan

Though the OECD and PISA have become powerful external references in Japanese education reform discourse since the turn of the twenty-first century, they were hardly part of the political discourse in the 1990s. The critical turning point was when the PISA 2003 findings were published in December 2004. The data were released in the middle of an intense national debate on declining academic achievement, which was triggered by the MEXT's new reform, generally called *yutori* (relaxing, low pressure) reform. Announced in 1998 and implemented in 2002, this reform introduced a complete five-day school week[1] and constructivist curricular change (a new conception of scholastic ability, a redefinition of teachers as facilitators and an introduction of an interdisciplinary 'integrated study period'), in addition to reducing curricular content by 30 per cent. Featuring student-initiated, problem-solving and inquiry-based interdisciplinary learning, the reform resembled the OECD's 'global curricular model', though the MEXT did not make any explicit reference to the OECD at the time.

Soon after the policy announcement, however, the new policy came under intense attack from cultural conservatives and nationalists. This was when the material consequences of social and economic restructuring of the 1990s started appearing with the widening economic disparity in the population. Nationalistic social movements 'from below' gained political momentum, as conservative politicians and associated intellectuals effectively exploited people's anxiety by rearticulating the consequences of structural economic and social changes into individualising and moralising discourses of discipline, order and patriotism (Takayama 2010b). They argued that *yutori* reform's 'soft' approach had 'feminised' the nation; it would undermine Japan's international competitiveness and turn it into 'a nation at risk' (Takayama 2007).

It was in December 2004, in the midst of this debate, that the MEXT released the PISA 2003 findings. Compared with their performance in PISA 2000, the rankings (and the mean test scores) of Japanese 15-year-olds dropped from 1st (557) to 6th (534) in mathematical literacy; from 8th (522) to 14th (498) in reading literacy; remained 2nd in scientific literacy (550 and 548, respectively); and achieved 4th place (548) in the newly created category of problem-solving literacy. These ranking drops – albeit statistically insignificant apart from reading literacy (Takayama 2008) – were generally perceived as a confirmation of the widespread fear of declining academic standards. Education Minister Nariaki Nakayama then wasted no time in signalling a sharp break from the contentious *yutori* reform. The Minister announced his intention to slash hours for the newly introduced integrated study period, resume classes on Saturdays, trim summer vacations and other holidays and introduce national achievement testing – all changes fundamentally nullifying the 2002 *yutori* reform (Takayama 2008).

The irony of the whole incident was the fact that the *yutori* reform was aligned with the OECD's proposed curricular and educational reform (Knipprath 2010). Recognising its mission as preparing member nations for the emerging knowledge economy, the OECD proposed curricular reforms promoting new forms of knowledge: 'know-why, know-how, and know-who' kinds of knowledge rather than 'know-what' or 'factual knowledge/recall' (OECD 2000: 3). The *yutori* reform's constructivist curricular focus, the elimination of the norm-referential assessment criteria and the redefinition of teachers as facilitators all responded to the curricular shift that the OECD promoted in the 1990s. Hence, one of the most logical responses to the 'PISA 2003 shock' would have been to call for more rigorous implementation of the reform. Instead, Minister Nakayama and other conservative critics blamed the 'soft' curricular reform for the 'national disgrace' and proposed a set of reforms that focussed on academic basics, discipline and competition.

Though the *yutori* reform closely responded to the OECD's curricular proposal for a knowledge economy, the MEXT made no references to the OECD or to PISA in the lead up to the 2002 implementation. Ken Terawaki, the top MEXT bureaucrat at the time and the spokesperson of the *yutori* reform, never discussed the OECD or PISA in his promotion of the reform. Even when it was vigorously criticised by conservative critics and others, he continued to justify the reform in terms of the domestic concerns that it was to address: that intense academic competition and rote memorisation characteristic of Japanese schooling had failed to nurture students' creativity, problem-solving skills, and joy and motivation for learning (Terawaki 2001).[2]

This lack of acknowledgment of policy borrowing from the OECD is conspicuous in light of the close relationship formed throughout the 1990s between the MEXT and the OECD. Ministry officials and researchers at the MEXT-affiliated National Institute for Educational Policy Research (NIER) – the administrative body of PISA in Japan – were involved in the initial development and the subsequent implementation of PISA throughout the 1990s (see Murata 2000: 172–173). The NIER, whose senior researcher

(Ryo Watanabe) currently serves as the chair of the PISA governing board, has closely worked with the OECD beyond its administrative responsibility for PISA in Japan. Besides, the Ministry regularly dispatches its most competent officials to the OECD for a one- to two-year internship, while top ministry bureaucrats frequently visit its Paris headquarters.[3] Jeremy Rappleye's (2011) interview with MEXT bureaucrats confirms the existence of a close relationship between the MEXT and the OECD before the PISA 2003 shock.

What Florian Waldow (2009) calls 'silent borrowing' captures the politics of this unacknowledged educational transfer. Waldow reports that in the case of Swedish education, when the country's education policy closely followed the OECD recommendation, the government chose not to make explicit the international origin of its education policies because doing so did not serve the strategic purpose of policy legitimisation. In Sweden, he explains, explicit reference to the global origin of policies was politically unwise in the context of the Swedish belief in its educational supremacy and its self-image of engaging in highly rational policy making. However, this national self-sufficiency could no longer persist, he concludes, when international comparative assessments such as PISA made national differences highly visible.

Just as in Sweden, before the first release of the PISA 2000 findings in 2001, the OECD did not provide the MEXT with much political purchase in Japanese education reform discourse. By then, a consensus, or what Takehiko Kariya (2002) calls an 'illusion', was formed around the belief that Japanese children were suffering under educational policies requiring didactic teaching, rote memorisation, excessive academic competition and mindless entrance exam preparation. The MEXT policy documents throughout the 1980s and the 1990s had identified the cause of 'educational pathologies' such as bullying, school refusal and youth suicide and violence in these rather rigid characteristics of Japanese schooling (Takayama 2009). The OECD's scientific discourse that closely links education to nations' economic productivity and competitiveness would have been ill-suited in this particular policy context. Instead, the MEXT chose such 'humanising' policy keywords as *yutori* (relaxing, low pressure), *kosei* (individuality) and *ikiru chikara* (zest for living) in its promotion of the reform. It was a strategy to 'indigenize' (Steiner-Khamsi 2002) the global curricular discourse into the existing domestic discourses so that it would directly speak to the particular domestic construction of the seeming policy problem: the so-called 'pathological' state of Japanese children.

This silent policy borrowing suddenly ended once the PISA 2003 findings (released in 2004) were publicised (discussed more fully below) in the midst of the national debate over declining scholastic standards. In response to the mounting public outcry over the reform immediately after the data release, the MEXT bureaucrats and the NIER researchers started stressing their reform's close alignment to the PISA data to minimise the damage to its political legitimacy (Tōyama 2004). Hereafter, the Education Ministers and bureaucrats consistently referred to PISA, the OECD, and Finnish education – whose exceptional performance in the last three rounds of PISA had turned it into a global symbol of educational excellence – to legitimise their policies (Takayama 2008, 2010a). PISA and the OECD had become powerful political symbols that politicians and policy makers now utilised as an external source of policy legitimisation.

The Media⁴

Upon the release of the PISA 2003 findings, all the major national daily newspapers emphasised the ranking drops in mathematics and reading in particular. The conservative *Yomiuri* reported the findings in three separate articles, with particularly startling headlines: 'Japanese 15-Year-Olds Fell from World Best', 'Plunging to 14th in Reading and 6th in Maths' and 'Children's Academic Achievement in Yellow Signal: Consequence of *Yutori* Reform? Decline in Thinking Ability Due to Cell Phone Emailing?' The newspaper reported that the Ministry had, for the first time, acknowledged that 'Japan is no longer at the world's top level' and was planning to introduce an emergency reading improvement programme. The *Yomiuri* article also noted the increased percentage of students occupying the lowest achievement level in reading. As for the drop in mathematical literacy, the newspaper quoted the National Institute for Educational Research (NIER) as stating that there was no statistically significant difference between Japan and the top-performing nation (Hong Kong), but quickly countered this with a re-emphasis of the decline: 'Japan, which was by far the number one nation, is now among the group of top nations'. The article also reported that study hours outside formal classroom settings in Japan was 6.5 hours per week, well below the OECD mean of 8.9 hours per week.

The progressive newspaper *Asahi* also spread its reporting of the findings over several pages, headlined with 'Reading Literacy 8th→14th, Mathematical Literacy 1st→6th', '14th in Reading, Shocking Fall from the Academic Top' and 'Japan Weak in Maths and Essay-Type Questions'. Citing Minister Nakayama's comment that 'Japan is no longer world best', the newspaper presented the league tables of the top 15 nations in mathematical and reading literacy, the two subjects where Japan dropped in ranking and mean test score, but excluded the tables for scientific literacy and problem solving where no decline had occurred. With only the top 15 nations shown, Japan appeared to be near the bottom of the table for reading; nowhere was it mentioned that Japan had actually performed 14th out of the 40 participating nations. The newspaper also noted Japanese students' low interest in mathematics and their significant achievement decline in reading, especially among low-performing students.

Nikkei, the leading business newspaper, for its part, featured the study results less extensively than the other two papers, devoting only one relatively small article to the matter, with the headlines 'Japan's Academic Achievement in Drastic Decline', 'Reading 8th→14th, Maths 1st→6th' and 'Ministry's Concession: No Longer Top Level'. Though the article quoted the Ministry bureaucrats' statistically valid explanation that Japan was among the top-ranking nations in mathematical and scientific literacy and was the second-ranking nation in reading literacy, placing it under the sensational announcement of a 'drastic decline' made it seem a desperate attempt by the Ministry to cover up scholastic waning.

In summary, without providing statistical information necessary to read the PISA findings accurately, the media reported on the ranking drops in a highly reductive and sensationalist fashion, confirming the 'crisis' of Japanese education and further promulgating the pervasive sense of fear and crisis. This created fertile ground for political uses of the PISA findings by various actors thereafter.

Education Minister

Appointed by nationalist Prime Minister Shinzo Abe in September 2004, three months before the release of PISA 2003, Education Minister Nariaki Nakayama, also an outspoken nationalist, wasted no time using the PISA 2003 rankings to shift the MEXT's education policy. Immediately after the PISA release, Nakayama announced the introduction of a national standard assessment, claiming that the measure would generate a healthy competitive spirit among Japanese children and thus bring the nation back to the top in international academic competitions. Nakayama also called for curricular reform that stressed didactic teaching of facts (*tatakikomi*), a move that clearly contradicted the curricular reform proposed by PISA (Takayama 2008).

Nakayama, along with Prime Minister Abe, had another political motive for introducing the national assessment testing. As self-proclaimed 'true' conservative politicians, they had been campaigning against the Japan Teachers Union (JTU), which in their views had corrupted children with its anti-nationalistic ideology, child-centred teaching philosophy and excessive egalitarianism, a charge that had been consistently made by nationalist politicians throughout the postwar period (Abe and Yamatani 2009; Nakanishi 2005; Nakayama and Yagi 2008). Continuing with the postwar tradition of nationalist politics, these political figures saw national assessment testing as a key strategy to expose and eliminate the JTU's ideological influence in schools, a strategy that they claimed to have learned from British education reform under Prime Minister Margaret Thatcher's leadership (Takayama and Apple 2008). In a later retrospection, Nakayama commented that he had hoped that the national standard testing would expose the inverse relationship between JTU's political activities and students' test scores in different prefectures (Nakayama and Yagi 2008).

Odds were against the Minister, however, regarding the timing for his introduction of the national standard assessment. The testing was not only costly but also redundant. By the time of the PISA 2003 rankings, virtually all the prefectural governments had introduced a similar standard assessment across the nation in response to rising public concerns about declining academic standards (Takayama 2008). In addition, the introduction of a nation-wide standard assessment (with its initial budget application of 5.7 billion yen) was not well received by other powerful Ministries (Ministry of Finance, Ministry of International Trade and Industry, Ministry of Internal Affairs and Communications and the Prime Minister's Cabinet Office) that had aggressively pursued a reduction in the state deficit (see Nitta 2008). In fact, the MEXT was under mounting pressure to eliminate an annual 850 billion yen subsidy as part of the fiscal decentralisation measure proposed by Junichiro Koizumi's government (Takayama 2008). What the Minister wanted was, therefore, a 'catastrophic event' that would legitimise the costly and redundant introduction of the national assessment.

To legitimise his controversial redirection of the *yutori* reform and the introduction of the national standard assessment, Nakayama consciously used the media to orchestrate such a catastrophe out of the PISA 2003 release. In fact, all of the three national newspapers quoted Nakayama openly acknowledging that Japan had lost its top-level ranking. *Yomiuri* quoted Nakayama's sensationalistic comment: 'While Japan slows down, other neighbouring nations are catching up. We will be sorry for our children and grandchildren if we are left behind'. *Asahi* quoted him as stating 'We must clearly recognise the declining scholastic trend as fact. We must be alert and sincere [about this fact]'. And finally, *Nikkei* quoted him as saying, 'Our nation's academic standing is no longer among the world's top nations'. The shocking newspaper headlines at that time clearly echoed the language employed by the Minister, a mark of his success in spinning a particular media image of the PISA 2003 findings. The manufactured crisis helped create popular consent that close monitoring of national scholastic trends was necessary.

MEXT

Minister Nakayama's public confirmation of the scholastic 'crisis' considerably undermined the Ministry bureaucrats' effort to counter the rising pressure against the *yutori* reform. Initially, the Ministry bureaucrats and the NIER researchers disagreed with the Minister's confirmation of the so-called crisis by insisting on a statistically accurate reading of the PISA findings (Ōshima et al. 2005). In the public outrage generated by the sensationalist media report on PISA 2003 and Minister Nakayama's comments, however, the Ministry bureaucrats had no choice but to break away from the *yutori* reform to prevent the further erosion of its political legitimacy.[5] In 2005 the MEXT stressed the importance of teaching basics, reintroduced schooling on Saturdays and increased curricular content: the three measures that not only undercut its *yutori* reform but had little to do with the general curricular orientation that PISA promoted.

However, the MEXT was not simply a passive agent merely responding to the mounting external pressures. The PISA 'shock' provided a convenient justification for the Ministry to introduce the national assessment testing, which has been on its agenda since the early 2000s (Takayama 2008). From the late 1990s onwards, the aforementioned powerful Ministries had pressured the MEXT to pursue its structural reform along the logics of decentralisation, marketisation and deregulation (Nitta 2008). Amid this mounting political pressure, the Ministry came to see its adoption of new public management–the 'Plan, Do, Check, Action' cycle that the OECD promoted as the global best practice of state governance (Nitta 2008: 139) – as a strategy to counter more radical marketisation, deregulation and decentralisation measures (e.g., tuition vouchers and corporate-run schools) that business communities vigorously demanded. After the turn of the millennium, the MEXT made a clear shift from the input to the output management mode of governance, or 'governing through numbers' wherein the Ministry concentrated on goal setting, assessment and auditing. Capitalising on the ranking crisis manufactured and then sensationalised by the media and Minister Nakayama's different political agenda, the Ministry managed to introduce national standard testing in 2007. Hence, Minister Nakayama and the MEXT became strange bedfellows; while the Minister and Prime Minister Abe saw the national standard testing as an ideological means to control educational inputs (leftist teachers), the Ministry bureaucrats saw it as part of its institutional shift towards a different mode of educational governance.

Progressive Scholars

Japanese progressive educational scholars welcomed the arrival of the PISA findings. At the time of the PISA 2000 and 2003 releases, there were little reliable, large-scale empirical data about a correlation between academic achievement and students' social, cultural and economic background (Knipprath 2010). This was partly because of the contested history over national achievement testing. Perceiving it as the Ministry's strategy to control curricular content and generate excessive competition among students and schools, the Japan Teachers Union vigorously challenged the MEXT's introduction of national standard testing throughout the postwar era. A series of legal challenges in the 1960s prevented the Ministry and conservative Liberal Democratic Party politicians from implementing the testing thereafter, resulting in the absence of a large representative national dataset. In the 1990s when a series of structural economic and social changes widened the class divide, progressive scholars had to assemble small-scale studies to demonstrate the consequences of widening economic disparity on students' learning (Kariya 2001; Kariya et al. 2002). Hence the PISA 2000 and 2003 datasets provided much needed large representative samples to assess socioeconomic disparity in educational outcomes.

As expected, progressive scholars carved a different narrative out of PISA, using it to highlight the negative consequence of the ongoing educational restructuring on equality. They focussed on the PISA findings regarding the percentage of students at different achievement levels (Category 1 to 6) in each tested area, a finding largely ignored by the mainstream media's preoccupation with the nation's declining rankings (Fujita 2009: 239). They pointed out that the percentage of Japanese 15-year-olds in the lowest achievement category 1 in reading literacy (7.4 per cent) was still above the OECD mean (6.7 per cent). They also pointed out that the percentage of children in this category had increased from 2.6 per cent in PISA 2000 (Fujita 2005, 2009; Shimizu 2005).

These scholars then related these undesirable PISA findings to the new policy measures that they identified as the cause of the widening disparity in educational outcomes. For instance, Hidenori Fujita (2009) linked the findings to two key reform measures – the introduction of ability grouping and five-day schooling – that he viewed as driven by the logic of economic rationalism and eroding the egalitarian foundation of Japanese education. Furthermore, reviewing the PISA 2003 findings, Fujita (2005) argued that top-performing nations had particular characteristics in their education systems, school operations, pedagogies and classroom organisation that were all carefully designed to minimise socioeconomic disparity. Then he warned that the recent introduction of integrated middle schools and school choice in Japanese education would encourage earlier selection and competition and thus more inequalities in educational outcome. In the context of exacerbated inequalities caused by neoliberal social and economic changes, these progressive scholars effectively accentuated PISA's social inclusion agenda and then disarticulated it from the OECD dominant human capital discourse.

These progressive scholars further capitalised on the positive representation of Finnish education that the PISA findings produced. Repackaging the Finnish system as the global symbol of progressivism in education reform, they attempted to reinvent the postwar social democratic discourse of equality, justice and democracy, which had been seriously eroded by the ongoing educational restructuring in Japan (see Takayama 2010a). This rearticulation was successful as it echoed the fears and concerns of the people at a time of radical economic and social restructuring and the resultant widening economic disparity in the nation. Through their active use of popular media outlets, these scholars effectively shifted public attention away from the nation's declining international academic rankings and refocussed it onto socioeconomic issues in education. In 2009 the MEXT, for the first time in its history, commissioned a research on the impact of socioeconomic status on children's learning (Yomiuri News 2009).

Politicising Studies of Education Policy Transfer

The above discussion of Japanese progressive scholars' rearticulation efforts demonstrates the critical role that researchers can play in the cultural politics of PISA. Researchers can either highlight PISA findings that are not picked up by the mainstream media or conduct a secondary analysis to stress the implication of PISA in terms of educational equality. Stephan Gorard and Emma Smith's (2004) secondary analysis of the PISA 2000 data, for instance, illuminates the statistically significant correlation between the differentiated provision of schools and social class-based test score gaps in European nations. They used the findings to counter the British government's plan to replace the comprehensive system with a tiered ladder of socioeconomically diverse schools. In the Czech Republic, Petre Mateju and Jana Strakova (2005) conducted a secondary analysis of the same PISA dataset to examine the effect of the highly selective multi-year gymnasia (elite middle schools) that cater to students of higher socioeconomic status. They used the PISA dataset to disprove egalitarian myths about the elite schools and called for the shift towards non-selective comprehensive schooling.

In Japan, Heidi Knipprath's (2010) secondary analysis of the PISA 2000, 2003 and 2006 datasets confirmed a widening achievement gap based on students' socioeconomic background. Knipprath further used the datasets to highlight the highly inequitable tracking system of Japanese high schools, which segregates students in terms of their academic achievement level. Further, his study shows that student achievement levels are closely correlated with social, cultural and economic background. Hence, Knipprath's secondary analysis demonstrates how the existing high school system is likely to segregate students in terms of socioeconomic status and reproduce social class disparity in educational outcomes.[6] Many other researchers in different countries, including Australia (De Bortoli and Cresswell 2004; De Bortoli and Thomson 2009) and Israel (Feniger et al. 2009), have used PISA datasets to generate counter-narratives that accentuate the OECD's social inclusion agenda, disarticulating it from its dominant human capital discourse. Unfortunately, however, unlike the progressive Japanese scholars, these scholars hardly influenced the mainstream public discourse on education reform, partly because their studies were circulated mostly in academic journals.

While these studies are important, the exclusive focus on domestic repackaging warrants some caution as it can lead to the problem of naive optimism: failure to acknowledge the discursive limitations acting on and through these studies (Ball 1993). By actively appropriating PISA findings to advance a social justice agenda, these scholars tend to accept the language, concepts and various subjectivities that PISA's policy discourse makes available. This, in turn, reinforces the discursive boundary that PISA sets up within which education policy can be debated. In the case of Japan, where divergent political interests, including progressive ones, use PISA as an external source of legitimisation, PISA has achieved uncontested legitimacy. This has narrowed the scope of policy debate, enabling the OECD to have considerable influence over the nation's educational reform discourse, with the MEXT adopting the OECD-based policy ensembles (national testing, test-based accountability, new public management and decentralisation) with little political opposition. The progressive scholars' rearticulation of PISA findings, therefore, is a double-edged sword; on one hand, it appropriates the hegemonic tool to generate a counter-hegemonic discourse, while on the other hand it can reinforce PISA's own discursive regime.

Hence, this local reappropriation needs to be augmented by critical macro analyses of PISA and the OECD that expose the effects that they create and thus illuminate possibilities beyond the discursive limits (e.g. Grek 2009; Nóvoa and Yariv-Mashal 2003; Ozga and Lingard 2007; Rizvi and Lingard 2006). At the same time, such macro – and often totalising – analyses of PISA and its impact must recognise the important strategic role of researchers who accentuate the international testing in ways to counter the OECD's dominant discourse. Along with quantitative researchers who identify serious methodological problems in the PISA findings (Goldstein 2004; Prais 2003; Torrance 2006), these two types of researchers must work together to challenge the unquestioned legitimacy that PISA currently enjoys in many nations and to highlight its possible adversarial effects on equality and democracy in public schools. These three types of scholarly engagement with PISA – 1) quantitative researchers' methodological critiques, 2) local reappropriations of the datasets for critical educational ends and 3) sociological macro analyses of PISA and the OECD's material and discursive effects on national education policies – speak to the notion of multiple 'games of truth' (Gergen 1999: 35–36) that educational researchers belonging to different epistemological communities and research traditions must pursue. Drawing on different methodological and epistemological assumptions of their respective research communities, they must contest the truth that the OECD's knowledge production constructs and demonstrate how things can be otherwise, while at the same time acknowledging the limitations of and contradictions among their separate epistemological interventions.

Such a careful consideration of strategic intervention into the process of transfer is relatively absent in the existing research on this topic. As discussed earlier, researchers on educational transfer have long focussed on understanding the processes of transfer – 'how and why educational knowledge – often educational policies – crosses national boundaries and what happens to it in the process' (Waldow 2009: 478; see also Beech 2006a, 2006b; Rappleye 2006; Steiner-Khamsi 2000, 2002). While this is a valuable scholarly pursuit, the exclusive focus on 'understanding' tends to treat the topic of transfer merely as a scholarly pursuit, removing researchers from the ethical and moral commitment to the subject of their research and the people affected by the phenomenon that they investigate. As feminist standpoint theorists have long demonstrated (Harding 2004), such a 'neutral', 'detached' and 'disembodied' approach to knowledge production actually keeps knowledge partial and distorted and serves to perpetuate existing unequal power relations in which educational transfer takes place. These feminist scholars help us question 'the conventional view that politics can only obstruct and damage the production of scientific knowledge' (Harding 2004: 1). The same 'detached' approach has afflicted the ongoing debate in comparative education between researchers with a system theory perspective and those with a neo-institutionalist theory (see the editors' introductory chapter; see also Rappleye 2011). The binary framing of global isomorphism on one hand, and local recontextualisation on the other, tends to focus on 'whether or not globalization is real' (Jules and Morais de Sá e Silva 2008: 48), and in so doing leaves unaddressed the questions central to critical social inquiries: whose interests does a given educational transfer serve, who are disadvantaged as a result and how can the regressive educational condition generated by the transfer be reversed for morally justifiable outcomes?[7]

Important lessons can be drawn from Apple's (2010) discussion of roles for socially committed, critical educational scholarship. He first argues that critical education scholars are committed to 'bearing witness to negativity' – 'to illuminate the ways in which educational policy and practice are connected to the relations of exploitation and domination in the larger society' (p. 15). These scholars view policy analyses as 'a form of political advocacy' (Henry 1993: 104) and thus recognise it as part of their responsibilities to make moral judgments on the subject of their scholarly inquiries. Second, Apple (2010) maintains that critical analyses of education must 'point to contradictions and to spaces of possible actions' (p. 15). Those engaged in critical educational research not only engage in 'deconstructing the obvious' but also 'give rise to analyses which possess a particular strategic edge or to identify those elements which have the potential to change or resist the "social reality" as it is articulated through the current educational reforms' (Troyna 1994: 81–82).

These proposals help us reconceptualise the existing comparative education scholarship on transnational educational transfer. When the dominant discourse of human capitalism and corporate managerialism considerably influences – though never completely determines – the very nature of PISA, when dominant groups are more likely to shape the interpretation and the circulation of PISA in national education discourse, and when they use PISA to legitimise policy ensembles that can erode public education's fundamental principle of democracy and equality, comparative education researchers cannot afford to study policy transfer simply to understand its mechanisms better. Nor can they afford to focus on the governments' responses to PISA, while ignoring the various efforts at rearticulation/translation that progressive organisations and scholars pursue on the ground. More effort is needed to articulate our desire for understanding with a scholarly commitment to witnessing the negativity generated by transnational movements of educational ideas and policies and, more importantly, to identifying the contradictory spaces for counter-hegemonic possibilities that are also created by the same global forces. At the same time, we must 'act as secretaries' (Apple 2010: 16) to the counter-hegemonic appropriation of the PISA datasets pursued by educational researchers and progressive advocacy groups, and provide resources and expertise to advance their political work. Furthermore, comparative education researchers must promote more collaboration and dialogue among the aforementioned different types of researchers who critically engage with PISA and the OECD and generate a more coherent critique of the global 'truth' that they naturalise. Just as Japanese progressive scholars have demonstrated, we must also circulate our critical insights into transnational education policy transfer outside conventional academic publication venues to intervene more effectively in the cultural politics that determine PISA's possible impact in different national contexts.

Acknowledgment

I would like to thank Brian Lagotte for his constructive criticism and editing of the earlier draft and Jeremy Rappleye for his comments.

Notes

1 The implementation of five-day schooling was incremental. It was partially introduced in 1992 when schooling was reduced from six days per week to five days once a month. Then, in 1995, it was reduced to five-day schooling every other week.
2 This view has been disproved by many studies. See Kariya (2001) for instance.
3 Japan is the second largest contributor to the OECD, following the US, with its contribution sharing approximately 23 per cent of the organisation's budget (Amiya-Nakata 2007).
4 This section is based on my earlier publication (Takayama 2008). Because it duplicates some of the material in that publication, I have omitted all the referencing to newspaper articles here. As three of Japan's most circulated newspapers, *Asahi, Nikkei* and *Yomiuri* were likely to have shaped public understanding of the PISA findings.
5 After the PISA 2003 'crisis', the MEXT discontinued the use of the term *yutori* in its policy documents. Instead, the Ministry featured *ikiru chikara* (zest for living), another keyword first introduced in the 1996 Central Council of Education report. Conspicuously, the term echoes PISA's definition of 'competencies' as 'ability to practically apply their skills in everyday life situations' (Grek 2009: 27). This keyword is now explicitly articulated with PISA's notion of competencies (see MEXT 2008).
6 While this has been well known by researchers both in and outside Japan (see Kariya 1995, Rholen 1983), reframing the same issue in the global language of PISA is of political importance, given the powerful symbolic authority that PISA currently enjoys in Japan.
7 Though drawing heavily on the existing conceptual work on educational transfer, Tavis Jules and Michelle Morais de Sá e Silva's (2008) discussion of South–South educational transfer acknowledges, albeit in passing, some of these questions. When critiquing the depoliticising effects of framing South–South cooperation as a form of transfer, they maintain that using transfer and cooperation interchangeably makes South–South cooperation 'a technical concept, a development technique, and loses political character that dependency theorists had attributed to it' (p. 57). By and large, however, the existing discussion on South–South cooperation informed by the transfer literature focuses heavily on understanding its mechanism within the existing conceptual paradigm (see Jules and Morais de Sá e Silva 2008; Rappleye 2008). This marks a clear contrast to the discussion of South–South cooperation that draws on critical social theories. For instance, Anne Hickling-Hudson's (2004) study of Cuban educators in Jamaica and Namibia explicitly defines the South–South transfer as a counter-hegemonic political project against the wealthy 'North'-driven development aid work. Her focus is not only on understanding the mechanism of cooperation but more importantly on advocating for South–South cooperation that promotes decolonising projects in formally colonised nations.

References

Abe, S. and Yamatani, Y. (2009) 'Hoshu wa konoshiren ni taerareruka' [Can conservatives withstand this hardship?]. *Seiron* (February): 50–59.

Amiya-Nakata, R. (2007) 'Global governance, Japan and the Organization for Economic Cooperation and Development', in G. D. Hook and H. Dobson (eds) *Global governance and Japan.* New York: Routledge.

Apple, M. W. (2006) *Educating the "right" way,* 2nd edn. New York: RoutledgeFalmer.

Apple, M. W. (2010) 'Global crises, social justice, and education', in M. W. Apple (ed.) *Global crises, social justice, and education.* New York: Routledge.

Ball, S. J. (1993) 'What is policy? Texts, trajectories and toolboxes'. *Discourse,* 13(2): 10–17.

Ball, S. J. (2008) *The education debate.* Bristol: The Policy Press.

Beech, J. (2006a) 'The theme of educational transfer in comparative education: a view over time'. *Research in Comparative and International Education,* 1 (1): 2–13.

Beech, J. (2006b) 'The institutionalization of education in Latin America', in D. P. Baker and A. Wiseman (eds) *The impact of comparative education research on institutional theory.* Burlington: Emerald Group Publishing.

Bieber, T. and Martens, K. (2011) 'The OECD PISA study as a soft power in education? Lessons from Switzerland and the US'. *European Journal of Education,* 46(1): 101–116.

De Bortoli, L. and Cresswell, J. (2004) *Australia's indigenous students in PISA 2000: Results from an international study.* ACER Research Monograph, No. 59. Camberwell, Victoria: Australian Council for Educational Research.

De Bortoli, L. and Thomson, S. (2009) *The achievement of Australia's indigenous students in PISA 2000–2006.* Camberwell, Victoria: Australian Council for Educational Research.

Ertl, H. (2006) 'Educational standards and the changing discourse on education: the reception and consequences of the PISA study in Germany'. *Oxford Review of Education,* 32(5): 619–634.

Feniger, Y., Livneh, I. and Yogev, A. (2009) *Globalization and the politics of international surveys of educational achievement: The case of Israel.* Unpublished manuscript, Tel Aviv University.

Fiske, J. (1986) 'Television: Polysemy and popularity'. *Critical Studies in Mass Communication,* 3(4): 391–408.

Fujita, H. (2005) *Gimukyōiku o toinaosu [Rethinking compulsory education].* Tokyo: Chikuma shobō.

Fujita, H. (2009) 'Yūgai muekina zenkoku gakuryoku tesuto' [Harmful without a merit, national standard testing]. *Sekai* (January): 232–240.

Gergen, K. J. (1999) *An invitation to social construction.* London: SAGE Publications.

Goldstein, H. (2004) 'International comparisons of student attainment: some issues arising from the PISA study'. *Assessment in Education,* 11(3): 319–330.

Gorard, S. and Smith, E. (2004) 'An international comparison of equity in education systems'. *Comparative Education,* 40(1): 15–28.

Gramsci, A. (1971) *Selections from the prison notebooks.* New York: International Publishers.

Grek, S. (2009) 'Governing by numbers: the PISA 'effect' in Europe'. *Comparative Education,* 24(1): 23–37.

Hall, S. (1996a) 'On postmodernism and articulation', in D. Morley and K. Chen (eds) *Stuart Hall: Critical dialogues in Cultural Studies.* London: Routledge.

Hall, S. (1996b) 'For Allon White: Metaphors of transformation', in D. Morley and K. Chen (eds) *Stuart Hall: Critical dialogues in cultural studies.* London: Routledge.

Harding, S. (2004) 'Introduction: Standpoint theory as a site of political, philosophic, and scientific debate', in S. Harding (ed.) *The feminist standpoint theory reader.* New York: Routledge.

Henry, M. (1993) 'What is policy? A response to Stephen Ball'. *Discourse,* 14(1): 102–105.

Hickling-Hudson, A. (2004) 'South–South collaboration: Cuban teachers in Jamaica and Namibia'. *Comparative Education,* 40(2): 289–311.

Jules, T. D. and Morais de Sá e Silva, M. (2008) 'How different disciplines have approached South–South cooperation and transfer'. *Society for International Education Journal,* 5(1): 45–64.

Kallo, J. (2009) *OECD education policy.* Jyvaskyla: Finnish Educational Research Association.

Kariya, T. (1995) *Taishū kyōiku shakai no yukue [The future of mass education society].* Tokyo: Chōkō shinsho.

Kariya, T. (2001) *Kaisōka nihon to kyōiku kiki [Stratification of Japan and crisis in education].* Tokyo: Yūshindō.

Kariya, T. (2002) *Kyōiku kaikaku no genso [Illusion of education reform].* Tokyo: Chikuma shobo.

Kariya, T., Shimizu, K., Shimizu, M. and Morota, Y. (2002) '"*Gakuryoku teika" no jittai' [The reality of achievement].* Tokyo: Iwanami Shoten.

Knipprath, H. (2010) 'What PISA tells us about the quality and inequality of Japanese education in mathematics and science'. *International Journal of Science and Mathematics Education,* 8: 389–408.

Lendvai, N. and Stubbs, P. (2007) 'Policies as translation: situating transnational social policies', in S. Hodgson and Z. Irving (eds) *Policy reconsidered.* Bristol: The Policy Press.

Lingard, B. and Grek, S. (2007) *The OECD, indicators and PISA: An exploration of events and theoretical perspectives.* Swindon: Economic and Social Research Council. Online. Available HTTP: www.ces.ed.ac.uk/PDF%20Files/FabQ_WP2.pdf (accessed 10 December 2010).

Mateju, P. and Strakova, J. (2005) 'The role of the family and the school in the reproduction of educational inequalities in the post-communist Czech Republic'. *British Journal of Sociology of Education,* 26(1): 17–40.

MEXT. (2008) *'Ikiru chikara' [Zest for living],* Tokyo: Ministry of Education. Online. Available HTTP: www.mext.go.jp/a_menu/shotou/new-cs/pamphlet/20080328/01-16.pdf (accessed 10 September 2010).

Murata, R. (2000) *OECD.* Tokyo: Chuōkōron shinsha.

Nakanishi, T. ed. (2005) *Sacchā kaikaku ni manabu [Lessons from Thatcher's reform].* Tokyo: PHP Shuppan.

Nakayama, N. and Yagi, H. (2008) 'Dewa kikō, nikkyōso ni mondai wa nainoka' [Let us ask, isn't there any problem with Japan Teachers Union?]. *Seiron* (December): 218–229.

Newman, J. and Clarke, J. (2009) *Publics, politics and power.* London: SAGE.

Nitta, K. (2008) *The politics of structural education reform.* New York: Routledge.

Nóvoa, A. and Yariv-Mashal, T. (2003) 'Comparative research in education: A mode of governance or a historical journey?'. *Comparative Education,* 39(4), 423–438.

OECD (2000) *Schooling for tomorrow: OECD scenarios.* Paris: OECD.

OECD (2001) *Knowledge and skills for life: First results from PISA 2000.* Paris: OECD.

OECD (2003) *Annual report 2003.* Paris: OECD.

OECD (2004) *Learning for tomorrow's world: First result from PISA 2003.* Paris: OECD.

OECD (2006) *Where immigrant students succeed: A comparative review of performance and engagement in PISA 2003.* Paris: OECD.

OECD (2009) *Equally prepared for life? How 15-year-old boys and girls perform in school.* Paris: OECD.

Ōshima, D., Nogami Y. and Yumioka, M. (2005) 'Seiji shudō no "datsu yutori"' [Politics driven 'shift away from yutori']. *Asahi News* (20 February): 2.

Ozga, J. and Lingard, B. (2007) 'Globalisation, education policy and politics', in B. Lingard and J. Ozga (eds) *The RoutledgeFalmer reader in education policy and politics.* London: RoutledgeFalmer.

Papadopoulos, G. S. (1994) *Education 1960–1990: The OECD perspective.* Paris: OECD.

Prais, S. J. (2003) 'Cautions on OECD's recent educational survey (PISA)'. *Oxford Review of Education,* 29(2): 139–163.

Rappleye, J. (2006) 'Theorizing educational transfer'. *Research in Comparative and International Education,* 1(3): 223–240.

Rappleye, J. (2008) 'Reflections on some challenges facing resurgent interest in South–South transfer in education'. *Society for International Education Journal,* 5(1): 65–78.

Rappleye, J. (2011) *Educational policy transfer in an era of globalization: History, spatiality, and comparison.* Frankfurt: Peter Lang.

Rautalin, M. and Alasuutari, P. (2007) 'The curse of success: the impact of the OECD's Programme for International Student Assessment on the discourses of the teaching profession in Finland'. *European Educational Research Journal,* 6(4): 348–363.

Rautalin, M. and Alasuutari, P. (2009) 'The uses of the national PISA results by Finnish officials in central government'. *Journal of Education Policy,* 24(5): 539–556.

Rizvi, F. and Lingard, B. (2006) 'Globalisation and the changing nature of the OECD's educational work,' in H. Lauder et al. (eds) *Education, globalisation and social change.* Oxford: Oxford University Press.

Rohlen, T. P. (1983) *Japan's high schools.* Berkeley: University of California Press.

Schriewer, J. (2000) 'World system and interrelationship network', in T. Popkewitz (ed.) *Educational knowledge.* Buffalo, NY: State University of New York Press.

Shimizu, K. (2005) *Gakuryoku wo sodateru [Fostering academic ability].* Tokyo: Iwanami shoten.

Stack, M. (2006) 'Testing, testing, read all about it: Canadian press coverage of the PISA results'. *Canadian Journal of Education,* 29(1): 49–69.

Steiner-Khamsi, G. (2000) 'Transferring education, displacing reforms', in J. Schriewer (ed.) *Discourse formation in comparative education.* New York: Peter Lang.

Steiner-Khamsi, G. (2002) 'Reterritorializing educational import', in A. Nóvoa and M. Lawn (eds) *Fabricating Europe.* Boston: Kluwer Academic.

Steiner-Khamsi, G. (2004) 'Globalization in education: Real or imagined?', in G. Steiner-Khamsi (ed.) *The global politics of educational borrowing and lending.* New York: Teachers College Press.

Takayama, K. (2007) '*A Nation at Risk* crosses the Pacific: Transnational borrowing of the U.S. crisis discourse in the debate on education reform in Japan'. *Comparative Education Review,* 51(4): 423–446.

Takayama, K. (2008) 'The politics of international league tables: PISA in Japan's achievement crisis debate'. *Comparative Education,* 44(4): 387–407.

Takayama, K. (2009) 'Is Japanese education the "exception"?'. *Asia Pacific Journal of Education,* 29(2): 125–142.

Takayama, K. (2010a) 'Politics of externalization in reflexive times: Reinventing Japanese education reform discourses through "Finnish success"'. *Comparative Education Review,* 54(1): 51–75.

Takayama, K. (2010b) 'From the Rightist "coup" to the new beginning of progressive politics in Japanese education', in M. W. Apple (ed.) *Global crises, social justice, and education.* New York: Routledge.

Takayama, K. and Apple, M. W. (2008) 'The cultural politics of borrowing: Japan, Britain, and the narrative of educational crisis'. *British Journal of Sociology of Education,* 29(3): 289–301.

Terawaki, K. (2001) *21 seiki no gakkō: yutori kyōiku no honshitsu wa koreda [School for the 21st century: This is the essence of yutori education].* Tokyo: Shinchōsha.

Torrance, H. (2006) 'Globalizing empiricism: What, if anything, can be learned from international comparisons of educational achievement?', in H. Lauder et al. (eds) *Education, globalisation and social change.* Oxford: Oxford University Press.

Tōyama, A. (2004) *Kōkawaru gakkō kōkawaru daigaku* [This is how school will change. This is how university will change]. Tokyo: Kōdansha.

Troyna, B. (1994) 'Critical social research and education policy'. *British Journal of Educational Studies,* 22(1): 70–84.

Waldow, F. (2009) 'Undeclared imports: silent borrowing in educational policy-making and research in Sweden'. *Comparative Education,* 45(4): 477–494.

Wiseman, A. and Baker, D. (2005) 'The worldwide explosion of internationalized education policy', in D. Baker and A. Wiseman (ed.) *Global trends in educational policy.* Emerald Group Publishing.

Woodward, R. (2007) 'Global governance and the Organization for Economic Cooperation and Development', in G. D. Hook and H. Dobson (eds) *Global governance and Japan.* New York: Routledge.

Yomiuri News (2009) 'Zenkoku gakuryoku tesuto bunseki, oyano nenshū takai hodo kōgakuryoku' (Analysis of the national achievement test, correlation between parents' educational level and test score). Online. Available HTTP: http://www.yomiuri.co.jp/kyoiku/news/20090805-OYT8T00352.htm?from=nwlb (accessed 5 August 5 2009).

9 International Benchmarking with the Best

The Varied Role of the State in the Quest for Regional Education Hubs in Malaysia and Hong Kong

Ka Ho Mok

The rise of transnational higher education in the Asia-Pacific region has undeniably reflected the growing pace of globalisation and the subsequent pressures imposed by it. Malaysia and Hong Kong, among others, are two notable cases in which states have explicitly declared their intentions to make their country/territory a regional education hub. Hence, we have witnessed rapid development of transnational higher education in these Asian societies in recent years. Apparently the pressing need for transformation into a knowledge-based economy has exceeded the capacity of many states to promptly expand their public institutions to offer sufficient opportunities for higher education to their population. The proliferation of higher-education providers, coupled with the global trends of marketisation and privatisation of higher education, have subsequently created a much diversified ecology of higher education; this development has also fundamentally blurred the line between the public and private. 'Transnational education' is being applied here as a term to denote education 'in which the learners are located in a country different from the one where the awarding institution is based' (UNESCO/Council of Europe 2001). It could therefore include both collaborative and non-collaborative transnational arrangements, such as franchising, twinning (dual degree) and joint degree programmes in the former, and branch campuses in the latter. Obviously, cross-border education has become a major component of the transformations taking place within the higher-education private-sector environment, as well as a central element of how quality is recognised within higher education (East–West Centre 2010).

This chapter critically examines the policy origins of the quest for global schoolhouse projects that have taken place in Malaysia and Hong Kong. In the light of policy learning and transfer perspectives, this chapter compares and contrasts the policies, strategies and practices adopted by these Asian societies. More specifically, this chapter critically evaluates the recent developments of the regional education hub projects, with particular reference to changing university governance and regulatory regimes monitoring transnational education in Malaysia and Hong Kong. After comparing and contrasting the role of the state in the promotion of regional education hubs between Malaysia and Hong Kong, this study discovers that although the economic dimension of higher education expansion has been well recognised by these

Asian states, we should also note the importance of the political dimension in the quest for regional hub status. The present study has found that the varied role of the state, in Hong Kong as opposed to Malaysia, is actively promoting regional education hubs as a solution to unequal access within the nation. In addition, the varied role of the state is clearly demonstrated in the quality assurance of the growing prominence of transnational higher education, especially when Malaysia has adopted a more centralised approach to assure quality while Hong Kong has relied on the providers to uphold the quality of their programme delivery. Most importantly, the quest for regional education hubs in Malaysia and Hong Kong is not only for the purpose of economic benefit but also for asserting 'soft power' and 'political influence' in the region.

Varieties of Regulatory Regimes in Governing Transnational Education

The emergence of transnational higher education in Malaysia and Hong Kong has been commonly prompted by the irresistible trend of globalisation, and fuelled by the inclusion of higher education as an industry under the GATS (General Agreement on Trade in Services) framework (Knight 2002). However, due to the diverse politico-economic contexts of these societies, it is promoted and developed under different considerations by each state, hence a variety of governance and regulatory systems are put in place between the state and transnational higher education providers. The following examination of transnational education in Malaysia and Hong Kong will draw on the theoretical framework adopted from Mok (2008a) for analysing the changing governance and regulatory framework of transnational education in these Asian economies.

Table 9.1 shows the varieties of regulatory regimes from the perspectives of state regulation, on the one hand, and from market regulation, on the other. A broad categorisation of four types of states, namely the market-accelerationist state, the interventionist state, the market-facilitating state and the market-coordinating state, can then be discerned in accordance with the context of strong or weak state and civil regulations. In the Asia-Pacific region, developmental states, while prevalent throughout the 1970s and 1980s, have to undergo decentralisation and deregulation

Table 9.1 Varieties of regulatory regimes

	Market regulation (planned)	*Market regulation (unplanned)*
State regulation (centralised)	• Authoritarian liberalism • **Market-accelerationist state** • State-corporatist regulatory regime	• State socialism • **Interventionist state** • Command-and-control regulatory regime
State regulation (decentralised)	• Economic liberalism • **Market-facilitating state** • Civil society regulatory regime	• Market socialism • **Market-coordinating state** • (Coordinated) Market regulatory regime

Source: Developed and modified from Levi-Faur (1998) by the author.

today in making themselves more competitive and entrepreneurial to face the growing challenge of globalisation. Yet a closer scrutiny of the states' capacity, as shown in cases of their governance upon transnational higher education, may reveal certain new possibilities that could actually sustain the pivotal role of the state.

Overall, the fundamental impetus behind the prosperity of transnational higher education in these two cases may well be economic. Though domestic demands for higher education (as in the case of Malaysia where non-Malays are discriminated against in their accessibility to public universities) could initially be the catalyst for the state to introduce or allow the advancement of transnational higher education, it finally boils down to 'the competitive rush for international students and their money' (Chan and Ng 2008: 291). In this sense, regardless of the nuance between the grand strategies/initiatives of the so-called 'Global Schoolhouse' or 'Regional Hub of Education', higher education as an exportable product of services should then be kept under strict supervision of quality control to achieve its sustainability and competitiveness in such a booming yet fiercely competed market. Thus, as McBurnie and Ziguras (2001) point out, Southeast Asia is now something like a laboratory in the development and regulation of transnational education. The region combines high demand and keen competition among service providers, and the regulatory regimes in host countries range from relatively laissez-faire to strongly interventionist. Let us first examine the policy contexts for the growing prominence of transnational education and then discuss the most recent developments of transnational education in these Asian economies.

The Rise of Transnational Education: Policy Contexts and Recent Developments

Malaysia: From Liberalisation of Higher Education to the Ambitious Goal of 'Regional Hub of Education'

The first reform effort made by the Malaysian government upon its higher-education system was liberalisation of the sector rather than deregulation of its public universities. The reason for this difference lies primarily in its subtler ethnic political context. The UMNO/Malay-dominated government was very keen on applying education as a tool to drastically promote the socio-economic status of its indigenous (*bumiputera*) population after the infamous incident of racial riots on 13 May 1969. The Universities and University Colleges Act was introduced in 1971 to enable direct state intervention in the running of higher education institutions. By the late 1980s, the state in fact determined not only financing and curriculum development of universities, but their student enrolment and staff appointment as well (Morshidi 2009b). Public higher-education institutions catered primarily to *bumiputera* students via the arrangement of ethnic quota, whereas a large number of non-*bumiputera* (basically refers to Chinese and Indian) students, in the face of a scarcity of domestic education opportunities, were forced to study abroad without any financial support from the state (Lee 2000, 2005, 2006; Agadjanian and Liew 2005).

The domestic private higher-education sector could only be activated after the mid-1980s when the global recession increasingly restricted the capability of both the non-*bumiputera* families and the government to finance students studying abroad.[1] As a result, the government reluctantly began to allow the establishment of private colleges[2] to act as vehicles for twinning programmes with foreign universities (Tan 2002). Yet a more drastic effort in reforming higher education was taken after the mid-1990s with further liberalisation of the private sector, on the one hand, and incorporation of public universities, on the other. A series of legislation governing both public and private higher education was passed in 1996, namely the Education Act, Private Higher Educational Act, National Council on Higher Education Act, National Accreditation Board Act and, finally, the Universities and University Colleges (Amendment) Act.

These regulatory frameworks, set by the above-mentioned legislation, actually reveal that the Malaysian public and private higher-education sectors are, by and large, regulated by different systems. Private higher-education providers, compared with their public counterparts, could enjoy much greater autonomy based mainly on the fact that they do not receive any government funding. However, as Morshidi (2009b) points out, once they are upgraded to fully fledged university status, their governance systems are still closely monitored by the state. The Private Education Act of 1996 was amended in 2003 precisely with the intention to provide a legal framework for governing local private colleges upgrading to private universities as well as branch campuses set up by those foreign universities in Malaysia.

In regard to public universities, the reforms also began with the process of incorporation of these statutory bodies. Starting in January 1998, University of Malay, the oldest university in Malaysia, was incorporated along with eight other public universities in the country. According to the original policy objectives, these public universities should therefore become more self-financing, especially when they become allowed to borrow money, enter into business ventures, establish companies and consultancy firms, as well as acquire and hold investment shares. In short, these incorporated universities are now expected to raise funds through all sorts of channels (Lee 1999b).

Under the favourable framework set out by the Private Education Act and the Universities and University College Act amendments, public universities began to franchise their programmes to local private colleges. For example, from 1996 to 1999, University Putra Malaysia expanded its franchising programmes from 1 to 33 in local private colleges, whereas the number of franchising programmes for University Tekonologi Malaysia increased from 11 to 32 (Tan 2002). Judging from this aspect as well as from the development of other flexible teaching, learning and research arrangements, public universities in Malaysia are indeed becoming more entrepreneurial. However, to date it seems that the strategy of incorporation may still not be able to address the long-standing issues of over-bureaucratisation and the powerful state intervention upon the governance of these public universities. The establishment of the Ministry of Higher Education (MOHE) in 2004 is, to some, yet another sign of the failed promise made by the government to endow more operational autonomy to public universities (e.g. Abdul Razak 2008; Morshidi 2009b).

The country's ambition to become a regional education hub was first briefly noted in the grand development blueprint of *Wawasan 2020* (Vision 2020) initiated by the Mahathir administration in 1991.[3] According to Vision 2020, the government is keen to meet the policy target of having 40 per cent of youth aged 19–24 admitted into tertiary education. By 2020, it hopes that 60 per cent of high-school students will be admitted into public universities, with the rest going to private colleges and universities. The publication of the *National Higher Education Strategic Plan 2020* and the *National Higher Education Action Plan, 2007–2010* (both launched in August 2007) are the most recent responses to the changing socio-economic and socio-political circumstances in Malaysia. Given that the global higher-educational environment has significantly changed, the *National Higher Education Strategic Plan 2020* outlines seven major reform objectives: widening access and enhancing quality; improving the quality of teaching and learning; enhancing research and innovation; strengthening institutions of higher education; intensifying internationalisation; enculturation of lifelong learning; and finally, reinforcing the MOHE's delivery system.

In December 2008 the Malaysian government again revealed its seriousness in pursuing that ambitious goal by amending the Universities and University Colleges Act significantly in order to further improve governance and reduce bureaucracy.[4] Among others, it introduced more prominent professionals into the composition of public university boards of directors. Also, selection committees were set up by the MOHE for the appointment of every Vice Chancellor of the public universities, and the Vice Chancellors were given the authority to extend the services of an academic beyond retirement age, on a contractual basis. Nevertheless, as pointed out by a World Bank report, the current governance regime of Malaysian public higher education is still restrictive, particularly in respect to three critical decision-making capacities: Malaysian universities' ability to select their students on their own terms; the freedom to offer competitive remuneration packages to attract the most talented faculty internationally; and the authority to appoint a highly qualified and capable university leader (World Bank 2007).

In terms of transnational higher education in Malaysia, the *Report by the Committee to Study, Review and Make Recommendations Concerning the Development and Direction of Higher Education in Malaysia (Halatuju Report)* was published in July 2005 and contained 138 recommendations. Though it was a controversial report (Wan Abdul Manan 2008), a central point is about the need for local higher-education institutions to engage in self-promoting activities in the outside world. In addition, the report also recommends that the government invest more in international student and staff-exchange programmes, which would promote more collaboration between local and transnational education institutions. Based on inputs from the Cabinet, another report named the *Transformation of Higher Education Document* was issued in July 2007 to combine the relevant elements in the Ninth Malaysia Plan and recommendations from the *Halatuju Report.* Subsequently, the latest publication for this long-term plan, the *National Higher Education Strategic Plan,* was released in August 2007. According to the plan, the Malaysia government was trying to attract 100,000 students from overseas by 2010.

As mentioned earlier, distance learning arrangements, notably twinning programmes, have been prosperous in Malaysia ever since the mid-1980s. Yet the establishment of international branch campuses could only become possible after the construction of new legal framework in 1996.[5] Since then, various forms of transnational higher education have swiftly emerged in Malaysia, especially in the Klang Valley where Kuala Lumpur is a major constituent. The development of international branch campuses across the country is particularly impressive. In Malaysia, branch campuses of foreign universities can only be established by an invitation from the Ministry of Education or the Ministry of Higher Education (after 2004). The invited foreign universities, however, need to establish themselves as Malaysian companies, with majority Malaysian ownership, to operate their campuses. For instance, the University of Nottingham has run its programmes in its Malaysia campus since 2000, with a new campus recently set up at Semenyih, Negeri Sembilan for the 2005–2006 academic year. The other three international branch campuses in Malaysia, to date, are all Australian universities, namely the Monash University (Petaling Jaya campus, 1998), Curtin University (Miri campus, 1999) and Swinburne University of Technology (Kuching campus, 2000). According to the Observatory on Borderless Higher Education (2002), Monash University cooperates with the Sunway Group – a pioneer of twinning arrangements in the field of education as early as the late 1980s – and the latter provides funding for its Malaysia campus. Similarly, the local partner of Swinburne University of Technology in Malaysia is the Sarawak state government, which cooperates indirectly with the university through its *Yayasan Sarawak* (Sarawak Foundation) and Sarawak Higher Education Foundation.

Malaysia's increasing cooperation with foreign universities has coincided with the increased regulation regarding transnational provision (Lee 1999a; McBurnie and Ziguras 2001). After establishing partnerships with local corporations, foreign university campuses in Malaysia have done well. For instance, Monash University was the first to build its overseas branch campus in Malaysia. With its five faculties including Medicine and Health Sciences, Engineering, Information Technology, Business, and Arts and Sciences, Monash University – Malaysia now offers various undergraduate and graduate programmes to almost 4,000 students. Its purpose-built campus was opened in 2007, providing a high-tech home for the University. The Nottingham Malaysia campus has also successfully recruited more than 2,700 international students from more than 50 countries. According to the Malaysian Qualifications Agency, as of 21 April 2009, there are altogether four branch campuses (one set up by the UK university and three by Australia), running 84 programmes in the country (interview conducted in Malaysia, April 2009). Official statistics also indicate that the private sector has played an increasingly important role in enhancing access to higher education in Malaysia. In 2004, 32 per cent of students were enrolled in private higher-education institutions in Malaysia. Furthermore, in the same year 27,731 international students were studying in Malaysian private higher-education institutions. I was also informed during my recent visit to the Malaysian Qualifications Agency that 19 UK universities are now running 110 twinning programmes accredited in the list of the Malaysian Qualifications Register (MQR); while 18 Australian universities are offering 71 programmes of this kind in the country. Institutions from other countries like New Zealand, the United States, Egypt and Jordan are also offering twinning programmes in Malaysia (interview conducted in Malaysia, April 2009).

Finally, the government has also initiated a general regulatory framework for quality assurance of higher education. In fact, the private-education sector was initially the only focus of this regulatory framework. *Lembaga Akreditasi Negara* (National Accreditation Board) was established under the *Lembaga Akreditasi Negara* Act of 1996 as a statutory body to accredit certificate, diploma and degree programmes provided by private institutions of higher learning. Yet in April 2002 the Ministry of Education also set up its own Quality Assurance Division to coordinate and manage the quality assurance system in public institutions of higher learning. With the rise of transnational education programmes and the rapid expansion of private higher education, the government eventually decided to streamline these existing regulatory frameworks in 2003, and thereafter adopted the unified Malaysian Qualifications Framework (MQF) in 2004, governed by the Malaysian Qualifications Agency (MQA), established in 2007 to accredit qualifications awarded by all institutions of higher education. In short, the most recent achievements of transnational higher education (TNHE) in Malaysia are as follows:

- Two major projects that the Malaysian government has engaged in to establish itself as a regional hub of education, namely, the development of Educity in Iskandar Malaysia, just next to Singapore, and the Kuala Lumpur Education City (KLEC), incorporating a new commercial and residential project in the Klang Valley south of Kuala Lumpur.
- Newcastle University in the UK is the first foreign institution signed on to be part of Educity and the Dutch Maritime Institute also plans to offer programmes with foreign degrees, while international schools such as Britain's Marlborough College will be set up in Educity (Pekwan 2009).
- In 2007 there were 47,928 international students from around 150 countries studying in Malaysia. Among them, 14,324 were enrolled in public HEIs, and 33,604 in private HEIs.
- In 2007 Indonesians represented 17.6 per cent (8,454) of the population of international students in Malaysia. It was followed by China 13.5 per cent (6,468), Iran 7.7 per cent (3,678), Nigeria 6 per cent (2,884) and Bangladesh 5.2 per cent (2,506).
- However, while the student population from Indonesia continued to expand from 2003 to 2007 (+ 50.1 per cent), the student population from China shrank significantly (−37.5 per cent).
- The growth of the student population from the Middle East has also been hindered by the latest higher-education developments in that region.
- The number of private universities/university colleges in Malaysia (branch campuses of foreign HEIs inclusive) increased dramatically from zero in 1998 to 37 in 2007, with a vast majority of them offering TNHE programmes, particularly in business and Science & Technology.
- Obviously, the two regional development projects mentioned above reveal Malaysia's ambition to develop a multi-use, commercial, academic, residential complex.

Hong Kong: From the Quest for Quality Education to an Exporter of Higher Education Services

It is notable that Hong Kong society, like its neighbouring countries, succumbs to the same pressures of globalisation and the pressing demands for the knowledge economy, and has undergone a series of educational reforms simultaneously since the mid-1990s. However, at the outset, the focus of these reform endeavours in Hong Kong was on the promotion of quality education in the context of expansion of its higher education rather than on the aspiration of becoming an exporter of higher education services (Chan 2008). After being hit by the Asian financial crisis in 1997, the government of the newly established Hong Kong Special Administration Region (HKSAR) conducted a comprehensive education review, and the consequential *Review of Education System Reform Proposal* highlighted education as a key factor in the global competitiveness of Hong Kong in its future development (Education Commission 2000). Thus in 2001, in order to improve both the quality and quantity of higher education, a new policy target of doubling enrolment by 2010 was set by then Chief Executive Tung Chee Hwa, aiming to provide 60 per cent of the secondary school leavers the opportunity of receiving tertiary education within a decade (Tung 2000).

The importance of quality education was reiterated when the University Grants Committee (UGC), the executive arm of the government tasked with planning and implementing higher education policies in Hong Kong, stated clearly in its review report of 2002 that:

> The ambition to be Asia's world city[6] is a worthy one, but there is no doubt that realization of that vision is only possible if it is based upon the platform of a very strong education and higher education sector. There are very good reasons for that which have to do with what universities are and what makes them excellent.
>
> (UGC 2002: 1)

This specifically commissioned review report, entitled *Higher Education in Hong Kong* (or the *Higher Education Review 2002*), had raised some controversial recommendations for the reformation of Hong Kong's higher-education system. Among others, it recommended that the government strategically identify a small number of institutions and highlight them to be the focus of support from both the public and private sectors, so as to assure their capacity to compete with others at the highest level internationally. It also proposed that the pay scale of academic staff should be detached from that of the civil service, so that the authorities of universities could enjoy more freedom and flexibility in determining their own terms and conditions of service. Moreover, in terms of quality assurance, the report recommended strengthening the existing system, and also increasing the proportion of public funding based on results of the Research Assessment Exercises (RAE) (UGC 2002).

A further step in restructuring higher education in Hong Kong was taken after the UGC released two other review reports in 2004 (2004a, 2004b). The emphasis of these two reports was on the differentiation of roles among the existing universities, while at the same time, they also sought to develop a deeply collaborative system of higher education. Thus each institution, under this 'differentiated yet interlocking system'

(2004a: 7) would now have its own role and mission, on the one hand, and, on the other, be committed to an extensive collaboration with others for a greater variety of programme offerings. Another noteworthy point raised by these reports was about the vision that the Hong Kong higher education sector – here referring primarily to the 'publicly-funded' higher education sector – should aspire to be '*the* education hub of the region' (2004a: 5). Yet, according to UGC, the strong competitive edge of Hong Kong over its regional competitors in this regard was first and foremost 'its strong links with Mainland China' (ibid.), followed by other elements such as its geographical location, cosmopolitan outlook and its internationalised and vibrant higher-education sector, which are also frequently claimed by Singapore in its bid for the Global Schoolhouse aspiration.[7]

In light of the previous discussion, it seems that as far as transnational higher education is concerned, it was initially regarded by the government as some sort of supplementary means to meet the domestic demands under the tide of massification of higher education (Chan and Lo 2007), rather than as a tool for another more aggressive strategy. With limited resources due to its low-tax policy and particularly after the Asian financial crisis, the Hong Kong government has to rely more on non-state financial sources as well as service providers (including overseas academic institutions) to cater to the further development of higher education. Another feature worth mentioning is the fact that institutional collaborations between Hong Kong and Mainland China had seized much attention from policy makers throughout the first decade of post-handover Hong Kong, which has resulted in a population of non-local tertiary students, consisting mainly of Mainland Chinese.[8] It was not until 2007 that Donald Tsang, the Chief Executive of Hong Kong, explicitly stated his intention to expand the population of international students by 'increasing the admission quotas for non-local students to local tertiary institutions, relaxing employment restrictions on non-local students, as well as providing scholarships' (Tsang 2007: 40). And most recently (June 2009), based on recommendations made by the Task Force on Economic Challenges set up after the distressing impacts of the global financial crisis, the government has declared its resolution to develop six economic areas where Hong Kong still enjoys clear advantages, one of which is 'educational services'.[9]

Differing from Malaysia, transnational education in Hong Kong is mainly provided in the form of joint programmes, distance learning and twinning programmes. In the context of financial constraints, all of the local publicly funded higher education institutions have had to develop more self-financing programmes or offer joint programmes with their overseas partners in order to recover costs and generate income (Yang 2006; Chan 2008).[10] For instance, continuing education units as well as community colleges have been established in turn by these institutions, and the full-time self-financing local programmes that they offer have steadily increased from 41 in 2001/02 to 347 in 2008/09, with academic qualifications ranging from higher diploma (128), associate degree (161) to bachelor's degree (58).[11] As for the non-local higher education and professional courses, the expansion of their numbers is even more impressive. Recognising that Hong Kong can offer very good market conditions for transnational higher education, especially with its geographical proximity to Mainland China, overseas institutions have become increasingly proactive in setting up their academic programmes in Hong Kong during the last few years to attract mainland students (Yang 2006). However, on the other hand, top universities from Mainland China have also begun to offer programmes in Hong Kong and expanded their market share (currently occupying 5 per cent of those registered courses and 7 per cent of exempted courses), which is a phenomenon that unequivocally reflects the closer ties between both sides, particularly after they struck a memorandum on mutual recognition of academic degrees in higher education in 2004. For example, Tsinghua University and Peking University, in collaboration with the HKU SPACE[12] and Hong Kong Shue Yan University, offer academic programmes ranging from professional certificates to master's degrees in law, economy, literature and architecture, respectively. Likewise, universities in Hong Kong have also started to export their education programmes to the mainland.

Yet despite the expansion of non-local courses, the Hong Kong government has, so far, set out only a code of practice for these courses (HKCAAVQ 2007) that is considered moderately liberal.[13] Foreign universities can easily enter or quit Hong Kong's market. Currently, all courses conducted in Hong Kong leading to the award of non-local higher academic qualifications (i.e. associate degree, degree, postgraduate or other post-secondary qualifications) or professional qualifications must be properly registered or be exempted from registration. Any overseas institution is required to obtain accreditation or other formal permission from the Education Bureau (EDB)[14] prior to its operation. However, this category is diverse, ranging from compulsory registration to formal assessment of academic criteria. The EDB will normally seek the independent expert advice of the Hong Kong Council for Accreditation of Academic and Vocational Qualifications (HKCAAVQ)[15] as to whether a course can meet the criteria for registration or be exempted from registration. Yet again, the relevant requirements are considered straightforward and non-burdensome.

Overall, it is noted that the Hong Kong government tends not to directly curb and regulate the quality, content, level and cost of courses offered by foreign educational institutions. Instead, the government relies heavily on the market mechanism, in which its main role is reduced to simply providing sufficient information for various consumers to choose (Yang 2006). In other words, dictated by the above principle, its regulation mechanism is largely about quality assurance in order to protect the consumers. Yet more specifically, three regular mechanisms of quality assurance, which function as certain means of regulation of the UGC towards tertiary institutions, include the following (Chan 2008):

1   Research Assessment Exercises. Each institution has to submit a self-appraisal and a Research Strategy Statement to UGC for assessment. These research outputs are then assessed by different panels to determine whether the works have satisfied the threshold requirements or not.
2   Teaching and Learning Quality Process Reviews. Special review panels would visit each higher-education institution for a number of days to meet with its academic staff, students and senior administrators, so as to get a comprehensive review of its teaching and learning performances.
3   Management Reviews. Again, special review panels would visit the higher-education institutions and conduct qualitative interviews with their academic and administrative staff, as well as with their student representatives.

In short, the most recent achievements of TNHE in Hong Kong are as follows (Hackett 2007):

- While to date, not a single foreign university has been approached and invited by the Hong Kong government to set up any branch campus in the territory, by the end of August 2009, a total of 1,230 non-local courses had become available to both local and overseas students, with a breakdown of 405 registered courses and 825 exempted courses.
- Among them, 49 per cent and 66 per cent, respectively, are offered by institutions from the United Kingdom, whereas Australian institutions take up another 30 per cent and 20 per cent.[16]

Comparing its hub project with neighbouring countries, Hong Kong could be seen as a latecomer, and the city state has to struggle against strong competition to achieve its goal of asserting its brain power in the region.

Changing Governance and Regulatory Regimes: A Comparison

Malaysia: Market-Accelerationist State with an Undecided Regulatory Regime of Simultaneous Centralisation and Decentralisation

In terms of the governance and regulatory reforms upon transnational higher education, the integrative framework constructed by the Malaysian government for quality assurance is arguably more comprehensive than that of Hong Kong. As mentioned, the *Lembaga Akreditasi Negara* (LAN or National Accreditation Board) was established in 1996 with the limited function of accrediting only programmes offered by private institutions of higher learning. Under this regulatory structure, these institutions were obliged to apply for approval from the Minister of Education (instead of the Ministry itself) to conduct a programme based on the recommendation of LAN. Various guidelines on the criteria and standards of programmes at different levels or in different modes were to be met, and LAN was even authorised to conduct site audit visits to ascertain the compliance of these institutions to minimum standards or, where required, accreditation. Moreover, LAN had also built a database concerning these private institutions, which included the evaluation of their staff qualifications and facilities, as well as their student–teacher ratio.

The Malaysian Qualifications Framework (MQF), a unified quality assurance structure that covers both private and public higher-education institutions, was adopted in 2004, and the framework has become even more centrally controlled since the founding of the Malaysian Qualifications Agency (MQA, or *Agensi Kelayakan Malaysia*) on 1 November 2007. The MQA is a merger of LAN and the Quality Assurance Division of the Ministry of Higher Education, which is now responsible for the implementation of MQF. Nevertheless, the MQA is still a subordinate agency placed directly under the Ministry of Higher Education. In terms of accreditation, a new feature worth noting is that under the MQA Act of 2007, there is now a possibility of the conferment of 'self-accrediting status' to mature higher education institutions that already have well-established internal quality assurance mechanisms. However, to be so conferred,

Figure 9.1 MQA quality assurance process

Source: the section on 'quality assurance system', official website of the MQA, Ministry of Higher Education Malaysia: www.mqa.gov.my/ (accessed on 3 September 2009).

the institution concerned needs to undergo an institutional audit, and if successful, all qualifications it offers will then be automatically registered in the Malaysian Qualifications Register (MQR).[17] Thus a complete process of the MQA quality assurance process, in theory, could be shown as in Figure 9.1.

The MQA claims that these processes are further supported by continuous monitoring in order to consistently ensure the quality of programmes offered by institutions of higher education. Moreover, the Ministry in Malaysia has a list of accredited overseas universities or, in some cases, a list of accredited programmes of certain universities. In other words, not only is the state involved in the assessment of all the domestic public and private tertiary programmes in Malaysia (transnational programmes included), but overseas programmes as well. Yet this seemingly impeccable framework obviously entails a powerful, significant and centralised bureaucracy to act as its administrative support, and a powerful bureaucracy may adversely imply more hassles than benefits. Moreover, in terms of execution, the lacklustre track record of the concerned Ministry of Education/Higher Education during the past few decades may also worry some observers regarding the effectiveness of the framework.[18]

The strong tendency to state intervention can also be found in other aspects of the governance of transnational higher education in Malaysia. While a series of decentralised policies, including the drastic liberalisation of the private higher-education sector and corporatisation of public universities, has been pushed forward since the mid-1990s, the Malaysian government has also paradoxically strengthened its governance – though in some cases indirectly – on higher education, particularly on those public institutions. For instance, Abdul Razak (2008) remarked recently that the Malaysian higher-education system is still very much dominated by the state to the point that it has virtually become part of the government bureaucracy. The establishment of the Ministry of Higher Education in 2004 clearly reveals the state's intention to retain its centralised control in this respect.[19] The Ministry, however, 'introduced new and superfluous bureaucratic procedures onto a system which has already been noted for its inefficiency' (Abdul Razak 2008: 9).

This paradoxical or rather undecided regulatory regime of simultaneous centralisation and decentralisation of higher education could again be epitomised by the recent conferment of the privileged position of 'Apex University' to Universiti Sains Malaysia (USM) and the subsequent developments. The Malaysian government designated four public universities in 2006 as 'Research Universities' based on their satisfactory track records in research.[20] Among them, the USM was further selected in 2008 to participate in the government's Accelerated Program for Excellence (APEX), which made it the first and only APEX University in Malaysia. Upon selection this university is then supposed to be adequately endowed and empowered so as to achieve world-class status and be included as one of the top 100 in global university rankings by 2013, and a member of the top 50 by 2020. However, as Morshidi and Abdul Razak (2009) worryingly point out, the government has yet to show its political will in offering a bold and liberal new legal and regulatory framework that is 'radically' different from the current framework practising under the Universities and University Colleges Act since 1996 (pp. 4, 9). Admittedly, as far as the private and transnational higher-education providers are concerned, it is, to date, still evident that the state's regulatory approach is comparatively liberal. However, the insistence of the Malaysian government in keeping its role for the promotion of 'national interest' is equally evident, thus resulting in a reservation of its regulatory powers through the existing legal framework even towards the sector of private and transnational higher education (Morshidi 2009b). Being asked to comment on the swing between centralisation and decentralisation in higher education governance during a regional conference on comparative education and development in Taiwan held in September 2009, Morshidi succinctly argued that the Malaysian government adopts 'selective decentralization', which is clearly reflected by 'policy yoyo' in education policy and management (Morshidi 2009a: 19).

Hong Kong: Market-Facilitating State with Comparatively More Liberal Regulation

As noted, the Hong Kong government initially tended to see transnational higher education as simply a supplement to the local universities. It was therefore a sector allowed to generate its own revenue and operate under a free-market mechanism, with hardly any public resources committed to, or proactive regulation imposed on, its development. While the government has become increasingly committed to the progress of transnational higher education since 2007, particularly since the Task Force on Economic Challenges pinpointed 'educational services' as one of the key industries for Hong Kong's future development in 2009, a closer scrutiny reveals that it still refrains from any direct intervention or regulation on either the content or quality of courses offered by foreign educational institutions.

The reliance on a market mechanism implies a regulatory regime of transnational higher education that focuses primarily on providing sufficient market information for the consumers to choose, as well as on defending their interests through quality assurance of the 'products'. Nevertheless, ever since the restructuring of the Hong Kong Council for Academic Accreditation (HKCAA), and thereafter the establishment of a more inclusive accreditation authority (HKCAAVQ) on 1 October 2007, a similar quality assurance mechanism has been constructed as in Malaysia. Though in comparison, HKCAAVQ is still not as inclusive or versatile as its Malaysian counterpart MQA, a more rigorous – at least formally – Qualifications Framework (QF)[21] and an associated Qualifications Register (QR)[22] are now in place and administered by the HKCAAVQ. This brand-new structure is made possible through the provision of the Accreditation of Academic and Vocational Qualifications Ordinance (Chapter 592), which became fully operational only as of 5 May 2008. One of the functional differences between HKCAAVQ and MQA is that the former only assesses academic and vocational programmes conducted by non-self-accrediting institutions, whereas the exempted list of self-accrediting institutions is indeed a significant one that includes all eight UGC-funded institutions[23] and the Open University of Hong Kong.[24]

Under this newly constructed Qualifications Framework, a four-stage quality assurance process, as delineated by the HKCAAVQ, could be shown as in Figure 9.2. This new quality assurance framework, as rigorous as it may seem, is still a fairly moderate approach as far as the 'non-local higher and professional education courses' are concerned. These courses are regulated by the Non-local Higher and Professional Education (Regulation) Ordinance (Chapter 493) through a system of registration, yet the registration criteria set for non-local higher academic qualifications, for instance, are rather lenient, consisting of only two points:

1   The awarding institution should be a non-local institution recognised in the home country.
2   Effective measures should be in place to ensure that the standard of the course is maintained at a level comparable with a course conducted in the home country leading to the same qualification. And it should as such be recognised by that institution, the academic community in that country and the relevant accreditation authority in that country (if any).[25]

Moreover, non-local courses conducted in collaboration with all the eight UGC-funded institutions and several other local institutions[26] are exempt from registration. Likewise, in respect to the standing of these courses in local society, the Hong Kong government has taken an approach that 'it is a matter of discretion for individual employers to recognise any qualification to which this course may lead'.[27] Thus as

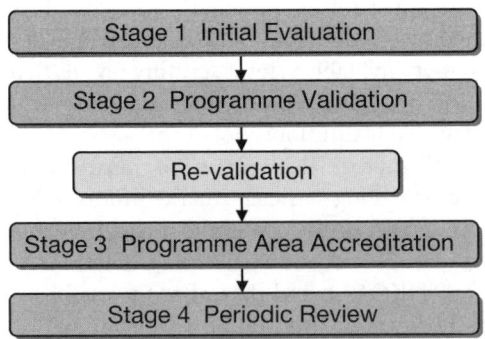

Figure 9.2 Four-stage quality assurance process, QF Hong Kong

Source: reconstructed from HKCAAVQ (2008: 2).

Note: Operators who have completed at least two cycles of programme re-validation in relevant programme area(s) can be considered for Programme Area Accreditation (PAA). With PAA status, the operators concerned can develop and offer new programmes within a defined scope of programme area and at specified QF level(s). Also, the qualification of these programmes can be included on the QR without being subject to external quality assurance by the HKCAAVQ within the PAA validity period.

McBurnie and Ziguras (2001) rightly observed, this government is adopting a far more liberal approach in dealing with transnational education. Unlike Malaysia, Hong Kong simply performs the role of 'market facilitator' instead of 'market generator' (p. 102).

The rationale behind this civil society regulatory regime is closely related to the tradition of the 'free market economy' that it has long committed to. Hence the objective of the Ordinance, as claimed by the official website of the Education Bureau, is 'to protect Hong Kong consumers by guarding against the marketing of substandard non-local higher and professional education courses conducted in Hong Kong'.[28] Further elaboration of this neoliberal approach came from Nigel French, then secretary-general of the Hong Kong University Grants Committee, when he suggested in 1999 that a key function of the regulatory regime was to provide the Hong Kong consumers with detailed information from providers regarding their offerings. Once this information was made publicly available, the government would leave individual consumers to decide, providing that their choices were informed ones (French 1999). Unlike Malaysia, even when the Government of the HKSAR has announced the policy intent to establish the city-state as a regional hub of education, the government has never come up with concrete plans or specific strategies but rather relies upon the market (private sector) to respond to the quest for the regional education centre project. Strongly believing in the market, the HKSAR government is rather reluctant to get involved in creating a 'governed education market' to compete with its regional competitors.

Between the State and the Market: Searching for New Governance in Asia

Analysing the recent developments of transnational higher education and the growing privateness in higher education in these two Asian societies, we can easily realise that they are experiencing fundamental changes in their governance and regulatory models, shifting to an interactionist focus (government with society), with a growing realisation of government–society interdependence, as Kooiman (1993) has suggested. With heightened expectations from their citizens for better and higher education, it is obvious that depending upon the provision of the states alone is no longer sufficient, particularly when most Asian states have experienced economic setback after the Asian financial crisis in 1997. Public universities in these societies thus began to diversify their funding sources from non-state actors or sectors since the 1990s, and the market, the community, as well as civil society at large have subsequently been revitalised by governments in Malaysia and Hong Kong to engage in higher-education financing and provision. Analysing these two cases in the light of the theoretical framework set out at the beginning of the chapter (see Table 9.1), the rise of transnational higher education, coupled with the growing importance of privateness in higher education, have suggested more or less a shift from the conventional centralised model of governance and regulation of these Asian states. Nevertheless, while they no longer monopolise the provision, financing and regulation of higher education, a further review and comparison among these two cases demonstrates that paradoxically, the states' capacity may not necessarily fade away, and there are varieties of regulatory regimes which indeed epitomise the dialectical conflicts between market efficiency and state capacity.

While government in Malaysia has played far more of a 'market generator' role, not only in setting out strategic directions but also proactively orchestrating developments in transnational higher education to meet their national agenda, the Hong Kong government is, conversely, far more committed to free-market economic principles, thus performing the role of 'market facilitator'. The Malaysian government stepped into a similar path of development to boost its transnational higher education, yet the lack of strategic and philosophical consistency in its planning has created the paradox of a regulatory regime of simultaneous centralisation and decentralisation (Mok 2010). Overall, the highly selective approach adopted by the government in directing developments of transnational higher education clearly shows that Malaysia is not altogether a market-embracing state. Rather, it is market-accelerationist state that operates to the logic of the market but intervenes in order to remove inefficiencies there. This new form of market-accelerationist state demonstrates that the developmental states in East Asia have not entirely given way to neoliberal globalisation. The Malaysian government now pursues 'regulation-for-competition' rather than 'regulation-of-competition', aiming to enhance the state's competitiveness through regulation in order to achieve its goals of economic nationalism (e.g. Malaysia's master plan of Vision 2020).

In comparison, the governance and regulatory approach taken by the Hong Kong government towards transnational higher education is the more liberal one; several significant changes, as mentioned earlier, can be identified over the last few years. These recent reforms all point to the direction of stronger state regulation, as well as a more proactive role played by the state. For instance, apart from the very new efforts of constructing a more inclusive Qualifications Framework, the government has also become more aggressive in providing financial incentives to lure international students with talent and expertise,[29] while at the same time relaxing immigration policies to facilitate their stay in Hong Kong. It has also planned to raise the international student rate in Hong Kong beyond the current 10 per cent threshold, and actively promotes business-related programmes, which are most popular among the Asian students.

It is thus intriguing for us to see that as far as the governance and regulatory regimes of transnational higher education are concerned, both the market-accelerationist state (Malaysia) and the market-facilitating state (Hong Kong), after roughly two decades of experiencing and adjusting to the rapid development of transnational higher education in their societies, have gradually approached a similar direction of reform: Malaysia may have to reduce its strong inclination towards state intervention in order to maintain the vitality and efficiency of the sector of transnational higher education; on the other hand, the Hong Kong government may be forced to wield its state capacity more proactively in industrialising the same sector, so as to make it more conducive to the territory's economy. After all, it is not easy either in theory or practice to strike a balance between a market economy and a strong regulatory state. More importantly, the variations regarding the regulatory regimes of these Asian transnational higher-education systems are closely related and the governments of Hong Kong and Malaysia have not decided which are the best and most effective governance/regulatory methods in monitoring the rapid growth of transnational education programmes. Such differences are clearly revealed by the ways these systems differ in terms of information provision/accreditation; programme delivery; and social issues such as equity/equality stemming from the rise of transnational education in these Asian societies.

Conclusion: Importance of Contextualisation for Policy Learning and Transfer

The above comparative study has clearly shown the exponential growth of knowledge, especially with the rise of transnational higher education, in Asia and the Pacific. The growing popularity of different forms of TNHE inevitably poses challenges to conventional universities/higher education institutions and undoubtedly drives the higher-education sector to continually transform to enhance the capacity to adapt to rapidly changing social and economic environments. We can therefore anticipate a continuous redefinition and reformulation of the 'university' into new and trans-formed roles, addressing research and relations to other social entities dedicated to research, technology development and innovation. The increasing blurring at the margins of the institutional forms of higher education, especially universities, and other organisations within society, such as business and financial firms, would become increasingly common features in higher education (Mok 2010). Against the backdrop of the growing prominence of TNHE, governments in Asia must develop appropriate policy frameworks to protect the interests of the students enrolling in these pro-grammes. We need to theorise more about why government has a role because: (a) student choices do not drive quality; (b) there is a risk of conspiracy over provider products; (c) issues of regional inequality and inequity exist; and (d) higher education is a time extensive product, and hence government needs to monitor financial security to protect students. In this regard, the question is not whether government has a role, but what should that intervention be to be effective.

This chapter has discussed the growing proliferation of providers in higher edu-cation, especially as transnational higher education has become increasingly popular in Malaysia and Hong Kong. The quest for becoming a regional hub of education has inevitably diversified educational programmes in these Asian societies and this development has also changed the relationship between the state and the market in educational provision and financing. In addressing the increasing complexity of the organisation and delivery of transnational education, comparative education researchers and analysts have to critically examine the changes taking place in gov-ernance and management of transnational higher education, with particular attention to analysing the regulatory regimes governing and assuring the academic quality of the newly emerging transitional education programmes. After close scrutiny of chang-ing governance and regulatory regimes of transnational higher education in Malaysia and Hong Kong, I have found a complexity of heterarchies and hybrid organisations where global education is rapidly expanding. Amid the proliferation of higher-education providers, coupled with the mobility of students and diversification of educational services, the conventional public–private distinction is rendered inappropriate. Further research should therefore be conducted to develop a better understanding/conceptualisation of changing governance and regulatory regimes of higher education in the context of questing for regional hubs of education in Asia (Mok 2011).

After witnessing the growing popularity of transnational higher education in general and the quest for regional education hubs in Asia in particular, Knight has highlighted the importance of developing a critical understanding of the notions of regional education hubs because the term may have different meanings to different countries/societies. According to Knight (2011), a regional education hub is:

> not an individual branch campus, or a large number of international students, or a science and technology park. It is more than that. Identifying the country as a hub involves a national effort to build a critical mass of local and foreign actors – including students, education institutions, training companies, knowledge industries, science and technology centres who through interaction and in some cases co-location, engage in education, training, knowledge production and innovation initiatives.
>
> (p. 2)

Analysing the above regional education hub projects orchestrated by Malaysia and Hong Kong, we should pay particular attention to the national plan and priority for a country/society to serve and be recognised as a centre of education expertise, excellence and economy. The present comparative study has clearly shown that the hub projects in Malaysia and Hong Kong are not purely for economic purposes but for asserting their political influence in the region. Contrasting the hub projects between Malaysia and Hong Kong, I have found that the states have performed varied roles in driving the policy objectives, while they have tried to differentiate their hubs by focusing on different targets. For Malaysia, their education hub has targeted students from the Middle East with similar cultural practices and religious backgrounds, whereas Hong Kong has attempted to expand its higher education market by capitalising on the pressing demands for internationalisation of higher education in Mainland China. In this regard, the strategies and practices adopted by Malaysia may not appropriately transfer to Hong Kong since there are marked differences between these two Asian societies in terms of history, culture, religion, politics and governance. More specifically, we should not underplay the importance of national agendas or priorities behind such regional education hub projects, i.e. special attention should be given to the political economy behind the quest for regional status initiatives.

The present chapter demonstrates the importance of proper contextualisation when making attempts for policy transfer or policy learning. Governments in Asia should not interpret the identification of 'good practices' from other parts of the globe as 'policy transfer' for the sake of improving public sector management or enhancing good governance by simply engaging in 'policy copying' without a proper contextual analysis before the policy or 'good practice' is adopted. When comparing the above case studies, it is clear that Malaysia and Hong Kong are different in terms of history, tradition, values in public administration, population size, etc. Strongly believing in the market, the public administration in Hong Kong has long adhered to the doctrine of 'big market, small government', whereby market ideas and practices have been adopted in running the public sector, including education. Nonetheless, the Malaysian government has selected a far more centralised model in running its public administration (especially in education management) although it is a democratic society. When conducting 'policy transfer' studies, we must be sensitive to the differences in the politics, economic system, governance philosophy and interactions between the state, market and civil society when public policy is conceived and implemented. A proper contextual analysis is deeply needed when governments try to identify good practices for the purpose of policy transfer to improve their governance.

Acknowledgement

The author wants to thank the Research Grant Council of the Government of the HKSAR for providing grant support to the project 'A Comparative Study of Transnational Higher Education Policy and Governance in Hong Kong, Shenzhen China and Singapore' (HKIEd7005-PPR-6). Thanks must be extended to those interviewees in Singapore and Malaysia for providing very useful insights to the author.

Notes

1 For the latter, this refers essentially to the Malay students who received official scholarships to study in Western countries, particularly in the UK and USA.

2 Prior to the mid-1980s, the Malaysian higher-education sector was almost exclusively a public affair (Morshidi 2009b). Moreover, the 1969 Essential (Higher Education Institution) Regulation had effectively barred private institutions from conferring degrees, not to mention the possibility of setting up branch campuses of foreign universities in Malaysia.

3 *Wawasan 2020*, as an ambitious national goal of development, was introduced by the then Prime Minister of Malaysia, Mahathir Mohamad, during the passage of the Sixth Malaysia Plan in 1991. The vision envisages the achievement of a self-sufficient, industrialised and well-developed Malaysia by the year 2020. In economic terms, it set the target of making the economy eightfold stronger by 2020 than it was in the early 1990s.

4 The amendment came into effect as of 1 February 2009.

5 Before 1996, private higher education institutions in Malaysia had no degree-awarding power. Even after the enactment of the Private Higher Education Act of 1996, the undergraduate degree programme could only be offered by private institutions with their degree-awarding foreign partners, with students being required to transfer between Malaysia and another country to complete their studies (Quality Assurance Agency for Higher Education 1999). It was only since 1998 that the Ministry of Education allowed private institutions to deliver degree programmes through the so-called '3+0' arrangement with their foreign partners.

6 The positioning of Hong Kong as Asia's world city was first put forward by then Chief Executive Tung Chee Hwa in his 1999 Policy Address. Subsequently, the Brand Hong Kong programme was launched in May 2001 to promote Hong Kong internationally as Asia's world city. Though some may scoff at the claim as somewhat exaggerated, *Time* magazine, in January 2008, did accredit the city of Hong Kong together with New York and London as the three exemplars for and explanations of globalisation ('A Tale of Three Cities', 17 January 2008).

7 Following the issue of the *Higher Education Review 2002*, the Closer Economic Partnership Arrangement (CEPA) between Hong Kong and Mainland China was signed on 29 June 2003. Hong Kong political leaders, thereafter, have worked towards the policy direction of broadening and deepening collaboration with Mainland China – particularly with the Pearl River Delta – across all sectors, including education.

8 For instance, there were 7,293 non-local students enrolled in the UGC-funded institutions in the academic year 2007/08, while 2,811 others attended various programmes at different higher-education institutions on a self-financed basis. For the former, only 542 of them (7 per cent) were students who came from countries other than Mainland China; while for the latter, only 619 of them (22 per cent) were non-Mainland Chinese (Cheng et al. 2009: 41, 45).

9 These six areas are educational services, medical services, testing and certification, environmental industry, innovation and technology, and finally cultural and creative industries (Task Force on Economic Challenges, Hong Kong 2009).

10 The budget cuts on government funding in higher education from 1999 to 2004, in particular, had driven the higher-education sector in Hong Kong to look to the market for additional funding.

11 Statistics provided by the Information Portal for Accredited Self-financing Post-secondary Programmes (IPASS), HKSAR: www.ipass.gov.hk/eng/stat_pg_index.aspx (accessed on 1 September 2009).

12 HKU SPACE refers to the School of Professional and Continuing Education at the University of Hong Kong.

13 For instance, in its preamble, the code of practice clearly states that it has 'no mandatory effect and institutions should be able to put in place policies and guidelines to reflect their own mission and philosophy' (HKCAAVQ 2007: 1).

14 EDB was previously the 'Education and Manpower Bureau' (EMB). Its manpower portfolio was transferred to the new Labour and Welfare Bureau in July 2007, thus streamlined to become the Education Bureau.

15 HKCAAVQ is a rather new statutory body established under the HKCAAVQ Ordinance (Chapter 1150) which came into effect on 1 October 2007. It was previously the 'Hong Kong Council for Academic Accreditation' (HKCAA). The new HKCAAVQ is appointed by the Secretary for Education as the Accreditation Authority and Qualifications Register (QR) Authority under the current Qualifications Framework (QF).

16 Statistics provided by the official website of the Education Bureau, HKSAR: www.edb. gov.hk/index.aspx?langno=1&nodeid=1250 (last accessed on 13 September 2009).

17 Information from the section regarding 'quality assurance system', official website of the MQA, Ministry of Higher Education Malaysia: www.mqa.gov.my/ (accessed on 3 September 2009).

18 Several historical cases may be drawn on to show the relative ineffectiveness of project execution of the Ministry when compared with its Singapore counterpart. For instance, the policy of switching the teaching medium of science and mathematics subjects in the Malaysian primary and secondary schools from Malay/Mandarin/Tamil to English since 2003 has been declared recently as a failure, and consequently was phased out and completely discarded. In terms of quality assurance, another noteworthy example is that prior to 2004, all lecturers in public tertiary institutions were required to have a certain postgraduate qualification. However, allegedly due to the shortage of lecturers, this prerequisite was removed in October 2004 by the Ministry of Higher Education to allow applications from industry professionals even though they did not possess any postgraduate qualification.

19 For instance, though as previously mentioned, the Ministry of Higher Education has introduced the mechanism of a search committee for the appointment of senior leaders of public universities in 2005, it is the Minister himself/herself that takes consideration of the committee's recommendations and makes the final decision. However, the fact that after more than a half century of nationhood, Malaysia has yet to see any non-Malay appointed as the Vice Chancellor of any public university indicates that this is still a highly biased selection process based primarily on domestic ethnic-political considerations rather than on the principle of meritocracy, and that the Ministry still holds final control. In fact, even the senior appointment of non-Malays as Deputy Vice Chancellors is rare, and it was not until 2007 that the Ministry decided to create another position of Deputy Vice Chancellor to accommodate the non-Malay candidates (Abdul Razak 2008: 14).

20 These are Universiti Sains Malaysia (Science University of Malaysia), Universiti Malaya (University of Malaya), Universiti Kebangsaan Malaysia (National University of Malaysia) and Universiti Putra Malaysia (Putra University of Malaysia).

21 The Qualifications Framework is a cross-sectoral hierarchy of qualifications (seven levels in total) covering both academic and vocational qualifications required by various industries.

22 The Qualifications Register is a centralised online database of qualifications and learning programmes as well as their providers/operators.

23 The eight UGC-funded institutions are: City University of Hong Kong, Hong Kong Baptist University, Lingnan University, the Chinese University of Hong Kong, the Hong Kong Institute of Education, the Hong Kong Polytechnic University, the Hong Kong University of Science and Technology and the University of Hong Kong. Among them, the Hong Kong Institute of Education's self-accrediting status is applicable to its teacher education programmes only.

24 Information from the section on 'quality assurance mechanism', official website of the Qualifications Framework, Education Bureau, HKSAR: http://www.hkqf.gov.hk/guie/QA_mech.asp (Last Assessed on 13 September 2009). It is also worth noting that since all these UGC-funded institutions are today increasingly involved in the provision of self-financing sub-degree programmes, they have formed a Joint Quality Review Committee (JQRC) to oversee the quality of such programmes and to assess them for classification onto the QR. (Information retrieved from the same section.)

25 Information from the Q&A section regarding 'non-local higher and professional courses', official website of the Education Bureau, HKSAR: www.edb.gov.hk/index.aspx?langno=1&nodeid=1251 (last accessed 13 September 2009).

26 These institutions are: Hong Kong Shue Yan University, the Hong Kong Academy for Performing Arts and the Open University of Hong Kong.

27 This is the statement that all advertisements of registered or exempted courses, by regulation, should contain.

28 Q&A section regarding 'non-local higher and professional courses', official website of the Education Bureau, HKSAR: www.edb.gov.hk/index.aspx?langno=1&nodeid=1251 (last accessed 13 September 2009).

29 The most recent example is the launch of the Hong Kong Ph.D. Fellowship Scheme by the Research Grants Council (RGC) in 2009. The Fellowship will provide a monthly stipend of HK$20,000, as well as a conference and research-related travel allowance of HK$10,000 per year for a maximum period of three years. A total of 135 Ph.D. Fellowships will be awarded for the 2010/11 academic year.

References

Abdul Razak, A. (2008) 'The university's governance in Malaysia – re-examining the role of the state', paper presented at the symposium on Positioning University in the Globalized World: Changing Governance and Coping Strategies in Asia, University of Hong Kong, Hong Kong, 10–11 December.

Agadjanian, V. and Liew, H. P. (2005) 'Preferential policies and ethnic differences in post-secondary education in peninsular Malaysia'. *Race Ethnicity and Education*, 8(2): 213–230.

Chan, D. K. K. (2008) 'Global agenda, local response: changing university governance and academic reflections in Hong Kong's higher education', paper presented at the symposium on Positioning University in the Globalized World: Changing Governance and Coping Strategies in Asia, University of Hong Kong, 10–11 December.

Chan, D. K. K. and Lo, W. (2007) 'Running universities as enterprises: university governance changes in Hong Kong'. *Asia Pacific Journal of Education*, 27(3): 305–322.

Chan, D. K. K. and Ng, P. T. (2008) 'Developing transnational higher education: comparing the approaches of Hong Kong and Singapore'. *International Journal of Educational Reform*, 17(3): 291–307.

Cheng, Y. C., Ng, S. W. and Cheung, A. C. K. (2009) *A Technical Research Report on the Development of Hong Kong as a Regional Education Hub.* Hong Kong: Hong Kong Institute of Education.

East–West Centre. (2010) 'The IFE 2020 tool kit', paper presented at the International Forum for Education 2010 Leadership Institute, Bangkok, 13–24 September.

Education Commission. (2000) *Review of Education System Reform Proposal: Excel and Grow.* Hong Kong: Government Printer.

French, N. J. (1999) 'Transnational education – competition or complementarity: the case of Hong Kong'. *Higher Education in Europe*, 24(2): 219–223.

Hackett, J. 2007. 'Hong Kong: the regional education hub: new kid on the block', Address to the 4th Asia-Pacific Conference on Continuing Education and Lifelong Learning, Hong Kong, retrieved on 10 July 2010 from www.hkuscape.hku.hk/apcell/PPT_files&papers/Jeanette-hacket_Paper.pdf.

Hong Kong Council for Accreditation of Academic and Vocational Qualifications (HKCAAVQ). (2007) *Code of Practice for Non-local Courses recommended by the Hong Kong Council for Accreditation of Academic and Vocational Qualifications* (December). Hong Kong: HKCAAVQ.

Hong Kong Council for Accreditation of Academic and Vocational Qualifications (HKCAAVQ). (2008) *Guidelines on Four-stage Quality Assurance Process under the Qualifications Framework: QF Levels 1–3* (Version 1.0, May). Hong Kong: HKCAAVQ.

Knight, J. (2002) 'Trade talk: an analysis of the impact of trade liberalization and the general agreement on trade in services on higher education'. *Journal of Studies in International Education*, 6(3): 209–229.

Knight, J. (2011) 'Education hubs: a fad, a brand, an innovation?'. *Journal of Studies in International Education*, 15(3): 221–240.

Kooiman, J. (1993) 'Socio-political governance: introduction', in J. Kooiman (ed.) *Modern Governance: New Government–Society Interactions*, pp. 1–8. London: SAGE.

Lee, H. G. (2005) 'Affirmative action in Malaysia'. *Southeast Asian Affairs*, 2005: 211–228. Singapore: Institute of Southeast Asian Studies.

Lee, H. G. (2006) 'Globalization and ethnic integration in Malaysian education', in S. S. Hock and K. Kesavapany (eds) *Malaysia: Recent Trends and Challenges*, pp. 230–259. Singapore: Institute of Southeast Asian Studies.

Lee, M. N. N. (1999a) 'Corporatization, privatization, and internationalization of higher education in Malaysia', in P. G. Altbach (ed.) *Private Prometheus: Private Higher Education and Development in the 21st Century*. New York: Greenwood Press.

Lee, M. N. N. (1999b) *Private Higher Education in Malaysia*. Penang, Malaysia: School of Educational Studies, Universiti Sains Malaysia.

Lee, M. N. N. (2000) 'The politics of educational change in Malaysia: national context and global influences', in T. Townsend and Y. C. Cheng (eds) *Educational Change and Development in the Asia-Pacific Region: Challenges for the Future*, pp. 107–131. Lisse: Swets & Zeitlinger.

Levi-Faur, D. (1998) 'The competition state as a neo–mercantalist state: understanding the restructuring of national and global telecommunications'. *Journal of Socio-Economics*, 27(6): 655–86.

McBurnie, G. and Ziguras, C. (2001) 'The regulation of transnational higher education in Southeast Asia: case studies of Hong Kong, Malaysia and Australia'. *Higher Education*, 42: 85–105.

Mok, K. H. (2008a) 'Varieties of regulatory regimes in Asia: the liberalization of the higher education market and changing governance in Hong Kong, Singapore and Malaysia'. *The Pacific Review*, 21(2): 147–170.

Mok, K. H. (2010) 'The changing role of university in promoting entrepreneurship and innovation: a comparative study of selected Asian economies', paper published online at www.undp.org.

Mok, K. H. (2011) 'The quest for regional hub of education: growing heterarchies, organizational hybridization, and new governance in Singapore and Malaysia'. *Journal of Education Policy*, 26(1): 61–81.

Morshidi, S. (2009a) 'Internationalization and the commercialization of research output of universities: emerging issues in Malaysian higher education 2006–2010', paper presented at the Regional Conference on Comparative Education and Development in Asia, National Chung Cheng University, Taiwan, 24–25 September.

Morshidi, S. (2009b) 'Strategic planning directions of Malaysia's higher education: university autonomy in the midst of political uncertainties', *Higher Education*, 59(4): 461–473.

Morshidi, S. and Abdul Razak, A. (2009) 'University governance structure in challenging times: the case of Malaysia's first APEX university (Universiti Sains Malaysia)', in K. H. Mok (ed.) *The Search for New Higher Education Governance in Asia*. New York: Palgrave.

Observatory on Borderless Higher Education. (2002) *International Branch Campuses: Scale and Significance*. London: Observatory on Borderless Higher Education.

Pekwan (2009) 'Global education hub in Johor: Marlborough College campus opens in 2010', *The Malay Mail*, retrieved on 15 July 2010 from www.mmail.com.my/content/17504-global-education-hub-johor.

Quality Assurance Agency for Higher Education. (1999) *Overview Report: Malaysia*. Gloucester, UK: Author. Retrieved on 29 August from www.qaa.ac.uk/reviews/reports/overseas/Overview_malaysia99.asp.

Tan, A. M. (2002) *Malaysian Private Higher Education: Globalisation, Privatisation, Transformation and Marketplaces*. London: Asean Academic Press.

Task Force on Economic Challenges, Hong Kong. (2009) *Recommendations from the Task Force on Economic Challenges for Promoting the Development of the Six Economic Areas* (22 June). Hong Kong: Author. Retrieved on 30 August 2009 from http://www.fso.gov.hk/tfec/eng/doc/TFEC%20-%20final%Recommendations%20_TFEC-INFO-13_%20_Eng_.pdf.

Tsang, D. Y. K. (2007) *The 2007–2008 Policy Address: The New Direction for Hong Kong*. Hong Kong: Government Printer.

Tung, C. H. (2000) *The 2000 Policy Address: Quality Education, Policy Objective for Education and Manpower Bureau*. Hong Kong: Government Printer.

UNESCO/Council of Europe. (2001) *Code of Good Practice in the Provision of Transnational Education*. Riga, Latvia: UNESCO–CEPES. Retrieved on 29 August 2009 from www.cepes.ro/hed/recogn/groups/transnat/ code.htm.

University Grants Committee (UGC). (2002) *Higher Education in Hong Kong: Report of the University Grants Committee*. Hong Kong: UGC.

University Grants Committee (UGC). (2004a) *Hong Kong Higher Education: To Make a Difference, to Move with the Times*. Hong Kong: UGC.

University Grants Committee (UGC). (2004b) *Hong Kong Higher Education Integration Matters: A Report of the Institutional Integration Working Party of the University Grants Committee*. Hong Kong: UGC.

Wan Abdul Manan, W. M. (2008) 'The Malaysian National Higher Education Action Plan: redefining autonomy and academic freedom under the APEX Experiment', paper presented at the ASAIHL Conference, University Autonomy: Interpretation and Variation, Universiti Sains Malaysia, Penang, 12–14 December.

World Bank. (2007) *Malaysia and the Knowledge Economy: Building a World-Class Higher Education System (Report No. 40397-MY)*. New York: Human Development Sector, East Asia and Pacific Region, the World Bank.

Yang, R. (2006) 'Transnational higher education in Hong Kong: an analysis', in H. Futao (ed.) *Transnational Higher Education in Asia and the Pacific Region*, pp. 41–67. Hiroshima, Japan: Research Institute for Higher Education, Hiroshima University.

10 Policy Borrowing and the Rise of a Vocational Education and Training System

The Case of Switzerland

Philipp Gonon

Policy transfer has a long tradition in vocational education and training. Debates about establishing reforms of vocational education and training have always referred to so-called successful examples. In the United States the efforts to establish an apprenticeship system like that in Germany led to various studies about this kind of vocational education and training (Gonon 2009a).

Today German-speaking countries such as Germany, Austria and Switzerland tend to be role models in this field (see Bierhoff and Prais 1997), while in the nineteenth century this part was reserved more or less for France, as will be developed in this chapter.

The quest for a modern education system that took industrial needs into account was a main driver for reform debates in all countries dealing with reform of trade and industrialisation. The rise of Switzerland's VET system at the end of the nineteenth century is of interest insofar as it shows the complex formation of a reform, following the pathway from 'cross-national attraction' to implementation and indigenisation as described by Phillips and Ochs (2004: 12).

Educational borrowing was of specific interest at that time because Switzerland faced an economic crisis, which was to be solved by educational reforms. Cross-national attraction that widened the scope of institutional alternatives to the established vocational education and training found in small enterprises was seen to further decision-making, implementation through different actors and indigenisation on a national level. The Swiss federal state and relevant economic actors collaborated to establish a coherent policy through which a modern vocational education could be established. In such a comprehensive model a reformed primary school and new organisations for the support of trade and industry played as important a role as a new model of vocational education and training.

The Birth of Modern Vocational Education from the Spirit of National and World Exhibitions

The ongoing progress of the industrial production of goods occurred differently in each country. This progress became visible for interested circles and the public particularly at trade fairs and exhibitions. Thus national and, especially, world exhibitions developed to mirror the state of the nations. They not only informed about the presence of inexpensively produced goods, works of art, inventions and discoveries but also, quite generally, about a country's level of modernisation. Just the same, in regard to the development of educational systems they played a role that cannot be underestimated.

It was the Vienna World Exhibition of 1873 that for the first time at the international level attributed an important role to the educational system itself and thus, just as at the following world exhibitions of Philadelphia (1876), Paris (1878), Chicago (1893) and Paris again (1900), supported debates on education reform. Government authorities and trade associations motivated and supported the visitors to these exhibitions, sometimes by funding them, especially as subject-related congresses, also on questions of education, were being held in connection to such events (see Guex 1903). Visitors were also obliged to inform authorities and the interested public about what they had seen, in order to uncover any deficits and stimulate reform in their education systems (Gonon 1998). The national economist Victor Böhmert, a professor at the Polytechnical University of Zurich, saw the positive influence of the Vienna World Exhibition of 1873 in the fact that not protective measures but 'good schools' and 'harmonic education' had pushed through as the essential message of economic progress and social well-being (1873: 3, 15).

The founding of artisan or technological museums also resulted from the debate in the wake of the world exhibitions (see Klimburg 1900), as did the readiness of several governments to increase their support of vocational and technical education. The commitment of the state was considered necessary, indeed urgent, to increase the general level of education as well as international competitiveness.

Just the same in Switzerland on a national level, according to the judgment by the Principal of the Fribourg College of Technology, Léon Genoud, the 1883 exhibition in Zurich was the main reason for the first amendment for artisan and industrial education of 1884 (1901); that is, it resulted in the first legal regulation on the support of vocationally oriented schools and organisations in Switzerland. Legislative steps at the levels of municipalities, cantons[1] and the federal state were meant to provide an organised framework for vocational education and training, which was developing in completely different ways across trades and regions.

Nevertheless, despite many individual attempts, apprentices and juvenile workers were often subject to arbitrary rules and exploitation by their superiors, as emphasised by a Vienna study on apprentices in 1900; this evil was said to be curable only by way of a 'state policy on apprenticeships'. As the heart of the reform the author suggested the extension of compulsory school education while including the *Fortbildungsschulen* (schools of further education for young adults and experienced workers in order to refresh general knowledge). Furthermore, the teaching of crafts and the establishing of craft shops at basic primary and secondary schools were supposed to make 'a kind of preparatory training workshops before master apprenticeship' possible (Pollitzer 1900: 124).

In the course of the nineteenth century a number of steps were initiated that were aimed at bringing schools more closely to the world of work and also resulting in the foundation of vocation-related and vocational-technological educational institutions. At the turn of the century these institutions were supposed to be systematised in line with the continuing generalisation of education, as had been established at the national level by the basic primary schools. This included, at least partly, the admission of women to vocational education (see Curtman 1836), following the demand to make the sciences and culture accessible to the labouring population (Peabody 1873). 'Educating towards manual skills' was a main demand of the 'modern school' (Haufe 1896: 5). The visits of national and especially international exhibitions furthered the willingness to learn from successful examples abroad or outside cantonal borders (Gonon 2004).

The Orientation of Basic Primary and Secondary School Towards The World of Work: Drawing and Manual Work

Thus, according to the almost unequivocal judgment both of those reporting on the world exhibitions and those calling for a reform of vocational apprenticeship, as well as the many supporters of the establishment of realistic, profession-related, trade-oriented, commercial and technological education, the entire educational system had increasingly to be oriented to the demands of the economy, more exactly of trade and industry, but also of the national state.

This demand called first of all on basic primary and secondary school. Traditionally, the focus of attention had been on the subject of drawing, as it was said to play the role of elementary teaching in respect to artistic skills and the development of general taste. Furthermore, after the Vienna World Exhibition policy makers and teachers looked increasingly at the teaching of manual work. Children's manual work was already supposed to prepare them for a life as labouring people, even more because schools of further education for young adults, which would have been able to take over such a task, were lacking (Schenckendorff 1894). German observers at the Paris World Exhibition of 1889 witnessed 'surprising achievements' which were connected to the introduction of new laws in France at the beginning of the 1880s, where the teaching of crafts was declared obligatory for basic primary and secondary school.

The Paris elementary schools impressed the visitors with their craft shops, equipped with carpenters' benches, lathes and vices, but also by their equipment for domestic business and health. It was the purpose of the exhibited handicraft products, the so-called *travaux manuels*, to make the children familiar with using tools, to develop their eyes for the crafts as well as a steady hand. Thus they were considered good preparation for apprenticeship and were said to be even 'suitable for reducing the latter's time' (Weigert 1890: 43). Many school reformers from different countries therefore urged their governments to introduce manual work in schools, like in France and Austria, as the 'improved practical preparatory education of the young people' would 'stimulate and perfect the industry' (Biedermann 1883: 125).

It was the first world exhibition on American soil, in Philadelphia, that initiated the introduction of crafts teaching at schools in the US. The idea of the systematic teaching of manual skills, illustratively presented by Russian Viktor Della-Vos at that exhibition, was immediately taken up and introduced in schools, also as a concept of progressive teaching, in order to remedy further flaws in the public-school system (Kliebard 1999). As Della-Vos, who had already participated in the Vienna World Exhibition as an observer and had since become Headmaster of the Moscow

Polytechnic Institute, stated, the age of industry needed a teaching method that was oriented to tasks of practical work, not only for engineers but also for instruction at factories and teaching at school (Ploghaus 2003).

In Switzerland, where the first crafts classes for teachers began in Basel in 1882, the attempts to firmly root manual work in schools were obviously and broadly supported by 1890, after its usefulness for vocational education had initially been judged sceptically (Weber 1882). From the 1880s, a pioneer magazine called the *Pionier*, with contributions from the progressive educationalist and Social-Democrat Robert Seidel, propagated the introduction of manual work that was in accordance with children's development (Seidel 1898). Similar to the teaching of drawing, the quite different motivations encountered by the activity or working school, the so-called *Arbeitsschule*, went far beyond the purpose of preparing for a vocation. However, the complete transformation of basic primary and secondary schools into work-preparatory or even exclusively vocational institutions was realistic neither in respect to the disparate agricultural, trade, commercial and industrial work environments nor in respect to competing educational goals, an insight gained already as the result of numerous studies in the nineteenth century. Following the 1896 national exhibition in Geneva, Léon Genoud, the previously mentioned Headmaster of the Fribourg College of Technology, could at least point to progress, in his report for the Department of the Interior, achieved by the reform of the teaching of drawing and particularly by the introduction of crafts teaching (Genoud 1897).

The Establishment of Institutions of Vocational Education as a Contribution to the Industrial Upswing: France as a Model

Apart from the teaching of drawing and crafts at basic primary and secondary schools, secondary schools as well as trade-related and technological institutions were also a topic of discussion at the national and world exhibitions. Again, France was the focus of attention, presenting impressive exhibits and even the results of individual educational institutions at the world exhibitions (see Mieussens 2004).

An overview of international reform efforts, written by the Zurich educationalist Eduard Aeberli, draws the conclusion that France stood out not only due to systematic training in craft skills but also because it had provided all branches of trade with 'the best trained and most intelligent workforce on the continent' (Aeberli 1892: 7). The goal of 'industrial upswing' demanded, as another observer of French education stated, that the entire system was saturated with organisation, from 'the temples of science as far down as to the vitally important classrooms of basic primary and secondary school' (Genauck 1882: 5).

In this respect, France was the model for Switzerland and other countries on the European continent, and for Russia beyond, as hardly any other country had such a wealth of experience or had taken steps to organise or reorganise vocational and technological education. According to the economist Karl Bücher (1878: 37), as in France the 'outdated crafts apprenticeship of the age of the guilds' had to be replaced by a variety of independent educational institutions. The École Polytechnique was considered the crown jewel of such institutions, and it was quickly copied and contributed to the 'progress of teaching', as the Austrians Beer and Hochegger stated in an early comparative study (1867: 235). In the less demanding fields of technological and vocational education it was almost inevitable to refer to France, even more because these forms of education were seen as improving the theoretical and practical vocational knowledge of the entire working class (Weigert 1890).

Just the same, the US in the nineteenth century was predominantly looking to France to thoroughly study its system of 'industrial education'. Schoenhof's report for the US government (1888) made the introductory remark that France had made its most comprehensive efforts in the course of the past few years: 'They made the public school system the instrument for laying the groundwork of technical knowledge in the make-up of the future workmen' (1888: XXI).

The most thorough analysis of the French educational system was carried out in Austria, and Armand Freiherr von Dumreicher, the foremost organiser of the Danube Monarchy's system of vocational education, became very familiar with it. The 'national wealth' was a 'result of education', which had helped France to her great upswing, as he explained in an extensive historical study (Dumreicher 1879: 193). For a modern industrial state the 'tasks of education policy' included the establishment of institutions of vocational education, and especially in this context the expansion of technical colleges and schools of further education. For industry and technology to flourish, he stated, the traditional apprenticeship of the guilds was no longer sufficient (Dumreicher 1881). Apart from the huge variety of technological institutions and museums, one type of school attracted the most attention of foreign visitors: the former *Écoles des arts et métiers* under the name of 'apprentice schools' or (public) training workshops. The future of the industrial states depended on this kind of full-time 'apprentice school', as was emphasised by the Viennese mechanical engineer Karl Göck, who travelled through Germany, Belgium and Switzerland to collect information about the state of vocational education and training (Göck 1882: 3).

Already in the nineteenth century a global discourse around the exhibitions and the comparative work of some politicians and school reformers emerged, who intended to borrow, implement and internalise appealing concepts and concrete school innovations (see Phillips and Ochs 2004).

The Path of School-based Apprenticeship: *Écoles des Arts et Métiers* as a Model for Industrial Training

With the emergence of a new world of work, characterised by industry and technology, it became apparent that a new kind of education and training had to be found. The increasingly popular opinion in France in the course of the nineteenth century was that the little formalised traditional apprenticeship was falling behind an *enseignement professionnel* characterised by an improved system of technical instruction and schooling. Thus apprenticeship at the master craftsman's workshop or in the factory came to be replaced by apprenticeship in schools. However, it was observed that educational institutions with an integrated apprenticeship were nothing new in the stricter sense but derived from existing types of schooling. They resulted from a new orientation towards the specific industrial needs of the time (Fouqué 1900).

However, even in France it was not easy to convince the public and the authorities to establish such a school-based vocational and technological education; some convincing by prominent figures was necessary. Outstanding pioneers in this regard included the founder of the *écoles des arts et métiers*, a philanthropist and adherent of physiocracy[2] by the name of François de La Rochefoucault-Liancourt, and Charles Dupin, a well-respected mathematician and engineer. Dupin was one of the first graduates from the École Polytechnique and constantly supported natural-scientific and technological matters. In the context of competition with Britain, Dupin stated, it was necessary, for the sake of France, to create, support and even 'glorify' vocational-educational and technological institutions (1825: 151).

At the beginning of the nineteenth century there had already developed a so-called 'technical education' besides the polytechnic. In the period from 1880 to 1900 an elementary technical curriculum followed this technical and professional education. However, at quite an early stage representatives spoke out against delegating vocational education to such *Écoles* and in support of the preservation of apprenticeship at factories instead (Corbon 1859). This opinion, however, which intended not to take the workshop to the school but rather the school to the workshop, remained in the minority (Pelpel and Troger 2001). In the second half of the century, the term 'vocational' was increasingly replaced by 'technological education' as the type of education that seemed to be more appropriate for the industry (Charmasson et al. 1987: 29). Under the aegis of the trade ministry, laws passed in 1887 and 1888 created a regulation for the establishment of schools of practical work with integrated workshops for industry and trade.

The *écoles des arts et métiers* which had been founded by La Rochefoucault at the beginning of the nineteenth century had been organised as boarding schools. The goal was to implement elementary knowledge of industrial production and to make a production site out of the school (Day 1987). In the course of the nineteenth century the first generation of these institutions, consisting of the three schools at Chalons, Aix and Angers, experienced a kind of 'academic drift'. They gradually increased their admission criteria and the minimum enrolment age. Also, these schools exclusively recruited academically trained mathematicians and engineers as teachers, so that they developed towards 'becoming technical colleges of the medium level' and restricted their original orientation to production (Meyser 1996: 59). Thus there developed a gap in respect to elementary vocational-technological education which was filled by various *Écoles industrielles*, *Écoles supérieures de commerce et d'industrie*, *Écoles nationales professionelles* and many other local and private institutions.

During the 1880s, the 'Apprentice School of Boulevard la Villette' in Paris, founded in 1873 and known also as École Municipale Diderot, was considered the perfect example. It was the prototype and initiated the founding of other schools. At this and at other 'Apprentice Schools', as an American observer called them, 300 apprentices each age 13 and older, most of them from the working class, were trained for three years. Every day they attended four theoretical lessons and six practical lessons in the fields of woodworking and metalworking. Apart from this, there were also military exercises (Schoenhof 1888: 27).

In their first year of this school-based apprenticeship, through a 'rotating system' the students were made familiar with iron, wood, steam and mechanics. Lessons in theoretical subjects covered mathematics, drawing, physics, chemistry and the repetition of primary school elementary subjects. Only in the second year did the apprentice choose a certain profession, and when leaving – according to reports by Swiss supporters of similar new institutions – he was preferentially hired due to his ability to change professions, as he had not been trained as a specialist (Riniker et al. 1884).

Apart from the Paris *écoles d´apprentissage*, there were other school-like apprentice workshops in France, but also institutions in Belgium, Baden, Württemberg, Saxony and Austria, which, as 'instructive experiences', would provide information about the future organisation of vocational education and training in Switzerland (GFS 1887: 66). In this context, the *écoles professionelles des arts et métiers* were attributed mostly the role of training a workers elite or a class of non-commissioned industrial officers. In this respect, as stated by another Swiss observer, the jury of the Department of Engineering Industry at the Paris World Exhibition suggested the spread of these schools beyond France (Tièche 1885).

Such public apprentice schools with integrated workshops also gained ground in Switzerland, by combining the advantages of planned teaching for apprentices found in the technical colleges and training on the road towards practical work (Schäppi 1887). However, public apprentice schools already existed in some regions, having developed predominantly from the demands of intensive and systematic training for certain professions, such as subject-related special schools for watch-makers. Accordingly, there were already alternative options to an apprenticeship in industrial workplaces. In Switzerland, however, it was precisely the trade association (*Schweizerischer Gewerbeverein*) that hoped the new foundation of public apprentice schools with integrated workshops would result in renewed economic flourishing of the trade (Scheidegger 1887). The new foundation of these institutions suggested such interest particularly among senior level workers, but also for the industrial cadre, for, similarly to a country's technological and engineering elites, systematic learning with a reference to practical work had to be combined with the provision of knowledge for trade and industrial leadership personnel.

School as a Completion of Apprenticeship at the Factory: The 'Combined Apprenticeship Systems'

It was the economist Karl Bücher who, in German-speaking countries, was the most determined supporter of the introduction of such apprentice schools following the French example. He considered them to be the 'educational institution of the future' (1877: 63) because they were most appropriate to the demands of modern economic life (1878). On the whole, however, in Germany, Austria and Switzerland the predominant opinion was that the introduction of technical colleges and such apprentice schools should be initiated only under certain conditions. Instead, people looked at the so-called 'continuation schools' as the kind of vocationally oriented further education that gave immediate reason to hope for the improvement of vocational education and training.

In Switzerland, Jakob Christinger, a member of the Commission of Further Schooling of the *Schweizerische Gemeinnützige Gesellschaft* (a Swiss charitable organisation), demanded that every canton should promote continuation schools of further education, including trade and agriculture subjects for boys as well as girls, in order to preserve wealth and competitiveness (Christinger 1877). Karl Göck made similar suggestions for Austria. Based on his travel reports and experiences in Dresden, Schaffhausen and other Swiss cantons, he concluded that the usual evening classes had to be given up and changed into weekly daytime classes of three to four lessons per day. Concerning subject-related content, the main emphasis should be on drawing, but also on individual trade-related subjects (Göck 1882).

Already several years earlier, the German Verein für Socialpolitik (Association of Social Policy) had made suggestions in the same direction, to combine apprenticeship at the factories with regular teaching at 'schools suitable for apprentices' (Wahle 2007: 145). The school of trade-related or vocational education was to be made mandatory, with day classes as 'combined teaching and learning systems' (Brentano 1875: 68).

This approach, suggested by economists and school reformers, gained more and more ground in Switzerland as well. Accordingly, the Winterthur teacher Gottlieb Hug spoke out, in a prize pamphlet for the Swiss trade association, for the creation of apprentice schools that would provide complete theoretical and practical training. The 'improvement of the crafts', he stated, was to be made dependent not only on training highly educated technicians but also common workers (Hug 1881: 31). Referring to Karl Bücher, he supported the introduction of school-based apprenticeships (i.e., apprentice schools), not generally, however, but just in those fields where the reorganisation of workshop apprenticeship was not sufficient.

The same attitude became obvious in the survey published by the Schweizerischer Gewerbeverein (Swiss Trade Association) in 1883 (Schweizerischer Gewerbeverein 1883). The Secretary of this association, Werner Krebs, argued that the economic upswing in Belgium, Saxony and Austria-Hungary showed that through technical colleges and apprentice schools with integrated workshops it was possible to achieve 'outstanding success'. These institutions, he stated, were to be considered the 'best way of trade-related vocational education' and the vocational education and training of the future. However, without losing sight of this final goal, one had to use 'those means more readily at hand', and this included theoretical education at continuation schools 'as an additional element of workshop apprenticeship' (Krebs 1888: 2).

Heinrich Bendel, the former Director of the Museum of Industry and Trade in St Gallen, marked the predominant position by his policies on vocational education: 'temporarily', trade-related technical colleges and apprentice schools provided an indispensable service, precisely for the training of an elite class of foremen and master craftsmen, mostly in declining trades. This was supposed to be a transitional system until a revived system of workshop apprenticeship would again be given its original significance (Bendel 1883: 39).

Thus both opinions, as far as the steps that followed, were in fact congruent with each other. At the Swiss Trade Association, after the mid-1890s the motto of giving priority to 'apprenticeship with a master craftsman' had finally pushed through as the main directive. Indeed, it was said, the exclusive preferential treatment of apprentice schools might still be possible, but workshop apprenticeship was far from being outdated or insufficient (Centralvorstand 1895: 19). This institution was seen as cheap and causing few extra costs, and thus almost all representatives of the Swiss Trade Association stipulated that apprenticeship with a good master craftsman in combination with continuation schools would be definitely sufficient.

If there were insecurities and differences in respect to the significance or the number and function of apprentice schools with integrated workshops and technical colleges, all reformers agreed that more schooling was necessary, but so were a number of measures to reorganise and re-direct apprenticeship. As a pragmatic and financially possible solution, a moderate degree of schooling seemed to be realistic, which would prove its worth also in the age of industry. This was the way that Swiss reformers adapted and implemented the idea of a further schooling of apprenticeship (see Gonon 2009b).

New Beginnings in Switzerland: Differentiated Institutions of Vocational Education and Exams for Apprentices as a Sign of Modern Vocational Education

For the reform of apprenticeship and the development of modern vocational education it was important that the state supported trade-related, but also industrial, vocational education. Austria, which in this respect was strongly oriented towards France, was the forerunner and thus received increasing attention in Switzerland. Hans Riniker, in his 1884 report to the Swiss Department of Trade and Agriculture, emphasised that in Austria the development of an industrial school system was far more advanced than in Switzerland. In this context, he stated, apart from 'trade-related technological schooling' and teaching 'across all classes and professions of the population as far as to the farthest periphery', apprentice schools with integrated workshops were also of significance (Riniker et al. 1884: 11).

One year earlier Heinrich Bendel had forcefully appealed to the federal government to ensure that, with the help of considerable federal contributions, schools of trade-related further education, technical colleges, apprentice schools, museums and collections of specimens, as well as an institute for the education of teachers would be created (Bendel 1883).

Expenses on subsidised institutions were rising year after year to a total of just over 284,000 Franks in 1889 for the 120 vocationally oriented institutions across Switzerland. This amount, however, did not satisfy Otto Hunziker, reporter and editorial staff member of *Die gewerbliche Fortbildungsschule*, the magazine for the teachers of such continuation schools. At least with respect to the broad measures of extending vocational education, he spoke of qualitative progress and beneficial results (Hunziker 1889). Since 1875 Hunziker had been the head of the 'Permanent School Exhibition' in Zurich, and in 1890 he became Professor of School History at the University of Zurich. Being an educated theologist and member of the Schweizerische Gemeinnützige Gesellschaft (a Swiss charitable organisation), as a publicist he supported vocational education and teacher training in particular, for example at the Verein von Lehrern an gewerblichen Fortbildungs-und Fachschulen (Association of Teachers at Schools of Trade-Related and Further Education and Technical Colleges).

In the context of an overview for the Swiss Department of the Interior on the occasion of the Chicago World Exhibition, Hunziker counted schools of further education, which were already considered partly responsible for 'developing those skills and kinds of knowledge as being necessary for working in a profession', among basic primary and secondary schools (Hunziker 1893: 19). Under 'vocational schools and technical colleges for trade-related and industrial education', however, he listed three technical colleges, two weaving schools, eight watchmaker schools, three schools for mechanics, one woodcarving school, seven schools of women's professions and seven other apprentice workshops, in addition to nine art schools and one railroad school. From the field of agriculture, this list was completed by five theoretical–practical schools, three winter schools and five dairy schools, whereas five subsidised business schools and the contributions to the expenses for classes of further education offered by 34 commercial associations and association sections were counted among commercial education.

Another matter was the inclusion of women in vocational education. While women often 'kept the books', for those of craftsmen for example, they still had to acquire appropriate knowledge. Other women had to be trained in the work of servant and household activities, and thus the federal decision of 1884 had to be interpreted in such a way that, according to Johannes Schäppi, member of parliament, 'the institutions for the practical training of the female sex, such as cooking schools, household schools, servants schools, sewing and knitting schools and classes', also had to be made subject to this decision (Schäppi 1895: 9).

The development of vocational education was also closely observed in the course of the following years. Accordingly, Heinrich Bendel on the occasion of the Great Swiss National Exhibition of 1896, and based on subject-related reports, stated that for the first time there was the opportunity 'to overview and evaluate the entire body of the trade-related and industrial educational system, according to its organisation, subject matter and performance' (Bendel 1899: 30). On the one hand, he acknowledged the positive results and the powerful effect of the decisions of the federal government in support of trade-related, industrial and commercial vocational education. On the other hand, he judged the cooperation of workshop practice and schools of trade-related further education as being in need of improvement and pointed out that – as in the Grand Duchy of Baden – it was possible to declare classes compulsory. This way, the training not only of teachers but also of schoolmasters would be made subject to state control. As the most effective and direct step, apart from the introduction of a written apprenticeship contract, Bendel suggested in particular the generalisation of examinations for apprentices (1899: 38).

Mandatory examinations for apprentices, which covered what had been learned at the workshop and the schools of trade-related or commercial further education, had had a positive effect in Baden and Württemberg, as the Secretary for the Swiss Trade Association Werner Krebs had also stated some years before. Thus already in 1888 the Swiss Trade Association decided on a regulation on examinations for Swiss apprentices, stipulating that the capability to work in a profession as well as school education should be examined, thus standardising and extending vocational education and also improving its quality (Krebs 1888).

Indeed, the examinations for apprentices, which were supervised by the Swiss Trade Association, and for which the latter was also subsidised, were considered the key to the reform of vocational education. Successfully piloted with seven candidates by the Basel Trade Association, this variant of trade support, which was acceptable for the many small businesses that hired apprentices, was gradually established also at the national level. In 1913, 7,686 male and 2,575 female apprentices applied for these examinations all over Switzerland, again supervised by the Trade Association (Surdez 2005).

In 1900 the number of Swiss apprentices holding a publicly accepted apprenticeship contract was 37,961 males and 14,906 females. The overwhelming majority was working in the textile and clothing industry. Apart from trades, from the 1890s vocational education was most significantly expanded in the industrial, commercial, and even domestic and agricultural fields. There was a consensus to support vocational education instead of protectionism, not only with respect to trade but also in agriculture and particularly in big industry. The latter, represented by the Association of Swiss Mechanical Industrials, stated that it was becoming ever more difficult to recruit a qualified workforce and thus also made the question of vocational education a matter for discussion (Widmer 1992).

Over the course of the twentieth century, apart from the written apprenticeship contract and examinations for apprentices, mandatory teaching at a vocational school was established as the 'normal case'. An apprenticeship of three to four years at a company was to be completed via daytime classes of eight to nine lessons each day, a system which – as stated by British and American supporters of a similar model – worked wonderfully. They observed that it successfully converted young people into 'capable workmen' and 'good citizens' (Snedden 1910: 81). Given its significance for education and the national economy in Switzerland, there were repeated demands for a comprehensive legal regulation, something that was realised only in the twentieth century. Indeed, the first law on vocational education in Switzerland became official in 1933, following France, Denmark, Hungary, Italy and several other Eastern European countries (Wettstein 2005).

Conclusion

It is remarkable that at the beginning of the twentieth century, across Europe as well as in the US and Russia, there was a series of similar efforts towards establishing profession-, economy- and society-related education. This 'policy interdependence' (see Simmons and Elkins 2004: 173) had established a mutual awareness of education policy in the nineteenth century, marked by a 'real' global dimension (Steiner-Khamsi 2004: 1). Educational frameworks, which had been developed during the nineteenth century, had to be transformed into a modern institution oriented to the demands of industries, the specialisation of trades and the basic supply of well-trained employees who were also capable of learning. In this context, each country attempted to borrow and develop its own national and economic logic.

In the Swiss case the establishment of a VET system was strongly based on a cross-national awareness of alternatives, especially from neighbouring countries, which were assessed and implemented in a specific context. As shown in this essay, policy transfer is not just an educational import of a model, but an assemblage of a variety of elements from an educational setting: from France, the vision of a state-driven industrial policy which included educational institutions like the full-time schools for trade as well as a modified primary school curriculum oriented towards industrial needs; from Württemberg and Baden, the concept of a continuation school and the idea of completion of work-based learning. After the first decade of the twentieth century, things had changed in so far as Swiss reformers of vocational education and training referred less to France and Paris than to German-speaking countries, and particularly to the 'Munich Model' (Best and Ogden 1914: 21). In this account the rise of a new educational (sub-)system (i.e. the VET system) is linked to such a policy transfer perspective, whereupon borrowed policies were adopted into the national context.

Notes

1 Switzerland is made up of 26 federated states or cantons, called *Kantone* or *Halb-Kantone*, which are partly sovereign, similar to the states in the United States.
2 Physiocracy was an economic approach and influential theory, developed in France in the second half of the eighteenth century. In contrast to mercantilism it emphasised productive work as the most important source for wealth and the welfare of a nation.

References

Aeberli, E. (1892) *Bericht über die Bedeutung und den gegenwärtigen Stand der Knabenarbeitsschulen insbesondere im Kanton Zürich.* Im Auftrage des zürcherischen Vereines für Knaben-Handarbeit. Zurich: Genossenschafts-Buchdruckerei.

Beer, A. and Hochegger, F. (1867) *Die Fortschritte des Unterrichtswesens in den Culturstaaten Europas.* Erster Band. Vienna: Carl Gerold.

Bendel, H. (1883) *Zur Frage der gewerblichen Erziehung in der Schweiz.* Winterthur: Bleueler-Hausheer.

Bendel, H. (1899) *Winke und Anregungen für das gewerbliche und industrielle Bildungswesen in der Schweiz.* Auf Grund der Gruppen-Fachberichte der Schweiz. Landesausstellung in Genf 1896. Berne: Schweizerischer Gewerbeverein.

Best, R. H. and Ogden, C. K. (1914) *The Problem of Continuation School and its Successful Solution in Germany.* London: King.

Biedermann, K. (1883) *Die Erziehung zur Arbeit, eine Forderung des Lebens an die Schule.* 2nd edition. Leipzig: Heinrich Matthes.

Bierhoff, H. and Prais, S. J. (1997) *From School to Work: Britain and Switzerland Compared.* Cambridge: Cambridge University Press.

Böhmert, V. (1873) *Der Einfluss der Wiener Weltausstellung auf die Arbeit des Volkes.* Vienna: Athenäum.

Brentano, L. (1875) 'Gutachten über das Lehrlingswesen', in Verein für Socialpolitik (ed.) *Die Reform des Lehrlingswesens. Sechzehn Gutachten und Berichte.* Leipzig: Duncker & Humblot, 49–71.

Bücher, K. (1877) *Die gewerbliche Bildungsfrage und der industrielle Rückgang.* Eisenach Bachmeister.

Bücher, K. (1878) *Lehrlingsfrage und gewerbliche Bildung in Frankreich.* Eisenach: Bachmeister.

Centralvorstand (des Schweizerischen Gewerbevereins) (1895) *Die Förderung der Berufslehre beim Meister. Bericht des Centralvorstandes über seine diesbezüglichen Untersuchungen, Verhandlungen und Beschlüsse.* Zurich: Schweizerischer Gewerbeverein.

Charmasson, T., Lelorrain, A.-M. and Ripa, Y. (1987) *L'Enseignement Technique de la Révolution à nos jours.* Tome I: 1789–1926. Paris: Economica.

Christinger, J. (1877) 'Die Fortbildungsschulen in Süddeutschland, Reisestudien, Vergleichungen und Vorschläge'. *Schweizerische Zeitschrift für Gemeinnützigkeit*, Volume XVI, 3: 232–272.

Corbon, A. (1859) *De l'Enseignement Professionnel.* Paris: Dubuisson.

Curtman, W. J. G. (1836) *Gewerbeschulen für das weibliche Geschlecht. Ein Blick in die Zukunft und ein Vorschlag für die Gegenwart.* Offenbach: Wächtershäuser.

Day, Ch. R. (1987) *Education for the Industrial World: The Ecole d'Arts et Métiers and the Rise of French Industrial Engineering.* Cambridge: MIT Press.

Dumreicher, A. F. v. (1879) *Über den französischen National-Wohlstand als Werk der Erziehung.* Studien über Geschichte und Organisation des künstlerischen und technischen Bildungswesens in Frankreich. Vienna: Hölder.

Dumreicher, A. F. v. (1881) *Über die Aufgaben der Unterrichtspolitik im Industrie-Staate Österreich.* Vienna: Hölder.

Dupin, C. (1825) *Hommage aux anicens élèves de l' École Polytechnique. Discours et leçons sur l'industrie, le commerce, la marine et sur les sciences appliquées aux arts.* Tome Second. Paris: Bachelier Libraire, 151–152.

Fouqué, J. (1900) *La crise de l'apprentissage et les progrès de l'enseignement professionnel.* (Thèse). Paris: Arthur Rousseau.

Genauck, C. (1882) *Die gewerbliche Erziehung durch Schulen, Lehrwerkstätten, Museen und Vereine im Königreich Württemberg.* Reichenberg: Schöpfer.

Genoud, L. (1897) *Rapport sur les travaux manuels à l'Exposition nationale de Genève en 1896.* Lausanne: Viret.

Genoud, L. (1901) *L'enseignement professionnel. Rapport présenté aux départements de l'instruction publique de la Suisse Française.* Fribourg: Imprimerie de l'oeuvre de Saint-Paul.

GFS – *Die gewerbliche Fortbildungsschule* (1887) (Blätter zur Förderung der Interessen derselben in der Schweiz): Lehrwerkstätten – Lehrwerkstätten des Auslandes, 3(9): 65–71.

Göck, K. (1882) Die gewerblichen Fortbildungsschulen und verwandten Anstalten in Deutschland, Belgien und der Schweiz. Vienna: Hölder.

Gonon, P. (1998) *Das internationale Argument in der Berufsbildungsreform.* Die Rolle internationaler Bezüge in den bildungspolitischen Debatten zur schweizerischen Berufsbildung und zur englischen Reform der Sekundarstufe II. Berne: Peter Lang.

Gonon, P. (2004) 'Travel and Reform', in D. Phillips and K. Ochs (eds), *Educational Policy Borrowing: Historical Perspectives.* Oxford Studies in Comparative Education. Oxford: Symposium Books, 125–144.

Gonon, P. (2009a) 'Efficiency and Vocationalism as Structuring Principles of Industrial Education in the USA'. *Vocations and Learning*, 1: 75–86.

Gonon, P. (2009b) 'The Internationalization of Vocational Education Reform Concepts – A Rhetorical Perspective', in A. Heikkinen and K. Kraus (eds), *Reworking Vocational Education: Policies, Practices and Concepts.* Berne: Peter Lang, 63–76.

Guex, F. (1903) *Éducation et Instruction. Rapport présenté au Haut Conseil Fédéral sur le Groupe I de l'Exposition universelle a Paris en 1900.* Lausanne: Payot.

Haufe, E. (1896) *Die Erziehung zur Arbeitstüchtigkeit eine Hauptforderung an die moderne Schule.* Znaim: Fournier & Haberler.

Hug, G. (1881) *Das gewerbliche Lehrlingswesen.* Winterthur: Westfehling.

Hunziker, O. (1889) 'Die Lehrlingsprüfungen im Jahr 1889'. *Die Gewerbliche Fortbildungsschule – Blätter zur Förderung der Interessen derselben in der Schweiz*, 5(12): 90–92.

Hunziker, O. (1893) *Das Schweizerische Schulwesen.* Herausgegeben aus Auftrag des Schweizerischen Departement des Innern anlässlich der Weltausstellung in Chicago 1893. Berne & Zurich: Union der schweizerischen permanenten Schulausstellungen.

Kliebard, H. M. (1999) *Schooled to Work: Vocationalism and the American Curriculum 1876–1946.* New York: Teachers College Press.

Klimburg, R. F. v. (1900) *Die Entwicklung des gewerblichen Unterrichtswesens in Oesterreich.* Tübingen: Mohr.

Krebs, W. (1888) *Organisation und Ergebnisse der Lehrlingsprüfungen im In- und Auslande, inklusive Anträge des Zentralvorstandes an die Delegirtenversammlung betreffend die künftige einheitliche Organisation derselben in der Schweiz.* Zurich: Schweizerischer Gewerbeverein.

Meyser, J. (1996) *Die berufspädagogische Genese des Produktionsschulprinzips. Von den Ursprüngen im 18. Jahrhundert zur aktuellen Situation.* Frankfurt a.M.: Peter Lang.

Mieussens, M. (2004) 'La participation des établissements techniques de la Seine-Inférieure aux expositions universelles, nationales et régionales', in T. Charmasson (ed.), *Formation au travail, enseigenement technique et apprentissage.* Paris: Édition du CTHS, 153–164.

Peabody, A. (1873) *The Scientific Education of Mechanics and Artizans.* Washington: Government Printing.

Pelpel, P. and Troger, V. (2001) *Histoire de l'Enseignement Technique.* Paris: L'Harmattan.

Phillips, D. and Ochs, K. (2004) 'Processes of Educational Borrowing in Historical Context', in D. Phillips and K. Ochs (eds), *Educational Policy Borrowing: historical perspectives.* Oxford Studies in Comparative Education. Oxford: Symposium Books, 7–24.

Ploghaus, G. (2003) *Die Lehrgangsmethode in der berufspraktischen Ausbildung. Genese, internationale Verbreitung und Weiterentwicklung.* Bonn: Schriftenreihe Bundesinstitut für Berufsbildung.

Pollitzer, J. (1900) *Die Lage der Lehrlinge im Kleingewerbe in Wien.* Tübingen: Mohr.

Riniker, H., Hunziker, J. and Wolfinger M. (1884) *Das gewerbliche Bildungswesen in Oesterreich, Würtemberg, Frankreich und der Schweiz.* Bericht und Anträge an das eidg. Handels- und Lanwirthschafts-Departement. Aarau: Sauerländer.

Schäppi, J. (1887) 'Organisation und Leistung bestehender Lehrwerkstätten und Fachschulen'. *Gewerbliche Zeitfragen,* 1: 1–12.

Schäppi, J. (1895) *Die Organisation des hauswirtschaftlichen und beruflichen Unterrichtes in unseren Mädchenschulen.* Zurich: Speidel.

Scheidegger, J. (1887) 'Errichtung von Lehrwerkstätten für die Bekleidungsindustrie'. *Gewerbliche Zeitfragen,* 1: 13–40.

Schenckendorff, E. v. (1894) *Die Ausgestaltung der Volksschule nach den Bedürfnissen der Gegenwart.* Berlin: Loewenthal.

Schoenhof, J. (1888) *Technical Education in Europe.* Washington: Government Printing Office.

Schweizerischer Gewerbeverein (1883) *Gewerbliche Enquête, II. Teil betreffend A. Resultate der Besprechungen in Gruppen-Zusammenkünften, B. Gutachten über verschiedene wirtschaftliche Themata's.* Winterthur: Bleueler-Hausheer.

Seidel, R. (1898) 'Die Bedeutung der Handarbeit für die Bildung und Erziehung'. *Schweizerische Blätter für Knabenhandarbeit,* 3(6): 71–73.

Snedden, D. (1910) *The Problem of Vocational Education.* Boston: Riverside Press Cambridge.

Simmons, B. A. and Elkins, Z. (2004) 'The Globalization of Liberalization: Policy Diffusion in the International Political Economy'. *American Political Science Review,* 98: 171–189.

Steiner-Khamsi, G. (2004) 'Globalization in Education: Real or Imagined?', in G. Steiner-Khamsi (ed.), *The Global Politics of Educational Borrowing and Lending.* New York: Teachers College Press, 1–7.

Surdez, M. (2005) *Diplômes et nation.* La constitution d'un espace suisse des professions avocate et artisanales (1880–1930). Berne: Peter Lang.

Tièche, A. (1885) *Über die gewerbliche und industrielle Berufsbildung.* Vortrag gehalten an der Versammlung der Gemeinnützigen Gesellschaft des Kantons Bern am 20. Oktober 1884. Berne: E. Krebs.

Wahle, M. (2007) *Im Rückspiegel – das Kaiserreich. Modernisierungsstrategien und Berufsausbildung.* Frankfurt a M.: G.A.F.B.

Weber, G. (1882) 'Preisarbeit', in Vorstand des zürcherischen kantonalen Handwerks- und

Gewerbevereins (ed.): *Preisaufgabe über folgende Fragen: Leistet der zürcherische Schul-Organismus das Nöthige in Bezug auf die gewerbliche Bildung oder aber nicht? Wenn nicht, wie kann geholfen werden?* Winterthur: Bleueler-Hausheer, 1–38.

Weigert, M. (1890) *Die Volksschule und der gewerbliche Unterricht in Frankreich. Mit besonderer Berücksichtigung des Schulwesens von Paris.* Berlin: Leonhard Simion.

Wettstein, E. (2005) *Die Entwicklung der Berufsbildung in der Schweiz.* Aarau: Sauerländer.

Widmer, Th. (1992) *Die Schweiz in der Wachstumskrise der 1880er Jahre.* Zurich: Chronos.

11 Education Policy Borrowing Across African Borders

Histories of Learner-centred Education in Botswana and South Africa

Linda Chisholm

During the 1970s, both Botswana and a neighbouring part of South Africa introduced learner-centred education into their educational systems. Thirty years later, the philosophy appears to be accepted by many teachers, but its meaning in practice remains highly variable and contested not only between the countries but also within them. Why and how this has come to be the case is in part linked to how the ideas have travelled to and settled within each context. How are these different travel histories to be understood?

'The classic problem of comparative education', writes Bob Cowen, 'is made up of three moments: (i) "*transfer*"; (ii) *translation* . . . and (iii) the *transformation* of the educational phenomenon as it "grows" socially, osmotically, in its new place' (Cowen 2009a: 339). African education has long been a site for exploration of this 'triad of relations', as colonial history provides the classic case of transfer, translation and transformation. It does so in a double sense: first in the sense of the borrowing, adoption and indigenisation of educational ideas from the colony during the period of colonialism, and second in the sense of the transfer, translation and transformation during the period of transition to the post-colony.

But exactly as the linking of the prefix 'post' to colony suggests the continued presence of the colony in its 'post'-manifestation, so the 'transformations' of the borrowed ideas over the borders of time are themselves imbued with the past, and something less than 'transformations'. Or, as Cowen once more puts it, continuities between past and present are often hidden, as comparativists concentrate on one or two aspects of the triad (p. 339). For this reason, comparativists have also criticised 'models of transformation with fixed points of departure . . . and arrival . . .' (Steiner-Khamsi 2005: 168). Such models ignore the strong legacies that carry through into the new and 'the ways in which new governments signal the beginning of a new era by deliberately distancing themselves from the . . . past' (Steiner-Khamsi 2005: 170). While Steiner-Khamsi was writing of socialist and post-socialist or capitalist societies, the same may be said of colonial and post-colonial or apartheid and post-apartheid societies.

Binary oppositions, of which this is but one example, have indeed come increasingly under attack in the comparative borrowing literature. Miriam Tag, in a review of the literature on globalisation, shows how several binary distinctions organise the debate in comparative education. The most prominent are the binaries of the global/ local, universal/particular, macro/micro, homogenisation/diversification, convergence/divergence and diffusion/reception. She argues that it is necessary to transcend not only their *oppositions* but also their presupposed *complementarities* (Tag 2010: 1) Her paper is, in a sense, a critique of the borrowing and lending literature, showing it to be implicated in a romantic celebration of the local, diverse and particular when in fact the global, macro and homogeneous are all deeply part of the local and particular and vice versa. A reflexive approach would, she argues, 'ask for how the globality and the locality of certain phenomena themselves are constructed, and how the one is first and foremost made possible by the other. It would thus conceptualise global and local as . . . relational categories . . .' (Tag 2010: 17). In this approach, processes of universalisation and localisation are intricately 'interrelated', 'borders 'are horizons of possibility'; changes in structures occur 'in the process of their "repetition"'.

Binary oppositions characterised dominant representations of the change from apartheid to post-apartheid education. When outcomes-based education (OBE) was introduced in South Africa in 1997, government presented it to teachers as being the antithesis of all that had gone before. These representations posited a Chinese wall between past and present. They counterposed (past) apartheid and (present) democratic pedagogies in terms that defined apartheid pedagogies as traditional, authoritarian, teacher-centred, exam-driven, syllabus-based, content and time-bound, based on assumptions of passivity among learners and curriculum development itself as a closed process. By contrast, outcomes-based education was presented as democratic and based on active learning, continuous assessment, learner-centredness and integrated, non-prescriptive curricula defined by teachers within flexible time-frames and with contributions from community members. Jansen was the first to show how the adoption of outcomes-based education in 1997 in South Africa was a symbolic distancing of the new regime from the old (Jansen 1997).

In practice, a gap was quickly visible between intended and enacted policy. The first generation of research in South Africa focused on the gap between ideal policy images and teachers' professional identities to explain the gap between policy and practice (Harley et al. 2000; Jansen 2001; Jita and Vandeyar 2006). A second generation has trained attention on the continuities in class-coded pedagogies of middle- and working-class schools to explain the gap (Harley and Wedekind 2004; Reeves and Muller 2005; Hoadley 2007, 2008) Both approaches have highlighted continuities rather than discontinuities between pedagogies in the past and present in black and white or middle-class and working-class schools; and how the 'translation' of the 'transferred' idea rapidly morphed into reproducing existing unequal conditions and differences in practice. 'Transformation' of the idea in many contexts quite literally became their domestication. Middle-class schools and teachers were seen as more successful in implementing new approaches while retaining former 'teacher-centred' practices intact, whereas working-class schools were less so, adopting 'learner-centred', constructivist approaches with disastrous consequences. Representations of the 'foreignness' and inappropriateness of the idea for local, especially working-class and rural school conditions abounded (Spreen 2004). Whereas official representations thus posed an old 'bad' and a new 'good', researchers have found the practical realisation of the new 'good' to be entrenching rather than transforming educational realities and outcomes and continuities, with past inequalities being stronger than discontinuities. The 'old' has thus become associated with the 'good', and the 'good' with the 'old'.

Research on classrooms in the wider region has similarly highlighted the gap between policy and practice and has also explored subtleties in teacher beliefs and strategies. In Botswana, Tabulawa (1997) has shown how practice has not conformed to policy intent and how teachers have *not* taken up learner-centred policy prescriptions. And Barrett, writing about teachers in Tanzania, uses Bernstein to show the opposite of what has been seen in South African classrooms: how teachers in low-income schools enact performative (whole-class, teacher-centred) rather than competency-based (learner-centred) pedagogies, despite professing sympathy for the latter and seeing themselves as doing the latter. She emphasises, though, that the 'polarization between teacher- and learner-centred approaches is an oversimplification of what actually happens in classrooms' and that polarised views of pedagogy fail to do justice to the educational values and teaching practices of many teachers working within contexts of scarcity (Barrett 2007: 274; see also Brodie et al. 2002). Her work demonstrates that although pedagogies in Tanzanian classrooms do not equate to a competency-based pedagogy, they nonetheless reveal that teachers in low-income societies use a mix of strategies to suit different contexts and purposes. This mix can still result in low learning outcomes. Here then, is an approach that emphasises the complementarity and hybridity rather than opposition of teacher- and learner-centred strategies. As such, it mirrors the state of the debate on globalisation and borrowing.

This chapter will draw on these approaches concerned with complementarity and hybridity to examine further the travel histories of learner-centred education in Botswana and Bophutatswana, now North West Province in South Africa. Rather than focusing on the gap between policy and practice per se, the concepts of transfer, translation and transformation are used to understand relationships between past and present, global and local, teacher- and learner-centred pedagogies. In concrete situations in historical time, each is found to be implicated in and constitutive of the other in complex ways. Central to the account is the notion of 'borders' as well as the content and meaning given in two historical periods and different geographical spaces to learner-centred education. Whereas meanings have differed from and between the points of origin and reception, the chapter shows how they have also differed and changed over time, at the point of local reception, in a process of continuous interaction between people and ideas across borders. These are however situated within specific local political economies, and so specific borders also become significant in whether and how ideas travel.

The chapter begins by situating the parallel initiatives in the 1970s in space and time, showing how history meant that each drew the idea of learner-centred education from different and sometimes similar sources in the UK and US. It then looks in greater detail at how 'border relations' over time between Botswana and South Africa determined relationships and the unfolding educational trajectories and form of borrowing or transfer (from the North) in the region, particularly in the 1980s. It goes on to explore the similarities and differences between the two programmes as they were translated into the Botswana and Bophutatswanan contexts, their origins, key

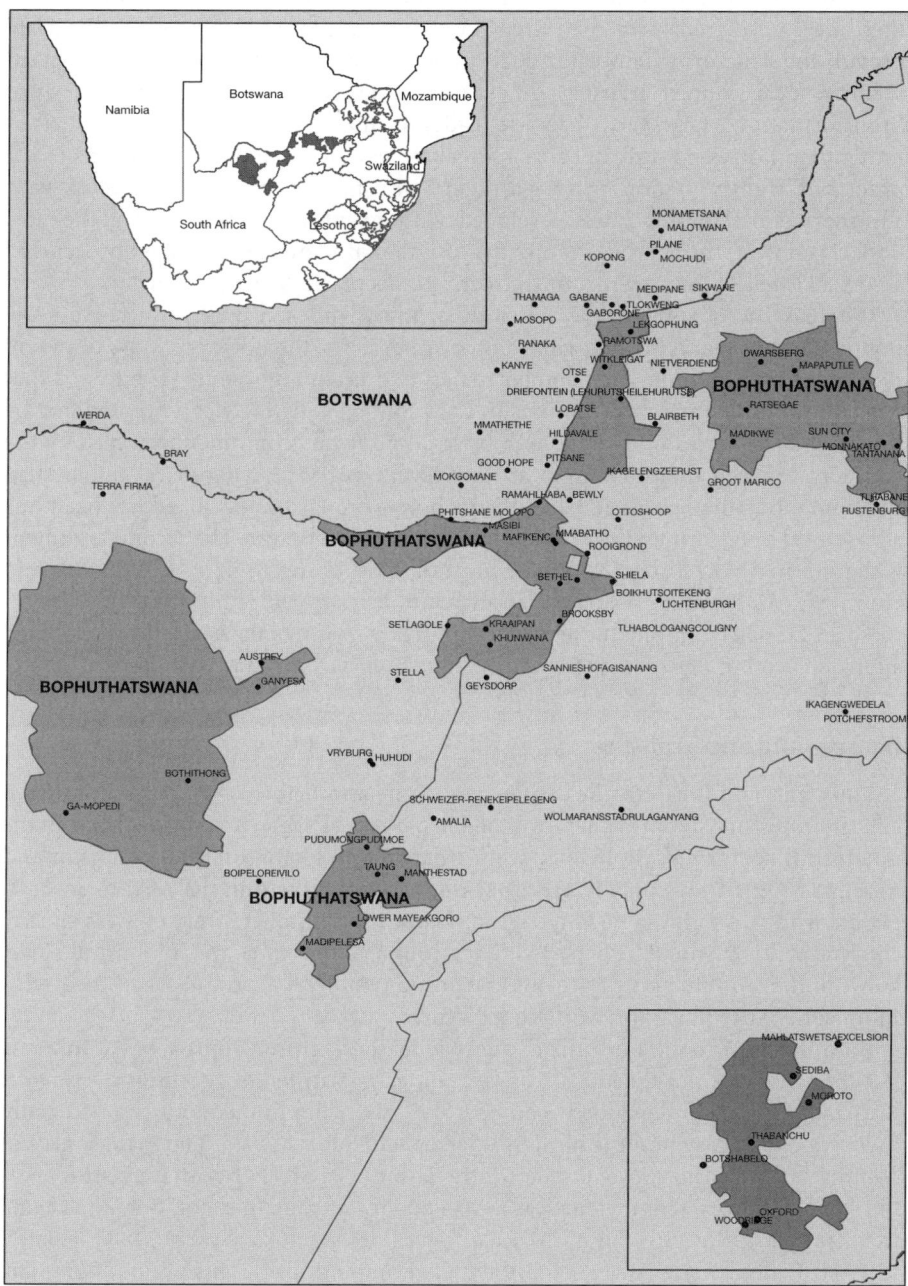

Figure 11.1 Map showing contiguity of Botswana and South Africa and Bophutatswana within South Africa bordering Botswana

foci and assessments of their success. The chapter finally examines the extent to which these ideas have 'transformed' in situ. Cowen's 'unit ideas of comparative education' provide the structuring template: space, time, the state, educational system, educated identity, social context, transfer and praxis (Cowen 2009b: 1285). In the analysis of 'transformation', however, I provide in-depth information on the South African rather than Botswana case, in part to reveal the paradoxes and contradictions of the process of 'transformation' in an apartheid Bantustan. For here, counter-intuitively, a learner-centred approach was developed, without substantial resources, in the most unlikely context: the heart of the apartheid system. Borrowing undoubtedly occurred across all levels of the system, but the focus in this paper is on schooling.

Whereas the chapter draws on both primary and secondary sources for the Bophutatswana story, including life-history interviews, the Botswana story draws on secondary sources only. The chapter makes two main arguments. The first is that educational policy and interventions in each context is strongly conditioned first by the colonial histories of each, second by local political economies and third by the conflicts between them. Conflict at local level has promoted vertical rather than horizontal borrowing relationships. Such borrowing as has occurred has been less across local borders than the historical axes of colonial power. The second argument is that meanings of learner-centred education have changed: in both Botswana and South Africa's Bophutatswana the approach to learner-centredness was both structured and teacher-centred; the learner-centred dimension of the later outcomes-based approach was but one aspect of a very different approach from what had come before.

Background and Transfer

South Africa and Botswana lie contiguous to one another, share a common mission education history, and were in fact joined in a political union for a brief period in the nineteenth century (for a history see Comaroff and Comaroff 1991; Manson and Mbenga 2009). They enjoy relatively strong economies within the African context, people who speak the same language and educational policies that express similar commitments. It would be expected that strong histories of cooperation would exist between the two, that borders would be porous. And yet a closer look at their educational histories illustrates a different picture.

Both Botswana and South Africa adopted learner-centred approaches at more or less the same time, in the late 1970s, but under very different conditions. The one, Botswana, was an independent country, the other, Bophutatswana, an artificially independent state within the borders of apartheid South Africa. The main source of conflict between the two countries in the latter part of the twentieth century was linked to this fact – that the one was independent and the other not. Botswana came to independence in 1966, South Africa achieved democratic rule some 28 years later, in 1994. Unlike South Africa's apartheid government during this period, Botswana under Seretse Khama consolidated a democratic, non-racial state. Botswana became fully integrated into development reforms, plans and projects as they swept the developing world in the 1970s and 1980s. South Africa was isolated from these trends, but experimented with them through its Bantustan policy. Bophutatswana formed a central pillar of South Africa's Bantustan policy. The Bantustan policy was central to apartheid's conception of separation of races and ethnic groups, but was distinctive in trying to create ethnic enclaves for African political expression within the overall borders of a South Africa that remained dominated by whites.

For Botswana, the key to the introduction of learner-centred education was the National Commission of Education, otherwise known as the Kagisano Report (Republic of Botswana 1977); for Bophutatswana it was the Commission of Inquiry into Education (Republic of Bophutatswana 1978), otherwise known as the Popagano Report. These Reports encompassed the entire spectrum of education, from early childhood to higher and adult education. Botswana's liberal-democratic, nation-building Kagisano ideals were reflected in the adoption of a learner-centred pedagogy. As Tabulawa puts it, a learner-centred pedagogy 'was seen as one way of extending democratic practice to the micro-level of the classroom'. (Tabulawa 1998: 250). This ideal found expression in the 1980s in Botswana's Primary Education Improvement Project (PEIP) and its Junior Secondary Education Improvement Project (JSEIP) (Tabulawa 2009: 93).

International participation in the policy and local programmes were present from the outset in Botswana. As far as policy was concerned, one of the Kagisano reports was chaired by Torsten Husén of Sweden. The other five commissioners included one each from Britain, America and Ethiopia. Botswana's subsequent PEIP and JSEIP programmes were the concrete expression of an agreement between the United States Agency for International Development (USAID) and the Government of Botswana (Yoder and Mautle 1991: 30). This project was primarily focused on teacher education and linking Botswanan with American counterparts principally from Ohio University. Placing the child, and the individual, at the centre of the educational enterprise, was at the core of this programme (Horgan et al. 1991: 77–103). Considerable synergies developed between this carefully planned and executed ten-year programme and a number of other initiatives supported by the United Kingdom and Scandinavian countries to improve primary education. Most important of these was a curricular innovation also undertaken in Bophutatswana, the British Council's Breakthrough to Setswana literacy programme.

Bophutatswana's Popagano was more closely linked to South African than international participation. It was similarly committed to nation-building, but within the context of Bantustan policy, it promoted a narrower ethnic nationalism. Like Botswana's Primary Education Improvement Project, Bophutatswana's Primary Education Upgrade Programme (PEUP) was introduced in 1979 after the Popagano Commission (Republic of Bophutatswana 1978) recommended the overhaul of the education system in the then-Bophutatswana. It proposed a clearly structured set of changes aimed at improving early childhood and primary education by 'imbuing it with what might be called the development spirit' (Republic of Bophutatswana 1978: 36). Unlike the Botswanan PEIP, Bophutatswana's PEUP was begun by a South African nursery and primary school teacher trainer in Rustenburg who had served on the Popagano Commission. At first inspired by the work of Pestalozzi, Froebel and Montessori, among others, and later by the work being conducted at Leeds University in the UK, she brought a mix of European and British child-centred educational traditions to bear on the PEUP educational experiment (Interviews conducted with Christel Bodenstein August 2009). Instead of the counterparts to Africans being

Americans, as in Botswana, here they were liberal white South Africans who worked with African teachers in local schools, the new university, local teacher education colleges, and anti-apartheid NGOS based in urban centres. Like Botswana's PEIP, child-centredness was fundamental to the programme. Christel Bodenstein, the driving force of the programme, herself had deep roots in German, missionary and child-centred education in South Africa's then all-white education system.

Funding for the Bophutatswana project was both local and external. Sources of finance other than the allocation from South Africa's Department of Foreign Affairs included the Development Bank of South Africa, Independent Development Trust, private-sector donations (such as from mining giant JCI), the homeland treasury, other government departments, school fees and local sources (Graaff 1992: 31). And additional funds were secured through the British Council for teacher exchanges with Leeds University with whom the PEUP organisers maintained close contact (Holderness interview, 5 August 2009). Key Britons involved in the programme included A. R. Thompson, Director of the Overseas Education Unit at Bristol University, Jimmy Taylor of the Overseas Education Unit at Leeds and Rick Collet, British Council Educator of Molteno Programmes and Inspector for Multi-Cultural Education in Kent. The project was successful in drawing additional funding from various sources outside the South African government, but the British link remained strong throughout.

This was clearly illustrated in one of the most significant aspects of the PEUP: the use of the Breakthrough to Literacy method for enliteration in the mother tongue. It was adapted from the British Breakthrough to Literacy Programme and prepared in the United Kingdom by the Schools Council Programme in Linguistics and English Teaching. In 1990, some 30 per cent of children in the UK were taught to read with the same method (MacDonald 1990a: 43). Breakthrough was an integrated approach of reading, writing, oral work and phonics, working with a child-centred method, as the child was expected to progress at their own individual rate in 50-minute lessons. Teacher-centred work was only done in phonics. By contrast with the Breakthrough to Literacy programme, Hans Bodenstein, Christel's husband, also developed a Decimal Board for primary mathematics, a learning aid for use with the whole class (MacDonald 1990a: 58).

In both countries, the primary education initiative was driven by states seeking to promote national or ethnic unity. The process of transfer of the ideas was intimately linked to the differently colonial histories of each, which continued into the present. The learner-centred approach was of a piece in Botswana with a liberal-democratic, nation-building project. In Bophutatswana it was a contradiction within an overall educational edifice in practice based on authoritarian repression but seeking legitimacy through the trappings of liberal democracy.

Border Relations and Borrowing: Transfer and Translation

Promotion of ethnic nationalism was central to the formation of the Bophutatswana Bantustan. The policy of grand apartheid was inaugurated with the Promotion of Bantu Self-Government Act of 1959. In terms of it, six territorial authorities were granted 'independence' in 1968 and 1969. They were all based on putative cultural and linguistic commonalities. One of these was for the Tswana under Chief Lucas M Mangope, a traditionalist in the battle between modernisers and traditionalists in the area (Lawrence and Manson 1994: 451). In 1977 he became 'President' of an 'independent Bophutatswana'. After a serious effort to promote Tswana ethnic nationhood in the 1960s, Mangope briefly flirted with non-racial liberal democracy from the mid-1970s to the mid-1980s. This was brought to a rapid close in 1988 when an attempted coup, from among the ranks of the homeland's military establishment, precipitated a drastic and repressive response. In this context, Bophutatswana now re-asserted an ethnic nationalism but sought closer alliance on this basis with its neighbour, Botswana, in a trans-regional alliance (Lawrence and Manson 1994).

As Magubane points out, Bantustans created all the trappings of states: they established development boards and parliaments, built capitals, inaugurated presidents, designed flags, composed national anthems and, above all, devised mechanisms of control and compulsion (Magubane n.d.: 754). Even histories of education were written for teachers to be trained in colleges and the new university, constructing a sense of a common Tswana history of education. One such, by African and Afrikaner academics, celebrated Bantu Education as heralding the expansion of education in the area, systematic introduction of mother tongue instruction and 'drive towards the indigenisation of education' (Lekhela et al. 1972: 37). At the same time, the mass removals of populations occurred under various statutes, and Bantustans became consolidated as reservoirs of labour migration to the cities. In this context, a liberal, child-centred project was an anomaly, but can be seen as part of Mangope's effort in the first phase of his rule to legitimate the Bantustan through assimilating to it the symbols of a liberal-democratic, non-racial state.

Despite the basis of the homeland being Tswana ethnicity, there was no common sense of nationhood among Tswana-speakers, there were many non-Tswana living in the region and many Tswana speakers outside the area. In as much as there was no common sense of ethnic nationhood within Bophutatswana, there was no common sense of nationhood on the basis of language and culture across the border, between Botswana and Bophutatswana. Indeed, throughout the apartheid period, Tswana-speakers in opposition to homeland authorities often fled into neighbouring Botswana where they found protection. This was the case after the baHurutshe revolt in 1957–8 and throughout the apartheid period, as the ANC established a military presence in neighbouring Botswana where it conducted training for underground cadres who would often return to mount organised resistance to the apartheid regime. Botswana was not sympathetic to the apartheid state.

Educational development in the region followed these trends of softening and hardening borders. Mission education in the area dates back to 1813 in South Africa and 1844 in Botswana. Schools were established first by the London and Wesleyan Missionary Societies, and then also the Berlin, Paris, American Board and Church Missionary Societies. In South Africa, they were later joined by the Hermannsburg-Lutheran and Hanoverian Free Church and Dutch Reformed missionaries. Borders for these missions were porous and stretched over the political borders. Tigerkloof near Vryburg in South Africa, and one of the most significant of the mission schools in the area, attracted not only the sons of local chiefs but also those from nearby Botswana. In the latter part of the nineteenth century it trained its students not only as evangelists, but also pupil-teachers (Lekhela et al. 1972: 16). By this stage, some of the *merafe* in Botswana also started to establish their own schools under the control of chiefs (Yoder and Mautle 1991: 13). In both South Africa and Botswana, the colonial state started to exercise control over curricula in the mission schools through grants-in-aid from the 1930s. By the middle of the twentieth century, state-supported mission education was in a state of crisis in both countries, even though it was attended by a tiny elite.

The introduction of Bantu Education in 1953 was a watershed for both countries as it brought all mission schools in South Africa, including Tigerkloof, under full state control operated on miserly budgets. From now on, and especially from 1959, Tigerkloof was closed to all non-Tswanans, including Botswanans. When Botswana attained its independence in 1966 it placed a high value on education for its population. In South Africa, this was the high point of segregated and unequal education for black and white. Whereas Botswana geared up to expand and develop education throughout the country, South Africa was keeping a tight lid on expansion. Development was, from this period, to be the Bantustan project. This paradox of casting the educational challenges of a society created through repression and predicated on separate development in an underdevelopment framework was not lost on all its participants in the society at the time (de Clerque 1994).

Not surprisingly, 'Botswana's independence in 1966', as Drummond and Manson (1993: 477) show, 'was accompanied by strict enforcement of the previously open and fluid border between Moiloa's reserve and the Bechuanaland Protectorate'. The closure of the border between Botswana and Bophutatswana in the 1970s was also manifested in the parallel but indifferent educational relationship that existed between the two countries during the apartheid period.

Popagano and PEUP were similar to what was being introduced in neighbouring Botswana, but there were no obvious links or borrowings between the two. Botswana borrowed its ideas from the US and UK as much as Christel Bodenstein and her colleagues took theirs from European and British progressive educational ideas and integrated these into a meliorative, liberal development approach. Both programmes were run from the centre, and had state support, but the Bophutatswana initiative differed in that it developed from a local initiative and worked closely with local NGOS and non-departmental personnel, which gave legitimacy to the larger project.

Teacher training was critical to the projects in both Botswana and Bophutatswana. Both followed similar strategies. In Botswana, the agreement with USAID involved the establishment of a new Department of Primary Education at the University's Faculty of Education. It was to offer an M.Ed, B.Ed and diploma course. The primary purpose was to produce trainers for the teacher-training colleges as well as supervisors for the schools. (Yoder and Mautle 1991: 31). In the then-Bophutatswana, whose borders were porous with those of South Africa, both the newly established University of Bophutatswana and the teacher education college where Christel Bodenstein was based became centres for the implementation of the Primary Education Upgrade Programme. In addition to introducing new courses from 1980, teacher training for the PEUP consisted of intensive one-week courses covering all the subjects in the primary school curriculum at any given level, observations of teaching practice in model school classrooms and coaching in the new methods by PEUP organisers (Holderness 1986: 5).

Despite the existence of these teacher training colleges, primary schools in both Botswana and Bophutatswana were relatively badly served. In 1981, when a range of diplomas were introduced in Bophutatswana for primary and secondary school teachers, the vast majority of black primary school teachers had no more qualification to teach than their own primary or junior secondary schooling, sometimes with and sometimes without a three-year diploma that in most cases was a repetition of the school content (Schlemmer 1982; Malao 1983: 158). Many teachers so qualified were also used at secondary school levels. Upgrading programmes were run by NGOs and the Bophutatswana government in the 1970s and 1980s, but with inconclusive success (Schlemmer 1982; Malope 1992: 70). In this context, the PEUP teacher training programme was closely integrated into the school improvement programme. It appears to have had moderate success as far as motivating teachers to do things differently was concerned.

But there were also differences in both style and substance. In style, the Botswana programme was professionally supported. The South African initiative had more of a missionary enthusiasm feel about it. Botswana's initiative appeared to have been more focused on building an infrastructure of supports for teacher development whereas the South African programme centred on a methodology of teaching. The Botswana programme for example developed and introduced Teaching Competency Instruments that school administrators and supervisors used to improve teacher practice in schools. They were based on the Teacher Performance Assessment Instruments (TPAI) which were developed by the University of Georgia Department of Education (Mogasha et al. 1991: 69). Built into the training and assessment instrument was an approach to teacher support based on the principle of collegiality and collaboration in identifying and correcting problems. The South African programme did not. Indeed, relationships between departmental officials and school supervisors differed markedly between Botswana and South Africa, with the former being consensual and the latter more conflictual. This was despite the close working relationship that Christel Bodenstein enjoyed with the Bantustan authorities.

Some insight into the process of translation of the programme and embedding of the ideas in the new context is provided by interviews with key actors who mediated the transfer of ideas and embedded the programme in South Africa. What emerges in the narrative is that this was a structured programme that was child-friendly in more than pedagogy. Its pedagogical strategies also conformed to neither the official post-apartheid stereotypes of what occurred in apartheid schools, nor did they conform to stereotypes of constructivist learning that have become prominent in the post-apartheid research. Planning, pacing and conceptual development, for example, were not in opposition to a child-friendly approach, but part of it.

The mediators or translators of new ideas were themselves both schooled in child- and child-centred ideas. Bill Holderness, who worked closely with Christel Bodenstein, used Unibo, as the University was called, as a base for the development and distribution of materials. He was born into a Grahamstown mission family and from 1974–5 studied Language and Literature in Education at the University of London's Institute of Education. After his training, between 1976 and 1980, he worked at the Johannesburg College of Education where he worked with the English Language Teaching and Information Centre, an NGO working in black schools to improve literacy. In 1980, in the midst of the discussion of the findings of the Popagano Commission and establishment of the PEUP, he was inspired to join Unibo.

Holderness describes the grassroots beginnings of the PEUP as arising from Christel Bodenstein's intensive in-service courses with a small number of schools from the Tlhabane and Molopo circuits near Rustenburg. In 1980 Bodenstein worked with principals and teachers to upgrade and renovate grade 1 classrooms, organise children into ability groups and encourage teachers to introduce more child-centred and discovery-learning approaches. By the end of the year, she had seven schools that became 'model schools'. Each year, additional schools were linked as satellite schools and began 'the upgrading journey moving from Grade 1 to std 4 which marks the end of primary education in Bophutatswana' (Holderness 1986: 2). The programme expanded dramatically: from 7 schools in 1980, it grew to 114 in 1981 and 625 in 1983. By 1985, 760 (over 90 per cent) out of a total 840 primary schools were involved (Holderness 1986: 3).

The objectives of the Primary Education Upgrade project (PEUP) were both infra-structural and pedagogical (see MacDonald 1993: 21). PEUP aimed to:

- turn the learning environment into a stimulating, rich environment for children by, for example, encouraging the painting of classrooms, improving the supply of adequate water and toilet facilities at schools;
- divide children into ability groups so that each child should be able to participate to learn at his/her own pace, become an active learner and participate in the learning process – this was to be achieved through the development, by the teacher, of activity cards;
- give each child an opportunity of learning from experience and expressing her-self, becoming creative and realising her full potential as a problem solver;
- help the child master new concepts and to explore these concepts;
- make learning a joyful and positive experience and to reduce harassment and confusion at this early stage of life and learning;
- help children build a good self-image, to be independent, self-reliant and to learn to share and be considerate towards others;
- plan the timetable in such a way that learning is more child-centred.

An important aspect of the programme was the elimination of end-of-the-year exam-inations up to and including standard 3. Throughout these grade levels there was automatic promotion of students. Released from the constraints of formal testing and the consequent cramming, teachers were free to institute child-centred methods at the lower end of the primary school. Not surprisingly, as students entered standard 4 (or the sixth grade, at the end of which there was an exam), there was a return to more didactic teaching.

In order to enter the project, schools had to demonstrate their commitment to an upgrading process. Schools were required to fulfil five conditions for entry into the programme. They had to commit themselves to having single sessions only; limit their class sizes to 50; admit pupils only if they were five and a half years old on entry; carry out certain classroom improvements, such as constructing shelves, at their own expense; and, finally, contribute on a rand-for-rand basis to the purchase of the project furniture. This cost was absorbed by parents.

Teacher and principal training combined theory and practice. Holderness recalls the excitement of the early days when he became involved. The process would begin with teachers and principals being introduced to new ideas in a community hall in the village. Thereafter they would observe demonstration classes in neighbouring grade 1 classes and return for discussions, having been 'inspired' in the classrooms (Holderness telephonic interview 5 August 2009). Through discussion they would prepare for the next day and the next school, so continuing the process of observation', reflection and preparation.

Central to the success of the project was its organisation. As it grew, Circuit Teams consisting of local programme education officers, principals, teachers and college lecturers were identified. They ran the in-service courses, prepared reading and writing materials, and conducted follow-up school visits. Christel Bodenstein, Bill Holderness, Nancy Motlala and Rosina and Molly Masimane worked with the 'Bop' department of education which then was still functioning. But their relationships with the department and school inspectors, despite official support from Mangope, were not easy. This was not least because of the low levels of education of inspectors them-selves. Christel Bodenstein said bluntly in 2009 that part of her programme involved teaching inspectors to read (Interview with Bodenstein Johannesburg 6 August 2009). As in the rest of the country, legacies and memories of now-dismantled systems of teacher supervision and evaluation still haunt teacher memory and make introduction of new systems extremely difficult (Jansen 2004).

Bodenstein retired in 1986, and PEUP was effectively closed down as a consequence of Mangope's authoritarian clampdown in 1988. From 1989, in the context of wide-spread resistance against apartheid authorities in schools, inspectors and subject advisors were routinely and often violently cast out of African schools when they attempted to set foot there, and teachers refused supervision and evaluation of their work. In the process, the entire inspectorate and function of inspection in African schools became dysfunctional (Jansen 2004). Some of these would have participated in the PEUP programme when it was running. Here then was another key difference from Botswana: the increasing conflict in the system that has impacted deeply on its functioning.

Although Bophutatswana's Popagano Commission and Primary Education Upgrade Programme shared much with the Kagisano Commission and its Education Improvement Projects in their learner-centred discourse, there was little relationship between Botswanans and Bophutatswanans in the formation or implementation of these educational policies and initiatives. This was linked both to the local political antagonisms from the side of Botswana, and colonial mentalities on both sides. Differences in the Tswana language spoken in Botswana and South Africa are prob-ably not inconsequential in accounting for this either. The language varies between the countries as well as within them. One of the key movers in the liberal education reform movement at the university, Bill Smith, reflecting on the contradictory relationship at the time between Bophutatswana and South Africa, observed that in general 'Botswana would have little or nothing to do with Bop at the official level'.

But likewise PEUP staff, who were mostly black teachers, were not interested in the local science solutions being explored in Botswana, and as represented in the then popular Zimsci programme. These they saw as a 'Third World solution' to science teaching inappropriate for what they wanted to develop (email exchange with Bob Smith 2 September 2009; see also Smith 1984). Links were thus always much stronger with the colonial power than the neighbour. This was not disconnected from the antagonisms created by local political differences. Ironically, closer relationships existed between the UK and South Africa and the UK and Botswana, in parallel processes, than between Botswana and South Africa or Bophutatswana.

But to what extent did these programmes become embedded or 'transformed' in the local context and how were they transformed as they grew into the new context? The next section explores this from the point of view of framers and participants as well as subsequent evaluations conducted by researchers.

Transformation

A signal of the 'transformation of a transferred and translated idea or programme, as it "grows" socially, osmotically in its new place' (Cowen 2009a: 339), are the assessments and evaluations made by participants and researchers. A decade after it was first introduced, the PEUP was described by those about to start playing a key role in crafting South Africa's post-apartheid education policy as having 'infused primary education in Bophuthatswana with a new spirit and orientation' (Taylor 1989: 38) and having made an impact on teacher–pupil ratios, classroom pupil ratios, school repetition and throughput rates and matric results (Graaff 1987, 1992; Hartshorne 1992: 134). The matric pass rate, despite significantly constrained resources, was considered to be substantially higher than in the other bantustans during the period 1987–1990 (NEPI 1993: 21). This was all ascribed to the PEUP.

Being part and parcel of South Africa, its political construction a mirage to all but its creators, Bophutatswana's relationship was always first and foremost with South Africa, rather than with either Botswana or the United Kingdom. In South Africa the dependent, unequal relationship of Bantustan or homeland governments to South Africa was central. Trying to construct an alternative vision within this context, those intellectuals associated with the PEUP had to grapple with the ambiguities of (in)dependence bequeathed by that relationship to SA. Some argued that the motivation for change and search for room for manoeuvre came from within these ethnic enclaves, and the resistance from above: 'always in the background Pretoria wielded its purse, showing clear disapproval and manipulating opposition when changes were envisaged that were contrary to South African education policy' (Hartshorne 1992: 133). Others argued that Bophutatswana was simply 'a laboratory' in which South Africa experimented with new ways of modernising apartheid or moving away from the more dysfunctional aspects of apartheid' (de Clerque 1994: 115).

Hartshorne's assessment is that while 'some changes were brought about in various homelands', 'the school systems in general continued to operate very much as in the rest of South Africa' (1992: 132). Ultimately, the whole approach was undermined by the squeeze on resources at the secondary and post-school level. Apartheid education policy in its broadest sense impacted fundamentally on the programme: the population resettlement programme, the emphasis on traditionalism, as well as a host of issues related to household poverty (Graaff 1992: 35–6).

The result was that despite this brief period of educational innovation, there was no long-term impact. The greater impact appears to have been the bigger political and socio-economic trajectory of the region, which was part of the overall apartheid grand design but also showed distinct particularities. At no point in the history of Bophuthatswana, for example, was the education budget allocated to it by Pretoria anything other than paltry. It was for many years way below that received by officially designated white, Indian, coloured or urban African schools (NEPI 1993). Additional resources allocated by national government and funds raised from external donors could not compensate for the deprivation and inequality imposed by national policy. And so the programme was translated and became embedded in the local context in practice for a brief period, but its long-term effects were more limited because it was not sustained beyond a ten-year period, if that. There is evidence, though, that it became firmly embedded in memory. As such, there were continuities between interpenetrations of pedagogical practice across successive historical phases.

In 2009, teachers who had been part of the programme remember it as bringing distinct educational benefits. I interviewed eight teachers, probing their understanding of what the PEUP was and their assessment of it. Mrs M, like her colleagues, harks back to a glorious past where teachers were trained properly and children learned to read and write. In contrast to the present, she sees PEUP as having provided a method and process to teach children to learn. 'When PEUP started,' she reminisces, 'teachers were a bit negative,' but 'that changed when they saw the results. Those learners could read and write compared with students now. Something wrong is happening in the Foundation Phase now. At that time our learners were so good we sent them to Batswana High School, the International school, Model C (former white) schools.'

Other teachers recalled the PEUP being introduced at a time when schools were massively overcrowded, classes full of over-aged children and teachers struggling with a lack of resources. The PEUP's benefits were associated with its strong coordination, scripted learning process, the teaching resources it provided (such as sentence makers, charts and teaching kits), as well as the systematic teacher training in PEUP methods in 'practical' workshops which consisted of demonstration lessons followed by reflection. Not surprisingly, these teachers believed, 'It was a good system because at the end of six months the learners could write'.

This golden age all came to an end with OBE in 1996/7 when teachers were told PEUP methods were 'a thing of the past'. For the teachers at these schools, the switch to outcomes-based education was distressing, but they also adapted what they knew to it, 'mixing' OBE with their already-known methods of teaching. Their words suggest a 'mix of strategies' as observed by Barrett (2007) in Tanzanian classrooms, and a complexity in the translation of ideas into practice belied by official representations of change from the old to the new.

The unbanning of political organisations in 1990 and ensuing preparations for a democratic South Africa provided the opportunity for several assessments of PEUP. A consideration of these assessments is instructive, for it highlights the ambiguity of the relationship to it as an initiative during 'the past' that had some 'positive' effects.

These assessments were vitally important for the future, but they were to all intents and purposes ignored as the Bantustan system and everything associated with it was to be swept away. Suggestions by writers like Jacklin and Graaff (1992), that 'bantustans have been something more than puppets of the apartheid system', and were deserving of close study, fell on deaf ears. It is significant that their book-length manuscript on education in the Bantustans, produced for the National Education Policy Investigation in 1992, was the only report not to see the light of day, the reasoning being that these systems were now consigned to the past and, as such, were dead.

At the end of the apartheid period, Bophutatswana was assessed as being better resourced, and having better developed staff and systems than the other so-called independent states, Transkei, Venda and Ciskei (Fehnel et al. 1993). An assessment by USAID of South Africa's primary education sector also compared Bophutatswana's throughput rates and pupil:teacher ratios favourably with the other authorities (Theisen et al. 1992; see also Donaldson 1989 and Taylor 1989). This was despite the fact that unemployment was by all accounts higher in this area than in other rural provinces and that it had the highest proportion of people without schooling in the agricultural and hunting sectors in 1996 (Orkin and Njobe 2000: 8). The difference between Bophutatswana and the rest was more often than not attributed to the PEUP.

Although the successes of PEUP did generate a sense that it was 'one of the best ventures ever to be introduced in the school system in black schools in the subregion' (Lehobye 1992: 48), other evaluations have pointed to more fundamental weaknesses in the approach adopted. Detailed evaluations were conducted by Lehobye (1992) and Carol MacDonald (1990a, 1990b, 1993). Lehobye's most significant finding was that although the programme enjoyed substantial success in the grades and first two standards, its success declined after standard 2 (grade 4). The major challenges hereafter were the demands on teachers and the ability of teachers to meet these demands given that the majority had academic qualifications below standard 10 plus two years' professional training, at a time when the requirement for teaching in a primary school was standard 10 plus three years' professional training (Lehobye 1992: 29). Whereas the same teacher could teach the whole curriculum up to the end of standard 2, the curriculum from standard 3 required specialised knowledge. It thus became increasingly more difficult for the teacher to address the curriculum while following a child-centred methodology. There was thus 'progressively less support for the aims and activities propagated for the programme by the senior classes' (p. 35). Although the first new corps of teachers was trained at colleges now working in association with the University of Bophutatswana, 'the new primary teachers' programme introduced in the colleges did not specifically cater for the needs of the primary schools in terms of relevance and content' (p. 36). There were complaints about the lack of alignment of training with what was to be taught and the neglect of the practical component of work experience. Had this been taken forward, there would have been more emphasis on the relevance and content of teacher education in the post-apartheid years. In the end, there was not.

Shortcomings of the programme identified by Lehobye thus related mainly to the senior phase or lower secondary schooling. Above and beyond teacher competence, they included the incompatibility of textbooks in this phase with the new philosophy and practices of learner-centred education, teachers' English language proficiency, and the lack of departmental and in-service support. These phases appeared to require something more than the learner-centred methods of the earlier phases (Hoadley and Muller 2009 also make the observation that learner-centredness may be appropriate for earlier grades but not for later).

Carol MacDonald's study (1990a) was interested in assessing the efficacy of the PEUP classroom in preparing children for standard three or the fifth grade. Like Lehobye (1992), she has nothing but praise for the coordinator and organisation of the PEUP. Like Lehobye, she also found that methods were more progressive in the early grades and 'almost wholly traditional by standard 3' (MacDonald 1990a: 25). Teachers in standard 3 (grade 5) had difficulty in using classic PEUP methods, mainly because the differentiation of children into three ability groups and the need to design lessons and materials for all three simultaneously imposed enormous demands on teachers (p. 27). The result was that teaching was simply not done regularly. But she found more mixed evidence of the use of a child-centred approach when it came to the role of the teacher, pupils, the nature of learning experiences and use of a cooperative approach. She found only the nature of testing and the accent on creative expression to be the truly progressive educational elements in PEUP classrooms (p. 19–21). Her most significant conclusion of all was that the particular style of differentiated learning adopted in the junior primary grades created a time-management problem for teachers who were thus unable to prepare children adequately for later standards in either process skills, concepts or language learning. Much of what PEUP set out to do it had achieved, she claims, with the exception of the development of the child as a problem-solver and learner of concepts (p. 90). A major additional problem she identified (MacDonald 1990b) was the transition from mother tongue to English in standard 3: by the time children reached the end of standard 2 they were inadequately prepared for suddenly learning ten subjects through the medium of English. Her proposal was not to adopt a 'straight for English' approach but to ensure a 'gradual transition' (1990b: 57). Again, there was no opportunity to build on these evaluative remarks.

Conclusion

Writing in 1998, Tabulawa notes:

> It is now more than a decade since a learner-centred pedagogy was introduced in schools (in Botswana). However, all research indications are that not much has changed in terms of the quality of teaching; teaching in schools is still didactic and authoritarian with little or no recognition of the learner's potential to actively construct classroom knowledge.
>
> (p. 250)

The same can probably be said for what was Bophutatswana and is now North West province. Here, by contrast, however, the experiment was brief, within an environment of extremely constrained resources, and was quickly snuffed out. Nonetheless, like learner-centred education in Botswana, there has been more evidence of learner-centred education in the theory than in the practice of teaching both in this innovation and in the later introduction of learner-centred education as part of outcomes-based education a decade later in the post-apartheid era. The irony of this is that at the very same time as the Bophutatswana experiment was closed down, and its strengths and limitations recognised, the democratic era saw the introduction of a new model of education, based on similar albeit not identical global ideas, but now extended to the whole country, as if nothing like the PEUP had ever existed.

At one level, some of the changes introduced into South African education after 1994 paralleled reforms introduced earlier in its own history as well as in Botswana. Learner-centredness was not, as new post-apartheid ideology would have it, a new phenomenon even at an official level where, for different reasons, it had found resonance among many educational reformers working within different parts of the system. But the form it took in the 1980s was highly structured and not the same as the form it took in the 1990s. The translation of the idea into practice in each context and over time demonstrated significant and substantial differences over time and space. Unofficially, the initial ideas and practices nonetheless subsequently fed into teachers' understandings and practices in the post-apartheid dispensation. Officially, these practices did not exist in the apartheid past. The continuities have therefore been hidden and are often cause for surprise when they have been encountered or observed.

The pre-1994 reform was crushed during the apartheid period and did not last, except in memory and in some practices in some classrooms. The post-1994 outcomes-based, learner-centred reforms were also borrowed adoptions, but in translation were linked to these past practices which themselves were varied. But both reforms, past and present, and across the region, took on their own locally informed dynamics, continuously interacting with a changing local political economy and global space. Changing power relations gave to each its significance and consequent insignificance. As a result, there was significant complexity, ambiguity and contradiction in the three moments of transfer, translation and transformation that Cowen describes as characteristic of colonial and post-colonial education.

In conclusion, then, binary oppositions constructed to distinguish past and present practices, the nature of local and global interactions or of pedagogies hold no water when examined against the concrete histories of education both under and after apartheid. The past has continuously left strong but also fragile and hidden legacies in ever-changing presents. Conflict and contradiction have been integral to the complementary positioning of countries, ideas and practices in processes of transfer, translation and transformation across time and space. And in this story the global and local have been as intertwined and inseparable as the past and the present or teacher- and learner-centred pedagogies. The implications are that efforts to construct 'purified' and polarised histories or pedagogies, from whatever angle, are bound to caricature and hide the complexity and diversity of educational practice. It is only through the recognition of this complexity and diversity, in the present as well as across time and space, that the full challenge and the scope of change can be grasped and provide the basis for adequate action.

Acknowledgements

The research for this chapter was made possible by a Spencer Foundation grant to Stanford University, the University of Botswana and Human Sciences Research Council, South Africa.

References

Barrett, A. (2007) 'Beyond the Polarization of Pedagogy: Models of Classroom Practice in Tanzanian Primary Schools', *Comparative Education,* 43(2): 273–294.

Brodie, K., Lelliott, A. and Davis, H. (2002) 'Forms and Substance in Learner-centred Teaching: Teachers' Take-Up from an In-service Programme in South Africa', *Teaching and Teacher Education,* 18(5): 541–559.

Comaroff, J. and Comaroff, J. (1991) *Of Revelation and Revolution. Christianity, Colonialism and Consciousness in South Africa,* Volume One. Chicago: University of Chicago Press.

Cowen, R. (2009a) 'Editorial Introduction: The National, the International and the Global', in R. Cowen and A. Kazamias (eds) *International Handbook of Comparative Education,* Volume 22. Dordrecht, Heidelberg, London & New York : Springer.

Cowen, R. (2009b) 'Then and Now: Unit Ideas and Comparative Education', in R. Cowen and A. Kazamias (eds) *International Handbook of Comparative Education,* Volume 22. Dordrecht, Heidelberg, London & New York: Springer.

de Clerque, F. (1994) 'High Skilled Manpower, Education and Work in Bophutatswana (1983)', in W. Flanagan, C. Hemson, J. Muller and N. Taylor (eds) *Vintage Kenton: A Kenton Education Association Commemmoration.* Cape Town: Maskew Millar, Longman.

Donaldson, A. (1989) 'Towards Progressive Education: Five Awkward Features of the Future'. In *Financing Education,* proceedings of a conference held by the Education Policy Unit, University of the Witwatersrand, Johannesburg, Workshop Series, No. 1.

Drummond, J. and Manson, A, (1993) 'The Rise and Demise of African Agricultural Production in Dinokana Village, Bophuthatswana', *Canadian Journal of African Studies,* 27(3): 462–479.

Fehnel, R., Bergman, R., Buckland, P., Jansen, J., Metcalfe, M. and Senkhame, Z. (1993) *Education Planning and Systems Management: An Appraisal of Needs in South Africa,* consultancy report. Johannesburg: World Bank.

Graaff, J. (1987) 'Rural Parents and School Enrolment Rates in Two Regions of Bophuthatswana: Subjects for Reconsideration', *Perspectives in Education,* 9(2): 25–43.

Graaff, J. (1992) 'Is Bop Better? A Case Study in Educational Innovation in Bophuthatswana', in H. Jacklin and J. Graaff, *Rural Education in South Africa. A Report on Schooling Systems in the Bantustans,* unpublished report.

Harley, K., Barasa, F., Bertram, C., Mattson, E. and Pillay, K. (2000) '"The Real and the Ideal": Teacher Roles and Competences in South African Policy and Practice', *International Journal of Educational Development,* 20(4): 287–304.

Harley, K. and Wedekind, V. (2004) 'Political Change, Curriculum Change and Social Formation, 1990–2002', in L. Chisholm (ed.) *Changing Class: Education and Social Change in Post-Apartheid South Africa.* Cape Town: HSRC Press.

Hartshorne, K. (1992) *Crisis and Challenge: Black Education 1910–1990.* Oxford: Oxford University Press.

Hoadley, U. (2007) 'The Reproduction of Social Class Inequalities through Mathematics Pedagogies in South African Primary Schools', *Journal of Curriculum Studies,* 39(6): 670–706.

Hoadley, U. (2008) 'Pedagogy and Social class: A Model for the Analysis of Pedagogic Variation', *British Journal of Sociology of Education,* 29(1): 63–78.

Hoadley, U. and Muller, J. (2009) 'Codes, Pedagogy and Knowledge: Advances in Bernsteinian Sociology of Education', in M. Apple, S. Ball and L. Gandin (eds) *The Routledge International Handbook of the Sociology of Education*. London: Routledge.

Holderness, B. (1986) 'Upgrading Primary Education in the Seventeen Circuits, 1980–1985: A Celebration of Achievement', occasional publication 2. University of Bophuthatswana. Institute of Education. Mafikeng.

Horgan, G., Moss, M., Kesupile, A., Maphorisa, J. and Haseley, L. (1991) 'Towards a Child-centred Classroom', in M. Evans and J. Yoder (eds) *Patterns of Reform in Primary Education: The Case of Botswana*. Gaborone: Macmillan Botswana.

Jacklin, H. and Graaff, J. (1992) *Rural Education in South Africa: A Report on Schooling Systems in the Bantustans*, unpublished report.

Jansen, J. (1997) *Why OBE Will Fail*, Mimeo. Westville, South Africa: Centre for Education Research, Evaluation and Policy, University of Durban-Westville.

Jansen, J. (2001) 'Image-ining teachers: Policy images and teacher identity in South African classrooms', *South African Journal of Education*, 21(4): 242–246.

Jansen, J. (2004) 'Autonomy and Accountability in the Regulation of the Teaching Profession: A South African Case Study', *Research Papers in Education*, 19(1): 51–66.

Jita, L. and Vandeyar, S. (2006) 'The Relationship between the Mathematics Identities of Primary School Teachers and New Curriculum Reforms in South Africa', *Perspectives in Education*, 24(1): 39–52.

Lawrence, M. and Manson, A. (1994) '"Dog of the Boers": The Rise and Fall of Mangope in Bophutatswana', *Journal of Southern African Studies*, 20(3), Special Issue: Ethnicity and Identity in Southern Africa, 447–461.

Lehobye, S. M. (1992) 'An Evaluation of the Primary Education Upgrading Programme in the Two Circuits of the Odi Region', University of Bophuthatswana, Institute of Education, 60.

Lekhela, E. P., Kgware, W. M., Vorster, T. and Rossouw, A. (1972) *Survey of the Development of Education among the Batswana of Bophuthatswana*. Mafikeng: South Africa: Tswana Territorial Authority, 1–51.

MacDonald, C. A. (1990a) *Swimming up the Waterfall: A Study of School-based Learning Experiences*. Pretoria: Human Sciences Research Council.

MacDonald, C. A. (1990b) *Crossing the Threshold into Standard Three in Black Education: the Consolidated Main Report of the Threshold Project*. Pretoria: Human Sciences Research Council.

MacDonald, C. A. (1993) *Towards a New Primary Curriculum for South Africa: The Main Report of the Threshold 2 Project*. Pretoria: Human Sciences Research Council.

Magubane, B. (n.d.) 'Resistance and Repression in the Bantustans', in South African Democracy Education Trust (ed.) *The Road to Democracy in South Africa: Volume 2 (1970–1980)*. Pretoria: UNISA Press.

Malao, J. (1983) 'Planning an Educational System for Bophutatswana', M. Ed. Potchefstroom University for Christian Higher Education.

Malope, L. (1992) 'Planning Educational Reforms in Bophutatswana: An Evaluation', M.Ed. Potchefstroom University for Christian Higher Education.

Manson, A. and Mbenga, B. (2009) 'The Immeasurable Wooden Plain: A History of the Bushveld Region of the NorthWest Province, South Africa. Introduction', in A. Manson and B. Mbenga (eds) *The Batswana in the Bushveld of the NorthWest Province, c. 1500–2000 AD. Essays and Portraits*. Unpublished MS.

Mogasha, M., Tsyang, G. and LeGrand, R. (1991) 'Improving Teaching in Primary Schools', in M. Evans and J. Yoder (eds) *Patterns of Reform in Primary Education: The Case of Botswana*. Gaborone: Macmillan Botswana.

National Education Policy Investigation (NEPI) (1993) *Education, Planning, Systems and Structure.* Cape Town: Oxford University Press.

Orkin, M. and Njobe, B. (2000) *Employment, Trends in Agriculture in South Africa.* Statistics South Africa and National Department of Agriculture. Pretoria: Government Publisher.

Reeves, C. and Muller, J. (2005) 'Picking Up the Pace: Variation in the Structure and Organization of Learning School Mathematics', *Journal of Education*, 37: 103–130.

Republic of Bophutatswana (1978) *Report of the National Education Commission.* Education for Popagano. Mafikeng.

Republic of Botswana Ministry of Education (1977) *Education for Kagisano.* Report of the National Commission on Education, Gaborone.

Schlemmer, L. (1982) *A Venture in Educational Development: An External Evaluation Report on the Bophutatswana Teacher Upgrading Project, Mounted by the SACHED Trust.* Centre for Applied Social Science. Durban: University of Natal.

Smith, B. (1984) 'Education: The Rural Poor: The Delusion of Basic Education', Carnegie Conference Paper No 98, Second Carnegie Inquiry into Poverty and Development in Southern Africa, Cape Town, 13–19 April.

Spreen, C. (2004) 'Appropriating Borrowed Policies: Outcomes-based Education in South Africa', in G. Steiner-Khamsi (ed) *The Global Politics of Educational Borrowing and Lending.* New York: Teachers College Press.

Steiner-Khamsi, G. (2005) 'Vouchers for Teacher Education (Non) Reform in Mongolia: Transitional, Postsocialist, or Antisocialist Explanations', *Comparative Education Review*, 49(2): 148–172.

Tabulawa, R. T. (1997) 'Pedagogical Classroom Practice and Social Context: The Case of Botswana', *International Journal of Educational Development*, 17(2): 189–204.

Tabulawa, R. T. (1998) 'Teachers' Perspectives for Classroom Practice in Botswana: Implications for Pedagogical Change', *Qualitative Studies in Education*, 11(2): 249–268.

Tabulawa, R. T. (2009) 'Education Reform in Botswana: Reflections on Policy Contradictions and Paradoxes', *Comparative Education*, 45(1): 87–107.

Tag, M. (2010) 'Rethinking Epistemological and Ontological Assumptions – Binary Distinctions and World Society Theories in Opposition, Complementarity and Beyond', draft paper for World Congress of Comparative Education Societies Conference, Istanbul, 14–19 June.

Taylor, N. (1989) 'Falling at the First Hurdle: Initial Encounters with the Formal System of African Education in South Africa'. Johannesburg South Africa: Education Policy Unit, University of the Witwatersrand. Research Report No 1.

Theisen, G., Cobbe, J., Jacklin, H., Lindsay, B., Plank, D., San Giovanni, R. and Wright, C. (1992) *South Africa: Primary Education Sector Assessment.* Washington: Academy for Educational Development in Washington, DC.

Yoder, J. and Mautle, G. (1991) 'The Context of Reform', in M. Evans and J. Yoder (eds) *Patterns of Reform in Primary Education: The Case of Botswana.* Gaborone: Macmillan Botswana.

Part III

Selective Borrowing and the Local Adaptation of Imported Reforms

12 Contested Meanings of Educational Borrowing

Iveta Silova

Educational borrowing is one of the central concepts in comparative education; yet, it is also one of the most contested. As Steiner-Khamsi (2004) observes, 'a large rift yawns between those implementing and those studying educational borrowing and lending' (p. 1). On the one hand, policy makers and practitioners are attracted to educational borrowing for its potential policy utility. From this perspective, educational borrowing is seen as a pragmatic tool for identifying and transferring 'best practices' from one context to another with the goal of improving educational systems in different national settings. Whether advanced by national governments or international development agencies (such as the World Bank, the Organization for Economic Cooperation and Development or the United Nations), the underlying assumption is that there exists a common and legitimate 'blueprint' of educational policies and practices, which would lead (if implemented properly) to increased educational opportunities and improved educational quality worldwide. On the other hand, many comparative educational researchers (starting from Sadler's famous Guildford lecture of 1900) have continuously warned against uncritical, de-contextualised educational borrowing. In particular, a growing number of scholars (Schriewer 2000; Phillips and Ochs 2004; Steiner-Khamsi 2004) have attempted to shift the focus from 'a normative preoccupation with policy borrowing and lending to a more analytical approach' (Steiner-Khamsi 2010: 323). Instead of examining 'what' can be imported from elsewhere, this type of research analyses the complex trajectories of educational borrowing and critically examines a variety of issues related to historical, political and economic dimensions of the educational borrowing process.

Notwithstanding the existing critique and shifting research foci, a normative (or policy- and practice-oriented) approach to educational borrowing research occupies a significant space in comparative education. Furthermore, this space continues to expand with the increase in global educational competition, the availability of cross-national student achievement data (such as PISA and TIMSS) and the involvement of many comparative educators in international development. And, while 'the community of researchers who critically analyze – rather than recommend – policy borrowing and lending is large', their impact on policy studies remains minimal (Steiner-Khamsi 2010: 335). As a result, these two strands of research – normative and analytical study of educational borrowing – continue to exist side-by-side, becoming increasingly at odds with one another.

Instead of obscuring this contradiction and complexity (or dismissing it as all too obvious), the purpose of this chapter is to analyse the contested meanings of educational borrowing and to discuss their implications for the broader field of comparative education. My general argument is that the normative, policy-oriented approach to educational borrowing has been rooted in a specific historical context – that of Western modernity and its accompanying logic of 'progress', 'rationality' and 'scientific expertise'. With the institutionalisation of comparative education as an academic discipline, the normative approach to educational borrowing not only gained strength in policy studies, but also increasingly permeated some strands of comparative education research (for example, cross-national student achievement studies, international development and world culture theory). Producing definitions of what constitutes 'good' educational policies and practices, this type of policy-oriented research has reinforced normative approaches to the study of educational borrowing. The significance of this research is immense, as evident in its contributions to shaping policy debates, setting discursive agendas and influencing educational reforms globally (Crossley 2002; Novoa and Yariv-Marshal 2003). As Popkewitz and Rizvi (2009) note, 'these rationalities are not merely discourses but generating principles that order what is seen, acted on, and thought about'; they emerge in con-crete education programmes, theories and systems of evaluation that circulate about education reform globally (p. 8). In this context, it is important to carefully examine the particular epistemological 'territories' and 'rationalities' being generated under the broader theme of educational borrowing.

Contextualising the analysis of the normative study of educational borrowing in a historical perspective, this chapter begins with an examination of the epistemological foundations of policy borrowing in comparative education, highlighting its ongoing commitment to the Western Enlightenment paradigm. It then locates the discussion of educational borrowing in the context of post-socialist education transformations, a context where the existing tensions between normative (policy-oriented) and ana-lytical (research-oriented) approaches to educational borrowing become clearly visible. In particular, the post-socialist education space illuminates the use of nor-mative borrowing as a strategy for normalising educational transformations and subsuming new realities into the familiar conceptual categories of modernity (now recast as globalisation paradigms). By focusing on the transfer of dominant ideas while glossing over the peripheral, normative approaches to educational borrowing thus potentially end up, in Cowen's (1996: 167) words, reading 'the wrong world' – a world regulated by the neoliberal logic of market capitalism and liberal democracy. Meanwhile, analytical (research-oriented) approaches to educational borrowing – when sufficiently distanced from the modernity paradigm – have the potential to avoid the tendency of collapsing difference in universal (and universalising) accounts of educational convergence by illuminating more nuanced, alternative readings of the world. This chapter thus highlights the importance of recapturing pluralities, dis-continuities and uncertainties through the critical study of educational borrowing in order to gain new comparative insights in comparative education.

Contextualising Educational Borrowing in the Modernity Project

From at least the times of Marc-Antoine Jullien comparative education has been 'an integral part of the modernity project in the West' (Hayhoe 2000: 426), with the ideas of Western Enlightenment and 'progress' laying the intellectual foundations of the field. At its core are several important assumptions, which intertwine with the theme of educational borrowing in interesting and complicated ways. For the purposes of this chapter, I will limit the discussion to the three themes that are perhaps most closely linked with the study of educational borrowing, including: (1) a belief in the possibility of educational progress and change; (2) a reliance on scientific rationality in achieving these goals; and (3) the emergence of the comparative education 'expert' in the broader context of international and national education reform. Combined, these themes have shaped the context within which a normative, policy-oriented approach to educational borrowing has emerged and become institutionalised in comparative education.

The Theme of 'Progress': Educational Borrowing from Jullien to Sputnik and Beyond

Historically, educational borrowing has been conceptualised as one of the key tools of pursuing progress and change in comparative and international education. As early as the 1800s, for example, Jullien conceptualised social change in mostly pragmatic terms, suggesting that educational borrowing was the primary means of perfecting society. Arguing that each generation 'should be the more perfect continuation of the generation it replaces', he believed that 'the human race [would] advance with firm and confident step[s] along the broad avenue of progress' if entrusted to teachers dedicated to their mission (quoted in Gautherin 1993: 757). Jullien's experience can thus be seen as one of the original attempts to conceptualise comparative education (and the study of educational borrowing) within the social science institution of modernity (Sobe 2002).

Since the times of Jullien, the theme of 'progress' has persistently echoed throughout comparative education scholarship, reflecting the melioristic purposes of the modernity project with varied degrees of intensity. When the first *Cyclopedia of Education* was published in 1911, for example, Paul Monroe stated that its purpose was to contribute to 'the solution of educational problems; if in no other way, at least through its direct aid to those engaged in practical work' (p. xii). For Kandel and Bereday, the study of educational borrowing was valuable primarily for internal self-reflection and analysis. For example, Kandel (1933) saw international comparison as a precondition for self-reflection, emphasising that the international study of educational systems means 'a critical approach and a challenge to one's own philosophy' and 'the development of a new attitude and a new point of view' (p. xx). Similarly, Bereday (1964) observed that 'it is self-knowledge born of the awareness of others that is the finest lesson comparative education can afford' (p. 6). For these scholars, the goal was not necessarily to change others but to reflect on one's own experience through the act of international comparison and transfer.

Yet this inward-looking purpose for the study of educational borrowing was eventually overshadowed by a more utility-oriented approach, where educational borrowing (and by extension the entire field of comparative education) came to be perceived as a 'tool' for achieving broader ends, directly 'relating education to economic growth, social amelioration, and political development' (Noah and Eckstein

1969: 116). In the post-World War II context, what educational borrowing offered comparative education was an 'instrumental value' for correcting the course of history:

> No longer were the horizons for comparative education limited to simple cross-national borrowing . . . by understanding forces and factors that molded education and society, men might be able to chart the course they were taking, and, if they did not like either direction or speed, conceivably they could hope to modify them.
>
> (Noah and Eckstein 1969: 41)

Perhaps not coincidentally, this normative, policy-oriented approach to educational borrowing intensified during the period of the Cold War. Following the launch of Sputnik by the Soviet government in 1957, the study of educational borrowing repositioned comparative education in the United States at the frontlines of the Cold War in order to 'keep the United States ahead of the Soviet Union through education' (Noah 2006: 10). With the funding available from the National Defense Education Act (NDEA) and Ford Foundation,[1] comparative educators in the US eagerly engaged in the study of 'best practices' to ensure the country's educational competitiveness globally, while at the same time pursuing other strategic interests of national importance – frequently expressed in the 'concern for the plight of less fortunate people' (Noah and Eckstein 1969: 38) – in non-aligned countries. Finally, the 'development turn' in comparative education extended opportunities for comparative educators to engage in technical assistance globally (Steiner-Khamsi 2006), further codifying the connection between normative educational borrowing and the ideal of 'progress' and thus giving comparative education a renewed (although strictly confined and ultimately conflicted) purpose in the world of policy making.

The Theme of Science: Perfecting the Methods of Educational Borrowing

Springing from a desire to improve education by studying foreign models in the context of modernisation, scholars in comparative education were expected not only to produce knowledge, but, more importantly, to provide practical guidance to educational policy makers. Cowen (2006) described it as 'the ideology of usefulness', a powerful legitimation motif in the history of the field (p. 561). And although early comparative education studies provided useful descriptive and interpretive analyses, utility alone was no longer sufficient by the 1960s. Comparative education was now expected to become 'scientific' in order to maintain its policy relevance. As Noah and Eckstein (1969) explained in *Toward a Science of Comparative Education,* 'If comparative education was to fulfill its potential as a tool for educational planning, it had to offer a means of reliable prediction' (p. 81). Without a quantitative basis, they argued, this could not be adequately achieved.

Those who advocated for infusing comparative education with social science methods and technique conceived comparative education as 'dealing with objectives, measurable and concrete levels of reality which, in principle, at least, existed independent of the observer' (Kazamias and Schwartz 1977: 167). Their conceptualisation of comparative education was based on the assumptions of 'linear evolution' (Anderson 1969: 28) and 'controlled inquiry' (Nagel 1969: 44). The technical side of it included hypothesis testing (falsification) and generalisations connecting variables, often using statistical tools or coding of quantitative data. In comparative education, the use of 'scientific' methods is perhaps best exemplified by the research initiated by the International Association for the Evaluation of Educational Achievements (IEA) in the early 1960s and by the Organisation for Economic Co-operation and Development (OECD) in the mid-1990s. As Wiseman et al. (2010: 6) observe, internationally comparative datasets – achievement studies such as the Trends in International Mathematics and Science Study (TIMSS) and the Programme for International Student Assessment (PISA) – have become 'ubiquitous components of educational decision-making processes at local as well as national policy levels':

> The increasing availability of internationally comparative educational information has had a profound effect on educational policymaking and governance worldwide. It has intensified an environment of extensive policy borrowing and model transfer from one nation to the next by providing internationally comparative benchmarks for educational, economic, and social development . . . This environment has led to widespread expansion of internationalized governance models for educational systems around the world. In some cases, this development has led to a gradual standardization of educational structure and delivery in otherwise diverse systems through the development of 'internationalized' models of educational governance and policy.
>
> (p. 4)

Although 'the scientific turn' legitimised comparative education as an academic discipline, it also reinforced the pragmatic, policy- and practice-oriented approach to the study of educational borrowing. Revolving around the belief in universal values, rules and policies, the search for 'best practices' became one of the main goals of international development agencies such as the World Bank, OECD, UNESCO and others (Beech 2009: 346). Backed by scientific data from robust experimental designs and empirically validated studies, international agencies have thus endorsed educational borrowing as a tool not only for solving national educational problems, but also for advancing educational 'progress' on a global scale through such initiatives as the Education for All (EFA) and Millennium Development Goals (MDGs). For the study of educational borrowing, this resulted in the narrowing down of a broadly conceptualised research agenda to the issues of method and technique: 'Could "transfer" be made predictable by a new "comparative method"?' (Cowen 2006: 564). Could transfer be made more effective? How could contextual factors be controlled and managed to ensure the success of educational transfer? In other words, the emphasis shifted from understanding the complexity of local contexts within which educational borrowing occurred to perfecting the technology of transfer with the help of scientific investigations. Notwithstanding multiple calls for problematising normative educational borrowing (Schriewer 2000, 2003; Steiner-Khamsi 2000, 2002, 2004; Phillips and Ochs 2004; Rappleye 2006, 2007, 2010; Beech 2009), the study of 'best practices' has remained central to comparative education research.

The Theme of Educational 'Expert'

The scientific turn of the 1960s and 1970s was accompanied by a re-thinking of what constituted authority and expertise in the field of comparative education. Noah and Eckstein (1969) argued that the traditional notions of authority were no longer appropriate because of their reliance on such 'unscientific' methods as travel to foreign countries, knowledge of the language and culture, understanding of the local context and intuition (pp. 87–88). While recognising that these methods contributed to 'intellectual progress in general and to substantive statements in comparative education' more specifically, Noah and Eckstein (1969) thought that a lack of scientific inquiry left comparative education 'peculiarly susceptible to the basic problems of bias' (p. 89). They argued for the need to institutionalise 'self-correcting devices' to prevent error in comparative education research:

> Ideally, what is required is a method of inquiry that is self-correcting, that minimizes the possibility of observer bias and maximizes the validity of data. Above all, it should be a method that opens to public scrutiny each step of the investigation and the logical and empirical bases for the researcher's conclusions. All this points towards what has come to be known as the method of science.
>
> (p. 89)

In other words, 'authority' in comparative education had been directly linked to 'scientific' knowledge, projecting the appearance of comparative education research not only as apolitical and unbiased but also as more 'efficient'. No longer were scholars expected to learn foreign languages and spend extended periods of time abroad, 'squirreling away data, ready to use the maximum of information on every possible occasion to explain or prove some point or other' (Noah and Eckstein 1969: 111). For Noah and Eckstein (1969), this was 'an inelegant and wholly pedantic approach to comparative education' (p. 111). Properly done, they argued, the empirical method of comparative education would offer the most economical way of doing comparative research, producing data that is 'systematic, controlled, and empirical' (p. 92).

What this re-definition of 'authority' implied was that the field of comparative education was now wide open to *anyone* who claimed expertise in scientific methods in narrowly professionalised areas of education, whether it be the economics of education, curriculum and teaching, educational assessment, school management, language learning or special education. As Phillips and Schweisfurth (2007) put it, 'we are all comparativists now' (p. 1). Equipped with the scientific knowledge of 'best practices', an 'expert' in any of these specialist areas could be easily catapulted to any part of the world, ready to diagnose the problems and prescribe solutions through professional consultancies in the world of international development. Such a radical re-definition of the term 'expert' made it possible for some scholars – see, for example, Eva L. Baker (2010), a former President of the American Educational Research Association – to believe that experts could produce 'dependable knowledge' that could be then synthesised into annual policy documents, released worldwide and replicated locally (p. x).[2]

The emergence of the education 'expert' has thus further codified the utility-oriented or the 'interventionist comparative education' (Cowen 1982: 108), highlighting the increasing intention of scholars to act upon – as opposed to understand – the educational world. Building on normative approaches to educational borrowing, 'experts' assumed the responsibility to first identify educational crises (periodically emerging 'Sputnik moments'), then scientifically analyse them, and, finally, efficiently fix them through the right combination of policies and practices.[3] Entering the field of comparative education, they gained power to define what was considered 'good' for society both locally and globally. They also gained the power to speak for those who supposedly lacked expert knowledge to 'help' themselves, thus re-inscribing an endless dependency of communities on 'expert' knowledge (Rancière 1991). In a way, the emergence of the education 'expert' both legitimised and spread – through the mechanism of normative educational borrowing – the values of Western Enlightenment in the name of 'progress'.

Combined, these three themes – the belief in 'progress', the reliance on 'science' and the increasing influence of the academic 'expert' – have shaped the context within which a normative, policy-oriented approach to educational borrowing has emerged and become institutionalised in comparative education. Generating particular epistemological 'rationalities' under the broader theme of educational borrowing, such normative, policy-driven research has contributed to the production of educational knowledge that not only attempts to explain education phenomena but also constructs 'norms' embedded in education theories, policies and practices. These newly emerging norms and conceptual categories – reflected in the themes of democracy, equality and economic progress – become distinctly visible in narratives of education reforms that 'shape and fashion what is possible' while making alternative futures non-existent (Lindblad and Popkewitz 2004). The emergence of new rationalities is, perhaps, most clearly evident during the periods of 'transitologies', when education plays 'a major symbolic and reconstructionist role' of destroying the past and redefining the future (Cowen 2000: 338). The discussion below will use one such transitology moment – the post-socialist transformation processes in Southeast/Central Europe and the former Soviet Union – to problematise discursive practices that have emerged under the broader theme of educational borrowing and to discuss their role in producing new consensuses about education and society.

Locating Educational Borrowing in Post-Socialist Education Space

Post-socialist transformations present a unique conceptual space to examine a rapid reconfiguration of discursive rationalities, norms and practices in the field of education. On the one hand, post-socialism appears to represent 'modernity's final bankruptcy as an intellectual and political project' (Outhwaite and Ray 2005: 99), undermining certainties associated with modernist culture and promising new forms of social and political organisation. On the other hand, however, post-socialism seems to be increasingly resembling the image of the 'West' – including the accompanying rhetoric of democracy and market economy – with a growing number of scholars noting the perceived convergence of post-socialist societies towards global norms. The puzzling aspect of post-socialism is that 'everything was tossed up into the air' in the early 1990s (Outhwaite and Ray 2005: 23), yet it all *seems* to be falling down into relatively familiar (Western) patterns. This raises many fascinating questions:

> How could futures which seemed so radically open, for better or worse, fall so quickly into familiar patterns? Were the apparent freedoms illusory, or just not exploited? Were the models adopted because they had proved themselves to be evolutionary or at least practically optimal, or just because they were familiar from the West and open to imitation?
>
> (Outhwaite and Ray 2005: 4)

Locating the discussion of education reform in the context of post-socialism helps us answer some of these questions, while illuminating the interplay between newly emerging discursive practices and the particular epistemological 'rationalities' generated under the broader theme of educational borrowing. A closer examination of this interplay reveals distinct, yet closely overlapping, strategies that define what is possible (and impossible) in education reform. First, post-socialism provides a unique space to examine discursive strategies that 'normalise' educational transformations (and its multiple mutations) by continuously relying on conceptual dichotomies such as global/local, real/imagined, convergence/divergence and others. Second, it reveals how narratives embedded in normative research on educational borrowing (with its intense focus on the transfer of 'best practices') are indeed re-ordering new realities into the familiar conceptual categories of modernity. And, finally, the post-socialist education space illuminates how dominant discourses construct ways of reasoning that undermine diverging visions for education reforms and limit possibilities of imagining any alternative trajectories of post-socialist transformations.

Normalising Post-Socialist Transformations: Educational Borrowing in the Context of Conceptual Dichotomies

The collapse of the socialist bloc in 1989–1991 triggered a wave of scholarship reporting triumphant accounts of the gradual (but monumental) replacement of the Soviet system with Western political, economic and social institutions, reflecting the principles of market economy, democratic pluralism and human rights (Silova 2010, 2011). Within a decade, policy rhetoric became remarkably similar across the region, signalling a move from socialist education policies to more Western-oriented ones. From the post-socialist countries of Central Europe to the post-Soviet republics of Central Asia, policy makers focussed (at least rhetorically) on the transfer of 'the post-education reform package', a set of policy reforms symbolising the adoption of Western education values (Silova and Steiner-Khamsi 2008). This package generally included such 'travelling policies' as student-centred learning, introduction of curriculum standards, decentralisation of educational finance and governance, privatisation of higher education, standardisation of student assessment and many others. In a way, post-socialist education reforms assumed characteristics similar (and sometimes identical) to those of the West.

Part of the explanation for the rapid adoption of these Western 'standards' throughout the former socialist bloc was undoubtedly the widespread perception that the whole *telos* of post-socialist transition was indeed a return to 'Europe' and to 'normality', with the EU accession processes accentuating the Westernisation trajectory (Silova 2010). In fact, any deviation from the Western 'norm' was immediately reflected in the emerging narratives of 'crisis', 'danger' and 'decline', which widely circulated in the academic scholarship on political, economic and social development in the former socialist region during the 1990s and 2000s (Silova 2011). For example, *Central Asian Survey* devoted an entire special issue of the journal to examining 'the discourses of danger', pointing to the tendency of 'the researchers, the development agencies, the experts' of Central Asia to discursively construct the region as rife with conflict and danger (Thompson and Heathershaw 2005: 1).

These narratives of 'crisis' became at once 'self-orientalizing' and normalising (Shevchenko 2009: 27), establishing dichotomous conceptual frameworks for dealing with post-socialist change. In comparative education, the emerging rhetoric of 'crisis' has meant that schools have needed to be normalised – redefined, recuperated and reformed – usually (but not exclusively) against the prevailing Western models (Silova 2010). In this context, the West has been unproblematically presented as the embodiment of progress, providing 'the normative affirmation of the Western modernity project' in academic terms (Blokker 2005: 504). Perry's (2009) analysis of scholarly publications examining education change in the former socialist countries highlights the use of 'normalizing' discourses, which construct conceptual dichotomies between education in the East and West. In particular, these dichotomies portray 'the West as tolerant, efficient, active, developed, organized, and democratic, and the East as intolerant, corrupt, passive, underdeveloped, chaotic, and undemocratic' (Perry 2009: 177). More importantly, alternatives are presented through the familiar narratives of 'progress', 'hope' and 'salvation', which the West is inevitably positioned to bring to the newly emerging societies of the post-socialist region. In other words, the promise of 'salvation' for post-socialist schools and societies lies in abandoning the socialist past and embracing the logic of Western modernity.

Conceptualising post-socialist transformations in such conceptual dichotomies illustrates a very particular way of theorising social change, treating 'non-Western societies as residual' and portraying 'Western societies as the seat of historical change and the apex of social development' (Outhwaite and Ray 2005: 201). In this context, the West (particularly the US) becomes identified as 'a forerunner in global institutional trends' (Baker and LeTendre 2005: 17), setting new global standards for education quality, equity and achievement. Educational borrowing (conceptualised as a normative practice) becomes a vehicle to catch up with the West, and international student achievement studies (such as TIMSS and PISA) function to streamline and manage the 'progress' of educational systems in accordance with global (Western) norms. Those who deviate must be brought into line; they must be disciplined – as 'the name, shame, and blame' strategy of the TIMSS and PISA studies exemplifies. These normalising discourses – justified through global data sets where local problems require global prescriptions (see Hwang 2006) – endow the West with 'the redemptive powers of human interference' (Ramaekers 2006: 249). As Lindblad and Popkewitz (2004) explain, these modern narratives of 'progress' and 'salvation' inevitably invoke 'social obligation to rescue those who have fallen outside the narratives of progress' (pp. xx–xxi). Within this logic, the post-socialist region is once again portrayed to be 'on a journey somewhere' – a predetermined journey towards the West, progress and modernity:

> The transition recalls the earlier historical positioning of the region as 'in between' east and west, a notion which not only redeploys the teleological construction of progress from east to west but also embeds the teleology (spatial and temporal) itself, focusing attention once again on the future and the west (then and there) rather than on the here and now of post-socialist Europe. In all of these ways, the diversity, depth and scale of the region's particular histories and geographies are erased as they become (just like) the west.
>
> (Stenning and Horschelmann 2008: 321)

(Mis)reading the World: Educational Borrowing in the Context of 'World Culture'

What the preceding discussion reveals is that research on post-socialist transformations has been increasingly subsumed by the existing globalisation frameworks, including theoretical debates over convergence/divergence, global/local and real/ imagined. Extending beyond post-socialism to explain educational convergence in the context of globalisation, one of the debates in comparative education has culminated around the idea of 'world culture'. Although not exclusively focussed on educational borrowing, the world culture debate has stimulated a rigorous exchange of ideas about the causes, processes and outcomes of 'travelling' education policies and practices. The key participants of the debate include scholars representing sociological neo-institutionalism (e.g. Meyer and Ramirez 2000), anthropology (e.g. Anderson-Levitt 2003) and systems theory (e.g. Schriewer 2000; Steiner-Khamsi 2004). Speaking from different theoretical perspectives and offering alternative explanations for the perceived educational convergence, they seem (surprisingly) to have one thing in common – their analyses consistently begin with the 'global', tracing the destiny of dominant education models as they spread worldwide.[4]

Recognising educational borrowing as real and substantive, world culture theorists have argued that borrowing has contributed to educational convergence through the dissemination of 'global scripts' or 'templates' that standardise national education arrangements at an increasing rate (Meyer and Ramirez 2000; Wiseman et al. 2010). Their main argument is that the rise of rationalised models of the nation-state and mass schooling in the nineteenth and twentieth centuries has produced institutions that are increasingly more homogeneous across countries. While world culture theory acknowledges instances of educational divergence as 'the evidence of loose coupling' (Drori and Krücken 2009: 20), the central focus is on the emergence of an increasingly similar world culture of standardisation, rationalisation and scientisation. Focussing on educational reforms that have gained popularity globally, world culture theory builds its arguments of global educational convergence using the following (familiar) themes: decentralisation, devolution, privatisation and marketisation of schools; standardised curriculum; national educational assessment and international testing; evidence-based education policy; and others.

The opposite side of the debate – which is usually referred to as 'culturalist' and includes diverse perspectives from anthropology, systems theory and other areas –

recognises the emergence of global models while re-interpreting them as primarily discursive or even imagined. In the case of anthropological research, for example, the focus is on local implementation of global reforms, with numerous case studies examining how global models are 'creolised' or 'indigenised' locally (for example, see an edited volume by Anderson-Levitt 2003). Scholars speaking from the systems theory perspective (e.g. Schriewer 2000; Steiner-Khamsi 2004) focus on the politics and economics of educational transfer, highlighting that educational borrowing does not necessarily occur because of global consensus on what constitutes best practices in education, but rather because of a range of locally determined (political) factors. In other words, this strand of research has produced numerous case studies highlighting contextual complexity, emphasising disjunctions between global norms and local meanings, and ultimately questioning the universality of the world culture (see edited volumes by Anderson-Levitt 2003; Steiner-Khamsi 2004).

What is important (yet rarely acknowledged) is that arguments on both sides of the world culture debate have been rendered possible by one another and have been increasingly perceived as 'complementary', suggesting that divergent findings may in fact reflect a more complete explanation of the complex interaction between the global and the local. For example, Anderson-Levitt (2003) explains that 'by looking at the whole world at once, world culture theorists have noticed an important phenomenon that anthropologists of education miss' when focussing on the local (p. 4). Similarly, Ramirez (2003) argues that, despite differing on the locus of research (from local communities to nation-state to world society), 'the focus on sense making constitutes more common ground between world culture research tradition . . . and the anthropological perspectives' (p. 240). Thus, the assumption is that a combination of the world culture and its local interpretations (or translations) provides a fuller explanation of globalisation phenomena than any one single theory alone could. The complementarity argument also echoes Schriewer's (2003) conceptualisations of the global/local nexus, which highlight 'the simultaneity of contrary currents', including, on the one hand, the increasing world-level interconnection of communication in one single world-society, and, on the other, the ongoing persistence of 'culture-specific' adoptions and interpretations of world-level forces (p. 273).

More critically, all sides of the theoretical debate (including the anthropologists) seem to use 'the global' as the starting point for their theoretical reflections. Notwithstanding their position on the world culture debate – whether endorsing the world culture (see world culture theory research) or critically examining its local meanings (see anthropological research) or re-conceptualising it (see systems theory) – the focus is always on 'big stories' and dominant paradigms. Examples abound. Studies on educational borrowing examine the trajectories of familiar education reforms that have spread globally (such as outcomes-based education, privatisation, decentralisation, child-friendly schools, etc.) as well as broader concepts circulating internationally (such as education for democracy, equality or civil society). Typically, the starting point is identifying a 'global' reform and tracing its complicated trajectory locally. Rarely do we begin the other way around by using local education experiences as a starting point for reflections on educational phenomena – whether the 'global' or the 'local'. And even when we do, the local is always compared against the global, further strengthening the established conceptual dichotomies and thus limiting our theoretical horizons.

We end up, in Cowen's words (1996: 167), 'reading the wrong world' – a world dominated by 'global norms' of reason, rationality and progress. And by the very act of engaging with the world culture debate, we contribute to stabilising dominant education models as valid, compelling and legitimate, thus firmly embedding them as meaningful narratives in comparative education research. What is not described – and thus negated – in the world culture debate becomes an important way to reveal its *telos*, its underlying ties to the modernity project, which allows it – consciously or otherwise – to normalise dominant (neoliberal) educational paradigms while silencing divergent voices.

Overlooking Alternative Visions: Educational Borrowing Outside the Global

Although the focus on dominant education paradigms is understandable – after all, the field has always been preoccupied with 'what works' in education reform – one of the outcomes is that alternative ideas may be easily overlooked. This is as critical for comparative education today as it was in the past. Reflecting on the historical development of the field, Cowen (1996) argues that the emphasis on the 'strongest themes of modernity' (for example, that the social sciences should be scientific and useful), 'rejected, bypassed, and marginalized' promising epistemological strands in comparative education such as historical, culturalist and post-structuralist perspectives (p. 152). Projected on globalisation debates, the emphasis on the dominant ideas and ideologies – offering a particular (mis)reading of 'the global' – makes what is outside the global impossible to imagine. As Stäheli (2003) explains:

> The rhetoric of globalization produces political and theoretical effects of closure that are often neglected by the practitioners of globalization theory. Accepting a notion of the global as a teleological figure of completeness precludes crucial politico-theoretical possibilities; it constitutes an exemplary case of a 'politics of the construction of the unthinkable' (Laclau 1981) that makes unthinkable that which does not fit in with the hegemonic definition of the global.
>
> (p. 2)

The implications of such an ongoing fixation on dominant paradigms (and the persistent desire to make them useful) are serious. When using 'singular Western models' as a yardstick for post-socialist transformations, we 'lose sight of alternatives, whether alternative capitalisms, alternative socialisms, or other utopias that offer novel lenses through which to interpret the present and the past, as well as future' (Burawoy 1999: 309). As earlier discussions of post-socialist transformations illustrated, it becomes almost impossible to 'see' the alternatives within the normative framework of globalisation and educational borrowing (Silova 2010). After all, the very language of educational borrowing implies deficit (or scarcity of some kind) and presupposes the existence of best practices (i.e. grand narratives) that are readily available to 'fix' an identified problem. Once again, we return to the construction of 'crisis'/'need' and presuppose the existence of universal solutions, leaving no hope for alternative visions to enter comparative education discourses. As Mehta (2009) observes, 'there is the erasure of voices as stories struggle to become part of a dominating discourse and the loss, or translated versions of those stories as they become part of the visible discourse' (p. 1193). It is as if the narrative embedded in the (normative) concept of educational borrowing functions as an epistemological gate-keeper, endlessly sorting stories into global/local, big/small, objective/subjective, thus re-enforcing the dominant (mis)reading of the world.

Globalisation narratives have thus incapacitated any attempts to question the established 'truths', to point to the limitations in mainstream theorising or to offer alternative readings of the world. They have set epistemological boundaries for comparative education, precluding critical questions from being asked, new realities from being seen and alternative visions from being articulated. After all, thinking about 'the unimaginable stories that await representation' is a fearsome, uncomfortable, unpredictable thing (Mehta 2009: 1203). This intolerance of uncertainty (stemming from the perceived dangers of difference and divergence) stalls our imagination, making the emergence of any new, alternative perspectives almost impossible:

> But what if there were other narratives that could resist being subsumed under [the] grandiose story of rising and falling expectations . . . ? What if, for a brief moment, the familiar music stopped, and the seats in the orchestra were occupied by players who insisted on making their own tunes, producing a new and unprecedented combination of aesthetic creativity and political activism?
>
> (Jay 2003: xvi)

Concluding Remarks: (Re)Thinking the Study of Educational Borrowing

Locating the discussion of educational borrowing in the context of post-socialist education transformations has raised many challenging questions for comparative education. In particular, it has highlighted how narratives embedded in the (normative) concept of educational borrowing have permeated broader research in comparative education, producing discourses (implicitly) linking comparative education to the modernity project and its values of reason, rationality and progress. Generating particular epistemological 'rationalities', policy-driven research (such as cross-national student achievement studies or world culture theory) has contributed to the production of educational knowledge that not only attempts to explain education phenomena but also constructs 'norms' embedded in education theories, policies and practices. These newly emerging norms appear as salvation themes that 'speak about saving or delivering the nation through the education of the child':

> These themes are today about democracy, equality, and economic progress. These are global discourses about change in curriculum and teaching as insuring the future of the nation in the new world that is called 'global' and 'a knowledge-based' society.
>
> (Lindblad and Popkewitz 2004: xx)

Generated under the broader theme of educational borrowing, these 'norms' function as strategies for normalising educational transformations and subsuming new realities into the familiar conceptual categories of modernity (now recast as globalisation paradigms). By focussing on the 'global', they construct ways of reasoning that undermine divergent visions for education reforms and limit possibilities of imagining any alternative trajectories of post-socialist transformations. In other words, thinking 'outside the global' becomes almost impossible (Stäheli 2003). This results in the ongoing (and uninterrupted) circulation of education discourses that sets the post-socialist education space on a predetermined journey towards the West, progress and modernity. At the same time, difference and divergence are collapsed in universalising accounts of educational convergence in an attempt to manage uncertainty. Narratives embedded in (normative) scholarship on educational borrowing thus tend to avoid both challenging the evolutionary scheme of thought and questioning the established concepts of Western modernity.

However, when difference and divergence become a starting point of comparative analysis, Westernisation frameworks begin to lose their explanatory power, failing to recognise sufficiently the essential ambiguity and complexity of post-socialist change (Silova 2010). As Burawoy (1999: 308) suggests, it is important to pursue this ambiguity in order to capture alternative 'post-socialist pathways' that re-order, re-constitute and re-configure dominant discourses and practices into new (and often unexpected) arrangements. As several edited volumes reveal (Burawoy and Verdery 1999; Silova 2010, 2011), post-socialist transformations have become no less uncertain two decades after socialism collapsed. In fact, post-socialist space has become even more complex and the post-socialist transformation processes have remained even more incomplete, open-ended and unpredictable. Further destabilising an ordering logic of Western modernity, these complex accounts of post-socialist transformations open an opportunity for theorisations that are 'open, full of potential, and marked more by beginnings than the endings so commonly associated with post-socialism' (Stenning and Horschelmann 2008: 330).

In this context, post-socialism becomes an intellectual space from which we can begin to challenge the established frameworks of Western modernity by critically interrogating globalisation narratives embedded in the (normative) study of educational borrowing, in order to ask difficult, timely and intractable questions about 'knowledge' in comparative education. Instead of focussing on the study of already formed (neoliberal) policies and practices, we can thus re-orient ourselves to the study of a complex set of education phenomena in the early stages of its formation. We thus avoid focussing on what Bakhtin (1986: 139) noted with regret as the 'readymade and finalized', and rather examine what is constantly in flux and shifting towards an open future. It is from this conceptual space that we may begin to critically re-think the study of educational borrowing in order to generate new comparative questions and insights, which will ultimately sustain the critical imagination necessary for alternative reading(s) of the world.

Notes

1 For more information on the role of comparative education during the Cold War, see the double issue of *European Education,* 'Post Cold-War Studies in Education', guest-edited by Gita Steiner-Khamsi and William deJong-Lambert (2006).
2 I would like to thank Noah W. Sobe for referring me to this example.

3 Perhaps the most recent 'Sputnik moment' for comparative education in the US coincided with the announcement of the 2009 PISA results, which indicated that Chinese students ranked the highest in mathematics, science and reading among 15-year-old participants from 65 participating countries. Following President Barack Obama's (2010) warning that 'in the race for the future, America is in danger of falling behind', comparative educators were once again called upon to assume their professional duty of 'fixing' the existing educational system through more targeted international comparisons and educational borrowing of 'best practices'. See also a related discussion on another 'Sputnik moment' by Jeremy Rappleye in this volume.

4 See Rappleye (2010) for a point-by-point review of the differences and a discussion about how the concept of 'transfer' is central to each of the perspectives.

References

Anderson, A. C. (1969) 'Methodology of comparative education', in M. A. Eckstein and H. J. Noah (eds) *Scientific investigations in comparative education: An anthropology illustrating the strategy and tactics of comparative education* (pp. 24–43). London: Macmillan.

Anderson-Levitt, K. M. (2003) *Local meanings, global schooling: Anthropology and world culture theory*. New York: Palgrave Macmillan.

Baker, E. L. (2010) 'Foreword', in D. K. Sharpes (ed.) *Handbook on international studies in education* (pp. ix–x). Charlotte, NC: Information Age Publishing.

Baker, D. P. and LeTendre, G. K. (2005) *National differences, global similarities: World culture and the future of schooling*. Stanford, CA: Stanford University Press.

Bakhtin, M. M. (1986) Speech genres and other late essays. (V. W. McGee, trans. and C. Emerson and M. Holquist, eds). Austin, TX: University of Texas Press.

Beech, J. (2009) 'Who is strolling through the global garden? International agencies and educational transfer', in R. Cowen and A. M. Kazamias (eds) *International handbook of comparative education* (pp. 341–358). Dordrecht: Springer.

Bereday, G. (1964) *Comparative method in education*. New York: Holt, Rinehart & Winston.

Blokker, P. (2005) 'Post-communist modernization, transition studies, and diversity in Europe'. *European Journal of Social Theory*, 8(4): 503–525.

Burawoy, M. (1999) 'Afterword', in M. Burawoy and K. Verdery (eds) *Uncertain transition: Ethnographies of change in the postsocialist world* (pp. 301–312). Lanham, MD: Rowman & Littlefield Publishers.

Burawoy, M. and Verdery, K. (eds) (1999) *Uncertain transition: Ethnographies of change in the postsocialist world*. Lanham, MD: Rowman & Littlefield Publishers.

Cowen, R. (1982) 'The place of comparative education in the educational sciences', in L. Cavicchi-Brouquet and P. Furter (eds) *Les sciences de l'éducation, perspectives et bilans Européens* (pp. 107–126). Geneva: CESE.

Cowen, R. (1996) 'Last past the post: Comparative education, modernity and perhaps post-modernity'. *Comparative Education*, 32(2): 151–170.

Cowen, R. (2000) 'Comparing futures or comparing pasts?' *Comparative Education*, 36(3): 333–342.

Cowen, R. (2006) 'Acting comparatively upon the educational world: Puzzles and possibilities'. *Oxford Review of Education*, 32(6): 561–573.

Crossley, M. (2002) 'Comparative and international education: Contemporary challenges, reconceptualization and new directions for the field'. *Current Issues in Comparative Education*, 4(2). Online. Available: www.tc.edu/cice/Issues/04.02/42crossley.pdf.

Drori, G. S. and Krücken, G. (2009) 'World society: A theory and research program in context', in G. Krücken and G. S. Drori (eds) *World society: The writings of John W. Meyer* (pp. 1–32). Oxford: Oxford University Press.

Gautherin, J. (1993) 'Marc-Antoine Jullien ("Jullien De Paris") (1775–1848)'. *Prospects: The Quarterly Review of Comparative Education*, XXIII(3/4): 757–773.

Hayhoe, R. (2000) 'Redeeming modernity'. *Comparative Education Review*, 44(4): 423–439.

Hwang, H. (2006) 'Planning development: Globalization and the shifting locus of planning', in G. S. Drori, J. W. Meyer and H. Hwang (eds) *Globalization and organization: World society and organizational change* (pp. 69–90). Oxford: Oxford University Press.

Jay, M. (2003) 'Foreword', in A. Erjavec (ed.) *Postmodernism and the postsocialist condition: Politicized art under late socialism* (pp. xv–xviii). Berkley and LA: University of California Press.

Kandel, I. L. (1933) *Comparative education*. Cambridge, MA: The Riverside Press.

Kazamias, A. and Schwartz, K. (1977) 'Intellectual and ideological perspectives in comparative education: An interpretation'. *Comparative Education Review* 21(2/3): 153–176.

Lindblad, S. and Popkewitz, T. S. (2004) *Educational restructuring: International perspectives on traveling policies*. Greenwich, CT: Information Age Publishing.

Mehta, S. (2009) 'Big stories, small stories: Beyond disputatious theory towards "multilogue"', in R. Cowen and A. M. Kazamias (eds) *International handbook of comparative education* (pp. 1189–1208). Dordrecht: Springer.

Meyer, J. W. and Ramirez, F. O. (2000) 'The world institutionalization of education', in J. Schriewer (ed.) *Discourse formation in comparative education* (pp. 111–132). Berlin: Peter Lang.

Monroe, P. (1911) *Cyclopedia of education*. New York: Teachers College Press.

Nagel, E. (1969) 'Forms of controlled inquiry', in M. A. Eckstein and H. J. Noah (eds) *Scientific investigations in comparative education: An anthropology illustrating the strategy and tactics of comparative education* (pp. 44–51). London: Macmillan.

Noah, H. (2006) 'U.S. social and educational research during the cold war: An interview with H. J. Noah by Gita Steiner-Khamsi'. *European Education: Issues and Studies*, 38(3): 9–18.

Noah, H. J. and Eckstein, M. A. (1969) *Toward a science of comparative education*. New York: Macmillan.

Novoa, A. and Yariv-Mashal, T. (2003) 'Comparative research in education: A mode of governance or a historical journey?' *Comparative Education*, 39(4): 423–438.

Outhwaite, W. and Ray, W. (2005) *Social theory and postcommunism*. Oxford, UK: Blackwell Publishing.

Perry, L. (2009) 'American academics and education for democracy in post-communist Europe', in N. Sobe (ed.) *American post-conflict educational reform: From the Spanish war to Iraq* (pp. 169–188). New York: Palgrave Macmillan.

Phillips, D. and Ochs, K. (eds) (2004) *Educational policy borrowing: Historical perspectives*. Oxford, UK: Symposium Books.

Phillips, D. and Schweisfurth, M. (2007) *Comparative and international education: An introduction to theory, method and practice*. New York: Continuum.

Popkewitz T. and Rizvi, F. (eds) (2009) *Globalization and the study of education*. Chicago: National Society for the Study of Education.

Ramaekers, S. (2006) 'No harm done: The implications for educational research of the rejection of truth'. *Journal of Philosophy of Education*, 40(2): 241–257.

Ramirez, F. O. (2003) 'The global model and national legacies', in K. Anderson-Levitt (ed.) *Local meanings, global schooling: Anthropology and world culture theory* (pp. 239–254). London: Palgrave Macmillan.

Rancière, J. (1991) *The ignorant schoolmaster: Five lessons in intellectual emancipation*. Stanford, CA: Stanford University Press.

Rappleye, J. (2006). 'Theorizing educational transfer: Toward a conceptual map of the context of cross-national attraction'. *Research in Comparative and International Education,* 1(3): 223–240.

Rappleye, J. (2007) *Exploring cross-national attraction in education: Some historical comparisons of American and Chinese attraction to Japanese education.* Oxford: Symposium Books.

Rappleye, J. (2010) 'Compasses, maps, and mirrors: Relocating episteme(s) of transfer, reorienting the comparative kosmos', in M. A. Larsen (ed.) *New thinking in comparative education: Honoring Robert Cowen* (pp. 57–80). Rotterdam: Sense Publishers.

Schriewer, J. (ed.) (2000) *Discourse formation in comparative education.* New York: Peter Lang.

Schriewer, J. (2003) 'Globalization and education: Process and discourse'. *Policy Futures in Education,* 1(2): 271–283.

Shevchenko, O. (2009) *Crisis and the everyday in postsocialist Moscow.* Bloomington, IN: Indiana University Press.

Silova, I. (2010) 'Rediscovering post-socialism in comparative education', in I. Silova (ed.) *Post-socialism is not dead: (Re)reading the global in comparative education* (pp. 1–24). Bingley, UK: Emerald.

Silova, I. (2011) 'Education and post-socialist transformations in Central Asia: Exploring margins and marginalities', in I. Silova (ed.) *Globalization on the margins: Education and post-socialist transformations in Central Asia* (pp. 1–26). Charlotte, NC: Information Age Publishing.

Silova, I. and Steiner-Khamsi, G. (eds) (2008) *How NGOs react: Globalization and education reform in the Caucasus, Central Asia and Mongolia.* Bloomfield, CT: Kumarian Press.

Sobe, N. W. (2002) 'Travel, social science and the making of nations in early 19th century comparative education', in M. Caruso and H.-E. Tenorth (eds) *Internationalisation: Comparing educational systems and semantics* (pp. 141–166). Frankfurt am Main: Peter Lang.

Stäheli, U. (2003) 'The outside of the global'. *The New Centennial Review,* 3(2): 1–22.

Steiner-Khamsi, G. (2000) 'Transfering education, displacing reforms', in J. Schriewer (ed.) *Discourse formations in comparative education* (pp. 155–187). Frankfurt am Main & New York: Lang Publishers.

Steiner-Khamsi, G. (2002) 'Re-territorializing educational import: Explorations into the politics of educational borrowing', in A. Novoa and M. Lawn (eds) *Fabricating Europe: The formation of an education space* (pp. 69–86). Utrecht: Kluwer.

Steiner-Khamsi, G. (ed.) (2004) *The global politics of educational borrowing and lending.* New York: Teachers College Press.

Steiner-Khamsi, G. (2006) 'The development turn in comparative education'. *European Education: Issues and Studies,* 38(3): 19–47.

Steiner-Khamsi, G. (2010) 'The politics and economic of comparison (Presidential address)'. *Comparative Education Review,* 54(3): 323–342.

Steiner-Khamsi, G. and deJong-Lambert, W. (eds) (2006) 'Special issue: Post–Cold War studies in education (Part I)'. *European Education: Issues and Studies,* 38(3): 1–94.

Stenning, A. and Horschelmann, K. (2008) 'History, geography and difference in the post-socialist world: Or, do we still need post-socialism?' *Antipode,* 40(2): 312–335.

Thompson, C. D. and Heathershaw, J. (2005) 'Introduction: Discourses of danger in Central Asia'. *Central Asian Survey,* 25(1): 1–4.

Wiseman, A. W., Pilton, J. and Lowe, C. J. (2010) 'International educational governance models and national policy convergence', in K. Amos (ed.) *International Educational Governance* (pp. 3–18). Bingley, UK: Emerald.

13 Teacher Licence Renewal System

Global and Local Influences on Teacher Accountability Policy in Japan

Motoko Akiba and Kazuhiko Shimizu

In 2007 a highly debated teacher accountability policy – the Teacher Licence Renewal System (TLRS) – was established in Japan. To accommodate the TLRS, the Educational Personnel Licence Law was revised for the first time since its establishment in 1949. This amendment changed the prior permanent licence for teachers to a temporary one that needs to be renewed every 10 years starting from 2009. To renew the licence, teachers are required to participate in 30 contact hours of university lectures called TLRS lectures approved by the Ministry of Education, Culture, Sports, Science and Technology (Ministry of Education hereafter). It even required the existing teachers who received a permanent licence before 2009 to renew their licences. Since April 2009, approximately 85–89,000 teachers across the country have been required to complete TLRS lectures each year to renew their licences, or else lose their teaching positions (Ministry of Education 2010a).

As a way to professionalise teachers who have been repeatedly criticised in the media, the Ministry of Education stated, 'The purpose of the Teacher Licence Renewal System is for teachers to have confidence and pride in teaching and to gain respect and trust of the general public through periodically obtaining the most recent skills and knowledge and maintaining needed quality and competence' (Ministry of Education 2008a:10).

The current study was conducted during 2010 in the second year of TLRS implementation. Based on a review of over 500 pages of policy documents, interviews of Ministry of Education officials and teachers, observations of the TLRS lectures, and a survey of 365 teachers who participated in TLRS lectures at the University of Tsukuba, a large national university in the central region surrounding Tokyo, this mixed-methods study sought to answer the following questions:

1   What are the backgrounds and processes in which the TLRS was introduced and implemented?
2   How did teachers react to the TLRS which required them to participate in 30 contact hours of TLRS lectures to renew their licences?

Teacher accountability led by market-driven, neoliberal thoughts characterises educational reforms in many countries around the world (Akiba and LeTendre 2009; Tatto 2007). Such a global trend in teacher accountability reforms has influenced

East Asian countries that are ranked among the top in international tests and where teachers have historically enjoyed a high social status. For example, Taiwan introduced the Teacher Evaluation Programme in 2005 and has encouraged all schools to implement teacher evaluation with financial support from the Ministry of Education (Liu et al. 2007). In South Korea, in addition to the nationwide implementation of teacher evaluation, teacher training programmes in teachers colleges and universities are being more rigorously evaluated and their results are tied to financial compensation from the government (Korean Ministry of Education, Science and Technology 2009). Teacher accountability discourse has also emerged in Japan since 2000 and the TLRS represents the country's first nationwide teacher accountability policy.

Such global discourses on teacher accountability, however, are transformed once they enter each national context through local interpretation and redefinitions (Phillips and Ochs 2003; Steiner-Khamsi 2004). We found that the development of the TLRS involved three stages: 1) internal criticism, 2) selection of a policy topic from reference societies using a cultural filter, and 3) development of its own policy scheme. As the sense of crisis about Japanese education and internal criticism towards teachers grew, a need for a new teacher reform emerged. The US licence renewal policies were referenced among other alternatives including teacher salary reform and teacher evaluation reform, and using a cultural filter, teacher licence renewal was considered the most culturally appropriate topic for a nationwide teacher reform. Once the topic was chosen, references to the US stopped and a new policy scheme was developed as its own policy. Thus the US origin disappeared in all the formal documents on the TLRS made available to the public.

The authors argue that in most educational reforms in Japan, international referencing is conducted only for the purpose of choosing a reform topic or general direction, not for finding the models to be followed or borrowed. This pattern of international referencing allows the country to develop its own policy that is more likely to be suitable to the national context and also accepted by the general public. However, the success of such a reform depends on the development of a new policy that fits into the existing system while adding a new element to improve the entire system. Our data show that, when the core idea of the new teacher policy – the requirement of professional development tied to the licence renewal in the TLRS in this case – does not fit into the existing teachers' professional development culture and system in Japan, it does not gain teachers' support and it is likely to fail.

In this chapter, we will provide detailed accounts of the three stages involved in the development of the TLRS described above. We will further show how the TLRS was perceived and experienced by teachers based on a survey and interviews. We will conclude the chapter with discussion of implications for international convergence and divergence.

Methods

This mixed-methods study was conducted from July to December 2010 in Tokyo and Ibaraki prefecture, which is located 50 miles north of Tokyo in the central region of Japan. First, to understand the background and development of the TLRS, we interviewed three Ministry of Education officials and reviewed over 500 pages of the minutes of TLRS-related meetings over the past 10 years. Second, to understand the lecture content, the first author attended 18 hours of TLRS lectures (12 hours of core lectures and 6 hours of elective lectures) offered by the University of Tsukuba, a major national university ranked within the top five in entrance selectivity.

Finally, to examine the perceptions and experiences of teachers, we conducted a survey of 365 teachers who participated in the TLRS lectures at the University of Tsukuba from 3 to 5 August. The survey asked teachers to indicate their level of agreement or disagreement with 14 items on three aspects of the TLRS: 1) purpose and effectiveness of the TLRS, 2) TLRS requirements, and 3) TLRS lecture content. Tables 2, 3, and 4 in the result section list these survey items. These items were developed based on the previous reports on teachers' opinions about the TLRS, and refined based on feedback from researchers in the field of teacher education and teacher policy/reforms and TLRS implementers at the University of Tsukuba. The survey also included an open-ended question that asked teachers to write down their comments or opinions about the TLRS.

This anonymous, one-page paper-and-pencil questionnaire was distributed to 513 teachers who were asked to complete the questionnaire during the break time and turn it into the survey box prepared by the researcher right after completing all the lectures at the University of Tsukuba. Out of 513 teachers, 365 turned in the questionnaire, for a response rate of 72 per cent. Among these 365 teachers, 242 teachers (66 per cent) also provided an open-ended comment or opinion about the TLRS at the end of the questionnaire. Of 365 teachers, 63 per cent were female and 37 per cent were male. Fifty per cent worked at elementary school, 20 per cent at middle school, 19 per cent at high school, and the remaining 11 per cent at various types of schools including secondary integrated schools, preschools, and special education schools. Eighty-nine per cent of them were regular teachers, 10 per cent contract-based teachers, and 1 per cent not currently working as teachers (but with a teaching licence). Among those who were teaching, the teaching experience ranged from zero to 35 years with an average of 20 years. Eighty-seven per cent of them hold a bachelor's degree, 5 per cent a junior college degree, and 8 per cent a master's degree.

After the survey we interviewed five middle school mathematics teachers to further understand their perspectives and experiences with the TLRS. We limited our interviews to middle school mathematics teachers for the purposes of: 1) understanding their perspectives on the elective maths-related lecture in which the first author participated, and 2) examining the variation in their opinions among same-subject teachers in the same type of school. These teachers were from five different middle schools. Four of these teachers were male and one was female. The teaching experience ranged from 20 to 32 years with a mean of 23 years.

Results

TLRS Development Process

Stage 1: Internal criticism

Female Judo club coach suspended for corporal punishment.
(Chiba, 1 March 2002)

Repeated teacher sex scandals, 4 teachers fired.
(Miyagi, 26 December 2004)

These are some headlines of teacher scandals reported in the media since 2000. The media coverage of teacher scandals reached its highest in 2004 with 89 cases in Asahi newspaper – a major national newspaper in Japan. These media reports influenced public opinions about the teaching profession and the sense of urgency to do something about teachers.

The most recent education reform debates in Japan since the 1990s have been characterised by the language of 'crisis'. Numerous problems including school bullying (*ijime*), school absenteeism (*futoko*), school violence (*kounai bouryoku*), and uncontrollable classrooms (*gakkyu hokai*) have been reported in the media, which created a sense of crisis in Japanese education among the general public. Around the same time, academic achievement crisis (*gakuryoku teika mondai*) became the focus of educational reforms, especially after Japan's international ranking in the Programme for International Student Assessment (PISA) dropped from 1st to 6th in mathematics literacy and 8th to 14th in reading literacy between 2000 and 2003 (Ministry of Education n.d., Takayama 2007, 2009).

In this climate, teacher quality has gathered media attention as a main problem for the educational crisis. The media started to report on teacher scandals and teachers lacking instructional ability (*shido ryoku busoku kyoshi*), which increased public concerns and criticism towards teachers. Gordon (2005) reported, based on interviews with teachers and parents, that Japanese teachers no longer receive the high social status and respect they had enjoyed in the past, mainly due to increased parental education and a changing teacher–parent relationship. The media also reported on 'monster parents' who do not hesitate to openly accuse teachers of any minor problems such as their child's minor injury during a PE class. Since 2000, the Ministry of Education has identified the teachers lacking instructional ability and required them to participate in intensive professional development for up to one year (Ministry of Education 2008b). The number of such teachers reached a high of 566 in 2004, gradually decreasing since then to 371 teachers in 2007 (Ministry of Education 2009a). Despite the public image and perceptions of teachers, these numbers account for less than 0.07 per cent of the population of over 900,000 teachers across the country.

Teacher accountability was also promoted through the influence of non-education sectors. As neoliberalism gained power in the political discourse in Japan, numerous social reforms promoted privatisation and decentralisation of social services including education. Accountability reforms including standardised national assessment and school evaluation have been implemented since 2000 and these reform trends further strengthened the need for a teacher accountability policy.

Stage 2: Selection of a policy topic from reference societies using a cultural filter

Whenever a need for an educational reform is expressed, Japan has always paid attention to educational systems in Western countries. Japan has a long history of voluntary policy borrowing. During the early Meiji era (1868–1912), the government sent a number of delegates to the US and Europe to learn from their education systems (Shibata 2004). Japan adopted the French system and some administrative structures from the US and Prussia to establish the first compulsory education system in 1872 (Shibata 2004). References to Western education, especially that of the US and Britain, and most recently of Finland, have become more frequent since the 1980s (Takayama 2009; Takayama and Apple 2008)

To respond to the urgent need for a new teacher reform, three major ideas for teacher accountability policy have emerged and been discussed by the Central Education Committee (CEC) – the committee under the Ministry of Education that consists of knowledgeable citizens including researchers, corporate leaders, and citizen group representatives. These three teacher policy issues are: 1) teacher salary, 2) teacher evaluation, and 3) teacher licence renewal.

Teacher salaries were criticised by the public for the fact that the Educational Personnel Law in Japan guarantees them to be higher than other civil servants' salary levels, including those working at local governments, police stations and fire stations. In 2006 the Teacher Salary Working Group was established under the CEC, and the group produced the report 'Future direction on teacher salary' (Ministry of Education 2007a). In this report the group concluded the importance of maintaining the Educational Personnel Law to keep the higher teacher salary level. At the same time, the group pointed out the lack of salary variability among teachers with the same number of years of teaching experience and recommended developing teacher leader positions with a higher salary scale. Furthermore, while pointing out the importance of teacher evaluation, the group made clear that the outcome-based merit-pay system used in private sectors was inappropriate for the teaching profession.

Teacher evaluation is another issue that emerged in response to the 2001 amendment of the Civil Servant System Reform Outline, which reformed the evaluation system for civil servants including teachers. The Ministry of Education requested the Prefecture Boards of Education (education agencies comparable to State Departments of Education in the US) to implement the new teacher evaluation system beginning in 2006. This new teacher evaluation system is characterised by the use of multiple data sources and multiple evaluators, and the opportunity to provide feedback to teachers (Senoo 2010).

The Ministry of Education further encouraged the use of evaluation results for professional development, promotion and salary consideration (Senoo 2010), although the decision was up to each Prefecture Board of Education. According to the Ministry of Education survey of 47 Prefecture Boards of Education and 19 Independent City Boards of Education on the implementation of the new teacher evaluation policy in

2010, 30 per cent of these educational agencies reported allowing the use of evaluation results for salary raise or reduction (Ministry of Education 2010b). No data exist on the actual implementation of salary raise or reduction, yet it is reported that such cases are extremely rare (Kariya and Kaneko 2010). In addition, no student achievement data are used as part of teacher evaluation, indicating this teacher evaluation reform is different from a popular model of outcome-based merit pay using student achievement.

Thus these two teacher accountability policy ideas were introduced and teacher evaluation methods were revised. However, neither of these policies was implemented as a nationwide policy. The responses of the Ministry of Education to these two popular teacher accountability policies are contrasted with two neighbouring countries – Taiwan and South Korea – where teacher evaluation is currently considered the most important teacher accountability policy and is nationally implemented. What caught the attention of the Ministry of Education was accountability through professional development. Teacher licence renewal policy tied to a professional development requirement was something in which the Ministry of Education saw the potential for success considering the strong professional development culture among Japanese teachers. Thus teacher licence renewal was the only reform idea that passed through the cultural filter to be considered appropriate and accepted as a national policy.

In late 2004 the Ministry of Education issued an appeal to the CEC to discuss the implementation of TLRS as a way to regain public trust in teachers. While the idea of a teacher licence renewal system was generally supported, no one knew at that point what such a system looked like. Thus the CEC requested one of its members, a university professor with expertise in US teacher policy, to produce a report on teacher licence renewal and advancement policies in the US. In early 2005 a four-page report was presented to the CEC and the US licence renewal policies with a professional development requirement, from the states of California, Florida, New York and Minnesota, were briefly introduced. The report also explained that teachers do not receive financial support or release time to attend professional development activities required for licence renewal or obtaining an advanced or secondary licence.

This four-page summary was the only document that introduced US licence renewal policies out of over 500 pages of TLRS-related documents. In this document, only four states' policies were introduced and no inquiry was made into how common this policy was across the US or regarding its effectiveness. This document provided no sufficient information to fully understand the US licence renewal policies. This was because the purpose of referencing the US policies was not to learn about the model they tried to emulate, but merely to justify that such policies exist in one of the reference societies. This justification was enough for the Ministry of Education to decide on the topic and start developing its own licence renewal policy.

Stage 3: Development of its own policy scheme

After this introduction a new TLRS working group consisting of 11 school leaders and university professors was established to discuss how to develop a licence renewal system in Japan. After 14 meetings of the TLRS working group and 20 CEC meetings over two years, in 2006 the CEC produced the report 'New teacher education and licensure system', which specified 30 contact hours of university lectures every 10 years to renew teaching licences (Ministry of Education 2006). In this final report there was no mention of the US licence renewal policies as the origin of the TLRS. In 2007 Prime Minister Abe established the Educational Renewal Council (*Kyoiku Saisei Kaigi*), consisting of 17 members including corporate and education leaders and researchers, for the purpose of establishing a new education system appropriate for the twenty-first century through various educational reforms. Their first report announced the amendment of the Educational Personnel Licence Law, which specified the licence renewal requirements under the TLRS and implementation of the TLRS beginning in 2009 (Educational Renewal Council 2007).

If the TLRS was developed as its own policy and not modelled after another, how do the TLRS and US licence renewal policies differ? There are two major differences between the US licence renewal requirements and the TLRS in Japan. First, the TLRS is a centralised national policy in which the Ministry of Education is in charge of its implementation, in contrast to the US system in which the implementers are local districts or schools working to meet the requirements set by the state departments of education. Thus the Ministry of Education determined the implementation details including who should be required to take the TLRS lectures and the specific content of TLRS lectures. The Ministry of Education probably chose this highly centralised approach for two reasons: 1) teacher licensing is a responsibility of the Ministry of Education in Japan, not of prefecture-level boards of education, and 2) the Ministry of Education needed a highly structured, centralised system to show its effort to improve teacher quality to the general public.

Second, the TLRS specified that universities are the major providers of the TLRS lectures to meet the licence renewal requirement, while in the US various providers including universities can offer professional development activities to meet the licence renewal requirements. This specification was unique to the TLRS as professional development activities are offered mainly by prefecture boards of education (offered through teacher professional development centres under the prefecture boards of education), teacher professional organisations, and school-based lesson study, not at Japanese universities. The Ministry of Education felt the need to specify the TLRS lecture content to ensure that every teacher learns the latest educational reforms and school context issues through university lectures approved by the Ministry. As universities have never offered professional development activities to practising teachers before, it was easier for the Ministry of Education to provide guidelines they could follow, rather than requiring an additional component or revising the well-established professional development curriculum developed by the prefecture-level teacher professional development centres.

Thus the specific requirements in the TLRS were developed based on the existing systems and cultures of teacher certification and professional development as well as for the Ministry of Education to improve the public image of the teaching profession through a visible, centralised approach. As a result, the TLRS is implemented quite differently from the licence renewal policies in US states.

With these organisational frameworks in mind, the CEC developed a detailed implementation plan. How to accommodate over 900,000 existing teachers for TLRS lectures across the country was a major concern for the Ministry of Education. Thus the CEC decided in its report titled 'How to implement TLRS' that approximately 10 per cent of existing teachers would take the lecture each year, completing all teachers' first licence renewal in 10 years (Ministry of Education 2007b). In 2009 those who were born in 1975, 1965 or 1955 were required to take 30 contact hours of TLRS lectures within two years (2009 to 2011).

The regulation of the TLRS lecture content provided by universities across the country was another concern for the Ministry of Education. Thus the course content was specified as shown in Table 13.1 and the Ministry of Education required the universities to go through the accreditation process to offer the TLRS lectures. Out of 30 hours, 12 hours need to be core lectures consisting of four topics: 1) teaching profession, 2) changing students, 3) educational policy, and 4) school partnership, and each topic has a required specific content (Ministry of Education 2007b). The remaining 18 hours are for elective courses on specific subject matters, instruction,

Table 13.1 Ministry of Education requirement for TLRS lectures

Courses	Required topic	Required content
Core lectures (12 hrs): Recent topics in education	Teaching profession	• Cover the recent changes in various environments surrounding schools. • Provide opportunities to reflect on teachers' work lives, and consider their own perspectives on children and education.
	Changing students	• Cover the most recent knowledge on child development such as brain science and psychology (including special education-related topics). • Cover the major issues in educating students considering the changes in their lives.
	Educational policy	• Include the content that facilitates understanding of the revisions in the course of study (national curriculum). • Cover educational law amendment and the issues on the national Central Education Committee.
	School Partnership	• Include the content that facilitates the understanding of organisational strategies to deal with various problems. • Cover emergency management at school. • Cover important instructional topics for infants, children and adolescent students.
Elective Lectures (18hrs): Instruction, student guidance and other education content matters		

Source: Translation of Table 1 on page 25 in the report by the Ministry of Education (2007a).

student guidance, and other topics. The accreditation process requires universities to submit a list of courses with details along with a checklist covering specific content areas required by the Ministry of Education and the credentials and qualifications of the lectures (Ministry of Education 2009b). In addition to the content requirement, the universities are required to give written exams on the lecture content and issue a TLRS lecture completion certificate to those who pass the exams. According to the TLRS steering committee at the University of Tsukuba, almost all teachers pass the exams and the other universities have similarly high pass rates.

In summary, despite the US origin of the TLRS, none of the finalised reports released to the policy implementers and teachers mentioned this origin. The TLRS was introduced as a new policy that addresses the need for improving teacher quality and gaining public trust in teachers. As a result, no teacher knew about the TLRS's origin. None of the 242 teachers who provided comments in the survey or five teachers we interviewed mentioned the US when they expressed their opinions about the TLRS.

Government action to conceal or obscure the international origin of an educational reform was reported by Spreen (2004), who studied outcome-based education in South Africa. Spreen found that governments concealed the international origin for the purpose of establishing local ownership and relevance to the particular national contexts. In the case of the TLRS, while it was more likely to be accepted and supported by the general public if it was presented as its own policy rather than as an imported or borrowed policy, there is no evidence to show the government purposefully concealed the US origin of the TLRS. There was only a four-page summary of US licence renewal requirements in four states, and no investigation into other states or whether these requirements were effective was conducted. The purpose of this referencing was just to show that it exists in another reference country in order to push the agenda; no more information was needed as policymakers are aware of the major contextual differences between the US and Japan. Since the TLRS was developed as its own policy, there was no need for the government to mention the US licence renewal policies in introducing this new policy to the general public.

Teacher Responses to the TLRS

Teachers' opinions about the TLRS

How did teachers respond to the TLRS developed as its own policy? Despite the fact that the TLRS was designed considering the national context, teachers were generally not happy with the core idea of being required to renew their licences. They received their permanent licences and went through the competitive process to become teachers. In Japan teachers receive licences after completing four years of teacher education courses including student teaching. Receiving a teaching licence is not difficult in that sense, yet becoming a teacher is another story. In 2007, 10,100 preservice teachers received a teaching licence and took the teacher hiring exam given by each hiring prefecture, and only 3,200 teachers were hired as regular teachers for a success rate of 32 per cent (Shimizu et al. 2008). Although the success rates have increased from 12 per cent in 2000 due to the decreasing number of teacher education students, teaching positions are still considered difficult to obtain.[1]

Table 13.2 Teacher opinions about the purpose and effectiveness of TLRS (N = 365)

		*Mean**	*SD*	*Min.*	*Max.*
1	It does not make sense that we are required to attend university lectures to renew our licences.	4.2	0.9	1	5
2	Teacher quality will improve as a result of the TLRS.	2.8	1.0	1	5
3	We need the TLRS to professionalise teachers.	2.4	1.0	1	5
4	We do not need the TLRS because we already have many professional development opportunities.	3.9	1.0	1	5
5	I don't think the TLRS will succeed.	3.9	0.9	1	5

Note: * Based on 1 = strongly disagree, 2 = disagree, 3 = neither, 4 = agree, 5 = strongly agree.

Thus teachers are understandably not pleased with their treatment by the media or with the establishment of the TLRS to gain public trust in teachers. Table 13.2 presents the level of agreement or disagreement with the statements regarding TLRS purpose and effectiveness. We can see that most teachers agree with the negative statements about the system such as 'It does not make sense that we are required to attend lectures to renew our licences' (mean of 4.2 on the scale of 1 = strongly disagree to 5 = strongly agree), 'We do not need the TLRS because we already have many professional development opportunities' (mean of 3.9), and 'I don't think the licence renewal system will succeed' (mean of 3.9). In contrast, most teachers' responses to positive statements such as 'Teacher quality will improve as a result of the TLRS' (mean of 2.8), and 'We need the TLRS to professionalise teachers' (mean of 2.4) were between 'disagree' to 'neither'.

Such disagreement with the TLRS was expressed in the written comments in the survey. Many questioned the purpose and effectiveness of the TLRS:

> I don't understand the purpose of TLRS. If it is for improving teacher quality, they should incorporate university lectures into 6th year and 11th year professional development requirements (rather than as a licence renewal system).
>
> (Middle school teacher with seven years of teaching experience)

A recent nationally representative survey of teachers and parents revealed that only 9.6 per cent of teachers believe that public trust and respect of teachers will be improved by the TLRS (Ministry of Education 2010c: 16). More importantly, only 31 per cent of parents believe that the TLRS will improve public trust and respect of teachers (Ministry of Education 2010c: 16).

Many teachers also questioned the fact that only teachers are required to renew their licences while other professions including medical doctors and lawyers are not required to do so. One teacher stated, 'I am against the TLRS when there is no renewal system for medical licences'. In the written comments in the survey, many also expressed frustration with the policymakers who blame teachers for all educational problems and who do not understand that they are constantly engaged in professional development.

I know that this system was created in response to teachers' low instructional ability. But I have never neglected professional development. I have been constantly engaged in various professional development activities. I don't understand why they (policymakers) don't get it.

(Elementary school teachers with 30 years of teaching experience)

The interview results also revealed that experienced teachers regularly participate in professional development in various formats. All five interviewed middle school mathematics teachers with teaching experience of 20 to 30 years were taking leadership roles such as professional development chair, grade-level chair, career placement chair, and special education chair. They are required to participate in leadership professional development seminars offered by the Ibaraki Prefecture Board of Education. In addition, there are meetings by subject-specific teacher research groups; for these teachers, there is a mathematics teacher research group that meets five or six times a year. The Prefecture Board of Education and local board of education also offer many professional development seminars on various subject topics, classroom management, and instructional technology, among others, for teachers to attend on a voluntary basis.

Inside schools, there are subject committees in which teachers meet frequently within each subject area during regular school hours to discuss instructional approaches or materials. Each school also has a research theme and organises professional development activities based on that theme. For example, in school A the current year's theme was 'instruction for student understanding' (*wakaru jugyo*) and each subject teacher committee analysed student assessment results and discussed instructional approaches. In addition, to involve all teachers the school decided to conduct a lesson study on ethics (*dotoku*) – a subject all homeroom teachers are required to teach. In school B the theme was 'integrated education', a new plan to integrate elementary and middle school in one building. This school conducted lesson studies in several subject areas throughout the year. In school C the theme was 'learning from one another' (*manabiai*) and a lesson was offered every month for teacher observation and to discuss the approaches among teachers.

These teachers are thus engaged in various professional development activities on a weekly basis. Being required to take 30 hours of university lectures beyond their weekly professional development activities for the purpose of improving teacher quality was upsetting to many teachers. Such teacher disagreement with the system is amplified when the system places a burden on teachers in terms of cost and time. Table 13.3 presents the results on teacher opinions about TLRS requirements in terms of time commitment, financial obligation, and test-taking requirement.

Many teachers agreed with the statements on the challenges the system creates such as a difficulty in finding time to attend the lectures (mean of 3.9) and financial burdens including tuition, lodging, and transportation (mean of 4.3). Many also reported that 30 hours of lectures are too many (mean of 3.9). In addition, many agreed that there is no need for a TLRS exam given to teachers each day after six hours of lectures (mean of 3.9).

National statistics reported that Japanese middle school teachers are spending an average of 11 hours each day at school (Ministry of Education 2007c). They also come to school at weekends to supervise club activities. All the other existing professional

Table 13.3 Teacher opinions about TLRS requirements (N = 365)

		Mean*	SD	Min.	Max.
1	It is difficult to find time to attend lectures.	3.9	1.0	1	5
2	This system causes a major financial burden including tuition, lodging, and transportation.	4.3	0.9	1	5
3	30 hrs of lectures is too much.	3.9	1.0	1	5
4	I don't think we need a TLRS exam.	3.9	1.1	1	5

Note: * Based on 1 = strongly disagree, 2 = disagree, 3 = neither, 4 = agree, 5 = strongly agree.

development activities are integrated into teachers' regular schedules. All of these professional development activities are free to them. Thus the TLRS, which is not integrated into teachers' work schedule and requires them to pay at least 30,000 yen ($350), is considered to be too much of a burden on teachers.

In addition to these burdens, many expressed the opinion that the cumbersome online application process took them all day to complete. One teacher stated, 'I wish the registration process could be a lot simpler. I spent all day facing a desk top to complete the registration for the TLRS courses' (elementary school teacher with 31 years of experience). This was the first time for teachers to individually register for professional development online. All other outside-school professional development (PD) activities are coordinated by school principals and board of education officials, so teachers simply need to communicate their PD participation plan to their principals. This also allows the principals to coordinate the work schedule of the participating teachers by asking other contract teachers to cover their teaching and other duties.

Teacher opinions about TLRS lectures

In contrast to their negative opinions about the system itself, teacher opinions about the lectures were generally positive. Many agreed that they gained new knowledge (mean of 3.8) and expanded their knowledge as a teacher (3.8). They also reported that they were glad to attend these lectures (3.7) and satisfied with the lecture content (3.7). Slightly fewer teachers agreed with the statement 'I learned something useful for my daily practice' with the responses falling between 'neither' and 'agree'. Yet overall, their opinions about the TLRS lectures were positive.

Such positive experience was expressed during the teacher interviews.

Q: What did you think about the TLRS lecture, 'History and Culture of Mathematics'?
A: It was very interesting. It is not about whether you can use the knowledge or not. It was a high-level content, so quite stimulating to me. I know some people would say this is useless, but I think useful content is not always interesting. Compared to the professional development offered by the Board of Education, it was very interesting because of the new content introduced in this lecture.

(Middle school maths teacher with 20 years of experience)

Table 13.4 Teacher opinions about TLRS lecture contents (N = 365)

		Mean*	SD	Min.	Max.
1	I gained new knowledge through the lecture.	3.8	1.0	1	5
2	I could expand my knowledge as a teacher.	3.8	0.9	1	5
3	I learned something useful for my daily practice.	3.4	1.0	1	5
4	I am glad to attend these lectures.	3.7	1.0	1	5
5	I am satisfied with the overall lecture content.	3.7	0.9	1	5

Note: * Based on 1 = strongly disagree, 2 = disagree, 3 = neither, 4 = agree, 5 = strongly agree.

Our observations of 18 hours of lectures taught by 10 different professors also confirmed their sincerity and sense of responsibility to offer high quality courses. They indeed developed these courses for experienced teachers, rather than just using the previous lectures for pre-service teachers. Such positive experience with the TLRS lectures made some teachers reconsider their perspectives toward the TLRS.

> I was 100 per cent against the TLRS, but the three lectures I attended were all interesting and useful for me. I don't like the requirement of 'take the TLRS lectures or lose the licence', but I feel conflicted because I couldn't have this learning opportunity without this system.
>
> (Middle school teacher with 10 years of experience)

In summary, a majority of teachers were against the TLRS as a system, yet their experiences with the TLRS lectures were generally positive. The TLRS was also the first national policy that challenged teachers' perceptions of the teaching profession and caused a major burden on their work lives. Their reactions to this system are based on the culturally and organisationally established professional development system and culture teachers that have been accustomed to for many years.

Discussion

This study uncovered the three stages involved in the development of the TLRS in Japan: 1) internal criticism, 2) selection of a policy topic from reference societies using a cultural filter, and 3) development of its own policy scheme. International criticism towards teachers led the Ministry of Education to implement a new teacher reform to gain back public trust in teachers. Three teacher accountability policy topics – 1) teacher salary, 2) teacher evaluation, and 3) teacher licence renewal – were considered, and only teacher licence renewal passed the cultural filter to be accepted as a national policy accompanied by legislative requirements.

The reference to the US licence renewal policies was made for the purpose of choosing and justifying the policy topic, not for the purpose of borrowing or importing the policy. Thus there was no need to carefully examine the US policies and the US origin quickly disappeared in the development process. The final documents released to the public included no mention of the US origin, and no teacher was informed of such origin. It was not the intentional concealment of the origin as explained in the South Africa case reported by Spreen (2004), however. Because the Ministry of Education developed the TLRS as its own, they saw no need to mention the US policies. It was a natural action not to mention the US as US policies were not even carefully examined or understood enough to be borrowed or imported. As a result, the TLRS was developed as a highly structured system with a detailed implementation plan, in contrast to the decentralised licence renewal systems implemented in most of the US states.

Despite the fact that the TLRS was developed considering the national context, a teacher survey and interviews revealed three critical issues the TLRS ignored despite the policymakers' awareness of them: 1) the fact that Japanese teachers are constantly engaged in professional development activities, 2) the fact that teachers are overworked, and 3) the TLRS was not designed to be integrated into the established professional development system and culture.

First, Japanese teachers engage in an extensive amount and range of professional development activities both outside and inside school (Akiba and LeTendre 2009; Shimahara 2002). Japanese teachers' engagement in lesson study is internationally known (Lewis 2002; Lewis et al. 2004; Stigler and Hiebert 1999) and many countries are attempting to establish this teacher-led professional development opportunity. Our interviews with teachers further revealed various types of professional development activities they are engaged in on a weekly basis. Thus the assumption of the TLRS that 30 hours of university lectures once every 10 years will improve teacher quality is ignoring the hundreds of hours they are spending on professional development each year. In addition, a majority of parents do not think that this system will improve teacher quality despite the fact that the Ministry of Education established this system to gain back public trust in teachers (Ministry of Education 2010c).

Second, the fact that teachers are overworked was not considered in the TLRS design and as a result created an extra burden on teachers. Many teachers struggled to find five days out of their tight schedule to complete 30 hours of lectures and they did so by giving up their weekends. They needed to find and register for courses that matched their schedule, which was often difficult. Some teachers needed to travel to another prefecture because all the courses were full or they missed the registration deadline for the nearby university. Even during the summer time when their schedule is less intensive, they were worried about who would supervise students on club activities and train them for major sports competitions while they were gone for the TLRS lectures. Thus the TLRS placed a major burden on teachers by forcing them to squeeze their already tight work schedule.

Finally, the existing professional development activities for teachers were already well established and integrated into teachers' work schedules when the TLRS was introduced. In 2002 a 40-day professional development programme was established for teachers in their 11th year. This intensive professional development for teachers after 10 years of teaching occurs during their regular work schedule. As a legislative requirement, all the expenses are covered by the prefecture board of education. Each school also has a system to allow teachers to participate in professional development offered by the prefecture or local board of education based on their interests or meetings by teacher-led subject research groups. All the professional development activities at school are integrated into the regular work schedule as well. Thus the TLRS was introduced without considering its integration into the existing professional development system and culture. If the TLRS was integrated into the 11th year professional development programme by offering university courses along with other programmes offered by the prefecture board of education, the system could avoid placing a major burden on teachers in terms of time commitment and expenses.

Thus even if the Ministry of Education developed the TLRS as its own policy, it failed to consider these critical issues. This is because the core logic of accountability manifested in the TLRS structure does not go well with the teacher professional culture in Japan. When the Ministry of Education considered possible reform directions, they chose only teacher accountability reforms: teacher salary, teacher evaluation and teacher licence renewal. They were aware of the teachers' extensive engagement in professional development and teachers' harsh working conditions, yet they did not consider other alternatives such as communicating the teachers' engagement in extensive professional development activities to the public or improving working conditions. They were influenced by the global trend towards teacher accountability because the teacher policies of the major reference societies are characterised by the logic of teacher accountability.

This shows the power of global trends to influence the policy direction in many countries around the world. Neighbouring East Asian countries including Taiwan and South Korea are engaged in teacher accountability policies whether it is through teacher evaluation, teacher education or initial licence or renewal policies. The policy development process used by Japan, however, characterised by developing the nation's own policy, leaves plenty of room for the new policy to be successful. Teacher responses to the TLRS revealed that they value university-based professional development, and this could be integrated into the existing professional development requirements for teachers, not as part of licence renewal. In this way the TLRS could be accepted by the teachers while improving the existing professional development system by adding the new element of university-based professional development.

The policy success depends on whether each country stayed focused on the central goal of improving teacher quality and developed a policy that can be integrated into the existing system and culture, while adding a new element to improve the entire system. When a country is blinded by the logic of accountability as a quick fix to a problem, as in the case of the TLRS in Japan, the policy will only have negative consequences for the teachers and students.

The examination of the TLRS development process in Japan produced important implications for the scholarly debate of global convergence or divergence. If we assume that many developed countries without direct pressure for policy borrowing tied to financial aid use a process of international referencing similar to Japan, then teacher reform topics would look similar across these developed countries due to the fact that most countries share the same Western countries as reference societies (mainly the US, Britain, France, Germany or Finland). There is sufficient evidence across the globe that teacher reforms are characterised by accountability logic whether it is through teacher evaluation, teacher education, compensation systems or licensure systems. Just by looking at the major teacher reform topics one can see the international convergence around teacher accountability reforms.

However, if the international referencing is conducted only for the purpose of choosing the topic or general direction as in Japan, the actual nature of the policies and their implementations and outcomes would largely differ across countries. This indicates divergence in teacher characteristics and practice as a result of teacher policies and reforms. Understanding the degree to which the content, implementation and outcomes of teacher policies differ across countries would require more in-depth country studies that reveal the policy development and implementation processes and outcomes.

This study shows that there was room for the TLRS to be developed differently if the Ministry of Education had paid closer attention to the existing professional development system and culture of teachers, instead of pushing the accountability agenda as a quick fix to solve the perceived problem of teacher quality. Thus the extent to which divergence could occur depends on each country's willingness to pursue the fundamental issue of improving teacher quality and developing a policy suitable for local contexts, instead of being influenced by the global trend of promoting teacher accountability logic.

Acknowledgement

We would like to thank Mr Masahiro Miyata and Mr Masato Suzuki in the TLRS Promotion Committee at the University of Tsukuba for their generous assistance with the survey and teacher interviews. Also, the assistance with data collection and entry from two graduate students, Mr Hiroyuki Sawada and Ms Kuanysh Tastanbekova, is greatly appreciated.

Note

1 The number of teacher education students decreased probably owing to two reasons: 1) an overall decreased number of college students due to the lower birth rates and 2) decreased popularity of teaching positions due to a difficult work schedule and many recent educational problems including school bullying, student absenteeism, and uncontrollable classrooms.

References

Akiba, M. and LeTendre, G. (2009) *Improving Teacher Quality: the U.S. Teaching Force in Global Context*, New York: Teachers College Press.

Educational Renewal Council. (2007) *Shakai Sougakaride Kyouiku Saiseiwo: Koukyouikuheno Daiippo [Educational Renewal as a Social Project: the First Step toward Educational Renewal]*, Tokyo: Educational Renewal Council.

Gordon, J. A. (2005) 'The crumbling pedestal: changing images of Japanese teachers', *Journal of Teacher Education*, 56: 459–70.

Kariya, T. and Kaneko, M. (2010) *Kyoin Hyokano Shakaigaku [Sociology of Teacher Evaluation]*, Tokyo: Iwanami Shoten.

Korean Ministry of Education, Science and Technology. (2009) *Major Policies and Plans for 2010*, Seoul: Korean Ministry of Education, Science and Technology.

Lewis, C. (2002) *Lesson Study: a Handbook for Teacher-led Instructional Change*, Philadelphia: Research for Better Schools, Inc.

Lewis, C., Perry, R. and Hurd, J. (2004) 'A deeper look at lesson study', *Educational Leadership*, 61: 18–22.

Liu, M., Huang, J. and Kang, Y. (2007) 'An analysis of teacher evaluation system in Taiwan', *Contemporary Educational Research Quarterly*, 15: 37–68.

Ministry of Education. (2006) *Kongono Kyouin Yousei Menkyo Seidono Arikatani Tsuite [New Teacher Education and Licensure System]*, Tokyo: Ministry of Education.

Ministry of Education. (2007a) *Kongono Kyouin Kyuyono Arikata Tsuite [Future Direction on Teacher Salary]*, Tokyo: Ministry of Education.

Ministry of Education. (2007b) *Kyouin Menkyo Koshinseino Unyouni Tsuite [How to Implement TLRS]*, Tokyo: Ministry of Education.

Ministry of Education. (2007c) *Kyouin Kinmu Jittai Tyousa [Teacher Working Condition Survey]*, Tokyo: Ministry of Education.

Ministry of Education. (2008a) *Miryokuaru Kyoinwo Motomete [Seeking Ideal Teachers]*, Tokyo: Ministry of Education.

Ministry of Education. (2008b) *Shidoga Futekisetsuya Kyoinni Taisuru Jinjikanri Shisutemuno Gaidorain [Guidelines for Human Resource Management System for Teachers with Problematic Instructional Quality]*, Online. Available HTTP: www.mext.go.jp/a_menu/shotou/jinji/08022711.htm (accessed 23 September 2010).

Ministry of Education. (2009a) *Monbu Kagaku Hakusho 2008 [Ministry of Education White Paper 2008]*, Online. Available HTTP: www.mext.go.jp/b_menu/hakusho/html/hpab200801/index.htm (accessed 23 September 2010).

Ministry of Education. (2009b) *Menkyo Koshin Konshu No Nintei Shintou Youryou [Teacher Licence Renewal Lecture Accreditation Process]*, Online. Available HTTP: www.mext.go.jp/a_menu/shotou/koushin/008/1267120.htm (accessed 1 September 2010).

Ministry of Education. (2010a) *Kyoin Menkyo Koshin Sei No Gaiyo [Summary of Teacher Licence Renewal System]*, Tokyo: Ministry of Education.

Ministry of Education. (2010b) *Kyoin Hyoka Shisutemuno Torikumi Jokyo [Implementation Status of Teacher Evaluation System]*, Tokyo: Ministry of Education.

Ministry of Education. (2010c) *Kyouinno Shishitsu Kojo Housakuno Minaoshi Oyobi Kyouin Menkyo Koushinsei No Kouka Kenshouni Kakawaru Tyousa Shuukei Kekka [Survey Results on Reconsideration of Teacher Quality Improvement Approaches and Effectiveness of TLRS]*, Tokyo: Ministry of Education.

Ministry of Education. (n.d.) *PISA OECD Seitono Gakushu Toutatsudo Tyousa [PISA OECD Student Achievement Assessment]*, Online. Available HTTP: www.mext.go.jp/b_menu/toukei/data/pisa/index.htm (accessed 23 September 2010)

Phillips, D. and Ochs, K. (2003) 'Processes of policy borrowing in education: some analytical and explanatory devices', *Comparative Education*, 39: 451–61.

Senoo, W. (2010) 'Zenkokuno "kyoinhyoka" jisshi doukoukara [Nation-wide implementation trend of 'teacher evaluation'], in T. Kariya and M. Kaneko (ed.) *Kyoin Hyokano Shakaigaku [Sociology of Teacher Evaluation]*, Tokyo: Iwanami Shoten.

Shibata, M. (2004) 'Educational borrowing in Japan in the Meiji and Post-War eras', in D. Phillips and K. Ochs (ed.) *Educational Policy Borrowing: Historical Perspectives*, Oxford: Symposium Books.

Shimahara, N. K. (2002) 'Teacher professional development in Japan', in G. DeCoker (ed.) *National Standards and School Reform in Japan and the United States*, New York: Teachers College Press.

Shimizu, K., Akao, K., Arai, A., Ito, T. and Sato, H. (2008) *Saishin Kyouiku Detabukku [Databook of Educational Statistics]*, Tokyo: Jijitsushinsya.

Spreen, C. A. (2004) 'Appropriating borrowed policies: outcomes-based education in South Africa', in G. Steiner-Khamsi (ed.) *The Global Politics of Educational Borrowing and Lending*, New York: Teachers College Press.

Steiner-Khamsi, G. (2004) 'Globalization in education: real or imagined?', in G. Steiner-Khamsi (ed.) *The Global Politics of Educational Borrowing and Lending*, New York: Teachers College Press.

Stigler, J. W. and Hiebert, J. (1999) *The Teaching Gap: Best Ideas from the World's Teachers for Improving Education in the Classroom*, New York: Free Press.

Takayama, K. (2007) 'A nation at risk crosses the pacific: transnational borrowing of the U.S. crisis discourse in the debate on education reform in Japan', *Comparative Education Review*, 51: 423–46.

Takayama, K. (2009) 'Politics of externalization in reflexive times: reinventing Japanese education reform discourses through Finnish PISA success', *Comparative Education Review*, 54: 51–75.

Takayama, K. and Apple, M. W. (2008) 'The cultural politics of borrowing: Japan, Britain, and the narrative of educational crisis', *British Journal of Sociology of Education*, 29: 289–301.

Tatto, M. T. (2007) *Reforming Teaching Globally*, Oxford: Symposium Books.

14 The Transformation of Education Policy in Israel

Julia Resnik

By comparing two large-scale reforms (Fullan 2000) in Israel – the 1968 reform and the proposed 2004 Dovrat reform – I intend to evaluate the transformations that took place in the country's process of educational policy making. Since the reforms in Israel strongly resemble reforms undertaken in many other countries around the world, the comparison of these two reforms will shed light on the evolution of educational policies globally.

In Israel, as in many countries, post-World War II education reforms focused on the expansion of compulsory education, the elimination of entrance exams for post-elementary education and the creation of lower secondary schools. The main target of Israel's first large-scale reform in 1968 was the transformation of the structure of the education system. This structural reform was developed by educational expert Moshe Smilansky, who was connected to global education networks, and whose research focussed on the 'inequality of opportunity'. He was strongly supported by Minister of Education Zalman Aran (Labour party), who succeeded in passing the reform in the Knesset and implementing it based on the need to solve the country's 'ethnic gap' social problem.

In 2004 the National Task Force for the Advancement of Education in Israel (Task Force) submitted its report. The reform proposed by the Task Force was similar to reforms of education systems throughout the world since the 1980s, including elements such as decentralisation, the search for efficiency based on cost/benefit ratios, school autonomy, parent choice, the incorporation of a managerial approach and greater accountability in schools, and the evaluation and assessment of student achievements. The main objective of this 2004 large-scale reform was to shift the mode of regulation of the education system from a bureaucratic to a post-bureaucratic managerial regime (Maroy 2008). The Task Force Committee was headed by Shlomo Dovrat, a high-tech philanthropic entrepreneur who was strongly supported by the former Prime Minister Ariel Sharon, his Minister of Education Limor Livnat (*Kadima* right-centre party) and the Minister of Finance Binyamin Netanyahu (*Likkud* party). This managerial reform was intended to solve the social problem of the 'interstate achievement gap' – referring to the low results of Israeli students in international surveys – formulated by the economist Ben David; it was not realised due to political changes that included the appointment of Yuli Tamir (Labour party) as head of the Ministry of Education.

Although the reform suggested in 2004 was not implemented, the neo-Weberian model I developed assumes that a large part of the reformist activity took place prior to 2004. This analytical approach views the reform as a long process of construction of a reformist discourse and focusses on the pervasion of this discourse into the academic and public arena. Whether the reform was partially or totally executed is less significant. The neo-Weberian theoretical model I employ includes three key concepts: reformist discourse structuration, knowledge producers as a status group and education global networks. The major advantage of this model is the ability to compare between two apparently dissimilar reforms, which in turn enables scholars to observe changes in the mechanisms that shape education policy.

My analysis shows similarities, but also important differences, between the two reforms. The lever of both reforms has been economic improvement. Nonetheless, the social problems and the discourse used to justify the reforms were dissimilar: the 'ethnic gap' and 'inequality of opportunity' in the 1968 reform and the 'interstate achievement gap' in the proposed reform of 2004. These social problems point to the first transformation in the reformist dynamic: a shift from a discourse focussed on social concerns – equality of opportunity – to a discourse that stressed economic competence between countries and the need to manage education in an efficient manner. In addition, the social objects that embodied each reform have a completely different nature. In the 1968 structural reform the social objects included comprehensive schools, streaming, school zoning maps and curriculum for lower secondary education, and primarily counselling and guidance services, all of them aimed at enabling access to secondary education by larger sections of the population. The proposed 2004 managerial reform was prompted by social objects such as decentralisation, accountability, efficiency, parent choice and school autonomy, constructed at schools of education but also economics and public policy departments. These social objects encouraged a discourse that prioritised managerial knowledge and paved the way for Dovrat's nomination as head of the Task Force Committee. Only after the submission of the report and instigation by the Dovrat Committee was the main social object 'evaluation, standards and measurement' instituted. The nature of the social objects shows a disciplinary change: education and social studies, and principally the sociology of education, have been displaced from reformist discourse structuration and replaced by public policies and management studies. An additional key transformation raised by the comparison concerns the character of reformist networks. In the past reformist structural networks included politicians, policy makers and knowledge producers. Although knowledge producers and political allies are still important actors in reformist networks, NGOs and philanthropic entrepreneurs play an increasingly significant role in the promotion of managerial reforms. This evolution sheds light on the new dynamics of policy borrowing and lending in education. While in the past social objects were constructed mainly by scholars who borrowed them from other education systems, in the present the 'evaluation, standards and measurement' social object has been borrowed by philanthropic entrepreneurs. On the other hand, the rising power of these entrepreneurs reflects the growing disempowerment of the state in educational policy making.

Two Different Reforms

The 1968 reform, also called the Integration reform, prolonged compulsory education until the age of 16 and exchanged the dual system (8 + 4) for a three-tiered system (6 + 3 + 3). Selection to secondary schools through entry examinations and through the National Survey Test was cancelled, allowing all pupils to continue on to lower secondary education; students were assigned by school counsellors to different streams (grouping) according to their past records. The counselling and guidance service determined which track (academic, vocational or agricultural) pupils would follow for their upper secondary education, according to their aptitudes, inclinations and wishes. The reform aimed at democratising the education system by reinforcing equality of educational opportunity. Encouraging a larger number of children to stay longer at school, entailing the improvement of the level of education of the population, was supposed to enhance economic growth.

Ben Gurion, the first Prime Minister of Israel, believed, like many modernist leaders of the 1950s, that education was the key to national development and economic improvement. For this purpose he appointed the public Prawer Committee to examine the expansion of compulsory education until the age of 16 or even 18. Aran, the Minister of Education at that time (1955–1960, 1963–1969), asked the members of the Committee to add the question of structural change to their debate.

In 1965, the Prawer Committee ended its term of office with the recommendation to extend compulsory education by one more year to the age of 15; the recommendation was premised on changing the educational structure. As soon as the recommendations were published the Primary Teachers Union launched an attack on the Committee's conclusions, undermining implementation of the reform. In 1966 the Knesset appointed a parliamentary committee (the Rimalt Committee) to investigate structural reform of the elementary and post-elementary education system in Israel (Resnik 2007). In July 1968 the Knesset approved the Committee's recommendations and immediately launched a massive and accelerated implementation of the reform.

The reform proposed by the Task Force in 2004 recommended the decentralisation of the system and the reorganisation of the Ministry of Education into three administrative echelons: the Ministry of Education, regional education administrations (REA) and the educational institutions themselves. The functions of the Ministry of Education would be policy making, budgeting and the monitoring and evaluation of the education system's performance based on standards set for achievements and abilities expected of the students. The REAs would run the schools in their region instead of the State. Pedagogical, administrative and budgetary autonomy would be granted to schools, led by the principals as leaders of educational activity. Public education under the responsibility of the State would be the backbone of the education system. All schools belonging to the different communities, and even independent Haredi schools, would teach the minimal national curriculum in order to be awarded public funding. Parents and children would be given the opportunity to choose an educational institution, within limits (Task Force, English summary 2004). All these measures were supposed to increase the quality of education for Israel's large population in order to improve the country's global competitiveness.

In light of the poor results of Israeli students in the 2002 PISA survey, Minister of Education Limor Livnat asked Shlomo Dovrat, a high-tech entrepreneur, to head a committee in order to examine the education system and suggest ways of improving it. After a few months of intensive work and the unconditional support of Prime Minister Ariel Sharon and Minister of Finances Binyamin Netanyahu, in 2003 the Task Force made public an interim report. Thereafter, the secondary education teachers' union launched a furious campaign attacking the report. In 2004 the Task Force submitted its final report and Livnat was convinced that she would be able to impose the reform despite teacher disapproval. In October 2004 the government coalition collapsed when the right wing party (*Israel Betenu*) abandoned the government because of Sharon's announcement to retreat from the Gaza strip. In March 2005 a new government including the Labour party was constituted and Yuli Tamir (Labour party), appointed Minister of Education, did not pursue the execution of the reform envisaged by Livnat.

It should be noted that in both cases, teachers' unions boycotted the reforms fostered by the ministers of education. However, the political stability of the 1960s permitted the final implementation of the 1968 reform whereas the political instability of the 2000s thwarted the Dovrat reform.

This section outlined the 1968 and the 2004 reforms and pointed to their political circumstances and to their main actors. However, both reforms were the result of a more complex dynamic that cannot be reduced to the will of a few local political actors. A theoretical neo-Weberian framework that also takes into account the knowledge producers and the influence of local and global education networks reveals the myriad of actors involved in each reform and the deeper implications of prospective reforms, including the long-term impact of the reforms on education policy mechanisms.

A Neo-Weberian Theoretical Perspective

Reformist Discourse Structuration

Wittrock et al. (1991) point to the increasingly significant role of the social sciences in policy making. They argue that after the late 1950s and 1960s, modernising political and social groupings that favoured more or less far-reaching reforms gradually came to embrace the notion that political action meant to alleviate the 'social question' (social problem) should be based on extensive, systematic and empirical analysis. At that time, new institutional mechanisms to secure appropriate links between social science research and policy making were established. Although similar in nature, the relationship between scholars and political actors was structured differently in each society. Wittrock et al. (1991) use 'discourse structuration' to explain the process of the historical institutionalisation of social science discourse into state institutions, namely, universities or national institutes.

The discourse structuration at the base of the reforms can be reconstructed by tracking the way the reformist discourse and the social problems have developed. Education policy responds to socio-political pressures but also to discourse structuration, meaning the scientific tradition of local institutions and the 'social problems' that have been institutionalised in knowledge production institutions over time. In recent decades, budgetary reductions and increasing community involvement in education decisions encouraged the participation of a new kind of institution – philanthropic associations – into discourse structuration.

Educational Knowledge Producers as a Status Group

Rather than being mere intermediaries between social reality and policy makers, knowledge producers (social scientists and experts), driven by their status group interests, actually emerged as the main agents of education reforms. As Max Weber (1968) stated, status groups are determined by the distribution of social honour or prestige, since people do not strive for power only for the sake of self-enrichment, and the motivation for power is frequently conditioned by the social honour it entails. The status group concept unveils a power factor usually disguised in impersonal forces, such as economic power or world culture. Advancing avant-garde theories and the homogenisation of education in a global context allow knowledge producers to further their professional careers. Following Bourdieu (1983), I argue that social scientists who are part of knowledge production try to impose their educational models locally in order to improve their academic capital, which in turn can be transformed into political and/or economic capital. Similarly, knowledge producers who participate in reformist networks – most of them global – are primarily motivated by their own professional interests, since advancing a reformist discourse means, simultaneously, increasing their own academic capital. By formulating social problems at the national level through the glocalisation of global educational models, encouraging the expansion of reformist networks, and becoming active partners of policy makers, knowledge producers enhance both the reformist discourse and their academic career at the same time.

Global Education Networks

According to Callon and Latour's (1992) studies of the ways in which scientific networks operate, objects of science owe their existence to actor-networks that include scientists, equipment, skills and theories. Similarly, objects of social sciences or 'social objects', such as 'counselling and guidance' or 'parent choice', owe their existence to reformist networks that include knowledge producers, policy makers, NGOs, psychological, social and economic theories (cultural deprivation, school based management) and statistical methods. Callon and Latour (1992) maintain that the success of the scientific approach is due to the ability of researchers to build a large and consistent network. In a similar vein, the success of education reforms in Israel and elsewhere has to be understood as a consequence of the ability of reformist actors – policy makers, knowledge producers and, more recently, philanthropists – to construct a large and influential reformist network. The recruitment of policy makers to their cause contributes to the funding of their projects and departments, and the alliance to scholars belonging to global networks contributes to the expansion of their local networks. By constructing their careers through international connections, knowledge producers contribute to the reinforcement of global education networks, whether they are centred in American universities or in intergovernmental organisations (UNESCO, OECD, World Bank), and the propagation of the educational models they diffuse.

The Construction of Reformist Discourses

The Structural Reformist Discourse

After World War II a wave of structural reforms to democratise education swept across the world; however, these reforms took root primarily in Western European countries. The structural reformist discourse in Israel and in many Western countries shared similar goals: first, to improve the level of education of the population in order to enhance economic growth; and second, to democratise the education system by reinforcing equality of educational opportunity (Resnik 2008). After World War II, scholars of economics of education included education as a key factor in economic development. Based mostly on human capital theory they constructed the 'education–economic growth' black box (in Latour's terms) which was adopted by international organisations such as UNESCO and the OECD. Once legitimised by the United Nations, the education–economic growth discourse became the basis of educational policies throughout the world. In order to increase economic development, developed countries were encouraged to democratise their secondary education system by extending the number of years of compulsory education (Resnik 2006).

Structural reform in Israel focussed on changing a dual system (primary and secondary education) to a three-tiered system (elementary education, lower secondary and upper secondary education). It was modelled after the education structure of the United States, which was established in the 1930s and 1940s and was considered more egalitarian and democratic. The basic American educational model prevailed in post-World War II global educational networks (Resnik 2008).

Reform was implemented in Israel after a long process of discourse structuration that underlined the 'inequality of opportunity' social problem between Ashkenazi and Oriental students and the construction of social objects, such as compensatory education programmes based on cultural deprivation approaches. The pervasion of this discourse in the professional and public sphere paved the way to formulation of the social problem of the 'ethnic gap', the construction of social objects needed for the implementation of reform – lower secondary schools and curricula, comprehensive schools and, mainly, counselling and guidance – and the final approval of the Knesset to execute structural reform.

Moreover, the economic discourse (economic growth, rates of return, planning) of structural reform was integrated into a discourse on equality of opportunity drawing on psycho-sociological approaches (cultural handicap, disadvantaged groups) and sociological approaches concerning social mobility and social reproduction (occupational gap and student achievement gap between Ashkenazi and Oriental groups).

The Managerial Reformist Discourse

The construction of the discourse that promotes managerial reforms began in the 1970s and 1980s as a reaction to structural reforms that took place in Western countries in the 1960s (Volansky 2007: 14). Scholars point to New Public Management (NPM) and the critical voices that arose against the inefficiency and wastefulness of state bureaucracy as the starting point of managerial reforms around the world (Ball 1998; Dutercq 2008). The US responded to critics of the administration by implementing NPM in the 1970s. The principles that led this type of modernisation in many countries include efficacy of public services, efficiency of investments in public services, improvement of service to the users, rigour and accountability (Bartoli 2005). The NPM approach shifts internal control to output control, defined according to standards and measurement of performance that can be quantified (Peters et al. 2000).

The critics attacking the inefficiency of state bureaucracy did not spare the education system and the solutions proposed represented the spirit of NPM. The search for rationality and efficiency in education resulted in the decentralisation of the system, control of student achievement through national standards and evaluation, increased parent choice and community involvement, school empowerment through the creation of autonomous schools and self-managed schools, and so forth.

Global networks in favour of managerial reforms in education, featuring participation by politicians, knowledge producers and businesspeople, were created in the UK, the US and New Zealand in the 1980s. International organisations such as the OECD and the World Bank (Jones 2004) also became central actors of the global reformist networks. They encouraged what Maroy (2008) refers to as post-bureaucratic education policies, which include two central models of post-bureaucratic regulation: one model represents 'the evaluator state' and the second represents the 'quasi-market' model. According to Maroy, nation-states integrate both models in practice.

The shift to a post-bureaucratic regime necessitates a new mode of control of the education system embodied in the 'evaluation, measurement and standards' social object, because standards aspire to ensure consistency and comparability in the everyday conduct that occurs at diverse locations (Fenwick 2010). As Ball (1998) argues, the control of schools by means of external standards and assessment practices represents the shift from direct state control to 'steering at a distance'. Global actors such as the World Bank, the OECD, the International Educational Assessment (IEA) and the American National Center of Educational Statistics participated in the construction of a discourse that encourages measurement and comparison of achievements in countries and between countries (Carnoy 1999). As Levin-Rozalis and Lapidot (2010) argue, the deep and costly involvement of financial and other international agencies in the evaluation field (in Bourdieu's terms) and their efforts for the incorporation of specific criteria and standards all over the world are politically driven. Evaluation, measurement and standards are not only a professional tool but also a means of controlling social, political and economic processes.

Similar to other countries, the reform proposed in the Dovrat Report in 2004 resulted from the construction of a managerial reformist discourse in the 1980s around social objects such as decentralisation, school autonomy and parent choice.

The pervasion of this managerial discourse in the academic and public arena paved the way for the formulation of the 'interstate education gap' social problem and the appointment of the Task Force Committee headed by Dovrat in order to advise the government on how to solve it. Despite the lack of formal implementation of the reform, the influence of the Task Force Report on the education system is undeniable. The ongoing construction of social objects, such as 'evaluation, standards and measurement', through the creation in 2005 of The National Authority for Measurement and Evaluation in Education (RAMA), is clear confirmation of its impact.

Comparing Reformist Discourses

We see that both reformist discourses were encouraged by international organisations: the structural reformist discourse, mainly by UNESCO and the OECD; and the managerial reformist discourse, mainly by the OECD and World Bank. In both cases, the structural and the managerial discourses that justified the proposed reforms were formulated in economic terms: the need to expand education in order to increase economic growth in the first case of 1968, and the need to raise the national education level in order to maintain or increase the economic competitiveness of the country in the latter case of 2004. While in both cases the objective was to raise the education level, in the structural reform it would be attained through expanding education to the entire population – a quantitative improvement – and in the managerial reform through enhancing the level of education – a qualitative improvement. Moreover, the economic discourse of the structural reform was integrated into a discourse on equality of opportunity drawing on psycho-sociological approaches first, and social reproduction theory further on. In the discourse justifying the managerial reform, the economic language has been applied to both the macro social level (high-tech industry, competitiveness between countries) and the micro level (school competition, education market, parent choice, privatisation of education). Furthermore, the latter economic discourse was integrated into an organisational and managerial discourse (decentralisation of the system, separation between steering/control and provision of education, delegating responsibilities, empowerment of principals). As Volansky and Friedman (2003) argue, one of the sources of the new management was business organisations. In a similar vein, the Dovrat Report determined that efficient management and appropriate organisation of the education system embodied the essence of the transformation needed to revolutionise the education system (Task Force 2004).

The Construction of Social Problems

The 'Ethnic Gap'

The call for equality of opportunity has a long history, but only after World War II, when it was linked to economic growth, did it become a significant element of education policies (Resnik 2008). In the early 1950s American scholars began to point out the 'wastage of the human pool of abilities' (Wolfle cited in Forquin 1990: 44) and its consequences regarding economic growth, and in the 1950s and 1960s developed countries started to conduct large national surveys in order to study the educational level of the population. The statistical data collected in different countries became unequivocal testimonies to the correlation between ethnic, racial or class origin and educational achievement. Inequality of opportunity – in a variety of local versions – was the social problem at the core of the reformist discourse. Thus, the discourse on the democratisation of education linked 'wastage' and 'drop outs' with the social problem of 'equality of opportunity'. The discourse emerged in leading American universities and spread to newly created intergovernmental organisations, namely, UNESCO and the OECD (Resnik 2008).

In Israel the National Survey Test,[1] administered since 1955 at the end of eighth grade, provided information about pupil achievement by countries of origin. Based on this data Smilansky (undated) showed the low achievement of Oriental students from Middle Eastern origins compared to that of Ashkenazi students from European-American origins. Smilansky, who was awarded his PhD at Ohio University in 1953 and lived again in the US in 1964, a period of lively debate on equality of opportunities and school desegregation, claimed that Israel should guarantee equality of opportunity for security, economic and social reasons.

Smilansky's studies were supported by the Szold Institute for Research in the Behavioral Sciences and the results were published in the Institute's *Megamot* journal. Since its inception in 1941, the Szold Institute has supported research and the publication of studies on Oriental children and their lower level of education. In 1953 Smilansky was appointed director of the Institute; since then the 'inequality of opportunity' social problem and compensatory education solutions became its central focus.

The achievement gap between Oriental and Ashkenazi children was explained using cultural deprivation theories developed in the US in the 1950s.[2] The Commission for the Disadvantaged, created by the Ministry of Education in 1962, implemented massive compensatory measures comprising a variety of frameworks at schools and boarding schools, such as enriching programmes and extra-curricular activities (Smilansky undated). A large local reformist network including a long list of scholars[3] developed around these projects orchestrated by Smilansky. He was convinced that the success of compensatory education showed that by transforming the education structure and creating lower secondary schools for all students, it would be possible to eliminate the correlation between low socio-economic status and social origin (Smilansky et al. 1960). Aran supported this reformist project and believed that, as Minister of Education, he was in a key position to transform Israeli society.

Ben Gurion, the first Prime Minister of Israel, was convinced that the educational lag of Oriental children represented a threat to Israel's national development. In 1963 he appointed the public Prawer Commission to examine the expansion of compulsory education. Aran interwove Ben Gurion's proposition with his own structural reformist agenda. The recommendations of the Prawer Commission in 1965 to extend compulsory education to the age of 15 and change the educational structure was strongly opposed by the Elementary Teachers' Union. Their protest prevented the implementation of the reform. Aran and Smilansky understood that in order to win the battle on the reform, it was necessary to go a step further, and they proceeded to formulate the ethnic gap social problem.

The formulation of the ethnic gap was based on Smilansky's previous studies. But instead of denouncing the inequality of opportunity for Oriental pupils on this occasion, he stressed the problem of social mobility, based on theories about social mobility and stratification developed in the US in the 1940s and 1950s.[4] Smilansky (1957) claimed that the educational gap between Oriental and Ashkenazi students would reproduce the occupational gap between the groups. According to Aran, a structural reform was the only way to prevent a permanent ethnic gap and the cleavage of Israeli society that threatened the nation (Schmida 1987). This new discourse presented the reform as the solution to a social problem that endangered Israel's future, namely, the unity of the nation and its economic and scientific development. In June 1966 the Knesset appointed the Rimalt Committee to investigate the structural reform of the elementary and post-elementary education system (Resnik 2007). The recommendations submitted by the Rimalt Committee were very similar to the recommendations of the Prawer Committee; the main difference was the emphasis of the latter on social integration (Schmida 1987), namely, the ethnic gap discourse (Report of the Parliamentary Committee 1971). In July 1968 the Knesset approved the recommendations and immediately launched a massive and accelerated implementation of the reform.

The 'Interstate Achievement Gap'

The construction of the managerial discourse has been pursued since the 1980s; however, it was the formulation of the 'interstate achievement gap' as a social problem, starting in 2000, that endangered the future of Israel and prompted the nomination of the Dovrat Committee and comprehensive education reform.

In many countries[5] the 'interstate achievement gap' social problem has been constructed through international standardised tests such as PISA, TIMMS and PIRLS, urging policy makers to adopt policies based on a managerial discourse, education standards and measurement of student achievement. Global actors such as the World Bank and the OECD encouraged the measurement and comparison of achievement between countries (Carnoy 1999) and urged states to found national institutes or centres of evaluation and assessment for this purpose.

In Israel the 'interstate achievement gap' social problem was formulated by Dan Ben-David, an economist in the Department of Public Policy at Tel Aviv University. Ben-David was awarded his PhD in economics at the University of Chicago, served as an adviser to the World Bank and in the Director-General's Office at the World Trade Organization, and was a member of the Taub Center for Social Policy Studies, a philanthropic association in Israel.[6] In the document 'National Socio-Economic Priorities', published in May 2000, Ben-David began to elaborate the 'interstate achievement gap' social problem. The poor results of Israeli students in the 2002 PISA tests enabled him to formulate this social problem more thoroughly:

> The level of knowledge attained by children in the basic subjects, as reflected in achievements scores in national and international examinations, is very low in comparison with other countries and also with the past (The E.L.A Committee, Executive Summary 2003: 2). . . . . Without dramatic improvement in the level of basic education and the provision of equal educational opportunities to its schoolchildren, Israel will have a hard time competing in a modern, competitive global economy.
>
> (ELA Committee, Executive Summary 2003)

The PowerPoint prepared by Ben-David, which clearly illustrated the 'interstate achievement gap', attracted philanthropic entrepreneurs – first, Meir Shani and then Shlomo Dovrat and Itzik Danziger – to the reformist network. They were convinced of the acuteness of the 'interstate achievement gap' as a social problem and the need to mobilise the government and public opinion to tackle the dire situation in Israel. In one of the multiple presentations attended by Limor Livnat, the Minister of Education, she asked Dovrat to chair a public committee to address the 'interstate achievement gap'. In October 2003 the Task Force for the Advancement of Education in Israel was appointed by the Government of Israel with the support of Prime Minister Ariel Sharon and Finance Minister Binyamin Netanyahu. In 2004 the committee submitted its report recommending comprehensive reform. The need for the proposed reform was justified by pointing to the low results of Israeli students compared to their counterparts in almost all OECD countries in the different disciplines (reading, mathematics and sciences). The report insisted on the fact that the low achievement of Israeli students would result in a decline of human capital which in turn threatened Israel's future and its ability to compete with more developed countries (Task Force 2004).

Comparing Social Problems

There are important differences concerning the social problems that prompted the reforms in Israel. The ethnic gap that fostered structural reform was formulated based on stratification theories adapted to social conditions in Israel. This local version of the inequality of opportunity social problem, developed in the 1950s and 1960s, represents a social issue linked to an economic target. The interstate achievement gap that prompted managerial reform was constructed in the 1990s based on theories of economic growth and job market needs. Equality of opportunity targeting poor families, ultra-orthodox Jews and Arabs aimed at preserving national unity but primarily responded to an economic issue.

Economic and political circumstances affect the nature of social problems. In the aftermath of World War II, a period of economic growth, most governments in Western countries, and that of Israel as well, were in the hands of labour coalitions. Social-democratic parties encouraged economic development as well as social justice. After the global economic crisis of the mid-1970s, rightist parties took power in an increasing number of Western countries. The managerial reformist discourse was initiated in the US and the UK through mandates by Bush and Thatcher, respectively, at the start of their administrations. Australia and New Zealand developed a strong managerial discourse and applied massive reforms in a period of rightist governments. Similarly, a rightist coalition in Israel, headed by Sharon as head of government, Netanyahu as Minister of Finances and Livnat as Minister of Education, appointed the Dovrat Committee and provided generous support.

Social Objects and Discourse Structuration

The implementation of these reforms required the construction of social objects that support the reformist discourse and embody the new policies. Tracking the way social objects were constituted allows a reconstruction of the reformist discourse structuration and the formation of the local networks that enhanced structural reform in the 1960s and managerial reform in the 2000s.

Many social objects were constructed in view of the structural reform: comprehensive schools, streaming, school zoning maps, curriculum for lower secondary education, counselling and guidance, and so forth. I examine 'curriculum for lower secondary education' but focus mainly on 'counselling and guidance', which I consider the main social object of the structural reform. Since discourse structuration of the structural reform has already been analysed in previous articles (Resnik 2007, 2008), in this chapter it will be presented only briefly. The expansion of the managerial reformist network analysed through the construction of social objects will be treated more extensively.

The Dovrat Committee discussed almost every issue concerning the education system, except for, according to many of its critics, values and pedagogical issues. The main topics included the restructuring of the Ministry of Education, teacher status and salary, the distribution of class hours per student, the optimal size of classrooms, the different resources used by the Ministry of Education, the need to reinforce pre-primary and primary education, the role of the headmaster, and accountability, among others. I focus on what I consider to be the main social objects in the construction of the managerial reformist discourse: 'decentralisation', 'school autonomy', 'parent choice' and 'evaluation, standards and assessments'.

Social Objects of the Structural Reform

Curriculum for Lower Secondary Education

The establishment of lower secondary schools required a new curriculum. The development of the new curriculum resulted not only in the selection of content for this new cycle but also in the adoption of a completely new concept of school curriculum planning. The new curriculum was 'pupil centred', conceived by professional curriculum planners and based on a quantitative 'scientific' methodology. Until the mid-1960s curricula content was determined by ad hoc inspectors and senior educator committees. Thereafter, the new curriculum was 'scientifically' based and represented an ongoing elaboration and evaluation process carried out by permanent planners (Sabar-Ben Yoshua 1988). This new perspective entailed the creation of a curriculum centre, and in 1962, the Ministry of Education founded a Curriculum Institute.

In 1963 Benjamin Bloom, a UNESCO curricular specialist from the University of Chicago and a friend of Smilansky, was invited to Israel, and in 1964 he submitted a project for the establishment of a Curriculum Institute, Bloom n.d. From 1965 to 1966, nine educational experts – including Shevah Eden, a member of the Pedagogic Secretariat of the Ministry of Education – attended one year of curricular studies in Chicago under Bloom's guidance. When they returned, the Curriculum Center, sponsored by the Ministry of Education, was founded (Yadlin 1971). According to Sabar-Ben Yoshua (1988), the curricula developed in Israel in the 1960s and early 1970s were largely influenced by the curricular approach developed by Tyler and Bloom in the US, which stressed inquiry, discovery and problem solving (Eden 1971).

The Curriculum Center accomplished a number of important activities: shaping the curriculum and streaming strategies for lower secondary schools; organising the tracks of upper secondary education in comprehensive schools; and delineating the school zoning map for lower secondary education (Eden 1968).

Counselling and Guidance

In order to improve equality of opportunities, international organisations recommended the elimination of entrance examinations for secondary education. The result was that secondary education became available to an increasingly large number of children, 'whose intellectual ability, social background and future occupation may be very varied' (UNESCO 1960 in Resnik 2002: 163). According to UNESCO, the selection of students for different types of schools (academic or vocational) or different tracks in the same school should respect individual freedom and be based on 'pupils' needs, interests and abilities'. National economic demands were used as criteria to help guide students into a particular track in order to satisfy specific economic needs. 'Counselling and guidance' provided the solution since, as OECD experts argued, 'no contradictions exist between the wishes of the individual and social requirements. On the contrary, professional observation and counseling linked between the individual choice and national educational policy' (Poignant 1966).

In Israel the selection process for secondary education based on the National Survey Test was also replaced by 'counselling and guidance'. The function of 'counselling and guidance' was to create a bridge between contradictory social demands, like student integration in order to narrow the ethnic gap, on the one hand, and the need to establish early differentiation in school in order to improve national educational levels, on the other. Similar to other countries, the counselling and guidance discourse was based on concepts such as the educational philosophy developed by Dewey on the different expressions of human capacity: intellectual capacity, aesthetic sensibility and manual ability (Klingman and Aizen 1990). This transformation involved adopting a mixed intellectual-technical-artistic orientation in lower secondary schools and establishing counselling and guidance service in all schools. Students would be assigned by school counsellors to different streams (groups) of the lower secondary cycle according to their past records. Determination of the type of schooling (academic, vocational or agricultural) in which pupils would continue their upper secondary education was made by the counselling and guidance service according to pupils' aptitudes, inclinations and wishes (Report of the Parliamentary Committee 1971).

Counselling and guidance entailed the creation of training tracks for education counsellors in teacher training institutes and universities. In Israel the first counsellors were trained in the School of Education at the Hebrew University, a firm ally of the Ministry of Education. The Department of Education at Tel Aviv University, headed by Smilansky, was founded in 1966. That same year the Educational Counselling Section was created at Tel Aviv University explicitly in order to train counsellor-teachers who would be needed for the implementation of the prospective reform (Klingman and Aizen, 1990). Similarly, educational departments were developed at Haifa University in order to train teachers and counsellors for northern Israel (Dror 1996).

Social Objects of the Managerial Reform

Decentralisation

The decentralisation of the Ministry of Education began formally in 1975 when the law to directly elect the heads of local authorities was enacted. Later, the recommendations of the public committee headed by the economist and statistician Moshe Zinbar[7] (1981) suggested delegating control from the central to the local governments, and delegating pedagogical responsibilities to local education authorities. This development fostered 'educational autonomy' in educational institutions and created an Education Public Council and a Pedagogical Secretariat at the local level. Furthermore, in 1988 the Education Administration of the municipality of Jerusalem was transformed into a Regional Education Administration (REA) of the Ministry of Education – the Jerusalem Education Administration (JEA *Manchi*) – according to the recommendations of Zinbar's committee and Michael Gal,[8] the Director of the Education Administration of Jerusalem, in cooperation with Shimshon Shohani,[9] then Director General of the Ministry of Education (Dror 2006).

In 2003 Victor Lavy, from the Department of Economics at the Hebrew University of Jerusalem, and well connected to local[10] and global networks including the World Bank,[11] and Ronit Tirosh, Director General of the Ministry of Education at the time, issued a position paper in which they encouraged the application of the Jerusalem model to the entire education system. The model focused on decentralisation, the constitution of regional education administrations (REAs) and reinforcement of the autonomy of the school and the principal. The ELA Committee, which included the economist Ben-David, made similar recommendations.[12] These ideas are reflected in and helped to shape the Dovrat Report (Dror 2006), to which both Lavy and Tirosh contributed: Lavy as a member of the steering commission and Tirosh as an external adviser. Indeed, the Dovrat Report suggests organising the education system into three administrative levels: the Ministry of Education, the REA and the school. The report recommends that the role of the Ministry of Education be reduced to shaping policies and monitoring their implementation; the REA would be responsible for the schools and other educational institutions in its area. The REA would inspect, control and evaluate the budgets and resources, the implementation of programmes and student output and performance (Task Force 2004).

School Autonomy and School-based Management

The construction of 'school autonomy' at its inception in the early 1970s intended to provide pedagogical autonomy to teachers.[13] In 1976 a ministerial circular announced school 'democratisation' and the need to train autonomous teachers for the development of school curricula. The report 'Education in the 1980s' was submitted by Elad Peled, the Director General of the Ministry of Education, and in 1984 another circular recommended increasing teacher pedagogical autonomy (Dror 2006).

In the 1980s, a period of budgetary reduction in education, middle-class parents began creating 'special schools' (art or nature schools) which were outside of the school zoning maps.[14] Scholars from Tel Aviv University involved with the study of these 'special schools' launched projects and experiments based on the scholarly discourse that was central to the education debate in the US at that time. Rina Shapira, well connected to global managerial networks,[15] and her colleagues David Reshef, Naama Sabar and Moshe Silberstein, affiliated with the School of Education at Tel Aviv University, were among the main actors in the construction of the school autonomy social object (Reshef 1990, Silberstein 1990, Shapira et al. 1995, Gibton et al. 2000). Policy makers financed and encouraged a large number of projects and programmes on school autonomy: a think-tank team addressing 'Thought on autonomous schools' in 1984;[16] a committee headed by Miriam Ben Peretz of Haifa University on teacher training in autonomous schools; a large project on school autonomy (200 schools) carried out between 1987 and 1992 supervised by teams of Schools of Education (Tel Aviv University, Ben Gurion University and the Hebrew University of Jerusalem) and education colleges (Dror 2006).[17]

School-based management (SBM), promoted mainly by Ami Volansky, was constructed as an expansion of autonomous schools already in place. Volansky had a long career at the Ministry of Education[18] (1985–2005) and at the end of his doctoral studies in the UK,[19] a country in which SBM flourished, he headed a committee for the creation of SBM appointed by the Ministry of Education in 1993. The steering committee encouraged further decentralisation by transferring responsibilities from the Ministry of Education, including planning, funding and control, to the local education authority that would in turn assist and support SBM. Teachers' autonomy and teachers' responsibilities would be reinforced if the ultimate responsibility for the student was in the hands of the SBM. SBM has gradually been introduced in all Israeli elementary schools, but as of 2002, it was practised in only 700 schools. Volansky and Friedman (2003) agree that the primary reason was the severe opposition to delegating authority to the schools and the unwillingness of key personnel to relinquish their own power in favour of the schools. Volansky later abandoned the Ministry of Education and started a new career as a scholar of the School of Education at Tel Aviv University.

The post-elementary teachers' union also participated in the construction of the school autonomy social object. In 2001 the union launched the experiment titled 'The force to change the education system' (*Oz letmura bema'arechet hachinuch*), which fostered autonomous self-managing schools. According to the project, school autonomy should include a feedback system, school management based on a school vision or philosophy, an organisational cooperative climate and the development and availability of resources for the team. The Szold Institute carried out the evaluation of this experiment (Dror 2006).

Parent Choice

Initially, scholars of the School of Education at Tel Aviv University and policy makers at the Tel Aviv Municipality participated in the construction of parent choice. Rina Shapira and her colleagues submitted a positional paper recommending controlled parents' choice in 1991, and in 1994, the experiment 'Controlled choice' was launched in Tel Aviv-Yaffo, headed by Shimshon Shoshani,[20] the head of the Tel Aviv Education and Culture Administration. This experiment included reinforcing school autonomy by fostering school specificity based on the development of a particular school philosophy (Dror 2006).

The parent choice question ignited a controversial public debate; it implied opening the school zoning maps, and therefore it was thought to harm the equality of opportunity. In the following years, a number of committees were appointed to deal with this delicate question: a commission headed by Kashti[21] (School of Education, Tel Aviv University) to examine the regional experimental schools; a commission for 'The Examination of Parent Choice Alternatives in the Education System in Israel', headed by Dan Inbar[22] (School of Education, Hebrew University of Jerusalem); and a commission headed by Victor Lavy[23] (Department of Economics, Hebrew University of Jerusalem). In general, the commissions agreed to parent choice but suggested implementing it in conjunction with several conditions that would preserve equality of opportunity for all the students.

It is evident that parent choice was constructed mainly by educational scholars from the major universities, but also by economics and public policy scholars. Nahum Ben-Elia, from the Department of Public Policy at Tel Aviv University, submitted a position paper in 2000 sponsored by the Floersheimer Studies Institute[24] in which he served as adviser on municipal policy and urban strategic planning. The paper, 'Restructuring Education Services in Israel: Deregulation, Democratization and Accountability',[25] recommended entirely restructuring the education system, taking into account parent choice as a basic human right and emphasising the need to involve different stakeholders in education policies.

Evaluation, Measurement and Standards

'Evaluation, measurement and standards' is at the heart of managerial reforms, but contrary to the rest of the social objects it was constructed mostly after submission of the Dovrat Report. Most national educational bureaucracies established international divisions, which deal with global education indicators and comparative performance measures (Rizvi and Lingard, 2009). In Israel the evaluation field has evolved very slowly[26] because of structural-historical conditions such as the paucity of funding for evaluation and the lack of academic recognition of the field (Levin-Rozalis and Shochot-Reich 2009). The National Authority for Measurement and Evaluation in Education (RAMA), founded in Israel only in 2005, was similar to those that already existed in many countries, measuring and comparing educational achievements in countries and between countries (Carnoy 1999).

The discourse on 'education standards', a predecessor of the 'evaluation, measurement and standards' social object, was constructed by the Ministry of Education. The Zinbar Committee Report (1981), which discussed the decentralisation of the education system, suggested that the Ministry of Education be responsible for the definition of standards, and encourage and control their implementation. Based on the Kobersky Committee's recommendations in 1976,[27] Shimson Shoshani, the Director General of the Ministry of Education at the time, founded the Department of Evaluation and Measurement in 1989. The objective of the new department was to provide data and practical recommendations to policy makers at the Ministry of Education to facilitate education planning and enhance the programmes and projects undertaken by the ministry. The responsibilities of the Department of Evaluation and Measurement include the evaluation and measurement of schools through GEMS tests (Growth and Effectiveness Measures for Schools – MEITZAV) and the evaluation of programmes, initiatives and projects carried out by the Ministry of Education.[28] The formulation of the interstate achievement gap, based on the low achievement of Israeli students in the 1999 TIMMS, enhanced the construction of standards. In 2000 the Ministry of Education initiated the development of standards for the different disciplines (Volansky 2007). The target, according to Ronit Tirosh, the Director General of the Ministry of Education, was manifold: to upgrade and advance the education system, to raise student achievement, to reinforce teachers' and headmasters' professional capabilities, to assist local authorities in organising their work more efficiently and economically and to monitor the implementation of local authorities' programmes and projects.[29]

But as the detractors as well as supporters of the Dovrat reform agree, the creation of the National Authority for Measurement and Evaluation in Education (RAMA) was the direct product of the Task Force's efforts.[30] This is not surprising since Dovrat, like the other leaders of the Force Task, Shani and Danziger – also philanthropic entrepreneurs – saw the need to transform the system of evaluation as one of the key targets of the reform, as highlighted in their interviews. In 2005 the Department of Evaluation and Measurement at the Ministry of Education was closed and replaced by RAMA, which enjoyed a statutory status that ensured independence in its activities. Michal Beller, former head of the National Institute for Testing and Evaluation (NITE), responsible for the Psychometric Entrance Test to universities and well-connected to global (mostly North American) networks, has been appointed Director General of RAMA. According to its website, the role of RAMA is to lead the process of measurement and evaluation of the education system through: 1) the evaluation of the education system and the examination of standards and objectives set by the Ministry of Education; 2) the evaluation of schools according to standards outlined by the Ministry of Education; 3) the execution of GEMS tests in 5th and 7th grades, the publication of the results and their submission to the government and Knesset; 4) the development and control of final examinations (*Bagruiot*) and the evaluation of the outcomes; and 5) the administration of international tests such as PISA and TIMSS.[31]

Following the Dovrat Committee recommendations, the Ministry of Education instructed that an evaluator should be incorporated into every school, a decision that implied training thousands of evaluators. Conferences were organised to encourage the incorporation of evaluation and assessment. Yitzhak Friedman, an expert on measurement and evaluation at Hebrew University and the director of the Szold Institute, was a central lecturer in these conferences. Dozens of various bodies jumped on the bandwagon and began training education evaluators (Levin-Rozalis and Shochot-Reich 2009).[32] The Israel Academy of Sciences and Humanities, the Rothschild Foundation (*Yad Hanadiv*) and the Ministry of Education jointly assumed the responsibility to prepare a training programme for evaluators.

Comparing Social Objects and Discourse Structuration

The ultimate and common objective of social objects of the structural 1968 reform – lower secondary schools and their curriculum, counselling and guidance, as well as comprehensive schools and school zone mapping, not analysed here – was a shift in the method of student selection at the entry of secondary education. The main social objects of the proposed managerial reform – including decentralisation, autonomous schools and SBM, parent choice and evaluation, standards and measurement evaluation – represent a shift in the type of control of the education system.

Social objects of the structural reform were constructed in departments of education with the direct support of the Ministry of Education. In the case of managerial reforms the picture is more complex. Economists were the first to speak in favour of decentralisation already by 1980 (e.g. Zinbar in 1981). Further on, though schools of education played a central role in constructing the managerial social objects, the contributions of economics (parent choice, SBM) and public policy[33] and departments were also significant. This is clearly illustrated by Ben-David, an economist in public policy and the knowledge producer that formulated the 'interstate achievement gap' social problem, or Lavy, coming from an economics department, who encouraged decentralisation and was on the steering committee of the Task Force. A number of managerial initiatives were supported by the Ministry of Education, in similarity to the case of the structural reform, but many of them were financed and fostered by local education authorities, and mainly in Tel Aviv and Jerusalem.

Another important difference between the discourse structuration of both reforms is that the main social object 'evaluation, standards and measurement' was not structured in local knowledge production institutions, due apparently to the weakness of the evaluation field in Israel. Instead, the leaders of the Task Force Committee, the social entrepreneurs Dovrat, Shani and Danziger, succeeded in establishing RAMA shortly after the committee submitted its recommendations. This shed light on the empowerment of philanthropic associations but also on the growing influence of international organisations.

As we have seen, international organisations in the past were also very influential in the development of the structural reformist discourse, in Israel as in many Western countries. However, social objects used to be constructed in local knowledge production institutions (Szold Institute, universities), based on the discourse and social objects constructed in the past (e.g. compensatory education, cultural deprivation). The urgency to build 'evaluation, standards and measurement', justified by being a crucial social object in the developed world without significant participation by education departments, proved the reach of international discourse and its powerful influence. Moreover, the lack of contribution of education studies in the construction of the main social object, and the foundation of RAMA despite it, points to the growing empowerment of philanthropic associations.

The growing participation of philanthropic associations in the construction of social objects is increasingly noted in the education field. Similar to their counterparts in the UK, philanthropic entrepreneurs in Israel, including businessmen, high-tech entrepreneurs and venture capitalists, invest money in demonstration stage projects, and if a project has proven its efficacy, they work closely with the government to try to secure nationwide support and funding (Ball 2008). Indeed, well-funded philanthropic associations in Israel such as IVN,[34] Karev Foundation, Rashi Foundation and Mandel Foundation[35] facilitate 'experimentation' and ad hoc activities by the state. Philanthropic entrepreneurs deal with education problems using their organisational experience and management expertise. In contrast with the burdensome and extricate view of the bureaucracy, these individuals 'get things done' and bring passion, drive, dynamism and a different kind of expertise to the tackling of social problems (Ball 2008). Thus, policy becomes subject to the supposed qualities of business, efficiency and cost-effectiveness in particular. Hence, as Ball (2008) notes, philanthropy is becoming incorporated into state policy.

Conclusions

The structural reform undertaken in 1968 and the managerial reform proposed in 2004 have been studied by means of a common neo-Weberian perspective. The analysis of these two large-scale reforms with the same analytical tools enables the comparison of these apparently very different reforms. This unique comparison sheds light on the evolution of the reformist dynamics and the transformation of education policy over time. I have followed the construction of the reformist discourses initiated decades before the structural and managerial reforms were made public. It seems that only when the reformist discourse pervades knowledge production institutions and the public arena is there a chance for the reform to be politically viable. This is a long process that includes the structuration of reformist discourse in knowledge production institutions, the construction of social objects that embody the reform and the expansion of reformist networks that enhance the reformist discourse.

In the case of the 1968 structural reform, 'inequality of opportunity' between Oriental and Ashkenazi children had been constructed as a social problem by Smilansky and his colleagues dating back to the 1950s at the School of Education at the Hebrew University. Both the social problem and its compensatory education solutions continued to be researched and developed by Smilansky and his colleagues at the Szold Institute and then at the School of Education at Tel Aviv University. Aran, the Minister of Education who believed in the need of the reform that Smilansky fostered, supported his research activities and the implementation of different social objects created in the spirit of a structural change that would allow access to secondary education for a larger student population. The reforms included comprehensive experimental schools, lower secondary schools and curriculum, zone school mapping and counselling and guidance. By transforming 'inequality of opportunity' to an 'ethnic gap' as an acute national social problem and through the spread of the reformist discourse over the years, the structural reform was finally approved in 1968. This long process was supported by Ben Gurion, who feared that the ethnic gap would impede Israel's economic development.

In the case of the Dovrat reform proposed in 2004, the construction of the managerial discourse began in the mid-1970s, first at Tel Aviv University and later at the Hebrew University of Jerusalem with the support of the local authorities of both cities. Decentralisation, school autonomy and SBM, and parent choice social objects were developed in education and economics departments at both universities. In the 2000s, based on the poor results of Israeli students in international surveys, the economist Ben-David formulated the 'interstate achievement gap' social problem and the economic risk it entailed for the country. Philanthropic entrepreneurs already active in the education field were associated with the diffusion of this social problem. Their public activity and the pervasion of the managerial discourse through the years brought about the designation by Livnat and the Ministry of Education of Dovrat, a high-tech entrepreneur, to head the Task Force Committee for transforming the education system. Political changes in 2005 prevented the implementation of the Dovrat reform. However, new social objects central to the recommended reform, such as 'evaluation, assessment and standards' and 'principals' empowerment', have since been implemented.

The key difference between the two reforms concerns their implementation. The first reform was approved in the Knesset in 1968 and then implemented in the education system, whereas the second reform has not been executed because of political changes and teacher union opposition. Nevertheless, we learned that after the first stage of implementation the execution of the structural reform slowed down because a number of local authorities opposed it (namely parent opposition to integration). Some districts or sectors (Orthodox Jewish and, partly, Arab sectors) today still run their schools according to the old structure (8 + 4). On the other hand, after the managerial reform was formally dismissed, we saw and continue to see today the continuous pervasion of the managerial discourse and the creation of social objects central to the Dovrat Report. The foundation of RAMA, the New Horizon reform (*Ofek Hadash*)[36] aimed at improving the status of teachers, and the creation of the Avnei Rosha Institute[37] targeting the empowerment of principals, reflect the impact of the Dovrat Report on education policy. Since the success or failure of a reform, according to the neo-Weberian model, depends mostly on the extent to which the reformist discourse pervades the public and professional arenas, there is not much difference between the two reforms.

In both cases the reformist discourse involved an economic concern – increase or maintain economic growth – but in the former (1968) it was linked to a social issue (equality of opportunity), while in the latter (2004) it was linked to organisational and managerial issues (efficiency). While the objective of the two reforms was to raise the education level, in the structural reform it was to be attained by expanding education to the entire population – a quantitative improvement – and in the managerial reform by enhancing the level of education – a qualitative improvement.

The social problem of the 'ethnic gap' was formulated as a domestic or a local problem (though very similar to local problems in many other countries) whereas the 'interstate achievement gap' was constructed as a global problem, or as a local problem in a global world. This difference between the local or global nature of the social problems has an important political implication. The ethnic gap was constructed based on surveys that took into account the Jewish population only, namely, Ashkenazi and Oriental students. Hence, the solution to the social problem, the structural reform, exclusively targeted equality of opportunity and integration of Jewish children. In contrast, the international surveys that constructed the interstate achievement gap included the whole Israeli student population, that is, Jewish and Arab students. International agencies conditioned the participation of Israel in the surveys on the inclusion of all social groups into the samples. Since both populations contribute largely to the low ranking of Israel on international surveys, the remedy – managerial reform – targeted all groups in the population.

The comparison between discourse structuration in both reforms also reflects the composition of reformist networks. The reformist discourse structuration in the first reform took place progressively in education institutes and education departments at universities; in the managerial reform the reformist discourse structuration also entered into public policy departments and philanthropic associations. Local reformist networks in both cases were integrated by knowledge producers well connected to global networks (to American universities but also to international organisations like the World Bank), ministers of education and key governmental figures (prime ministers and ministers of finances). However, since the 1990s there has been increasing involvement of local policy makers (in Jerusalem and Tel Aviv). More interestingly, a new type of actor, the philanthropic entrepreneur, is perceived as an active member of the reformist education network. Dovrat, Shani and Danziger are part of an expanding network of Israeli businessmen and high-tech entrepreneurs[38] engaged in improving education.

This evolution is not unique to Israel. Ball (2008) notes that new communities of social entrepreneurs and business philanthropists influence, to varying degrees, the education policies in the UK. The appointment of Dovrat as the head of the Task Force Committee and the deep involvement of Shani and Danziger in the steering committee and its numerous sub-committees legitimised the managerial discourse and laid the foundation for a larger and stronger engagement of philanthropic associations in education decisions. Not surprisingly, the association *Hakol* Hinuch,[39] in which Dovrat and Danziger are involved, was 'founded in response to the needs for reform in the education system in Israel'.[40] It is currently working hard on the preparation of a Public Education Bill, which is meant to organise the entire education system according to the Task Force report recommendations (Interview with Piron). But as Ball (2008) argues, new kinds of actors in the policy process also disable, disenfranchise or circumvent some of the established policy actors and agencies. By privileging managerial knowledge, the new dominant discourse disables scholars and experts in education as legitimate actors in decision-making in the education field.

The main conclusion of comparing the structural and the managerial reform is of a general nature and refers to the educational policy borrowing and lending process and the changes it underwent over time. This comparison sheds light on two main transformations in educational policy in Israel and elsewhere: first, education disciplines, primarily the sociology of education, have been displaced from reformist discourse structuration and replaced by public policy, economics and management studies; and second, the role of knowledge producers as being responsible for borrowing educational 'global models' (Steiner-Khamsi 2004: 215) is decreasing and the role of NGOs and philanthropic entrepreneurs is increasing. Hence, this study points to the growing irrelevance of education studies and social sciences in defining goals and desirable changes in the education system and the increasing significance of philanthropic associations in shaping education reforms and policies.

Notes

1 Gina Ortar (Hebrew University and Szold Institute) headed this National Survey Test that operated between 1955 and 1972 (Resnik 2002).

2 A large body of literature on cultural deprivation developed in the US in the 1950s but was enhanced anew after the Sputnik affair. Several studies, including 'Society and Education' (Havighurst and Neugarten 1957), 'The Children of Sanchez' (Lewis 1961) and 'Children of Bondage' (Davis and Dollard 1964), stressed the link between class features and children's cognitive abilities following Basil Bernstein's (1960) 'linguistic or cognitive deficit' concept. Bernstein's conception enhanced a larger theoretical discussion that expanded to the US. Deutsch (1966), Bereiter and Engelmann (1966) and Jensen (1968), among others, stressed the consequences of children's cognitive deficiencies on their success in school. Based on these 'cultural handicap' approaches, several large compensatory education programmes, mainly at the pre-primary level, were organised in the US, the largest being the Head Start Program.

3 Among the scholars: Adar, Adler, Chen, Eiger, Feitelston, Arieh, Minkowitz, Sharan, Shtal and Simon.

4 The work of well-known scholars such as Talcott Parsons (1949, 1954, 1959) and Seymour M. Lipset and Reinhard Bendix (1959), as well as the research undertaken by Kingsley Davis and Wilbert Moore (1944), Pitirim Sorokin (1959), Peter Blau (1956) Otis D. Duncan (1966) and Blau and Duncan (1967), were at the centre of American sociological inquiry at that time. Although Smilansky did not apply the sophisticated methodology developed by these scholars, and did not study social mobility in Israel either, he used their insights to reframe his findings.

5 See the example of Canada on this question in Davidson-Harden and Majhanovich (2004).

6 Established in 1982 under the leadership and vision of Herbert M. Singer, Henry Taub and the American Jewish Joint Distribution Committee (JDC), the Center is funded by a permanent endowment created by the Henry and Marilyn Taub Foundation, the Herbert M. and Nell Singer Foundation, Jane and John Colman, the Kolker-Saxon-Hallock Family Foundation, the Milton A. and Roslyn Z. Wolf Family Foundation and the JDC. The Center's operating budget comes from the JDC and the generous donations of its supporters. The Taub Center and JDC are committed to continuing the Taub Center Endowment fundraising campaign. Since November 2008, Ben-David has been the Executive Director of the Taub Center for Social Policy Studies in Israel.

7 Moshe Zinbar used to teach at the Hebrew University of Jerusalem and Tel Aviv University and carried out research in the Institute of Applied Research in Jerusalem.

8 Michael Gal was director of the Mandel Institute (1993–1996), a large foundation dealing with education issues; he was also directly involved with other educational organisations, often playing a central role.

9 Shimshon Shohani was awarded his PhD at the University of New York in Buffalo (1975) and served as director of the Tel Aviv Education Administration from 1978 to 1986. He was appointed Director General at the Ministry of Education (1986–1989), when Yitzhak Navon was Minister of Education, and again under Amnon Rubinstein (1993–1996). He presently serves under Gidon Saar, the current Minister of Education (2009–present). In 2002 he headed the Public Committee for the revision of the method of financing elementary education in Israel (Shoshani Committee).

10 Victor Lavy served as Policy Adviser in the Israel Energy Ministry, Deputy Director General (1980–1983) and as Policy Adviser in the Israel Education Ministry, Director General (1999–2003). He collaborated with the Milken Family Foundation and authored two papers on education supported by the foundation: Milken Center for Education Systems Research at the Jerusalem Center for Public and State Affairs. The Jerusalem Center's programme on Israel's Educational System, initially a joint venture of the Jerusalem Center for Public Affairs and the Milken Family Foundation, conducts applied research on educational problems from a systematic perspective to better deal with the educational needs of the twenty-first century (www.jcpa.org/mises.htm).

11   Victor Lavy obained his MA and PhD in Economics at the University of Chicago. He worked for many years for the Research Department of the World Bank. He is a Board Member of the Bureau for Research in the Economic Analysis of Development (BREAD), a research associate in the National Bureau of Economic Research (NBER), in the Center for Economics and Policy Research (CEPR), and research fellow at the Center for Economic Performance (CEP) (http://economics.huji.ac.il/facultye/lavy/cv.pdf).

12   The ELA Committee submitted the 'Proposal for Structural Reform of Israel's Educational System' in 2003 (www.achrayutleumit.org.il/edu).

13   For this reason the Ministry of Education appointed a committee for the 'Teacher initiative in primary education' in 1972.

14   The school zoning maps were defined in order to implement the 1968 structural reform and aimed to regulate the integration of children from different social backgrounds in the same school. Children were ascribed to a particular school by the authorities and no choice was possible. Special schools were not subjected to this regime and could enrol students outside of the particular school-zoning map in which the special school was implanted (Shapira et al. 1995).

15   Shapira obtained her PhD at Columbia University in 1965. One of her mentors with whom she was in further contact was Robert Dentler, a specialist on magnet schools (see, e.g., Fleming et al. 1982). James S. Coleman was a colleague and close friend of Shapira since the 1960s. Coleman's work in the 1980s was very influential on the tendency to privatisation of education in the US and elsewhere (see Coleman et al. 1982; Coleman and Hoffer 1987).

16   The think-tank team 'Thought on autonomous schools' reunited senior officials from the Pedagogical Secretariat at the Ministry of Education and the scholars mentioned above belonging to the School of Education at Tel Aviv University.

17   Oranim, Lewinsly and Seminar Hakibuztim colleges.

18   First, as adviser to the ministers and then as Director General of the Planning Department.

19   PhD at University of Oxford, Wolfson College (1988–1991).

20   Shoshani was director general of the Ministry of Education in the period during which Ytzhak Nvon was Minister of Education.

21   Kashti was appointed by the Minister of Education, Itzhak Navon, whose recommendations were submitted in 1991.

22   Inbar was appointed by the Pedagogical Secretariat and the Minister of Education at that time, Amnon Rubinstein, whose recommendations were submitted in 1994.

23   The committee submitted its recommendations in 2003. Report of the Commission for the Examination of Equality of Opportunity, Zone Mapping, Parent School Choice in the Education System of Jerusalem, March 2003, Municipality of Jerusalem (www.jerusalem.muni.il/pages/vaada_takzir.pdf).

24   Floersheimer Studies at the Hebrew University in Jerusalem is a research unit operating under the auspices of the Institute for Urban and Regional Studies. The programme is the successor of the Floersheimer Institute for Policy Studies, a non-profit organisation active in Jerusalem from 1991 to 2007 that was founded and supported by Dr. Stephen H. Floersheimer (www.hunews.huji.ac.il/articles.asp?cat=3&artID=902).

25   Deregulation, democratisation and increased public accountability – all three principles are enveloped in the idea of civic education, namely shifting the focus of responsibility for educational institutions from the government (and local authorities) to civil organisations (communities, parent groups, educators, societies with a defined educational ideology, albeit diverse at times). The idea of civic education is not an abstract one. This publication presents examples of sound international experience whether as a means to expand the possibilities within the framework of local education (as in the US) or as a basis for national structural reform (as in New Zealand) (www.fips.org.il/site/p_publications/item_en.asp?doc=&iss=&iid=564).

26   The Israeli Association for Program Evaluation (IAPE) was founded in 1998 (Levin-Rozalis and Shochot-Reich 2009).

27   Haim Kobersky was the founder of the Department of Education and Culture of the Municipality of Jerusalem and its Director General until 1970.

28 http://cms.education.gov.il/EducationCMS/Units/Haaracha/OdotHagaf/default.htm.
29 Source: The Director General's speech in the booklet: The standards based education system. Jerusalem, the Ministry of Education (http://cms.education.gov.il/EducationCMS/Units/MinhalPedagogi/Agafim/Mosadot/standrtimbhinuk.htm).
30 All the persons interviewed for the study were convinced that RAMA was created as a result of the Dovrat Report.
31 http://cms.education.gov.il/educationcms/units/rama/odotrama/odot.htm
32 Karev Program, a joint initiative of the Ministry of Education and Karev Foundation, which was established by Charles Bronfman, a Jewish Canadian businessman in the 1990s, is one of the organisations that has recently begun to offer evaluator training programmes.
33 Departments of public policy have been created in Israeli universities relatively late compared to Western countries. Tel Aviv University's Department of Public Policy was founded in 1985 and enlarged in 1994, Hebrew University's was founded in 1996 and further developed in 2003 and Haifa University's was founded in 2004.
34 IVN is a venture philanthropy network of high-tech entrepreneurs, business executives, venture capitalists, corporations, and philanthropists from Israel and the US. IVN was established in 2002, and it defined educational intervention initiatives as part of its core activities (www.israelventurenetwork.org/).
35 The Mandel Foundation in Israel is responsible mainly for the Mandel Leadership Institute and the Mandel Institute of Jewish Studies at the Hebrew University of Jerusalem. The Mandel Leadership Institute trains social and educational leaders from all walks of Israeli society, and leaders in Jewish education from communities outside Israel. The Institute's programmes include the Mandel School for Educational Leadership, the Mandel Jerusalem Fellows, and programs for Senior Civil Servants in Israel. The Mandel Institute of Jewish Studies is responsible for coordinating the teaching departments and research centres devoted to the pursuit of Jewish Studies at the University (www.mandelfoundation.org/).
36 The New Horizon reform has been implemented gradually since 2008 and deals with one of the central topics tackled by the Dovrat Commission – the improvement of teacher level/skill. Among others, New Horizon has increased teachers' salary in exchange for additional work hours and has transformed the occupational and salary ladder by stressing in-service training.
37 The principals training course was a pilot programme conceived and implemented in 2004 by IVN (in which Dovrat and Danziger were members of the IVN Board) with the cooperation of Yad Hanadiv Foundation and Check Point 'based on the belief that school principals must become the primary change agents in schools'. In 2007 the Ministry of Education agreed to take ownership of the programme and accordingly founded the Avnei Rosha Institute (www.israelventurenetwork.org/).
38 Among the most active education entrepreneurs in Israel we can mention Shlomo Dovrat, Dov Lautman, Itzik Danziger, Ofer Brandeis and Avi Naor.
39 Founded in 1998, *Hakol Hinuch*, which means 'it's all education', is the Movement for the Advancement of Education in Israel and includes leading lecturers from the academic world, together with leading business figures actively involved in civil society, school principals, teachers, education activists, foundations and NGOs. Among the founders are many prominent businesspeople in Israel: Eli Horowitz of TEVA pharmaceutical industry, Ofra Strauss, General director of the Strauss corporation, and Dov Lautman who is also the President and Chairman of the Board of Directors. Rabbi Shay Piron, the Executive Director, is an educator and public figure, and was a member of the Dovrat Commission. Avi Naor, Shlomo Dovrat and Izhak Dantziger are members of the board of the association (www.hakoled.org.il/?p=376).
40 www.hakoled.org.il/?p=369

References

Ball, S. (1998) 'Big policies/small world: an introduction to international perspectives in education policy'. *Comparative Education*, 34(2): 119–130.

Ball, S. (2008) 'New Philanthropy, New Networks and New Governance in Education'. *Political Studies*, 56: 747–765.

Bartoli, A. (2005) *Le management dans les organisations publiques, 2ème édition*, Collection Management Public. Dunod: Paris.

Bereiter, C. and Engelmann, S. (1966) *Teaching disadvantaged children in the preschool*. Englewood Cliffs, NJ: Prentice Hall.

Bernstein, B. (1960) 'Language and social class'. *British Journal of Sociology*, 11(3), 271–276.

Blau, P. M. (1956) 'Social mobility and interpersonal relations'. *American Sociological Review*, 21(3), June, 290–295.

Blau, P. M. and Duncan, O. D. (with the collaboration of A. Tyree) (1967) *The American occupational structure*. New York: Wiley.

Bourdieu, P. (1983) 'The field of cultural production, or: The economic world reversed'. *Poetics*, 12: 311–356.

Callon M. and Latour, B. (1992) 'Do not Throw out the Baby with the Bath School', in A. Pickering (ed.), *Science as Practice and Culture*. Chicago: Chicago University Press, 343–368.

Carnoy, M. (1999) *Globalization and educational reforms: what planners have to know*. Paris: UNESCO, International Institute of Educational Planning.

Coleman, J. S. and Hoffer, T. (1987) *Public and private high schools: The impact of communities*. New York: Basic Books.

Coleman, J. S., Hoffer, T. and Kilgore, S. (1982) *High school achievement: Public, Catholic, and private schools compared*. New York: Basic Books.

Davidson-Harden, A. and Majhanovich, S. (2004) 'Privatisation of education in Canada: A survey of trends'. *International Review of Education*, 50 (3–4), 263–287.

Davis, A. and Dollard, J. (1964) *Children of bondage. The personality development of Negro youth in the urban south*. New York: Harper & Row.

Davis, K. and Moore, W. E. (1944) 'Some principles of stratification in social theory'. *American Sociological Review*, 10(April), 242–249.

Dutercq, Y. (2008) 'Administration de l'éducation', in van Zanten (dir.) *Dictionnaire de l'éducation*. Paris: PUF, 1–5.

Dror, Y. (1996) *The university school between the "academy" and the "field" – establishment of the School of Education at Haifa University 1963–1883* (in Hebrew). Oranim, Haifa University and Tel Aviv University.

Dror, Y. (2006) 'Past reforms in israel education system. What can we learn from history on the Dovrat reform?', in D. Inbar (ed.) *Likrat mahapecha hinujit?* [Towards an educational revolution?] Van Leer Jerusalem Institute and Hakibbutz Hameuchad Publishing House, 35–60.

Eden, S. (1968) *Principles and guidelines for junior high school curriculum*. Jerusalem: Ministry of Education and Culture.

Eden, S. (1971) 'New Curricula – Principles and processes', in S. Eden (ed.), *On the new curricula*. Jerusalem: Ministry of Education and Culture, Curriculum Center, 21–69.

ELA Committee (2003) 'Citizens for the advancement of education in Israel'. Proposal for a structural reform in the education system in Israel. Chair of the committee: Herzl Bondinger. Online. Available: http://www.achrayutleumit.org.il/edu.

Fenwick, T. J. (2010) '(un)Doing standards in education with actor-network theory'. *Journal of Education Policy*, 25(2): 117–133.

Fleming, P., Blank, R., Dentler, R. A. and Baltzell, D. (1982) *Survey of magnet schools: Interim report*. Washington, DC: James H. Lowry & Associates.

Forquin, J. C. (1990) 'La sociologie des inégalités dans l'éducation: principales orientations, principaux résultats depuis 1965', in J. C. Forquin (ed.), *Sociologie de l'éducation – Dix ans de recherché – Recueil de synthèse par la Revue Francaise de Pédagogie.* Paris: INRP, L'Harmattan.

Fullan, M. (2000) 'The return of large-scale reform'. *Journal of Educational Change,* 1: 5–28.

Gibton, D., Sabar, N. and Goldring, E. B. (2000) 'How principals of autonomous schools in Israel view implementation of decentralization and restructuring policy: Risks, rights, and wrongs'. *Educational Evaluation and Policy Analysis,* 22(2): 193–210.

Havighurst, R. J. and Neugarten, B. L. (1957) *Society and education.* New York: Allyn & Bacon.

Jensen, A. R. (1968) 'The culturally disadvantaged: psychological and educational aspects'. *Educational Research,* 10, 4–20.

Jones, P. (2004) 'Taking the credit: financing and policy linkages in the portfolio of the World Bank', in G. Steiner-Khamsi (ed.), *The global politics of educational borrowing and lending.* New York: Teachers College Press, 188–199.

Klingman, A. and Aizen, R. (1990) *Psychological counseling.* Ramot: Tel Aviv University.

Levin-Rozalis, M. and Lapidot, O. (2010) 'Evaluation in teacher training colleges in Israel: Do teachers' colleges stand a chance?' *Journal of Assessment and Accountability Systems in Educator Preparation,* 1(1): 16–28.

Levin-Rozalis, M. and Shochot-Reich, E. (2009) 'Professional identity of evaluators in Israel'. *Canadian Journal of Program Evaluation,* 23(1): 141–177.

Lewis, O. (1961) *The children of Sanchez: autobiography of a Mexican family.* New York: Random House.

Lipset, S. M. and Bendix, R. (eds) (1959) *Social mobility in industrial society.* Berkeley: University of California Press.

Maroy, C. (2008) 'Convergences and hybridization of educational policies around "post-bureaucratic" models of regulation'. *Compare,* 39(1): 1–15.

Parsons, T. (1949) *The structure of social action.* Glencoe, IL and New York: Free Press.

Parsons, T. (1954) *Essays in sociological theory.* New York: Free Press.

Parsons, T. (1959) 'The school class as a social system: some of its functions'. *American Society Harvard Educational Review,* 29, 297–318.

Peters, M., Marshall, J. and Fitzsimons, P. (2000) 'Managerialism and educational policy in a global context: Foucault, Neoliberalism, and the doctrine of self-management', in N. C. Burbules and C. A. Torres (eds), *Globalization and education Critical perspectives.* London, New York: Routledge, 109–132.

Poignant, R. (1966) *The role of educational plans in economic and social development programmes,* in OECD Study Group in the economic of education organizational problems in planning educational development.

Report of the Parliamentary Committee for the Examination of the Structure of Elementary and post-Elementary Education in Israel (1971) Jerusalem: Adiel, 134.

Reshef, S. (1990) 'Ha'otonomia shel beit sefer: idan hadash bahinuj hamamlachti' [School autonomy: A new era in national education], in I. Friedman (ed.), *Otonomia behinuj – Misgarot musagiot vetahalichei bitzua* [Autonomy in education – Conceptual frames and implementation processes] (13–31). Jerusalem: Szold Institute.

Resnik, J. (2002) *Globalization of educational models: Structural reforms of the education system in Israel and France,* PhD dissertation, Department of Sociology and Anthropology, Tel Aviv University.

Resnik, J. (2006) 'International organizations, the "education-economic growth" black box, and the development of world education Culture'. *Comparative Education Review,* 50(2): 173–195.

Resnik, J. (2007) 'Discourse structuration in Israel, democratization of education and the impact of the global network'. *Journal of Education Policy,* 22(3): 215–240.

Resnik, J. (2008) 'Introducing a neo-Weberian perspective in the study of globalization and education: Structural reforms of the education systems in France and Israel after WWII'. *Oxford Review of Education*, 34(4): 385–402.

Rizvi, F. L. and Lingard, B. (2009) *Globalizing Education Policy*. London: Routledge.

Sabar-Ben Yoshua, N. (1988) *Curriculum metamorphoses* (in Hebrew). Tel Aviv: Yachdav Publisher.

Schmida, M. (1987) *Equality and Excellence – Educational reform and the comprehensive school* (in Hebrew). University of Bar-Ilan.

Shapira, R., Haymann, F. and Shavit, R. (1995) 'Autonomy as ethos, content as commodity: An Israeli model of controlled choice of autonomous schools', in R. Kahane (ed.), *Educational advancement and distributive justice between equality and equity*. Jerusalem: Magnes Press, 358–374.

Silberstein, M. (1990) 'The autonomous school: A combination of planning approaches', in I. Friedman (ed.), *Autonomy in education* (in Hebrew). Jerusalem: Szold Institute, 100–129.

Smilansky, M. (undated) *Ministry of Education confronting culturally disadvantaged pupils' needs*. School of Education, Institute of educational experiment, the laboratory of nourishing research, Ministry of Education Planning Committee for the advancement of disadvantaged in the decade 1975–1985.

Smilansky, M. (1957) 'Education and the in-gathering of the Diasporas', *Megamot*. Vol. VIII, 3 (in Hebrew).

Smilansky, M., Weintraub, S. and Hanegbi, Y. (eds) (1960) *Child and Youth Welfare in Israel*. Jerusalem: Szold Institute.

Sorokin, P. A. (1959) *Social and cultural mobility*. New York: Free Press.

Steiner-Khamsi, G. (2004) 'Conclusion: Blazing a trail for policy theory and practice', in G. Steiner-Khamsi (ed.), *The global politics of educational borrowing and lending*. New York: Teachers College Press, 201–220.

Task Force (2004) Koah hamesima aleumi lekidum hahinuj beisrael. Hatochnit haleumit lehinuj (Doh sofi) [The National Task Force for the Advancement of Education in Israel. The National Educational Program, Final Report (Dovrat Report)]. Online. Available http://cms.education.gov.il/educationcms/units/ntfe/hdochhsofi/dochsofi.htm.

Task Force (2004) Taktzir hadoh beanglit (English Summary Report). Online. Available http://cms.education.gov.il/educationcms/units/ntfe/hdochhsofi/dochsofi.htm.

Volansky, A. (2007) 'School autonomy for school effectiveness and improvement: The case of Israel', in T. Townsend (ed.) *International handbook on school effectiveness and Improvement*. New York: Springer, 351–362.

Volansky, A. and Friedman, I. A. (2003) 'Introduction', in A. Volansky and I. A. Friedman (eds), *School-Based Management, An International Perspective*. State of Israel Ministry of Education.

Weber, M. (1968) *Economy and society: An outline of interpretive sociology*. New York: Bedminster Press.

Wittrock, B., Wagner, P. and Hollman, H. (1991) 'Social sciences and the modern state: policy knowledge and political institutions in western europe and the united states', in P. Wagner, C. H. Weiss, B. Wittrock and H. Wollmann (eds), *Social Sciences and the modern states: National experiences and theoretical crossroads*. Cambridge: Cambridge University Press, 28–85.

Yadlin, A. (1971) 'The turning point in curriculum development', in S. Eden (ed.), *On the new curricula* (in Hebrew). The Ministry of Education and Culture, Curriculum Center, 9–20.

Zinbar Committee Report (1981) Havaada Hamamlachtit leinyanei hashilton hamekomi [The national committee for the local authority's questions].

15 In the Shadow of Global Discourses

Gender, Education and Modernity in the Arabian Peninsula

Natasha Ridge

In the past 20 years there has been a strengthening of the global discourse on modernity, disseminated not only through the United Nations agencies and the World Bank but also through the Organisation for Economic Cooperation and Development (OECD), the World Economic Forum (WEF), and other transnational bodies. While the actual term *modernity* appears far less frequently than in the past, the underlying rationale of modernisation for economic development persists but is now increasingly framed through the use of terms such as best practices, international or global. In the education sector the United Nations, the World Bank and the OECD have been responsible for crafting what has been described as a universal set of education priorities and best practices that now define the modern nation state (Jansen 2005; Porter and Webb 2008; Mahon 2009). The use of international assessments and global comparison indexes by new global players, such as the OECD, has produced a discourse on modernity that is disseminated and strengthened not through aid conditionality, as has been the case with the World Bank and the International Monetary Fund (IMF) (Escobar 1994; Samoff 2000; Jansen 2005), but rather through what has been termed *governance by information* (Porter and Webb 2008).

A concern with gender, or more particularly with women and girls, has also become an integral part of the modernity prescription, especially with regard to education (Escobar 1994; Abu-Lughod 1998). This concern began in earnest with the introduction of the Education for All targets and the Millennium Development Goals in the early 1990s, both of which emphasised the importance of focusing on women and girls in education, in particular gender parity in school enrolment (Jansen 2005; Tilak 2005). Girls' education since then has been institutionalised as a key part of the education strategy of aid-dependent countries (Ali 2002; Chabbott 2003). Despite global trends showing that boys are now performing more poorly than girls in international and national assessments (Baker and LeTendre 2005; Gurian and Stevens 2005), a specific focus on boys' education has yet to appear in any international organisations' education goals and boys remain largely excluded from the policy menu.

In the Arabian Peninsula boys are failing at ever increasing rates, and they are less likely than girls to go on to higher education (Mullis et al. 2008; UNESCO 2008). Policy makers in the region, however, continue to highlight the successes of girls and as yet have no policies to target the widening gap between the two genders.

The limited framing of gender, provided by international agreements such as the Millennium Development Goals (MDGs), has enabled countries like Saudi Arabia, the United Arab Emirates (UAE) and Qatar to declare successes in terms of gender and education. This is particularly the case as a greater proportion of girls attend higher education institutions in these countries (UNESCO 2008) and girls perform better than boys in national and international assessments (Mullis et al. 2004). Saudi Arabia points to these achievements and declares that it has 'paid special attention to [the education of] girls' (Ministry of Education, Saudi Arabia 2008: 19) despite the fact that women cannot leave the country without the permission of their guardian, drive a car or work in a mixed gender environment (Howden and Shields 2008). In the UAE much is made of the fact that girls outperformed boys in all subjects in the final year exams, according to the annual *UAE Yearbook* (UAE Ministry of Information and Culture 2008), while in Qatar the achievement of women in all fields, including education, is highlighted on the Ministry of Foreign Affairs website. Thus in the Gulf the successes of women in the education sector have helped to signal modernity to the outside world and to present a positive image vis-à-vis human rights advocates in the region. In the meantime, however, the failings of boys in education, stemming from a combination of poor quality schools and a perception that employment will be easy to find regardless of how well they are educated, are largely ignored.

This chapter begins with an examination of the development of universal education priorities, with a focus on gender. It then considers how these global gender and education priorities have become linked to notions of modernity. I look at the cases of the United Arab Emirates, Qatar and Saudi Arabia, which despite the declining achievement and poor retention of boys are pursuing gender-blind approaches to education. I also examine the inherent tensions that exist in these resource-rich yet developing countries that need to appear to be simultaneously both modern and traditional. The chapter concludes with a discussion of how even discursive borrowing of policies which privilege certain targets over others has had a heavy cost for both boys and girls in the Gulf States.

The Establishment of Universal Policy Education Priorities

The establishment of universal priorities for education, Samoff (2000) argues, has in some sense been in development since colonising nations first transplanted their own education systems into their colonies. It has, however, only been since the establishment of the United Nations Education, Scientific and Cultural Organization (UNESCO), the IMF, the OECD and the World Bank that global norms for education truly began to coalesce and spread internationally (Samoff 2000; Chabbott 2003; Heyneman 2003; Jones 2004,). The World Conferences on Education for All (EFA) have been highly influential in the construction of global norms and best practices for education, largely through the EFA *Frameworks for Action* and the yearly EFA *Global Monitoring Reports* by UNESCO (Chabbott 2003; Jansen 2005; Tilak 2005). They have developed a discourse that problematises certain areas of development, often those only relevant to Sub-Saharan Africa (Heyneman 2003). Jansen (2005) claims that the EFA and MDG priorities spread rapidly because, for a variety of reasons, countries wanted to be seen to be actively engaging with the new global discourses. He argues that 'not to be part of the EFA consensus is to appear to be out of line, illogical or even rebellious in the context of what seems to be a very rational and reasonable set of goals' (p. 375). By defining education and development priorities in scientific terms, the World Bank, UNICEF and UNESCO have constructed a knowledge regime, wherein only experts are permitted to define the problems and only experts have the solutions to solve them (Escobar 1994; Parpart et al. 2000).

While EFA and the MDGs set targets for nations to reach in terms of enrolment and gender parity, typically enforced through various loan conditionalities, other international organisations such as the OECD and the International Association for the Evaluation of Educational Achievement (IEA) have used soft law (Morgan 2009), or governance by information (Goldmann 2008), to indicate their own set of global education priorities. These priorities have been established through both the use of international league tables and the publication of reports such as *Education at a Glance*. Through the use of the PISA league tables, the OECD 'calls attention to leaders and laggards among countries in their adoption of OECD norms' (Porter and Webb 2008: 4). Porter and Webb (2008: 4) assert that 'ultimately what the OECD identifies as a good policy or best practice becomes part of the identity of the ideal modern state, an identity to which western governments aspire, as do many non-western governments'. Mahon and McBride (2008: 87) point out that the dominant norms and ideas in the OECD are largely derived from the West and consequently emphasise cultural norms such as individual human rights and modern bureaucracy as the 'paramount form of political organization'. Thus the OECD not only offers best practice solutions but, like the World Bank and the UN agencies, it also defines the problems or areas that countries should be concerned about.

While the various international organisations have been active in promoting their particular set of education priorities, their adoption at the country level is also determined by how well they resonate locally. Scholars such as Steiner-Khamsi (2004), Schriewer and Martinez (2004), Silova (2004) and Spreen (2004) believe that policies (such as those relating to girls' education) become widespread not merely due to isomorphism resulting from a common world culture (Meyer et al. 1997), but also because political actors often see compatibility between certain global policies and their own domestic interests. The timing of a nation's agreement to institute particular reforms, these scholars argue, often coincides more with its own internal political situation and needs than with any external forces (see also Phillips 2004). They state that it is often the case that policy change is only at the discourse level, with very little actually changing on the ground, and that only discursive borrowing of policies is occurring. In the case of the Gulf nations, choosing to focus on girls' education at the policy discourse level helps to signal alignment with global education priorities (and thus modernity) that keeps less conservative local interest groups happy. In order to placate the more conservative elements in their populations, however, very little is done to address the quality of schools or to make any substantive changes to existing educational and social structures.

Modernity and Girls' Education in the Middle East

> The development of women is more important for measuring the development
> of a country than its construction of sky high buildings and wide boulevards.
>
> (M. Brahim, Beirut, 1952)

Interestingly, the strength of the gender and education discourse has often been greater in regions that have been characterised and stereotyped as traditional and misogynist by development organisations, such as the Middle East (Abu-Lughod 1998; Ali 2002). The Middle East has long been perceived as a region where women are particularly oppressed (Said 1979; Abu-Lughod 1998; Sabbagh 2003; Sonbol 2006). Not only are there countless media reports detailing the horrors of life as a woman in the Middle East (Sabbagh 2003; Sonbol 2006), but there are also many biographies and autobiographies dealing with the subject (Sasson 1992; Souad 2003). Academia has not been immune to stereotyping either, with some Western academics (Doumato and Posusney 2003; Moghadam 2003) subscribing to and promoting the narrative of the oppressed, Muslim, Arab woman portrayed, according to Abu Lughod (2002), as in need of saving.

This narrative, coupled with the rise and spread of global ideologies about girls' education and its benefits for national development, has led to the production of a slew of development reports on gender in the Middle East. Reports such as the *Arab Human Development Report* (AHDR) (UNDP 2005), the World Bank Middle East and North Africa (MENA) report (World Bank 2008), its *Gender and Development Report* (World Bank 2004) and the *EFA Arab States Regional Report* (UNESCO 2002) all present the same story of the marginalisation of girls and the oppression of women. While concerns about women and girls are well founded, boys rarely receive a mention in any of these global reports despite recent figures from the TIMSS 2007 study and EFA Global Monitoring reports showing the increasingly poor academic performance of boys and the low retention rates at secondary and tertiary levels in the Middle East.

In the Middle East the gender and modernity discourse is particularly pervasive and relatively unchallenged. Both the World Bank and the UNDP utilise a narrow framing of gender limited to girls and neglect to consider any imbalances in enrolment or achievement that may adversely affect boys. The 2005 AHDR (UNDP 2005), *Towards the Rise of Women in the Arab World*, states that Arab girls are deprived of education because they are held back by discriminatory traditions and customs, as well as by obstructive family situations. A concern with girls' education is part of modernising education in the Middle East and by implication a concern with boys' education is not. Throughout the AHDR (UNDP 2005), modernity in education is set in opposition to what it refers to as 'traditional teaching methods', 'traditional values' and traditional pedagogical practices. The AHDR (UNDP 2005: 267) states that the history of education reform in the MENA region is 'the story of the interaction of competing visions of the purpose and ends of education, pitching global trends in education strategy and content against age-old educational traditions'. The AHDR does not clarify what exactly the 'age-old education traditions' are and how they are in opposition with the also undefined 'global trends' (p. 297).

The World Bank Middle East North Africa development report, *The Road Not Traveled: Education Reforms in the Middle East and North Africa* (World Bank 2008), is also preoccupied with modernity and emphasises the term *modern* in the context of having a modern curriculum, a modern education system and becoming a modern nation-state. The report makes cross-national comparisons of performance on international tests in order to highlight the failings of the region. With regard to gender, however, *The Road Not Traveled* does not share the concern of the AHDR (UNDP 2005) and dismisses gender inequality in education from the beginning of the report, stating, 'Since the early 1960s, the MENA region has registered tremendous gains in terms of more equitable access to formal education . . . Moreover, the region no longer has severe gender disparities in secondary and tertiary education' (World Bank 2008: xvi).

In the Middle East a number of international and domestic reports have shown that girls are outperforming and outrepresenting boys in education (UAE Ministry of Education 2005; UNDP 2005; World Bank 2008). Baker and LeTendre (2005: 30) state that globally, 'instead of sustained gender-inequality in favor of males, there is growing evidence that females are actually doing better than males in many aspects of attainment of education credentials'. Rather than being concerned by the declining performance of boys, however, many international organisations reward it. Countries that achieve a positive Gender Development Index (GDI), exceed the Millennium Development Goals or exceed EFA targets with respect to gender are presented as success stories to the international community (UNESCO 2002). They are considered to have met the targets and therefore solved the problem of girls' education.

Global Discourses, Local Appropriations

> By relying on signals of mass opportunity and meritocratic rules of getting ahead, the state can display Western ideals without directly attacking pre-modern economic interests and social organization.
>
> (Fuller 1991: xvii)

The problem of dominant discourses and knowledge regimes that privilege certain priorities and solutions over others becomes more apparent in those countries that are most different from the norm. The oil-rich, aid-free Gulf States are an anomaly; they are classified by the IMF (2009) as 'developing' countries although they have some of the highest per-capita incomes in the world (IMF 2008) and are thus free of the aid regimes that exist in their poorer Middle Eastern neighbours. They are also eager to position themselves as beacons of modernity and progress in the Middle East but lack the internal capacity to implement many of their desired reforms. As a result of this lack of capacity and a desire to distance themselves from other, less affluent Middle Eastern countries, the Gulf States tend to align their policy approaches not with the World Bank and UN agencies but rather with the member states of the OECD (Ridge 2008). To that end many of the Gulf States hold education conferences that focus on addressing global issues in education, such as the Bahrain Education Project and the Qatar WISE (World Innovation Summit for Education) project, in order to position themselves as purveyors rather than receivers of education reforms.

However, the Gulf States are in essence tribal monarchies, and thus rely on the support of various groups to ensure that they remain in power. There is a tacit bargain made in which, as Fuller (1991: 21) describes, 'The state, collaborating with local elites, *signals* the provision of opportunity and equity. In turn, this process enhances the legitimacy and authority of traditional, local leaders who now align themselves with the central state'. The oil-rich Gulf States are therefore caught in a similar situation to that of many aid-dependent countries in that they are forced to play a delicate balancing game in order to maintain the political status quo. On the one hand, governments must placate conservative allies who wish to protect religious and national identity through as little change as possible, while on the other hand they need to satisfy more liberal groups and international allies through ambitious modernisation programmes with the aim of creating a so-called knowledge-based economy.

To date, the modernity project in the UAE, Qatar and Saudi Arabia has been typically evidenced through ambitious infrastructure and real estate projects, framed in superlatives: the world's tallest, biggest, longest and most expensive. Nevertheless, governments of all three countries struggle with the poor educational achievement of their citizens and the popular (mis)perception of Gulf Arabs as being spoiled, lazy and culturally conservative (Arabian Business 2008). In addition, growing unemployment levels among young people in the Gulf (Kabbani and Kothari 2005) have put pressure on governments to provide increased job opportunities for their citizens. Doing so has been difficult, however, with employers finding that many job seekers lack even the most basic skills. This in turn has put pressure on the education system, which has been blamed for the shortcomings.

As a result, governments in all three countries have been spending heavily on efforts to improve the quality and skills of secondary and tertiary graduates in order to promote employment of nationals in the private sector and ease the burden on the public sector. Some of the most recent educational projects include the ambitious RAND-led school reform in Qatar, the creation of the King Abdullah University of Science and Technology (KAUST) in Saudi Arabia and the Madares Al Ghad (Schools of the Future) initiative in the UAE. However, more than five years after implementation, these reforms there have yet to produce any measurable improvements in the quality of education in these countries, especially at the school level, as evidenced on the PISA, TIMSS and local higher education assessments.[1]

Notable also in the overall performance of Gulf students has been the poor performance of males. In a study comparing the quality of secondary schools for boys and for girls in the United Arab Emirates, I found that boys lagged behind girls in terms of academic performance and persistence in schooling. Boys' schools were also inferior in terms of teaching quality (as measured by classroom observations), leadership and ethos. Girls were taught with lessons that were more engaging, they had more opportunity to have a say in school affairs, they used the library more frequently and they were less likely to be subjected to corporal punishment (Ridge 2008). However, despite clear differences in the quality of education and in achievement and retention, the UAE does not have a single policy that addresses the challenges faced by boys. While data on schools are scarce for Saudi Arabia and Qatar, the 2003 and 2007 TIMSS results show similar patterns in achievement and other studies have also shown high levels of male dropouts for both countries.

Education and Gender Discourses in the Gulf: The Cases of Qatar, the United Arab Emirates and the Kingdom of Saudi Arabia

This section considers the specific education, gender and modernity discourses of three Gulf countries: Qatar, the United Arab Emirates and Saudi Arabia. These countries were selected because they have all made much of the educational achievements of women, all struggle with the poor performance of males and all have been aggressively pursuing education reform over the past 10 years, though to different degrees. The most ambitious reformer has been Qatar, which in 2001 hired the RAND Corporation to oversee the transformation of its education system. This involved 'a system-wide structural reform plan that encouraged qualified persons with innovative ideas (including non-educators) to apply to run new independent schools under contracts with the government' (Larson 2009: 1). The UAE, rather than taking a single unified approach to education, chose to adopt a number of different reform measures from a variety of countries and implemented by different federal and state government entities. Finally, Saudi Arabia, after September 11, has been under increasing international pressure to reform its education system but, due to a far more complex political environment, has taken much more gradual steps towards education reform, involving textbook revisions, increased spending and improvements for girls' education (Al Munajjed 2008).

Table 15.1 provides an overview of each of the three countries. All have high per capita GDPs, with Qatar having the highest GDP per capita in the world. Qatar and the UAE have minority populations with nationals accounting only for roughly 20 per cent of the population, while Saudi Arabia has a much larger percentage of nationals at 80 per cent. In terms of gender parity, data from the Millennium Development Goals database reveals that all countries have a gender parity index in favour of females at the tertiary level, and both Qatar and the UAE also have gender parity indexes in favour of females at the secondary level.

Table 15.1 Population and education statistics for Qatar, Saudi Arabia and the United Arab Emirates

Country	Per capita GDP[1] (USD)	Population[2]/ est. percentage of Nationals	Gender Parity Index (Secondary)[3]	Gender Parity Index (Tertiary)[4]
Qatar	85,000	1,280,862 (20%)	1.46	6.05
Saudi Arabia	20,000	24,645,686 (80%)	0.85	1.65
United Arab Emirates	36,000	4,484,935 (20%)	1.02	2.05[5]

Notes:
1 IMF (2009)
2 World Bank, World Development Indicators (2008)
3 Millennium Development Goals Database (2008)
4 Millennium Development Goals Database (2008)
5 Figures from the UAE Ministry of Higher Education estimate this to be higher for Emiratis, stating that over 75 per cent of students studying at public universities are female (Abdulla and Ridge 2011).

One important reason why all three countries have become concerned with education reform is the presence of a youth bulge in their populations (Dhillon and Yousef 2009). This bulge, coupled with a strong preference for public sector employment, is resulting in rising youth unemployment levels (Janahi 2010), estimated to be at 43 per cent in Saudi Arabia (Maktoob Business 2010), and a growing discontentment in the younger generation, which has been clearly evidenced in the recent regional uprisings in the Middle East. Education is seen as key to promoting private sector employment for nationals and has become increasingly tied to modernity discourses in this context in particular. However, in the rush towards modernity and a thriving public sector, gendered differences are ignored and/or marginalised.

Gender Realities and Discourses

Qatar

With regard to gender differences in education, Qatar has nearly triple the number of girls than boys in higher education, the highest in the Gulf States and over twice that of the UK and USA (UNESCO 2008). In 2001/02 the dropout rate for boys at the secondary level was twice that of females and males were much more likely to repeat grades than females, with around 14 per cent of all males in public secondary schools repeating (Menne 2008). Also of note is the fact that there has actually been a decline in the number of males with a higher education degree over the past five years (Menne 2008). In the 2007 TIMSS girls outperformed boys in both maths and science; overall, however, Qatari students were among the poorest performers of all participating countries and scored well below the international averages for both maths and science (Mullis et al. 2004; Mullis et al. 2008).

Despite the poor performance and retention rate of boys, girls continue to receive far more attention from policy makers, with the recent establishment of the Centre for Girls' Creativity being a prime example. In official discourses on gender special emphasis is given to women throughout the *Qatar National Vision 2030*, especially in the section on social development where it states that 'Women will assume a significant role in all spheres of life, especially through participating in economic and political decision-making' (General Secretariat for Development Planning Qatar 2010: 23). Men are only mentioned once in this document and that is in the context of healthcare. On the website of the Embassy of Qatar a full section is dedicated to Qatari women, detailing their achievements in the various sectors and highlighting the role of Sheikha Moza (wife of the Emir) in promoting the role of women in society. The site emphasises the role of women in the development of Qatar and highlights the fact that there are more women than men in university. The site also provides a link to the Freedom House report *Women's Rights in the Middle East and North Africa* which lauds the achievements of Qatar in promoting the rights of women (Kelly and Breslin 2010).

United Arab Emirates

In the United Arab Emirates girls currently outperform boys in all subjects for grades 10–12, the dropout rate for girls averages around 3 per cent while for boys the figure ranges up to 20 per cent (Lewis 2010). Despite the poor performance of boys, in English in particular, but also in mathematics and science (Ridge 2008), little attention has been given to them by the education or other authorities, while the educational achievements of girls are often noted.

Official discourses on gender in the UAE, similar to Qatar, emphasise the importance of women. While there is a section dedicated to education in the *UAE Yearbook* (UAE Ministry of Information and Culture 2008), it is followed by a section dedicated specifically to women. In the education section, gender is not mentioned at all, but in the section dedicated to women the successes of women in education are identified briefly. In particular, the high enrolment percentages of Emirati women in tertiary education are cited. Similarly, the *National Strategy of the Ministry of Education for 2008–2010* (UAE Ministry of Education 2008) and *Vision 2020* make no references to gender, girls or boys. In the most recent national strategy document, *Ministry of Education Strategy 2010–2020* (UAE Ministry of Education 2010), a reference is made to both male and female dropouts; however, the strategy highlights the fact that there has been an overall decrease in the number of dropouts while failing to mention that in fact the number of male dropouts is increasing.

Saudi Arabia

In Saudi Arabia gender imbalances are not as acute as in Qatar or the UAE. However, the number of girls attending school is steadily increasing and since 2006 the combined enrolments for primary, secondary and tertiary education for girls have exceeded that of boys (Ministry of Economy and Planning, Saudi Arabia 2009). In terms of academic achievement, girls significantly outperformed boys on the 2007 TIMSS tests at the grade 8 level in both maths and science. At the national level data are scarce but a Booz and Co. report on girls' education in Saudi Arabia stated that there is a 37 per cent dropout rate overall at the high school level (Al Munajjed 2008). Given that nearly 50 per cent more girls go on to higher education than boys, it could reasonably be assumed that the majority of the dropouts are males.

With regard to the official discourses surrounding gender, there is a full section on the Ministry of Education's website dedicated to addressing the role of women in Saudi culture in general, and in the education system in particular. Further, within a 2003 Ministry report, *The Development of Education*, a section titled 'Eliminating Gender Discrimination' highlights the fact that 'the Kingdom has given special emphasis to the education of girls, who occupy a special position in Saudi society' (2003: 16). Another report, *National Report on Education Development in the Kingdom of Saudi Arabia* (Ministry of Education, Saudi Arabia 2008: 18), goes a step further, claiming that 'the Kingdom of Saudi Arabia has eliminated any differences between the genders in the elementary and high school [levels of] education'. This same report goes on to explain that 'Saudi Arabia [has] paid special attention to girl[s'] education', even providing free housing and transportation to school (2008: 19). It is not mentioned however if these services were equally provided for male students and males are not addressed as a separate or distinct group in any of these documents.

Education and Modernity Discourses

Qatar

Evidence of the modernisation and education discourse can be found in the *Qatar National Vision 2030* where there is a strong emphasis on having a world-class infrastructure but at the same time maintaining Islamic values and culture. One major target identified is the 'modernization and the preservation of traditions' (General Secretariat for Development Planning 2010: 7), which refers to shaping modernisation around local culture and traditions. The first pillar of the vision, Human Development, states that 'Qatar aims to build a modern world-class educational system that provides students with a first-rate education, comparable to that offered anywhere in the world' (General Secretariat for Development Planning 2010: 17). The page continues to indicate that the education system will also 'promote social cohesion and respect for Qatari society's values and heritage'. The website of the Supreme Education Council states that 'Qatar seeks to build a world-class education system by incorporating the best education practices from around the world while simultaneously placing a priority on the teaching of religion, Arabic, Islamic values, and culture' (Supreme Education Council Qatar 2009).

In appropriating discourses and reforms from abroad, Qatar has had to play a delicate balancing game with local interest groups. An article in the *Wall Street Journal* discussed how 'radio talk shows and imams here [Qatar] have held fiery discussions about whether the schools are "un-Islamic" for teaching some subjects in English, not Arabic, and for providing music classes' (Coker 2010). In other media outlets academics warned of the loss of the Arabic language and the corresponding threat to national identity (Lepeska 2010).

United Arab Emirates

While references to gender and education are limited in official documents, references to modernity and international best practices with regard to education are much more common. The UAE's *National Strategy of the Ministry of Education for 2008-2010* also contains many references to international best practices and the importance of having a modern curriculum and using modern techniques to teach students. Its emphasis is on transforming the UAE education system into one that is world class through the use of modern approaches that are to be guided by international standards. In the most recent Ministry of Education *Strategy 2010–2020* there is again an emphasis on best practices, international education systems and staff and references to meeting world-class standards. However, unlike earlier documents that did not focus on national identity, this document states that the goals of the strategy are to meet world-class standards 'while promoting national identity' (UAE Ministry of Education 2010: 15).

Tensions between the desire to embrace modern education practices and the preservation of local traditions in the UAE are also evident. Some were highlighted when members of the Federal National Council called for a greater focus on local identity, traditions and culture (Khalaf and Habboush 2009). In response to parental concerns about the latest reforms, education authorities have begun to include more emphasis on Arabic and Islamic studies. In Dubai, for example, the 2009/2010 school inspections run by the Knowledge and Human Development Authority for the first time included inspections of Arabic and Islamic Studies, downgrading the ratings of international schools that did not perform adequately in these inspections and boosting those of otherwise poor quality public schools that taught those classes well.[2] In addition, the newly introduced curriculum in the emirate of Abu Dhabi now includes a focus on national identity. Finally, in the most recent federal government strategy (UAE Prime Minister's Office 2009: 4) there is also a strong emphasis on national identity and culture, with the preface speaking of 'building a modern and progressive nation' while preserving the 'fabric of their [Emirati] society' and the 'strength of their [Emirati] culture'. So while there exists tension between some of the aspects of the modernity prescription such as a focus on English, the issue of gender imbalances in educational achievement goes unmentioned and unaddressed.

Saudi Arabia

Saudi Arabia has also embraced modernity discourses in education with its *Ten-Year Plan 2004–2014* (Ministry of Education, Saudi Arabia 2005: 5) that states, 'It is imperative for the ten-year plan to raise the standards of education and to ensure the improvement of its outcomes . . . so that it can compete with other international systems in the field'. The Plan goes on to say that 'through [educational reform], the Kingdom has achieved – with Allah's assistance – a deep physical structure and civilised experiences with distinguished standards and international measures of high degrees of excellence'. Again, however, the tension between embracing modernity and appeasing traditionalists is felt via an entire separate section of the Plan dedicated to *The Cultural Invasion and its Results*. This section stresses the importance of protecting traditional Saudi culture while introducing new methods for education; it asserts that due to the 'threat to the Kingdom's national identity and culture' that can come with interaction with an outside world, 'a balanced approach [is required] that will allow students to enjoy the benefits of modern technology . . . while maintaining the Kingdom's values and faith' (p. 6).

In wider discourses in Saudi Arabia, outside of the education sector, there is a frequent clash between, on one side, modernisation efforts by the government that seek to improve the quality of graduates and promote employment of nationals, and, on the other, religious conservatives who seek to maintain the status quo or implement more restrictions, in particular with respect to women's rights. A recent example can be found in the case of the female cashiers in grocery stores. In an effort to promote employment opportunities for women the government decreed that women may work as cashiers in grocery stores, and stores began to hire them; however, almost immediately a fatwa was issued by the Grand Mufti[3] forbidding women to work in these positions (Hilabi 2010).

Gender, Modernity and Education

Governments in all three countries emphasise market style reforms and the importance of a modern, world-class education sector. Again, despite the failings of boys, their high drop-out rates and high repetition rates, policy makers in all three countries are silent on education for males. While there are some nascent efforts underway to address the high levels of male dropouts (Ameinfo 2010), males are still not identified publicly as the focus of these efforts.

In addition, while the successes of girls are important and commendable, it is necessary to recognise that they are only performing well relative to boys in their respective countries. Indeed, overall both boys and girls in Qatar, the UAE and Saudi Arabia are performing poorly on international assessments such as the PISA and TIMSS, with all of them scoring well under the international mean. For girls, comparatively better performance has meant that questions regarding the quality and suitability of their education have been ignored. Moreover, given that around 85 per cent of job seekers in government employment agencies in the UAE are women (Janahi 2010), there are clearly issues related to education, gender and employment that need to be addressed. In Saudi Arabia girls are still not allowed to take physical education and their school curriculum is different from that of males (Doumato and Posusney 2003), designed in many ways to keep them focused on becoming the ideal housewife (Najmabadi 1998). Once they complete their education they are also much more likely to be unemployed than men (Doumato and Posusney 2003). In addition they will be denied many fundamental human rights including the right to drive or leave the country without a male relative's permission (Middle East Online 2010).

Thus the appropriation of gender-blind education discourses reflects the Qatari, Emirati and Saudi governments' decision to adopt educational reforms that are drawn from an amorphous body of international best practices. However, these reforms, through their failure to include gender issues, do not address the specific problems facing Qatar, the UAE and Saudi Arabia in their education sectors. On the one hand, girls are short-changed as their relatively better performance compared with boys obviates a closer look at the quality of their education. On the other hand, the narrow framing of gender has enabled these governments to ignore the growing failure rates and increasing dropout rates of boys at both the secondary and tertiary levels. The restriction of the definition of gender equality to the enrolment rates of girls has benefited policy makers in Saudi Arabia but it has silenced the debate on quality for both boys and girls. Meanwhile the rhetoric of becoming a knowledge-based society, a world-class economy and having an international standard education sector continues.

Conclusion

The governments of Qatar, the UAE and Saudi Arabia are keen to signal modernity in education both to local constituents and the world at large. One of the globally accepted hallmarks of modernity in education is a focus on girls. However, through the development of universal education goals and best practices a focus on girls has been limited to enrolment rates and achievement relative to boys. Global gender and education priorities, as framed by Education for All, the Millennium Development Goals, Education at a Glance and the various TIMSS and PISA reports have served to focus attention on areas where these countries face relatively few problems (girls' enrolment and relative academic achievement) and away from those areas that are in greatest need (boys' performance and retention, and education quality in general). The *Millennium Development Goals Report for Saudi Arabia* (Ministry of Economy and Planning, Saudi Arabia 2009: 11) states that Saudi Arabia has a 'good' supporting environment to achieve gender equality (defined as '[e]liminating the gender disparity in primary and secondary education, by 2005, and in all levels of education by 2015'). This report fails to mention, however, that at the tertiary level women already outstrip men and in terms of achievement girls also perform better than boys on international assessments such as the TIMSS (Mullis et al. 2008). The unexpected, and, I would argue, unintended, educational achievements of girls[4] have enabled the countries of Qatar, the UAE and Saudi Arabia to declare success in terms of education and gender equality, while ignoring the fact that boys are falling further and further behind.

Qatar, the UAE and Saudi Arabia are now ranked with the most developed nations in terms of girls' enrolment and achievement in comparison with that of boys (UNESCO 2008). The World Economic Forum's *Global Gender Gap Report* states that the countries of the Gulf States have reached gender parity levels in education (World Economic Forum 2009).[5] Thus governments of the Gulf States are able to signal modernity to the West through the positive achievements of girls in relation to boys, while at the same time keep local constituents happy by maintaining the social and cultural status quo that limits women's opportunities to work, pass their citizenship on to their children, divorce or even drive (Middle East Online 2010).

The particular challenges facing boys can be easily ignored as they are not a part of the modernity benchmark, but doing so results in negative educational and employment outcomes for them. The OECD and the World Bank disregard in large measure the education of boys while many other international development organisations often view males as a hindrance to development (Bannon and Correia 2006). Thus for states that have been traditionally cast as oppressors of women, there is a double disincentive to focus on the achievement and retention of boys. If these states do decide to pay attention to boys they will appear to be, in the words of Jansen (2005), 'illogical' or, worse, patriarchal and misogynistic; and will appear out of line with conventional discourses on modernity, gender and education. Such a focus would give credence to the claim that they are indeed nations who only care about men.

While larger questions may be raised about the general purpose of education in the Gulf States, the growth in the number of youth attending private schools in the Gulf suggests that the belief in and the desire for a high quality education persists, even in the face of many disincentives to education. In Dubai more Emiratis now attend private schools than public schools (KHDA 2009) and with the introduction of school inspections parents are becoming much more aware of the differences between public and private schools. Across the region the failings of the various education systems have been clearly evidenced in the uprisings stretching from Egypt to Libya to Bahrain. All of these uprisings involved large numbers of unemployed and under-employed young males. While this chapter only looks at three countries in the Gulf region, the issue of poor quality education in the entire Middle East is very real and its impact on young men in particular is still largely unexplored and misunderstood.

Despite a spate of education reforms over the past 10 years, very little has changed in terms of what and how students are taught in Qatar, the United Arab Emirates and the Kingdom of Saudi Arabia. Modern education reforms, such as new curricula, environmentally friendly school buildings or investments in the latest ICTs, are announced, but little effort is focused on improving the quality of education at the classroom level and very little persists in terms of tangible achievement once the 'announcement effect' is over. Combined with the perception that parents' traditions and identity are under threat, reforms that become too unpopular are quickly undermined and scrapped. The impact of this situation, however, is not evenly felt among boys and girls, and yet education systems fail to acknowledge this fact. As long as modernity is, at least in part, defined as a focus on girls' education and measured through attainment of EFA and MDG targets or standardised test scores, then countries such as Qatar, the UAE and Saudi Arabia can continue to ignore boys and to evade tough questions about the quality of education for all.

Notes

1 An example of the poor quality of secondary schooling is evidenced by the fact that over 80 per cent of Emirati students need to attend a foundation year before they are accepted into regular courses at local universities, let alone to go abroad.
2 Given that both Arabic and Islamic Studies emphasise memorisation and rote learning it is unlikely that the teachers of these subjects are being assessed in the same way as teachers of other subjects, and thus it is unclear what this means in terms of accurately reflecting the overall quality of teaching and learning at these schools.
3 The Grand Mufti is the highest official of religious law in a Sunni country. In Saudi Arabia the current (2011) Grand Mufti is Abdulaziz Al Sheikh.
4 Other than providing schools for girls to attend, these states have not targeted girls' education explicitly.
5 Of note is Qatar, which ranks 53rd in terms of education but overall ranks at 125th out of 135 countries. There is no penalty, however, for countries that have a gender gap in favour of females on the WEF (2009) report, as it uses a single-sided measure.

References

Abdulla, F. and Ridge, N. (2011) *Where are all the men? Gender, participation and higher education in the United Arab Emirates.* Dubai School of Government. Online. Available www.dsg.ae/PUBLICATIONS/PublicationDetail.aspx?udt_826_param_detail=3015 (accessed March 2011).

Abu-Lughod, L. (ed.). (1998) *Remaking women: Feminism and modernity in the Middle East.* Princeton, NJ: Princeton University Press.

Abu-Lughod, L. (2002) 'Do Muslim women really need saving? Anthropological reflections on cultural relativism and its others'. *American Anthropologist,* 104: 783–790.

Al Munajjed, M. (2008) *Women's employment in Saudi Arabia: A major challenge.* Booz and Company. Online. Available www.booz.com/media/uploads/Womens_Employment_in_ Saudi_Arabia.pdf (accessed 12 May 2010).

Ali, K. A. (2002) *Planning the family in Egypt: New bodies, new selves.* Austin: University of Texas Press.

Ameinfo (2010) DSG Hosts Task force examining reasons why students drop out of school. *AMEINFO.* Online. Available www.ameinfo.com/237161.html (accessed 15 August 2010).

Arabian Business (2008) Gulf Arabs 'lazy' and 'spoilt', blasts Minister, *Arabian Business.* Online. Available www.arabianbusiness.com/509425-gulf-arabs-lazy-and-spoilt-blasts-minister (accessed 5 March 2010).

Baker, D. and LeTendre, G. (2005) *National differences, global similarities, world culture and the future of schooling.* Stanford, CA: Stanford University Press.

Bannon, I. and Correia, M. (eds). (2006) *The other half of gender.* Washington, DC: World Bank.

Chabbott, C. (2003) *Constructing education for development: International organizations and Education for All.* New York: Routledge.

Coker, M. (2010) Qatar rewrites ABCs of Mideast Education. *Wall Street Journal.* Online. Available http://online.wsj.com/article/NA_WSJ_PUB:SB1000142405274870424790457524 0083760987978.html (accessed 11 August 2010).

Dhillon, N. and Yousef, T. (eds) (2009) *Generation in waiting: The unfulfilled promise of young people in the Middle East.* Washington, DC: Brookings Institution Press.

Doumato, E. and Posusney, M. (eds) (2003) *Women and globalization in the Arab Middle East: Gender, economy and society.* Boulder, CO: Lynne Rienner.

Escobar, A. (1994) *Encountering development: The making and unmaking of the Third World.* Princeton, NJ: Princeton University Press.

Fuller, B. (1991) *Growing up modern: The Western state builds Third World schools.* New York: Routledge.

General Secretariat for Development Planning Qatar (2010) *Qatar National Vision 2030.* Online. Available www.investinqatar.com.qa/about/qatar%20vision (accessed 30 June 2010).

Goldmann, M. (2008) 'The accountability of private vs. public governance "by information": A comparison of the assessment activities of the OECD and the IEA in the field of education'. *Rivista trimestrale di diritto pubblico,* 58(1): 41–69.

Gurian, M. and Stevens, K. (2005) *The minds of boys.* San Francisco: Jossey-Bass.

Heyneman, S. P. (2003) 'The history and problems in the making of education policy at the World Bank 1960–2000'. *International Journal of Educational Development,* 23: 315–337.

Hilabi, A. (2010) Saudi stores defy fatwa banning female cashiers. *The National,* Online. Available www.thenational.ae/news/worldwide/middle-east/saudi-stores-defy-fatwa-banning-female-cashiers (accessed 8 November 2010).

Howden, D and Shields, R. (2008) Saudi women appeal for legal freedoms, *Independent.* Online. Available www.independent.co.uk/news/world/middle-east/saudi-women-appeal-for-legal-freedoms-812657.html (accessed 10 July 2010).

IMF (2008) *World Economic Outlook Database.* Online. Available www.imf.org/external/pubs/ft/weo/2008/02/weodata/index.aspx (accessed 8 August 2010).

IMF (2009) *World Economic Outlook: Sustaining the Recovery.* Online. Available www.imf.org/external/pubs/ft/weo/2009/02/ (accessed 8 August 2010).

Janahi, S. (2010) Do not stereotype Emiratis, says skills official. *The Gulf News.* Online. Available http://gulfnews.com/news/gulf/uae/employment/do-not-stereotype-emiratis-says-skills-official-1.664808 (accessed 20 July 2010).

Jansen, J. D. (2005) 'Targeting education: The politics of performance and the prospects of "Education for All"'. *International Journal of Educational Development,* 25: 368–380.

Jones, P. (2004) 'Taking the credit: Financing and policy linkages in the education portfolio of the World Bank', in G. Steiner-Khamsi (ed.) *The Global Politics of Educational Borrowing and Lending.* New York: Teachers College Press.

Kabbani, N. and Kothari, E. (2005) *Youth employment in the MENA region: A situational assessment.* Washington, DC: World Bank.

Kelly, S. and Breslin, J. (2010) *Women's rights in the Middle East and North Africa: Progress amid resistance.* Freedom House, New York. Online. Available http://freedomhouse.org/uploads/specialreports/womensrights/2010/womensrights2010.pdf (accessed 5 January 2011).

Khalaf, H. and Habboush, M. (2009) FNC presses educators on protection of national identity. *The National*. Online. Available www.thenational.ae/apps/pbcs.dll/article?AID=/2009 1117/NATIONAL/711169839&SearchID=73400341559996 (accessed 10 July 2010).

Knowledge and Human Development Authority (KHDA) (2009). *Key education statistics for Dubai*. Dubai: Knowledge and Human Development Authority. Online. Available http://www.khda.gov.ae/CMS/WebParts/TextEditor/Documents/Key%20EDU%20Stats%20Sheet_English.pdf (accessed 9 December 2010).

Larson, J. (2009) *Qatar's K-12 Education Reform has Achieved Success in its Early Years*, Research Brief, Rand-Qatar Policy Institute. Online. Available www.rand.org/pubs/research_briefs/2009/RAND_RB9455.pdf (accessed 10 November 2010).

Lepeska, D. (2010) Qatari Professor urges massive effort to prevent the death of Arabic. *The National*, Online. Available www.thenational.ae/news/worldwide/middle-east/qatari-professor-urges-massive-effort-to-prevent-death-of-arabic (accessed 14 January 2011).

Lewis, K. (2010) Alarm over school dropout rate. *The National*. Online. Available www.thenational.ae/news/uae-news/education/alarm-over-school-dropout-rate (accessed 20 December 2010)

Mahon, R. (2009) *Transnationalizing (child) care policy: The OECD and the World Bank*. Online. Available www.cccg.umontreal.ca/RC19/PDF/Mahon-R_Rc192009.pdf (accessed 1 July 2010).

Mahon, R. and McBride, S. (2008) *The OECD and transnational governance*. Vancouver: UBC Press.

Maktoob Business (2010) Saudi youth unemployment over 40%, *Maktoob Business*. Online. Available www.business.maktoob.com/20090000460774/Saudi_youth_unemployment_over_40_pct/Article.htm (accessed 20 August 2010).

Menne, A. (2008) *Challenges of Qatar's male deficit in education, policy implications*. General Secretariat for Development Planning. Online. Available www.gsdp.gov.qa/portal/page/portal/GSDP_Vision_Root/GSDP_EN/GSDP_News/GSDP%20News%20Files/Challenges_of_Qatar_Male_Deficit_in_Education_Policy_Imp.pdf (accessed 3 June 2010)

Meyer, J. W., Boli, J., Thomas, G. M. and Ramirez, F. O. (1997) 'World society and the nation-state'. *American Journal of Sociology*, 103: 144–181.

Middle East Online (2010) Women's rights in Saudi lag behind Gulf nations, Online. Available www.middle-east-online.com/english/?id=37671 (accessed 22 August 2010).

Ministry of Economy and Planning, Saudi Arabia (2009) *Millennium Development Goals*, Online. Available www.undp.org.sa/sa/index.php?option=com_content&view=article&id=26&Itemid=49&lang=en (accessed 15 August 2010).

Ministry of Education, Saudi Arabia (2003). *The Development of Education*. Online. Available www.ibe.unesco.org/International/ICE47/English/Natreps/reports/sarabia_en.pdf (accessed 25 May 2010)

Ministry of Education, Saudi Arabia (2005) *The Executive Summary of the Ministry of Education Ten-Year Plan* (2004–2014), Online. Available http://planipolis.iiep.unesco.org/upload/Saudi%20Arabia/Saudi%20Arabia%20Education%20Plan%20English%20summary.pdf (accessed 7 June 2010).

Ministry of Education, Saudi Arabia (2008) *National Report on Educational Development in the Kingdom of Saudi Arabia*, Education International Conference Geneva. Online. Available www.ibe.unesco.org/National_Reports/ICE_2008/saudiarabia_NR08_en.pdf (accessed 20 May 2010).

Moghadam, V. (2003) *Modernizing women: Gender and social change in the Middle East*. Boulder, CO: Lynne Rienner.

Morgan, C. (2009) 'Transnational governance: The case of the OECD PISA', paper presented at the Annual Conference of the Canadian Political Science Association, Ottawa, May 27.

Mullis, I., Martin, M. and Foy, P. (2008) *TIMSS 2007 International Mathematics Report: Findings from IEA's Trends in International Mathematics and Science Study at the Fourth and Eighth Grades.* Boston: International Association for the Evaluation of Educational Achievement.

Mullis, I., Martin, M., Gonzalez, E. and Chrostowski, S. (2004) *TIMMS 2003 International Mathematics Report: Findings from IEA's Trends in International Mathematics and Science Study at the Fourth and Eighth Grades.* Boston: International Association for the Evaluation of Educational Achievement.

Najmabadi, A. (1998) 'Crafting an educated housewife in Iran', in L. Abu-Lughod (ed.) *Remaking women: Feminism and modernity in the Middle East.* Princeton, NJ: Princeton University Press.

Parpart, J., Connelly, P. and Barriteau, V. (eds) (2000) *Theoretical perspectives on gender and development.* Ottawa: International Development Research Center.

Phillips, D. (2004) 'Towards a theory of policy attraction in education', in G. Steiner-Khamsi (ed.) *The Global Politics of Educational Borrowing and Lending.* New York: Teachers College Press.

Porter, T. and Webb, M. (2008) 'Role of the OECD in the orchestration of global knowledge networks', in R. Mahon and S. McBride (eds) *The OECD and Transnational Governance.* Vancouver: UBC Press.

Ridge, N. (2008) *Privileged and penalized: The education of boys in the United Arab Emirates* (doctoral dissertation). Teachers College, Columbia University, New York.

Sabbagh, S. (2003) *Arab women: Between defiance and restraint.* Northampton, MA: Olive Branch Press.

Said, E. (1979) *Orientalism.* New York: Random House.

Samoff, J. (2000) 'Institutionalizing international influence', in N. Burbules and C. A. Torres (eds) *Globalization and education: Critical perspectives.* New York: Routledge.

Sasson, J. (1992) *Princess: A true story of life behind the veil in Saudi Arabia.* Atlanta: William Morrow Press.

Schriewer, J. and Martinez, C. (2004) 'Constructions and internationality in education', in G. Steiner-Khamsi (ed.) *The global politics of educational borrowing and lending.* New York: Teachers College Press.

Silova, I. (2004) 'Adopting the language of new allies', in G. Steiner-Khamsi (ed.) *The global politics of educational borrowing and lending.* New York: Teachers College Press.

Sonbol, A. (2006) 'Women, Islam and education', in R. Zia (ed.) *Globalization, modernization and education in Muslim countries.* New York: Nova Science.

Souad. (2003) *Burned alive: A victim of the law of men.* New York: Warner Books.

Spreen, C. (2004) 'Appropriating borrowed policies: Outcomes-based education in South Africa', in G. Steiner-Khamsi (ed.) *The global politics of educational borrowing and lending.* New York: Teachers College Press.

Steiner-Khamsi, G. (Ed.) (2004) *The global politics of educational borrowing and lending.* New York: Teachers College Press.

Supreme Education Council Qatar (2009) *Annual Symposium Stresses Importance of Maintaining Cultural Identity in a Global Era.* Supreme Education Council Press Release. Online. Available www.english.education.gov.qa/content/resources/detail/7342 (accessed 23 October 2010).

Tilak, J. B. (2005) 'Critique: UNESCO. 2003. Gender and education for all: The leap to equality'. *International Review of Education,* 51: 73–83.

UAE Ministry of Education (2004) *Vision 2020.* Dubai: UAE Ministry of Education.

UAE Ministry of Education (2005) Unpublished statistics on education and achievement in the United Arab Emirates.

UAE Ministry of Education (2008) *National Strategy of the Ministry of Education 2008–2010.* Abu Dhabi: UAE Ministry of Education.

UAE Ministry of Education (2010) The *Ministry of Education Strategy 2010–2020: Aiming at accomplishing a score of 10/10 in all its initiatives.* Abu Dhabi: UAE Ministry of Education.

UAE Ministry of Information and Culture (2008) *UAE yearbook 2006–2008.* Online. Available www.uaeinteract.com/uaeint_misc/ pdf_2008/index.asp (accessed 5 May 2008).

UAE Prime Minister's Office (2009) *Vision 2021: United in Ambition and Determination.* Abu Dhabi: United Arab Emirates. Online. Available www.vision2021.ae/downloads/UAE-Vision2021-Brochure-English.pdf (accessed September 1, 2010).

UNDP (2005) *Arab human development report 2005: Towards the rise of women in the Arab world.* New York: United Nations Publications.

UNESCO (2002) *Arab States regional report.* Quebec: UNESCO Institute for Statistics. Online. Available www.uis.unesco.org (accessed 22 November 2005).

UNESCO (2008) *Education for All global monitoring report: Education for all by 2015: Will we make it?* Oxford: Oxford University Press.

World Bank (2004) *Gender and development in the Middle East and North Africa: Women in the public sphere.* Washington, DC: World Bank.

World Bank (2008) *MENA development report: The road not traveled, Education reform in the Middle East and North Africa.* Washington, DC: World Bank.

World Economic Forum (2009) *Global Gender Gap Report,* World Economic Forum. Online. Available www.weforum.org/pdf/gendergap/report2009.pdf (accessed 22 August 2010).

16 Conditional Cash Transfers

Paying to Keep Children in School and Conquering the World. Three Selected Case Studies[1]

Michelle Morais de Sá e Silva

This chapter addresses an educational/poverty reduction policy that has been involved in many instances of policy borrowing and lending over the past 15 years: conditional cash transfer (CCT) programmes. These programmes have become a global reform model that has currently been adopted by at least 40 countries. They are intended to improve the income of poor families in the short term, but at the same time are expected to break the intergenerational cycle of poverty by increasing the educational attainment of poor children.

This chapter explains in detail the nature of CCTs and their relationship to education. It then addresses their international diffusion, presenting the results of a quantitative appraisal of the existing programmes in various countries. Finally, the chapter presents three case studies – *Bolsa Família* in Brazil, *Subsidios Condicionados a la Asistencia Escolar* in Bogotá (Colombia), and Opportunity NYC in the United States – selected because of their different structures of education conditionalities. Bolsa Familia makes cash transfers to families dependent upon children's school attendance; Subsidios adds the condition of completing the school year; and Opportunity NYC conditions some payments on children's academic performance. Bolsa Familia is the typical case, because most CCTs include required enrolment and a minimum level of school attendance. Subsidios and Opportunity NYC, with more conditions, are rather exceptions in this regard, although they do comply with other CCT standard characteristics: they are cash-based and targeted programmes. In essence, the idea was to look at variations within a global model.

Despite their differences and commonalities, the three selected cases have had their conception and implementation marked by interesting processes of policy borrowing and lending. This chapter analyses those processes by attempting to answer the following research question: 'What contribution can the apparent globalisation of the CCT model bring to the borrowing and lending theoretical framework?'

The Basic Features of CCT Programmes

With few exceptions, most countries with high poverty also suffer from a lack of educational opportunities for youth. Poor families often cannot afford the direct and indirect costs of sending their children to school and, even when they can, the children face adverse conditions that hinder their performance and motivation to remain enrolled. In a vicious cycle, poor children's limited access to schooling prevents them from accumulating human capital (Schultz 1961) and from taking advantage of the liberating potential of education (Freire 1970). Empirically, the correlation between poverty-level income and lack of schooling is strong (Fiszbein and Psacharopoulos 1995).

Scholars acknowledge that breaking this vicious cycle is not an easy task. On the one hand, as concluded by Levin and Kelley (1994), education cannot do it alone. On the other hand, even if an immediate reduction in poverty by means of handouts helps the poor cope with the challenges to daily survival, it does not ensure that they will escape the poverty trap. In the mid-1990s, conditional cash transfers were conceptualised in Brazil and Mexico to deal with this dilemma.

The idea of giving poor families a certain amount of cash on the condition that they send their children to school or frequently visit health clinics was a strategy to reconcile short-term needs with long-term human capital development. In the wake of structural adjustment programmes and the deteriorating social conditions that followed in developing countries, CCTs arose as an alternative to universal and unconditional social programmes, especially food subsidies. Different from government subsidies, which benefit anyone who purchases a certain good or service, conditional cash transfers are only provided to a targeted population. According to Grosh et al. (2008), 'the last 20 years have seen a marked move away from generalized, universal food subsidies toward more targeted programs, and from the use of food toward the use of cash' (p. 254). Besides, CCTs are not only cash grants meant to reduce income poverty. They also work as incentives or 'rewards' for people to look after their education and health. From an education perspective, CCTs are a step beyond the elimination of school fees in efforts to universalise basic education (United Nations Educational, Scientific and Cultural Organization (UNESCO) 2008). Besides eliminating the direct barriers to enrolment, they serve as financial support so that students can remain in school and eventually graduate.

CCTS around the World

As of late 2009, there were 43 CCT programmes spread across 40 countries (see the Appendix for a list of the programmes). Interestingly, most of them share some basic characteristics, making CCTs resemble a global model at first sight. Every CCT programme in the world has at least the following three features: 1) they are cash based; 2) they are targeted; and 3) they require family compliance with conditions related to the acquisition of human capital.

In addition, 35 out of the existing 43 programmes (81.3 per cent) have a national scope. It is a fact, however, that among national programmes the total number of beneficiaries widely varies. In the case of Brazil, for instance, Bolsa Familia reaches about a quarter of the country's total population. Moreover, from their predominantly national scope, we can infer that CCTs are implemented by central governments rather than by regional, provincial or city governments.

Even though programmes appear not to be as homogenous with respect to funding, variation is mostly concentrated around four categories: of the 43 programmes, 22 programmes (51.16 per cent) are exclusively funded by the government, 10 (23.26 per

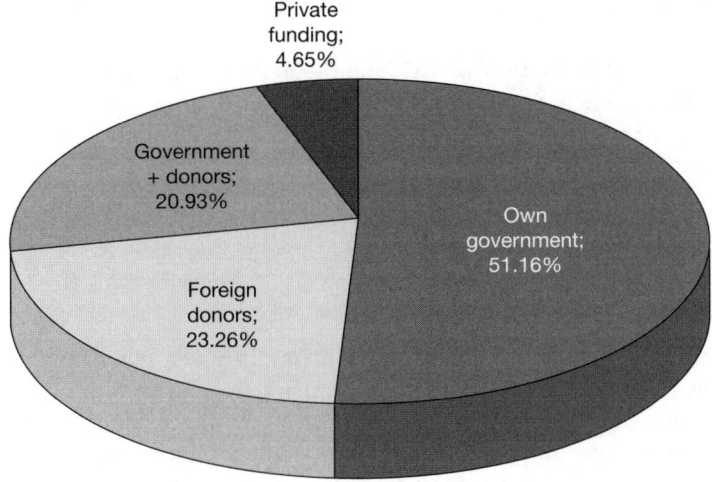

Private funding; 4.65%

Government + donors; 20.93%

Foreign donors; 23.26%

Own government; 51.16%

Figure 16.1 CCT funding by source (percentage)

cent) are exclusively funded by multilateral organisations or bilateral agencies, 9 (20.93 per cent) have a mix of government funds and foreign loans, and 2 (4.65 per cent) are based on private funds.

Figure 16.1 signals the considerable presence of foreign donors involved in CCT funding. Comparing the programmes that are externally funded to those that receive both government and foreign funds, the international presence reaches 44.19 per cent of all catalogued CCTs. That finding testifies to the fact that those programmes have been globally promoted as 'best practices' by various international organisations, such as the World Bank, the Inter-American Development Bank (IDB), the United Nations Development Program (UNDP), UNESCO and the UN Children's Fund (UNICEF). The World Bank alone has organised three international conferences for the exchange of experiences among CCT countries (World Bank 2006). Just recently, private phil-anthropies have also joined the legion of CCT supporters. The most compelling example is the Rockefeller Foundation, which has taken the lead in supporting, both financially and politically, the adoption and implementation of New York City's CCT programme, Opportunity NYC.[2] The influence of those advocates, who usually have funding on their side to make the case for CCTs, is an important factor for the under-standing of how those programmes achieved their current global reach.

In the majority of programmes (35 out of 43) transfers are made conditional upon school attendance. Exceptions include some African countries, where minimum attendance is not required.[3] In a few other countries, more ambitious conditions and goals have been added to the attendance-only conditionality, including the require-ment of grade completion (i.e. Colombia) and improved performance in standardised tests (i.e. the US).

Despite their educational conditionalities and goals, most CCT programmes are managed by non-education government institutions, most of them in the field of welfare and social development. In only five of the 40 countries are CCTs under the responsibility of the Ministry of Education or of a city's Department of Education.

Those exceptions are the city of Bogotá (Colombia), New York City (US), Bangladesh, Cambodia and Mozambique.

Despite this apparent globalisation of CCTs and standardisation of poverty-reduction programmes, at the national level CCTs have actually been quite heterogeneous. Their underlying discourse, education goals and mode of operation vary considerably across countries.

The Three-Case Study

Research Design

The selection of cases for the study was guided by an interest in better understanding typical cases, since so many programmes share basic characteristics such as scope, source of funding and education-related conditionalities. However, 'outliers' are equally interesting, since a few programmes appear as stark exceptions for most of the appraised characteristics. Case selection was also based on the fact that the programmes are diverse in terms of the education conditionalities to which their cash benefits are tied: Bolsa Familia is the typical case, being only conditional upon school attendance; the Subsidios programme has attendance and graduation conditionalities; and Opportunity NYC makes transfers dependent upon attendance and improved performance on tests.

This research made use of qualitative methods for the analysis and comparison of cases. Data collection was carried out in three research sites – New York City, Bogotá and Brasilia – from February 2009 to March 2010. Collection methods were similar across the three cases, involving semi-structured interviews, collection of policy documents and appraisal of press materials and institutional websites. A total of 66 semi-structured interviews were conducted across the three cases over one year of data collection. Data obtained from interviews are referenced by means of codes in order to assure participant anonymity. Each case study was assigned a letter code: A for Opportunity NYC, B for Subsidios Condicionados a la Asistencia Escolar, and C for Bolsa Familia. Each participant was then assigned a letter code and a number, which corresponds to the chronological order of interviews. In referencing interview data, the exact date when the interview was carried out is also presented.

Case A: Opportunity NYC (New York City)[4]

Programme Overview

For those who thought that CCTs were exclusive remedies of the developing world, the adoption of Opportunity NYC in the world's financial capital came as a surprise. Officially, the programme was a response to the recommendations issued by the Commission for Economic Opportunity (CEO; the 'Poverty Commission'), which had been formed by Mayor Michael Bloomberg to advise him on how to mitigate poverty in the city. In the midst of discussions about possible strategies to face the city's poverty problems, representatives of the Rockefeller Foundation and some other members of the commission recommended the adoption of a conditional cash transfer programme (UN Webcast Archives 2007). The Rockefeller Foundation then coordinated a study tour to Mexico so that Mayor Bloomberg and Deputy Mayor Linda Gibbs could get to know the *Oportunidades* programme and borrow its CCT model (Morais de Sá e Silva 2008c).

The idea of a cash transfer tied to education-seeking behaviour resonated with the ideas that Harvard Professor Roland Fryer had been promoting for some time. Fryer had based his views on the argument that disadvantaged children lack the motivation to perform better in school because they do not have close examples of the future benefits of investing time and effort in education. Consequently, they need a material incentive that would influence their behaviour and boost their performance. In 2004 Fryer convinced then NYC Schools Chancellor Joel Klein to let him expand an experiment that he had been running in Public School 70 in the Bronx, where he had introduced small prizes to reward students for achieving better grades. Even though the data for P.S. 70 had been inconclusive, Chancellor Klein allowed the experiment to be taken to more schools, with the replacement of small prizes by cash incentives (Dubner 2005).

Thus the idea of adopting a CCT to tackle poverty in the city was coupled with the ideas and practices that Fryer had been promoting in education. The end result of this merger is reflected in the way that NYC's CCT – *Opportunity NYC* – was structured when launched in 2007. The bulk of the programme, called Family Rewards, would be managed by CEO and include a plethora of different conditions, which, if met in their entirety, could allow a beneficiary family to receive cash benefits of as much as US$ 6,000 per year. The Department of Education was expected to oversee the Spark sub-programme, which targeted only fourth and seventh graders in 60 pre-selected low-performing schools. Table 16.1 contrasts Family Rewards and Spark in greater detail.

Opportunity NYC had a total budget of US$ 50 million, meant to fund a two-year pilot that started in September 2007. The budget was entirely funded by private institutions such as the Rockefeller Foundation, the Starr Foundation, the Robin Hood Foundation, the Open Society Institute, the American International Group and Mayor Bloomberg himself (Office of the Mayor 2007).

In 2009 Family Rewards was renewed for a third year. The renewal included the revision of some of its conditionalities, especially in the areas where early evaluation results showed the programme had had no impact (i.e. school attendance during elementary and middle school). In April 2010 comprehensive evaluation results were launched and programme managers confirmed the unexpected: Opportunity NYC had a dismal performance, with no substantial impact on the beneficiary's school performance (Riccio et al. 2010). Since then it has been unclear whether the programme will be terminated or reformed.

Was the Policy Really Borrowed from Mexico?

Opportunity NYC had been announced and advertised as an import from Mexico. CEO's 2009 annual report included a section, 'From Oportunidades to Opportunity NYC', suggesting that the New York programme was named after its Mexican inspiration. According to the World Bank's latest book on CCTs, 'Opportunity NYC was modelled explicitly on Mexico's Oportunidades' (Fiszbein and Schady 2009: 144).

Table 16.1 Opportunity NYC Family Rewards and Opportunity NYC Spark

Programme elements	Family Rewards		Spark
Development and management	CEO, Seedco, MDRC and selected community-based organisations		NYC Department of Education and the EdLabs (Harvard University).
Beneficiaries	2,500 families residing in Central and East Harlem in Manhattan, Brownsville and East New York in Brooklyn, and Morris Heights/ Mount Hope and East Tremont/Belmont in the Bronx		8,000 kids from 60 schools located all over the city have been chosen to participate. They are either 4th or 7th graders.
Activities and rewards	*Condition*	*Reward*	
	95% of school attendance per month	$25 per month (elementary and middle school students) $50 per month (high school students)	'Students in the fourth grade will receive up to $25 for a perfect score on each of 10 interim assessment tests taken throughout the year, up to a total of $250' (Seedco 2007). 'Seventh graders can earn up to $50 per test for a maximum payment of $500 per year' (Seedco 2007).
	Attending parent–teacher conferences	$25	
	Obtaining a library card	$50	
	Improvement in scores or proficiency on standardised tests at the elementary and middle school levels	$300 per test (elementary school) $350 per test (middle school)	
	Passing grade on individual Regents exams	$600	
	Parental review of the test and discussion with teachers	$25	

Source: Morais de Sá e Silva (2008c).

In addition, among the 209 newspaper articles found on Opportunity NYC, 109 (52.15 per cent) made reference to Mexico and 76 (36.36 per cent) to Oportunidades.

In the early stages of the New York programme there were indeed numerous exchanges between Opportunity NYC's designers and Oportunidades' officials. Joint workshops and study tours were organised. However, upon looking at how the two programmes operated, it becomes apparent that Opportunity NYC preserved only a few characteristics of its Mexican counterpart. It also diverged from the Brazilian and the Bogotá experiences in many respects, as shown below.

At the discourse level, Opportunity NYC kept the ideas of breaking the intergenerational cycle of poverty and of investing in human capital. Nonetheless, if one compares its documents to international papers and reports on CCTs, it is interesting to notice the great difference in the language used. Whereas CCT experts in Mexico, Brazil, Colombia and other countries talk about 'conditionalities' and 'stipends' (*bolsa* in Portuguese, *bono* or *subsidio* in Spanish), Opportunity NYC had 'activities' and 'rewards' or 'incentives'. Opportunity NYC interviewees used expressions such as 'customer service', 'reward menu' and 'claims processing', which were not part of the language used by Bolsa Família's and Subsidios' interviewees. The open and direct reference to reducing poverty and inequality was also subtle in Opportunity NYC, which insisted instead on 'behavior change' and 'creating opportunities'. Thus if one considers the distinction between policy talk, policy action and policy implementation (Tyack and Cuban 1995), the kind of policy borrowing that took place in Opportunity NYC had not been complete even at the minimum level of policy talk, being closer to what the literature calls 'brand-name piracy' (Steiner-Khamsi 2004).

Differences in terms of programme operations abound. First, there was a deliberate process of searching for eligible families and having them apply to the lottery. In most CCTs there are only public information campaigns to let eligible families know that they should apply. Programme managers do not pursue families to convince them to participate. Second, the hiring of neighbourhood partner organisations to do the recruitment work and support families throughout the programme was also a feature unique to New York City. As mentioned above, Opportunity NYC had a long list of conditionalities and families only received payments if they were able to properly hand in coupons to prove compliance. Those aspects added complexity to the programme and made it more time-consuming for participating families.

The above comparison makes it clear that even though there has been great emphasis on following the Mexican experience and on South–North learning, Opportunity NYC was an experiment that was actually very different when compared with most existing CCTs. The reasons behind that deviation from the standard CCT *modus operandi* may have to do with the fact that the programme was not dependent upon international funding. Therefore, it did not need to strictly follow a certain model or hire the same consultants.

Also, in the US it appears that there is a different understanding about the causes of poverty and how it should be tackled. Whereas internationally those reasons are seen as structural, related to the history and development of each country, in the US they are approached as a consequence of individual effort and behaviour. That may be why Opportunity NYC was less about providing additional income to poor families – as in the case of Oportunidades, Bolsa Família, and other programmes – and more about incentivising behaviour.

The emphasis on the idea that Opportunity NYC borrowed its policy model from Mexico can be explained by the borrowing and lending literature through the concepts of 'externalization' and 'certification strategy' (Steiner-Khamsi 2004). According to that literature, governments declare plans to borrow policy models from other countries in order to legitimise policy ideas that have been domestically grown. As previously reported, the proposal of an incentives programme to induce behaviour, such as improved academic performance, had already been introduced in the US by

Professor Fryer. But as Spark was included under the umbrella of Opportunity NYC, it became part of the 'borrowing from Mexico' package and consequently received the certification and legitimisation that comes with policy borrowing from elsewhere.

Also, as City Hall expected to face opposition to its incentive programme, it used the reference to Oportunidades as a shield. Interestingly, the 'borrowing from Mexico' idea backfired and ended up being criticised, with many pointing the finger at how poverty conditions were different in New York City as compared with rural Mexico (Gelinas 2006). Consequently, programme managers eventually had to emphasise that they were aware of the contextual differences and that adaptations had been duly carried out. The following paragraph from Opportunity NYC's evaluation report exemplifies this process:

> In 2006, mindful of the differences between Mexico's rural poor (where the most evidence had been amassed) and the urban poor in this country, but impressed by the success of Oportunidades and other countries' CCT programs, Mayor Michael Bloomberg's Center for Economic Opportunity (CEO) began to explore whether a CCT program could be adapted for use in New York City's poorest neighborhoods.
>
> (Riccio et al. 2010: xv)

Policy Lending: It Is Never Too Early for Policy Transfer

Interestingly, there have been efforts to disseminate Opportunity NYC's experience since the early stages of the programme's pilot, even in the absence of evidence of its impact. According to the borrowing and lending literature, the above can be interpreted as an attempt to obtain legitimacy for the programme through policy lending (Steiner-Khamsi 2004). As other countries import the NYC model, this is used as proof of the programme's value. Why would Opportunity NYC need to be legitimised? First, because the media initially created the impression that the programme was too controversial. Second, because the continuation or replication of Opportunity NYC after the three-year pilot depended on public funding. More than that, it is likely that the programme will depend on federal dollars.

In December 2007, only three months after Opportunity NYC started operating, the City government participated in a UN Conference about South–South learning. A few months later the Rockefeller Foundation gave a grant to MDRC for the establishment of the Conditional Cash Transfer Learning Network, whose purpose was to allow other cities and countries to learn from the Opportunity NYC experience (interviewee A9, 12 May 2009). During the launch of the Network, Mayor Bloomberg said: 'We are encouraged by the interest generated in Opportunity NYC, and look forward to sharing our expertise with others as they seek to tackle the issue of poverty in their respective countries and cities' (Rockefeller Foundation 2008). In the framework of the CCT Learning Network, the Rockefeller Foundation funded a seminar on CCT experiences in July 2008. The seminar brought to Rockefeller's Bellagio Center in Italy CCT experts from several countries, including Colombia, Brazil, Indonesia, Turkey and South Africa. Representatives of the World Bank, Seedco, CEO, MDRC and Harvard were also present.

Later in 2009 another initiative that would work as a platform to help disseminate New York City's experience was created: the Inter-American Social Protection Network (IASPN). 'The objective of the IASPN is to promote cooperation and information-sharing among countries and institutions on social protection practices that provide real solutions to help reduce social inequality and poverty' (Organization of American States 2009). During the launch of the Inter-American Social Protection Network, Secretary of State Hillary Clinton praised CCTs for their impact on reducing poverty and inequality (Organization of American States 2009).

Interestingly, Opportunity NYC's managers and funders readily listed the programme's best practice elements, even though evaluation results were not available by that time. Interviewees from CEO, MDRC, the Rockefeller Foundation and the World Bank were unanimous about the set of programme aspects that they considered innovative and that could inform policies in other cities and countries: the work component, incentives for academic performance, established alliances with local organisations for family guidance and the operation in a large urban setting (interviewees A7, A8, A9, and A10). Mayor Bloomberg, in his words of endorsement for the World Bank's most recent book on CCTs, said: 'We look forward to adding our evaluation results to an important body of research and continuing our work with partners worldwide to reach our shared goal of breaking the cycles of intergenerational poverty' (Bloomberg 2009, quoted in Fiszbein and Schady 2009, back cover).

Opportunity NYC's lending drive has been met with much enthusiasm by the international community. The World Bank, which was initially an important source of CCT expertise during the design of the programme, has now turned into a main broker for its lending to other countries. For instance, the Bank has organised study tours for foreign delegations to learn from the New York experience. That was the case of a visit by a Nigerian delegation and of a workshop with representatives of Latin American countries (Chile, Colombia, Mexico and Brazil) in June 2009 (interviewee A7, 8 May 2009).

Does the above narrative mean that Opportunity NYC has already become a 'best practice'? Will its cash-for-performance model be disseminated to developing countries by means of World Bank loans and consultants? Will the CCT Learning Network become a school for policy makers around the globe to replicate Opportunity NYC at home? If so, what supposedly started as South–North learning may end up turning again into the traditional North–South learning of the past.

Case B: Subsidios Condicionados a la Asistencia Escolar (Bogotá, Colombia)[5]

Colombia counts on a nationwide conditional cash programme called *Familias en Accion*. The programme was especially designed for rural areas and follows the pattern of making transfers conditional upon children's school attendance (see the Appendix). Even so, in 2005 the Inter-American Development Bank (IDB), along with researchers from some universities in the US, designed a project to introduce a separate CCT in the capital, Bogotá. The CCT project '*Subsidios Condicionados a la Asistencia Escolar*'[6] had a budget of US$ 20.3 million and was part of a broader loan agreement of US$ 92.9 million for the overarching 'Bogotá Equity in Education Program' (IDB 2006).

The creation of the Subsidios CCT was based on evidence that, despite superior net enrolment in basic education (85 per cent in primary education and 80 per cent in secondary), Bogotá faced a severe dropout problem. In 2003 it was estimated that there were 89,000 dropouts among children and adolescents, 98 per cent of them from SISBEN[7] 1 and 2, the poorest social strata (IDB 2005). Thus, with the aim of fostering retention and increasing graduation rates, IDB and the City Department of Education (SED) designed a CCT that was targeted at the upper grades of primary education and at secondary education.

Besides working as a direct intervention, the project was also an experiment. It encompassed three payment schemes involving different conditionalities and cash benefits. The idea was to evaluate which scheme would be more effective in keeping beneficiaries in school. Initially, the programme was implemented in only two of the city's 20 districts: Suba and San Cristobal. As explained in Mayer and Morais de Sá e Silva (2008), the different payment schemes were organised into 'modalities', which comprised the following characteristics:

- Modality 1: A bi-monthly transfer of 60,000[8] pesos for up to two years for students in 6th to 11th grade in San Cristobal and 6th to 8th grade in Suba.
- Modality 2: A bi-monthly transfer of 40,000 pesos plus 100,000 pesos received from a savings account upon grade completion for up to two years. Beneficiary students had to be in the 6th to 11th grade and reside in San Cristobal.
- Modality 3: A bi-monthly transfer of 40,000 pesos plus 100,000 pesos received from a savings account upon grade completion for up to three years. An additional 600,000 pesos upon enrolment in post-secondary education. Beneficiary students had be in the 9th to 11th grade and reside in Suba.

A year after the concurrent implementation of the three modalities, a new programme was 'attached' to the CCT experiment. Modality 3 beneficiaries who were in 11th grade in 2005 and fulfilled the requirement of graduating from high school were offered a full scholarship for post-secondary education. The additional bonus that had been offered for enrolment in higher education was replaced by a scholarship covering tuition and a stipend for six semesters. Students were offered a range of technical and technological careers in a set of private institutions certified by the Department of Education (Mayer and Morais de Sá e Silva 2008).

In 2006, besides the addition of the post-secondary scholarship, the decision was made to expand the Subsidios programme to all areas of the city with high concentrations of low-income students. Despite such expansion and the positive results identified by a quantitative evaluation (Barrera-Osorio et al. 2008), modality 3 was dropped from the CCT programme and its participants became modality 2 beneficiaries.

By mid-2008 the Subsidios programme went through a second, now qualitative, evaluation. Study findings indicated that the programme was strongly valued by families, especially with regard to its post-secondary scholarship component. Also, it had some positive spillover effects on the siblings[9] of beneficiary students, who saw the programme as a source of encouragement to remain in school. Still, it was apparent that both the cash transfer for high school completion and the scholarship for post-secondary education did not offset all costs that students faced to remain enrolled, not to mention opportunity costs. Even so, families had stretched their budgets and students had made all necessary efforts to graduate. In cases where beneficiaries dropped out, the reasons were external circumstances such as pregnancy, illness of a family member or military service (Mayer and Morais de Sá e Silva 2008).

Institutionally, the Subsidios programme was managed by Bogotá's Department of Education and funded and monitored by the Inter-American Development Bank. Its design and evaluations were meant to inform CCT programmes in other countries, especially in Latin America, about the effectiveness of different payment schemes.

Policy Borrowing: From Mexico and Brazil

According to interviewees B2 and B6, Subsidios was modelled after Mexico's Oportunidades and Brazil's Bolsa Escola (which at the time had already become Bolsa Familia). The programme's savings component was specifically inspired by *Jovenes con Oportunidades*, a component of the Oportunidades programme. *Jovenes* benefits adolescents and young adults in Oportunidades families who are enrolled in lower and upper secondary school (the last year of *secundaria* and the two years of *bachillerato*). As beneficiaries complete each of those grades, they accumulate 'points' in the programme, which are turned into cash once the beneficiary completes high school. This strategy was devised to reduce the dropout rate, increase high school completion and also support enrolment in higher education (Oportunidades 2010).

As for Bolsa Escola/Bolsa Familia, it also had a savings component, which was called School Savings (*Poupança Escola*). Yonemura (2005: 52) explains that:

> One minimum wage was deposited into a savings account for each child whose family was a beneficiary of the scholarship program if the child successfully completed the grade and was promoted to the next grade. . . . Half of the deposit could be withdrawn if the child reached the 4th grade or the 8th grade, depending on when they started the program. The balance could be withdrawn only when the student completed high school.

Borrowing from the Mexican and Brazilian programmes can be explained as a consequence of the economics of policy borrowing (Steiner-Khamsi 2004). According to the literature, one of the reasons why governments borrow policy models from abroad is to please donors and thus receive funding. In the case of Bogotá, the city government wanted to obtain an external loan, especially from the Inter-American Development Bank. Since both Oportunidades and Bolsa Escola/Bolsa Familia were favourites among the international community of donors, reference to those programmes could facilitate the approval of funds. Thus policy borrowing was not a result of external pressure, but rather a mechanism to impress donors.

Even though Oportunidades and Bolsa Escola/Bolsa Familia were used as models in the design of the Subsidios programme, Subsidios was not created as an exact copy of those two programmes. The direct involvement of school personnel in its operation, the use of three different payment schemes and the signing of 'terms of commitment' by participating families were among its peculiar features. Programme designers had room for innovation and that may be associated with the fact that among them were US-based researchers who pushed for making Subsidios a new experiment.

Policy Lending: Not Internationally Prominent

For both the IDB and the involved US-based researchers, Subsidios was purposefully designed and evaluated to inform other countries about the effectiveness of different payment schemes. Even though the programme had operated for five years, it was still portrayed as an experiment in international publications such as Barrera-Osorio et al. (2008) and Fizsbein and Schady (2009). However, little had been done to promote Subsidios in other countries. It received no media coverage outside of Colombia. Of the four articles published on the programme, none was from a foreign newspaper. In addition, a search of the World Bank's and the IDB's websites for *Subsidios Condicionados a la Asistencia Escolar* found only three pages of results on the former and six on the latter. Compared with the other two case studies analysed here, the results were, respectively: 1,210 and 83 pages for Bolsa Familia, and 96 and 1 for Opportunity NYC.

According to an IDB representative, Subsidios' low profile internationally derived from the absence of efforts by the Department of Education to give international exposure to the programme (interviewee B21, 25 June 2009). However, neither the World Bank nor the IDB itself has included Subsidios in international exchanges such as visits by foreign delegations or the frequent videoconferences with representatives of CCT programmes in Latin America (in which managers of Familias en Accion participate).

The reason behind both Banks' lack of effort to export Subsidios may be related to some 'reverse' politics of policy lending. As in the case of policy borrowing, borrowing and lending theory argues that policy lending occurs when a policy is in need of legitimisation at home. The export of that policy is used as a sign of its value, as a certification strategy. In that case, political factors contribute to the promotion of policy lending (Steiner-Khamsi 2004). In contrast, 'reverse' politics would mean that politics work as a constraint to policy lending. In Bogotá political disputes between the national government and the city government led to a prevalence of Familias en Accion (the national programme) in the international arena. Both the IDB and the World Bank, as providers of large annual loans to finance Familias, could not 'upset' the national government by internationally promoting the CCT implemented by its opponent party in the City of Bogotá. Consequently, there were minimal efforts to promote the Subsidios' model and experience outside of Colombia.

Case C: Bolsa Família (Brazil)

Despite its current status as a federal programme, Bolsa Familia has municipal and state origins. Its conditional cash transfer model first emerged in Campinas and in the Federal District[10] in 1995 (Britto 2004). In the former, the programme was called Guarantee of Minimum Family Income. In the latter, it was named *Bolsa Escola* (School Stipend) and had been conceptualised by then governor Cristovam Buarque.

In 2001 the Ministry of Education decided to adopt a CCT programme at the national level, naming it Bolsa Escola. It was mostly an educational programme, as it was meant to help poor families cope with both the direct and opportunity costs of sending their children to school. Poor families received a fixed amount of cash every month if they sent their children to school regularly. It was a strategy designed to reduce the number of out-of-school children, reduce child labour and increase enrolment, especially in primary education. The programme was quickly scaled up to virtually all Brazilian municipalities and reached over five million families in a short time.

In 2003 newly elected President Luis Inacio Lula da Silva maintained Bolsa Escola and launched a major poverty-reduction programme, *Fome Zero* (Zero Hunger), as his flagship social initiative. Zero Hunger comprised different elements, among them a cash transfer for the purchase of food (*Cartão Alimentação*/Food Card). Yet it soon faced various implementation difficulties and had a hard time demonstrating positive results. Against that backdrop, there were a number of other cash transfer programmes that were inherited from the previous administration. They were scattered around different line ministries: *Bolsa Escola* at the Ministry of Education, *Bolsa Alimentação* (Food Stipend) at the Ministry of Health, and *Vale Gás* (Cooking Gas Stamp) at the Ministry of Mines and Enegy.

By the end of 2003 the federal government decided to consolidate all of the cash transfers into a single programme: *Bolsa Familia* (Britto 2008). By early 2004 a new ministry was created, the Ministry of Social Development and Fight against Hunger (MDS), which became responsible for the implementation of the programme. From then on the Ministry of Education became responsible only for assisting MDS in obtaining attendance records of Bolsa Familia's beneficiary children. Similarly to the former Bolsa Escola, Bolsa Familia transferred a certain amount of cash to the female head of the household provided that children demonstrated minimum school attendance of 85 per cent if they were six to 15 years old and 75 per cent for adolescents age 16 or 17. In addition, the programme had health-related conditionalities, such as the immunisation of children younger than age seven and monthly visits to health clinics by expectant women (MDS 2008).

By 2010 Bolsa Familia had reached 13 million families from every Brazilian municipality, which corresponds to about a quarter of the country's total population. Previous studies and evaluations found that the programme had a positive impact on reducing poverty and inequality (Soares et al. 2007). It terms of its education outcomes, the 2008 Global Monitoring Report on Education for All found that it led to 'reduction of drop out by 75% among beneficiaries' (UNESCO 2008: 115).

Policy Borrowing: No Need to Borrow

CCTs have existed for the longest time of any country in Brazil and they did not emerge out of a process of policy borrowing from abroad. However, that does not mean that Bolsa Familia might not have been influenced by foreign models. In fact, the very decision to create Bolsa Familia by unifying previously existing CCTs was to some extent influenced by advice from Oportunidades' creator Santiago Levy (interviewee C6, 6 June 2009). Also, Bolsa Familia officials had been part of the international network of CCT specialists, who met regularly in countless meetings for experience sharing.

Even so, there is no explicit evidence of policy borrowing from a particular country. MDS officials considered that Brazil had numerous peculiarities and had been attempting to cope with them on their own. Only recently had the Bolsa Familia team made a concession to import some aspects of Chile's CCT programme, particularly the processes of family follow-up and case management (interviewee C17, 5 March 2010). Such a lack of effort to borrow from elsewhere may be explained by Bolsa Familia's strong legitimacy in Brazil. Just as the borrowing and lending literature indicates that policy makers borrow from other countries in order to obtain legitimacy at home, governments that enjoy significant support for their policies may be in the comfortable position of not having to borrow. That seems to be the case of Bolsa Familia.

The absence of policy borrowing does not mean that Brazil has not received foreign support, particularly from donors. The World Bank has been the programme's most important external partner. The Bank played an important role in Bolsa Familia's creation by helping convince the Brazilian government to base its poverty reduction strategy on targeted conditional cash transfers rather than on unconditional food support (interviewee C2, 6 May 2009; interviewee C6, 6 June 2009).

Following the unification of programmes and the creation of Bolsa Familia, the World Bank negotiated and approved a loan to support the new comprehensive programme. The 'Bolsa Familia First Adaptable Program Loan', with a total budget of US\$ 520 million, was approved in June 2004 (World Bank 2004). Most of the loan funds – US\$ 500 million – were to be directly used for family cash transfers (interviewee C2, 6 May 2006). The Inter-American Development Bank (IDB) also provided the programme with financial support in its early stages (Hall 2008). In 2009 the IDB approved a new Bolsa Familia-related project, this time aimed at knowledge building and sharing in the broader field of social protection. The project, with a budget of only US\$ 1 million, is described thus:

> The Technical Cooperation [TC] will support the definition of the country's mid and long-term strategy in social protection. The TC will finance studies, seminars and workshops that will feed into a Knowledge Agenda for (i) the evaluation of the social safety net in Brazil; (ii) the definition of strategies for including families in vulnerability in urban areas and metropolitan regions; and (iii) identification and analysis of best practices for the economic inclusion of beneficiaries in productive and income-generating activities.
>
> (IDB 2010)

The United Kingdom's Department for International Development (DFID) has been another constant partner of Bolsa Familia. DFID has offered direct technical assistance and has hired consultants to work in the programme. Lately it has provided technical and financial support for the sharing of social protection experiences between MDS and African countries (see below).

Interestingly, donors have changed their approach towards Brazil and Bolsa Familia in recent years. According to interviewee C17 (5 March 2010), in the beginning of the

Lula administration donors used to approach MDS to offer technical assistance and financial support. In some cases there were strings attached to their offers and they presented specific demands about how projects should be developed. Lately, however, the Ministry has been given a greater voice in cooperation initiatives. Besides, donors such as DFID and the World Bank have increasingly asked MDS to share its experience with other countries. As concluded by interviewee C17, this new situation reflects how Bolsa Familia in particular and the government of Brazil as a whole have gained international respect in recent years.

Policy Lending: High Demand

As the idea of a CCT programme has existed in Brazil since the 1990s, there have been countless opportunities for policy lending involving Brazilian CCT policy makers. In fact, proponents of the different variations of cash transfer schemes have made use of policy lending to earn legitimacy for their ideas. For instance, Bolsa Escola creators claim direct influence over the establishment of similar CCTs in Latin America, such as those in Mexico, Ecuador and the city of Buenos Aires (Aguiar and Araújo 2002). In the case of Mexico's Progresa/Oportunidades, Brazilian interviewees reported that Mexican officials visited Brazil to get to know the Bolsa Escola experience (interviewee C4, 20 May 2009; interviewee C15, 26 February 2010).[11] In addition, Cristovam and his supporters created the NGO *Missão Criança* (Mission Child), aimed at the promotion of the Bolsa Escola model. This NGO has supported the creation of pilot Bolsa Escola programmes in other countries, such as Mozambique, Guatemala, Sao Tome and Principe and Tanzania (Missão Criança 2010).

Since the creation of Bolsa Familia, the government of Brazil has received various cooperation requests from other developing countries. As the programme has been well documented in the international CCT literature, governments around the world have received information about it. Many have developed an interest in learning about it in greater detail and, possibly, in importing its model. Bolsa Familia's policy lending initiatives have also been a result of the president's foreign policy agenda. During his visits to other developing countries, as well as during visits by other presidents and prime ministers, Lula has often offered technical cooperation in the field of social development and poverty reduction. As a result, various bilateral Protocols of Intention have been signed. Then, if the other country maintains its interest, specific cooperation projects are designed by the Brazilian Cooperation Agency (ABC) and the Ministry of Social Development.

Different from Bolsa Escola's proponents, Bolsa Familia's managers and supporters have not had to actively seek to promote the programme abroad. The first reason is that Bolsa Familia is politically strong in Brazil, as discussed above. Thus the programme does not need the seal of approval that comes with policy lending (Steiner-Khamsi 2004). Second, foreign demand for Bolsa Familia is such that MDS has worked mostly in a responsive manner. Third, the Ministry counts on limited human resources to manage the programme: about 200 people, as compared with almost 1,000 working for Mexico's Oportunidades (interviewee C17, 5 March 2010). Consequently, MDS cannot devote much personnel and energy to replicating Bolsa Familia elsewhere. The priority is working on the programme at home. According to interviewee C17, the Minister of Social Development will not make more human resources available to international cooperation before concrete results of international efforts are presented.

Donors have played an important role in encouraging the international diffusion of the Bolsa Familia model. The World Bank, for instance, has worked as a broker in that regard, linking Brazil to other countries that are interested in establishing a CCT. That was the case of India and Peru. Besides providing resources to fund exchanges between countries, the Bank also offers a loan to help fund the creation of a CCT in the recipient country (interviewee C1, 1 May 2009).

The UK's Department for International Development (DFID) has been also very active in supporting cooperation between Brazil and other developing countries in the field of social protection. Specifically, DFID finances the 'Africa–Brazil Cooperation Program on Social Development'. DFID's programme has facilitated cooperation efforts between Brazil and selected African countries, constituting a so-called 'triangulation' initiative in South–South cooperation. Although the programme's mission is broadly defined in terms of social development, there have been initiatives specifically focused on Bolsa Familia. According to the Africa–Brazil website, housed by the International Policy Center for Inclusive Growth (IPC-IG):

> In 2006, representatives of Ghana, Guinea Bissau, Mozambique, Nigeria, South Africa and Zambia undertook a study tour to Brazil on conditional cash transfer programs. In 2007, Brazil provided the government of Ghana with technical cooperation in the design of a pilot social grants program entitled Livelihood Empowerment Against Poverty.
>
> (IPC-IG 2010)

Despite such a high demand from other countries and interest from donors, Bolsa Familia has not received as much international exposure as Mexico's Progresa/ Oportunidades, especially in the academic literature (interviewee C3, 20 May 2009). Major CCT funders, such as the World Bank and the Inter-American Development Bank, have also featured the Mexican CCT many more times than Brazil's Bolsa programmes (Bolsa Escola and Bolsa Família). Figure 16.2 presents the number of entries found on the banks' websites for Brazil's and Mexico's CCTs.

When asked about why Progresa/Oportunidades is better known internationally than Bolsa Família, interviewees indicated the following reasons:

1   'Bolsa Familia is so Brazilian'. It works in a decentralised way and only uses the self-declared family income as its targeting criterion (interviewee C1, 1 May 2009).
2   Most evaluations of Bolsa Familia have been done on a small scale and quietly, whereas Oportunidades/Progressa set up an evaluation unit from its beginning and has made its evaluations internationally available (interviewee C3, 20 May 2009; interviewee C18, 7 March 2010).
3   Most Mexican policy makers have studied in US universities. Upon their return they are very serious about applying what they learned in terms of methods and new ideas. Consequently Mexico ends up becoming a 'policy laboratory', which,

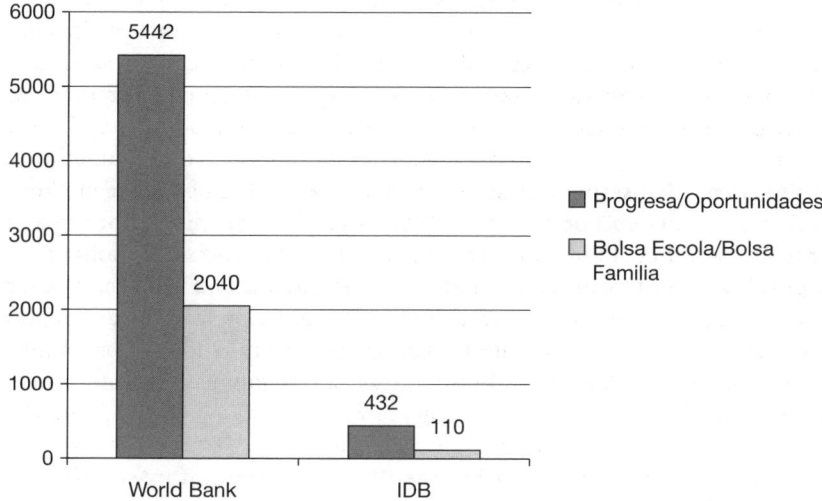

Figure 16.2 Progresa/Oportunidades and Bolsa Escola/Bolsa Familia on the banks' websites

Notes: Data for Progresa/Oportunidades corresponds to: the number of pages with the name Progresa + the number of pages with the name of Oportunidades – the number of pages with both names. Data for Bolsa Escola/Bolsa Familia corresponds to: the number of pages with the name Bolsa Escola + the number of pages with the name Bolsa Familia – the number of pages with both names.

due to its link to the US, gets significant international visibility (interviewee C7, 10 September 2009).

4   Progresa/Oportunidades has been more dependent on international funding than Bolsa Familia (interviewee C7, 10 September 2009).

5   Progresa/Oportunidades has strictly conformed to the CCT model that international experts have advocated for; it is completely focused on building human capital, which is reflected in the programme's design, documents and discourse.
                                                    (Interviewee C18, 7 March 2010)

Furthermore, interviewee C7 argued that Progresa/Oportunidades has faced greater political challenges at home than has Bolsa Familia. Even though Mexico is also a federation, its CCT was designed and implemented in a centralised way. In order to obtain legitimacy, especially in the relationship with different states, the programme has needed the 'international seal of approval'. Conversely, the decentralised implementation of Bolsa Familia allowed for the sharing of 'political dividends' between the federal, state and municipal governments, and, consequently, the programme was supported by a multi-partisan network and less in need of external legitimisation.

A Comparison of the Cases

Rather than conforming to that human capital CCT model, the three CCTs studied have shown various peculiarities in their design, mode of implementation and policy discourse. By comparing interviews with the managers of the three cases to those with representatives of international organisations (as well as with the international literature on the topic), it was surprising to find that the programme managers did not completely reproduce the international discourse on conditional cash transfers. As a matter of fact, the idea of building human capital was not mentioned by programme managers in any of the three cases.

In Brazil the dominating discourse was that of citizenship, with conditionalities on fund transfers seen as 'co-responsibilities' and even as rights. In Bogotá, the predominant idea was one of promoting student well-being by providing children and adolescents with additional income to cover school expenses and satisfy other daily needs. Opportunity NYC worked around the idea of rewards and incentives for increased student effort and parental participation. As an example of the disconnect between the international focus on human capital and the individual national discourses, here is an excerpt of how the Ministry of Social Development officially defines Bolsa Familia:

> The Bolsa Familia Program is based on the articulation among three dimensions that are essential to overcome poverty and hunger: immediate poverty relief through the direct transfer of income to families; the reinforcement of basic social rights in the fields of Health and Education, by means of the compliance with conditionalities, which help families break the intergenerational cycle of poverty; and the coordination with complementary programs, which are aimed at families' development, so that Bolsa Familia's beneficiaries will be able to overcome their situation of vulnerability and poverty.
>
> (MDS 2008)

Thus, although the borrowing and lending literature indicates that policy borrowing occurs mostly at the level of 'policy talk' (Steiner-Khamsi 2004), in this case even policy talk has been just partially borrowed. The reproduction of the CCT jargon only takes place when it is convenient, such as in international meetings, publications and loan documents. Domestically, however, each government has produced its own way of conceptualising and communicating CCT fundamentals.

Considering that the three cases have either worked with international funding (Subsidios and Bolsa Familia) or have capitalised on the seal of approval of international organisations (Opportunity NYC), the above finding would be unexpected from the point of view of the economics of policy borrowing. However, this research was able to demonstrate that in countries like Brazil and Colombia, which are not extremely poor, governments have some room to impose their will because it is also in the banks' interest to lend money. Such a 'reverse dependence' (bank dependence on borrowing governments) was clear in the Colombian case, where the banks' ties to the national government generated constraints for the international promotion of Bogotá's CCT programme.

When it comes to whether each of the three CCTs officially borrowed from other countries and whether it exported its own model, the study found that all three cases partially conformed to what the borrowing and lending literature would predict. But beyond that, each case also showed peculiar aspects related to their borrowing and lending processes.

In the case of Opportunity NYC, the 'borrowing from Mexico' discourse was used as a strategy to obtain legitimacy for the programme at home. For the same reason, there has been a desire for policy lending to other countries. Initiatives to promote the programme abroad were begun even before its impact was known. The peculiar aspect about Opportunity NYC, however, is that eventually critics attacked the idea of using a programme in NYC that was inspired by a poverty-reduction experience in Mexico, where poverty conditions are supposedly very different. Consequently, programme managers needed to reassure the public that the model had been adapted to the different situation in NYC.

In Bogotá, Subsidios was a clear case of the economics of policy borrowing, where reference was made to CCT model programmes in Mexico and in Brazil in order to please donors. However, it was very interesting to find that Subsidios was a case of reverse politics of policy lending. The political dispute between those in the city government and those in the national government constrained policy lending. International banks did not promote the programme outside of Colombia to prevent upsetting the national government, which had its own CCT programme – Familias en Accion – and which took out annual international loans to maintain it.

Finally, the case of Bolsa Familia shows a close connection between findings related to the programme's strong political sustainability and its near lack of policy borrowing. Besides the initial influence of Mexico's experience, Bolsa Familia managers have made little effort to borrow from other CCTs. In theory they do not have the political need to do so. Similarly, there have not been major efforts in policy lending except for those in response to demands that come directly from other countries or that are intermediated by international organisations.

Contributions of this Study to Borrowing and Lending Theory

The detailed study of three cases of CCT programmes presented here revealed new conceptual possibilities of how borrowing and lending processes can develop. First, the study revealed that not only can politics play a role in triggering policy lending, it can prevent such lending from taking place. Due to political disputes, an interesting policy experience may be kept hidden from international eyes so as not to give exposure and credit to its creators.

Also, if a certain government counts on strong political support at home, it will not borrow from elsewhere and will not feel the need to market its policy abroad. So far, the borrowing and lending literature has documented various cases where policy transfer took place because legitimacy and a seal of approval were needed. This study, conversely, presents evidence that the counterfactual to that finding is also true: when there is no political need, there is no borrowing and lending.

Finally, the study's findings speak to those who are true believers in evidence-based policy making and in the possibility of 'speaking truth to power' (Henig 2008). CCT cases, especially the Opportunity NYC experience, indicate that evidence of impact and positive results is not necessarily a condition for the international spread of a policy model. In other words, policy experiences may be called best practices without having been proven to be best.

Appendix: Conditional Cash Transfers around the World

Region	Country	Programme(s)	Government Institution	Funding Source	Scope	Educational Conditionalities
Americas	1. Argentina (World Bank 2006, IPC-IG 2008c)	Ciudadania Portena	Government of Buenos Aires	City government	Municipal	School attendance
		Jefes de Hogar	Ministry of Labor and Social Security	Central government and World Bank Central	National	School attendance
	2. Brazil (World Bank 2006)	Bolsa Familia	Ministry of Social Development	government, supported by past loans from the World Bank and the Inter-American Development Bank (IDB)	National	School attendance
	3. Chile (IPC-IG 2008c)	Chile Solidario	Ministry of Planning	Central government	National	Tailored conditionalities for each family
	4. Colombia (IPC-IG 2008c Mayer and Morais de Sá e Silva 2008)	Familias en Accion	Agency for Social Action and International Cooperation	Government and IDB	National	School attendance
		Subsidios Condicionados a la Asistencia Escolar	Bogotá Department of Education	IDB and Department of Education	Municipal	Attendance, grade promotion, and high school graduation
	5. Costa Rica (IPC-IG 2008c)	Avancemos	Ministry of Housing and Human Settlements	Central government	National	Attendance and grade promotion
	6. Dominican Republic (World Bank 2006)	Solidaridad	Social Policies Bureau	Central government	National	School attendance
	7. Ecuador (World Bank 2006)	Bono de Desarrollo Humano	Ministry of Social Welfare	Government and World Bank	National	School attendance
	8. El Salvador (World Bank 2006)	Red Solidaria	Social Area at the President's Office	Central government	National	School attendance

Country (reference)	Program	Implementing agency	Funding	Coverage	Outcome
9. Guatemala (Fiszbein and Schady 2009)	Mi Familia Progresa	Department of Executive Coordination, President's Office	Government and World Bank	National	School attendance
10. Honduras (World Bank 2006)	Programa de Asignacion Familiar	Ministry of the Presidency	IDB and World Bank	National	School attendance
11. Jamaica (World Bank 2006)	PATH	Ministry of Labor and Social Security	Central government	National	School attendance
12. Mexico (World Bank 2006, Oportunidades Press and Media Office 2008).	Oportunidades	Secretariat for Social Development	Government and IDB	National	Attendance and high school graduation
13. Nicaragua (World Bank 2006)	Red de Proteccion Social	Family Ministry	Central government	National	Attendance and grade promotion
14. Panama (IPC-IG 2008c)	Red de Oportunidades	Ministry of Social Development	Central government	National	School attendance
15. Paraguay (Soares and Britto 2007)	Tekopora	Secretary of Social Action	Government, supported by past IDB loan	National	School attendance
16. Peru (World Bank 2006)	Juntos	Ministry of Women and Social Development	Central government	National	School attendance
17. Uruguay (IPC-IG 2008c)	Ingreso Ciudadano	Ministry of Social Development	Central government	National	School attendance
18. US, NYC (Morais de Sá e Silva 2008a, 2008b, 2008c)	Opportunity NYC	City Department of Education and Center for Economic Opportunity	Various private sponsors	City-wide	School attendance and academic achievement
Asia and the Pacific 19. Bangladesh (World Bank 2002, Tietjen 2003)	1. Primary Education Stipend Program (Food for Education) 2. Female Secondary School Assistance	1 & 2. Ministry of Education	1. Government Budget 2. World Bank loan	1 & 2. National	1 & 2. Student attendance and performance, and school performance.

Region	Country	Programme(s)	Government Institution	Funding Source	Scope	Educational Conditionalities
	20. Cambodia (Filmer and Schady 2009)	Cambodia Education Support Project	Ministry of Education	World Bank	National	Enrolment, attendance and grade promotion
	21. India (IPC-IG 2008b)	Conditional Cash Transfer Scheme for Girl Child	Ministry of Women and Child Development	Central government	Some states	School attendance
	22. Indonesia (Fiszbein and Schady 2009)	Keluarga Harapan	Ministry of Social Welfare	Central government	National	School enrolment and attendance
	23. Mongolia (IPC-IG 2008b)	Child Money Program	Ministry of Social Welfare and Labor	Asian Development Bank	National	School enrolment
	24. Pakistan (World Bank 2006)	Child Support Program	Ministry of Social Welfare and Special Education	Central government	National	School attendance and passing final exam
	25. Philippines (IPC-IG 2008b)	AHON	Department of Social Welfare and Development	Central government World Bank	National	School attendance
	26. Turkey (World Bank 2006)	Social Risk Mitigation Project	General Directorate of Social Assistance and Solidarity	World Bank	National	School attendance
Africa	27. Botswana (IPC-IG 2008a)	Orphan Care Program	Ministry of Local Government	Central government	National	Unconditional
	28. Burkina Faso (Fiszbein and Schady 2009)	Orphans and Vulnerable Children	National Council against HIV/AIDS and STDs	World Bank and other donors	Regional	School attendance
	29. Burundi (Devereux et al. 2005)	Children in Distressing Situations Scheme		UNICEF	National	Unconditional
	30. Egypt (IPC-IG 2008a)	Ain el-Sira Project (Cairo)	Ministry of Social Solidarity	Ministry of Social Solidarity	Municipal	School attendance

Country (reference)	Program	Implementing agency	Funding source	Coverage	Conditionality
31. Ghana (IPC-IG 2008d)	Livelihood Empowerment against Poverty	Ministry of Manpower, Youth and Employment	Central government	National	School enrolment and attendance
32. Kenya (World Bank 2006, Andrade 2007)	Cash Transfer Program for Orphans and Vulnerable Children	Ministry of Home Affairs	UNICEF	National	School attendance
33. Lesotho (Devereux et al. 2005)	Cash Transfer Program for Orphans and Vulnerable Children	Ministry of Health and Social Welfare	Central government	National	Unconditional
34. Malawi (Andrade 2007)	Malawi Social Cash Transfer Scheme	Department of Poverty and Disaster Management	UNICEF	National	Unconditional
35. Mozambique (Andrade 2007)	Bolsa Escola	Ministry of Education	Brazil/Missao Crianca	District (Maputo)	School attendance
36. Namibia (Devereux et al. 2005)	Child Maintenance Grant	Ministry of Health and Social Services	Central government	National	Unconditional
37. Nigeria (IPC-IG 2008a)	In Care of the Poor	National Agency for the Poverty Eradication Program	Central government	National	School attendance
38. South Africa (World Bank 2006, Andrade 2007)	CCT to Support Vulnerable Children in the Context of HIV/AIDS and Poverty	Ministry of Social Development	South African Government	National	School attendance
39. Tanzania (IPC-IG 2008a)	Save the Children	Department of Social Welfare	Central government	National	Unconditional
40. Zambia (Andrade 2007)	Kalomo Social Cash Transfer Scheme	District Social Welfare Office	GTZ (German cooperation)	District (Kalomo)	Unconditional

Notes

1 This chapter derives from my PhD dissertation, 'Conditional Cash Transfers and Education: United in Theory, Divorced in Policy', Columbia University, 2010. The dissertation analyses conditional cash transfer programmes from four theoretical perspectives, one of which is policy borrowing and lending.
2 See www.rockfound.org/efforts/nycof/opportunity_nyc.shtml.
3 In most cases, the reason why minimum attendance is not required, even though the programme has educational goals, is that countries lack the administrative capacity to verify attendance and enforce compliance.
4 This sub-section is based on Morais de Sá e Silva (2008a, 2008b, 2008c).
5 This sub-section is based on Mayer and Morais de Sá e Silva (2008).
6 The title translates as Conditional Subsidies for School Attendance.
7 SISBEN stands for System for the Identification of Potential Beneficiaries of Social Programs. A unified measurement system of citizens' standard of living, it classifies them into six different strata. The lower the family scores in the system, the poorer it is and the more eligible for participation in social programmes.
8 The exchange rate between the US dollar and the Colombia peso fluctuates around 1:2,000.
9 Different from the majority of CCT programmes, where more than one school-age child is entitled to the transfer in each family, most families who participated in the Subsidios program had only one child benefiting from the programme because participation was defined through a lottery system randomised at the child level and not at the family level.
10 The Federal District, where Brasilia is located, is the size of a city but has the status of a federated state. It elects its own governor and state legislature but has no municipal-level elected officials.
11 However, Santiago Levy, the founder of Progresa/Oportunidades in Mexico, did not mention Bolsa Escola as a source of inspiration in his book (Levy 2006).

References

Aguiar, M. and Araújo, C. H. (2002) *Bolsa Escola: Education to confront poverty*. Brasilia: UNESCO.
Andrade, M. (2007) *Social protection schemes in selected African countries*. [Unpublished manuscript].
Barrera-Osorio, F., Bertrand, M., Linden, L. and Perez-Calle, F. (2008) Conditional cash transfers in education: Design features, peer and sibling effects. Evidence from a randomized experiment in Colombia. Retrieved on 15 November 2008, from http://web.worldbank.org/WBSITE/EXTERNAL/TOPICS/EXTEDUCATION/0,,contentMDK:21631004~isCURL:Y~menuPK:2448393~pagePK:210058~piPK:210062~theSitePK:282386,00.html.
Britto, T. F. (2004) *Conditional cash transfers: Why have they become so prominent in recent poverty reduction strategies in Latin America?* The Hague: Institute of Social Studies.
Britto, T. F. (2008). 'Brazil's Bolsa Familia: Understanding its origins and challenges'. *Poverty in Focus*, 15: 6–7.
Devereux S., Marshall J., MacAskill, J. and Pelham, L. (2005) *Making Cash Count: Lessons from cash transfer schemes in east and southern Africa for supporting the most vulnerable children and households*. London: Save the Children UK, HelpAge International and IDS Sussex.
Dubner, S. (2005) 'Toward a unified theory of black America'. *New York Times Magazine*, 20 March 2005. Retrieved on 15 July 2008, from www.nytimes.com/2005/03/20/magazine/20HARVARD.html?pagewanted=all.
Filmer, D. and Schady, N. (2009) *In school but not learning: The impact of a scholarship program on school enrollment and achievement*. Washington, DC: The World Bank.

Fiszbein, A. and Psacharopoulos, G. (1995) 'Income inequality trends in Latin America in the 1980s'. In N. Lustig (ed.), *Coping with austerity: Poverty and inequality in Latin America.* Washington, DC: The Brookings Institution.

Fiszbein, A. and Schady, N. (2009) *Conditional cash transfers: Reducing present and future poverty.* Washington, DC: The World Bank Group.

Freire, P. (1970) *Pedagogy of the oppressed.* New York: Herder & Herder.

Gelinas, N. (2006) 'New York isn't Mexico'. *City Journal,* 17 (4). Retrieved 25 October 2007, from www.city-journal.org/html/eon2006-10-20ng.html.

Grosh, M., del Ninno, C., Tesliuc, E. and Ouerghi, A. (2008) *For protection and promotion: The design and implementation of effective safety nets.* Washington, DC: The World Bank.

Hall, A. (2008) 'Brazil's Bolsa Familia: A double-edged sword?', *Development and change,* 39 (5): 799–822.

Henig, J. (2008) *Spin cycle. How research is used in policy debates: The case of charter schools.* New York: Russell Sage Foundation.

IDB. (2005) *Documento conceptual de proyecto. Programa de Equidad en Educacion en Bogota.* Retrieved on 15 November 2008, from http://idbdocs.iadb.org/wsdocs/getdocument. aspx?docnum=571342.

IDB. (2006) *Bogota Equity in Education Program.* Retrieved on 2 March 2008, from www.iadb. org/projects/Project.cfm?project=CO-L1010&Language=English.

IDB. (2010) *BR-T1080: Knowledge Agenda – Social Protection.* Retrieved on 8 March 2010, from www.iadb.org/projects/project.cfm?id=BR-T1080&lang=en.

IPC-IG. (2008a) *Cash transfer programs in Africa.* Retrieved on 15 October 2008, from www. undp-povertycentre.org/cctafrica.do.

IPC-IG. (2008b) *Cash transfer programs in Asia and the Pacific.* Retrieved on 28 October 2008, from www.undp-povertycentre.org/cctasia.do.

IPC-IG. (2008c) *Cash transfer programs in Latin America and the Caribbean.* Retrieved on 28 October 2008, from www.undp-povertycentre.org/cctlac.do.

IPC-IG. (2008d) *Cooperation Brazil-Ghana.* Retrieved on 28 October 2008, from www.undp-povertycentre.org/africa-brazil/brasilganaeng.do.

IPC-IG. (2010) *Africa–Brazil Cooperation Programme on Social Development.* Retrieved on 5 March 2010, from www.ipc-undp.org/ipc/africa-brazil.jsp.

Levin, H. and Kelley, C. (1994) 'Can education do it alone?'. *Economics of Education Review,* 13(2): 97–108.

Levy, S. (2006) *Progress against poverty: Sustaining Mexico's Progresa-Oportunidades program.* Washington, DC: Brookings Institution Press.

Mayer, P. and Morais de Sá e Silva, M. (2008) *Bogotá Equity in Education: Conditional subsidies for school attendance and postsecondary study. A qualitative evaluation.* [Unpublished manuscript].

MDS. (2008) *Programa Bolsa Familia.* Retrieved on 2 November 2008, from www.mds.gov.br/ bolsafamilia/.

Missão Criança. (2010) *Atuação internacional* [International action]. Retrieved on 5 March 2010, from www.missaocrianca.org.br/saibamais.html.

Morais de Sá e Silva, M. (2008a) 'Opportunity NYC: A performance-based conditional cash transfer programme. A qualitative analysis'. *International Poverty Centre Working Paper,* n. 49.

Morais de Sá e Silva, M. (2008b) 'Opportunity NYC: A controversial cash transfer in the North'. *Poverty in Focus,* 15: 16–17.

Morais de Sá e Silva, M. (2008c) 'New York's brand-new conditional cash transfer programme: What if it succeeds?' *International Poverty Centre One Pager,* n. 60.

Office of the Mayor. (2007) *Mayor Bloomberg Welcomes First Opportunity NYC Program Participants and Announces Partnerships with Eight Local Banks and Credit Unions to Offer Them "No Fee" Accounts*. Retrieved on 20 October 2007, from www.nyc.gov/portal/site/nycgov/menuitem.c0935b9a57bb4ef3daf2f1c701c789a0/index.jsp?pageID=mayor_press_r elease&catID=1194&doc_name=http%3A%2F%2Fwww.nyc.gov%2Fhtml%2Fom%2Fht ml%2F2007b%2Fpr33007.html&cc=unused1978&rc=1194&ndi=1.

Oportunidades. (2010) *Jovenes con Oportunidades*. Retrieved on 26 January 2010, from www.oportunidades.gob.mx/jovenes/jovenes.html.

Oportunidades Press and Media Office. (2008) *Oportunidades: A program of results*. Retrieved on 29 October 2008, from www.oportunidades.gob.mx/e_oportunidades/publicaciones/Oportunidades a_program_of_resullts_PDF.pdf.

Organization of American States. (2009) Inter-American social protection network launched. *Summit of the Americas Newsletter,* October 2009. Retrieved on 6 January 2010, from www.summit-americas.org/Newsletter/2009/nl_en_1009_iaspn.htm.

Riccio, J., Dechausay, N., Greenberg, D., Miller, C., Rucks, Z. and Verma, N. (2010) *Toward reduced poverty across generations: Early findings from New York City's conditional cash transfer program*. Retrieved on March 30, 2010, from http://www.mdrc.org/publications/549/full.pdf.

Rockefeller Foundation. (2008) *Mayor Bloomberg and the Rockefeller Foundation announce the launch of a learning network to share design and implementation of a conditional cash transfer program*. Retrieved on 24 January 2010, from www.rockefellerfoundation.org/news/press-releases/mayor-bloomberg-rockefeller-foundation.

Schultz, T. S. (1961) 'Investment in human capital'. *American Economic Review*, 51: 1–17.

Seedco. (2007) *Mayor Bloomberg Releases Incemtives Schedule for Opportunity NYC Aimed at Helping New Yorkers Break the Cycle of Poverty*. Retrieved on 12 November 2007, from http://www.seedco.org/newsreleases/newsrelease.php?id=49.

Soares, F and Britto, T. (2007) 'Confronting capacity constraints on conditional cash transfers in Latin America: The cases of El Salvador and Paraguay'. *International Policy Center for Inclusive Growth Working Paper 38*.

Soares, F., Ribas, R. and Osório, R. (2007) 'Evaluating the impact of Brazil's Bolsa Família: Cash transfer programmes in comparative perspective'. *IPC Evaluation Note, 1*.

Steiner-Khamsi, G. (2004) *The politics of educational borrowing and lending*. New York: Teachers College Press.

Tietjen, K. (2003) The Bangladesh Primary Education Stipend Project: A descriptive analysis. [Manuscript]. Retrieved on October 27, 2008, from http://siteresources.worldbank.org/EDUCATION/Resources/278200-1099079877269/547664-1099080014368/BangladeshStipend.pdf.

Tyack, D. and Cuban, L. (1995) *Tinkering toward utopia: A century of public school reform*. Cambridge, MA: Harvard University Press.

United Nations Educational, Scientific and Cultural Organization (UNESCO). (2008) *EFA Global Monitoring Report. Education for All by 2015. Will we make it?* Oxford: Oxford University Press.

UN Webcast Archives (2007) Eyes on the South as a knowledge hub. Retrieved on 25 November 2007, from www.un.org/webcast/SE2007.html.

World Bank. (2002) Project appraisal document on a proposed credit to the People's Republic of Bangladesh for a Female Secondary School Assistance Project II. Retrieved on 27 October 2008, from www-wds.worldbank.org/external/default/WDSContentServer/WDSP/IB/2002/03/08/000094946_0202230403505/Rendered/PDF/multi0page.pdf.

World Bank. (2004) *Project Information Document. Bolsa Familia First Adaptable Program Loan*. Retrieved on March 8, 2010, from www-wds.worldbank.org/external/default/WDS

ContentServer/WDSP/IB/2004/05/11/000104615_20040513125107/Rendered/PDF/BF0PI
D0100MAY02004.pdf.

World Bank. (2006) *Conditional cash transfers*. Retrieved on 15 October 2008, from http://web.
worldbank.org/WBSITE/EXTERNAL/TOPICS/EXTSOCIALPROTECTION/EXTSAFETY
NETSANDTRANSFERS/0,,contentMDK:20615138~menuPK:282766~pagePK:148956~pi
PK:216618~theSitePK:282761,00.html.

Yonemura, A., (2005) *The changing social agenda in Brazil: An analysis of the policymaking
process in the case of Bolsa Escola.* Unpublished doctoral dissertation, Teachers College,
Columbia University.

Part IV

Diffusion, Travelling Reforms and Policyscapes

17 Imagining Globalisation

Educational Policyscapes

Stephen Carney

Comparative education has been reinvigorated but also fundamentally challenged by the contemporary desire for international policy borrowing and lending. In no other era have we seen such intense cross-national attraction, adaptation and imposition of education policies. This mania of learning from, and out-manoeuvring, our allies, partners and competitors has strong origins in the intensified relations between nations made necessary by the so-called global knowledge economy. Here, the logic of capitalism requires that nations maximise their advantage, and policy makers operationalise this effort by connecting to – usually uncritically – the distinct fields of educational attainment and economic growth. Irrespective of the forces driving this passion for policy reform, the implications for comparative education have been profound. On the one hand, the field has seen a resurgence of interest in terms of new university programmes, growing participation in formal academic societies and a revitalised relationship to policy making. Each of these concerns carries a range of potential but also dangers: the institutionalisation and trivialisation of intellectual work into schools of thought (and dogma); a dilution of our focus as many new and different types of participants enter and influence the field; and the threat of corruption as rivers of money attract what Stephen Ball (1995) has called policy *entrepreneurs* with their hasty linkages between schooling and the workplaces of the future.

These threats are common to many practice-oriented disciplines and can be countered by what Ball calls policy *scholarship*. However, the threat to comparative education is much greater than the existence of disciplinary rivalries, unchecked standards or the vulgarities of penetrative market capitalism. I argue that the world has simply moved on, leaving the discipline of comparative education in its wake. Unless it is able to read the world anew, find new units of analysis and new purpose, comparative education will become an ornament to the rich and diverse struggles of nation- and system-building that characterised the nineteenth and twentieth centuries, and the positivist certainties that fuelled them.

In the first part of this chapter I attempt to unsettle the taken-for-granted place of the nation-state in contemporary comparative education via the construction of a cross-national policy space that I refer to as an educational 'policyscape' (Carney 2009). My aim is to establish new ways of approaching educational phenomena. I do this through the *optique* of globalisation, giving certain approaches within that literature my own particular treatment. While doing so opens up a range of ways to reconsider the nature of educational policy formation and practice in contemporary times, I make clear that these global policies are understood and enacted in quite different ways depending on one's position within the new and emerging discursive spaces made available by the 'postmodernization of the global economy' in which 'the economic, the political, and the cultural increasingly overlap and invest one another' (Hardt and Negri 2000: xiii). Not only must comparative education as a discipline come to terms with the new landscape of policy formulation across borders, but it must also develop innovative methodologies to identify, understand and come to terms with the diverse ways in which global educational visions and practices are being experienced. It is these *experiences* of globalisation that form the basis of this chapter.

Decentring the Nation State in Comparative Study: Educational Policyscapes

It is common in the field of comparative education to refer, albeit fleetingly, to the concept of 'globalisation'. In many cases this loose signifier aims to capture the role of economic and political forces in reshaping public education (Dale 1999, 2000; Welch 2001). Relatively few researchers have focused on cultural processes of identity formation and subjectivity (Marginson and Mollis 2001) and fewer still analyse the mutually constitutive nature of economics, politics, and culture as they reshape modernity (Rizvi 2010).

Notwithstanding this criticism, comparativists have been much exercised by the conversation between the so-called universalist and culturalist schools of thought (e.g. Anderson-Levitt 2003; Ramirez 2003; Steiner-Khamsi and Stolpe 2006). For the former, global reform movements manifest both inherent and universal modes of being, as well as strikingly similar processes of bureaucratic rationalisation. For the latter, global education reform is placed in history and context in order to understand the ways that policy comes to life as specific, often unpredictable, practices. At the edges of this debate we can find the once mighty neo-Marxist tradition of analysing education and the state in terms of intranational power inequalities (Burbules and Torres 2000; Carnoy 1974). In many instances this rich theoretical tradition has been usurped by the Foucauldian approach to conceptualising power through techniques of surveillance, discipline and normalisation. Here, we find a different way to understand the subject and subjectivity as scholarship explores the various (usually seductive) policy regimes that are simultaneously repressive *and* productive (Foucault 2008). It is this emphasis on the *production* of new normative understandings of state, citizen and learner/learning that have inspired my initial analyses of education in the global era (Carney 2006, 2007, 2008, 2009).

Even though these theoretical ideas enable us to conceptualise power, governance, society and social action under conditions of globalisation, we are still left with the fundamental challenge of how to theorise 'place' and 'space'. Here, cultural anthropology has provided us with new understandings of the nature of 'field' as physical locality and the role of global processes in the de-territorialisation of phenomena (Gupta and Ferguson 1997). Perhaps the most influential scholar in this regard has been Arjun Appadurai (1996, 2000), who challenges us to rethink our tendency to treat as fixed social phenomena that are actually highly dynamic:

the apparent stabilities that we see are, under close examination, usually our devices for handling objects characterized by motion. The greatest of these apparently stable objects is the nation-state, which is today frequently characterized by floating populations, transnational politics within national borders, and mobile configurations of technology and expertise.

(Appadurai 2000: 5)

Appadurai suggests that we think of globalisation as sets of 'flows' that are both rapid and disjunctive, and which result in 'intensely local forms' of action that 'have contexts that are anything but local' (p. 6). Such flows bring to life cultural worlds of possibility that simply redefine what it means to live and imagine in a particular place. However, rather than unfolding an unproblematic world of opportunity, such global flows embody inconsistencies and contradictions as well:

Media flows across national boundaries that produce images of well-being that cannot be satisfied by national standards of living and consumer capabilities; flows of discourses of human rights that generate demands from workforces that are repressed by state violence which is itself backed by global arms flows; ideas about gender and modernity that circulate to create large female workforces at the same time that cross-national ideologies of 'culture', 'authenticity', and national honor put increasing pressure on various communities to morally discipline just these working women who are vital to emerging markets and manufacturing sites.

(Appadurai 2000: 5)

This dynamism and complexity is central to his understanding of the new global cultural economy, which he then conceptualises in terms of a number of 'scapes': ethno, media, techno, finance and ideo. These imaginative and material worlds, albeit presented in overly functional terms (Tsing 2000) and without deep regard for power relations (Ong 1999), hold key ideas and processes that have broken free from the confines of regional and national places. One example is the emergence of 'diasporic public spheres' where communities in far flung places maintain and strengthen their ties to home and culture via media, technology, and sheer willpower. Such 'ethnoscapes', Appadurai (1996) suggests, provide a glimpse of a coming 'postnational political order' (p. 22) and, while surely still in their infancy, may emerge as coherent partners (or challengers) to the beleaguered state. More likely, though, is their taking form as 'relations and networks between heterogenous units' as diverse as 'some social movements, some interest groups, some professional bodies, some non-governmental organizations, some armed constabularies, some judicial bodies' (p. 23).

For the purposes of the study reported here, the notion of 'ideoscape' is particularly well suited for capturing the power of global policy messages in the field of education. With its enlightenment heritage, 'ideoscape' becomes a new 'building block' (Appadurai 1996: 33) for the reassembly of concepts such as 'freedom, welfare, rights, sovereignty, representation, and the master term democracy'; once set free from local/national referents, these terms swirl around within the new global cultural economy and provide a basis for (seemingly) coherent narratives and programmes of action (Appadurai 1996: 36).

While Appadurai's notion of global flows has been largely bypassed by mainstream educational policy research, some within the field of comparative education have begun to explore the consequences arising from the contemporary de-territorialisation of phenomena. Here, national governments are simultaneously 'de-centered' by international reform movements, but also 'strengthened' by their new mandates in 'organizing the field of possibilities, and laying the boundaries for local policy' (Kamat 2002: 116). Rather than thinking of state power as being diluted by new global processes and systems, it is perhaps better to think of it as being *reconfigured* by them. From this perspective the state draws on global discourses – in Sangeeta Kamat's case related to decentralisation and democratisation – to craft a package of technologies and subject positions with which to consolidate and extend its reach. This is the 'deliberate production of state space':

> In everyday political and administrative routines the state may be less present than before, strengthening instead its role in producing consensus for the normative framework that determines much of how decentralized relations will be self-governed and self-regulatory.
>
> (Kamat 2002: 116)

This is an important point. While the state may now be, in some senses, dislodged from its national context and sucked into the disjunctive forces and imaginative regimes of different global 'scapes', developmental agencies, and their vested interests, it nevertheless mediates the terms on which new regimes and technologies can be received. For my research this has been a helpful way to retain the state as an important object for analysis without being beholden to it. It moves us beyond those studies that lament the decline of the state in the field of education and, instead, provides us with a lens through which to see state action in a new light. This recalibration of our understanding of the state has been buttressed by James Ferguson's call to reconsider the transnational nature of political relations. Rather than perpetuating the 'intensively managed fiction' of thinking in 'levels' from 'top' to 'bottom' he challenges us to explore the practices of government at the 'top' and within grassroots organisations at the 'bottom' and to tease out the ways in which they are actually deeply connected to and formed by global and cross-national phenomena. The instruments and techniques of contemporary governance may be wielded by national governments and their agencies (as far as we can tell), but they are very much conditioned by and connected to transnational relations *across* levels (Ferguson 2006: 10). Such conditioning maintains our gaze on national and international political entities but also brings into the frame diverse and disparate social movements empowered in new, often unpredictable, ways by the forces of global interconnectivity.

While much policy scholarship considers transnational policy making through the lens of *economic* globalisation (i.e. Dale 2000; Henry et al. 2001; Moutsios 2009, 2010), my starting point is broader. Clearly, the ideology of economic liberalism and its embodiment in key international institutions such as the OECD, World Bank, IMF and WTO, and transnational bodies such as the European Union, plays a major role in shaping the field of possibility (see Moutsios 2010 for a fuller discussion of the role of these bodies). Others, however, have sought to view the economic sphere as interconnected with much deeper-running *cultural* and *political* processes, not all of which can be easily subordinated to economics. Tikly (2003), for example, describes the ongoing development of the nation-state in terms of its role in the protection of individual liberty. Neo-institutionalist scholars have identified processes of professionalism and bureaucracy that are clearly linked to the capitalist mode of production, but speak to processes of, if not desires for, universalism and democratisation that reflect an emphasis on issues of participation, equity and identity formation (Ramirez 2003). Others, notably those inspired by Foucault's notion of governmentality, have explored genealogies of subjectivity where 'no single point of origin or principle of unification' is posited (Rose 1999: xvii). Within our field of educational studies, scholars have built on these ideas to examine processes of self-regulation and freedom inherent in modern educational ideologies, often in ways that have only subtle connections to theories of political economy (Baker and Heyning 2004; Popkewitz 2000). As such, the slogans of self-determination, ownership and choice and those of value, efficiency and competition must be seen as part of an overall 'advanced liberal' understanding of society (Dean 1999) in which discourses of global economic neoliberalism must be seen in *relation to* ongoing and deep-running cultural and political changes.

Irrespective of our different vantage points in this discussion, we can identify policies and practices at three levels that can be seen as part of a coherent educational policyscape. They seek to combine political interest in access, participation and engagement with concerns for efficiency and value.

At the level of *visions and values* we can identify a focus on curricula that conceptualise learning in terms of individual skills and competencies. From the perspective of *management and organisation* we are currently confronted with a plethora of policies of decentralisation, choice and, for example, executive leader models of control. Finally, at the level of *learning processes* classrooms are increasingly shaped by strategies for child-centred pedagogy, classroom democracy and active learning. These policies and the narratives that sustain them are transnational messages that reach into diverse and far-flung educational spaces. While adapted to fit particular contexts, they nevertheless possess coherence by virtue of a narrative that centres the cosmopolitan individual in learning processes (Popkewitz 2008) and prioritises the market logic of efficiency and effectiveness. In the process the state is dislodged from its hitherto unchallenged position as provider of education and focus for learning.

This educational policyscape – at least in terms of the contours I have marked out here – provides one way to experiment in the new world of comparative education, and if there is leverage in such a construction we can begin to bring together disparate country 'cases' and look afresh at educational phenomena through the lens of globalisation. Indeed, given our interest in globalisation as interconnectivity, it must be possible to explore phenomena not only in different *types* of countries but at different *levels* of the educational systems within these cases.

Taking up this challenge, I have aligned three very different empirical studies – management reform in Danish universities, school curriculum reform in the west of China and community schooling in Nepal – and subjected them to comparative analysis (Carney 2009). At first glance the only thing to bind these dissimilar dramas together is their complete lack of resonance! However, as 'transitologies' – what

Robert Cowen (2000) calls societies in the midst of processes of 'collapse and reconstruction' – we can see education as playing a central role in 'social processes of destroying the past and redefining the future' (p. 338). This is globalisation 'institutionalized as a program' (Tsing 2000: 329). The rapid shift to the ideology of managerialism in consensus-oriented Danish universities, learner-centred pedagogy in teacher-dominated Chinese schools and community involvement in school management in hierarchical Nepal opens up the possibility of seeing actually existing global reform as it is enacted. Importantly, I take nothing for granted and favour no single 'program of global-future commitments', only the 'uneven and contested global terrain of global promotion' (p. 330). Thus I focus on contestation and resistance as well as tension and rupture; what Tsing (2005) prefers to label as 'the productive moment' of 'misunderstanding' (p. 4). Doing so promised something quite different from the assumptions of 'equilibrium' and 'equilibrium theorizing' on which much comparative education rests (Cowen 2000: 339) and provided the basis for an innovative 'experiment' in method.

Experimenting, Comparatively: Three Places, One Space

> If globalization can be predicted in advance, there is nothing to learn from research except how the details support the plan. And if the world centres provide the dynamic impetus for global change, why even study more peripheral places?
>
> (Tsing 2005: 3)

The different studies that make it possible to construct the policyscape are part of an ongoing research programme (Carney 2006, 2007, 2008, 2009; Carney and Bista 2009, Carney et al. 2007). Brought together, they illustrate some of the possibilities that this conceptualisation of education reform makes possible. Unlike other studies that become quickly bogged down as they try to unpick the multiple criss-crossings of reform – what Noah Sobe (2008) calls the 'reciprocal, reversible, and multiple vectors of movement and exchange' – my aim in bringing these studies together is to present some of the lived consequences of these 'entanglements' (p. 4) and, importantly, to chart some of the forms of response and reworking that emerge in the newly de-territorialised spaces of education.

This interest in the entangled and co-produced experience of global education reform is lacking in many recent analyses of education policy. While much work acknowledges the changed role of states in the production and promotion of reform, it is often conceptualised as the 'universalizing quality of capitalism' (Tsing 2005: 4) and delivered via a poetics of loss and longing. For some, we have entered the age of the 'quasi-state' where political decisions are being removed from the public domain and are subject to the interests of business, primarily because nations and their political bodies 'accede to take part in the global production system':

> Politics then is being eliminated by the dominance of policy-making, exercised through national, and increasingly transnational bureaucracies and steering mechanisms of objective setting and performance measurement. As a consequence, education politics as the activity of teachers/academics, learners and

parents to question and reflect on the purpose, the contents and the pedagogic mode of learning, is superseded by transnational policy-making, which aims primarily at generating the cognitive and human resources required by the labour markets.

(Moutsios 2010: 128)

This view is increasingly common in our field. However, while there is general agreement that 'nomadic, footloose global capital' is broadly ascendant (Henry et al. 2001: 27), some note the difficulty in locating the centre of this social maelstrom: what Bauman (1998) calls the 'indeterminate, unruly and self-propelled character of world affairs', which defies location in terms of a 'controlling desk, of a board of directors, of a managerial office' (cited in Henry et al. 2001: 65). For Hardt and Negri (2000), this view enables us to reimagine the global via the emergence of an 'Empire' of 'autonomous movement', interconnectivity and social activism that might undermine the hegemonic position of the metropolitan centres and their institutions, and herald a new era where the coordinated voices of the 'multitude' will reappropriate space and constitute itself as an active subject, challenging and ultimately dismantling the old order (p. 397):

The passage to Empire emerges from the twilight of modern sovereignty. In contrast to imperialism, Empire establishes no territorial center of power and does not rely on fixed boundaries or barriers. It is a decentered and deterritorializing apparatus of rule that progressively incorporates the entire global realm within its open, expanding frontiers.

(Hardt and Negri 2000: xiii)

Both narratives – totalising projects of different kinds – speak to our base fears and desires but could benefit by reference to the 'worldly encounters' (Tsing 2005: 4) that *make* globalisation. On the one hand we have generic capitalism spreading its exploitative arms across hitherto unimagined places, shaping all social life in its apparently vulgar image. On the other, we see the mobilisation of the very same universal as the 'key to effective opposition to exploitation' (Tsing 2005: 4). For the former, education politics is 'practically eliminated' because power 'lies in a transnational space of de-territorialised economic and political rule' (Moutsios 2010: 137). For the latter, 'collective labour power' is being transformed by global interconnectivity from the logic and confines of the 'industrial factory' to a 'communicative, cooperative, and affective' force for social progress (Hardt and Negri 2000: xiii). We are left, it seems, with neoliberalism from (somewhere) above carpet-bombing communities into conformance *or* labour power from (somewhere) below 'wielding' its 'experiences of resistance' into concerted action against the nerve centres of imperial command' (p. 399). Perhaps a more productive alternative lies in exploring the 'friction' of global connectivity between these imagined worlds where 'heterogeneous and unequal encounters' shape 'new arrangements of culture and power' (Tsing 2005: 5). This orientation provides inspiration not only to explore regimes of 'liberal sovereignty and biopower' (p. 5) *and* diverse and disruptive social movements, but to be conscious of the dramas of compromise, coercion and conflict that constitute global educational reform projects and that work to reconfigure state power, identities and localities in ways that are *mutually constitutive* and *dialectically constructed*.

While Denmark, Nepal and China have very different histories and positions in the global policyscape, they are nonetheless linked by a shared vision for education in the emerging global knowledge economy, especially in terms of efforts to orient their educational visions and systems to the needs of the market, the individualised learner, and the empowered consumer. In Denmark the rhetoric of benchmarking and best practice leads to policies that evoke the signifiers of 'quality', 'elite' and 'world-class'. Much of this spectacle is driven by regional dreams and directives in which the European Union's Lisbon Declaration aims to reshape Europe into the world's most competitive and dynamic knowledge-based economy. Even war-torn Nepal aims to develop schools that 'keep[ing] abreast of emerging, new knowledge and skills in the "global society"' (MOES 2006: 18–19). For China education is central to its 'go global' ambition, in which life-long learning, advanced technological study and education for economic success dovetail neatly into the prevailing global-speak (*People's Daily* 2001).

The ideologies of individualism and self-determination – central to the emerging policyscape – require the invention of new actors to promote reform. In Denmark a radical new university law has replaced inclusive decision-making processes with elected boards and an appointed (not elected) chief executive model of institutional leadership. Government now talks of students as 'customers' and institutions as 'service-providers'. In the Nepali case, school management committees have been reinvented with the explicit logic of reaching out to 'stakeholders' and 'service-seekers' (World Bank 2003). For China a new curriculum attempts to prioritise the student as learner, all with the aim of promoting the forms of innovation, creativity and curiosity needed to drive the next phase of the country's industrial development; what the state calls its 'glorious modernization' (MOE 2001).

Global reform is facilitated by a range of pervasive administrative techniques (Foucault 1978). For example, Danish university boards must write detailed development contracts in agreement with the ministry. Rectors must do the same with their boards. Community schools in Nepal must satisfy a host of new demands and conditions from a Ministry of Education that has not lost its centralist zest. Chinese teachers battle to treat the learner as unique, but within a context of continued hysteria about the (quite uniform) entry requirements for the country's exclusive universities.

Notwithstanding the similarities embedded into this reform context, the empirical studies have highlighted much resistance and contestation. Academic staff at Danish universities have manoeuvred within the discourse of 'world-class' to pressure the government for the additional funding and greater autonomy that is characteristic of those institutions that lead international league tables (Carney 2007). Danish students – as learners *and* consumers – have once again become politically active on university campuses. In Nepal state and donor efforts to involve local communities in schooling have been driven by concerns for equity and social justice. However, rather than limiting their focus to schools, the poor are using their newfound voice to engage in broader critiques of society and the political process (Carney et al. 2007). In China student-centredness has, perversely, intensified processes of rote learning, exam preparation and teacher authoritarianism (Carney 2008). In these processes of policy imposition we are actually seeing groups within each country find new resources, arguments and strategies with which to reconfigure many of the initiatives that were supposed to have enabled them. The results are not necessarily 'progressive'. Instead, they speak to the multiplicity and complexity of experiences of globalisation.

The newly emerging space of global educational reform is making it possible to re-imagine locality as the embodiment of the practices that make possible certain de-territorialised displays of identity. In Denmark this new idea of locality emerges through efforts to maintain democratic engagement in education and actors strive towards this by aligning with international ideas, colleagues and social movements at least as much as they do with new groups within the borders of the country. For Nepal, locality is signified by the battles within and around school management committees and communities that, having entered the spaces made by international development agencies and their liberal elite backers at 'home', begin to articulate their unrest at the perpetuation of historical inequalities. In China locality takes form as conflicts between loyalty to idealised notions of what it means to be 'Chinese' and fascination with partially grasped images of the Enlightenment subject. In all cases we are witnessing passions unhinged from places!

New Directions and Challenges

A feature of the approach adopted here was to focus not only on what Hardt and Negri (2000) call the 'biopolitical *production*' of social life (p. xiii) but also on the ways that global images, messages and artifacts are *consumed*. Much work within the Foucauldian governmentality tradition tends to focus upon human subjectivity in its totality. As such, we have *the* cosmopolitan citizen (Popkewitz 2008), *the* self-managing school (Peters et al. 2000), *the* child (Baker 1998), *the* performative teacher (Ball 2003), and so forth. Notwithstanding the service they provide in alerting us to the fundamentally new conditions under which we live, such analyses run the risk of over-generalising and homogenising the complexity and hybridity of practices and processes within educational spaces. While the policyscape study identifies a host of new subjectivities and subject positions that are conditioned by biopower and the 'technologies of domination' that structure it (Peters et al. 2000: 121), I suggest that we are also beginning to see the emergence of a quite different type of global cultural economy: one shaped by processes of confusion and uncertainty.

Like Baudrillard (1987) I have tried to question the Marxist logic of production that lingers in many Foucault-inspired policy studies. By this I mean the tendency of humans to 'act[ing] upon and transform[ing] the material world into commodities with surplus value' (Luke and Luke 1990: 77). Inspired in part by Marcel Mauss's analysis of gift exchange in earlier societies, Baudrillard argues that 'objects' were once 'inseparable from the concrete relations in which [they are] exchanged' and were thus part of a 'transferential pact' between people. Instead of embodying 'use value' or 'economic exchange value', such objects possessed a 'symbolic exchange value' (Baudrillard 1981: 64). This type of value is in 'fundamental opposition to both economic exchange-value and the economy of the sign, for it rests upon an order of culture which is radically other to the ideologies of scarcity, need, wealth and function which legitimate capitalist exchange' (Gane 2004: 134). This recognition drives Baudrillard's critique of consumer society. Here, objects must gain signification in order to be consumed. With the transformation of the commodity into a sign, it becomes 'immersed within the endless stream of signs'. In time, the separation of signifier and signified leads to a 'proliferation' of signs and the 'violence' of the image which 'entails the eclipse – even death – of the real' (Norris 2006: 468). This is perhaps the most fundamental characteristic of the emerging era of global consumer modernity but one largely ignored by theorists of education policy.

In perhaps his most influential early work, Baudrillard (1981) outlines a genealogy of simulation via stages in the transformation of the sign from a time when it attempted to mirror 'basic reality', through an Enlightenment project based on the 'textual duplication of the real' – in effect 'perverting' a notion of basic reality – to the rise of modernity and 'technicist rationality' with the production of 'goods', 'subjects', 'selves' and 'desires'. For Baudrillard, the many inscriptions of the self that characterised nineteenth-century social science bear 'no resemblance to the familiar, to the visibly "real" of bodily surfaces' which in contemporary society takes form as the pure simulacrum: 'a proliferation of myths of origin and signs of reality; of second-hand truth, objectivity and authenticity'. Here, we are left with 'floating intertextual sets of fragmented, and ultimately non-rational signs' (pp. 80–82).

This analysis requires that we rethink our conventional ways of looking at the world. When citizens can barely define what their country stands for, or what is distinctive about its 'culture'; when 'education' has vastly different meanings for corporate leaders, teachers, students and laypersons; when young people imagine themselves part of a global polity that is distinguished mainly by its masterly capacity to exclude, marginalise and exploit those on its periphery, we would be well-advised to go beyond issues of multiplicity, unpredictability and rupture so as to take in not only complexity but incompatibility, incoherence and confusion. It was clear during the study that university workers in Denmark shared no common understanding of what, for example, the new category of departmental 'leader' meant. For some a leader was a resource to support autonomy and freedom of research; for others it was a selfish managerialist to be avoided. In Nepal many parents made a connection between the World Bank as a global facilitator of help to the poor, decentralisation as a democratisation strategy, and thus community schooling as a form of social justice. Others saw the same policy as an invitation to exclude the poor further, to consolidate local power hierarchies and turn their 'public' school into a poor substitute for a 'private' one. Many Chinese teachers understood the national reform of pedagogical method as a willingness by the centre to let autonomy and thus cultural diversity flourish in the provinces. Others read the very same policy as a call to intensify the country's singular Han chauvinist push for economic ascendency via the tried and true methods of teacher-dominated classrooms, rote learning and summative assessment.

Within the policyscape it was evident that, at a certain scale, sign and signifier appeared relatively stable. This seemed especially so for educational policy makers and administrators who spoke a common set of linguistic codes and interacted in immediate and direct ways (e.g. shared policy frameworks; joint documentation and terminology; personal relations developed through participation in shared events such as conferences, workshops). Ministry officials in Denmark appeared fluent, for example, in the effectiveness language of the OECD. In the same way it was often hard to distinguish between the world view of education ministers, senior civil servants and university leaders. In Nepal donor ideology appeared so embedded in the national ministry of education that it was often difficult to distinguish who in fact was talking; not surprising given that many senior staff were trained to graduate level in donor countries at donor expense and then went on to careers within the donor community itself. In remote Lhasa senior spokespeople for Tibet's educational development strategy spoke only in terms of national(ist) development goals and their relation to the global-speak of access, quality and efficiency. Indeed, for a host of reasons, not all of which could be traced to China's crude political strategy in that region, 'Tibet' was rarely mentioned in 'Tibetan' educational reform.

For others, though, and especially those at some distance from the table at which such visions were initially drafted, the norm was fragmentation and mis-recognition. In particular, line managers, teachers and young people struggled to create their own logic from the stream of signifiers that comprise the contemporary global cultural economy. This was perhaps most dramatic in the Nepali context where parents, emboldened by the related but distinct discourses of participatory liberal democracy and free market choice, embraced community schooling because their involvement on school management committees (SMCs) could shape school policies in the image of the much-cherished private model. English language instruction, compulsory school uniforms and selective admittance were described by parents as important for identification with cosmopolitan city life: a world alien from the very 'community' in whose name these reforms were legitimised. As one parent explained: 'Why should our children be forced to learn our language? Let them speak English and leave this place'. In the process, the spate of government-funded 'boarding schools' (a loose signifier for 'community school') contributed to a devaluation of the entire private sector; a catastrophe for middle-class parents investing in their child's future by sending them to 'real' private schools, but a victory of sorts for the excluded poor who had never dreamed that they could shape in their own image something as mighty as modern schooling. At the level of the classroom such misrecognition was equally dramatic. Here, teachers would scream at docile children to be the 'active' subject of child-centred pedagogy (Madsen and Carney 2010). For one school management committee chair, the incentive funding that accompanied the transition to community-managed status led to 'modern' pedagogical methods: namely the purchase of a 'rotating chair' from which the head teacher could 'now give[s] instruc-tion' (Carney et al. 2007: 624). In such cases the unending stream of reform led to attempts to create an 'authentic copy' (Ferguson 2006: 20) from partially transmitted, hybrid policy concepts made less decipherable by the multitude of political, economic and cultural forces they embodied. In the process, though, they created productive – though not necessarily progressive – strategies for voices on the periphery to take part in the new global cultural economy, and to shape it.

For the purposes of this chapter the inclusion of such empirical richness enables us to see the multitude of ways that globalisation is practised in different contexts. We see coherence, coercion *and* confusion with the final result never more than a work in progress. Such fragments attune us not only to the necessity of incorporating divergent voices in our analyses but also to questioning our methods. Perhaps the confusion that appears so blatant on the edges of the new global order is equally present at the so-called centre but strategically ignored as part of 'Western culture's triumphal stories of progress, reason and order' (MacLure 2006a: 226).

As 'scientists' we do our best to iron out, if not avoid, the types of incoherence identified here; what Ferguson (1999) calls the elimination of ethnographic 'noise' from the 'sign' system of 'information transmission'. Education policy studies, especially those attempting to bridge empirical cases across wildly divergent settings, are no exception, and may need to develop an 'analytic of noise' (p. 210) if they are to capture the 'details and decorations' of entangled experiences, rather than 'rise above them' (MacLure 2006b: 731).

Conclusion

In the policyscape study described here I have attempted to recalibrate space and place in order to capture the divergent and contradictory experiences of actors engaged in creating nation and locality as well as self and subjectivity. Whether we take our inspiration from concepts such as 'scapes' and 'flows' (Appadurai 1996), 'friction' (Tsing 2005), or 'mobilities' (Rizvi 2010), we have an inspiring range of concepts with which to destabilise phenomena that are often presented as firm and secure. Such work can only deepen and enrich our understanding of the spread of education policy globally. However, much work remains.

It is assumed that these flows are contained within bounded and knowable spaces. I have suggested one way to structure such space but there are undoubtedly other ways to capture the 'economy of appearances' (Tsing 2005) that constitutes contemporary educational experiences. Perhaps the most urgent task is to address issues of scale. Clearly, some reforms resonate across certain spaces and among certain actors with considerable degrees of clarity and mutual reinforcement. Those transnational dynamics need elaboration. Within the policyscape, however, these major policy moments are nevertheless brought to life in quite distinct and unpredictable ways and it is thus perhaps unwise even to think about splitting our work into large- and small-scale reforms. Understanding processes of policy formation in a global era should probably proceed on a broad canvas and maintain a commitment to entangled forms of knowing and acting.

The notion of 'policyscape' is built on the suggestion that phenomena are constituted mutually and dialectically although much more empirical work – of quite different types – is required before we can flesh out the dynamics of this connectivity. Some education reforms appear to be mediated through transnational bodies and agencies, only then to be transferred *down* into contexts. Others appear to arise from the new forms of connectivity *across* de-territorialised spaces. These observations speak to the limitations of our methodologies and field methods as much as they do to our conceptual insights. Innovative approaches to ethnography (e.g. Wright and Shore 1997; Vavrus and Bartlett 2009) provide one important element in a project of exploring the co-constitution of educational life.

On what basis should such ethnography proceed? With my evocation of Baudrillard's notion of simulation (1981), I suggest that we challenge the ontological and epistemological basis on which we read a world shaped by unprecedented complexity. Rather than remain embedded in the 'salvationist, redemptive, and reform rhetoric' (Baker and Heyning 2004: 1) that structures so much of the education field, I recommend that we remain open to the possibility that the most profound and stimulating consequences of the globalisation of modernity (and of schooling in particular) might just be confusion and dissonance. Rather than a call to dismiss the modes of conceptualisation and analysis that have structured our understanding of policy transfer, borrowing and the like, this is a call to rethink how these tools could be enhanced to better fit the task at hand. At the very least, it is a call for more diversity in methodologies and an insistence that these methodologies resist the urge of our discipline towards forced acts of coherence and closure. In the process we may find not only new empirical spaces and objects but also different concepts and dispositions with which to engage in the world (Carney 2010).

References

Anderson-Levitt, K. (2003) 'A world culture of schooling?', in K. Anderson-Levitt (ed.), *Local meanings, global schooling: Anthropology and world culture theory*, New York: Palgrave Macmillan: 1–26.

Appadurai, A. (1996) *Modernity at large: Cultural dimensions of globalization*, Minneapolis: University of Minnesota Press.

Appadurai, A. (2000) 'Grassroots globalization and the research Imagination', *Public Culture*, 12(1): 1–19.

Baker, B. (1998) 'Child-centered teaching, redemption, and educational identities: A history of the present'. *Educational Theory*, 48(2): 155–175.

Baker, B. M. and Heyning, K. E. (2004) *Dangerous coagulations? The use of Foucault in the study of education*. New York: Peter Lang.

Ball, S. J. (1995) 'Intellectuals or technicians: The urgent role of theory in educational studies', *British Journal of Educational Studies*, 43(3): 255–271.

Ball, S. J. (2003) 'The teachers' soul and the terrors of performativity', *Journal of Education Policy*, 18(2): 215–228.

Baudrillard, J. (1981) *For a critique of the political economy of the sign*, trans. C. Levin, St. Louis: Telos Press.

Baudrillard, J. (1987) *Forget Foucault*, Semiotext(e), New York: Columbia University Press.

Bauman, Z. (1998) *Globalization: The human consequences*, Cambridge: Polity Press.

Burbules, N. C. and Torres, C. A. (2000) 'Globalisation and education: An introduction', in N. C. Burbules and C. A. Torres (eds), *Globalization and education: Critical perspectives*, New York: Routledge: 1–26.

Carney, S. (2006) 'University governance in Denmark: From democracy to accountability', *European Educational Research Journal*, 5(3 & 4), 221–233.

Carney, S. (2007) 'Neo-liberal reform of higher education and the return of "heroic" leadership: The case of Denmark', *Management Review: the International Review of Management Studies* (Special Issue on Managing Higher Education), 18(2): 174–186.

Carney, S. (2008) 'Learner-centered pedagogy in Tibet: Understanding international education reform in a local context', *Comparative Education*, 44(1): 39–55.

Carney, S. (2009) 'Negotiating policy in an age of globalization: Exploring educational "policyscapes" in Denmark, Nepal and China', *Comparative Education Review*, 53(1): 63–88.

Carney, S. (2010) 'Reading the global: comparative education at the end of an era', in M. Larsen (ed.), *New thinking in comparative education: Honouring the work of Dr. Robert Cowen*, Amsterdam: Sense Publishers: 125–142.

Carney, S. and Bista, M. B. (2009) 'Community schooling in Nepal: A genealogy of education reforms since 1990', *Comparative Education Review*, 53(2): 189–211.

Carney, S. Bista, M. B. and Agergaard, J. (2007) '"Empowering" the "local" through education? Exploring community managed schooling in Nepal', *Oxford Review of Education*, 33(5): 611–628.

Carnoy, M. (1974) *Education as cultural imperialism*, New York: David McKay.

Cowen, R. (2000) 'Comparing futures or comparing pasts?' *Comparative Education*, 36(3): 333–342.

Dale, R. (1999) 'Specifying globalization effects on national policy: A focus on mechanisms', *Journal of Education Policy*, 14(1): 1–17.

Dale, R. (2000) 'Globalization: A new world for comparative education', in J. Schriewer (ed.), *Discourse formation in comparative education*, Frankfurt am Main: Peter Lang GmbH: 87–110.

Dean, M. (1999) *Governmentality: Power and rule in modern society*. London: SAGE.

Ferguson, J. (1999) 'Global disconnect: abjection and the aftermath of modernism', in *Expectations of modernity: Myths and meanings of urban life on the Zambian Copperbelt*, Berkeley: University of California: 234–254.

Ferguson, J. (2006) *Global shadows: Africa in the neo-liberal world order*, Durham: Duke University Press.

Foucault, M. (1978) *The history of sexuality, Vol. 1, An introduction*, New York: Random House.

Foucault, M. (2008) *The birth of biopolitics: Lectures at the College De France, 1978–1979*, trans. Graham Burchell, London: Palgrave Macmillan.

Gane, N. (2004) *Max Weber and post modern theory: Rationalization Versus Re-enchantment*, London: Palgrave Macmillan.

Gupta, A. and Ferguson, J. (1997) 'After "peoples and cultures"', in A. Gupta and J. Ferguson (eds), *Culture, power and place: Explorations in critical anthropology*, Durham: Duke University Press: 1–29.

Hardt, M. and Negri, A. (2000) *Empire*, Cambridge: Harvard University Press.

Henry, M., Lingard, B., Rizvi, F. and Taylor, S. (2001) *The OECD, Globalisation and Education Policy*, Oxford: Permagon.

Kamat, S. (2002) 'Deconstructing the rhetoric of decentralization: The state in education reform', *Current Issues in Comparative Education*, 2(2): 110–119.

Luke, A. and Luke, C. (1990) 'School knowledge as simulation: Curriculum in postmodern conditions', *Discourse*, 10(2): 75–91.

MacLure, M. (2006a) '"A demented form of the familiar": Postmodernism and educational research', *Journal of Philosophy of Education*, 40(2): 221–239.

MacLure, M. (2006b) 'The bone in the throat: Some uncertain thoughts on baroque method', *International Journal of Qualitative Studies in Education*, 19(6): 729–745.

Madsen, U. M. and Carney, S. J. (2010) 'Education in an age of radical uncertainty: Youth and schooling in Urban Nepal', *Globalisation, Societies and Education*, 8(4): 115–133.

Marginson, S. and Mollis, M. (2001) 'The door opens and the tiger leaps: Theories and reflexivities of comparative education for a global millennium', *Comparative Education Review*, 45(4): 581–615.

Ministry of Education (MOE) (2001) '*Guidelines for Curriculum Reform of Basic Education, Document 17*', Beijing: Ministry of Education, People's Republic of China.

Ministry of Education and Sports (MOES) (2006) '*Concept Paper on School Sector Approach*', Kathmandu: MOES.

Moutsios, S. (2009) 'International organisations and transnational education policy', *Compare*, 39(4): 467–478.

Moutsios, S. (2010) 'Power, politics and transnational policy-making in education', *Globalisation, Societies and Education*, 8(1): 121–141.

Norris, T. (2006) 'Hannah Arendt & Jean Baudrillard: Pedagogy in the consumer society', *Studies in Philosophy and Education*, 25: 457–477.

Ong, A. (1999) *Flexible citizenship: The cultural logics of transnationality*, Durham, NC: Duke University Press.

People's Daily Online. (2001) '*Editorial: Tamping Foundation Work for Strategy of Rejuvenating Nation with Science and Education*'. Available online at: www://English.peopledaily.com. cn/English/200106/14eng20010614_72604.html (accessed 9 January 2007).

Peters, M., Marshall, J. and Fitzsimmons, P. (2000) 'Managerialism and educational policy in a global context: Foucault, neoliberalism, and the doctrine of self-management', in N. C. Burbules and C. A. Torres (eds), *Globalization and education: Critical perspectives*, New York: Routledge: 109–132.

Popkewitz, T. (2000) 'Reform as the social administration of the child: Globalization of knowledge and power', in N. C. Burbules and C. A. Torres (eds), *Globalization and education: Critical perspectives*, New York: Routledge: 157–186.

Popkewitz, T. (2008) *Cosmopolitanism and the age of school reform: Science, education, and making society by making the child*, New York: Routledge.

Ramirez, F. O. (2003) 'The global model and national legacies', in K. Anderson-Levitt (ed.), *Local meanings, global schooling: Anthropology and world culture theory*, New York: Palgrave Macmillan: 239–254.

Rizvi, F. (2010) '*Mobilities paradigm and its challenges for comparative education*', keynote address to Comparative Education Society of Europe, Uppsala, 16–19 August.

Rose, N. (1999) *Governing the soul: The shaping of the private self (second edition)*, London: Routledge.

Sobe, N. (2008) 'Entanglements and intercultural exchange in the history of education: Mobilizing John Dewey in the interwar era'. Unpublished paper, 15 November.

Steiner-Khamsi, G. and Stolpe, I. (2006) *Educational Import: Local encounters with global forces in Mongolia*, New York: Palgrave Macmillan.

Tikly, L. (2003) 'Governmentality and the study of education policy in South Africa', *Journal of Education Policy*, 18 (2): 161–74.

Tsing, A. L. (2000) 'The global situation', *Cultural Anthropology*, 15(3): 327–360.

Tsing, A. L. (2005) *Friction: An ethnography of global connection*, Princeton and Oxford, Princeton University Press.

Vavrus, F. and Bartlett, L. (eds) (2009) *Critical approaches to comparative education: Vertical case studies from Africa, Europe, the Middle East, and the Americas*, New York: Palgrave Macmillan, Comparative and Development series.

Welch, A. (2001) 'Globalisation, post-modernity and the state: Comparative education facing the third millennium', *Comparative Education*, 37(4): 475–492.

World Bank. (2003) *Project appraisal document for a community school support project*, Human Development Sector Unit Report no. 25789-NEP, World Bank, Kathmandu.

Wright, S. and Shore, C. (eds) (1997) *Anthropology of policy: Critical perspectives on governance and power*. EASA Series. London: Routledge.

18 Policy Tourism and Policy Borrowing in Education

A Trans-Atlantic Case Study

Geoff Whitty

International policy tourism and policy borrowing in education have become common occurrences. They are now worldwide phenomena but the focus in this chapter is on trans-Atlantic policy exchanges, as they have a particularly long history and are also particularly important today. They are used here as a case study, which in Stake's (1995) terms is both 'intrinsic' and 'instrumental' – that is, it is interesting in its own right, but also illustrates a range of factors involved in policy exchange more generally. Rather like Steiner-Khamsi, Silova and Johnson (2006) and Phillips and Ochs (2003), I shall use the term 'policy borrowing' to describe the activities I am discussing here, while recognising that there is a continuing debate about the appropriateness of that term in relation to possible alternatives. For the moment, I believe it remains the 'least bad' option, although those writers' own use of the complementary concepts of 'policy lending' (Steiner-Khamsi et al. 2006: 217) and 'policy attraction' (Phillips and Ochs 2003: 451) provide additional insights into the nature of the processes at work.

This chapter will describe a long tradition of trans-Atlantic policy tourism and policy borrowing from the mid-nineteenth century to the present day and then consider why the US and England have found each other's education policies so attractive, even in recent years when the educational performance of both countries has been relatively unimpressive in international terms. It will argue that shared assumptive worlds among policy makers are more of an explanation rather than evidence that the policies in question actually 'work' on the ground. Indeed, much of the evidence invoked by politicians to justify the borrowing of policies is shown to be highly questionable. However, the chapter goes on to point out that the questionable use of evidence is also a feature of policy justification at a national level and that the growing use of examples of 'what works' elsewhere is a product of the increasing globalisation of education policy rather than a distinct phenomenon. It concludes that greater emphasis should now be put upon sharing evidence of 'what doesn't work' to provide a form of 'inoculation' against what Ben Levin (1998) once termed 'policy epidemics'.

The Tradition of Trans-Atlantic Policy Borrowing

Although policy tourism and policy borrowing have become more common in the context of globalisation, they are by no means new. Horace Mann – whose travels to

Europe in the 1840s when he was Secretary of the Massachusetts Board of Education are a very early example of education policy tourism – advocated policy borrowing in the following terms:

> I do not hesitate to say that there are many things abroad which we at home should do well to imitate; things some of which are here, as yet, mere matters of speculation and theory, but which, there, have long been in operation, and are now producing a harvest of rich and abundant blessings.
>
> (Mann 1844)

More recently, in one of his last actions before his death in 1995, Ernest L. Boyer, then President of the Carnegie Foundation for the Advancement of Teaching, wrote a foreword for a Carnegie Foundation special report by Kathryn Stearns of the *Washington Post* entitled *School Reform: Lessons from England* (Stearns 1996). Boyer concluded on the basis of that report that 'there may be some aspects of the British reforms [especially with regard to school choice and school autonomy] that may be worthy of adaptation, if not downright imitation, in the United States'. In the field of school governance in particular, he said, 'England . . . might just be the place to turn to learn some important lessons' (Boyer in Stearns 1996: xviii).

In fact, this was not the first instance of US policy tourists alighting on English neoliberal school governance reforms as a possible model to emulate at home. In 1991 the Brookings Institution sent John Chubb and Terry Moe to England soon after the publication of their *Politics, Markets and America's Schools* (Chubb and Moe 1990) to look at school choice and autonomous schools. Their report on the visit, entitled *A Lesson in School Reform from Great Britain* (Chubb and Moe 1992), concluded:

> In fundamental respects . . . Britain is not unique. What is happening there is happening in the United States . . . The only real difference is that Britain, owing to its parliamentary form of government, has been able to move farther and faster toward a radical overhaul of its educational system – and is far more likely to succeed. We can only hope it does, and that America can someday follow in Britain's footsteps.
>
> (p. 50)

In his introduction to the report, Bruce K. MacLaury, President of the Brookings Institution, commented that 'one would think that the British experience would be receiving careful scrutiny by participants in the emerging American debate. So far, it has not' (Chubb and Moe 1992: v).

However, coming just after the publication of Stearns' book and Boyer's advice, the education summit of US state governors held in Palisades, New York, in 1996 certainly knew about the English reforms and some of their deliberations were informed by this knowledge. In particular, the expansion of charter schools, and the move to give them increased autonomy in some states, was influenced by the English experience of grant maintained schools which had been allowed by the Thatcher government to opt out of local authority (or school district) control. Up to that time, there were only 300 charter schools in the US (Nathan 1996) and they generally had significantly less autonomy than even mainstream schools in England. From that point on they gained wider support, received Presidential encouragement and took on forms that now make at least some of them a model for those calling for yet greater freedoms for schools in England.

In the 1990s, the defence of states' rights meant that some of the other English experiments, such as the National Curriculum and a national system of assessment at ages 7, 11, 14 and 16 were likely to be less attractive in the US context, though the developing language of standards and high stakes testing already showed some similarities with the English approach. Indeed, Roy Romer, Governor of Colorado, actually made reference to the English experience at the National Goals Panel in connection with America 2000 and Goals 2000 (see Whitty and Edwards 1998) and, subsequently, *No Child Left Behind* and the Obama Administration's recent *Blueprint for Reform* have brought the US approach closer to the English one in these areas as well.

Even in the 1990s, there was some traffic in the opposite direction.[1] David Green (1991), in a paper entitled 'Lessons from America' for the free-market think tank the Institute of Economic Affairs, commended Chubb and Moe (1990) for the boldness of their arguments in favour of deregulating educational supply and cited Minnesota and East Harlem as successful examples of doing so. From a different point on the political spectrum, David Miliband (1991), then a rising star in what was soon to become New Labour, identified the management of school placements in Cambridge, Massachusetts, as a demonstration of the power of 'controlled parental choice' to reconcile parental preferences with the public goal of 'voluntary' desegregation. In 1990, Her Majesty's Inspectorate of Schools went to study teaching and learning in New York City Schools (HMI 1990), while a year earlier they had visited New Jersey to look at 'alternative routes' to teacher training (HMI 1989). Then, early in this century, *Teach for America* became the inspiration for London's *Teach First*.

There was even some academic interest in the process of trans-Atlantic policy borrowing at that time, with the Brookings Institution and the University of Warwick hosting a conference to explore the subject, which in turn led to a collection of papers entitled *Something Borrowed, Something Learned? The transatlantic market in education and training reform* (Finegold, McFarland and Richardson 1993) being published on both sides of the Atlantic. This identified 'government ministers, seconded advisers, local government politicians, private sector companies, travelling fellowship programmes and the managers of education institutions' (p. 8) as among the policy tourists implicated in this policy borrowing process.

Nevertheless, despite these precursors in the 1990s, the English interest in US reforms has recently assumed new proportions. A keynote speaker at the Conservative Party conference in October 2010 was New York's Geoffrey Canada, who talked about his work at the Harlem Children's Zone, which provides a range of social services to families and children and runs two charter schools. Canada is one of the stars of Guggenheim's film on the merits of charter schools, *Waiting for 'Superman'* (see Weber 2010), which has been hailed by many in the US although subjected to a damning critique by Diane Ravitch in the *New York Review of Books* (Ravitch 2010). It has subsequently been promoted by *Teach First* in the UK.

The following extract from Canada's speech to the Conservative Party neatly illustrates many of the points that will be made in this chapter about policy borrowing and how it works.

Thank you so much for that warm introduction and good morning everybody.

I was really very excited to come. I actually couldn't wait to come here because there are no two countries that have a closer relationship than the UK and the United States *[applause]* . . . and . . . I really felt obligated to share with you what we're doing and what we are struggling with. *[topical joke about the Ryder Cup omitted]*

When I told my wife I was coming here she said to me 'so Geoff you're friends with President Obama and he's an education reformer' and I said 'that's exactly right'. 'And he's a Democrat', I said 'that's right'.

'And Mayor Bloomberg in New York City he's an Independent and you're friends with him' and I said 'that's right honey, that's right'.

'And just last week, you were with the Republican Governor of Newark,[2] Governor Christie, and you say he's your friend also', I said 'that's right honey, that's right'.

She said 'so please explain the Conservative Party to me' *[laughter]*. I said 'well, I hear they're education reformers and if they are I'm going to have a bunch of new friends in the UK'. *[applause]*

Here's why everyone in America is upset with me. I have been making sure our nation knows that we have lost our way. That we have allowed our country – the last remaining superpower on the face of the Earth – to offer our children a third world education system *[applause]*. We have failed. We are not in the top ten, in many cases we are not even in the top twenty.

If you look down the road and you say 'what is going on in the US?' you see a nation in decline that is quietly allowing itself to deteriorate because it will not face some tough truths. The fact of the matter is, we have mishandled the education system in our country and now we are at a fork in the road. And I am determined even if the right, the left, the conservatives, the liberals – even if they all are angry at me – I am simply going to tell the truth. If you have a system that is failing your children there is no way that you will remain a great power if you allow your children to get an inferior education *[applause]* . . .

(www.conservatives.com/Get_involved/Conference/Conference_2010.aspx)

In his own speech on this occasion, Michael Gove, the Conservative Secretary of State for Education, presented charter schools as a model for academy schools and free schools in England, seemingly forgetting that charter schools had themselves been justified by reference to grant maintained schools in England (although he would probably have argued that Labour had reduced their freedoms over the previous 13 years).

Picking up on Canada's comments about common themes in the education policies of opposing political parties, Michael Gove also spoke positively about the policies of President Obama:

In America, President Obama is pressing ahead with radical school reform to close the gap between rich and poor . . .

He is promoting greater autonomy by providing cash and other incentives to encourage more charter schools, the equivalent of our free schools and academies.

He has offered extra support to programmes designed to attract more great
people into teaching and leadership.

And he has encouraged states and school districts to provide greater accountability through improved testing and assessment.

(Gove 2010)

In November 2010, US Education Secretary Arne Duncan was invited by Michael
Gove to a breakfast meeting with key English education stakeholders, including
sceptical union leaders, to persuade them that charter schools (or academies and free
schools in England) were the way to go. During Duncan's visit, the UK government
announced the establishment of an Education Endowment Fund to which groups
could bid with ideas about how to turn round under-performing schools. Gove
explicitly compared this fund with Barack Obama's *Race to the Top* initiative, under
which states compete for federal cash, saying:

> America is a bigger country and there are differences between us, but I have been
> impressed by what Race to the Top has done, and impressed by many of the
> things that President Obama and Arne Duncan have been fighting for.
>
> (Gove quoted in Vasagar 2010)

In January 2011 Gove invited Mike Feinberg from the Knowledge is Power
Programme (KIPP), one of the most successful chains of charter schools in America,
and Joel Klein, former Chancellor of New York City Schools, to address a major
conference in London to promote free schools.

Even at the Labour Party conference in September 2010, its first in opposition for
13 years, there were positive references to the US experience, especially KIPP schools,
which had been visited by Labour politicians during that summer.

It seems then that neoliberal and neoconservative education policies are not
partisan in a narrow party political sense. In England, there has been considerable
continuity at least in direction of travel between Conservative, New Labour and now
Coalition education policies, while the same is often true of Democrat and Republican
policies in the US. Nor is policy borrowing carried out along entirely predictable lines.
Democrat administrations in the US have borrowed from Conservative governments
in Britain and vice versa.

Why Policy Convergence between the UK and the US?

I was already trying to make sense of this in some work undertaken in the 1990s. It
began with a paper I gave with Tony Edwards to the American Educational Research
Association annual meeting in 1992, which was partly based on my own policy
tourism in the US, aided by policy entrepreneur Bruce Cooper of Fordham University,
who managed to get visits onto my itinerary that I would not easily have arranged
myself, including one to the White House under the first President George Bush.

The paper was substantially revised for publication in *Comparative Education* in
1998, and examined the reasons for policy borrowing between the US and the UK in
the field of school choice (Whitty and Edwards 1998). It explored two different

approaches to explaining the apparent convergence of policy. On the one hand, there was evidence of direct policy exchange between the two countries through shared policy networks, some of which are reflected in the examples given above. In other cases, similar policies – or at least similar *sounding* policies – could be identified but without there being any evidence of knowledge on the part of the alleged borrower. We suggested that, superficially at least, there were parallels between the assisted places scheme in England and the Milwaukee choice experiment which also subsidised access to private education for 'poor' children (Witte 1993); between local management of schools and site-based management; and between England's city technology colleges and the New American Schools Initiative.

We therefore wondered whether there was a policy zeitgeist associated with post-modernity that could be invoked to explain such similarities in the absence of direct linkages in advance of the policies emerging in both places. Stephen Ball, the journal's guest editor on that occasion, summarised our conclusions as follows:

> Whitty and Edwards . . . argue that proposals and justifications for reform in one country provide resources for advocates and politicians interested in promoting change in others. This is not so much a matter of policy exchange but the rein-forcement of shared assumptive worlds.
>
> (Ball 1998: 119)

This process made use of mutually reinforcing versions of reality which reflected shared assumptions and shared reference groups. We were made aware of some personal links between US policy makers and officials and their British equivalents, through family ties and common educational experiences. These are typical of net-works of influence and they reinforced the tendency for the US to look to England (rather than, say, Japan or Germany) in discussions of how best to improve national performance, even though those and other countries were performing better educa-tionally at that time. To that extent, broad political affinity and similar ideological preferences seemed to take precedence even over a concerted search for more effective policies. One Bush government staffer remarked:

> Whereas you heard more about Japan about five years ago, I think you're hearing more people look at England, not Germany so much now. Since the issue is standards and choice, you hear more people talking about England and you guys have done more on the role of unions and things.
>
> (Interview, June 1991)

While economic and social changes put education reform high on the political agenda in both nations, the similarity of response and the interest in sharing New Right ideas derived from a distinctively neoliberal faith that 'choice and competition' was indeed the answer. In that sense Phillips and Ochs' (2003) 'theoretical' basis for deciding what overseas policies were attractive was very much in evidence, albeit alongside examples that also fitted their 'phoney', 'realistic/practical' and 'quick fix' reasons for borrowing (pp. 454–455).

Although we did not refer to it at the time, our analysis had something in common with Paul Sabatier's Advocacy Coalition Framework (Sabatier and Jenkins-Smith

1993; Sabatier and Weible 2007). Our paper was also an example of what Steiner-Khamsi et al. (2006), drawing on the work of Jürgen Schriewer (1990), call an analytical rather than a normative approach to the study of policy borrowing. The same is true of this chapter – at least until towards the end.

Steiner-Khamsi et al. (2006) themselves write cogently about the reasons for policy borrowing, particularly between rich and poor countries in the context of international aid. However, one of the things that is superficially puzzling is why there has been a continuing US–UK nexus in education policy reform that has extended well beyond the close political ties of the Reagan–Thatcher years. It has not apparently been linked to aid, nor is it an obvious example of so-called 'PISA-tourism'.

The rise of the importance of PISA in education policy discourse has certainly been significant over the last ten years. It is rare to hear a speech on education by a British politician without reference to England's place in the international league tables. Colleagues at Edinburgh University in Scotland have undertaken a project looking at the role international comparison surveys are increasingly playing in our education policy. They have found that both policy makers and the media 'unequivocally accept' PISA and other OECD research findings with little interrogation or further exploration.

PISA results (and others) have become 'an event that no-one can afford to miss – it requires answers and demands action' (Grek 2008). Even in the US, the pressures of globalisation and the need for a competitive American workforce mean that OECD data feed into President Obama's rhetoric. For example, in his introduction to *A Blueprint for Reform* reference is made to 'world-class' education in these terms:

> Today more than ever, a world-class education is a pre-requisite for success. America was once the best educated nation in the world. A generation ago, we led all nations in college completion, but today, 10 countries have passed us.
>
> (Obama 2010: 1)

One impact of international surveys such as PISA has been a focus on education systems that have topped the league tables. There has been increased interest in systems that are shown by PISA results to be succeeding – often on both 'excellence' (high attainment overall) and 'equity' (low influence of socio-economic background on attainment) measures. Finland has, up to now, been the well-known star of the show in this respect and it is understandable why it has had to limit the numbers of foreign delegations it can receive as politicians search for the magic bullet. Other countries, and provinces such as Ontario in Canada, have also been the focus of much policy tourism and it is likely that, following the latest round of PISA tables, the province of Shanghai in China will become the new destination of choice for education policy tourists.

However, PISA and similar surveys do not really provide an explanation for the flow of traffic between the UK and the US. Both countries continue to perform embarrassingly badly in many of these tables, so it cannot be that their performance to date justifies the interest they take in each other's reforms. It may be, of course, that the interest in each other's policies is driven by the fact that they are more similar to each other socially and economically than they are to Finland. An explanation could thus be that their reforms are more likely to work in each other's countries than the Finnish ones because the context is more similar. Yet the continuing mutual interest in each other's reforms probably remains as much to do with those shared assumptive worlds described above – and, of course, a common language in which to describe their reforms.

Dominant Discourses of Reform

It is, however, possible to overestimate the extent to which similar terms – or even similar substantive policies – are necessary to make reference to other countries' reforms attractive to governments. As already mentioned, there are some clear parallels between grant maintained schools in England and charter schools in the US and now between charter schools in the US and free schools and academies in England. In these cases the names are different but the content similar. Steiner-Khamsi et al. (2006) argue that the language of reform may sometimes be the same but the actual content different. Even between the US and the UK, there are cases where the language is similar but the content significantly, though not entirely, different. *No Child Left Behind* and *Every Child Matters* would be one example. *Race to the Top* and *Aimhigher* would be another. In both these cases, any cross referencing would indicate a shared ambition rather than a shared policy prescription.

Steiner-Khamsi et al. (2006) also argue that policy borrowing, or rather, reference to practice elsewhere, takes place even when similar reforms already exist in the local context (Steiner-Khamsi and Quist 2000). This points to the conclusion that it is the discursive and legitimatory work that other people's reforms do for one's own that is important rather than that they are necessarily new ideas or whether they would actually work in your own context.

Yet this is not how it is often made to appear. One phrase that percolates through much of the education system at both macro-policy level and at classroom level in both countries is 'what works' and this also applies to the discourse of policy borrowing. We are encouraged to learn 'what works' from other countries. Sometimes, this reflects what Phillips and Ochs (2003) describe as 'realistic/practical' reasons for borrowing, although sometimes it is more of a search for their 'quick fix'.

Superficially, an international policy interest in 'what works' should be good news for those who work in research-intensive university schools of education. However, much of the evidence produced by politicians in support of so-called 'evidence-informed' policy is not what university-based researchers would recognise as research. Often it is *quasi*-research carried out by think tanks and advocacy groups.

Observers often do not distinguish between different types of research and the distinctive missions of different types of institutes and foundations.[3] In the context of international policy borrowing, this may be even more of an issue than at home. In the UK, for example, most politicians would know that the Institute of Economic Affairs or the Centre for Policy Studies were neoliberal think tanks and very different from, say, the Nuffield Foundation. They would not necessarily know that the Manhattan Institute or the Bradley Foundation in the US were very different from the Spencer Foundation. Nor would they realise that, in Canada, the Hudson Institute was a different type of operation from the Ontario Institute for Studies in Education.

North American politicians would probably be similarly confused by the UK examples.

Media stories carry details of research but rarely distinguish between different types of research and their varying degrees of robustness. Media reports themselves become the source of evidence for policy in their own right. There are also crossovers between these various types of evidence. Chubb and Moe undertook their policy tourism as a commission from the *Sunday Times* and, about the same time, the *New York Times* sent Susan Chira, its then education correspondent, on the same journey. Interestingly, Chira made more use of academic research findings in her reports than did Chubb and Moe and, possibly because of this, she produced a more nuanced verdict on the English reforms. But one of the features of media reporting, and herein perhaps lies its appeal to politicians and advocacy groups, is that it tends not to distinguish between anecdote and peer reviewed research findings when weighing up evidence.

The following example relates to the earlier discussion of the way in which the current government in England is using US charter schools to justify its own policy of freeing up the system by creating academies and free schools outside the control of local authorities. This use of anecdote comes from policy tourism on the part of the person who now runs the New Schools Network, a charity that has been engaged by the government to promote free schools and which models itself partly on the New York City Charter School Center. This particular account comes from the *Sunday Times* on 21 February 2010:

> Wolf says her inspiration to set up the New Schools Network, which will act as a 'back-room operation', providing administration and advice, came from a trip to New York. She flew there after working as a researcher for Michael Gove, the Conservative party's education spokesman. The party has championed the new movement, promising . . . to permit as many as 3,000 [new free] schools, which are modelled on Sweden's 'free schools' and America's charter movement . . .
>
> 'I was reasonably convinced the new schools the Tories were talking about would work. But I wanted to see for myself,' says Wolf.
>
> In New York she saw the contrast between dysfunctional public schools and some of the disciplined, creative charter schools. Sometimes both types of school were housed in one block. 'On one floor of a building I visited, a girl was being told to put on her hat. I watched her fling it at the staff,' says Wolf. 'When the lift doors opened on the floor of the charter school, by contrast, an 11-year-old came over and asked, ever so politely, would I like to be escorted around.
>
> 'I came back to Britain and decided this was what I wanted to do,' she continues. 'I can't think of any other idea that excites me so much.'
>
> (Griffiths 2010)

Nevertheless, despite the use of such anecdotes in policy borrowing, appeals to the findings of mainstream education research also feature as a key element of policy legitimation. Indeed, in a posting on the *Guardian* website, Wolf herself cited research from Sweden, the US and Alberta, Canada, as evidence that 'new schools perform better, that they have a positive effect on neighbouring schools and that the poorest benefit most' (Wolf 2010). However, a review of research on Swedish free schools has presented a much more nuanced picture (Allen 2010), while doubts have now been raised in the press about the link claimed by Wolf (and by Secretary of State Gove) between school autonomy and the high levels of educational attainment in Alberta (Evans 2011).

In another example of the selective use of research, almost as soon the coalition government had been elected in Britain in May 2010 and announced its policies, a document appeared on the website of the UK Department of Education, entitled 'Mythbuster'.[4] It included, along with selective use of UK and Swedish research findings, the following references to research on US charter schools:

The Case for School Freedom: National and International Evidence

Free Schools Raise Standards

- A recent study concluded that Boston's charter schools 'have a consistently positive impact on student achievement' . . .
- New York has instituted a 'report card' system . . . The charter schools have performed better than other schools, with the majority received (*sic*) As and Bs . . .
- Recent studies from Chicago and Florida indicate that charter school students have higher ACT scores, higher graduation rates and a greater probability of attending college than students who attend traditional public schools . . .

Free Schools Help the Disadvantaged

- Charter schools in New York have been shown to dramatically close the gap separating inner-city neighbourhood students from those of the wealthiest suburbs . . .
- The Harlem Children's Zone charters have completely closed the black-white achievement gap at both elementary and middle school level . . .
- Charter schools in Chicago close half of the achievement gap between disadvantaged inner-city public school students and middle-income students in suburban districts . . .

Debunking Myths About School Freedom

Myth: Free Schools will only benefit the well-off

Reality:

91 percent of New York charter school students participate in the Free or Reduced-Price lunch program (compared with 72 percent of students in the traditional state schools) . . .

Myth: Free Schools will covertly select the most able pupils

Reality:

The major report on Chicago charter schools found that the charters studied drew students who were, on average, lower achieving than public school students in the neighbourhoods where the schools were located . . .

> (Extracted from *Mythbuster*, Department for Education 2010)

This document was sent to some US researchers to gauge their reactions and the following response was typical of the comments received:

> Most of what they are claiming is technically true, but quite skewed in selection and interpretation. They only select from the minority of studies – like the study of New York City – that support their claims. Some of those localities indeed have some very good charter schools. However, *Mythbuster* ignores the many larger and more representative studies, like the recent national study out of Stanford [CREDO], that show charter schools, on average, underperforming compared to other public schools. I don't think that any of the studies they cite were peer-reviewed, and almost all were done by charter advocates.
>
> They are not only selective in choosing studies, but make claims from those studies without including the usual caveats and cautions. For instance, the claims about higher test scores – while technically correct – show no indication that the authors are aware that charter schools often exclude more difficult to educate students. The tenuous assertion that charter schools do not select more able students is drawn from a 2005 magazine article, which was in fact based on 3 schools in one city. There are a number of peer-reviewed studies that show the opposite.
>
> (Lubienski 2010)

Policy Borrowing or Just Policy Making on a Global Scale?

However, this use of research is probably merely an example of the globalisation of education policy making rather than something that is peculiar to policy *borrowing*. While it may be harder to scrutinise the validity of claims about the impact of policies being implemented elsewhere, there is nothing unusual in the selective use of research findings in policy making. Indeed, there have been many examples in UK policy making over many years (Whitty 2006). Ravitch's review of *Waiting for 'Superman'*, entitled 'The Myth of Charter Schools' (Ravitch 2010), identifies a similar phenomenon in the US. She points out that the Guggenheim film quietly acknowledges that only one in five charter schools achieves 'amazing results', but fails to explore why there are twice as many failing charter schools as there are successful ones, despite the wide availability of the CREDO study from Stanford that showed this. Similar concerns about the use of research evidence have actually been expressed by both sides of the debate about charter schools (Henig 2008).

More generally, the use of research in claims about 'what works' is particularly interesting. The language of 'what works' has been influential in the US since the

1980s and was adopted enthusiastically in the UK as part of Tony Blair's modernisation of the Labour Party and its abandonment of supposedly outdated ideologies. It remains a key part of the coalition government's discourse in the UK and seems to have been a crucial element of *Race for the Top* in the US, which President Obama stated would 'not be based on politics, ideology, or the preferences of a particular interest group. Instead, it will be based on a simple principle . . . whether a state is ready to do "what works"' (cited in Mathis and Welner 2010: 2). The *Blueprint* similarly makes reference to prioritising approaches to reform 'on the strengths of their evidentiary base' (ibid.).

However, the way in which academic research is actually used as part of that 'evidentiary base' by politicians is disturbing. A publication from the National Education Policy Center in Boulder, Colorado, by William Mathis and Kevin Welner concludes that criticisms made by Gene Glass of the evidence cited in the 1986 report *What Works* (US Department of Education 1986) also apply to the six summaries of research issued by the Obama government to support the Obama Education *Blueprint for Reform* in 2010. Glass had said of *What Works*:

> The selection of research to legitimize political views is an activity engaged in by governments at every point on the political compass . . . *What works* does not synthesize research, it invokes it in a modern ritual seeking legitimation of the Reagan administration's policies . . . and, lest one forget, previous administrations have done the same.
>
> (Glass 1987: 9)

Mathis and Welner and the researchers who reviewed the six *Blueprint* reports suggest that the same is true of the present US administration. They conclude that:

> The overall quality of the [research] summaries is far below what is required for a national policy discussion of critical issues. Each of the summaries was found to give overly simplified, biased, and too-brief explanations of complex issues.
>
> (Mathis and Welner 2010: 3)

None of this should be surprising either in the context of national policy or its use of research evidence from overseas. The contributors to the Mathis and Welner book seem very disappointed to find governments doing this sort of thing. But as Glass pointed out years before, that disappointment should be leavened with a cynical expectation that it is par for the course. While researchers may ideally wish policy to be based on robust research findings, in reality policy is driven by all sorts of considerations and the findings of education research will sometimes be rather low down the list. Other influences include the vicissitudes of the moment, the requirements of staying in office and the beliefs, commitments and prejudices of policy makers and their advisers and constituents. More fundamentally, we have to acknowledge that politics is significantly shaped by symbolic considerations that may have little to do with the real effects of policies. While this does not excuse blatant misrepresentation of research findings, it does indicate a need to be realistic about the context in which research is often used.

Particularly frustrating is the fact that politicians looking for evidence to support what they already think or want to do may not be interested in the more profound questions researchers want to ask. Researchers quite reasonably want to ask questions that go beyond 'what works' and it is often the answers to these questions that explain why 'what works' sometimes does not work. Always important, but particularly so in the context of cross cultural research and policy borrowing, are questions about 'what works where with whom' and why. So it was somewhat reassuring to read recently that the new official research agenda for the US Institute of Education Sciences gives greater priority to putting research findings into context by asking 'how, why, for whom, and under what conditions' policies are effective (National Board for Educational Sciences 2010). Some research can also have a role in helping people to think about questions such as whether what policy makers are trying to do is worthwhile and what constitutes socially just schooling. Politicians though tend to see that as their job rather than that of education researchers.

For all these reasons and more, achieving consensus on the evidence needed to establish 'what works' and to base education policy on that is unlikely to be an attainable goal even if such a technicist utopia were desirable. This is not to suggest that there is no role for a 'what works' approach to education research, but the notion that this is the only type of research that should be encouraged or funded certainly needs to be resisted (Whitty 2006). On policy borrowing, Andy Hargreaves (2008) rightly suggests that policy *principles* may travel better than policies and that they are 'much more transposable and transportable if they are interpreted intelligently within communities of practice among and between those who are their bearers and recipients' (p. 118). But the fact that they may be transposable among communities of *political* practice in the manner described earlier in this chapter does not ensure that they are transposable to communities of *educational* practice within which sensitivity to context is crucial to success. And it is this element that is obscured by the sort of political grandstanding described earlier and, in particular, its tendency to disregard the nuances that research properly records.

Conclusions

I have argued in this chapter that there has been a long tradition of trans-Atlantic policy tourism and policy borrowing since the mid-nineteenth century, reflecting shared assumptive worlds among policy makers in Britain and the US. I have also suggested that, in the discourse of policy making at all levels, questionable use of evidence is often part of policy justification. However, in the context of globalisation, there has been an increasing tendency to invoke claims about 'what works' in other countries and I have pointed here to some of the dangers and limitations of this approach.

So what might be the alternative to policy borrowing as it is currently practised? Given the host of initiatives that have been launched and abandoned over the past 30 years, there may be value in a more modest goal of reaching some agreement on 'what doesn't work', even across national contexts. In this connection, the Canadian commentator Ben Levin (1998) uses the notion of 'policy epidemic' as a tool for thinking about cross-national policy sharing and asks whether the 'prevention' of disease could be a similarly useful idea to apply to inappropriate education policies.

This provides a somewhat different perspective on cross-national policy sharing and is reminiscent of something else said by Horace Mann about his policy tourism in Europe when he was Secretary of the Massachusetts Board of Education. As well as leading Mann to advocate policy borrowing, his experiences also led him to reflect that

> if we are wise enough to learn from the experience of others rather than await the infliction consequent upon our own errors, we may yet escape the magnitude and formidableness of those calamities under which some other communities are now suffering.
>
> (Mann 1844)

In fact, Edwards and I identified an example of 'negative' policy borrowing in our 1998 paper (Whitty and Edwards 1998: 214), when we noted that:

> Britain's independent National Commission on Education (1993: 185) cited the Carnegie Foundation's (1992) study of school choice to justify its own warning that similar reforms in England's steeply tiered education system could have the 'unacceptable consequence' of increasingly unequal opportunities.

In this case, there is a clear recognition both of the possibilities of learning lessons from abroad and of the importance of context. Such an approach would probably not appeal to politicians looking for magic bullets, but it might be more appealing to a wider public who tend, like many researchers, to be sceptical about magic bullets.

Although pointing out the limitations of charter schools, for example, to policy makers can sometimes seem fruitless, education researchers also have a wider job as public intellectuals in addressing broader public attitudes to education policy and reform. Henig (2008) concludes a fascinating, and not entirely depressing, account of how research has been used in US policy debates on charter schools with the encouraging claim that 'shifting the center of gravity of public discourse towards a higher level of sophistication seems within grasp, and seems likely also to generate positive results' (p. 245).

In the UK, the Fabian Society, which in view of my earlier comments I should clearly identify as a left-of-centre think-tank, recently published a report on narrowing the attainment gap between pupils from different socio-economic backgrounds (Bamfield and Horton 2010). What made this piece of research stand out was its emphasis on the need to address public opinion in relation to educational inequality and counter the way in which this has too often been shaped by misleading political narratives around 'educational failure'.

Education researchers can help in challenging such narratives and changing the terms of the debate by reinforcing messages, not just about what works, but also about what *doesn't* work and why it doesn't work. In Levin's terms, cross national comparisons of reform may provide a way of strengthening the public mind on education to increase 'resistance' to superficial but seemingly attractive policies.

Policy inoculation may thus be a more appropriate metaphor than policy borrowing and such work might in time come to be seen as at least as legitimate a form of impact for education researchers as the questionable 'quick fixes' encouraged by too narrow a 'what works' philosophy. But it should be clear from what has been said in this chapter that, in a globalising world, this work will need to take place on a global as well as a national scale.[5]

Acknowledgements

This chapter is based on lectures delivered at Teachers College, Columbia University, New York City, on 8 November 2010, and the Ontario Institute for Studies in Education, University of Toronto, on 11 November 2010. I am most grateful to Sarah Tang of the Institute of Education, University of London, for her help in preparing it for publication.

Notes

1   There were, of course, earlier examples in that direction as well. Beresford-Hill (1993) cites Board of Education visits to America in 1900 on behalf of Michael Sadler.
2   Governor Christie is in fact Governor of the State of New Jersey.
3   Britain has a much weaker tradition than the US of philanthropic organisations being involved in education research and advocacy, but it is now becoming an increasingly important feature of the UK landscape (Ball 2009).
4   It is unclear whether this document was originally intended to be made publicly available, at least in the form it was, as it was not presented in the usual high standard of official documentation. Interestingly, it is no longer available on the UK Government's website now that the legislation to implement the free schools policy has been successfully passed. However, a similar type of document, but one that was more professionally produced (DfE 2010a), appeared alongside the Government's 2010 schools White Paper (DfE 2010b).
5   Of course, when policy borrowing involves West–East, North–South, developed–developing country interchange, additional considerations enter into the picture, such as those mentioned above in relation to Steiner-Khamsi's work. In seeking to understand the ways in which 'British Educational Reform' has been used in the Japanese education context, Takayama and Apple (2008) point to the need to employ not only the literature of policy borrowing, but also that of postcolonial studies and cultural studies.

References

Allen, R. (2010) 'Replicating Swedish free school reforms in England', *Research in Public Policy*, 10: 4–7.

Ball, S. J. (1998) 'Big policies/small world: An introduction to international perspectives in education policy', *Comparative Education*, 34(2): 119–130.

Ball, S. J. (2009) 'Privatising education, privatising education policy, privatising educational research: network governance and the "competition state"', *Journal of Education Policy*, 24(1): 83–99.

Bamfield, L. and Horton, T. (2010) *What's fair? Applying the fairness test to education*. London: Fabian Society. Online at: www.fabians.org.uk/images/stories/publication_/Whats_Fair_web.pdf [accessed 15 November 2010].

Beresford-Hill, P. (1993) 'Teacher education, access and quality control in higher education: Lessons from America for Britain's policy-makers', *Oxford Review of Education*, 19(1): 79–88.

Carnegie Foundation (1992) *School Choice*. Princeton, NJ: Carnegie Foundation

Chubb, J. and Moe, T. (1990) *Politics, Markets and America's Schools.* Washington, DC: Brookings Institution.

Chubb, J. and Moe, T. (1992) *A Lesson in School Reform from Great Britain.* Washington, DC: Brookings Institution.

Department for Education (DfE) (2010a) *The Case for Change.* London: The Stationery Office.

Department for Education (DfE) (2010b) *The Importance of Teaching.* London: The Stationery Office.

Evans, R. (2011) 'Is the Canadian model right for UK schools?', *Guardian,* 4 January.

Finegold, D., McFarland, L. and Richardson, W. (eds) (1993) *Something Borrowed, Something Learned? The transatlantic market in education and training reform.* Washington, DC: Brookings Institution.

Glass, G. V. (1987) 'What works: Politics and research', *Educational Researcher,* 16: 5–1.

Gove, M. (2010) Speech by Michael Gove to Westminster Academy, 6 September 2010. Online at: www.education.gov.uk/inthenews/speeches/a0064281/michael-gove-to-westminster-academy [accessed 15 November 2010].

Green, D. (1991) 'Lessons from America' in D. Green (ed.) *Empowering the Parents: How to break the schools' monopoly.* London: Institute of Economic Affairs.

Grek, S. (2008) PISA in the British media: Leaning tower or robust testing tool? *CES Briefing No. 45,* April 2008. Online at: www.ces.ed.ac.uk/PDF%20Files/Brief045.pdf [accessed 15 November 2010].

Griffiths, S. (2010) 'Me and my 350 schools', *Sunday Times,* 21 February. Online at: www.timesonline.co.uk/tol/life_and_style/education/article7034772.ece [accessed 15 November 2010].

Hargreaves, A. (2008) 'Engaging policy: Neither a borrower nor a lender be', *European Training Foundation Yearbook,* 113–118. Luxembourg: European Training Foundation.

Henig, J. R. (2008) *Spin Cycle: How research is used in policy debates – the case of charter schools.* New York: Russell Sage Foundation.

Her Majesty's Inspectorate of Schools (HMI) (1989) *The Provisional Teacher Program in New Jersey.* London: HMSO.

Her Majesty's Inspectorate of Schools (HMI) (1990) *Teaching and Learning in New York City Schools.* London: HMSO.

Levin, B. (1998) 'An epidemic of education policy: (what) can we learn from each other?', *Comparative Education,* 34(2): 131–141.

Lubienski, C. (2010) Personal Communication, 22 June.

Mann, H. (1844) *Mr. Mann's Seventh Annual Report; Education in Europe.* Boston: Massachusetts Board of Education.

Mathis, W. and Welner, K. (2010) *The Obama Education Blueprint: Researchers Examine the Evidence.* Boulder, CO: National Education Policy Center.

Miliband, D. (1991) *Markets, Politics and Education: Beyond the Education Reform Act.* London: Institute for Public Policy Research.

Nathan, J. (1996) *Charter Schools: Creating Hope and Opportunity for American Education.* San Francisco: Jossey Bass.

National Board for Educational Sciences (2010) Director's Final Proposed Priorities for the Institute Of Education Sciences, November 1. Online at: http://ies.ed.gov/director/board/priorities.asp [accessed 31 January 2010].

National Commission on Education (1993) *Learning to Succeed: A radical look at education today and a strategy for the future.* London: Heinemann.

Obama, B. (2010) 'A letter from the President' in United States Department of Education (2010) *A Blueprint for Reform: The Reauthorization of the Elementary and Secondary*

Education Act. Washington, DC: US Department of Education. Online at: www2.ed.gov/policy/elsec/leg/blueprint/blueprint.pdf [accessed 15 November 2010].

Phillips, D. and Ochs, K. (2003) 'Processes of policy borrowing in education: Some explanatory and analytical devices', *Comparative Education*, 39(4): 451–461.

Ravitch, D. (2010) The myth of charter schools. *New York Review of Books,* 11 November. Online at: www.nybooks.com/articles/archives/2010/nov/11/myth-charter-schools/ [accessed 15 November 2010].

Sabatier, P. A. and Jenkins-Smith, H. (eds) (1993) *Policy Change and Learning: An advocacy coalition approach*. Boulder, CO: Westview Press.

Sabatier, P. A. and Weible, C. M. (2007) 'The advocacy coalition framework. innovations and clarifications' in P. A. Sabatier (ed.) *Theories of the Policy Process*. Boulder, CO: Westview Press, 189–220.

Schriewer, J. (1990) 'The method of comparison and the need for externalization: methodological criteria and sociological concepts' in J. Schriewer, in cooperation with B. Holmes (eds) *Theories and Methods in Comparative Education* (pp. 25–83). Frankfurt am Main, Bern, New York, Paris: Peter Lang.

Stake, R. (1995) *The Art of Case Study Research*. Thousand Oaks, CA and London: Sage.

Stearns, K. (1996) *School Reform: Lessons from England*. Princeton, NJ: Carnegie Foundation for the Advancement of Teaching.

Steiner-Khamsi, G. and Quist, H. (2000) 'The politics of educational borrowing: Reopening the case of Achimota in British Ghana', *Comparative Education Review*, 44(3): 272–299.

Steiner-Khamsi, G., Silova, I. and Johnson, E. M. (2006) 'Neoliberalism liberally applied: Educational policy borrowing in Central Asia' in J. Ozga, T. Seddon and T. S. Popkewitz (eds) *World Yearbook of Education 2006*. Abingdon: Routledge.

Takayama, K. and Apple, M. W. (2008) 'The cultural politics of borrowing: Japan, Britain, and the narrative of educational crisis', *British Journal of Sociology of Education*, 29(3): 289–301.

US Department of Education (1986) *What Works: Research about Teaching and Learning*. Washington, DC: US Department of Education.

Vasagar, J. (2010) Free meals scrapped to pay for school improvement scheme, *Guardian*, 2 November 2010. Online at: www.guardian.co.uk/politics/2010/nov/02/free-meals-school-improvement-scheme [accessed 15 November 2010].

Weber, K. (ed.) (2010) *Waiting for 'Superman': How we can save America's failing public schools*. New York: Public Affairs.

Whitty, G. (2006) 'Education(al) research and education policy making: Is conflict inevitable?', *British Educational Research Journal*, 32(2): 159–176.

Whitty, G. and Edwards, T. (1998) 'School choice policies in England and the United States: An exploration of their origins and significance', *Comparative Education*, 34(2): 211–227.

Witte, J. (1993) 'The Milwaukee Parental Choice Program: The first thirty months', paper delivered at the Annual Meeting of the American Educational Research Association, Atlanta, Georgia.

Wolf, R. (2010) 'New schools and real parental choice', *Guardian* website, 20 February. Online at: www.guardian.co.uk/commentisfree/2010/feb/20/education-choice-new-schools [accessed 15 November 2010].

19 Flowing Discourses and Border Crossing

The Slogan of 'Respect for Diversity' in Latin America

Jason Beech and Emmanuel Lista

This chapter is aimed at analysing the ways in which the notion of 'respect for diversity', disseminated through global discourses, is interpreted in different educational systems in Latin America. It will be argued that as respect for diversity is promoted through global policy networks it is rendered as an abstract and malleable slogan that can be interpreted and rearranged in a multiplicity of diverse meanings, depending on the context of reception. It will also be suggested that the case of respect for diversity is especially relevant to analyse the flow and recontextualisation of global educational discourses.

In comparative education, theories that analyse global flows of educational ideas and their recontextualisation are based on the notion that as discourses are adopted in different contexts they are translated and transformed. It is the crossing of borders from one context to another that defines if and how a certain discourse will be translated. So, in order to further understand the effects of global discourses, comparative education needs theories that can interpret these cultural borders and the ways in which discourse changes as it passes through them, avoiding the pitfall of falling into a reified notion of cultures as if they were fixed, static and coherent wholes. This chapter is aimed at contributing to the reading of this complex puzzle.

The content of the transfer analysed in this chapter adds another layer of complexity to the puzzle of understanding cultural borders, because, as will be shown, the notion of respect for diversity has the potential to alter existing cultural, ethnic and political identifications, questioning cultural borders in specific places. Furthermore, in places where the homogenisation of the population was considered an important strategy in the construction of the nation, respect for diversity can weaken homogenising approaches, and empower some of the groups whose culture and knowledge was excluded or treated as inferior in educational systems and in society at large.

Thus, through a comparative analysis of the ways in which the slogan of respect for diversity was interpreted in Bolivia and Argentina, this chapter will argue that it is important to understand how different groups within a country appropriate, translate and transform global slogans to use them in their struggles to attain recognition and political power within a given society.

The chapter is divided into five sections. The first will briefly discuss notions of policy borrowing, transfer and the flows of educational discourse, and suggest some theoretical propositions about ways of understanding processes of border crossing and recontextualisation. The second section will analyse the slogan of respect for diversity in global discourses, reflecting upon the tensions that these concepts create in the definition of cultural borders. Based on the concept of 'colonial difference' (Mignolo 2008a: 18), the third section will examine the specificity of colonialism and post-colonialism in Latin America to understand the particular ways in which Eurocentric views and modernisation processes were interpreted in this region. Against this historical backdrop, current interpretations of the slogan of respect for diversity in Argentina and Bolivia will be analysed in the fourth section. In the last section, some concluding remarks about the theoretical puzzles that were opened up to think about processes of educational borrowing and lending and recontextualisation will be offered.

Educational Transfer, Recontextualisation and Cultural Assumptions

Education is a global phenomenon. It is global in the sense that every human community needs education to preserve and transmit its culture and to provide the newly arrived with the 'means of orientation' (Elías 1994: 55) that will help them interpret and act upon the world. But education is also global in the sense that definitions of what it means to be educated (what means of orientation are needed to inhabit the world) and of how people should be educated have been exchanged and diffused around the world resulting in certain global common sense about the aims of education and the means to attain those aims. The growth of global interconnectedness in current times has intensified the global character of educational ideas that manifests itself in global policy spaces (Beech 2009) and through global speak (Steiner-Khamsi 2000) or global educational discourses.

However, the practice of formal education is strongly localised, in the sense that schools are attached to a given territory and influenced by the specific experiences and identities of the communities they serve and help to construct. As global discourses move into a locality they transform (and are transformed by) local discourses and available meanings in the context of reception.

Understanding the movement of ideas about education and the ways in which they transform and are transformed by contexts of reception has been (and still is) one of the most relevant puzzles in comparative education and studies of globalisation in education. Notions of indigenisation (Schriewer 2000), recontextualisation (Steiner-Khamsi 2000; Beech 2009) and shape-shifting (Cowen 2009) have been used to analyse these transformations. Overall, the logic of these analyses is that every time a discourse moves, 'there is a space in which ideology can play . . . [as a] discourse moves, it is ideologically transformed; it is not the same discourse any longer' (Bernstein 1996: 47). It is the moving between contexts, and, thus, the crossing of borders between contexts that defines these transformations.

International borders are most commonly considered in studies of educational transfer (Ravitch 1983; Shibata 2005; Tanaka 2005). But international borders are not the only type of border that defines the transformation of educational discourses. These borders are still important, especially because formal education is a national enterprise in most nation-states. However, concentrating only on international borders misses some of the complexities of educational interactions under the current system of global relations and networks.

One of the problems with using nation-states as the unit of analysis in studies about flows and recontextualisation of discourses is that it assumes certain unity within national borders by reifying national cultures as fixed, static and coherent wholes. However, different groups within a national territory could in principle appropriate the abstract and malleable slogans contained in global discourses, making specific interpretations of its postulates that would strengthen their positions and arguments in order to pursue their own interests (Popkewitz 1980). In such a case, generalisations about how global discourses are interpreted in a given country cannot be made. Instead, it is necessary to examine how different groups within a given country interpret in practice global slogans to capture the complexity of processes through which global discourses are decoded.

In the next sections it will be argued that interpretations of the slogan of 'respect for diversity' are especially relevant to analyse ways in which different groups use global slogans for their own purpose, given that this notion has the potential to destabilise ethnic affiliations and question existing power relations between groups, opening up the possibilities for negotiations and repositioning of sub-national groups and identities.

The Slogan of Respect for Diversity and Cultural Borders

The notion of respect for diversity has gained much visibility in global policy discourses about education. It is promoted by most of the actors that participate in global policy spaces, and it has become part of a common sense in education that has influenced state policy discourses in many educational systems (Silova 2006). International agencies such as United Nations Educational, Scientific and Cultural Organization (UNESCO), United Nations Children's Fund (UNICEF) and the World Bank consider cultural diversity to be a basic human right. These agencies have established numerous international agreements, recommendations and guidelines intended to support states in the design of policies that are more responsive to cultural pluralism. In line with this position, UNESCO's Universal Declaration on Cultural Diversity (2001) states: 'The defence of cultural diversity is an ethical imperative, inseparable from respect for human dignity. It implies a commitment to human rights and fundamental freedoms, in particular the rights of persons belonging to minorities and those of indigenous peoples' (UNESCO 2001: 13).

The World Bank follows a similarly broad approach and works with two definitions of culture which cover a wide range of issues:

> The first, wider, definition describes particular shared values, beliefs, knowledge, skills and practices that underpin behavior by members of a social group at a particular point in time (with potentially good and bad effects on processes of poverty reduction). The second definition describes creative expression, skills, traditional knowledge and cultural resources that form part of the lives of people and societies, and can be a basis for social engagement and enterprise development.
>
> (World Bank 2008)

Similarly, the Inter-American Development Bank (2007) presents the issue of cultural diversity in the context of economic and social exclusion.

In addition to 'culture' there are other terms such as 'ethnicity' and 'race', which are often used interchangeably by international organisations when talking about similar issues. In UNICEF's 2006 State of the World's Children report on the 'Excluded and Invisible', for example, exclusion is discussed on the basis of ethnicity rather than cultural identity. In this report the term 'ethnicity' is defined as 'a set of characteristics – cultural, social, religious and linguistic – that forms a distinctive identity shared by a community of people' (UNICEF 2006: 23).

Thus, the promotion of respect for diversity in the recommendations of international agencies shows that there is a lack of conceptual clarity in terms of what type of diversity should be respected and how. The definitions discussed thus far suggest that the notion of cultural diversity spans a wide range of issues, and that depending on the context it can be associated with race, ethnicity, socioeconomic inequality or religion, among others (Aragón 2008). Furthermore, concepts such as 'respecting' or 'recognising' are ambiguous and open up to very different interpretations in practice.

In this way, respect for diversity follows the typical characteristics of global discourses that are coded through complex processes of collaboration in global networks, in which institutions with different ideological positions and specific objectives have to produce proposals that could be attractive and applicable in very different cultural, ideological, socio-economic and political contexts.

> [E]ducational discourse is transformed in the global policy space of education into a discourse that combines in an elaborate way certain stability with malleability and adaptability that allow for its persuasive imaging and its acceptability in very different contexts. This discourse is abstracted from place-based historical experience, and thus its postulates are stripped of their specific meaning and they become a kind of 'floating signifier' that can be interpreted and rearranged in a multiplicity of diverse meanings, depending on the context of reception.
>
> (Beech 2009: 355)

Respect for diversity implies a substantial rupture with previous modern-nationalistic visions that were dominant in mainstream Western educational discourses. In modern narratives the nation 'was seen to have fixed geographical boundaries, to contain one identifiable language and culture, to be itself part of a progressive history through its emergence, liberation, unification or conquest, to be identical with the state and to be, in its initials and so many subsequent formulations, in danger' (Coulby and Jones 1996: 172). From this perspective, diversity was seen as an obstacle standing in the way of the progress of the nation. The obstacle had to be managed and eradicated, mainly by homogenising the population through a common national culture. In this way, symbolic borders of identification would coincide with geopolitical international borders and social cohesion and political legitimation of the state would be attained. As Rousseau (1966) suggested:

> It appears that the feeling of humanity evaporates and grows feeble in embracing all mankind, and that we cannot be affected by the calamities of Tartary or Japan,

in the same manner as we are by those of European nations. It is necessary in some degree to confine and limit our interest and compassion in order to make it active. Now, as this sentiment can be useful only to those with whom we have to live, it is proper that our humanity should confine itself to our fellow-citizens . . . It is certain that the greatest miracles of virtue have been produced by patriotism: this fine and lively feeling, which gives to the force of self-love all the beauty of virtue, lends it an energy which, without disfiguring it, makes it the most heroic of all passions.

(p. 142)

The notion of political nationalism promoted by Rousseau was very influential in post-revolutionary France, as the educational system was organised to promote a unifying language and culture (Barnard 1969; Green 1990). The idea that all schools should function in exactly the same way was also reinforced by the French notion of equality, which implied giving all citizens a homogeneous education, disregarding their differences.

This overall approach to the organisation of the educational system as a means to contribute to nation-building was later very influential in South America. Indigenous peoples and populations of African descent were considered to be inferior and therefore, they had to be 'civilised' through Western modern education. Following the French model, the state centralised strong control over the curriculum, teacher training and text books, with the aim of offering very similar educational experiences to all students (Gvirtz and Beech 2008). The effects of this overall logic varied significantly from country to country; the consequent degree of homogenisation and Westernisation was very strong in countries such as Argentina and Uruguay, but much weaker in other countries, such as Bolivia, Guatemala and Paraguay. Similarly, while the principle of *laïcité* was strictly followed in Uruguay, the power of the Catholic Church over education was (and remains) very strong in other countries such as Colombia (Saenz Obregón and Saldarriaga Vélez 2008).

The slogan of respect for diversity is strongly linked to the post-modern critique of the grand narratives of the Enlightenment (Lyotard 1984). The term post-modernity will be simplified in this chapter as being a cultural perspective in which the great narratives of the Enlightenment are questioned for being culturally, class and gender biased; in which the capacity of human reason to understand the world is doubted; and in which positional knowledges are growing in opposition to grand narratives. Thus, in post-modern philosophy, there is no place for an ideal human condition or for a generalised aim for society, and respect for diversity is essential (Lyotard 1984; Bauman 1992, 1995).

The post-modern critique is still European, still Western (Dussel 2008). It is a critique from within the European colonial project that travels to places like Latin America promoting a rupture with a modern, Enlightened vision of the world that was also foreign, incomplete and diverse. As the concept of 'colonial difference' (Mignolo 2008b) suggests, the influence of European Enlightenment ideas (and Eurocentrism in general) was not uniform. It resulted in different manifestations of modern institutions and visions. In that sense, when analysing processes of modernisation, external influences have to be considered in relation to local historical trajectories (Sachsenmaier 2010). Furthermore, within these trajectories, the ways in which different groups have appropriated and adapted modern reason are fundamental in order to capture the complexity of global/local specificities in different modernisation processes.

Stressing the Eurocentric perspective of post-modernity does not imply a lack of non-Western critiques of modernity and its messianic colonial project. But there is an essential difference between critiques of modern reason from within and critiques enunciated by those in subaltern positions, such as dependency theories, subaltern studies and philosophy of liberation, amongst others (Dussel 2008; Mignolo 2008a). We suggest that the geopolitics of knowledge (Mignolo 2008a) are central in the analysis of educational flows, including the examination of ways in which specific subaltern critiques of (and resistance to) modern reason interact with globally diffused slogans such as respect for diversity that can repress or strengthen these localised struggles.

The notion of respect for diversity is also strongly linked to the promotion of multiculturalism in the US and in Europe. In the US, initiatives to promote multicultural education started in the 1960s and 1970s through different movements that promoted the inclusion of contents linked to different ethnic groups in school curricula (Gay 1983; Banks 1993; Sleeter 1996). These initiatives were the result of 'new directions in the civil rights movement, the criticisms expressed by textbook analysts, and the reassessment of the psychological premises on which compensatory education programs of the late 1950s and early 1960s had been founded' (Gay 1983: 560). In the case of Europe, the patchwork settlement of Europe by different linguistic, ethnic and religious groups as a result of immigration from former colonies that took place mainly after the Second World War displaced the problem of multiculturalism from the international to some of the national European agendas (Lynch 1983). The increasing presence of ethnic minorities within the borders of Western nation-states created tensions that eventually destabilised national symbolic borders of identification and opened up the question of 'who legitimately belongs to the nation, who are the real citizens, and where immigrants and the children of immigrants fit in relation to such conceptions' (Gibson and Rojas 2006: 69).

Even though other attributes were later associated with 'multicultural' education – gender, social class, special needs – the strong discursive link between multiculturalism and ethnicity is important to this chapter for two reasons. First, it reduces the concept of culture to an equivalent of ethnicity, resulting in an oversimplification of the notion of culture and processes through which cultural borders are constructed and interpreted. Second, a multicultural education that equates culture and ethnicity can strengthen the idea of a homogeneous nation-state, reinforcing the notion that differences always reflect the outside (immigrants, peoples of other colour, of other habits, other languages) and not the inside. In that sense, multiculturalism and respect for diversity can be seen as strategic discourses that are still based on the notion of diversity as a problem that needs to be managed and domesticated.

It is also interesting to emphasise the strong link that was (and is) made between multicultural education and immigration, to reflect upon cases such as Latin America, in which minorities are not always immigrant groups, but rather the peoples who lived in that territory before the European conquest (this problem will be further developed in the next section). Finally, it is important to stress that the different groups struggling for recognition are not necessarily 'cultures', but they sometimes strategically define themselves as a culture to gain legitimacy (García Castaño et al. 1997). In that sense, multiculturalism cannot be analysed outside of power struggles between different groups to attain status, recognition and political power within a given society.

Thus, when analysing the recontextualisation of respect for diversity in Latin America, the first puzzle is to understand the ways in which this slogan is interpreted and enacted differently in different countries. On the other hand, given the potential destabilisation of existing borders of identification, it is possible that different groups within the same country will make specific interpretations and uses of the abstract and malleable slogan of respect for diversity.

What types of diversity should be respected? How and how much should diversity be respected? Where is the limit? Furthermore, what does 'respect' mean? It is clear that different groups will have different views about the answers to these questions. For example, in 2010 the Argentine Congress passed a law authorising same-sex marriages. Respect for diversity was used discursively by gay movements and their supporters to confront the Catholic Church, which defined the law as a 'destructive attack on God's plan' (Barrionuevo 2010). According to the Catholic Church in Argentina, sexual orientation is not a type of diversity that should be respected (at least not to the point of allowing for same-sex marriage), but groups within that same institution use respect for diversity as a discursive tactic to promote religious Catholic education in schools.

The Colonial Difference and Respect for Diversity in Latin America

Starting from the concept of 'colonial difference' (Mignolo 2008a), this section will discuss the specificities of the Latin American colonial experience. As Rizvi (2009) suggests, in order to understand global movements of capital, people and ideas it is necessary to consider how colonial histories have affected the patterns of global flows since these current movements emerge 'out of a historical architecture that is already in place' (p. 104). Then, the Argentine and Bolivian processes of modernisation will be briefly described to show the significant differences between these two places, which, it will be argued, are central to understanding the different ways in which the slogan of respect for diversity has been interpreted and enacted by specific groups within these countries.

The concept of 'colonial difference' questions simplistic and generalised interpretations of colonialism and post-colonialism that reduce very complex and diverse cultural and political practices to binary categories such as coloniser and colonised, centre and periphery that dissolve internal differences and lead 'to an inevitable homogenization of entirely different phenomena' (Chanady 2008: 417). Following Moraña, Dussel and Jáuregui (2008), we 'use the term *colonial difference* . . . in order to emphasize the *specificity* of Latin America's colonial history, that is, its particular historical, political, social, and cultural modes of articulation within the world-system of colonial domination throughout the centuries' (p. 18).

Given the specificities of the Latin American colonial experience, the use of post-colonial theories, mostly developed from Asian and African perspectives, to understand the Latin American situation is problematic. One of the problems with the use of post-colonial theories in Latin America is that the rupture between the colonial system and independence was quite weak. Creole oligarchies replaced the Spanish and the Portuguese authorities, but the overall colonial social structure was continued, keeping indigenous peoples and epistemologies in subaltern and marginal positions (Dussel 2008; Moraña et al. 2008). As Mignolo explains:

> The singularity of the Americas, seen from the perspective of coloniality, also resides in its being the space where a population of Creoles of European descent gained independence from the imperial metropolis, and reproduced the logic of coloniality in the new independent governments in both the North and the South against the Indigenous and Afro populations. Thus, the Creole population of European descent became, in South America and the Caribbean, the master while remaining the slave with respect to Western Europe and the US.
>
> (2008b: 47)

These national elites acted as a class of mediators controlling the connection of Latin American countries with the world-system, and acting as translators of Western modern episteme and institutions that were rendered as the only possible option (Mignolo 2008a) for the advancement of national projects. These Creole groups were often 'involved in "neocolonial pacts" with international powers (mostly England, France and the United States), which strengthened economic and political dependency and deepened inequality in Latin American societies' (Moraña et al. 2008: 9).

Thus, the colonial logic did not end with independence. During the nineteenth century Great Britain had neo-colonial control of the Latin American economy, while France had a strong cultural influence in the region. As international power shifted to the US in the twentieth century, there were military and political interventions in Cuba, Mexico, Guatemala, Honduras, Nicaragua, Panama, Colombia, Haiti and the Dominican Republic. Other more recent and somehow disguised interventions, such as the support for Pinochet's coup d'état, Plan Colombia and Plan Condor in the Southern Cone, reveal the continuity of colonialism that has marked Latin American history (Moraña et al. 2008).

Quijano has coined the concept of 'coloniality' to refer to the global hegemonic power that was imposed on the Americas since the Conquista and continued throughout Latin American history (Castro-Gómez 2008, Moraña et al. 2008; Quijano 2008). One of the main characteristics of the coloniality of power is that it not only included domination by force, but it was also strongly based on the repression of indigenous epistemes and the simultaneous positioning of Western knowledge as superior and as the only valuable option to apprehend the world. Repression and seduction functioned as two sides of the same coin:

> European culture became a seduction; it gave access to power. After all, besides repression, seduction is the main instrument of all power. Cultural Europeization turned into an aspiration. It was a means of participating in colonial power.
>
> (Quijano 2008: 439)

The aspiration to cultural 'Europeization' was shared both by dominated and dominators. As Castro-Gómez (2008: 282) notes, the 'imaginary of whiteness' was internalised as an aspiration in the subjectivity of all social actors in colonial society. But whiteness was not so much a question of skin colour, but rather a certain disposition of the mind, forms of dress and customs that represented 'cultural signs of distinction' and civilisation (Castro-Gómez 2008). Thus, the classification of populations using the concept of race was (and still is) the epistemic base of the coloniality of power.

Coloniality in Latin America originated with the transoceanic voyages from which European modernity was born. The 'discovery' of the Americas happened in a time of religious (Catholic) expansionism in the Iberian Peninsula. It was not the 'expression of the logistics of an imperial search for transnational markets implemented from the centers of advanced capitalism – as it would be the case with English and French territorial appropriations during the nineteenth and twentieth century' (Moraña et al. 2008: 8). The 'New World' placed Europe in the centre of the world. Thus, Eurocentrism reached the Americas, much before the Enlightenment. Americans were defined as human beings, but barely so. They were considered to be 'peoples without history' (Mignolo 2008b: xii), as an immature *tabula rasa* on which Christianity and European epistemes could and should be inscribed.

Thus, the difference between indigenous populations and Creole elites acting as mediators between Latin America and the world-system is essential to understand the distribution of power, knowledge and education in the region. This difference – defined by a combination of ethnicity and cultural dispositions – is also critical in order to analyse interpretations and enactments of the slogan of respect for diversity in Latin America.

The remaining part of this section offers an historical overview of education in Bolivia and Argentina, showing the strong influence that the classification of population had in the construction of the nation-state and the educational system in these two countries. It will be argued that the distinction between white/mestizo Creoles and indigenous peoples was important in both countries, but had very different effects and manifestations in each one of them.

Bolivia is one of the countries in Latin America with the highest proportion of indigenous people (62.2 per cent) (López and Murillo 2006). 'Though far from being the "dominant group" politically, indigenous people dominate Bolivia's cultural landscape, urban as well as rural, by sheer force of numbers and the cohesion of a distinctive complex of cultural traits' (Luykx 1999: 2). According to the 2001 census there are 30 different indigenous communities in Bolivia (CEPAL and BID 2005). This shows that ethnic and cultural diversity in Bolivia is much more complex than the binary 'indigenous/Creole' suggests.

The history of education in Bolivia has been strongly marked by the coloniality of power. After independence, Creole elites continued with the same logic and principles of the colonisers, subordinating the indigenous population and expropriating their land. Thus, Bolivians attained independence from Spain, but internally the colonial structure of power was maintained with Creoles occupying the place of the Spanish conquerors (Albó 2005; Albó and Barrios Súbelas 2006). The imposition of the Spanish language, the repression of indigenous languages and knowledge in the educational system, the differences between rural education for the indigenous people and urban education for the Creole elites, and the exclusion of indigenous cultures and people from higher education have been strategies used by the colonial powers and, later, by the elites to dominate, civilise and/or assimilate indigenous communities.

The language of instruction has been in the centre of educational struggles and a 'crucial obstacle to national unity' from the perspective of Bolivian policy makers (Luykx 1999: 13). Throughout history, on the one hand, indigenous communities opposed the imposition of the Spanish language that was seen as one of the homogenising strategies aimed at repressing indigenous cultures and enforcing Western knowledge and habits. But, on the other hand, access to the Spanish language was also seen as a strategic element that could help indigenous communities fight for their land and rights within dominant institutions established by Western elites. Similarly, Creole dominant groups saw rural education and the teaching of Spanish as instrumental to the assimilation and control of indigenous groups, but also as a potentially dangerous strategy that could empower indigenous resistance.

The 'nation' has been another contentious element used by indigenous groups and elites in different ways. Through a position described as 'bourgeois nationalism' elites defined the Bolivian nation as rooted in the cultural heritage of Spanish colonisers. Meanwhile, the lower classes and the indigenous and mestizo people comprising them defended what was known as 'revolutionary nationalism', based on the notion that the essence of Bolivia is rooted in the cultural heritage of indigenous peoples (Luykx 1999: 25). Thus, in Bolivia, Creole elites appropriated modern ideas about Western reason and education. Yet within these groups there was a permanent debate between the need to modernise and civilise the indigenous majority in order to have a modern nation integrated into the world-system, and the risk that educating the indigenous peoples presented in terms of empowering these groups that could (and some times did) rebel against the domination of the Creole minority.

On the other hand, indigenous groups debated between the acceptance of Western indoctrination on the principle that having access to the Spanish language and Western knowledge could give them power in their political struggle for recognition, and the defence and development of indigenous epistemic and educational options that would contribute to the preservation of their cultures. In this context, educational expansion was slow, unstable and fragmented; at least when compared with Bolivia's southern neighbour, Argentina, where the percentage of indigenous peoples in the population is much smaller (around 1.7 per cent) due to very different historical trajectories.

Since Argentina's independence from Spain in 1816, immigration has been a fundamental trait in the construction of the nation. During the nineteenth century, the promotion of European immigration was used as one of the main strategies to 'civilise' and 'modernise' the newborn nation, and in this way immigrants became co-protagonists of national progress. Argentina has been described as a country *of* immigrants (not a country *with* immigrants) (Oteiza and Novick 2000). Between 1880 and 1930, massive immigration deeply restructured the profile of Argentine society. The 1.8 million inhabitants present in 1869 became 7.8 million in 1914, and, during that same period, the population of the city of Buenos Aires rose from 180,000 to 1.5

million. In 1895, two out of three inhabitants of the city were immigrants and by 1914, when many of these immigrants had children born in Argentina, 30 per cent of the total population was foreign-born, 28 per cent from Europe and only 2 per cent from other American countries (Romero 2001; INDEC 2009).

The educational system was designed with the aim of homogenising the population under the new 'Argentine culture' that would guarantee political stability and legitimise the power of the central state. *Civilización o barbarie* was the slogan of the time that expressed in binary terms the essential difference between modern European epistemes and indigenous cultures that were considered inferior. Consequently indigenous people needed to be given even more 'education' than the other children, 'at least as much as the abnormal' (Naboulet, cited in Artieda 1993: 313). Primary schools expanded rapidly through most of the Argentine territory. Under the firm control of the state, each and every school in Argentina had to function in exactly the same way, offering the same content, at the same time, with the same methods and using the same didactic materials (Gvirtz et al. 2008). At the time, the French Republican ethos of equality had a strong influence on the educational system, reinforcing the notion that all students should receive exactly the same education in order to assimilate into the invented 'Argentine culture' (Bravo-Moreno and Beech forthcoming).

Overall, the historical narratives that were promoted in schools and other institutions in order to construct and develop national identity were based on the idea that Argentina was an ethnic melting pot. However, this imagined melting pot included only people with different European origins. Indigenous people have been almost invisible in these narratives, and when they were considered, they were portrayed as backwards people that were an obstacle to progress and civilisation. Thus, popular images in Argentina sustain that 'Argentinians descend from boats'; a statement that is based on the idea that they do not have any indigenous blood (Grimson 2006). In this way, Argentina, and especially Buenos Aires, was constructed discursively as a European enclave in South America. The 'virtues' of European immigration have been idealised in Argentina. Consequently, an image of superiority was constructed, differentiating Argentina from other Latin American countries.

Thus, Bolivia and Argentina have very different demographic, ethnic, cultural and educational historical trajectories that, to a certain extent, represent the two extremes of the Latin American spectrum. In the next section some vignettes about how the abstract and malleable global slogan of 'respect for diversity' was interpreted in these two places will be discussed.

Respect for Diversity in Bolivia and Argentina

When 'respect for diversity' entered Bolivia it affected ethnic and cultural tensions that, as has been discussed, were very strong. Creole elites that acted as mediators between Bolivia and the world-system had historically used Western knowledge to support their dominant position and their superiority with respect to 'backwards' indigenous cultures. By the 1990s, global discourses, influenced by changes in Western philosophy, were promoting the slogan of respect for diversity. The source of knowledge/power of Bolivian elites turned against them, weakening their dominant position, while at the same time empowering claims of recognition and political power of the indigenous movements.[1]

In this context, Bolivia initiated an educational reform that was 'the most comprehensive effort to date to break with the civilizatory project that made the destruction of indigenous identity one of the school's central objectives' (Luykx and López 2008: 45). The reform, launched in 1994 and based on the notion of interculturality, changed official curricula and produced new textbooks in different indigenous languages in which contents and activities associated with indigenous communities were included. Intercultural Bilingual Education (EIB), which up to that time had been used as a localised policy for specific regions and communities, was consolidated as a state policy that, in theory, should have had an impact on all schools, giving non-indigenous students the option to learn an indigenous language (López and Murillo 2006). Those changes, which were not only expressed in the educational system, paved the way for more radical political restructuring that would substantially alter the notion of Bolivia and Bolivian culture.

In 2005 Evo Morales was elected as the first indigenous president of Bolivia (Morales is of indigenous Aymara descent). He comes from a rural background and started his political career as the leader of the union of coca producers, from where he led the opposition to pressures by the US to eliminate all coca plantations from Bolivia. His presidency has been strongly resisted by the Creole elite that is even proposing (unsuccessfully) the division of Bolivia by transforming the departments of Santa Cruz and Tarija (were Creoles are still dominant) into a separate country. Under the leadership of Morales a Constitutional reform stressed the linguistic and cultural plurality of Bolivia and even changed the country's official name, to what is now called the Plurinational State of Bolivia (Bolivia 2009). This symbolic change shows the strong emphasis that is being placed on the recognition of the different indigenous groups in Bolivia. In terms of education, Morales, who was re-elected in 2009, has emphasised the teaching of indigenous languages in all schools and started several literacy campaigns for indigenous peoples in rural areas.

The recognition of indigenous cultures and languages in the educational system that started with the reform of 1994 has faced many problems in practice and 'entrenched racism, sexism, and linguistic discrimination persisted at all levels of the system' (Luykx and López 2008: 45). Interestingly, the teaching of indigenous languages in schools has been resisted by some indigenous groups (López and Murillo 2006) that claim that Spanish is the language that gives access to power and that children can learn indigenous languages at home. This shows that even within indigenous movements there are groups with different ideologies and interests: some fought for and then accepted bilingual intercultural education, while others were against it. Nevertheless, Bolivia is moving steadily in the direction of empowering indigenous groups vis à vis Creole elites. The weakening of this group by the global slogan of respect for diversity seems to have had a fundamental role in this realignment of political power.

Meanwhile, in Argentina, the effects of the slogan of respect for diversity were much weaker and more localised. In the 1990s an all-encompassing reform of the educational system made some references to respect for diversity (Beech 2011). This implied a big rupture with the traditional approach based on homogenisation. The National

Educational Law of 2006 strengthened and consolidated the move towards respect for diversity in official rhetoric. Consequently, in Argentine policy discourse in education there has been strong rhetoric about the recognition of indigenous cultures. However, this discursive emphasis on cultural recognition was translated into a few projects aimed at introducing intercultural bilingual education for the indigenous peoples, and at improving the material conditions in which these communities live and study (Cippolloni 2004). This shows that there was a localised approach to respect for diversity: as something that is done to 'diverse' populations such as the indigenous peoples if they are present, not as a philosophical change that should affect the overall approach to education in all institutions.

In Argentina, respect for diversity has clashed with the persistence of the French Republican ethos of equality and with historical narratives of admiration for European culture and disrespect for indigenous knowledge. This is very noticeable in the city of Buenos Aires where changes in immigration profiles have revitalised ethnic tensions. Since the 1990s South American immigrants had become more visible in the city. Economic growth in Argentina and a favourable exchange rate attracted regional migrants, especially from Peru, Bolivia and Paraguay, while European immigration had decreased significantly. In addition, migrants from neighbouring countries, who had traditionally settled in areas close to the borders, started to move into Buenos Aires and other big cities (Ceva 2006). As social networks expanded in the metropolitan area, the costs of migrating to Buenos Aires were reduced, and a process of territorial segregation started in which migrants tended to settle in certain areas that became Bolivian, Paraguayan or Peruvian enclaves. This process of segregation also included a cultural dimension: the neighbourhood is given a specific name (such as the Bolivian *Barrio Charrua*), religious, national and ethnic celebrations are organised, and newspapers, radios and restaurants that cater to that specific community are opened (Sassone and Mera 2007).

As a result of the growth of ethnic plurality in a city that defined itself as 'European', immigration started receiving much attention in the media and in public debates. Overall, there were two types of reactions and positions in the debate. One position was reflected in the passing of Law 25871 in 2004 that defined a new political approach to immigration, based on the ideal of an 'inclusive, multicultural society, integrated to the region, that respects the rights of foreigners and values their cultural and social contribution' (Novick 2005: 11). It grants immigrants and their families equal access to social services such as education, health, justice, work and social security. In education, all foreigners, regardless of their legal status, are granted the right to enrol in public and private institutions at all levels under the same conditions as nationals.

On the other hand, racist and xenophobic discourses blamed immigrants from other South American countries for the high unemployment rates, for the 'overload' of public services (health and education), and for the growth in criminality (Aruj et al. 2000). Such views, combined with the political and economic collapse of 2001, and a huge increase in poverty rates and in the gap between the income of rich and poor (Gasparini and Cruces 2008), were translated into a typical phrase in public opinion: 'We are now really Latin Americans'. There was a strong feeling that the distinctive characteristics of Argentina in relation to other Latin American countries (a strong middle class, low poverty rates and 'European flavour') were gone.

In the educational system migrant students tend to concentrate in state schools (80 per cent). Argentine parents do not want their children to go to a school were there is a significant presence of immigrant students and this reinforces the concentration of migrant children in certain schools. In this way, many migrant children (and the Argentine children of immigrants) attend schools in which they form the majority of the school population (Bravo-Moreno and Beech forthcoming).

The institutional response to immigrant students at the macro level has been limited to granting immigrants access to institutions, regardless of their legal status, and giving foreign-born students the possibility of applying for scholarships that help economically disadvantaged students pay the costs of books, travel and other expenses. No special pedagogic or institutional devices have been designed to attend to the specific needs of immigrant students (Bravo-Moreno and Beech forthcoming). Furthermore, teachers and principals who were interviewed in a study about the school experiences of migrant students[2] consistently said that they did not adapt to the needs of immigrant students, since they believed that treating all their students in the same way was the fairest way to deal with differences. Given this assimilationist perspective, foreign students have to participate in nationalistic rituals, singing the national anthem, learning Argentine history and geography, etc.

Teachers in Buenos Aires schools with a strong presence of immigrant students tended to have nostalgic views about European immigrants and their old students. This shows how migration from neighbouring countries in Buenos Aires revitalises ethnic tensions linked with the coloniality of power. The head of a school emphasised with pride the great number of students from the Jewish community they had in the past. When we suggested that those were also immigrant families, she immediately reacted: 'No, no, that was something else', and explained how their 'old' graduates had become 'important people', doctors, lawyers and so on. Implicit was the notion that their current students had no chance of becoming 'important people', that they had some kind of deficit.

'We have become Latin Americans', said another teacher disdainfully. The alleged deficit was associated with stereotypes such as the slowness and quietness of Bolivians and Peruvians, with their socio-economic origins (that included deficits in their families, their homes and their previous education, among other things) and with ethnicity. One teacher, for example, emphasised how the colour of the skin was more important than the nationality in terms of defining which students had academic difficulties: 'There are kids here that come from the [Argentine] provinces of the north that look very similar to Bolivians, they have the same physiognomy . . . in general you can see that those with [academic] problems are the ones with dark skin'. Nationality, social class and ethnicity were muddled up in the discourse of adults in schools that overall were not happy with the type of students they had.

Therefore, in Argentina the global slogan of respect for diversity has had an influence, but it has not altered significantly the overall definition of 'Argentina' or 'Argentine culture'. Given the localised approach to respect for diversity (diversity has to be managed and respected only when it is present), and the historical legacy of the French Republican ethos and of historical narratives that defined Argentina as an European enclave in South America, the educational system has been mostly impermeable to the type of cultural reconfiguration that respect for diversity has contributed to produce in Bolivia.

Conclusion

This chapter has shown that global discourses and their slogans are not only coded in very complex ways in global policy spaces (Beech 2009), but they are also decoded and enacted in intricate ways in different places. Global discourses require a sophisticated elaboration in order to combine some stability that would allow for their persuasive imaging with a degree of malleability and adaptability that would make them appealing to people and institutions with different ideologies and positions (Beech 2009). 'Their communicative power comes from their capacity to be interpreted and re-arranged in a multi-vocality of meanings, depending on the receiver, and on the interactor' (Castells 2000: 22).

Global discourses are abstracted from place-based historical experience, and consequently they are stripped of their specific localised meaning and they become slogans whose specific meaning depends on the characteristics of the contexts of reception. The origins of respect for diversity, for example, are difficult to track. They can be associated with post-modern political philosophies, with multiculturalism, with the civil rights movement in the US, with feminism and with many other political struggles for recognition in different parts of the world. Nevertheless, whichever influence is considered, what is clear is that as respect for diversity takes on a global status it is semantically disconnected from the specific localised political struggles on which it was based. As this global slogan is then taken up in specific places it enters into arenas of other political struggles, opening up the possibilities for different groups to strategically use this slogan to support their own political projects.

The slogan of respect for diversity is prone to very different interpretations in different contexts of reception because both the concepts of 'respect' and of 'diversity' are very abstract and malleable. Also because this slogan affects ethnic, cultural and political affiliations, and has the potential of opening up possibilities for strong renegotiations in terms of definitions of cultural/political borders of identification. Different countries will be more or less willing to open up these renegotiations and, furthermore, different groups within a given place will have specific (and sometimes opposed) views about which diversities should be respected and how.

In the case of Latin America, given its specific colonial and post-colonial (or neo-colonial) situation, respect for diversity has a strong potential to contribute to a redefinition of local, national and regional identities and cultural definitions. But as has been shown, the borders between Western epistemes/Creole elites and indigenous knowledges/populations that are common to the region have had very specific manifestations in the historical trajectories of each country. Thus even while respect for diversity has been taken up overall at the discursive level, especially in policy discourses, in similar ways at the level of practice the effects have varied significantly in different places.

As has been shown, in Bolivia respect for diversity was functional to the interests of indigenous movements. Creole elites that acted as mediators between Western and Bolivian knowledge, using the historical architecture of knowledge/power to position themselves as superior to indigenous peoples, were weakened by the notion of respect for diversity that came from their own traditional source of power. At the same time, indigenous groups were strengthened and this has resulted in the opening up of significant renegotiations in the social structure of the country. Furthermore, the new indigenous leadership that has placed the recognition of Bolivia's multiple cultures in the centre of the political agenda is disputing the concept of Bolivia itself, by changing the country's original name. Meanwhile, in Argentina, the slogan of respect for diversity has resulted in significant changes in official rhetoric that has started to include the need to recognise indigenous cultures in schools. But these changes have not had a significant impact in practice. Given the size and lack of power and visibility of indigenous movements, the notion of respect for diversity has not opened up a major renegotiation of the social structure nor of ethnic and political affiliations.

Consequently, it is very difficult to make generalised judgments and critiques of multiculturalism and respect for diversity. Žižek (2003), for example, claims that multiculturalism over-simplifies and caricatures differences, and implies a move into identity politics that are, from his perspective, the end of politics proper. Even though for some specific cases this critique may be sustainable, it is clear that for the Bolivian indigenous movements the multicultural slogan has represented a great opportunity to bend their opponent's arm with their own force and has empowered their position, contributing to what is starting to resemble a radical renegotiation of Bolivian social structure and identity.

Thus, as researchers, we need to be aware of how global slogans are used by different groups to support very different power struggles with very different results in specific places. In this way, we would avoid falling into misleading generalisations and assumptions about the effects of global discourses. As has been shown in this chapter, assuming common interpretations and effects even within a national territory can be problematic and misleading. In other words, in order to further understand processes of educational flows and their recontextualisation we need to refine our own theories and interpretations of the ways in which global educational discourse is transformed as it is localised.

Notes

1   An example of how Western sources of knowledge/power of Bolivian Creole elites turns against their position can be seen in different discourses of international organisations that were cited in the first section of this chapter that define respect for cultural diversity as a human right.

2   The following analysis of the education of immigrant students in Buenos Aires is based on the analysis of data collected for the study '*Migración, Educación e Integración: un estudio comparativo de las experiencias escolares de estudiantes inmigrantes latinoamericanos en Buenos Aires y en Madrid*' [*Migration, education and integration: a comparative study of school experiences of Latin American immigrant students in Buenos Aires and Madrid*], directed by Jason Beech and Ana Bravo-Moreno and financed by AECID (Spanish Agency for International Development Cooperation).

References

Albó, X. (2005) Ciudadanía étnico-cultural en Bolivia. La Paz: Corte Nacional Electoral. Sucre: ACLO, CIPCA y Foro Constituyente. (Edición preliminar limitada para uso de los miembros de la Asamblea Constituyente.)

Albó, X. and Barrios Súbelas, F. (2006) Por una Bolivia plurinacional e intercultural con autonomías. Documento de Trabajo, Informe Nacional sobre Desarrollo Humano en Bolivia, programa de Las Naciones Unidas para el Desarrollo (PNUD) en Bolivia.

Aragón, M. J. (2008) *Making Sense of Cultural Diversity: A Comparative Analysis of Local Perspectives in Buenos Aires and New York*. Tesis de Maestría en Educación con orientación en Gestión Educativa, Universidad de San Andrés.

Artieda, T. L. (1993) 'El magisterio en los territorios nacionales: el caso de Misiones', in A. Puiggros (ed.) *La educación en las Provincias y territorios nacionales (1885–1945)*. Buenos Aires: Editorial Galerna.

Aruj, R, Novick, S. and Oteiza, E. (2000) *Inmigración y Discriminación Políticas y Discursos*. Buenos Aires: Grupo Editor Universitario.

Banks, J. (1993) 'Multicultural education: historical development, dimensions and practice', *Review of Research in Education*, American Public Association, 19: 3–49.

Barnard, H. C. (1969) *Education and the French Revolution*. London: Cambridge University Press.

Barrionuevo, A. (2010) 'Argentina approves gay marriage, in a first for region,' *New York Times*, 15 July. Retrieved from www.nytimes.com/2010/07/16/world/americas/16argentina.html.

Bauman, Z. (1992) *Intimations of Postmodernity*. London: Routledge.

Bauman, Z. (1995) *Legislators and Interpreters: On Modernity, Post-Modernity and Intellectuals*. Cambridge: Polity Press.

Beech, J. (2009) 'Policy spaces, mobile discourses, and the definition of educated identities', *Comparative Education*, 45(3): 347–365.

Beech, J. (2011) *Global Panaceas, Local Realities: International Agencies and the Future of Education*. Frankfurt am Main: Peter Lang,

Bernstein, B. (1996) *Pedagogy, Symbolic Control and Identity: Theory, Research, Critique*. London: Taylor & Francis.

Bolivia (2009) Decreto supremo N° 0048. Gaceta Oficial de Bolivia.

Bravo-Moreno, A. and Beech, J. (forthcoming) 'Migration, educational policies & practices: constructing difference in Buenos Aires & in Madrid', in Z. Bekerman and T. Geisen (eds) *International Handbook of Migration, Minorities, and Education – Understanding Cultural and Social Differences in Processes of Learning*. New York: Springer.

Castells, J. M. (2000) 'Grassrooting the space of flows', in J. O. Wheeler, Y. Aouama and B. Warf (eds) *Cities in the Telecommunications Age: The Fracturing of Geographies*. New York: Routledge.

Castro-Gómez, S. (2008) '(Post)coloniality for dummies: Latin American perspectives on modernity, coloniality, and the geopolitics of knowledge', in M. Moraña, E. Dussel and C. A. Jáuregui (eds) *Coloniality at Large: Latin America and the Postcolonial Debate*. Durham, NC: Duke University Press.

CEPAL and BID (2005) *Los pueblos indígenas en Bolivia: diagnóstico sociodemográfico a partir del censo del 2001*. Publicación de Las Naciones Unidas, Santiago de Chile.

Ceva, M. (2006) *La migración limítrofe hacia la Argentina*. Buenos Aires: Prometeo libros.

Chanady, A. (2008) 'The Latin American postcolonialism debate in a comparative context', in M. Moraña, E. Dussel and C. A. Jáuregui (eds) *Coloniality at Large: Latin America and the Postcolonial Debate*. Durham, NC: Duke University Press.

Cippolloni, O. (2004) *Programa Nacional de Educación Intercultural Bilingüe* [National programme for intercultural bilingual education]. Ministerio de Educación, Ciencia y Tecnología.

Coulby, D. and Jones, C. (1996) 'Postmodernity, education and European identities', *Comparative Education*, 32(2): 171–184.

Cowen, R. (2009) 'The transfer, translation and transformation of educational Processes: and their shape-shifting?', *Comparative Education Review*, 45(3): 347–365.

Dussel, E. (2008) 'Philosophy of liberation, the postmodern debate, and Latin American studies', in M. Moraña, E. Dussel and C. A. Jáuregui (eds) *Coloniality at Large. Latin America and the Postcolonial Debate*. Durham, NC: Duke University Press.

Elías, N. (1994) *Conocimiento y poder*. Madrid: La Piqueta.

García Castaño, F. J., Pulido Moyano, R. A. and Montes del Castillo, A. (1997) 'La educación multicultural y el concepto de cultura', *Revista Iberoamericana de Educación*, 13.

Gasparini, L. and Cruces, G. (2008) *A Distribution in Motion: The Case of Argentina. A Review of the Empirical Evidence*. CEDLAS, Universidad de La Plata.

Gay, G. (1983) 'Multiethnic education: historical development and future prospects', *The Phi Delta Kappan*, 64(8): 560–563.

Gibson, M. and Rojas, A. (2006) 'Globalization, immigration and the education of "new" immigrants in the 21st century', *Comparative Education*, 9(1): 69–76.

Green, A. (1990) *Education and State Formation: The Rise of Education Systems in England, France and the USA*. London: The Macmillan Press Ltd.

Grimson, A. (2006). 'Nuevas xenofobias, nuevas políticas étnicas en Argentina', in A. Grimson and E. Jelin (eds) *Migraciones regionales hacia la Argentina: Diferencias, desigualdades y derechos*. Buenos Aires: Prometeo.

Gvirtz, S. and Beech, J. (eds) (2008) *Going to School in Latin America*. Westport, CT: Greenwood Press.

Gvirtz, S., Beech, J. and Oria, A. (2008) 'Schooling in Argentina', in S. Gvirtz and J. Beech (eds) *Going to School in Latin America*. Westport, CT: Greenwood Press.

INDEC (2009). Retrieved November 2009 from www.indec.gov.ar/.

Inter-American Development Bank (2007) *¿Los de afuera? Patrones cambiantes de exclusión en América Latina y el Caribe*. Washington, DC: Inter-American Development Bank.

López, E. and Murillo, O. (2006) *La Reforma Educativa Boliviana: Lecciones aprendidas y sostenibilidad de las transformaciones*, Documento elaborado en el marco del convenio Corporación Andina de Fomento/Organización de Estados Iberoamericanos para la Educación, la Ciencia y la Cultura (OEI).

Luykx, A. (1999) *The Citizen Factory: Schooling and Cultural Production in Bolivia*. Albany, NY: State University of New York Press.

Luykx, A. and López, L. E. (2008) 'Schooling in Bolivia', in S. Gvirtz and J. Beech (eds) *Going to School in Latin America*. Westport, CT: Greenwood Press.

Lynch, J. (1983) 'Multiethnic Education in Europe: Problems and Prospects', *The Phi Delta Kappan*, 64(8): 576–579.

Lyotard, J. (1984) *The Postmodern Condition: A Report on Knowledge*. Manchester: Manchester University Press.

Mignolo, D. W. (2008a) 'The geopolitics of knowledge and the colonial difference', in M. Moraña, E. Dussel and C. A. Jáuregui (eds) *Coloniality at Large: Latin America and the Postcolonial Debate*. Durham, NC: Duke University Press.

Mignolo, D. W. (2008b) *The Idea of Latin America*. Malden, Oxford & Victoria: Blackwell Publishing.

Moraña, M., Dussel, E. and Jáuregui, C. A. (2008) 'Colonialism and its replicants', in M. Moraña, E. Dussel and C. A. Jáuregui (eds) *Coloniality at Large: Latin America and the Postcolonial Debate*. Durham, NC: Duke University Press.

Novick, S. (2005) 'La reciente política migratoria argentina en el contexto del MERCOSUR', in *El proceso de integración Mercosur: de las políticas migratorias y de seguridad a las trayectorias de los inmigrantes*. Buenos Aires: Instituto de Investigaciones Gino Germani, Facultad de Ciencias Sociales, UBA.

Oteiza, E. and Novick, S. (2000) *Inmigración y derechos humanos: Política y discursos en el tramo final del menemismo*. Buenos Aires: Instituto de Investigaciones Gino Germani, Facultad de Ciencias Sociales, Universidad de Buenos Aires, Documento de Trabajo 14.

Popkewitz, T. (1980) 'Global education as a slogan system', *Curriculum Inquiry*, 10(3): 303–316.

Quijano, A. (2008) 'Coloniality of power, eurocentrism, and social classification', in M. Moraña, E. Dussel and C. A. Jáuregui (eds) *Coloniality at Large: Latin America and the Postcolonial Debate*. Durham, NC: Duke University Press.

Ravitch, D. (1983) *The Troubled Crusade: American Education, 1945–1980*. New York: Basic Books.

Rizvi, F. (2009) 'Mobile Minds', in J. Kenway and J. Fahey (eds) *Globalizing the Research Imagination*. Abingdon: Routledge.

Romero, L. A. (2001) *Breve historia contemporánea de la Argentina*. Buenos Aires: Fondo de Cultura Económica de Argentina S.A.

Rousseau, J. J. (1966) 'A discourse on political economy', in *The Social Contract and Discourses*. London: J.M. Dent & Sons Ltd.

Sachsenmaier, D. (2010) 'El concepto de modernidades múltiples y sus áreas subyacentes', in J. Schriewer and H. Kaelble (Comp.) *La comparación en las ciencias sociales e históricas*, Barcelona: Ed. Octaedro – ICE.

Saenz Obregón, J. and Saldarriaga Vélez, O. (2008) 'Schooling in Colombia', in S. Gvirtz and J. Beech (eds) *Going to School in Latin America*, The Global School Room. Westport: Greenwood Press.

Sassone, S. and Mera, C. (2007) *Barrios de migrantes en Buenos Aires: Identidad, cultura y cohesión socioterritorial*. Presented at the European Congress of Latin American Studies.

Schriewer, J. (2000) 'World system and interrelationship networks: the internalization of education and the role of comparative Inquiry', in T. S. Popkewitz (ed.) *Educational Knowledge: Changing Relationships between the State, Civil Society, and the Educational Community*. Albany, NY: State of University of New York Press.

Shibata, M. (2005) *Japan and Germany under the U.S. Occupation: A Comparative Analysis of the Post-war Education Reform*. Lanham, MD: Lexington Books.

Silova, I. (2006) *From Sites of Occupation to Symbols of Multiculturalism. Reconceptualizing Minority Education in Post-Soviet Latvia*. Charlotte, NC: Information Age Publishing.

Sleeter, C. E. (1996) 'Multicultural education as a social movement', *Theory into Practice*, 35(4): 239–247.

Steiner-Khamsi, G. (2000) 'Transferir la educación y desplazar las reformas', in J. Schriewer (comp.) *Formación del discurso en la educación comparada*. Barcelona: Pomares.

Tanaka, M. (2005) *The Cross-cultural Transfer of Educational Concepts and Practices: A Comparative Study*. Oxford: Symposium Books.

UNESCO (2001) *Universal Declaration on Cultural Diversity*, Adopted by the General Conference of the United Nations Educational, Scientific and Cultural Organization at its 31st session. Retrieved December 2010 from: http://unesdoc.unesco.org/images/0012/001271/127160m.pdf.

UNICEF (2006) *The State of the World's Children 2006. Excluded and Invisible*. New York: UNICEF. Retrieved December 2010 from: www.unicef.org/sowc06/pdfs/sowc06_full report.pdf.

World Bank (2008) *Poverty: Culture and Public Action*. Retrieved December 2010 from: http://

web.worldbank.org/WBSITE/EXTERNAL/TOPICS/EXTPOVERTY/0,,contentMDK:2024 6138~pagePK:210058~piPK:210062~theSitePK:336992,00.html.

Žižek, S. (2003) 'Multiculturalismo, o la lógica cultural del capitalismo multinacional', in E. Jameson and S. Žižek (eds) *Estudios culturales: reflexiones sobre el multiculturalismo.* Buenos Aires: Paidós.

20 Facilitating Transfer

International Organisations as Central Nodes for Policy Diffusion

Anja P. Jakobi

This chapter analyses the role of international organisations in policy diffusion.[1] Research in international relations has frequently identified international organisations as sources for national political change (Finnemore 1993, 1996; Finnemore and Sikkink 1999). In particular, constructivist theorising, more specifically new institutionalism, has underlined the importance of international society and international organisations for the diffusion of global policies and values (Meyer et al. 1997a; Boli and Thomas 1999; Meyer 2000). In line with these arguments, this chapter analyses the role of international organisations in the diffusion of lifelong learning, a currently prominent concept in education policy.[2] By developing and promoting lifelong learning, international organisations have become important parts – central nodes – in the process of policy diffusion. As such, they enable and channel how policies are transferred across countries; they support the borrowing of policies by identifying 'best practices'; and they monitor how countries develop with regard to similar policy goals, e.g. by providing statistical analyses.

The case of lifelong learning is particularly suitable for examining the role of international organisations. Throughout the history of international lifelong learning policies, these agencies have always been prominent in its diffusion: a global emphasis on adult education and lifelong learning could first be observed in the 1960s, mainly in the context of the United Nations Educational, Scientific and Cultural Organization (UNESCO) and the Organisation for Economic Cooperation and Development (OECD) (UNESCO 1972; Papadopoulos 1994: 112–113; Sutton 1996: 28). The International Labour Organization also dealt with lifelong learning, in particular by setting up the paid educational leave standard (ILO 1974; Salt and Bowland 1996). However, other than small steps towards success, the debate had not caused major changes in national education systems (Kallen 1979: 50), which sharply distinguished the situation from today – governments at present widely appreciate this idea and try to incorporate it into national education policy development (e.g. Papadopoulos 2002; Schuller et al. 2002. From a policy perspective, the current debate on lifelong learning differs from earlier proposals in several ways. Today's emphasis is much more on learning than on education, which also means that the role of the state and in particular the financing of lifelong learning has been shifted from a governmental to a more private responsibility. The ongoing debate is also very functionalistic, so that lifelong learning today is often narrowed down to its economic potential (Kallen 2002), while in the 1970s the discussions were concerned with the right to education and self-development. Furthermore, discussions nowadays integrate all educational stages from early age to later life, while the earlier debate focused exclusively on adult education. As a last difference, lifelong learning today often integrates several forms of learning, ranging from a more formal setting to more informal learning processes (e.g. EU Commission 2000: 8–9).

In the remainder of this chapter, I first outline different concepts linked to policy transfer and diffusion, highlighting in particular the crucial role of international organisations. I then turn to the activities of several international organisations on lifelong learning. In the third step, I show the impact of these activities, distinguishing the idea of lifelong learning and reforms linked to it. In the conclusions, I sum up the article's main findings and outline further research areas linked to education policy transfer and diffusion processes. To assess the diffusion of lifelong learning, I primarily rely on textual material that is transformed to a binary-coded variable. The textual data has been accessed from the UNESCO International Bureau of Education (IBE), specifically policy reports submitted to the International Conference on Education as well as the 'World Data on Education' (UNESCO 2003). Assessing the spread of the idea of lifelong learning is based on a standardised content analysis. It is counted whether or not an education policy report contains a reference to the idea of lifelong learning, operationalised by the terms 'lifelong learning' or 'lifelong education'. The inquiry of lifelong learning reforms is carried out by a non-standardised text analysis of the same policy reports plus the World Data on Education (WDE) with the pre-defined categories pre-primary education, adult education and higher education. In total, the data set includes original information on 99 countries in the time span from 1996 to 2004.

Theoretical Concepts Linked to Policy Transfer and Diffusion

Emphasising the role of international organisations as nodes in policy diffusion requires conceptual clarifications. As the introduction to this yearbook outlines, different disciplines emphasise different terms, and these have partially overlapping meanings. To link international organisations to these processes, Table 20.1 lists different concepts related to policy transfer.[3] Although there is necessarily a conceptual overlap between them, and they are used to a different extent in different disciplines, it is nonetheless possible to distinguish specific emphases of the terms. The first ones are derived from the idea of the policy cycle (de Leon 1999): policy adoption refers to the process of adopting a law or a programme, while policy implementation concerns the subsequent realisation of a policy in practice. Both notions are not necessarily linked to a comparative perspective; policy studies often concern single countries or issue areas. Policy learning is a relational concept. It refers to the adoption or the implementation of a policy, also considering available experiences with the policy – either in the past, in other policy fields or, most importantly in our context here, with experiences that other countries have. Policy borrowing is even more explicit in assuming another source for policy change. Here, too, states may borrow from other policy fields or from other countries' experiences. The invention of an OECD education assessment for adults (PIAAC – Programme for International Assessment of Adult Competencies) was borrowed from student assessment (PISA –

Programme for International Student Assessment), while the introduction of school vouchers in African countries was borrowed from other countries, mediated by World Bank advice (Rose 2003). While borrowing presupposes the perspective of the borrower, lending is the reverse – in particular international organisations, being important policy disseminators, 'lend' policies across countries, often in the form of blueprints.

The process of borrowing and lending can also be summarised as 'policy transfer'. Here, the focus is on the exchange process, both sender and recipient can be considered, as well as the structures that facilitate transfer – for example international organisations. Policy diffusion is the observed pattern that results from a row of subsequent policy adoptions or implementations of the same policy in different countries (compare Rogers 2003). Policy convergence, finally, is a growing similarity of countries. Different concepts of convergence exist, depending on whether researchers focus on overall similarity, similarity to specific models or decreasing variance (Heichel et al. 2005; Knill 2005). Also, sharp differences may exist in whether countries converge with respect to policy adoptions, implementations and practice. This short description of concepts also outlines how these notions are interlinked. Adoption and implementation are different stages of the policy cycle that may be part of any of the other concepts. Policy learning, lending and borrowing are part of policy transfer. Finally, transfer may be part of policy diffusion – a large number of transfers constitute a diffusion pattern. Diffusion, finally, may result in policy convergence.

International organisations can be linked to any of these concepts: they may foster policy adoption, for example when financial support is linked to the introduction of specific policies; or they support implementation when providing technical assistance. They support policy learning and policy borrowing when they assemble meetings that are concerned with common policy problems and identify the results of best practices and lessons learned. They themselves transfer policies from one place to another when taking up a best practice and benchmarking other countries against it. By all these practices, international organisations are part of global governance in the field of education, exceeding global or international influence on national policy processes (compare, e.g., Barnett and Finnemore 2004; Jakobi 2009a; Avant et al. 2010). They can thus move to central stage in processes of policy diffusion and convergence. By being central nodes in a network of interrelated states, international organisations support the communication process among countries. This includes a selection of priorities, e.g., through agenda-setting processes, and may lead to worldwide diffusion of these selected policies. Moreover, by identifying common policy problems, benchmarks or policy templates, international organisations may act as important sources of policy convergence, facilitating common orientations, targets and policies of nation-states.

While so far I have focused on transfer processes themselves, very different theoretical frameworks can be used to explain what actually causes these phenomena. Rationalist approaches foremost consider the characteristics and aims of national policy actors. From such a perspective, policy transfer would be the outcome of a purposeful adoption of policies that have succeeded in other places. In particular the notion of 'policy learning' is linked to such a framework, since it presupposes a more or less rationalist learning process (for a comprehensive perspective, see Steiner-

Table 20.1 Conceptual clarifications related to policy transfer

Notion	Observation	Relation	Perspective
Policy adoption	State/government adopts specific law or programme	Not necessarily related to other states or policies	Focus on specific/single state/government
Policy implementation	State/government aims to establish policy in practice	Not necessarily related to other states or policies, but to adoption	Focus on subunits of specific state/government
Policy learning	State/government discusses/adopts/implements policy	Related to experiences in other states, policy fields, past experiences	Focus on relation between two/more actors or policy fields
Policy borrowing	State/government discusses/adopts/implements policy	Related to experiences in other states or policy fields	Focus on relation between two/more actors or policy fields
Policy lending	State/government/organisation provides good example	Related to experiences of states or other actors	Focus on the 'good properties' of a policy
Policy transfer	State/government discusses/adopts/implements policy	Related to experiences in other states or policy fields	Focus on relation between two/more actors or policy fields, on structures that facilitate transfer
Policy diffusion	Different states/governments discuss/adopt/implement same policy	Related or not related to other governments' activities	Focus on the pattern of cross-national policy adoptions and implementations
Policy convergence	Different states become more similar in policy adoption/implementation/outcomes	Related to other governments' activities; related to other factors	Focus on reasons for this similarity

Khamsi 2004 and Waldow 2009). Theorists subsume such factors under the heading of 'internal conditions' (Berry and Berry 2007), or 'independent problem-solving' (Knill 2005), pointing at the state level as an important cause of finding similar policies in different countries. From this perspective, countries follow a rational logic and adopt policies that seem to be most promising. Indeed, lifelong learning is not only the subject of international promotion and norm development, but it is also an important policy linked to current developments in national economies and societies. One argument in this context is that new needs are linked to new forms of work in a knowledge-based economy (e.g. Hasan 1996: 36).

But analyses of the policy process have also shown that such rationalist assumption does not always hold true. Policy makers select from given and restricted alternatives, consider other than rational factors, and implementation may fail altogether (Lindblom 1959; Pressman and Wildavsky 1973, Kingdon 2003). Besides, states also pursue other aims than strictly rational problem solving. Research in international relations scholarship has found that states often adopt policies for reasons of legitimacy (e.g. Finnemore 1993). In particular research that builds on new institutionalism and the idea of a world society (e.g. Meyer et al. 1997a) has analysed such patterns of policy adoption. From the perspective of new institutionalism, world politics is based on a shared world culture and exposing an organisational structure that causes the diffusion of policy ideas across countries (e.g. Meyer et al. 1997a, 1997b). This means that states are increasingly relying on the same principles and values, and that the structure of the world society, its international exchange and the existence of global forums support the transfer and diffusion of these principles.

While new institutionalists have assessed various examples of diffusion processes, education has been identified as a particularly widely shared and central societal institution. Education systems have become increasingly similar across countries and contain many standardised procedures, beginning with classroom teaching but going far beyond (Meyer and Ramirez 2003). Mass schooling and common curricula are disseminated across the world (Fuller and Rubinson 1992; Meyer et al. 1992). University systems have been established and identified as important elements of national development (Ramirez and Riddle 1991). Schooling is successively introduced all over the world, and school curricula often follow the logic of universalism and are detached from local circumstances. Over time and space, the value of education has been acknowledged widely and has become something taken for granted. At the same time, educational targets have been pursued across countries in an increasingly similar way. Moreover, education is also closely linked to other central ideas in society, such as individual and collective progress, which heavily supports its wide and unanimous spread. International organisations are key actors in disseminating these world cultural ideas and policies. For example, despite being a 'hard instrument', a conference can nonetheless influence national policy development, and UN meetings have been a ritual in disseminating world cultural perspectives to countries (Lechner and Boli 2005: 81–109). International organisations also have other means at hand to disseminate policies. The following section elaborates on how international organisations have used these means with regard to lifelong learning promotion.

International Organisations and the Diffusion of Lifelong Learning

Policy diffusion and other transfer activities involve several actors. On the one hand, forums need to be identified where policies are actually discussed and may eventually be diffused. On the other hand, the results should also be visible, e.g. a pattern of diffusion of changed political discussions or policy implementation. With a view to international organisations, we can identify several tools – governance instruments – by which they facilitate transfer (Jakobi 2009b). First, international organisations disseminate ideas, for example, what are the most important aims of an education system or which elements it includes. Here, organisations can differ widely – while UNESCO mainly perceives education as a public good, the World Bank regularly stretches the concept of education to the private sphere, most recently to include a most diverse set of actors under the common roof of a 'national education system'

(World Bank 2010). A second instrument is standard setting, either implicit or explicit. For example, UNESCO conventions form an explicit and binding standard, while PISA rankings are more implicit. Yet binding or non-binding is not necessarily linked to being more or less successful. In particular, the recent wave of league tables created non-binding, yet powerful standards of how 'the best education system' should perform. A third instrument is policy coordination. This instrument builds upon sharing expertise in policy forums provided by international organisations, but it may also include more explicit coordination between different actors with a view to common policy aims. Policy networks or public–private partnerships that prominently involve international organisations are an important element of this coordinative function. Financial incentives are a fourth instrument. In this case, the international organisation directly sponsors specific national implementation efforts or the development of new policy programmes. The most prominent example of education financing is the World Bank, but other organisations like the European Union (EU) or the ILO also finance specific education programmes. Finally, international organisations can also provide technical assistance, for example in setting up schools or teacher training or in building up a functioning education administration. In such case, the practice of 'good' education policy implementation is transferred in a very practical way. Together, international organisations thus have important tools at hand to move countries in preferred policy directions.

Lifelong learning has been promoted by international organisations by all these means and quite intensively. UNESCO had already been involved in early debates in the 1970s; in the 1990s, the organisation continued its work on the subject. For example, in 1991, the UNESCO General Conference decided to establish a commission assigned to reflect the future of education systems. The 'International Commission on Education for the 21st Century' published a major report in 1996, emphasising the importance of lifelong learning for future education systems (UNESCO 1996: 111). In a related standard setting activity, the 2001 revision 'Recommendation concerning Technical and Vocational Education' conceptualised vocational education and training as being one element of lifelong learning (UNESCO 2001: I). In this conceptualisation, barriers between different levels and kinds of education should be abolished, and flexible structures would be needed that guarantee individual entry and re-entry to education as well as continuous learning. Summarising these and other activities that UNESCO has carried out over the years, one can say that the organisation invested many efforts in promoting lifelong learning (Gerlach 2000). UNESCO emphasises its importance both for developed and for developing countries (UNESCO 2005: 24–25). Standard setting instruments, declarations at world conferences and publications have continuously highlighted the value of lifelong learning.

The OECD began working on lifelong learning at the end of the 1960s, but without triggering national policy change. The visible re-emergence of lifelong learning began in the 1990s. The 1994 'OECD Jobs Study' emphasised the need for further qualifying the labour force and the results of the 'Adult Literacy Survey' further illustrated a quite serious lack of competencies of adults, which underlined the importance of further qualification (OECD 1995: 15, 1996: 237–238). The OECD's education ministers' meeting in 1996 was concerned with 'Lifelong Learning for All', constituting an initial event for the success of lifelong learning within the OECD, its members and beyond.

Since then, the OECD has published a variety of issues linked to lifelong learning, ranging from issues of financing to the role of school buildings and education policy reviews (OECD 2000, 2002a, 2002b; Istance 2003). Furthermore, the OECD is well connected to other international education policy actors, which secures a wide dissemination of its perspectives and a sensitive taking up and framing of emergent issues. OECD representatives promote lifelong learning, for example, in the context of the European Bologna Process or at ASEM meetings (Wurzburg 2003; ASEM 2005; Norwegian Ministry of Education and Research 2005). In sum, the organisation has carried out a wide range of initiatives, trying to bring lifelong learning closer to member countries. For example, recent changes in the German law on financing adult education have been prepared in collaboration with an OECD project on financing lifelong learning. The country established an Expert Commission on Financing Lifelong Learning in 2001 (Expertenkommission zur Finanzierung Lebenslangen Lernens 2004).

A further important international actor is the EU, which initiated activities in the early 1990s. A major public event was the European Year of Lifelong Learning in 1996, which was followed by a strategy on lifelong learning adopted by the council, including diverse areas of education, from pre-school to accreditation of teachers (European Council 1996). Since 1997, lifelong learning has been part of the European employment strategy, and the Lisbon agenda further reinforced the central role of education and qualifications (EU Commission 2000: 5; European Council 2000, 2002a: 1). The Memorandum on Lifelong Learning, published in 2000, included thoughts on indicators, benchmarks and best practices for lifelong learning policies (EU Commission 2000: 24–36). It was followed by the Commission's 'Making a European Area of Lifelong Learning a Reality' in 2001, emphasising the role of lifelong learning in empowering citizens and serving the economic goals of the Union (EU Commission 2001: 5). In their 2002 work programme on education and training, the European Council and the Commission again underlined the importance of lifelong learning and set the target that, by 2010, 'for the benefit of citizens and the Union as a whole . . . Europeans at all ages should have access to lifelong learning (European Council 2002b: 3). In the same year, a council resolution on lifelong learning was adopted, emphasising a 'cradle-to-grave' principle of education and provision in different settings (European Council 2002a: 2). A common qualification framework was later created, the implementation of which began in 2007 (EU Commission 2005: 4). An additional peak was the 2006 decision of the European Parliament and the Council on establishing a lifelong learning action programme. The agenda included programmes linked to educational phases from pre-primary and secondary to higher education, vocational education and adult education. From 2007 to 2013, more than 6.9 billion euros are planned to be invested and the programme has enabled the Commission to develop wide-ranging education policies at the European level, including financing of programmes and technical assistance or the exchange of policies and their evaluation (European Union 2006: 2–10). In sum, lifelong learning has become a major issue in European education policy, and the EU has pursued this concept through several means and in different policy contexts.

Lifelong learning has also become an issue of interregional activity, as the Asia–Europe–Meeting (ASEM) shows. In 2001, the meeting of foreign ministers approved a proposal on the 'ASEM Lifelong Learning Initiative', to be carried out during the following year. It held three international conferences in 2002 and presented conclusions to the head of the ASEM states in September 2002. The initiative resulted in a shared commitment and understanding of the different states regarding lifelong learning (ASEM 2002: 9). Additional international organisations that promoted lifelong learning include the World Bank and the ILO. The Bank worked on concepts of lifelong learning for developing countries, and has been financing related projects (World Bank 2003). The 2004 renewed ILO Recommendation on Human Resource Development underlines the importance of lifelong learning for countries across the world, and this organisation has also financed related projects (e.g. ILO 2005).

We can thus observe very different instruments by which international organisations have supported the diffusion of lifelong learning (see Table 20.2). Conferences like the 1996 OECD meeting 'Lifelong Learning for All' or the UNESCO Commission have been important for establishing the idea of lifelong learning. Standard setting took place with regard to UNESCO and ILO recommendations, but also other frameworks like the EU Open Method of Coordination. Financial incentives have been provided, for example in the case of World Bank projects or the EU Lifelong Learning Program. Coordination has taken place, for example in monitoring processes and in data collection exercises. Finally, countries have also received technical assistance in case they needed external support for policy adoption or implementation.

All these organisations and activities deliver important examples of how countries are continuously involved in discussions, working groups, projects and communication concerning lifelong learning, representing additional forums in which countries not yet drawn to the idea of lifelong learning can be convinced that it is an important issue to address. There has thus been a great deal of international activity on lifelong learning, ranging from official standards as recommendations to meetings on special issues such as financing. As such, international organisations have actively contributed to the diffusion of this idea and corresponding reforms, facilitating learning and borrowing processes. As a consequence, we could reasonably expect countries to adopt lifelong learning policies and to converge in that respect.

Table 20.2 Instruments used for the diffusion of lifelong learning

Instrument:	Ideas	Standard setting	Financial means	Coordination	Technical assistance
Examples:	OECD Meeting 'Lifelong Learning for All'	UNESCO Recommendation concerning technical and vocational education	World Bank project financing	UNESCO/EFA Monitoring reports	ILO Projects supporting, e.g., the Albanian Government
	UNESCO Commission on Education for the 21st Century	ILO Recommendation on human resource development	EU Lifelong Learning Action Programme	OECD PIAAC ILO Qualification Framework Project	

From Diffusion to Adoption: Differentiating Lifelong Learning Ideas and Reforms

Only by focusing on national adoption patterns can one tell whether the international attempts to promote lifelong learning have actually been successful. Indeed, in line with international activity, countries have recently turned to lifelong learning policies.[4] An analysis of an early UNESCO collection of education policy reports dating from the late 1960s (UNESCO 1971) reveals that there was hardly any reference to the idea of lifelong learning some decades ago – only six of 136 countries mention the idea. Their number was still low even in the early 1990s; however, from the mid-1990s until 2004, countries have more and more frequently referred to lifelong learning in the context of education policy (Table 20.3). Nearly 80 per cent of the countries mention lifelong learning at least once in this period, including many developing countries.

Countries thus clearly converge with respect to whether or not lifelong learning is an important principle in education policy. These figures, however, only refer to whether or not countries mention lifelong learning, not whether they start policy implementation. While the spread of the idea alone might be impressive, implementation might be very different. For this purpose, I analysed the same set of countries with regard to the diffusion of lifelong learning policies in the fields of pre-primary, adult and higher education.

Pre-primary education is the earliest stage of education, and, like 'kindergarten', it is also a very widely known concept (Rogers 2003: 63–64). However, the original idea linked to kindergartens – children should enjoy learning through playing – has changed in the course of lifelong learning discussions. Early learning in pre-primary education is emphasised because it introduces learning activities and prepares for continuing learning – which is assumed to be a pre-condition for success in contemporary and future society. The emphasis on lifelong learning thus includes a new idea of early childhood and the need to prepare the ability of lifelong learning during that period. On the one hand, the intervention into early childhood can be justified by

Table 20.3 Diffusion of the idea of lifelong learning, 1996–2004 across countries

	1996	2001	2004
Percentage of countries referring to lifelong learning:			
– in the respective year	62.8	70.6	72.0
– accumulated (from 1996)	62.8	71.8	78.8
Number of countries referring to lifelong learning:			
– in the respective year	27	36	59
– accumulated (from 1996)	27	51	78
Number of countries analysed:			
– in the respective year	43	51	82
– accumulated (from 1996)	43	71	99

Source: Policy reports submitted to ICE 1996, 2001, 2004; author's own calculations.

giving opportunities to children, in particular to those from disadvantaged back-grounds. On the other hand, the argument that learning processes should take place early also strictly complies with human capital theory (Becker 1964). On the national level, increased attention to pre-primary education is mirrored in different facets of policy reforms. Firstly, countries are increasingly introducing compulsory pre-primary education, even if it is difficult for them to enforce it. International activities and exchange further reinforce this trend. For example, Swaziland observed the South African debate on the introduction of one year of compulsory pre-primary education before schooling and evaluated how this could be adopted to the country's own needs (Report Swaziland 2004: 2). A further element of structuring early childhood edu-cation is the establishment of learning goals through a pre-school curriculum. Other policy reforms to extend pre-primary education include, for example, increased state financing of such education. Moreover, the emphasis on early education is evident by the renaming of institutions. In 1996, Brazil reformed the organisation of its education system. One of the changes was that day-care and pre-school were now called 'early childhood education', and that this stage was now a part of basic education, along with primary and secondary education (Report Brazil 2001: 7). As the analysis of the policy reports shows, the pre-primary education sector has under-gone a major restructuring process since the beginning of the 1990s. Although compulsory schooling has still only been established in a minority of countries, it has become a common occurrence in education policy that the government regulates that phase of life and the learning taking place therein.

Adult education is the core field in which lifelong learning had been discussed already since the 1970s. While earlier debates focused on individual development, current political ideas mainly refer to the need for up-to-date qualifications. Countries try to support the individual learning efforts of adults with different political instru-ments. Qualification frameworks are a comprehensive measure, categorising learning achievements according to a list of possible qualifications. They can assess and, in case of qualification gaps, stimulate learning in adult life. These frameworks are often linked to discussions on lifelong learning because they enable the description, analysis and comparison of individual learning records, even when the learning process took place in very different settings. Depending on its specific characteristics, such a frame-work also allows the accumulation and transfer of achieved learning across diverse sectors, including higher education. It is best understood as a credit accumulation system like the ones used in higher education contexts, but extended to – theoretically – all forms of learning, all educational stages and all education and training sectors. Despite individual differences in the frameworks, this idea has spread around the globe to very different countries since New Zealand introduced the first framework in 1990. Besides establishing qualification frameworks, another possibility to extend adult education is setting up laws and programmes related to lifelong learning. For example, the 1999 Thai National Education Act refers to lifelong learning extensively, defining it as 'education resulting from integration of formal, non-formal and infor-mal education so as to create ability for continuous lifelong development of quality of life', and the act additionally stipulates that 'educational provision shall be based on the principle of lifelong education for all' (Report Thailand 2001: 46, 49). Moreover, countries can, in principle, provide additional funding for learning efforts in adulthood or they can try to stimulate the establishment of private institutions to foster lifelong learning. Analysis of all the reports shows that adult education has been extended across the countries and, by means of qualification frameworks, this diverse field is increasingly regulated. While education has, for a long time, been linked mostly to children, recent developments in the sector show substantial changes and the regular establishment of education during adulthood.

Higher education has undergone a massive increase all over the world (Ramirez and Riddle 1991) and discussions about lifelong learning are likely to reinforce this phenomenon. Traditionally, the university is seen as the unique place that can create new knowledge and, in the meantime, can disseminate it to its students, who are often assumed to come directly from school to higher education. Higher education in this traditional sense thus constitutes the preparation of students for their first entry to the labour market. This educational sector, however, can also be understood as one among several opportunities to gain qualifications, for instance while working, or during a temporary leave. In that sense, higher education institutions develop in places where qualifications of an already skilled workforce can be further updated. Consequently, borders between higher education and other educational pathways are increasingly blurring, as illustrated in the case of the Scottish Qualification Framework. This framework integrates all pathways and draws no elementary distinction between continuing education obtained elsewhere and grades obtained in universities (ILO 2005). Such cases signify a move towards higher education as a form of a standard further education, and countries cope differently with the challenge to expand this stage. A first opportunity is to set up laws and programmes or found new institutions to increase access. Countries vary widely concerning such measures. In 1994 Austria established its first university for post-graduate studies, the Danube University in Krems, which offers courses for post-graduate and continuing professional education (Report Austria 2001: 161; UNESCO 2003). Moreover, private institutions and private or individual funding are a further governmental means for increasing participation rates without raising public investment in education. Egypt, for example, encourages the establishment of private providers because it reduces government investments (Report Egypt 2004: 117). In sum, the analysis of the reports shows that, although higher education is still often seen as prolonging the period of formal schooling, being the final stage of an educational career, the sector is increasingly being expanded as a place for updating knowledge beyond being the classical student. As a special form of adult education, higher education offers specialised knowledge to older age groups in society – either those at the university for the first time or for returnees. Countries have invested different efforts to ensure this provision.

Evaluating all reforms undertaken by countries in the period of 1996 to 2004 reveals diverse outcomes with regard to lifelong learning policies. Only a total of 53 countries have introduced lifelong learning reforms – a rather low figure when considering that the indicator is quite broad and includes many different reforms (see Table 20.3). Among these countries, 34 have reformed the field of pre-primary education to increase coverage by compulsory education, to structure learning by a curriculum or by other means. In the field of adult education, a total of 33 countries have initiated reforms such as qualification frameworks, new laws concerning adult education for lifelong learning and others. Reforms in the higher education sector, for example the

Table 20.4 Number of lifelong learning reforms, 1996–2004

Reform	Number of Countries
Pre-primary Compulsory pre-primary education or introduction of curriculum and other reforms	34
Adult Education Qualification frameworks, new laws, programmes and institutions, increased financing and other reforms	33
Higher Education New laws, programmes and institutions, increased financing and other reforms	19
Number of countries with at least one of the reforms	53

Source: Author's own account based on policy reports submitted to ICE (International Conference on Education) 1996, 2001, 2004 and the WDE.

establishment of new institutions or new laws for expanding access, have been carried out by 19 countries. These figures show that countries are generally active in the area of lifelong learning. However, compared to the spread of the idea of lifelong learning, there is obviously more talk than action. While nearly 80 per cent of the countries mentioned the idea in their policy reports, countries are less eager to introduce corresponding reforms.

In sum, the analysis of national policies worldwide illustrated that there is a growing consensus on lifelong learning and a majority of countries are also intensively trying to reform their education systems in order to implement lifelong learning measures. However, given the fact that the indicator for lifelong learning reforms has been rather broad, there is obviously a difference between the acknowledgement of the idea of lifelong learning and the introduction of reforms, indicating a decoupling of the lifelong learning discourse and corresponding activities. We can thus speak of a global consensus on lifelong learning, but a large divergence in its realisation. The diffusion of an idea may thus vary significantly from the diffusion of related reforms, and international organisations may be stronger actors in the former process than in the latter. It is the adoption and implementation where national factors outweigh the international activities (Jakobi 2011).

Conclusions: International Organisations and a Global Policy Process

This chapter has analysed education policy diffusion through international organisations. I first identified different concepts related to policy transfer and diffusion. Explanations for these processes can be found in rationalist accounts of policy making but also in world society theory and the importance of legitimacy. As I showed, international organisations have indeed promoted lifelong learning intensively, in various contexts and by different instruments. As a result, countries have increasingly referred to lifelong learning in the development of their national education policies (compare also Jakobi 2009b, 2011). As nodes of diffusion – central points at which transfer of policies originates or crosses – international organisations fulfil an important function in generating political exchange and the building of common aims and goals. Therefore, much research on world society puts them at the centre.

Research related to international influences is likely to become more important in the coming years, given the growing number of international activities, the increase in available information on other education systems and the rhetorical emphasis on national competiveness in a global knowledge-society. But this also results in difficulties – it is not easy for policy makers to consider whether or not policies are really transferrable in practice, even if they seem to be promising. Even more severe, important stakeholders (like students or parents) may feel they lose significant and legitimate influence on education policy if most ideas are actually transferred from external contexts and are not developed on a case-by-case basis in a local context. It also remains to be seen whether the growth of exchange actually results in better education outcomes.

There are also still major research gaps to be tackled from a more theoretical perspective. For example, it is unclear what the most effective instrument of organisations is in policy transfer. Often, standard setting instruments, or also financial incentives – like in the case of the World Bank – seem to be the strongest instruments, but this is yet to be shown empirically and in contrast to other ways of influence. Also, it is still unclear how policies are actually disseminated among international organisations. These organisations are not only central nodes for diffusion with regard to countries, but are themselves subject to trends and react to policies that other organisations develop and promote. Finally, future research could examine more closely how far international influence reaches. While I focused on two levels – the diffusion of the idea of lifelong learning and reforms linked to it – I have not considered whether these reforms are actually implemented and how successful they are. In principle – although data problems are yet severe – one could distinguish these levels and look at which of them is most influenced by international developments. It is not necessarily the case that the closer one approaches the implementation level, the less influence exists. New institutionalism would predict a strong influence on the individual level, but due to other causal factors (see Meyer 2000). In sum, much remains to be done at the intersection of international organisations, policy diffusion and global as well as national policy processes.

Notes

1 The article is based on a finished book project (see Jakobi 2011, 2009a, 2009b). The research project was supported by the German Research Foundation (DFG).
2 In this article, the term 'lifelong learning' refers to the policy concept, not to a comprehensive educational framework or a biographical experience.
3 For literature in education science, see Steiner-Khamsi (2004), Kallo and Rinne (2006) or Waldow (2009); for political science see, e.g., Dolowitz and Marsh (1996, 2000), Dolowitz (2003), Jahn (2006), Simmons et al. (2008), Meseguer and Gilardi (2009); for early discussions see Walker (1969), Collier and Messick (1975), Eyestone (1977); for a new institutionalist approach, see Strang and Meyer (1994).
4 While I focus here on a presentation of national policies, thus showing a correlation between international and national activity, Jakobi (2011) shows a quantitative analysis of how both levels are causally linked.

References

ASEM (2002) *Lifelong Learning in ASEM Countries: The Way Forward.* Singapore: ASEM.

ASEM (2005) Asia–Europe Education and Research Hub for Life Long Learning: Programme of the Opening Conference. Copenhagen, 1–4 May.

Avant, D., Finnemore, M. and Sell, S.K. (eds) (2010) *Who Governs the Globe?* Cambridge: Cambridge University Press.

Barnett, M. and Finnemore, M. (2004) *Rules of the World: International Organizations in Global Politics.* Ithaca: Cornell University Press.

Becker, G. S. (1964) *Human Capital: A Theoretical and Empirical Analysis, with special Reference to Education.* New York: Columbia University Press.

Berry, F. S. and Berry, W. D. (2007) 'Innovation and Diffusion Models in Policy Research', in P. A. Sabatier (ed.) *Theories of the Policy Process.* Boulder: Westview Press. 223–260.

Boli, J. and Thomas, G. M. (eds) (1999) *Constructing World Culture.* Stanford: Stanford University Press.

Collier, D. and Messick, R. E. (1975) 'Prerequisites versus Diffusion: Testing Alternative Explanations of Social Security Adoption'. *The American Political Science Review,* 69: 1299–1315.

de Leon, P. (1999) 'The Stages Approach to the Policy Process: What Has It Done? Where Is It Going?' in P. A. Sabatier (ed.) *Theories of the Policy Process.* Boulder: Westview Press. 19–32.

Dolowitz, D. P. (2003) 'A Policy-Maker's Guide to Policy Transfer'. *The Political Quarterly,* 101–108.

Dolowitz, D. P. and Marsh, D. (1996) 'Who Learns What from Whom: A Review of the Policy Transfer Literature'. *Political Studies,* 44: 343–357.

Dolowitz, D. P. and Marsh, D. (2000) 'Learning from Abroad: The Role of Policy Transfer in Contemporary Policy-Making'. *Governance,* 13(1): 5–24.

EU Commission (2000) *A Memorandum on Lifelong Learning.* SEC (2000) 1832.

EU Commission (2001) *Making A European Area of Lifelong Learning A Reality.* COM (2001) 678.

EU Commission (2005) *Towards a European Qualification Framework for Lifelong Learning.* SEC (2005) 957.

European Council (1996) *Council Conclusions of 20 December on a Strategy for Lifelong Learning* (97/C 7/02).

European Council (2000) *Presidency Conclusions of the Council of the European Union.*

European Council (2002a) *Council Resolution of 27 June 2002 on Lifelong Learning.* 2002/ C163/01.

European Council (2002b) *Detailed Work Progamme on the follow-up of the Objectives of Education and Training Systems in Europe.* 2002/C142/01.

European Union (2006) *Decision of the European Parliament and the European Council on the Establishment of a Lifelong Learning Action Programme.* Online at http://eur-lex.europa.eu/ LexUriServ/site/en/oj/2006/l_327/l_32720061124en00450068.pdf (last accessed December 2008).

Expertenkommission zur Finanzierung Lebenslangen Lernens (2004) *Finanzierung Lebenslangen Lernens – der Weg in die Zukunft.* Bielefeld: Bertelsmann.

Eyestone, R. (1977) 'Confusion, Diffusion, and Innovation'. *American Political Science Review,* 71(2): 441–447.

Finnemore, M. (1993) 'International Organizations as Teachers of Norms: The United Nations Educational, Scientific, and Cultural Organization and Science Policy'. *International Organization,* 47(1): 565–597.

Finnemore, M. (1996) *National Interests in International Society*. Ithaca: Cornell University Press.

Finnemore, M. and Sikkink, K. (1999) 'International Norm Dynamics and Political Change', in P. J. Katzenstein, R. O. Keohane, and S. D. Krasner (eds) *Exploration and Contestation in the Study of World Politics*. Cambridge, MA: MIT Press. 247–277.

Fuller, B. and Rubinson, R. (eds) (1992) *The Political Construction of Education: The State, School Expansion and Economic Change*. Westport: Praeger.

Gerlach, C. (2000) *Lebenslanges Lernen. Konzepte und Entwicklungen 1972 bis 1997*. Cologne and Weimar: Böhlau.

Hasan, A. (1996) 'Lifelong Learning', in A. C. Tuijnman (ed.) *International Encyclopedia of Adult Education and Training*. Oxford: Pergamon. 33–41.

Heichel, S., Pape, J. and Sommerer, T. (2005) 'Is There Convergence in Convergence Research? An Overview of Empirical Studies on Policy Convergence'. *Journal of European Public Policy*, 12(5): 817–840.

ILO (1974) C 140 Paid Educational Leave Convention.

ILO (2005) *Project on National Qualification Frameworks*. Online at www.logos-net.net/ilo/ngf/topics/ow/htm (last accessed 7 August 2005).

Istance, D. (2003) 'Schooling and Lifelong Learning: Insights from OECD analyses'. *European Journal of Education*, 38(1): 85–98.

Jahn, D. (2006) 'Globalization as "Galton's Problem": The Missing Link in the Analysis of Diffusion Patterns in Welfare State Development'. *International Organization*, 60(2): 401–431.

Jakobi, A. P. (2009a) 'Global Education Policy in the Making: International Organizations and Lifelong Learning'. *Globalisation, Education and Societies*, 7(4): 473–487.

Jakobi, A. P. (2009b) *International Organizations and Lifelong Learning: From Global Agendas to Policy Diffusion*. Houndmills: Palgrave.

Jakobi, A. P. (2011) 'International Organizations and Policy Diffusion: The Global Norm of Lifelong Learning'. *Journal of International Relations and Development*, forthcoming.

Kallen, D. (1979) 'Recurrent Education and Lifelong Learning: Definitions and Distinctions', in T. Schuller and J. Megarry (eds) *Recurrent Education and Lifelong Learning*. New York: Kogan Page. 45–54.

Kallen, D. (2002) 'Lifelong Learning Revisited', in D. Istance, H. G. Schuetze and T. Schuller (eds) *International Perspectives on Lifelong Learning: From Recurrent Education to the Knowledge Society*. Buckingham: Open University Press. 32–38.

Kallo, J. and Rinne, R. (2006) *Supranational Regimes and National Education Policies – Encountering Challenge*. Helsinki: FERA.

Kingdon, J. W. (2003) *Agendas, Alternatives and Public Policies*. New York: Longman.

Knill, C. (2005) 'Introduction: Cross-National Policy Convergence: Concepts, Approaches and Explanatory Factors'. *Journal of European Public Policy*, 12(5): 764–774.

Lechner, F. J. and Boli, J. (2005) *World Culture: Origins and Consequences*. Oxford: Blackwell.

Lindblom, C. E. (1959) 'The Science of "Muddling Through"'. *Public Administration Review*, 14 (Spring): 79–88.

Meseguer, C and Gilardi, F. (2009) 'What Is New in the Study of Policy Diffusion?' *Review of International Political Economy* 16(3): 527–543.

Meyer, J. W. (2000) 'Globalization. Sources and Effects on National States and Societies'. *International Sociology*, 15(2): 233–248.

Meyer, J. W., Boli, J., Thomas, G. M. and Ramirez, F. O. (1997a) 'World Society and the Nation-State'. *American Journal of Sociology*, 103(1): 144–181.

Meyer, J. W., Frank, D. J., Hironaka, A., Schofer, E. and Tuma, N. B. (1997b) 'The Structuring of a World Environmental Regime, 1870–1990'. *International Organization*, 51(4): 623–651.

Meyer, J. W., Kamens, D. and Benavot, A. (1992) *School Knowledge for the Masses.* Washington: Falmer.

Meyer, J. W. and Ramirez, F. O. (2003) 'The World Institutionalization of Education', in J. Schriewer (ed.) *Discourse Formation in Comparative Education.* 2nd edn. Frankfurt/Main: Peter Lang. 111–132.

Norwegian Ministry of Education and Research (2005) *Conference Programme of the 2005 Bergen Conference.*

OECD (1995) *The OECD Jobs Study: Implementing the Strategy.* Paris: OECD.

OECD (1996) *Lifelong Learning for All.* Paris: OECD.

OECD (2000) *Motivating Students for Lifelong Learning.* Paris: OECD.

OECD (2002a) *Completing the Foundations for Lifelong Learning – An OECD Survey of Upper Secondary Schools.* Paris: OECD.

OECD (2002b) OECD Programme on Educational Building: International Seminar on Educational Infrastructure. Guadelajara, Mexico, 24–27 February.

Papadopoulos, G. (1994) *Education 1960 – 1990: The OECD Perspective.* Paris: OECD.

Papadopoulos, G. (2002) 'Lifelong Learning and the Changing Policy Environment', in D. Istance, H. G. Schuetze and T. Schuller (eds) *International Perspectives on Lifelong Learning: From Recurrent Education to the Knowledge Society.* Buckingham: Open University Press. 39–46.

Pressman, J. L. and Wildavsky, A. (1973) *Implementation: How Great Expectations in Washington are Dashed in Oakland.* Berkeley: University of California Press.

Ramirez, F. O. and Riddle, P. (1991) 'The Expansion of Higher Education', in P. G. Altenbach (ed.) *International Higher Education: An Encyclopedia.* New York: Garland.

Report Austria (2001) *National Education Policy Report submitted to the International Conference on Education.* Online at www.ibe.unesco.org/International/ICE/ 46english/46natrape.htm (last accessed July 2005).

Report Brazil (2001) National Education Policy Report submitted to the International Conference on Education. Online at www.ibe.unesco.org/International/ICE/ 46english/ 46natrape.htm (last accessed July 2005).

Report Egypt (2004) *National Education Policy Report submitted to the International Conference on Education.* Online at www.ibe.unesco.org/International/ ICE47/English/Natreps/Nrep_ main.htm (last accessed July 2005).

Report Swaziland (2004) *National Education Policy Report submitted to the International Conference on Education.* Online at www.ibe.unesco.org/International/ ICE47/English/ Natreps/Nrep_main.htm (last accessed July 2005).

Report Thailand (2001) *National Education Policy Report submitted to the International Conference on Education.* Online at www.ibe.unesco.org/International/ICE/ 46english/ 46natrape.htm (last accessed July 2005).

Rogers, E. M. (2003) *The Diffusion of Innovations.* London: Free Press.

Rose, P. (2003) 'From Washington to the Post-Washington Consensus: The Influence of International Agendas on Education Policy and Practice in Malawi'. *Globalisation, Societies and Education,* 1(1): 67–86.

Salt, A. and Bowland, D. (1996) 'International Labour Organization', in A. C. Tuijnman (ed.) *International Encyclopedia of Adult Education and Training.* 2nd edn. Oxford: Pergamon. 704–709.

Schuller, T., Schuetze, H. G. and Istance, D. (2002) 'From Recurrent Education to the Knowledge Society: An Introduction', in D. Istance, H. G. Schuetze, and T. Schuller (eds) *International Perspectives on Lifelong Learning: From Recurrent Education to the Knowledge Society.* Buckingham: Open University Press. 1–21.

Simmons, B. A., Dobbin, F. and Garrett, G (eds) (2008) *The Global Diffusion of Markets and Democracy.* Cambridge: Cambridge University Press.

Steiner-Khamsi, G. (ed.) (2004) *The Global Politics of Educational Borrowing and Lending.* New York: Teachers College Press.

Strang, D. and Meyer, J. W. (1994) 'Institutional Conditions for Diffusion', in W. R. Scott, J. W. Meyer and Associates (eds) *Institutional Environments and Organizations.* Thousand Oaks: SAGE. 100–112.

Sutton, P. J. (1996) 'Lifelong and Continuing Education', in A. C. Tuijnman (ed.) *International Encyclopedia of Adult Education and Training.* Oxford: Pergamon. 27–33.

UNESCO (1971) *World Survey of Education V: Educational Policy, Legislation and Administration.* Paris: UNESCO.

UNESCO (1972) *Learning to Be: The World of Education Today and Tomorrow.* Paris: UNESCO.

UNESCO (1996) *Learning: The Treasure Within.* Paris: UNESCO.

UNESCO (2001) *Revised Recommendation Concerning Technical and Vocational Education.* Paris: UNESCO.

UNESCO (2003) *World Data on Education.* 5th edn (CD-ROM). Geneva: UNESCO/IBE.

UNESCO (2005) *Towards Knowledge Societies.* Paris: UNESCO.

Waldow, F. (2009) 'Undeclared Imports: silent borrowing in educational policy-making and research in Sweden'. *Comparative Education*, 45(4): 477–494.

Walker, J. L. (1969) 'The Diffusion of Innovations among the American States'. *American Political Science Review*, 63 (September): 880–899.

World Bank (2003) *Lifelong Learning in the Global Knowledge Economy: Challenges for Developing Countries.* Washington: World Bank.

World Bank (2010) *Draft Education Sector Strategy.* Online at http://go.worldbank.org/ DTQZ9EKJW0 (last accessed December 2010).

Wurzburg, G. (2003) *Charts of the Lifelong Learning Workshop sponsored by the World Bank and the Slovak Governance Insitute: Lifelong Learning – What Lessons from Experience in the OECD?* December. Online at www.worldbank.org/education/lifelong_learning (last accessed 7 July 2005).

Conclusions

21 Standardisation and Legitimacy

Two Central Concepts in Research on Educational Borrowing and Lending

Florian Waldow

In recent decades, the transfer of ideas, policies and organisational models from one place to another has become a hot topic in several academic disciplines, including education. There has been a proliferation of approaches and labels, ranging from 'policy learning' (Hall 1993) via 'lesson-drawing' (Rose 1991), to 'diffusion' (Jakobi and Martens 2007), 'policy attraction' (Phillips 2000) and 'borrowing and lending' (Steiner-Khamsi 2004c). Each of these approaches refers to the study of processes 'in which knowledge about policies, administrative arrangements, institutions and ideas in one political setting (past or present) is used in the development of policies, administrative arrangements, institutions and ideas in another political setting' (Dolowitz and Marsh 2000: 5). In recent years borrowing and lending have become the terms most commonly used when studying such processes in the field of comparative education (Perry and Tor 2008: 510). The separation of the transfer process into the borrowing and lending sides is an analytical one: with lending, one is typically more interested in the context from which a given idea, policy or organisational model *originates*; with borrowing, one is usually more concerned with the context in which it is *received*. That the former has attracted more interest among researchers is a fact mirrored in the composition of this volume.

The chapters in this book show that borrowing and lending occur in numerous formats, with important differences such as which actors are involved, and whether or not the process is voluntary. It is not easy to draw clear boundaries between these different forms, and it also can be difficult to distinguish forms of policy making where transfer plays a role from other forms. Even the fact that 'nothing happens' in a given context may be the result of 'learning from abroad', as 'policy makers' preference for the status quo in their own jurisdiction could be seen as implicitly involving negative lessons about alternatives in other countries or in other times' (James and Lodge 2003: 181). Also, references to 'elsewhere' may have effects in the receiving context without necessarily involving the transfer of content. This type of effect has also sometimes been placed under the label of 'borrowing'.

Different approaches to educational borrowing and lending have specific advantages and disadvantages, strengths and weaknesses. Several authors in this volume discuss the various concepts and terms used within this field of study (e.g. Beech and Lista, Dale and Robertson, Jakobi, Rappleye, Silova). In this concluding chapter I will not go into the details of each approach. Rather, I will focus on two key issues that surfaced in the chapters of this volume, and also commonly appear in research in the field.

The first is *standardisation.* Globalisation has had a considerable impact upon how we study and understand processes of standardisation in education. Among the central questions is whether the processes of educational borrowing and lending connected to globalisation make education more standardised around the globe or not. An interesting aspect here is the similarities between the processes of standardisation at work currently and the processes of standardisation that could be observed when national systems of education first emerged.

The second issue is the production of *legitimacy* for certain policy measures and policy actors through educational borrowing and lending. This, even if it is couched in a variety of terms and conceptualised in different ways by different approaches, is a fundamental feature of research on educational borrowing and lending. One important, though often only partially understood contribution to this area, has been the so-called 'externalisation' thesis, which conceptualises the use of external reference points in the educational system. I will begin by discussing some aspects of this thesis and how it is connected to issues of legitimacy. Next I will discuss the similarities and differences between borrowing and lending in a geographical/political sense (i.e. across national borders) and borrowing from other social sub-systems, such as the economic system, into the education system, and vice versa.

Standardisation

The term 'standardisation' is not used in any uniform way in the social sciences (Brunsson and Jacobsson 2000: 14–15). According to Craig Calhoun's definition, 'standardisation' means the 'imposition of uniformity on a good or measure, generally in cases where data or products are unique or produced according to different criteria' (Calhoun 2002). Often, the term is used in a slightly weaker sense, i.e. not signalling *achieved* uniformity, but rather the movement *towards* uniformity or similarity, in the direction of a shared standard, or the *intention* of creating a certain degree of uniformity, regardless of whether or not this process is successful.[1] In this chapter I use the term to denote increasing convergence towards a shared standard, whether intentional or not.

Global Convergence or Perseverance of Local Differences?

Today there is a tendency to attribute any change in the field of education to globalisation. While globalisation is indeed influential in many ways, indiscriminate use of the term reduces its analytical value. One way to avoid this problem is to treat globalisation in terms of its manifestations, such as standardisation, and the processes of borrowing and lending attached to it. Breaking globalisation down into smaller, more manageable bits may lead to a better understanding of what the phenomenon as a whole actually entails. Even if there is disagreement among researchers about what globalisation is (see Dale and Robertson in this volume), most scholars would probably agree that processes of standardisation of one type or another are a central component. Depending on the theory, standardisation can refer to different aspects:

material goods such as industrial products, as well as organisational arrangements, cultural patterns such as markets, life-worlds, discourses and 'scripts' for individual and organisational behaviour, culture or curricula, to name but a few aspects that have been highlighted by different theorists (see, e.g., the contributions in Lechner and Boli 2008). Different approaches also give different answers to the question of how much coercion is involved in these processes of standardisation.

Education is fundamentally affected by most aspects of globalisation named in the preceding paragraph. Unsurprisingly, the standardisation of educational provision has been a central concern for scholars of comparative education. A great deal of research has centred on the question of whether or not globalisation has led to increased global convergence in education. The question has often been framed even more broadly, to ask not just about the effects of globalisation, but about effects of the emergence of the modern world. Does modernity mean local particularities are weakened, or do they persist, possibly in a changed, but not a standardised form?

Answers have differed widely. One approach to analysing the global dynamics of education over the course of the past 200 years that has become increasingly popular is the theory of a 'world culture' (a.k.a. 'world polity'), first developed by John Meyer, Francisco Ramirez and their colleagues at Stanford University. The world culture framework originated in the field of neo-institutionalist organisational sociology. It studies the emergence and global diffusion of a common world culture with Western roots. Among its principles are a belief in progress, rationality, individuality and certain models of state, society and actorship (Thomas et al. 1987). In its wake, the 'world culture' brings certain structural patterns such as systems of mass schooling (Ramirez and Boli 1987). Proponents of the world-culture approach have primarily studied the diffusion of this culture and its attendant structural forms using quantitative methods on large samples of countries (Krücken 2002).

The world-culture approach has become one of the most widely used (or at least widely cited) theories in comparative education, but it has also attracted a fair amount of criticism (Schriewer 2005). For example, critics have claimed that it pays too little attention to issues of power and coercion and overestimates the role of values while underestimating the role of the needs of the global capitalist system in the production of isomorphism between countries (Anderson-Levitt 2003; Dale 2000). A line of critique that has sometimes been labelled 'culturalist' (Spring 2009: 14) stresses that the diffusion of the world culture produces a much murkier image than proponents of world culture would imply. The culturalists point to the importance and perseverance of local contexts, showing how world culture may be resisted or processed, adapted and appropriated to local conditions, leading to hybridisations and new local particularities. A number of authors in this volume criticise the findings and assumptions of the proponents of the world culture-approach from a culturalist position (e.g. Carney, Rappleye, Silova).

The stance of the world culture approach on the one hand and the position(s) of the culturalists on the other have sometimes been presented as being mutually exclusive. However, while both sides view social reality differently, their approaches may not be impossible to reconcile. One must bear in mind that studies following the pattern of the world culture approach and studies following the culturalist pattern produce very different types of results. Studying a large sample of countries, using fairly standardised indicators, will inevitably yield a different *type* of result on a different *level of aggregation* than a case study focusing on one country or a small number of countries, using a wide variety of sources. Advocates of world culture look at large global developments while *systematically* not looking at heterogeneity, internal differences, tensions and ambivalences (Krücken 2002: 230), i.e. the exact topics that most interest culturalists.

Parallel differences among various approaches can be observed if we look at studies investigating individuals or groups of individuals: a large-scale survey study using a large sample of individuals and treating the results with statistical methods will yield a different type of result than in-depth interviews with a few individuals, interpreted by qualitative methods. A similar relationship exists between the results produced by the world culture approach and the in-depth local studies produced by culturalists. Both approaches capture a valid aspect of social reality, however what is captured differs significantly. These differences make it difficult to *falsify* the results of one type of study with the results of the other.

It is possible, however, to *qualify* and *nuance* the results of one type of approach by the results of the other. Local developments can thus be seen in a wider, international context (for a number of interesting examples, see Baker and LeTendre 2005). Conversely, it is possible to see how global developments play out locally, in context, with particular conditions. It is also possible to understand the extent to which global tendencies impact on how educational provision actually functions. Sometimes isomorphisms to world culture might be confined to the level of 'policy talk' (Steiner-Khamsi and Stolpe 2006) (although the fact that isomorphism remains on the level of policy talk of course does not mean that it is insignificant). Thus, these two approaches to studying whether the emergence of the modern world and/or globalisation have led to an increased standardisation of education may be seen as *complementary*, rather than opposed. The discussion between culturalists and proponents of the world culture approach has produced interesting insights, but if taken to the extreme, the dichotomisation of the two approaches leads into a dead end. The following may seem fairly obvious, but it is a point that is sometimes forgotten in the heat of the argument: both large global developments *and* heterogeneity, internal differences, tensions and ambivalences must be explained.

Space and Standardisation

Space is an important issue in studies of educational borrowing and lending. Research in this area has usually been concerned with transfer across space, i.e. policies, programmes, organisational models etc., travelling from one (geographical) location to another and crossing national boundaries in the process (Beech 2006: 2). Recently, however, space has been used to refer to much more than geography. Public discourse and policy-making, as well as the social science and humanities disciplines, have become increasingly 'spatialised' (Therborn 2002: 15). Not only have issues connected to geographic space become important, social dynamics and 'social futures' are now often presented in spatial terms (Therborn 2002: 16). Geographic imagery has spread to all kinds of areas, not least to educational research. Some scholars speak of a 'spatial turn' in social sciences like education (see the contributions in Gulson and Symes

2007). Scholars use terms like 'policy landscapes' (Herschbach 2009; Wolf and Bokhorst-Heng 2008) and 'policyscapes' (Stephen Carney, in this volume). There is an increased awareness of how geographic and social space overlap, and how they are 'integral to each other rather than space being an undifferentiated spatial backdrop against which social relations take place' (Robertson and Dale 2008: 28–29; see also Lawn and Nóvoa's conception of a 'European educational space', 2002).[2]

The spaces and -scapes within which educational borrowing and lending take place are not only occupied by nation-state actors. In recent years, borrowing and lending from entities that transcend the level of individual nation states has moved to the foreground of interest of researchers. Increasingly, 'reference societies' in the sense of individual nation states serving as a model (a concept going back to Reinhard Bendix; see Bendix 1978) are being accompanied and partly supplanted by international points of reference, such as various types of international organisations, transnational processes such as the Bologna Process and international studies such as PISA (see Dale and Robertson, Grek, Jakobi, Takayama in this volume).

However, that these international points of reference have become more important does not mean that they have completely replaced national reference societies. On the contrary, some reference societies would never have achieved their position without reinforcement from international points of reference. What has happened to Finland since the publication of the first round of PISA results is a good example. Finland would hardly have achieved the status of an educational utopia in countries such as Germany and Japan if not for the OECD PISA study and the league tables generated from it (see Takayama 2010; Waldow 2010; see also Takayama's contribution to this volume). Thus, the function of national and international points of reference is tightly connected, as international and national points of reference influence and reinforce one another.

International and National Standardisation: Processes and Mechanisms

Much of the standardisation taking place is not strictly the result of direct coercion. It is also the product of various forms of 'soft power', such as the provision of organisational models and statistical categories, the offering of problem definitions plus fitting solutions and the setting of 'standards' or 'benchmarks' (Grek 2009; Kalló 2009; see also Grek, Maroy, Ridge, Sobe in this volume). On the surface, conforming to these usually seems voluntary (Brunsson and Jacobsson 2000); however, in practice this is often not the case. Sometimes loans or other types of support are made conditional to compliance with certain standards. But even if there is no direct coercion, actors may find it hard not to comply (see Nóvoa and Yariv-Mashal 2003: 429). Standards and benchmarks set by highly legitimate organisations such as certain IOs are difficult to ignore, even for entities not belonging to the organisation setting the standards and defining the benchmarks (c.f. Ahrne and Brunsson 2008: 153). Standards and benchmarks are often particularly effective when it is possible to *quantify* the degree to which individual nation states, regions, etc., conform to them, and if these quantifications can be arranged in league tables (Ahrne and Brunsson 2008: 153; Steiner-Khamsi 2003).

In recent years there has been tremendous interest in these processes of standardisation among researchers, again possibly partly triggered by the processes of standardisation attached to globalisation (Brunsson and Jacobsson 2000). However, these processes of international exchange and standardisation have a history that well precedes the latest round of globalisation. While it is true that globalisation makes it obvious that certain ways of conceptualising the world no longer work (see Dale and Robertson in this volume), some of these conceptualisations were always exaggerations and simplifications. The national never was as 'national' as social scientists and historians claimed in the high age of nationalism. 'Methodological nationalism', i.e. the assumption that 'nation states and their boundaries are the "natural" containers of societies and hence the appropriate unit of analysis for social sciences' (Dale 2005: 124), never was a wholly accurate description of the social world (see also Wimmer and Glick Schiller 2002).[3]

As Bernd Zymek (2007: 309) has reminded us, the history of education in the last couple of centuries should not be seen as a linear development from local to regional to national and finally international structures. National educational systems did not evolve in isolation; rather, 'looking abroad was instrumental in building a national education system' (Zymek and Zymek 2004: 26; see also Gonon in this volume). It has never been possible to draw a neat distinction between the inside and outside of national education systems. National education systems have not evolved as neatly delimited, self-contained, largely independent entities. Rather, as Zymek has put it, there has been 'a complex sequence of ever-changing processes of regional and trans-regional, national and international systematisation and rationalisation in education, sometimes replacing, sometimes overlapping one another' (Zymek and Zymek 2004: 26).

It is probably true that globalisation changes – or, if you wish, destroys – local particularities. However, the nation state – with the help of the educational system – did the same thing within its own boundaries. And just as globalisation has not succeeded in creating a uniform world (so far at least), the nation state was not totally successful in eradicating the local. Local particularities survived the advent of the nation state and national educational systems. Zymek's notion of overlapping and interacting processes on local, regional, national and international levels also applies to today's globalising processes. However, this is often not evident, because in the 'wider literature on globalization, the spatial is binarised – as either global or local' (Robertson and Dale 2008: 28).

One of the distinct features of globalisation is denationalisation (Robertson and Dale 2008: 19). However, there are striking parallels between the methods, instruments and concrete processes of standardisation at work within national states when national education systems first formed, and those currently functioning globally. When forging their educational systems in the nineteenth century, states like Prussia also employed 'best-practice' models and relied on the more or less voluntary self-standardisation of educational institutions along the lines offered, e.g. by the statistical offices (Zymek 2007: 316). Offering categories to which institutions could align was an incentive for self-standardisation – first of institutions, increasingly also of results (Zymek 2007: 329).

All of this is not to say that current processes of standardisation and globalisation are exactly the same as those that occurred when nation states developed. The world was very different from today in the nineteenth century, not least in terms of the size and inclusiveness of educational systems. Change in quantity is connected to change in quality; today's standardisations often occur on a vastly different level than those that went on inside emerging nation states. The latest round of globalisation has certainly had an impact on the processes of borrowing and lending (see Dale 1999; Robertson 2005). However, the tension between standardising forces, on the one hand, and local resistance and locally contingent configurations of actors, on the other, is much older than globalisation (and probably older than the nation state, for that matter) (Zymek 2007: 310). We should not forget that some of the processes involved in the system-building of national educational systems bear strong resemblance to many of the global standardising processes going on today, a fact that is often not acknowledged by students of globalisation. That 'soft power' and benchmarking have a long history is just one of several important reasons why research and teaching in comparative education should have a historical dimension.

The Production of Legitimacy

Today there seems to be almost universal agreement – at least among those *studying* rather than *promoting* educational borrowing (see Steiner-Khamsi 2004b: 1) – that whether borrowing takes place, and in what form it does so, depends on the *borrowing* context, not the place of origin of what is borrowed. The model is in the eye of the beholder. A key issue in this respect is that borrowing can be used to gain legitimacy for (or to de-legitimate) political actors, propositions, or agendas in the borrowing country (Halpin and Troyna 1995: 307–308; Steiner-Khamsi 2004a). Conversely, the urge to lend is also connected to issues of legitimacy; being a policy lender can also provide legitimacy. Gita Steiner-Khamsi has termed this 'export for survival' (Steiner-Khamsi 2004a: 204). Due to the central role aspects of the production of legitimacy play for both borrowing and lending, a concern for these issues is common to many studies in the field of borrowing and lending.

The concept of legitimacy owes much to the work of Max Weber, who discussed legitimacy in the context of how the moral grounding for different types of political authority is provided (see Uphoff 1989). Today the concept is applied to many more phenomena than political authority, e.g. to organisations in general. Organisations must be perceived as legitimate by their environment. In a seminal article, Mark Suchman defined organisational legitimacy as a 'generalized perception or assumption that the actions of an entity are desirable, proper, or appropriate within some socially constructed system of norms, values, beliefs, and definitions' (Suchman 1995: 574).

Analogous to the application to organisations, the concept of legitimacy can also be applied to policy agendas and social structures; they, too, must be legitimated as 'desirable, proper, or appropriate', and this takes place in a process of social construction. This is what I term the 'production of legitimacy'.

Externalisation

One approach that lends itself well to studying issues of legitimacy production and that has been used by many scholars in the field of comparative education in recent years (including the editors of and some of the contributors to this volume) is the so-called 'externalisation' thesis.

The concept of externalisation goes back to the German sociologist Niklas Luhmann (1927–1998). Luhmannian systems theory forms a complex conceptual universe that is not easily accessible (two of the theoretical cornerstones of his oeuvre: Luhmann 1995, 1997). The fact that only a small portion of Luhmann's writings (and he was extremely prolific) are available in English, has not made things easier. As a result, the concept of externalisation has often been used in a truncated way. Crucial points of the externalisation thesis perhaps bear re-stating here. It should be noted that it is impossible to do full justice to Luhmannian systems theory in the context of this chapter. What follows is an extremely simplified account of just a few aspects of his rich conceptual world.

According to Luhmann, modern society is functionally differentiated into several sub-systems (education, law, politics, religion, etc.) that follow their own codes and programmes. Each sub-system fulfils a certain function for society as a whole. In contrast to what 'system' often means in everyday language, social systems in Luhmann's sense are made up not of human beings or organisations, but internally linked *communications*. A crucial feature of Luhmann's theory is that communications can only connect directly with each other *within* the boundaries of each social sub-system. Communications from outside a sub-system, i.e. its environment, *cannot* directly link up with communications inside the sub-system. What they can do, however, is 'irritate' the sub-system from outside. This irritation is then processed *within* the sub-system. Luhmann calls this the 'principle of operative closure' (Luhmann 2005: 26–37).

However, systems can use *external* points of reference from their environment, which are then processed within the system (according to the principle of operative closure). This is what Luhmann terms *externalisation*.[4] Externalisation does not come to the system from the outside: it is both instigated from within and processed within the system. Luhmann (together with his co-author Karl Eberhard Schorr) identifies several possible external points of reference – i.e. forms of externalisation – that are employed in the educational system. These include externalisation to values, to organisation or to the principles and results of science (*Wissenschaftlichkeit*) (Luhmann and Schorr 1988: 340–342; English translation: Luhmann and Schorr 2000). Different forms of externalisation can (and often do) occur simultaneously, and can be mutually reinforcing (Schriewer 1990: 69).

Luhmann and Schorr allow that there may be more types of externalisation than those they cover (Luhmann and Schorr 1988: 342), and Jürgen Schriewer has added another to their list. Schriewer categorises references to other countries or the international as 'externalisation to world situations' (Schriewer 1990: 62–72). This type of externalisation for obvious reasons has attracted the most interest among students of educational borrowing and lending.

Externalisation to world situations is not the only type of externalisation employed in the educational system. Externalisation is also not synonymous with borrowing narrowly defined, i.e. borrowing as the transfer of content. Rather, externalisation is a discursive formation that can become relevant in the context of borrowing, and lends itself easily to the purpose of producing legitimacy. Some examples may clarify this.

Educational reforms can be legitimised by being described as 'evidence-based', in the sense that the reform measures have been established as effective by scientific methods. This constitutes an externalisation to the principles and results of science (*Wissenschaftlichkeit*). Reforms can also be legitimised by being portrayed as in line with a certain set of values (i.e. externalisation to values). Externalisation can also be used to shift the blame for failure by attributing it to organisational constraints – 'If only we didn't have to conform to the demands of the administration, our school could be so much better!' – which is an externalisation to organisation. Finally, we have the 'externalisation to world situations' so familiar to students of educational borrowing. This model provides ample opportunities for legitimation and de-legitimation and also for combination with other forms of externalisation, e.g. when following the model of a particular reference society is presented as being supported by scientific evidence (externalisation to world situations *plus* externalisation to the principles and results of science).

It is important to keep in mind that the 'external' in 'externalisation' is *not* meant in a geographic/political sense (i.e. external in relation to the boundaries of a particular geographical entity such as a nation state). Rather, it refers to that which is external to the education system, as a social system made up of communications linking up with each other, and operating according to the principle of operative closure. While it is certainly possible to use the externalisation thesis in a fruitful way without applying a full-fledged Luhmannian theoretical framework (educational researchers do it all the time), it is important to keep in mind this original meaning of 'external' in externalisation. Thinking in terms of the different forms of externalisation makes it possible to put them alongside one another and consider the different ways they produce legitimacy, and how they are intertwined. If externalisation is only used with reference to world situations, this aspect is lost. We miss the opportunity to compare the *different* forms of externalisation, which is – or could be – among the primary virtues of the systems-theory approach. Treated in a non-truncated way, the externalisation thesis can be fruitfully applied whenever external (that is, to the educational system) points of reference appear in education discourse.

Once again, externalisation to world situations is not synonymous with borrowing in the sense that some content has presumably been transferred. Rather, the concept denotes a form of *reference* to an external point, either a national reference society, or an international organisation, process or discourse. 'Reference' simply indicates the allusion to, or citation of, something external. It does not necessarily mean that something has been transferred. In fact, reference can even serve to disguise that nothing is being transferred.

Thinking metaphorically, we may imagine references to elsewhere as screens onto which positive images – the ideal school, the model system of education – can be projected. Whether or not these pictures actually portray anything 'real' is beside the point (Takayama 2010; Waldow 2010). Research has regularly demonstrated that borrowing is always selective, and that the reason something is borrowed is not that it is 'good', but that it serves some function in the context of reception (see Halpin and Troyna 1995). Conceiving reference societies as a 'projection screen' takes this argument one step further, realising that in some cases, saying that borrowing is selective is an understatement. Rather, what appears to be borrowed does not necessarily need to have much to do at all with what seems to be its place of origin.

Meanwhile, educational transfer does not require reference. In fact, sometimes the process of legitimising a given programme or reform is facilitated if its geographical origin is suppressed (Lundahl 2005; Waldow 2009), or 're-territorialised' during the policy implementation process (Spreen 2004; Steiner-Khamsi 2002). Just as it is important to realise there is more to externalisation than externalisation to world situations, it seems wise to differentiate between 'reference' and borrowing/lending. The crucial questions then become how reference is processed, why it occurs, and what effect it has. To focus only on borrowing in a narrow sense, i.e. occasions where content is actually transferred, occludes some of the most interesting questions. Borrowing is a potential – but by no means necessary – effect of reference.

Borrowing from Other Social Sub-Systems

Borrowing and lending are usually used to denote transfer in a geographical/political sense. Policies, programmes, etc. travel from one (geographic) location to another, crossing national boundaries in the process (Beech 2006: 2). In the preceding section, I underlined that externalisation to world situations is not synonymous with borrowing, but that it can become important in the context of borrowing, especially as a legitimising device. The existence of several other forms of externalisation, proximate and parallel to externalisation to world situations, raises the question of whether it might make sense to see 'imports' from other social sub-systems into the educational system as a kind of borrowing as well. The boundaries crossed in this case would not be those of a geographical or political entity, but those of a social system.

As mentioned above, many authors have noted the usefulness of applying geographic concepts and imagery to the analysis of social issues. With this in mind, I will examine what happens if borrowing and lending are conceived not just geographically, but as a process of crossing the borders separating social sub-systems. Gita Steiner-Khamsi has labelled this 'cross-sectoral transfer' (Steiner-Khamsi 2004a: 204). There are many similarities between borrowing across national boundaries and borrowing from other social sub-systems.

Borrowing from 'reference societies' or international points of reference often serves the purpose of creating *legitimacy* for certain policy agendas at home. The import from other social sub-systems can accomplish this as well. For instance, arguing that a policy measure is 'evidence-based' (externalisation to principles and results of science), is a powerful way of legitimising educational policy measures. Here, legitimacy is established by partaking of the prestige and perceived objectivity of the hard sciences, not to mention the quasi-religious status science and its principles enjoy in the modern world (see Drori et al. 2003: 2). Scientific modes of justifying conclusions are imported into the education system.

Another similarity concerns the *standardising* effects of educational borrowing (see first section of this chapter). Importing modes of thinking and acting from other social systems can serve a unifying function in the educational system. Christian Lundahl and myself have described this with the notion of 'quick languages', i.e. languages that offer a shared medium of communication, facilitating dialogue within the educational system (Lundahl and Waldow 2009: 366). One example is the quick language derived from psychometrics – including terms like 'intelligence' as a conceptual tool for sorting and selecting pupils – enlisted in numerous countries during the first half of the twentieth century. This quick language served as a shorthand for dealing with pressing educational problems, such as efficiently choosing pupils for higher secondary education. The resulting 'efficiency', or rather, reduction in complexity that this entailed, was at the same time the reason the quick language was successful, and the price to be paid for its success.

Just as borrowing from reference societies and international points of reference is always selective, quick languages make *selective* use of theories and concepts originating in other social sub-systems and process them. Again, the quick language derived from psychometrics is a good example. The science of psychometrics was not imported as such – in toto – into the educational system. Rather, concepts, methods and data offered by the science of psychometrics were used selectively.

There are clear parallels here to Luhmann's principle of operative closure mentioned above. What is borrowed comes from outside the social sub-system and is not imported neatly and directly. It is processed within and according to the rules of the educational domain. Just as imports from elsewhere in a geographical/political sense are changed in the process of appropriation into the receiving context, imports into the educational system are not imported unaltered. They are remoulded according to the logic of the educational system.

Just as reference societies may change over time, what seems a promising field for borrowing into the educational system can evolve as well. When mass schooling in nation states first emerged, the religious system was an important external reference point (Tenorth 2010: 69). Today, other sub-systems, such as the economic system have become more relevant for the purpose of externalisation (Brüsemeister 2002; Radtke 2009; Waldow 2007).

As was mentioned above, it has sometimes seemed opportune to hide the geographical origins of a certain policy, as was the case with the decentralisation and marketisation reforms in Sweden since the early 1990s (Lundahl 2005: 158–159). Parallels to this phenomenon can also be found when looking at borrowing from other social sub-systems. For instance, many proponents of standards-based reform are likely to be unaware that in the beginning of the twentieth century, standards in education bore a strong relationship to and often were used analogous to industrial 'standards', e.g. when John Franklin Bobbitt tried to apply Frederick Taylor's principles of 'scientific management' to education (Waldow forthcoming). Just as emphasising the Reaganite and Thatcherite connections of the decentralisation and marketisation reforms in Sweden in the 1990s probably would not have increased their popularity, the connection to 'industrial standards' might also reduce acceptance for educational standards among progressively minded reformers.

Imports from other social sub-systems can also be linked with borrowing in a geographic/political sense. This is the case when an international body, such as the OECD or the World Bank, recommends a marketisation reform which is accepted and implemented by a nation state. In this case, recommendations cross both national and systemic boundaries. A related case can be observed when a particular country that supposedly has already implemented a certain reform is used as a model, e.g. for the implementation of markets in education (e.g. Chubb and Moe 1992).

I pointed out above that the practice of learning from elsewhere has been in evidence since the genesis of national systems of education (here in the more conventional sense of a system of organisations), and continues to play a crucial role in how they function today. The delimitation of the international, the national and the regional is only analytical, with borrowing and lending between the different levels occurring constantly. There is a close parallel here to imports to the educational system from other social sub-systems. Imports from outside the educational system have always occurred from the beginning of formal education, and continue to play a crucial role. However, as indicated by the example of economics supplanting religion, where the imports come from has changed over time. So, just as the way formal education is organised is the result of imports from other geographic locations, it is also the outcome of imports from other social sub-systems. This should not be seen as a usurpation or colonisation of the 'genuinely pedagogical'. Ever since institutions offering formal education emerged, it has been genuinely pedagogical to import and incorporate concepts, ways of thinking, and rationales for action from other social domains.

This is of course *not* to mean that any kind of import is to be welcomed by everyone; that would mean committing the naturalistic fallacy. The fact that imports from other social sub-systems into the educational system have occurred, and continue to occur, does not mean that all concerned should indiscriminately welcome and support any import. This is, once again, similar to what is the case with educational borrowing in the geographic sense.

It is also important to keep in mind that the educational system is not just a borrower, it is also a frequent lender. This process has sometimes been labelled the 'educationalisation' of society and life-worlds (Lüders et al. 2010; Smeyers and Depaepe 2008). This is a phenomenon which gained particular momentum during the 1960s, but started long before. Social problems were problematised as educational, in the sense that education was offered as a solution to them. Today, there are educational professionals for all stages and areas of life (Rüttgers 2010: 22–23). One example is how juvenile delinquency is viewed by the judicial system. Delinquents are no longer 'punished', they are 'educated' to make better choices and improve their behaviour. A more recent example is the development of fields like 'educational gerontology', wherein the problem of securing 'sustainable senior living for the 21st century' (Ingman and Amin 2011) is no longer seen primarily as a medical problem, but as an educational one. The academic discipline of education has benefited tremendously from educationalisation, because it has come with a massive expansion in funding for research to cover these new areas where education is now regarded as relevant.

In sum, it has become clear that there are many similarities between educational borrowing and lending in a geographic/political sense, and educational borrowing and lending from other social sub-systems into the education system. Just as borrowing and lending in a geographic/political sense takes place constantly, boundary-crossing between social systems also occurs all of the time. Borrowing and lending in a geographic/political sense belongs to the larger family of imports and transfers from and into the education system, moulding and changing it along with other social systems in the process.

Conclusion: Standardisation and the Production of Legitimacy

As we have seen, borrowing and lending are basic components of educational change. Education evolves according to a process of constant exchange in an environment consisting of other geographical/political entities and social systems. One potential effect is an increased standardisation of educational arrangements, programmes, or policies. Issues of legitimacy are always involved, though it is not necessarily easy to identify who is doing the standard-setting, or if a standard has been consciously set by anyone at all. For instance, processes of standardisation may be fuelled by certain, highly legitimate principles that need not be codified by any one actor to achieve a dynamics of their own (Drori et al. 2003: ix). The evolution of mass schooling as a standard component of modern nation states is one example (see Ramirez and Boli 1987).

In other cases, prospective policy lenders actively seek to enhance their legitimacy as standard-setters. Anyone can attempt to set standards, but the standards will only be followed if the standard-setter is perceived as legitimate and the standards as legitimate. One device for legitimisation is externalisation. Andreas Schleicher, head of the Indicators and Analysis Division of OECD's Directorate for Education (the unit responsible for PISA), usually ends his presentations with the sentence: 'Remember, without data you are just another person with an opinion' (see, e.g., Schleicher 2008). Following talks that typically contain large amounts of data, often in conjunction with policy recommendations, this statement implies that Schleicher and the OECD are uniquely positioned to be policy lenders, and set the standards others should follow. This is a classic example of externalisation to the principles and results of science, as a way of legitimising oneself and undermining one's critics' legitimacy.

The OECD is not the only actor seeking legitimacy as a policy lender and standard-setter. Others include inter- and transnational bodies, as well as nation states and organisations within nation states. Policy borrowing and lending carries on at all these levels. International benchmarks, best practices and league tables with attendant guidelines for how to improve one's rank proliferate. Seeing these developments as (not always successful) processes of standardisation and attempts at standard-setting in a field where different actors struggle for legitimacy, is one way to perhaps gain a better understanding of these processes.

Acknowledgements

I would like to thank Barbara Schulte, Gita Steiner-Khamsi, Johannes Bellmann, Stephen Carney, Matthias vom Hau, Florian Kiuppis and Thomas Müller for their very valuable comments on an earlier draft of this chapter.

Notes

1 This is not exactly the same use of the term 'standards' as in the concept of 'educational standards', where 'standards' usually refer to certain normative expectations concerning the outcome of pupils' learning (content and performance standards); c.f. Ravitch (1995).
2 There are predecessors for this line of thinking, such as Fernand Braudel's (1949) classic study of the Mediterranean during the time of Philip II.

3 Having said that, it has to be acknowledged that 'methodological nationalism' is an analytical simplification that has proved and continues to be of great heuristic value in many instances.
4 Placed in the conceptual universe of Luhmannian systems theory, externalisations serve as 'interruptions of interdependence' of communications within social sub-systems (*Interdependenzunterbrechungen*); see Nassehi (2002: 454), Schriewer (1990: 64).

References

Ahrne, G. and Brunsson, N. (2008) *Meta-organizations*. Cheltenham: Edward Elgar.

Anderson-Levitt, K. (2003) 'A world culture of schooling?', in K. Anderson-Levitt (ed.) *Local meanings, global schooling: Anthropology and world culture theory*. New York: Palgrave Macmillan. 1–26.

Baker, D. P. and LeTendre, G. K. (2005) *National differences, global similarities: World culture and the future of schooling*. Stanford: Stanford University Press.

Beech, J. (2006) 'The theme of educational transfer in comparative education: A view over time', *Research in comparative and international education*, 1(1): 2–13.

Bendix, R. (1978) *Kings or people: Power and the mandate to rule*. Berkeley: University of California Press.

Braudel, F. (1949) *La Méditerranée et le monde méditerranéen à l'époque de Philippe II* [The Mediterranean and the Mediterranean world in the age of Philip II]. Paris: A. Colin.

Brüsemeister, T. (2002) 'Myths of efficiency and the school system: Observed at the levels of interaction, organisation and society', *European Educational Research Journal*, 1(2): 234–255.

Brunsson, N. and Jacobsson, B. (2000) *A world of standards*. Oxford: Oxford University Press.

Calhoun, C. J. (2002) 'Standardization', in C. J. Calhoun (ed.) *Dictionary of the social sciences*. New York: Oxford University Press. Online. Available HTTP: www.oxfordreference.com/views/ENTRY.html?subview=Main&entry=t104.e1589 (accessed 15 June 2011).

Chubb, J. E. and Moe, T. M. (1992) *A lesson in school reform from Great Britain*. Washington, DC: Brookings Institution.

Dale, R. (1999) 'Specifying globalization effects on national policy: A focus on the mechanisms', *Journal of Education Policy*, 14(1): 1–17.

Dale, R. (2000) 'Globalization and education: Demonstrating a "common world educational culture" or locating a "globally structured educational agenda"?' *Educational Theory*, 50(4): 419–426.

Dale, R. (2005) 'Globalisation, knowledge economy and comparative education', *Comparative Education*, 41(2): 117–149.

Dolowitz, D. P. and Marsh, D. (2000) 'Learning from abroad: The role of policy transfer in contemporary policy-making', *Governance*, 13(1): 5–23.

Drori, G. S., Meyer, J. W., Ramirez, F. O. and Schofer, E. (2003) *Science in the modern world polity: Institutionalization and globalization*. Stanford: Stanford University Press.

Grek, S. (2009) 'Governing by numbers: the PISA "effect" in Europe', *Journal of Education Policy*, 24(1): 23–37.

Gulson, K. N. and Symes, C. (2007) *Spatial theories of education: Policy and geography matters*. New York: Routledge.

Hall, P. A. (1993) 'Policy paradigms, social learning, and the state: The case of economic policymaking in Britain', *Comparative Politics*, 25(3): 275–296.

Halpin, D. and Troyna, B. (1995) 'The politics of education policy borrowing', *Comparative Education*, 31(3): 303–310.

Herschbach, D. R. (2009) 'Overview: Navigating the policy landscape: Education, training and work', in R. Maclean and D. Wilson (eds) *International handbook of education for the changing world of work*. Dordrecht: Springer Netherlands. 869–890.

Ingman, S. and Amin, I. (2011) 'Introduction to the theme issue on sustainable senior living for the 21st century', *Educational Gerontology*, 37(6): 441–449.

Jakobi, A. and Martens, K. (2007) 'Diffusion durch Internationale Organisationen: Die Bildungspolitik der OECD' [Diffusion through international organisations: The educational policy-making of the OECD], in K. Holzinger, H. Joergens and C. Knill (eds) *Politische Vierteljahresschrift, Sonderband Transfer, Diffusion und Konvergenz von Politiken*. Wiesbaden: VS Verlag für Sozialwissenschaften. 247–270.

James, O. and Lodge, M. (2003) 'The limitations of "policy transfer" and "lesson drawing" for public policy research', *Political Studies Review*, 1(2): 179–193.

Kalló, J. (2009) *OECD education policy: A comparative and historical study focusing on the thematic reviews of tertiary education*. Jyväskylä: Finnish Educational Research Association.

Krücken, G. (2002) 'Amerikanischer Neo-Institutionalismus: Europäische Perspektiven' [American neo-institutionalism: European perspectives], *Sociologia Internationalis*, 40(2): 227–259.

Lawn, M. and Nóvoa, A. (2002) 'Introduction: Fabricating Europe – The formation of an education space', in M. Lawn and A. Nóvoa (eds) *Fabricating Europe: The formation of an education space*. Dordrecht: Kluwer. 1–13.

Lechner, F. J. and Boli, J. (2008) *The globalization reader*, 3rd edn. Malden, MA: Blackwell.

Lüders, C., Kade, J. and Hornstein, W. (2010) 'Entgrenzung des Pädagogischen' [The pedagogical transcending its boundaries], in H.-H. Krüger and W. Helsper (eds) *Einführung in die Grundbegriffe und Grundfragen der Erziehungswissenschaft*, 9th edn. Opladen: Barbara Budrich. 223–232.

Luhmann, N. (1995) *Social systems*, trans. John Bednarz Jr. with Dirk Baecker. Stanford: Stanford University Press.

Luhmann, N. (1997) *Die Gesellschaft der Gesellschaft* [Society of society]. Frankfurt am Main: Suhrkamp.

Luhmann, N. (2005) *Soziologische Aufklärung 6: Die Soziologie und der Mensch* [Sociological enlightenment 6: Sociology and man], 2nd edn. Wiesbaden: VS Verlag für Sozialwissenschaften.

Luhmann, N. and Schorr, K. E. (1988) *Reflexionsprobleme im Erziehungssystem* [Problems of reflection in the system of education]. Frankfurt am Main: Suhrkamp.

Luhmann, N. and Schorr, K. E. (2000) *Problems of reflection in the system of education*, trans. Rebecca A. Neuwirth. Münster: Waxmann.

Lundahl, L. (2005) 'Swedish, European, global', in D. Coulby and E. Zambeta (eds) *World yearbook of education 2005: Globalization and nationalism in education*. London: RoutledgeFalmer. 147–164.

Lundahl, C. and Waldow, F. (2009) 'Standardisation and "quick languages": The shape-shifting of standardised measurement of pupil achievement in Sweden and Germany', *Comparative Education*, 45(3): 365–385.

Nassehi, A. (2002) 'Die Organisationen der Gesellschaft: Skizze einer Organisationssoziologie in gesellschaftstheoretischer Absicht' [The organisations of society: Sketch of an organisational sociology as a contribution to a theory of society], in J. Allmendinger and T. Hinz (eds) *Organisationssoziologie*. Wiesbaden: Westdeutscher Verlag. 443–478.

Nóvoa, A. N. and Yariv-Mashal, T. (2003) 'Comparative research in education: A mode of governance or a historical journey?', *Comparative Education*, 39(4): 423 – 438.

Perry, L. and Tor, G.-H. (2008) 'Understanding educational transfer: Theoretical perspectives and conceptual frameworks', *Prospects*, 38(4): 509–526.

Phillips, D. (2000) 'Learning from elsewhere in education: Some perennial problems revisited with reference to British interest in Germany', *Comparative Education*, 36(3): 297–307.

Radtke, F.-O. (2009) 'Ökonomisierung' [Economisation], in S. Andresen, R. Casale, T. Gabriel, R. Horlacher, S. Larcher Klee and J. Oelkers (eds) *Handwörterbuch Erziehungswissenschaft*. Weinheim: Beltz. 621–636.

Ramirez, F. O., and Boli, J. (1987) 'The political construction of mass schooling: European origins and worldwide institutionalization', *Sociology of Education*, 60: 2–17.

Ravitch, D. (1995) *National standards in American education: A citizen's guide*. Washington, DC: Brookings.

Robertson, S. L. (2005) 'Re-imagining and rescripting the future of education: Global knowledge economy discourses and the challenge to education systems', *Comparative Education*, 41(2): 151–170.

Robertson, S. L. and Dale, R. (2008) 'Researching education in a globalising era: Beyond methodological nationalism, methodological statism, methodological educationism and spatial fetishism', in J. Resnik (ed.) *The production of educational knowledge in the global era*. Rotterdam: Sense. 19–32.

Rose, R. (1991) 'What is lesson-drawing?', *Journal of Public Policy*, 11(01): 3–30.

Rüttgers, P. (2010) *Die Pädagogisierung der Gesellschaft im Spannungsfeld funktionalistischer und machttheoretischer Perspektiven* [The educationalisation of society seen in a functionalist perspective and a perspective of a theory of power], Dr. phil.-thesis, University of Duisburg-Essen. Online. Available HTTP: http://deposit.d-nb.de/cgi-bin/dokserv?idn= 100317079x&dok_var=d1&dok_ext=pdf&filename=100317079x.pdf (accessed 15 June 2011).

Schleicher, A. (2008) *Seeing quality and equity of education systems through the prism of international comparisons*, presentation at the 48th International Conference of Education, Geneva: International Bureau of Education. Online. Available HTTP: www.ibe.unesco.org/ fileadmin/user_upload/Policy_Dialogue/48th_ICE/Presentations/IBE_ICE_Research_ Findings_EN_Andreas_Schleicher_Nov08.pdf> (accessed 15 June 2011).

Schriewer, J. (1990) 'The method of comparison and the need for externalization: Methodological criteria and sociological concepts', in J. Schriewer and B. Holmes (eds) *Theories and methods in comparative education*, 2nd edn. Frankfurt am Main: Peter Lang. 25–83.

Schriewer, J. (2005) 'Wie global ist institutionalisierte Weltbildungsprogrammatik? Neo-institutionalistische Thesen im Licht kulturvergleichender Analysen' [How global are institutionalised educational programmes? Neo-institutionalist theses in the light of analyses comparing cultures], in B. Heintz, R. Münch and H. Tyrell (eds) *Weltgesellschaft: Theoretische Zugänge und empirische Problemlagen*. Stuttgart: Lucius & Lucius. 415–441 (*Zeitschrift für Soziologie* 34, special issue 1).

Smeyers, P., and Depaepe, M. (eds) (2008) *Educational research: The educationalization of social problems*. Dordrecht: Springer Netherland.

Spreen, C. A. (2004) 'Appropriating borrowed policies: Outcomes-based education in South Africa', in G. Steiner-Khamsi (ed.) *The global politics of educational borrowing and lending*. New York: Teachers College Press. 101–113.

Spring, J. H. (2009) *Globalization of education: An introduction*. New York: Routledge.

Steiner-Khamsi, G. (2002) 'Re-territorializing educational import: Explorations into the politics of educational borrowing', in A. Nóvoa and M. Lawn (eds) *Fabricating Europe: The formation of an education space*. Dordrecht: Kluwer. 69–86.

Steiner-Khamsi, G. (2003) 'The politics of league tables', *Journal of Social Science Education*, 2003–1. Online. Available HTTP: www.jsse.org/2003/2003-1/pdf/khamsi-tables-1-2003. pdf (accessed 15 June 2011).

Steiner-Khamsi, G. (2004a) 'Blazing a trail for policy theory and practice', in G. Steiner-Khamsi (ed.) *The global politics of educational borrowing and lending*. New York: Teachers College Press. 201–220.

Steiner-Khamsi, G. (2004b) 'Globalization in education: Real or imagined?', in G. Steiner-Khamsi (ed.) *The global politics of educational borrowing and lending*. New York: Teachers College Press. 1–6.

Steiner-Khamsi, G. (ed.) (2004c) *The global politics of educational borrowing and lending*. New York: Teachers College Press.

Steiner-Khamsi, G. and Stolpe, I. (2006) *Educational import: Local encounters with global forces in Mongolia*. New York: Palgrave Macmillan.

Suchman, M. C. (1995) 'Managing legitimacy: Strategic and institutional approaches', *Academy of Management Review*, 20(3): 571–610.

Takayama, K. (2010) 'Politics of externalization in reflexive times: Reinventing Japanese education reform discourses through "Finnish PISA success"', *Comparative Education Review*, 54(1): 51–75.

Tenorth, H.-E. (2010) *Geschichte der Erziehung: Einführung in die Grundzüge ihrer neuzeitlichen Entwicklung* [History of education: Introduction to the basics of the modern history of education], 5th edn. Weinheim: Juventa.

Therborn, G. (2002) 'Foreword: Space and learning', in A. Nóvoa and M. Lawn (eds) *Fabricating Europe: The formation of an education space*. Dordrecht: Kluwer. 15–17.

Thomas, G. M., Meyer, J. W., Ramirez, F. O. and Boli, J. (1987) *Institutional structure: Constituting state, society, and the individual*. Newbury Park, CA: SAGE Publications.

Uphoff, N. (1989) 'Distinguishing power, authority & legitimacy: Taking Max Weber at his word by using resources-exchange analysis', *Polity*, 22(2): 295–322.

Waldow, F. (2007) *Ökonomische Strukturzyklen und internationale Diskurskonjunkturen: Zur Entwicklung der schwedischen Bildungsprogrammatik, 1930–2000* [Structural economic cycles and international discursive swings: On the development of educational policy in Sweden, 1930–2000]. Frankfurt am Main: Peter Lang.

Waldow, F. (2009) 'Undeclared imports: "Silent borrowing" in educational policy-making and research in Sweden', *Comparative Education*, 45(4): 477–494.

Waldow, F. (2010) 'Der Traum vom 'skandinavisch schlau Werden'' [Dreaming of 'getting smart the Scandinavian way'], *Zeitschrift für Pädagogik*, 54(4).

Waldow, F. (forthcoming) 'Taylorismus im Klassenzimmer: John Franklin Bobbitts Vorschläge zur *standards-based reform*' [Taylorism in the classroom: John Franklin Bobbitt's suggestions concerning standards-based reform], *Zeitschrift für Pädagogik*.

Wimmer, A. and Glick Schiller, N. (2002) 'Methodological nationalism and beyond: nationstate building, migration and the social sciences', *Global Networks: A Journal of Transnational Affairs*, 2(4): 301–334.

Wolf, J. and Bokhorst-Heng, W. (2008) 'Policies of promise and practices of limit: Singapore's literacy education policy landscape and its impact on one school programme', *Educational Research for Policy and Practice*, 7(3): 151–164.

Zymek, B. (2007) 'Nationale und internationale Standardisierungsprozesse in der Bildungsgeschichte: Das deutsche Beispiel' [National and international processes of standardisation in educational history: The German example], *Jahrbuch für historische Bildungsforschung*, 13: 307–334.

Zymek, B. and Zymek, R. (2004) 'Traditional – national – international: Explaining the inconsistency of educational borrowers', in D. Phillips and K. Ochs (eds) *Educational policy borrowing: Historical perspectives*. Didcot: Symposium. 25–35.

Index